South of France

Provence & the Côte d'Azur

Penguin Books

PENGUIN BOOKS

Published by the Penguin Group
Penguin Books Ltd, 80 Strand, London WC2R ORL, England
Penguin Books USA Inc., 375 Hudson Street, New York, New York 10014, USA
Penguin Books Australia Ltd, 250 Camberwell Road, Camberwell, Victoria 3124, Australia
Penguin Books Canada Ltd, 10 Alcorn Avenue, Toronto, Ontario, Canada M4V 3B2
Penguin Books (NZ) Ltd, cnr Rosedale and Airborne Rds, Albany, Auckland, New Zealand

Penguin Books Ltd, Registered Offices: Harmondsworth, Middlesex, England

First published 2000
Second edition 2002
10 9 8 7 6 5 4 3 2 1

Reprographics by Quebecor Numeric, 56 bd Davout, 75020 Paris
Cover reprographics by Precise Litho, 34-35 Great Sutton Street, London EC1
Printed and bound by Cayfosa-Quebecor, Ctra. de Caldes, Km 3 08 130 Sta Perpètua de Mogoda, Barcelona, Spain

**Edited and
designed by
Time Out Paris**
100 rue du Fbg-St-Antoine
75012 Paris
Tel: +33 (0)1.44.87.00.45
Fax:+33 (0)1.44.73.90.60
Email: editors@timeout.fr

**For
Time Out Guides Ltd
Universal House
251 Tottenham Court Road
London W1T 7AB**
Tel: +44 (0)20 7813 3000
Fax:+44 (0)20 7813 6001
Email: guides@timeout.com
www.timeout.com

Editorial

Editor Natasha Edwards
Production Editor Alison Culliford
Sub Editor Rosalind Sykes
Editorial Assistant Natalie Whittle
Additional research Frances Dougherty, Sophia Khan, Cara Young

Editorial Director Peter Fiennes
Series Editor Ruth Jarvis
Deputy Series Editor Jonathan Cox

Design

Art Director Paris Richard Joy
Ad Design Philippe Thareaut

Group Art Director John Oakey
Art Director Mandy Martin
Picture Editor Kerri Miles

Advertising

Sales & Administration Manager Philippe Thareaut
Advertising Executive (Cannes) Sarah Fraser

Group Commercial Director Lesley Gill
Sales Director Mark Phillips
International Sales Co-ordinator Ross Canadé

Administration

Managing Director Paris Karen Albrecht

Chairman Tony Elliott
Managing Director Mike Hardwick
Group Financial Director Kevin Ellis
Marketing Director Christine Cort
Marketing Manager Mandy Martinez
US Publicity & Marketing Associate Rosella Albanese
Group General Manager Nichola Coulthard
Production Manager Mark Lamond
Production Controller Samantha Furniss
Accountant Sarah Bostock

Features for the second edition were written or updated by: Introduction Natasha Edwards. **History** Natasha Edwards (*Provençal People: Petrarch* Isabel Pitman; *Provençal People: Marquis de Sade* Stephen Mudge; *How the glamour turned into glitz* Natalie Whittle). **The South of France Today** Natasha Edwards (*Full-speed Med* Alexander Lobrano). **Art & Modernism in the South** Natasha Edwards. **Provençal Food & Drink** Natasha Edwards (*Foodie festivities* Isabel Pitman; *Pastis goes ladylike* Susan Bell). **Arts & Entertainment** Natasha Edwards, Stephen Mudge (*Electrocity* Muriel Fourlan). **The Festive South** Natalie Whittle (*Cannes* Toby Rose; *Festival crazy* Isabel Pitman). **Nîmes & the Pont du Gard** Rosemary Bailey (*Uzès & the Gardon* Susan Bell). **St-Rémy & the Alpilles** Nicola Mitchell (*Beaucaire & Tarascon*; *Salon-de-Provence* Stephen Mudge). **Arles** Rosemary Bailey. **The Camargue** Stephen Mudge. **Avignon** Isabel Pitman. **Orange & Around** Stephen Mudge. **Carpentras & Mont Ventoux** Stephen Mudge (*Blue highways* Isabel Pitman). **The Drôme Provençale** Isabel Pitman. **The Luberon** Natasha Edwards (*Provençal People: Olivier Baussan* Isabel Pitman). **Marseille** Rosa Jackson (*Provençal People: Robert Guédiguian* Isabel Pitman). **Aix-en-Provence** Natasha Edwards. **Cassis to Toulon** Inger Holland. **Hyères to the Maures** Natasha Edwards. **St-Tropez** Kate Horne, Toby Rose (*It's a fair cop* Natasha Edwards; *Yacht etiquette* Isabel Pitman; *Loft conversion* Toby Rose). **St-Raphaël & the Estérel** Sarah Fraser. **Brignoles & the Sainte Baume** Inger Holland. **The Var Heartland** Nicola Mitchell (*Provençal People: Bruno* Inger Holland). **The Gorges du Verdon** Natasha Edwards. **Cannes** Sarah Fraser. **Antibes to Cagnes** Tanya Cagnoni (*Walks on the wild side* Inger Holland). **Nice** Lanie Goodman (*Provençal People: Ben* Tanya Cagnoni). **The Corniches** Lanie Goodman. **Monaco & Monte-Carlo** Lanie Goodman (*Banco* Michael McCarthy). **Roquebrune to Menton** Lanie Goodman (*Gardens of Eden* Nicola Mitchell). **Grasse & the Gorges du Loup** Sarah Fraser. **Vence & St-Paul** Tanya Cagnoni. **The Arrière Pays** Stephen Mudge. **Into the Alps** Stephen Mudge (*White out* Sarah Fraser). **Directory** Natalie Whittle. **Additional listings** Olivier Baenninger, Alexander Lobrano, Toby Rose. **Index** Natalie Whittle.

Maps by J S Graphics, 17 Beadles Lane, Old Oxted, Surrey RH8 9JG (john@jsgraphics.co.uk)
Street plans are based on material supplied by Thomas Cook Publishers.

Photography Adam Eastland, Inger Holland. **Additional photography** Fabienne Caulet, Bruno Contesse, V Coutant (CDT Vaucluse), Tom Craig, Philippe Delacroix, Jacques Foudraz, Daniel Gorgeon (CDT 13), J Guillard (CDT 13), N & F Michel (CDT Vaucluse). **Additional photos courtesy** Office de Tourisme d'Aix-en-Provence (CDT 13), Bridgeman Art Gallery, Galerie Lara Vincy, Galerie Yvon Lambert/Collection Lambert, Donation Jacques-Henri Lartigue, Musée de la Marine, Musée Pétrarque, Laurent Philippe/Ballets de Monte-Carlo, Mairie de Tarascon.

Contents

Introduction

Picasso has a lot to answer for: all those enduring images of bathers running along long, sandy beaches and then you arrive to discover there's only two feet between you and your neighbour, that the beach might actually be pebbles and that the bougainvillea-dripping villas have been replaced by a long concrete block of *résidences* all with sea-view-hogging balconies. But then the very words 'Provence' and 'Côte d'Azur' are as much about evocative images and a way of life as any physical reality.

The South of France does have glorious beaches, with all the posing and preening you can want, but there's also a vibrant urban culture in the streets of Marseille, sophisticated Aix or bull-crazy Nîmes; you can head a few miles inland and discover mountains with magnificent scenery where it's just you and a few sheep, the unbeatable watery reflections and birdlife of the Camargue or centuries-old hill villages, where centuries-old habits of *pétanque*, *pastis* and long hours on café terraces endure.

It's perhaps in the South of France that the French have really got the *art de vivre* sewn up: an enviable climate, a delicious, healthy diet and a winning *mélange* of the authentic and the mondaine, simplicity and sophistication. Take eating out: it can be as snobby or as simple as you wish. As well as internationally famed restaurants, we've tried to include the little local places where the French themselves head, where a love of food and wine knows no boundaries and where (*vive la Révolution!*) you really will find all sorts, from local farmers to artists to smart second-homers and film producers, rubbing shoulders in a uniquely French social mix.

ABOUT THE TIME OUT CITY GUIDES

The *Time Out South of France Guide* is one of an expanding series of *Time Out* guides produced by the people behind London's and New York's successful listings magazines. This second edition has been thoroughly revised and updated by writers resident in France who have striven to provide you with all the most up-to-date information you'll need to explore the region, whether you're a local or a first-time visitor.

The *Time Out South of France Guide* was the first in which the dynamic, critical approach of Time Out's successful city guide series was applied to a whole region. Whereas most general guides to the South concentrate on sightseeing, the *Time Out South of France Guide* adds a distinctively cultural slant, covering today's arts scene and a wide selection of the best places to stay, eat and unwind, from the glitziest Riviera hotel to the humblest village brasserie.

THE LIE OF THE LAND

The South of France is as much about an image and a lifestyle as technical boundaries. The main area we cover coincides with the southern portion of the modern French administrative region of Provence-Alpes-Côte d'Azur, taking in the *départements* of Bouches-du-Rhône, Vaucluse, Var and Alpes-Maritimes, as well as the south of the Alpes de Haute-Provence. But we also spread westwards to Nîmes and Uzès, which fell within the historic Roman region of Provincia, and Aigues-Mortes, which marks the western boundary of the Camargue, as well as

adding for this second edition, the south of the Drôme *département*, an area commonly dubbed 'the Drôme Provençale', where the characteristic vegetation of olives and herbs already augurs in the South. Our regional sections are arranged roughly in a west-east order.

All the areas covered, from big cities to rural backwaters, follow a similar format, starting with the background and sightseeing information, followed by where to eat, where to stay and visitor information, including the addresses of the relevant tourist offices. We give essential road and public transport information at the end of chapters, but sometimes suggested routes between villages are detailed in the main

The euro

The euro came into circulation in France on 1 January 2002; the franc was withdrawn on 17 February. Prices in this guide are given in euros; all prices were checked before going to press, and when necessary were translated into euros using the official rate of 6.55957. The transition to the new currency is bound to cause some fluctuation, with many businesses succumbing to the temptation to round prices upwards, while some astute marketers have rounded down.

text. Bear in mind that public transport in inland rural areas is often extremely limited.

PRICES & PAYMENT
The prices we've supplied should be treated as guidelines, not gospel, especially in the light of the changeover to the euro. If you encounter prices that vary wildly from those we've quoted, ask whether there's a good reason. If not, go elsewhere. Note that for hotels we have listed the price for a double room as the best indication for the price bracket within which a hotel falls (although these hotels may well equally have single rooms or, indeed, triples, quadruples or suites). The range for a double takes in different categories of room and/or variations between low- and high-season prices. For restaurants, we have given the price range for set menus (referred to in French as *formule*, *menu* or *prix-fixe*); note that the lowest-priced menu is often available only at lunch. Where no menus are served, we give an average price for a three-course meal without drinks, for one person. In main cities we have noted whether restaurants, hotels and cafés take credit cards – American Express (AmEx), Diners Club (DC), MasterCard (MC) and Visa (V). The most widely accepted credit card in France is Visa. Note that museums and tourist sites often do not take credit cards and that shops, restaurants and cafés often do not accept credit cards for less than €15.

TELEPHONE NUMBERS
All French phone numbers have ten digits. Numbers for the whole area covered in this guide – with the exception of Monaco – start with 04. From outside France, dial the country code (33) and leave off the zero at the beginning of the number. Numbers prefixed by 06 are mobile phones, 08.36 numbers are premium rate and 08.00 are freephone numbers (sometimes available from outside France at standard international rates). The Monaco code is 00 377.

POSTCODES
All addresses in France have a five-figure postcode, starting with the two figures that indicate the *département* (eg. 06000 Nice, 06400 Cannes). For questions of space and readability, we have not put postcodes in each address, but have included them, should you need to write to a particular town or village, in the address of tourist information offices.

THE LOWDOWN ON THE LISTINGS
Above all, we've tried to make this book as useful as possible. Addresses, phone numbers, transport information, opening details and admission prices are all included. However, owners and managers can change their arrangements at any time. Note that seasonal

closures for restaurants and hotels can vary from year to year. Before you go out of your way, we'd strongly advise you to phone ahead to check opening times and other particulars. While every effort and care has been made to ensure the accuracy of the information contained in this guide, the publishers cannot accept responsibility for any errors it may contain.

ESSENTIAL INFORMATION
For all the practical information you might need for visiting the area, before and during your trip, including emergency numbers, car and bike hire information, and an essential vocabulary, turn to the Directory chapter at the back of this guide.

MAPS
Regional maps to the different areas covered are at the back of the guide – starting on *p320*. Central street maps for the key cities of Nîmes, Arles, Avignon, Marseille, Aix-en-Provence, Cannes and Nice are in the relevant chapters.

LET US KNOW WHAT YOU THINK
We hope you enjoy the *Time Out South of France Guide* and we'd like to know what you think of it. We welcome your tips for places that you consider we should include in future editons and we value and take notice of your criticisms of our choices. There's a reader's reply card at the back of this book – or you can simply email us on editors@timeout.fr.

In Context

History

The proverbial land of lavender, light and the good life has also known anarchy, persecution and bloodshed.

Evidence from sites near Nice and Monaco show that our ancestors lived here half a million years ago, perhaps earlier. Even before the last ice age, hunter societies had left propitiatory animal paintings on the walls of caves such as the Grotte Cosquer near Cassis (*see p162*). After the last ice age, neolithic man took up residence in this fertile region as well as in the cave-pocked Verdon gorges (a past now reflected in the new Musée de la Préhistoire in Quinson, *see p206*).

Around 1200BC, the Gauls – a Celtic people – began to migrate from the Rhine Valley into France and Italy. The southernmost front of this advance developed into the Ligurian culture, which stretched from Spain into Italy. Skilled metal workers and stone carvers, the Ligurians lived in *oppidiums* – fortified villages such as that at Entremont (*see p154*).

Western civilisation first came to Provence in the form of the Greeks from the Ionian city of Phocaea, who founded the colony of Massalia (modern-day Marseille) in about 600BC. By the beginning of the fifth century BC, Massalia had become so powerful that it was minting its own money and had begun to plant colonies along the coast, at Nikaia (Nice), Olbia (Hyères), Taureontum (Les Lecques) and Agde, and inland at Arles. The Greek innovations of wine, olive oil and other goods traded around the Mediterranean soon filtered through to neighbouring Celtic areas.

ROMAN 'PROVINCIA'

Marseille took the Roman side during the Carthaginian Wars, a smart move that stood it in good stead when Rome went annexing beyond the Alps towards the end of the second century BC. Called in by Marseille to help the city repulse a Celtic attack, the Romans stayed on, destroying the Celto-Ligurian *oppidium* of Entremont and founding the city of Aquae Sextiae (Aix-en-Provence) in 122BC. In recognition of its support, Marseille was allowed to stay an independent state within Roman territory. The main reason, however, for expansion into the south of France was the need to secure the land route to Spain. From around

120BC, Roman Consul Cneus Domitius Ahenobarbus created the Via Domitia (Domitian Way) with staging posts at Nîmes, Beaucaire, Cavaillon and Apt. By 118BC Rome controlled the whole coast westwards to the Pyrenees and a large swathe of the hinterland. In time-honoured fashion, the Romans subdued by colonisation: vast numbers of settlers, many of them army veterans, were attracted by a promise of free land. The Celtic town of what is now Vaison-la-Romaine became a federated city, rather than a colony, with semi-autonomous status. Narbonne, in the south-west, became the capital of Gallia Narbonensis, also known, more simply, by its former name of 'Provincia'.

To the north, the Celts had not yet conceded defeat. After 115BC, the northern Celtic tribe of the Cimbri and the Germanic Teutons mounted a series of raids on Provence, culminating in a humiliating defeat for the Romans at Orange in 105BC. The Roman general Marius went in to repair the damage in 102BC.

Under the *pax romana*, Gallia Narbonensis became a model province. Even after Julius Caesar had subdued the rest of Gaul in the Gallic Wars (58-51BC), this remained the most Roman of the empire's transalpine possessions. The lower Rhône Valley bristled with fine cities: Aix, Arles, Nîmes, Orange, Glanum (St-Rémy) and further east the major port of Fréjus, probable birthplace of the historian Tacitus.

Marseille was eclipsed after it chose the wrong horse, supporting Pompey against Caesar in the Civil Wars. Besieged in 49BC, it lost its independence, and its possessions were transferred to Arles, Narbonne and Fréjus – though it continued to be a centre of scholarship, the last outpost of Greek culture in the west.

Provence became an important supplier of grain, olive oil and ships for the ever-hungry empire. In return, it was treated more as an extension of the motherland than a colonial outpost. The aqueducts, baths, amphitheatres and temples that serviced the citizenry of burgeoning centres such as Arles and Nîmes often surpassed those of similar-sized Italian cities. The Rhône became the trading river par excellence, with Arles acting as the northern European port of entry for goods from Spain, Africa and Arabia; it was often quicker and cheaper to trade even with Britain via the Rhône and the Seine rather than on the dangerous Atlantic route. The imperial connection with Provence was reinforced under Antoninus Pius (emperor from AD138 to 161), whose family came from Nîmes; and with Constantine, the first Christian emperor, Arles became a favoured imperial residence in the early fourth century.

MONKS & INVADERS

The Christian community came into the open with the foundation of the monasteries of St-Honorat on the Iles des Lérins and St-Victor in Marseille in the early fifth century. The latter was the centre of a monastic diaspora that gave the South a generous sprinkling of abbeys from Le Barben to Castellane, ensuring the land was worked even in times of crisis – though the monks could be as tyrannical in exploiting the peasantry as any feudal landlord.

When the Roman empire finally fell apart in 476, the bishoprics maintained some semblance of order in the face of successive invasions by Visigoths and Ostrogoths. It was the Franks – who originally came from the west bank of the Rhine – who eventually gained the upper hand, after a period of anarchy during which Roman embellishments such as aqueducts, bridges and theatres fell into ruin and drained fields returned to swampland. In addition, the new rulers looked north rather than south, and the Mediterranean trade that had provided a living for cities like Arles or Marseille gradually dried up.

The three-way partition of the Carolingian empire in the Treaty of Verdun in 843 made the

Top ten Antique ruins

Maison Carrée, Nîmes
Elegant house of imperial worship. See p51.

Pont du Gard
Triple-decker water carrier. See p57.

Glanum, St-Rémy-de-Provence
Already a chic site to plant a villa. See p60.

Les Arènes, Arles
Vast gladiatorial amphitheatre. See p71.

Théâtre Antique, Orange
Still perfectly preserved for opera. See p99.

Quartier de la Villasse, Vaison-la-Romaine
Prosperous shopping centre. See p111.

Jardin des Vestiges, Marseille
Massilia's Greek origins. See p135.

Lanterne d'Auguste, Fréjus
Watchtower over the naval base. See p183.

Musée d'Archéologie, Nice
The remains of Cemenetum. See p236.

La Trophée des Alpes, La Turbie
Augustus' victory call. See p252.

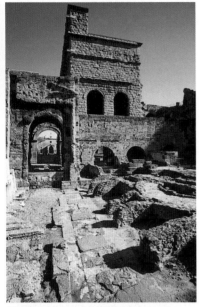

Orange: one more city under Roman rule.

Rhône a frontier and provided the basis for the later division between Provence and Languedoc. Over the next couple of centuries, imperial rule gave way to out and out feudalism, with a succession of local lords using brute force and taxes to subdue the territory around their castle strongholds. In the eighth and ninth centuries, the Saracens terrorised the coast and launched raids on the surrounding countryside from their base at La Garde-Freinet in the Massif des Maures.

COUNTS & CONSULATES

In around 931 the kingdom of Provence – one of many fragments of Charlemagne's former empire – was allied with Burgundy. A century later, as the kingdom of Arles, it became part of the Holy Roman Empire, thus establishing the Rhône as its western limit.

The Church's influence was stronger than ever before. From the end of the 11th century more efficient agriculture, the revival of trade and the rise of the guilds provided the money for the construction of new religious foundations such as the magnificent abbey of St-Gilles, with its richly carved facade, on the edge of the Camargue, and the restoration and embellishment of pre-existing ones at St-Trophime in Arles and the cloisters at Aix cathedral. A sober, pared-back style of

Romanesque also evolved in the 12th century at the great Cistercian foundations of Silvacane, Senanque and Thoronet. Northern French Gothic (which had its beginnings at St-Denis in the 12th century) was slow to percolate the South where Romanesque continued to hold sway, though a few fine Gothic edifices were built, notably the flamboyant 14th-century Gothic of the Palais des Papes in Avignon, the Cathédrale St-Suffrein in Carpentras and the magnificent Basilique Ste-Maximin-la-Ste-Baume.

Sometime in the 11th century, a small local dynasty had felt confident enough to award itself the title of Counts of Provence. When the line died out in 1113, the title passed to the House of Barcelona, which became the nominal ruler of the area. However, the larger cities were soon asserting their independence, setting up governments known as Consulates. In the country, local bosses such as the lords of Les Baux and count of Forcalquier reigned supreme and put up fierce resistance to those claiming higher authority.

The Catalan sway over Mediterranean France was helped along by language. Provençal, the eastern dialect of Occitan or *langue d'Oc,* was a close cousin of Catalan. Out of the apparent anarchy and the frequent shifts in the balance of power among the warring seigneuries, a distinctive local culture was being formed, which reached its fullest expression in the poetry and ballads of the troubadours, or itinerant love poets.

ANJOU COUNTS, BABYLONIAN POPES

Provence was spared the destruction and slaughter visited upon south-western France during the Albigensian Crusade against the Cathars. But the crusade altered the balance of power in the south: the Counts of Toulouse were crushed, and the whole of Languedoc passed to the French crown in 1271.

The Counts of Provence emerged as sole rulers of the land between the Rhône and the Alps. The last Count of Provence, Raymond Berenger V, was also one of the shrewdest and most cultured. He gave his territories an efficient administration and dealt with the increasingly muscular power of France by marrying his daughter Béatrice to Charles d'Anjou, brother of Louis IX, in 1246.

Angevin rule lasted two and a half centuries, bringing a new degree of stability, though the Anjou princes at first preferred to reside in Palermo or Naples, the other poles of their Mediterranean empire, until chased out of Sicily in 1282. Louis II of Anjou, however, founded the University of Aix in 1409, and from 1471, Good King René (1434-80) established his court at Aix. His reign was longer and more stable than most, and the poet-king encouraged a minor artistic revival from his court. The administrative reforms introduced by the last Count of Provence were continued with the establishment of the *Etats généraux*, a regional assembly that had the power to raise taxes and take over the reins of government in times of crisis. The last of the local warlords, the Baux family, retreated to Orange, setting off the dynastic daisy chain that would lead to this becoming a corner of Protestant Holland in the 16th century.

Other interlopers were of a very different stamp: the Comtat Venaissin around Carpentras, Avignon, Cavaillon and Fontaine de Vaucluse was a territorial overspill of the Comté of Toulouse. In 1274, three years after the Counts' main territory was annexed to the French crown, this enclave – whose borders had the shape, and the territorial logic, of an inkblot – was given to the papacy by Philippe III (the Bold). In 1306, the French pope Clément V made good use of this bolthole, transferring his whole court first to Carpentras and then to Avignon, and ushering in the papacy's 70-year 'Babylonian captivity'. When the Jews were expelled from France, first in 1306 by Philippe

Provençal People: Petrarch

Petrarch should be at the top of the reading list of every romantic, especially those unrequited in love. The great Italian classical scholar, humanist and lyric poet of undying love, did enough pining and soul-searching in his masterpiece *Canzoniere* to keep even the most heartbroken in good company.

The object of his affections is a literary mystery, buried in Provençal folklore. The story goes that on 6 April 1327 in the church of Ste-Claire in papal Avignon, Francesco di Ser Petrarca spotted a beautiful, noble blonde, allegedly known as Laure. He fell immediately and profoundly in love.

Sadly the romance didn't develop much further – he never saw her again, nor perhaps even discovered her real name. Some say she never existed at all. Most claim she was Laure de Noves, wife of Hugues de Sade and mother of 11 children. Progress was further stumped by her death from the Plague in 1348. And then there was the issue of Petrarch becoming chaplain to the Colonna family in Avignon, and taking vows of celibacy.

Imaginary or not, that fleeting glimpse was enough to fuel a lifetime of helpless longing, and 366 sonnets and ballads addressed to this enigmatic muse. *Canzoniere* is in the tradition of courtly love poetry, expressing Petrarch's passion as a spiritual journey. Racked with agony, penitence and lofty oxymorons, it established him as one of the greatest Renaissance poets and, along with Dante (busy adoring Beatrice), among the first to write in vernacular Italian.

Brought to Avignon aged nine by his father, Petrarch became enchanted by the rugged tranquility of the Vaucluse, his 'fair transalpine solitude'. Between campaigning to restore the papal seat in Rome where he

was crowned poet laureate, and travelling Europe as a celebrity genius and father of Humanism, he returned here regularly to write and meditate.

The emerald source of the River Sorgue was another great inspiration. Petrarch lived near the water's edge at Fontaine-de-Vaucluse for nine years until his definitive departure from France in 1353. His little house had two gardens, planted with bay trees – *lauriers* – in remembrance of his beloved. Pillaged and burnt, the original site is now the Musée Petrarque. Yet the romantic giant already foresaw his endowment to local tourism, describing the fountain as 'famous in its own right, but now a lot more famous due to my long stay here and my poems'.

le Bel and again in 1394 under Charles VI, they found refuge in the Papal enclave, where fine synagogues still survive at Carpentras and Cavaillon.

The Avignon Papacy spurred an economic, intellectual and cultural renaissance in the region, from new industries like glass-making, paper manufacture and melon growing, to the rise of an artistic school, now known as the Provençal Primitives, as Siennese painters like Simone Martini flocked to produce altarpieces for the rash of new religious edifices. In the 15th

Heresy

The Vaudois, also known as the Pauvres de Lyon – and in English Waldensians – were founded in 1180 by Pierre Valdès, a Lyon merchant, who gave up all his possessions to preach the Bible and the virtues of poverty. In 1184 Valdès was excommunicated by the Pope for preaching in the vernacular and the Vaudrois hid out in the Alpine valleys around Briançon and in northern Italy. During the 15th century, encouraged by feudal landlords who wanted to repopulate farmlands decimated by the Black Death, Vaudois peasants arrived in the Luberon villages of Mérindol, Lourmarin, Buoux, Lacoste and Cabrières d'Aigues. The settlers kept a low profile, their preachers travelling discreetly in pairs, but the heresy split the area: other villages, such as Curcuron, Lauris, Bonnieux and Oppède remained fervently Catholic. Persecution arrived with the condemnation of Protestantism. From the start the Vaudois were receptive to Luther's reforms, and when papal inquisitor Jean de Roma arrived in Apt in the 1530s on the trail of Lutherans, it was the Vaudois who were there to take the flak. In 1540, in the Decree of Mérindol, the Parlement d'Aix condemned the Vaudois as heretics to be burned alive, their goods confiscated and families banished. It was only after royal assent from François 1er that Jean de Meynier, president of the Parlement d'Aix and Baron of Oppède, could implement the decree. On 16 April 1545 he sent in his troops: within six days 22 villages were pillaged and burned and an estimated 2,500 were dead. Mérindol was razed to the ground and its ruined citadel, now bearing the plaque of the Mémorial des Vaudois, remains a potent symbol of the massacre.

century, homegrown talent, notably Enguerrand Quarton, evolved a more local, Flemish-influenced style of crystalline painterly detail. A rival artistic pole of attraction, centred on the patronage of the comtal court at Aix, especially around Good King René, with artists including Nicolas Froment and the Flemish painter Barthélémy van Eyck. To the east, in the territory of Nice (grabbed by the House of Savoy in 1388) – and especially its mountainous hinterland – Niçois painter Louis Bréa and Piedmontese imports Giovanni Canavesio and Jean Baleison would found a distinctive school in the mid-15th to mid-16th centuries.

The Black Death hit Provence in 1348, entering through the port of Marseille (which had regained its maritime power thanks to the Crusades and the revival of Mediterranean trade) and decimating the population.

UNION WITH FRANCE & THE WARS OF RELIGION

Charles du Maine, René's nephew, survived his uncle by only a year. Dying without an heir in 1481, he bequeathed the territory of Provence (excluding Savoy, Monaco and the Comtat Venaissin) to portly King Louis XI of France. Not only Provence but Roussillon, Burgundy, Lorraine and parts of northern Italy came under the sway of this fat controller.

After trying strong-arm tactics for the first three years, France decided to allow Provence at least the illusion of independence for the time being, with the Act of Union (1486) granting the region substantial autonomy within the French state. A *parlement* was established at Aix in 1501, but within the region it was supposed to govern there were still several pockets of autonomy – notably Marseille, which stoutly defended its republican traditions. François 1er subdued the city with the fort on the Ile d'If and used the Marseille shipyards in his Italian wars against his arch-enemy, the Holy Roman Emperor Charles V, who replied by besieging the city in 1523. He added similar fortifications on the Ile de Porquerolles and at St-Paul-de-Vence, where the fortifications survive pretty much intact.

But on the ground the dominant issue became that of religious difference. Protestantism had achieved a firm foothold in Provence and eastern Languedoc, especially among the rural poor. Even before Luther, the Waldensian or *Vaudois* sect – whose tweaking of Catholic doctrine was more than enough to have it branded heretical – had put down roots in the South (*see left* **Heresy**) but was brutally put down in 1545.

This, though, was only the opening salvo of the Wars of Religion, which really kicked in

Marseille already one of the finest ports in the land when painted by Joseph Vernet.

when French Calvinism – or Huguenotism – spread throughout France in the 1550s. There were Protestant enclaves in Orange, Haute Provence and the Luberon, but the main seedbed of the new faith was west of the Rhône: in Nîmes, three-quarters of the population became Huguenot. In 1560, a wave of factional violence spread through the region, with atrocities on both sides. Most of the Huguenot population of Orange was massacred in 1563; in reprisal, the notorious Baron des Adrets, who had converted from Catholicism only the year before, went on the rampage; he specialised in throwing Catholic prisoners from the top of the nearest castle (two years later he converted back and retired to the family estate).

> **'Most of the Huguenot population of Orange was massacred in 1563'**

But in general these were less turbulent times: châteaux such as Lourmarin, La Tour d'Aigues and Grignan were designed with an eye to new Renaissance standards of comfort, rather than defence.

Henri IV's Edict of Nantes (1598), guaranteeing Protestants civil and religious liberties, marked the formal end of hostilities. In the South its main effect was to reconfirm the Rhône split – this time as a religious rather than

political frontier. To the east, Provence had demonstrated its essential loyalty to France and the French crown; the French language, too, was becoming more dominant in the region, with Occitan resisting mainly west of the Rhône or in the more remote Alpine valleys. When Louis XIV revoked the Edict of Nantes in 1685, the main effect was to deprive Nîmes and Uzès of their industrious Huguenot manufacturers, who were forced to emigrate in their thousands (though a few stayed on to make silk and the blue linen 'de Nîmes' that English merchants referred to as 'denim').

DICTATORSHIP & ENLIGHTENMENT

By the 17th century, the history of the South had become bound up with the history of France. Of use to Paris mainly as a source of fruit, olive oil, wine, textiles and taxes, and as a builder of ships for royal wars, the Midi was drained of funds and, at the same time, kept firmly in line by an increasingly centralised state. When restless Marseille dared to set up a rebel council in 1658, Louis XIV turned the town's cannons on itself and built an additional fort designed above all to keep an eye on the unruly citizens. The port of Toulon was expanded and turned into the main base of the Mediterranean fleet. Louis XIV's military architect Vauban added his characteristic star-shaped defences in both Toulon and Antibes.

Fine Baroque edifices were also put up – local sculptor and architect Pierre Puget built his masterpiece La Vieille Charité in Marseille, and flamboyant Baroque churches were built at L'Isle-sur-la-Sorgue, Martigues and in Italian-ruled Nice.

Marseille took a further body blow in 1720, when a visiting Syrian ship caused one of the last big outbreaks of plague in the West, which killed 50,000 people in the city alone. A plague wall was built that stretched as far as the Luberon to try and restrict the disease but it spread all the same.

The 18th century was also a time of increasing prosperity, when the South – especially the fertile, mercantile triangle of Provence between Arles, Avignon and Aix –

1930s jet-set photographer **J-H Lartigue** found ideal subjects on the Côte d'Azur, *see p15*.

benefited from being largely left to its own devices. A prosperous bourgeoisie developed around the main industries – textiles around Nîmes, salt at Aigues-Mortes and Hyères, furniture at Beaucaire (site of the most important fair in the South), faïence in Marseille and Moustiers, perfumery and tanning in Grasse. In the 'parliamentary' city of Aix (capital of the *Etats généraux* administrative area of Provence), a wealthy caste of politicians with plenty of time on their hands built themselves sumptuous townhouses and lavish country *bastides*.

REVOLUTIONS & RESTORATIONS

Resentment of distant, uncaring Paris – and royal taxes – continued to simmer, the appetite for change whetted by a couple of bad harvests and rising urban unemployment. When the Revolution broke out in 1789, the South joined in enthusiastically – among its primary movers was the Conte de Mirabeau, elected as *député* of Aix when the Third Estate was finally convened in 1789. The dockers of Marseille were particularly active, taking the Forts of St-Jean and St-Nicolas in an echo of the Bastille – though the battle-hymn of the republic, *La Marseillaise*, was in fact written by Rouget de l'Isle, an Alsatian captain in Strasbourg, and only associated with Marseille when adopted by the city's Jacobin national guard (*les Féderés*) on their march to Paris in July 1792.

Religious foundations and churches became state property and many châteaux were destroyed. A few places had lucky escapes: Toulon cathedral survived as an arms depot, St-Maximin-la-Sainte-Baume was saved by a gutsy rendition of *La Marseillaise* on the organ by Napoléon's brother Lucien. The papal enclave of the Comtat Venaissin was reincorporated into France in 1791 and in 1792 Revolutionary forces took Nice, which was handed back to Italy only in 1814. Anarchy soon set in all over France, with counter-revolutionary uprisings and the White Terror of 1795 setting faction against faction. The British took advantage of the confusion to occupy Toulon in 1793; they were sent packing by artillery commanded by a rising military star, 24-year-old Napoléon Bonaparte.

Though he hailed from Corsica and had served his military apprenticeship in Antibes and Toulon, Bonaparte had little affection for Provence, and the feeling was mutual. His return from exile on Elba and flight north to Paris in 1815 are today commemorated by the Route Napoléon, a scenic drive promoted by local tourist boards. But at the time, this roundabout mountain road via Grasse and Sisteron was chosen as the safest and quickest way out of a potentially hostile area.

FROM RESTORATION TO REPUBLIC

Perhaps the main legacy of the Revolution was a further weakening of regional autonomy with the abolition of the *États généraux* and the carve-up of France into centrally administrated *départements*. But the radical spirit endured, nurtured in the shipyards of Toulon and Marseille, and most of the South threw its weight behind the 1848 Revolution.

At the same time, an ever-present current of Catholic fundamentalism created a reactionary minority that would take different forms, from the revival of the Provençal language and traditions promoted by Frédéric Mistral – author of epic Provençal poem *Mirèio* (Mireille) and one of the seven young poets who founded the Félibrige movement in 1854 – to the proto-Fascist Action Française movement founded in Paris in 1899 by Southerner Charles Maurras. Even the more recent strength of the Front National in the region may partly be explained by this strong Provençal undercurrent in which wounded pride mingles with nostalgia for a mythical purity of language or race.

The last of the major territorial reshuffles took place in 1860, when Napoléon III received Nice and its mountainous hinterland from the House of Savoy in return for his diplomatic neutrality during the unification of Italy. Monaco was now a one-town state, having lost Roquebrune and Menton in 1848 when the inhabitants revolted against the Grimaldis'

Provençal People: the Marquis de Sade

'No kind of sensation is keener and more active than that of pain...' The Marquis de Sade was born in 1740 to Marie-Eléonore de Maille de Carman and the Conte de Sade, lord of the manors of Saumane and Lacoste and co-Lord of Mazan. Entrusted to his paternal uncle for his education, the Marquis spent most of his childhood at Saumane-de-Vaucluse near Fontaine-de-Vaucluse. Here, in a 15th-century castle complete with dungeons and moats, were born the Gothic fantasies of the highly sexed young man.

Sade's outrageous lifestyle began early, with the young soldier dividing his energies between his pursuit of physical pleasure and his army career. 1763 found him engaged to two young ladies simultaneously and, until two weeks before wedding Renée-Pelagie de Montreuil, he was still undecided.

Sade's true nature was quickly revealed and by October the same year he found himself in prison for 'excesses' in a local brothel. This was the start of a long series of very public scandals, which lent his name to sadomasochistic sex for eternity. Sade used the château of Lacoste to hold wild parties that produced a mixture of offence, jealousy and curiosity among local aristocrats.

No doubt history would have forgotten Sade had he not been a great writer too. It was during periods behind bars that he found most time to put pen to paper. Most of his works were considered obscene and unpublishable: *Justine* (1791), *Juliette* (1798), *The 120 Days of Sodom* (written in 1785 but not discovered until 1904), *Aline and Valcour* (1795), *Philosophy in the Boudoir* (1795) and *Crimes of Love* (1800). From 1803 until his death in 1814 Sade was confined to the asylum in Charenton, near Paris, paid for by his by then ex-wife. He became friends with the prison governor, and was allowed to put on 'therapeutic' plays with the patients; was he something of a therapist before his time?

The Marquis' arrogant hedonism can still produce a gasp of incredulity. It was his refusal to repent in the face of universal condemnation that earned him his place among the great antiheroes of history: 'Imperious, choleric, irrascible, extreme in everything, with a dissolute imagination the like of which has never been seen, atheistic to the point of fanaticism, there you have me in a nutshell, and kill me again or take me as I am, for I shall not change.'

exorbitant taxes; after a period as independent republics, the towns were formally transferred to France in 1860. Ironically, it was his principality's increasing isolation and threatened bankruptcy that spurred Charles III to reinvent Monaco as the gambling capital of Europe.

Meanwhile, industrialisation was transforming the region. The opening of the Suez Canal in 1869 and the spread of colonial France quadrupled Marseille's port traffic, and the coastal railway, an engineering feat with its tunnels and viaducts, had reached Nice by 1865, Monaco by 1868. Development of the coast and the Rhône estuary proceeded apace, to the detriment of the mountainous hinterland, which went into a decline not reversed until the modern era of second homes and bijou restaurants.

THE TWENTIETH CENTURY

The early 20th century was the era of the great waterfront hotels, built in response to a surge in tourism: between 1890 and 1910 the number of

How the glamour turned into glitz

Blame it on the weather. The Rivierans have always had it good, with gentle winters and uninhibited sunshine in summer. For a long time this meteorological good fortune was best known to themselves. Its discovery involved more than two centuries and an international cast of aristocrats, politicians, artists and entrepreneurs who used it to cultivate their health, fortunes and suntans.

The South of France's first regular visitors were 18th-century English gentlemen, making it a stop on the knowledge-polishing Grand Tour. Although the milords did not linger, they left behind them the beginnings of the modern hotel, providing comfort *à l'anglaise*. But the real boom was unwittingly started by Tobias Smollett, a Scottish writer and doctor who specialised in complaining. The sickly Smollett grumbled his way around France and Italy, stopped only by the mild winter climate

of Nice, shielded by the Maritime Alps. In 1765 he declared: 'There is less rain and wind at Nice than in any other part of the world that I know.' Smollett noted improvements to his health, but also the charms of narcissi blooming in mid-winter.

For those with money and bad health, a winter sojourn abroad became commonly recommended, even fashionable. Between October and May, Nice and Hyères were filled with delicate Brits and a few Swiss, Russians and Polish. *Les Anglais* carved out their own colony in Nice, an area called La Croix de Marbre, which they simplified to 'Newborough'. The promenade des Anglais was built in 1822 for seaside walks – tourism at this point had yet to reach the beach.

Further down the coast, Lord Brougham, former Lord Chancellor of England, chanced upon the small fishing village of Cannes in

foreigners visiting Nice grew almost sixfold to over 150,000. Amused by these eccentric milords, the French bourgeoisie continued to winter in the country; only in the 1920s did French artists, designers and socialites began to descend on Le Midi in any great number.

World War I was a distant, rain-soaked northern affair, although it took its toll of Provençal conscripts and Fréjus played a curious role as acclimatisation zone for colonial troops. In the 1930s, France saw its first socialist

government under Léon Blum's Front Populaire – and the arrival of paid holidays for all.

World War II did impinge on the South. After the fall of Paris in June 1940, when France was ruled by Maréchal Petain from Vichy, the South was originally part of the *zone libre* or free France, not that this stopped the creation of a number of internment camps for aliens, notably at Les Milles, just outside Aix (*see p154*, **The writing on the wall***)*; Marseille served as an important escape route. From autumn 1942, the South was occupied by German troops. Hardest hit were the strategic naval ports of Marseille and Toulon, ravaged both by Allied bombing raids and by the retreating Germans in 1944. Groups of *maquis*, or resistants, hid out in the hills.

The liberation of Provence by Allied forces based in North Africa came on 15 August, in a two-pronged attack centred on the Var. Airborne troops were parachuted into Le Muy, but most troops landed on the beaches from Toulon to the Estérel, notably at the Plage du Dramont, where 20,000 GIs from the 36th Texan Division landed on the beach in under ten hours, with tanks and heavy artillery, liberating the town the next day.

Post-war reconstruction was responsible for some of the architectural horrors that dog the South; lax or corrupt planning departments did the rest, suffocating the Côte d'Azur in concrete – a combination of the arrival of mass tourism and the urban housing shortage in main towns.

'Corrupt or lax planning departments suffocated the Côte in concrete.'

Heavy industry, too, has done its share of environmental damage, especially west of Marseille where the salt marsh of the Etang de Berre became a huge oil dump. The proud radicalism of the ports was becoming tinged by corruption and by a new kind of reactionary radicalism, reflecting poor white workers' fears of the new immigrants from North Africa who began to pour in after 1945, along with *pieds noirs,* former French colonials from North Africa, but important leftist fiefdoms remained, including Nîmes, long under Communist rule.

It was only in the 1980s – when Mitterrand granted the regions a limited form of autonomy – that the centralising impetus of the previous two centuries began to be reversed. There has been a rediscovery of regional identity and dialects, with school courses in Provençal and the appearance of dual-language street signs, although there is no real separatist movement, and the regional assembly is less to do with regional identity than a degree of economic power.

1834. He liked it enough to knock up a nice villa, and a winter resort for his aristocratic circle was born. Beaulieu and Antibes were also colonised, and the Côte began to balloon with luxury.

The extension of the railway from Marseille to Nice in 1864 spelled irreversible change for the Riviera. Trainloads of rich Americans arrived, along with fresh supplies of English and numerous Russian aristocrats, who added to the architectural jumble of the coast by installing orthodox churches, notably the Cathédrale St-Nicolas in Nice. The Côte d'Azur was prime celebrity-spotting turf; Queen Victoria wintered throughout the 1880s in Nice's grand Cimiez *quartier*.

The Americans were not to be outdone. Juan-les-Pins owes its beach to railroad magnate Frank Jay Gould and socialites Sara and Gerald Murphy (the models for Dick and Nicole Diver in Fitzgerald's *Tender is the Night*) practically invented the bohemian chic holiday. They built Villa America on the Cap d'Antibes, invited all their friends and pioneered horizontal sunbathing. Artists and writers arrived, settling in smaller, quieter havens: Picasso chose Vallauris, Aldous Huxley and Thomas Mann were neighbours in Sanary.

By 1931, all the Côte's hotels opened in summer and the winter season gradually declined. The summer holiday was born. In 1936 the French were given a chance to get in on the act, when they were granted paid vacation under the Front Populaire.

After World War II, the glamour was replaced by Hollywood glitz at the Cannes Film Festival and flashy yachts in the harbours. But, as thousands of tourists agree, it continues to be a great place to catch the sun, provided you can find space on the beach.

The South of France Today

The South is in transition, but along with high-tech modernity has come a return to the values of small-scale production.

If the South of France has a popular hero for today, it is no longer Pagnol's land-greedy peasant, nor Giono's swashbuckling hussard, but Jean-Claude Izzo's middle-aged Marseille cop Fabio Montale: independent, incorruptible, with a passionate love of his city and an enormous appetite for its food. Izzo's is a multicultural city where Montale, son of Italian immigrants, battles against gangsters, racists and corrupt officials in scenarios that go from Le Panier to the Calanques, from luxury villas to tower blocks, all impregnated with the tangy air and the aroma of freshly caught fish.

Curiously Nice and Marseille (respectively, the fifth and second urban agglomerations in France) seem to have exchanged their reputations in recent years. Whereas Marseille was long considered dodgy, a declining industrial power marked by crime, dock strikes and the mob, it is now perceived as one of the most dynamic cities in France and – apart from the ongoing Olympique Marseille/Bernard Tapie saga – relatively scandal free. Marseille is à la mode. Its change of image has accelerated with the arrival of the TGV, but had started earlier with the 1998 football World Cup and a new international export in the form of Zinedine Zidane, and with its 2,600th birthday celebrations, a reminder of the cultural heritage of France's oldest city.

Nice, in comparison, seems to be stagnating. Although it remains a favourite location for high-powered conventions, the city is still tarnished by the memory of late, former mayor

Full-Speed Med

On 10 June 2001, Provence turned into a day-trip from Paris when the TGV Méditerranée, the latest branch of the ever-expanding French high-speed train network, went into service. The new 250km line, which took 11 years and roughly 4 billion euros to build, extends dedicated TGV track from Valence in the Rhône valley south to Avignon, Nîmes, Marseille and Aix-en-Provence. With trains running at 300km an hour, Avignon is now two-and-a-half hours from Paris, and the other three cities three hours from the capital. Not surprisingly, real estate values in Marseille rose a record 18% in 2001, as the new train line effectively redraws the map of France and accelerates the French run for the sun.

A little less than a year after its much-hyped and rather rocky debut (fewer than 75% of trains ran on time during the first six months), the jury's still out on the glamorous-looking but impractical Avignon station (it's oven-like in summer and a bus-ride from the city centre). But on the grander scale there's no doubt that this extraordinary public works project is a huge success. By the end of December 2001 over 11 million passengers had already used the new TGV and rail had replaced air as the main means of transport between Paris and Marseille.

'Aside from being a vital link in the expanding high-speed rail service in France, the real importance of the TGV Méditerranée is that it's changed the way major public works projects will be executed in Europe in the future', says Michel Pronost, director of communication for the SNCF's Grandes Lignes. There were, not surprisingly, fierce protests by environmentalists, farmers and archaeologists when the project was first announced in 1993, but instead of being dismissed in the name of national interests, their concerns were made part of the project.

'It was, of course, a huge challenge to cross Provence, due not only to the beauty of the landscape, but also because so many powerful media people and politicians have homes in Les Alpilles and the Luberon,' says Pronost. Suffice to say that few public works projects in history have ever been subjected to such scrutiny, with the result that this is the first one in France where landscape architects were part of the original team.

The passage of the TGV Méditerranée through Tavel, a region famous for its rosé wines, illustrates how the landscaping

respected local land use patterns. Avignon-based landscape architect Sébastien Giorgis explains, 'We built terraces with dry-stone walls that mimicked the local vineyard terraces, and planted them with trees so that the train would pass through the area almost invisibly.' Bridges and underpasses were built for the movements of wild boar, deer and even toads, and 60m was added to a railway viaduct that crosses the Drôme to protect marshlands important for birdlife.

The project was also bound to have an archaeological dimension. Aside from the remains of the oldest Neolithic village ever discovered, near Lamotte-du-Rhone in the northern Vaucluse, the archaeological finds were not extraordinary, but the fact that 300 archaeologists were recruited to examine an area of 250km^2 in 14 months was.

'Ultimately, 250km of new track isn't in itself enormous, but it will be the catalyst for many other changes,' says Pronost. 'In the years to come, the TGV Med will lead to a cultural, sociological and economic re-alignment of France. Avignon is at the centre of a revived East-West corridor; eventually Barcelona and Marseille will be linked and the high-speed train service will be extended to the big cities of northern Italy. It's a new era for the whole northwestern arc of the Mediterranean littoral.' Studies have already begun for the extension of dedicated TGV tracks to Nice, a project that will surely have a huge future impact on Provence, since the coastal strip where the trains currently run is so crowded that the trace will likely have to go through the rural back country.

Jacques Médecin (who remains curiously loved by a certain breed of niçois) and more recent legal scandal and drug and prostitution rings. An estimated 400 Eastern European prostitutes ply their wares in the Riviera city in a less-than-glamorous return from the East after the Russian aristocrats who helped build Nice's reputation in the 1860s. Behind the private beach concessions along the promenade des Anglais lie spates of car muggings and no-go *cités* (housing estates), following decades when local government embellished the tourist facade of the city and forgot about public housing. After the taint of favouritism and botched planning that hangs over much of the coastline, if the worst of *bétonnage* (concretisation) now seems to be over in favour of more considered development, a question mark still hangs over two key projects in Nice that will be telling for the direction the coast is to take in the 21st century: the Palais de la Méditerranée, once one of the most brilliant art deco casinos on the coast, now due to resurface as a casino/hotel/apartment complex after being shamefully gutted, and the Vieux Port, a testing ground for developers and environmentalists.

Between them, Marseille and Nice show a South in a state of transition but they also give only a very partial picture of a region with startling contrasts. The South remains both a major agricultural producer and an area where industry ranges from the petrochemicals of Fos and Etang de Berre to the high-tech industry and scientific research of Sophia Antipolis. Then there is the Euroméditerranée redevelopment project in Marseille, where the image of striking dockers is being replaced by tertiary sector service industry.

The agricultural fruit basket of France, with its long growing season and huge range of crops, is also evolving as urban sophisticates rediscover lavender, olive oil and the joys of artisanal production. The success of the Occitane group (*see p118*) and the rebirth in artisanal olive oil production is due largely to the foresight, dedication and marketing skills of small producers determined to keep their tradition and community alive. In this changing agricultural world peasant-scale production has had to fight to survive, but José Bové's anti-globalisation Confédération Paysanne and 'small is beautiful' are beginning to be heard after decades of factory farming.

The TGV may have opened up the Rhône corridor but many other parts of the region remain cut off. Behind the conspicuous consumption of Cannes or Monte-Carlo, the landlocked mountainous *département* of the Alpes de Haute-Provence is one of the most sparsely populated in France, where villages struggle to keep their bistro/bar/tobacconist/newsagent/shop alive. In the more trendified areas, like Les Alpilles or the Luberon, there's still a startling contrast between the done-up villages of second homers and those that have been left behind. Even on the coast, excesses of wealth hide an unemployment rate well above the national average (12.9% in 2000 for the region, against 9.6% in France as a whole) and a higher than average population living below the poverty line. As Michelle Casanove, *sous-préfete* in Nice, told French daily *Libération* in October 2001, 'Poverty in the sun isn't better than poverty elsewhere. And the problems seem even greater because next door you have that enormous display of wealth.' For all its advantages, tourism also means imbalance. Once the media circus has left, Cannes reverts to a provincial town with an ageing population, and the thousands of visitors who throng St-Tropez in summer give way to a winter town of just 6,000 inhabitants. A seasonal imbalance is reflected not only in a summer-heavy cultural programme but also seasonal unemployment. It's a situation that may improve: with the TGV and Jospin's 35-hour week giving many French employees longer holidays, it may be that the winter season comes back into vogue.

Art & Modernism in the South

For artists discovering the South, the endless sun and bright colours were enough to drive most of them crazy.

For a crucial period of post-Impressionism and modern art, the South of France became a pivot of the art world, when for the first time what the South could offer coincided with the research going on at the forefront of art's avant garde. Previously, Provençal landscapes had often featured in the background of paintings – but it was only after the painters *en plein air* and the Impressionists that landscapes and the outdoors became acceptable subjects in their own right. The South offered sparkling colours, authentic subject matter, and, no doubt also, the advantages of low rents and an aristocratic and avant-garde clientele.

The Impressionists, however, were more interested in capturing the changing light of northern France and the signs of modern life, with its steam trains, buses and busy boulevards. (Southern summers were considered too hot; when the Impressionists painted beach society it was in Normandy.)

TRUTH VERSUS EMOTION

It took Cézanne, native of Aix-en-Provence, to focus on the southern landscapes themselves, as he alternated stays in Paris and Auvers-sur-Oise with long periods in the South. Cézanne sought the permanent truth behind the landscape, as opposed to the transient impressions of the Impressionists. In 1871, escaping the Franco-Prussian war, he painted the fishing village and the coast at L'Estaque near Marseille, returning frequently in the 1870s and 80s. It was 'red roofs on a blue sea'

Above: **Paul Cézanne** *Farm at Jas de Bouffan.*

that drew him here, until put off by the arrival of 'progress', when first gas and then electric lights were installed along the quays. From the 1880s he turned increasingly to the area around Aix and above all to the unspoilt savagery of Montagne Ste-Victoire (*see p158*), which he painted over and over again, searching for the key to its structure: 'to paint a landscape well; I must first discover its geological characteristics.' Influenced by Poussin's rationalism, Cézanne's ordering of nature on canvas – 'Nature must be treated by the cylinder, the sphere, the cone...' – led towards a new conception of perspective. When painter and critic Emile Bernard visited Cézanne in 1904, 'We didn't go up to the studio. Cézanne picked up a portfolio in the entrance and led me "to the motif"... to the foot of the Ste-Victoire, rugged mountain that he didn't cease to paint in both oil and water and which filled him with admiration.'

Van Gogh arrived in Arles in February 1888 where he painted many of his most celebrated works, staying first in a hotel, then renting a room at the house depicted in *The Bedroom at Arles* and *The Yellow House*. His copious correspondence with beloved brother Theo shows both his bouts of depression and moments of exaltation and excitement at discovering the intense Southern light and landscapes, in letters that describe everything he sees in terms of colours and pigment: sea is ultramarine, the shore violet and russet, infinity 'the richest, intensest blue I can contrive'.

'I have tried to express the terrible passions of humanity by means of red and green.'

Van Gogh found in the blossoming trees and blazing colours a substitute for the Japan he had discovered in Japanese woodcuts, using boiling colours and new vigorous brushstrokes that signified both foreignness and unrest. His rapport with the South was far more visceral than Cézanne's as he sought to understand not structure but the underlying emotion of these burning Provençal landscapes. 'I should not be surprised if the Impressionists soon find fault with my way of working, for it has been fertilised by the ideas of Delacroix rather than by theirs. Because, instead of trying to reproduce exactly what I have before my eyes, I use colour more arbitrarily so as to express myself more forcibly,' he wrote or, later, describing *The Night Café*: 'I have tried to express the terrible passions of humanity by means of red and green'. Van Gogh longed to

found a new artistic school down south and begged Gauguin to join him, although they soon fell out. On 23 December, Van Gogh cut off his ear, and was taken the Hôtel Dieu hospital (now **Espace Van Gogh**, *see p75*).

In May 1889 he had himself admitted to the asylum at St-Rémy de Provence. After a fit when painting at Glanum, he was confined to the hospital and thereafter painted numerous pictures of flowers, such as the famous Irises, views of the asylum garden and colourful, individualised versions of works by Delacroix, Daumier, Rembrandt and Millet.

Van Gogh failed to establish the school he had hoped for but his Arles period influenced Fauvism nonetheless – via the intermediary of Paris, where Matisse and Derain had discovered his works in an exhibition at Galerie Bernheim Jeune in 1901. Using colour for its expressive value, they found authenticity in the fishing boats and village houses of Collioure, on the southwestern coast near the Spanish border, and around Marseille where Derain painted L'Estaque, La Ciotat and Martigues in 1906. Their unnatural use of colour created scandal at the 1905 Salon d'Automne and led to their being dubbed Fauves (savages) by the critic Vauxcelles.

In 1906-08 Braque visited L'Estaque in what proved a crucial transition in his art between his brief Fauve period and Cubism. His first Fauvist paintings of L'Estaque are a rhythm of waves of pink, but in 1907 in Paris, Braque visited Picasso's studio at the Bateau Lavoir and saw *Les Demoiselles d'Avignon*. By 1908 when he again spent the summer in L'Estaque, this time joined by Othon Friesz and Raoul Dufy, his paintings show a new concern with structure, in pictures built up of planes, and a more sober palette dominated by greens and ochres that show the influence of Cézanne.

Further along the coast, keen yachtsman Paul Signac had discovered St-Tropez, then a simple fishing village as early as the 1890s. Attracted by the wildness of the Var coast, accessible largely by sea, his paintings of the port move away from the tiny dots of Seurat's *pointillisme* to larger blocks of colour. Signac stayed, bought a house and in 1904 he was joined by Albert Marquet, Henri Manguin, Henri-Edmond Cross, a fellow disiple of Seurat, and Henri Matisse, whose early canvas *Calme, Luxe et Volupté* is clearly influenced by Signac's divisionism and reveals part of his continuing attempt to resolve the relationship between line and colour.

Renoir also visited the coast from the late 1890s. for medical reasons. Suffering from rheumatism, he was advised by doctors to spend his winters in the south, first at Le Cannet, Villefranche and Antibes, later at Cagnes-sur-Mer. In 1907 he bought the Domaine des Collettes, where he built himself a house and studio (now **Musée Renoir**, *see p228*). Although he painted his late, almost garish *Les Grandes Baigneuses* here, he complained of the sun as too dazzling and concentrated in his last years on sculpture. For Pierre Bonnard the 'affolant' (maddening) southern light accentuated the Nabis tendency of patterns with a chromatic rhythm which broke down the solidity of outlines and perspective. In 1926, he bought a house at Le Cannet, where his large canvases of the garden and intimist interiors of domestic life are marked by the vibrant dematerialisation of form.

BATHERS & ODALISQUES

The inter-war period heralded in a new age of sun worship and a new cult of the body. What had begun as winter resorts became summer ones, and the mode for Le Midi was born. As the avant-garde mixed with the jet set, the Riviera – in constant dialogue with Paris as artists moved between the two – became a place of exchange between artists, writers and photographers, including Man Ray, Paul Eluard, Roland Penrose, Lee Miller, Pablo Picasso, Dora Maar, Robert Capa and Marcel Duchamp, who drew varying inspirations from a coast as yet untramelled by mass tourism: light, Mediterranean culture and the Riviera set's lack of restraint and unconventional behaviour.

Society playboy and photographer Jacques-Henri Lartigue snapped fast cars and the rich at

Van Gogh: *The Park at the St-Paul Hospital.*

play. Picabia was both satirist of jet set society and part of it with his passion for cars (he owned 127) and the extravagant fancy-dress balls that he organised in the Casino at Cannes. In 1925 he designed himself a house at Mougins which he called the Château de Mai, constantly transforming it as he added more terraces, a swimming pool, turrets and an atelier, moving away in his paintings from the machine-like inventions to a dreamy mythology. Giacometti, Picasso, Man Ray, Stravinsky, Poulenc and Buñuel were among those who holed-up at the avant-garde **Villa Noailles** in Hyères (*see p168*) designed by Robert Mallet-Stevens for aristocrats Charles and Marie-Laure de Noailles.

In 1917 Matisse paid his first visit to Nice and from 1919 on spent half the year there, finding here both light and calm, but fed also by Classical and Oriental art and visits to North Africa. Despite his long friendship and frequent contact with Bonnard and Picasso, Matisse essentially remained isolated on the hill of Cimiez from the frivolity going down on the beaches below, developing in his interiors, still lifes and Odalisques his interest in colour and pattern, the breaking down of perspective and the simplification of forms marked in his cut outs and the arabesque line of *La Danse*. The **Chapelle du Rosaire** in Vence (*see p277*) designed by the elderly Matisse when recovering from illness, is in a sense the ultimate expression of his dual conclusions, the simplified line drawings in black on the white tiled walls representing the stations of the cross, the virgin and child and St-Dominic and the purity of colour of the stained glass.

'Picasso was less interested in southern light than in people…'

Picasso was less interested in southern light than in people and his output was ever linked to his life and lovers. As early as the 1910s, he spent summers in the South. Bathers and the human body became a recurrent subject, whether in the South or in his Paris studio, from simple oil sketches on cardboard to the elongated bronze sculptures and tin cut-outs of the 50s. His *Baigneuses regardent un avion*, painted in 1920 at Juan-les-Pins, or his curious sand-covered tableaux-reliefs of the 30s (at much the same time as André Masson's automatic sand paintings produced in Antibes) show his affinities with the Surrealists, in parallel with his classical period. Other works celebrate the Mediterranean and mytholgical themes like Pan, fawns, goats, centaurs and the Minotaur, or the local fishermen. In 1936-38,

Paul Signac *The Cote d'Azur*, 1889.

with new love and model Dora Maar, herself
part of the St-Germain arty set, he spent the
summer in Mougins (a town he returned to in
the 60s with Jacqueline). In 1946, Picasso passed
several months in the Château Grimaldi at
Antibes (*see p220*, **Musée Picasso**), then the
local archaeology museum where he was given
a studio. He later donated many of the drawings
and paintings to Antibes as well as the panels
on the theme *La Joie de Vivre*.

From 1947 Picasso moved to Vallauris, just
outside Cannes, with Françoise Gilot, where he
discovered pottery at the atelier Madoura,
sometimes making over 20 pots in a day. While
here he painted the allegorical panels *La Guerre
et La Paix* for the château's deconsecrated
chapel (*see p218*, **Musée National Picasso**),
but the period was particularly fertile for his
sculpture. Often these works were
'assemblages', making use of whatever found
objects came to hand: *Petite Fille sautant à la
corde* (Little Girl Skipping) of 1950 with a
basket for her body, *Le Chèvre* (Goat) or the *Ape*
whose head is made from a toy car.

During World War II, numerous artists,

many of foreign birth, gravitated south as until
November 1942 this was France Libre. Some,
like Arp, Magnelli and Sonia Delaunay, were
based around Grasse. The Surrealists mostly
went to Marseille, congregating at the house of
young American Varian Fry, who had been sent
by the Emergency Rescue Committee to help
artists and intellectuals leave the country.
While they were waiting for their ticket to
freedom, André Breton, Max Ernst, Victor
Brauner, Wilfredo Lam, Marcel Duchamp, Hans
Bellmer, André Masson, Tristan Tzara and
others devised a card game, *Le Jeu de Marseille*,
and drew *cadavres exquis*, a sort of pictorial
Surrealist version of the game of consequences.

Other artists returned to the South of France
after the war: Cocteau painted the Salle des
Fêtes in the town hall at Menton; Chagall
moved to Vence, encouraged by his dealer Aimé
Maeght; Picasso moved between Cannes,
Mougins and Vauvenargues; the Nouveaux
Réalistes and Support-Surface groups had their
offshoots in Nice, but the focus of art had
shifted across the Atlantic as new concepts and
new media went in search of new subjects.

LA TERRASSE A MOUGINS

RESTAURANT

L'HOTEL DU VILLAGE

Enjoy a simple and authentic stay at L'Hôtel du Village in the heart of Mougins. The two suites and two bedrooms of the Villa Lombarde retain all the charm of this Provençal village, to make a heaven of peace!

La Terrasse à Mougins is a new-style restaurant with its old-style rotisserie and an outstanding view of the bay of Cannes.

**31 boulevard Courteline – 06250 Mougins
Tel: 33 (0)4.92.28.36.20 – Fax: 33 (0)4.92.28.36.21
la-terrasse-a-mougins.com
laterrassemougins@lemel.fr**

Provençal Food & Drink

The South of France is a cornucopia of glorious produce, from the sea to the Alps, herb-covered garrigue to fertile plain.

Seasons and age-old tradition remain at the heart of Provençal cuisine. Long a poor region, thrift is at the heart of its cooking, as in *daube de boeuf*, beef simmered in red wine for hours to make it tender and flavourful; vegetables are prominent and meat is often used sparingly. The less noble parts of the beast are used, too, as in the *pieds et paquets* of Marseille (stuffed tripe cooked in wine and served with sheep's trotters).

The natural goodness of Provence's signature ingredients has made its fame abroad. Garlic purifies the blood and is a universal panacea. Olive oil strengthens the bones, heart and liver. And herbs, in wild and cultivated profusion everywhere, have long been appreciated for their therapeutic qualities. The celebrated Provençal sauces and condiments – *aïoli, pistou, rouille* and *tapenade* – work variations on these basic ingredients. *Anchoïade* or *aïoli* is often a special weekly dish in many cafés: a boat of anchovy sauce or garlic sauce accompanied by a big basket of chopped raw vegetables, perhaps with hard-boiled eggs and potatoes. Thyme, rosemary, bay leaves, lavender and honey find their way as flavourings on everything from lamb or rabbit to crème brûlée.

FAUNA & FLORA

Sheep- and goat-farming from the Alpine foothills and the Crau produce tender free-range meat. The region's game includes rabbits from the garrigue (brush hillsides), hares, wild boar and birds such as snipe, plover and thrush, which find their way into rich stews and *saucissons*. As with anywhere in France, you'll always be able to find a *steak-frites*, but in the

Camargue look out in particular for bull's meat (*taureau*), simply grilled, stewed in hearty *daubes* or in *boeuf à la gardiane*.

Along the coast, Provence has developed a splendid battery of fish and seafood dishes, the most famous of which is *bouillabaisse*. You'll find this celebrated soup all along the coast, though Marseille is its acknowledged home; a group of restaurateurs has even signed a *bouillabaisse* charter to defend the authentic recipe. *Bouillabaisse* is traditionally served in two courses, first the saffron-tinted soup, accompanied by toasted baguette, fiery *rouille* and a sprinkling of gruyère, then the fish. The correct array of fish and shellfish is hotly contested; purists insist on 12, but the three essentials are *rascasse* (scorpion fish), *grondin* (red gurnet) and *congre* (conger eel). Less well-known but equally delicious is *bourride*, a creamy garlic-spiked fish soup made with John Dory, sea bass and monkfish. If you're lucky, you may find *poutargue* (or *boutargue*), a speciality of Martigues, made with grey mullet roe that has been pressed and salted the same way since Phoenician times. Other typical fish preparations include marinated sardines, *loup au fenouil* (sea bass baked with fennel) and red mullet with basil. *Brandade de morue*, salt cod creamed with potato purée, is a speciality of

Fruit fans will have a feast in Provence.

Nîmes. Some of the best meals may consist of just-out-of-the-sea fish grilled on charcoal at a beachside restaurant – pure simplicity.

One of the pleasures of travelling in the South of France is discovering the variety of cuisine from one area to the next. The Italian kitchen had a strong impact in Nice, long part of the kingdom of Genoa. Marseille cuisine goes well beyond *bouillabaisse*; the city boasts a superb selection of ethnic restaurants, reflecting the kaleidoscopic variety of people who've settled there from all over the Mediterranean and its large Italian, Spanish, North African, Greek and Armenian communities. If much Provençal cuisine remains delightfully traditional, you'll also see these influences making their mark on many chefs.

The quality and variety of the vegetables and fruit in Provence is superb, whether they come from fields and orchards along the Durance (irrigated since the 12th century) and Var rivers or tiny coastal gardens, making this part of the world a rare paradise for vegetarians – although specifically vegetarian restaurants and menus are rare. As well as *ratatouille*, other favourites include *poivrade d'artichauts* and courgette flower fritters. There are all manner of stuffed vegetables and baked *tians*, types of gratins named after the earthenware dish in which they are cooked. And what could be simpler – or more delicious – than grilled red peppers, served cold and drizzled with olive oil? In spring, the region produces some of the best asparagus in France, followed by a summer abundance of aubergines, courgettes, tomatoes and artichokes. Autumn brings wild mushrooms, pumpkins and squash, while mesclun, that distinctly Provençal salad of tender mixed leaves and herbs, is available all year round. Winter truffle hunting is a serious affair in the Drôme, Luberon and the Var.

Fruit production includes the delicious orange-fleshed melon de Cavaillon, grown here since being introduced by the Avignon papacy, cherries, apricots and table grapes, and a sumptuous glut of figs in late summer.

Among the most common cheeses are banon, made with ewe's or goat's milk, wrapped in chestnut leaves and aged to a pungent runniness; picodon, small, young, tangy goat's cheese from north Provence; pelardon, similar to picodon, but aged and very firm; and brousse, a soft, mild, fresh cheese used to fill ravioli or eaten drizzled with olive oil or honey.

A whirlwind of local sweets and snacks includes the *calissons* of Aix, *berlingots* of Carpentras and *socca* (chickpea crêpes) of Nice.

Fortunately, Provence's thriving tourist scene has not corrupted its famous open-air markets, where the stands selling scented candles and lavender sachets remain squarely outnumbered

Foodie festivities

Food is a major player in the annual calendar, tracing the harvests throughout the fruit 'n' veg capitals of the south. The lemon is honoured in **Menton** with a citrus sculpture fest, paraded through the town each Sunday during February on gigantic, kitsch, fruity floats based on popular cartoon and fairytale characters (the 2002 theme was Pinocchio). The **Uzès** garlic fair on 24 June, when the village is piled with bulbous, purple cloves and a flame is carried at night from village to village up to Mont Ventoux, has wafted through Provençal history since 1571, when it received its letters patent from Charles IX.

The melon mafia, or rather the 'Brotherhood of the Knights of the Order of the Melons of **Cavaillon**', are solemnly enthroned in July for the Melon Festival in the town where Alexandre Dumas offered 300 copies of his work for an annuity of 12 Cavaillon melons a year. **Arles** welcomes the start of the Camargue rice harvest in September with the **Fêtes des Prémices du Riz**, staging bullfights in the ancient arena, and a grand *corso* – a parade of decorated floats led by the Ambassadrice du Riz on a Camargue pony. The Soup Festival in **Vaison-la-Romaine** will keep you going through October and November. The autumn chestnut harvest in the Maures is celebrated in **Collobrières**, *marrons glacés* capital of France.

Winter truffles are big news. The *Marché aux truffes* at **Rognes** features costumed minstrels, no doubt cheered by the astronomical truffle prices, while in January, St Antoine, patron saint of truffle hunters, is blessed in the church at **Richerenches** in the Drôme, by the Confrérie des Chevaliers du Diamant Noir. In November, the start of the olive oil pressing season is accompanied by costumed *arlésiennes*, *gardians* on horseback and an olive-spitting competition at **Mouriès** in the Vallée des Baux, later holding Huiles-Primeurs in December, when the new oil harvest is baptised.

In January and February, the fishing villages of **Sausset-les-Pins** and **Carry-le-Rousset** on the Côte Bleue – the rocky stretch of coast between Marseille and Martigues – celebrate the prickly sea urchin in the Oursinades, spiny communal feasts on the quayside.

Wine flows freely, especially during the September *récoltes*, with the wine festival in **Cassis** and blessing of the vines. Look out also for opportunities to taste at the Fête de

la Vigne et du Vin in **Châteauneuf-du-Pape** and other prime Côtes du Rhône villages at the end of May/early June (Sunday after Ascension). On the first Sunday in December, the Fête du Millésime is held in the port of **Bandol**. The 52 vintners of the region bring keg-loads of their three-month-old wines for a public tasting, before putting them to bed in wooden casks for 18 months.

The ultimate foodie fest is **Christmas**. For the traditional Christmas Eve, the Provençal table is laden with the *treize desserts* – 13 desserts that symbolise Christ and the 12 apostles, but are in effect a gathering of the region's fruits and sweets. The classic 13 are: the *pompe à l'huile* (a form of sweet biscuit made with olive oil and orange flower water); white nougat; dark nougat; *les quatres mendiants* (the four mendicant orders – hazelnuts for Augustine friars, figs for Franciscans, almonds for Carmelites, raisins for Dominicans); and fresh fruits: dates, oranges, mandarins, apples, pears and grapes. Local specialities, such as *calissons d'Aix*, melon or candied fruits, are often substituted for one element or other.

The best for...

Troglodyte or terrace? Go with the
seasons: **Le Fournil** in Bonnieux. *See p119.*

Gleaming fresh fish: **Poissonnerie Laurent**
on the port at Cassis. *See p160.*

Delicious and design, the latest haunt at
Marseille: **Le Peron**. *See p142.*

Classic, old-fashioned grandeur: **Auberge
La Régalido** at Fontvieille. *See p66.*

Gourmet with a view: Jacques Chibois at
La Bastide St-Antoine, Grasse. See p268.

Provence revisited with imagination: **La
Tonnelle**, Bormes-les-Mimosas. *See p170.*

Great seafood and conviviality: **Maurin des
Maures** at Le Rayol-Canadel. *See p173.*

Ducasse's mountain eyrie: **La Bastide de
Moustiers**, Moustiers-Ste-Marie. *See p205.*

Perhaps the best *bouillabaisse* on the Med:
Miramar, Vieux-Port, Marseille. *See p141.*

A sumptuous vegetarian spread: **La Zucca
Magica**, Nice. *See p240.*

Timeless, luxury fish house: **Bacon**, Cap
d'Antibes. *See p223.*

Young chef with panache: Daniel Hebert at
elegant **La Mirande**, Avignon. *See p93.*

For a fantastic, died-in-the-wool *daube de
boeuf*: **Farigoulette**, Aups. *See p190.*

Grade A people-watching: **Le Farfalla**,
Cannes. *See p210.*

Rustic mountain fare and *truite au bleu*:
L'Auberge Tendasque, Tende. *See p283.*

Bruno's latest truffle offering: **Terres des
Truffes**, Nice. *See p240.*

Unforgettable brasserie ambience: **Les
Deux Garçons**, Aix-en-Provence. *See p155.*

Hip young culinary talent: **Bistrot
d'Eygalières**. *See p66.*

Bistro cooking and a great atmosphere:
La Forge, Ramatuelle. *See p179.*

Chef's annexe, under the wing of Jacques
Maximin: **Mirazur**, Menton. *See p262.*

Herb-packed invention: Edouard Loubet at
Le Moulin de Lourmarin. *See p120.*

Breathtaking, spot-on, home-cooked
simplicity: **Casa Bella**, Nîmes. *See p54.*

by farmers touting goat's cheeses, stout ladies
selling tightly bound bunches of fresh herbs,
and table after table of perfectly ripened
tomatoes and glossy aubergines. You'll also
find stalls specialising in olives, dried fruit and
nuts, jam and honey, cured meat and sausages.
In larger towns, there are daily markets; in
smaller towns and villages they're often once or
twice a week, usually in the morning. A growing
trend is for farmers' markets, sometimes in the
evening, where you buy direct from the producer.

Organic (*biologique*) produce is also
burgeoning. At Correns in the Green Var, 95% of
the wines and farm-produce are now grown
organically, while the Luberon has a successful
scheme, *Le Luberon a bon goût*, in which
participating restaurants produce one *prix-fixe*
menu based on organic ingredients.

WINE & SPIRITS

Some of the most glorious of all French wines
come from the South of France, and the quality
of the region's wines, from the Rhône Valley to
the Italian border, has improved dramatically
over the past few years.

The Rhône Valley produces superb reds, and
you'll rarely go wrong with the Côtes du Rhône
appellations. Châteauneuf-du-Pape, a complex
blend of at least eight different *cépages* (grape
varieties), is perhaps the most famous, but other
potentially excellent full-bodied reds from the
region include Gigondas, Rasteau and Cairanne.
Lesser known, but a real treat, is white
Châteauneuf-du-Pape, which goes beautifully
with fish and shellfish, while Beaumes-de-Venise
is famed for its sweet white dessert wine. North
of Avignon, Tavel is one of the best rosés in the
world. Many lists include Costières de Nîmes,
Côtes du Luberon and Côtes de Ventoux, known
as easy-drinking, inexpensive reds, but with
some up-and-coming young producers in each
area who are doing much to improve quality.

Further south, 13 traditional grape varieties
are grown in the Provence area, including rolle,
clairette and sémillon (white) and syrah,
grenache, mourvèdre, carignan and cabernet
sauvignon (red). *Appellations* to look for are
Coteaux d'Aix, Côtes de Provence, Cassis
(known for crisp white wine that goes well with
seafood), Bandol, dominated by mourvèdre, and
the small Bellet area round Nice. The biggest
area is taken up by Côtes de Provence which
covers much of the Var from Cap Benat and St-
Tropez to around Draguignan and Les Arcs and
produces 70% rosé wines.

Wine-tasting at source can be one of the
delights of a Provençal holiday, though cellar-
door prices are often not a great deal cheaper
than their high-street equivalents. With the
exception of a few big-name producers, who

Bandol is just one among many Provençal *appellations* to sample during your wine-tastings.

may offer cellar tours and *son et lumière* frills in addition to the tasting, it is worth ringing ahead to confirm opening days and times, and – if you are interested in a particular vintage – availability, as limited-edition *crus* often sell out weeks after bottling. In many areas the cooperative tradition remains strong, where small individual cultivators bring their grapes to the central village *cave* for production.

The best areas for wine-touring in the South are the Châteauneuf-du-Pape enclave on the eastern bank of the Rhône (*see chapter* **Orange & Around**), the coastal Bandol *appellation* (*see chapter* **Cassis to Toulon**) and the heartland of the Côtes de Provence *appellation* around Les Arcs (*see chapter* **The Var Heartland**).

RESTAURANT LORE

The South of France is heaven for the restaurant junkie, offering meals to suit all levels and moods, from celebrated haute cuisine temples and showbiz *spectacles* via picturesque village bistros to the inimitable village bar-cum-*tabac*-cum-café-cum-restaurant where all sorts pile in for a *pastis*, gossip and, often, a surprisingly good *menu du jour*.

At the grandest establishments with famous chefs, you'll eat sublime food and pay sublimely ridiculous prices. And tune in to the international babble on the other tables, since the locals patronise these places only on special occasions, or for lunch, when many renowned kitchens offer relatively affordable lunch

menus. The French themselves are more likely to seek out good-value local establishments, where there may be less silverware on the table and only one waiter or waitress, but the home-cooking can still be spot on.

The southern restaurant scene is not standing still. If many restaurants delight in died-in-the-wool Provence, with print cloths and the comforting reassurance of age-old *daubes* and *tians* or dead-simple, classic fresh fish, there is also a host of good-value restaurants that are renewing southern cuisine in creative use of regional produce. On the one hand there's a whole legion of rising young chefs going out on their own; on the other the trend of super-chefs opening bistro annexes and rural retreats continues. After Alain Ducasse, whose southern antennae take in Monte-Carlo, Moustiers and La Celle, or Bruno Clément with his new truffle restaurant-cum-deli in Nice, St-Tropez celeb chef Christophe Leroy has taken over restaurants in Ramatuelle and Mougins, while the Pourcel twins of Montpellier have opened a new outlet in Avignon.

Restaurants are generally relaxed. Although you shouldn't come to the table in a bathing suit unless you're right on the beach, ties are rarely required and T-shirts and shorts are just fine, although note that grand haute cuisine establishments, even in a tiny country village, can be as dressy, if not more so, as Paris. Children are almost always welcome.

By law, the menu must be posted outside the

Provençal menu lexicon

Agneau lamb. **aiglefin** haddock. **ail** garlic. **aïoli** garlic mayonnaise. **airelle** cranberry. **allouettes sans têtes** literally headless skylarks, actually small stuffed veal parcels. **amande** almond; **– de mer** small clam. **ananas** pineapple. **anchoïade** anchovy and olive sauce, served with raw vegetables. **anchois** anchovy. **andouillette** sausage made from pig's offal. **anguille** eel. **artichauts à la barigoule** small purple artichokes braised in white wine. **anis** aniseed. **asperge** asparagus. **aubergine** aubergine (GB); eggplant (US).

Bar sea bass. **barbue** brill. **baudroie** coastal monkfish. **bavarois** moulded cream dessert. **bavette** beef flank steak. **béarnaise** sauce of butter and egg yolk. **beignet** fritter or doughnut; **– de fleur de courgette** courgette flower fritters. **belon** smooth, flat oyster. **betterave** beetroot. **biche** venison. **bifteak** steak. **bisque** shellfish soup. **blanc** white; **– de poulet** breast. **blanquette** 'white' stew made with eggs and cream. **blette** swiss chard; **tourte de –** swiss chard pie with pine nuts and raisins. **boudin noir/ blanc** black (blood)/ white pudding. **boeuf** beef; **– à la gardiane** (Camargue) bulls' beef stewed with carrots and celery; **– gros sel** boiled beef with vegetables. **bouillabaisse** (Marseille) Provençal fish soup. **bourride** thick *bouillabaisse*-like fish soup, without shellfish. **brandade de morue** (Nîmes) purée of salt cod, potatoes, cream, garlic and olive oil. **brébis** ewe's milk cheese. **brousse** soft, mild white cheese. **bulot** whelk.

Cabillaud fresh cod. **caille** quail. **caillette** pork terrine with herbs and spinach or chard cooked in caul. **calmar** squid. **calisson d'Aix** (Aix-en-Provence) diamond-shaped sweet of almonds, sugar and preserved fruit. **canard** duck. **cannelle** cinnamon. **cardon** cardoon (edible thistle). **câpre** caper. **carrelet** plaice. **cassis** blackcurrants, also blackcurrant liqueur. **cassoulet** stew of haricot beans, sausage and preserved duck. **catégau d'anguilles** (Camargue) eels cooked with red wine and garlic. **céleri** celery; **– rave** celeriac. **cèpe** cep mushroom. **cerise** cherry. **cervelle** brains. **champignon** mushroom. **charlotte** moulded cream dessert with biscuit edge. **châtaigne** chestnut. **chateaubriand** thick fillet steak. **cheval** horse. **à cheval** with an egg on top. **chèvre** goat's cheese. **chevreuil** young roe deer. **chichis** (Nice) deep-fried dough sticks. **chou** cabbage. **choucroute** sauerkraut, usually served *garnie* with cured ham and sausages. **chou-fleur** cauliflower. **ciboulette**

chive. **citron** lemon. **– vert** lime. **citronelle** lemongrass. **civet** game stew. **clafoutis** baked batter tart filled with fruit, usually cherries. **cochon de lait** suckling pig. **coco** large white bean. **colin** hake. **confit de canard** preserved duck. **congre** conger eel. **contre-filet** sirloin steak. **coquille** shell; **– st-jacques** scallop. **côte** chop; **– de boeuf** beef rib. **crème chantilly** whipped cream. **crème fraîche** thick, slightly soured cream. **cresson** watercress. **crevette** prawn (GB), shrimp (US). **croquante** crunchy; **– de Nîmes** (Nîmes) hard nut biscuit. **croque-monsieur** toasted cheese and ham sandwich. **en croûte** in a pastry case. **cru** raw. **crudités** assorted raw vegetables. **crustacé** shellfish.

Daube meat (beef or lamb) braised slowly in red wine with lardons, onions, garlic and herbs. **daurade** sea bream. **désossé** boned. **dinde** turkey.

Echalote shallot. **écrevisse** freshwater crayfish. **endive** chicory (GB), Belgian endive (US). **entrecôte** beef rib steak. **entremêts** milk-based dessert. **épeautre** wild barley. **épices** spices. **épinards** spinach. **escabèche** sautéed, marinated fish, served cold. **escargot** snail. **espadon** swordfish. **estocafinado** (Nice) salt cod stewed with garlic and tomato. **estouffade** meat, usually beef, braised with carrots, onions, garlic and orange zest.

Faisan pheasant. **farci** stuffed. **fenouil** fennel. **faux-filet** sirloin steak. **feuilleté** 'leaves' of (puff) pastry. **fève** broad bean (UK), fava bean (US). **filet mignon** tenderloin. **fines de claire** crinkle-shelled oysters. **flageolet** small green kidney bean. **flambé** flamed in alcohol. **flétan** halibut. **foie** liver; **foie gras** fattened goose or duck liver. **forestière** with mushrooms. **fougasse** flat bread made with olive oil, flavoured with lardons or olives, also sweet versions. **au four** baked. **fraise** strawberry. **framboise** raspberry. **fricassé** fried and simmered in stock, with creamy sauce. **frisée** curly endive. **fromage** cheese; **– blanc** smooth cream cheese. **fruit** fruit. **fruits de mer** shellfish. **fruits rouge** red summer berries.

Galette flat flaky pastry cake, potato pancake or buckwheat savoury *crêpe*. **galinette** tub gurnard fish. **garni(e)** garnished. **gelée** aspic. **gésiers** gizzards. **gibier** game. **gigot d'agneau** leg of lamb. **gingembre** ginger. **girolle** chanterelle mushroom. **glace** ice cream. **glacé(e)** frozen or iced. **goujon** breaded, fried strip of fish; also small catfish.

gras fat. **gratin dauphinois** sliced potatoes baked with milk, cheese and garlic. **grenouille** frog; **cuisses de – ** frogs' legs. **grondin** red gurnet. **groseille** redcurrant; **à maquereau** gooseberry.

Haché minced. **hachis Parmentier** shepherd's pie. **hareng** herring. **haricot** bean; **– vert** green bean. **homard** lobster. **huile** oil. **huître** oyster.

Ile flottante whipped egg white floating in vanilla custard.

Jambon ham; **– cru** cured raw ham. **jarret de porc** ham shin or knuckle. **joue** cheek.

Langouste spiny lobster. **langoustine** Dublin bay prawn/scampi. **langue** tongue. **lapin** rabbit; **– à la provençale** rabbit in white wine with tomato and mustard. **lard** bacon. **lardon** small cube of bacon. **laurier** bay leaf. **légume** vegetable. **lentilles** lentils. **lieu** pollock. **lièvre** hare. **limande** lemon sole. **lisette** small mackerel. **loup** sea bass. **lotte** monkfish.

Mâche lamb's lettuce. **magret** duck breast. **maquereau** mackerel. **marcassin** wild boar. **mariné** marinated. **marmite** small cooking pot. **marquise** mousse-like cake. **marron** chestnut. **merguez** spicy lamb/ beef sausage. **merlan** whiting. **merlu** hake. **mesclun** salad of tiny leaves and herbs. **miel** honey. **mirabelle** tiny yellow plum. **moelle** bone marrow; **os à la –** marrow bone. **morille** morel mushroom. **moules** mussels. **morue** dried, salted cod. **mulet** grey mullet. **mûre** blackberry. **muscade** nutmeg. **myrtille** bilberry (UK), blueberry (US).

Navarin lamb and vegetable stew. **navet** turnip. **noisette** hazelnut; small round portion of meat. **noix** walnut; **– de coco** coconut. **nouilles** noodles.

Oeuf egg; **– en cocotte** baked egg; **– en meurette** egg poached in red wine; **– à la neige** see *Ile flottante*. **oie** goose. **oignon** onion. **onglet** cut of beef, similar to *bavette*. **oseille** sorrel. **oursin** sea urchin.

Pageot pandora, similar to sea bream. **pain** bread; **– perdu** French toast. **palombe** wood pigeon. **palourde** type of clam. **pamplemousse** grapefruit. **pan bagnat** (Nice) bread roll filled with tuna, tomatoes, onions, egg, olive oil. **panais** parsnip. **en papillote** cooked in a packet. **pastèque** water melon. **pâte** pastry. **pâtes** pasta. **paupiette** slice of meat or fish, stuffed and rolled. **pavé** thick steak. **pêche** peach. **perdrix** partridge. **persil** parsley. **petits farcis or farcis niçois** (Nice)

vegetables stuffed with meat or mushrooms and herbs. **petits pois** peas. **petit salé** salt pork. **pied** foot (trotter). **pieds et paquets** (Marseille) stew of stuffed tripe and sheep's feet. **pignon** pine kernel. **piment** hot pepper or chilli. **pintade** guinea fowl. **pissaladière** pizza-like onion and anchovy tart. **pistou** pesto-like basil and garlic sauce served with vegetable soup. **pleurotte** oyster mushroom. **poire** pear. **poireau** leek. **pois chiche** chickpea. **poisson** fish. **poivre** pepper. **poivron** red or green (bell) pepper. **pomme** apple. **pomme de terre** potato. **porc** pork. **potage** soup. **potiron** pumpkin. **poulet** chicken. **poulpe** octopus. **poutargue** (Martigues) preserved grey mullet roe. **pressé** squeezed. **prune** plum. **pruneau** prune.

Quenelle light, poached fish dumpling. **quetsche** damson. **queue de boeuf** oxtail.

Rabasse truffle. **raie** skate. **raisin** grape; **– sec** raisin. **rascasse** scorpion fish. **ratatouille** Provençal stew of onion, aubergine, courgette, tomato and peppers. **réglisse** liquorice. **reine-claude** greengage plum. **ris de veau** veal sweetbreads. **riz** rice. **rognon** kidney. **romarin** rosemary. **roquette** rocket. **rouget** red mullet. **rouille** spicy red pepper, garlic and olive oil sauce, served with *bouillabaisse*.

Sablé shortbread biscuit. **St Pierre** John Dory. **salade niçoise** (Nice) salad of tuna, lettuce, green beans, egg and anchovies. **salé** salted. **sandre** pike-perch. **sanglier** wild boar. **saucisse** sausage. **saucisson** small dried sausage. **saumon** salmon. **seiche** squid. **socca** (Nice) thin pancake made with chickpea flour. **souris d'agneau** lamb knuckle. **stockfisch** dried cod. **supion** small squid.

Tapenade Provençal olive and caper paste. **tartare** raw minced steak (also tuna or salmon). **tarte Tatin** caramelised apple tart cooked upside-down and served warm. **taureau** (Camargue) bull's meat. **tête de veau** calf's head jelly. **thon** tuna. **thym** thyme. **tian** vegetable gratin baked in an earthenware *tian*. **topinambour** Jerusalem artichoke. **tourte** covered pie or tart, usually savoury. **travers de porc** pork spare ribs. **tripoux** dish of sheep's tripe and feet. **tropézienne** (St-Tropez) sponge cake filled with custard cream. **truffe** truffle. **truite** trout.

Vacherin dessert of meringue, cream, fruit and ice cream; a soft, cow's milk cheese. **veau** veal. **velouté** stock-based white sauce; creamy soup. **venaison** venison. **viande** meat. **violet** sea potato. **volaille** poultry.

restaurant. Depending on the establishment, there is usually a choice of one or more *menus prix-fixe*: ranging from a basic, inexpensive, two- or three-course *formule*, with a limited choice, that may sometimes include wine, via the classic *entrée*, *plat*, cheese and dessert, to the *menu dégustation*, an extravagant multiple-course gastronomic splurge of the chef's party pieces. The *menu-carte* is an increasingly popular formula, with all *entrées*, *plats*, *desserts* at the same price. Note that bread is always included and that French tap water is perfectly drinkable – it's perfectly acceptable to ask for a *carafe d'eau* if you don't want to buy mineral water. By French law, service is included in the price of a meal: it's customary, however, to leave some change, up to around 5% of the bill.

We list *menus prix-fixe* prices rather than average *à la carte* prices, as the former are a pretty accurate indication of the latter – though in the gourmet temples, a meal *à la carte* may cost significantly more than the priciest menu.

You could invade France at noon, when nothing can distract the nation's attention from lunch. Most restaurants serve until around 2pm. Dinner service usually runs from 7.30pm to 10.30pm, when the last orders are taken. When you book the table it's generally yours for the evening, as there is rarely more than one sitting. If you've missed lunch, you can usually get a salad or a sandwich in a café, while brasseries in larger towns are good bets for a late meal, often serving until midnight or later.

For most upmarket places, reservations are recommended; some top restaurants ask clients to reconfirm on the day, as they invariably have a waiting list. Even in simpler bistros, especially during the peak summer season, it's always worth ringing ahead to reserve a table, even if only for the same evening.

Pastis goes ladylike

Pastis – the very word conjures up images straight out of a Marcel Pagnol film... elderly *paysans* clinking glasses on the *terrasse* of their local café after a hard game of *boules*, or tatooed Marseille dockers standing round a zinc bar, as they knock back a glass – or two, or three – of the stuff. This aniseed- and herb-flavoured apéritif is the traditional tipple of the south and its macho image has remained unchallenged for generations. But in the new millennium, even *pastis* is being forced to move with the times.

In November 2001, the world's biggest *pastis* producer, Marseille-based firm Ricard, did the unthinkable by introducing ready-mixed *pastis* in cans. Each can contains the official proportion of one volume of *pastis* to five of water (a ratio which goes largely unrespected in the cafés and bars of the south where one to four or one to three is more often the norm). Hardened aficionados agree that one of the main pleasures of *pastis* is the ritual that accompanies it – the adding of water to the glass of clear yellow liquor which turns the drink cloudy.

Now, as if canned *pastis* were not shocking enough, a controversial new version of the apéritif is rapidly becoming the latest hip tipple in trendy Mediterranean cafés. Pastis Bleu (literally, blue *pastis*) is the proud creation of Etablissements Germain, a small factory at St-Florent-sur-Auzonnet near Nîmes which has been producing *pastis* since 1881. The idea was born when the four-year-old son of one of the directors asked his father if he could have blue grenadine drinks at his birthday party. Much to his son's delight, Philippe Pot granted his wish by adding blue food colouring to colourless syrup, before going on to experiment with *pastis*. He then took the bright-blue prototype into a local bar, where the crowd could hardly believe their eyes. The idea was adopted as a marketing project by one of France's top business management schools and Etablissements Germain went into production. Le Pastis Bleu comes in an elegant engraved bottle and enjoys particular success among women and young people. 'For ladies, it has the added advantage that if they are seen sitting outside a cafe with a glass of blue *pastis*, no one can tell what they are drinking. *Pastis* is a bit macho, it's a bloke's drink. There are women who like it, but is not considered a very ladylike thing to order,' said factory director Jean Hegy. Some drinkers, apparently reminded of mouthwash, swear the blue *pastis* has a minty aftertaste, while others say it is sweeter or that it has a more pronounced aniseed flavour. Rumours are also circulating that it gets you drunk faster than the original. 'In fact, it has exactly the same taste as the traditional version, only the colour has changed,' confided Hegy. At 45 degrees proof, it also shares the power of the original to leave drinkers who over-indulge under the strong Midi sun with a memorable hangover.

Arts & Entertainment

From installation art to opera to video-infused dance: where to find the South's creative juices in action.

The Southern arts calendar – Avignon, Aix, Orange, Cannes, Juan-les-Pins... – offers an endless parade of international performers and more festivals than you can fit into a lifetime. All that southern sun and all those millions of visitors, a potentially captiv(ated) audience. What could be wrong with that? Well, it means a summer-heavy cultural scene and a season that, outside the principal metropolises of Aix, Marseille, Toulon, Nice and Monte-Carlo, can be disappointingly limited the rest of the year. Creation there is, but you have to look for it. For more on annual festivals, *see p41.*

CONTEMPORARY ART

The South of France is associated above all with the Modern Movement in art, from forefathers like Cézanne to Modernist icons like Picasso (*see chapter* **Art & Modernism in the South**). But contemporary artists down South don't let this weighty legacy get to them; the Provence-Alpes-Côte d'Azur region today has a thriving and highly international art scene, with a large number of institutions from museums and private galleries to artist-run associations and studio schemes. While every *village perché* seems to have its dabbling daubers and pottering potters, the main art hubs are Marseille and to a lesser extent Nice. In Avignon, the opening of the **Collection Lambert** in 2000 has at last given it a contemporary art collection on a par with its historical treasures, putting on summer theme

Above: Jean-Christophe Maillot has got **Les Ballets de Monte-Carlo** moving.

exhibitions (contemporary photography-based art for 2002), and a rotating selection from the collection, the rest of the year.

Several young artists from the region have recently emerged at the forefront of the current French scene, including Gilles Barbier, whose work treats technology and genetics, Stéphane Magnin, whose paintings using industrial materials embrace and reflect techno culture, or the complex actions and soundpieces of Francesco Finizio.

Beyond the contemporary art museums in Nice and Marseille, the principal body in the region is the **Frac Paca** (Fonds Régional d'Art Contemporain Provence-Alpes-Côte d'Azur), which runs an extremely active programme of exhibitions in its gallery in Le Panier district of Marseille as well as in museums, châteaux and schools across the region; it also develops external projects with young local artists. Marseille's contemporary art museum, the **MAC**, in a hangar-like space on the eastern hills, has a wide-ranging international collection that includes Rauschenberg, César, Roth, Balkenhol, Absalon and Laffont, and varied exhibitions.

But the South's most dynamic city also has several artist-run associations. The first stopping-off point for those keen to catch up on the more alternative scene has to be **La Friche la Belle de Mai**, a disused industrial complex up in the scruffy Belle de Mai quarter west of the centre. First an artists' squat, now home to numerous artistic, musical and theatrical groups, its gallery is used for exhibitions put on by its resident artists and associations, often installation-based projects in varied media. The commercial gallery that has long set the agenda with its international roster of artists is the **Galerie Roger Pailhas**.

In the 1960s, Nice was a satellite of the Nouveaux Réalistes, the French version of Pop Art – leading members Yves Klein, Martial Raysse and Arman were all based in the Riviera city – as well as Neopolitan Fluxus *emigré* Ben (*see p239*). In the 1970s, the Support-Surface group also had its Nice outpost with Viallat, Pagès and Toni Grand. Both movements feature strongly in the collection of the city's **Musée d'Art Moderne et d'Art Contemporain**, which also stages temporary exhibitions. **Villa Arson** has a more adventurous conceptual bent, with exhibitions that reflect the latest international trends, and an art school and programme of residencies for both artists and critics on the premises. Nice also has its own contemporary art fair, **Art Jonction**, originally run by, but now separate from, the art magazine of the same name. One other essential Nice address for contemporary art buffs is the **Hôtel Windsor**, where owner Bernard Redolfi-

Strizzoli has taken art out of the museum and given contemporary artists, including Ben, Jean Le Gac, Gottfried Honegger, Lawrence Weiner and Glen Baxter, the freedom to decorate a bedroom as they wish.

In Nîmes, the **Musée d'Art Contemporain** in the minimalist high-tech glass Carré d'Art designed by Norman Foster, has a permanent collection that is strong on New Realism, Support-Surface, *figuration libre* and Italian Arte Povera. Arles becomes a centre of pilgrimage for creative photographers each summer during the **Rencontres Internationales de la Photographie**.

As so often in France, funding comes from an enormous number of public sources, from national to local level, and many regional arts boards have their own galleries, such as the **Hôtel des Arts** in Toulon, while the stunning **Villa Noailles** in Hyères is used for everything from the spring fashion and summer electronic music festivals to a show of funky Dutch designers Droog Design. There is some action outside the major towns, too. The **Musée Picasso** in Antibes alternates classic modern art with contemporary exhibitions, as does the **Hôtel Donadeï de Campredon** in L'Isle-sur-la-Sorgue and **Le Crestet Centre d'Art**.

The modern masterpieces at the **Fondation Maeght** in St-Paul-de-Vence have inspired an army of private art galleries of varying quality, but **Galerie Catherine Issert** is well worth a visit, as is the **Galerie Beaubourg** in Vence, which moved south from Paris in the 1990s and has a chapel by Tinguely and a permanent sculpture garden. In Mouans-Sartoux, north-west of Cannes, the **Espace de l'Art Concret** centres on a core collection of geometrical abstraction and minimalism (Albers, Honegger, Bill, Twombly, Judd, etc) donated by Swiss painter Gottfried Honegger and the widow of artist Josef Albers. Its three themed exhibitions a year make imaginative links between historic greats and young artists or new media.

DANCE

It was the pioneer of modern movement, **Isadora Duncan**, who started the French Riviera dance trend in the early years of the 20th century. In her celebrated performance studio on the promenade des Anglais in Nice and extravagent happenings at the Hôtel Negresco, she created works with Jean Cocteau and other avant-garde artists.

After Duncan's death in 1927, **Les Ballets de Monte-Carlo** (successors to the legendary Ballets russes, founded by Diaghilev in 1909) continued the tradition, helped by princely subsidies. Today, the talented **Jean-Christophe Maillot** has rejuvenated the

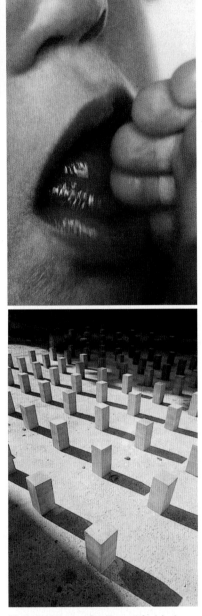

company, creating new works, inviting choreographers like Lucinda Childs and reviving historic productions, notably by Balanchine. The Ballets also organises the **Nuits de la Danse** in summer, and the new **Monaco Dance Forum** in December, with a mix of prestigious established companies and opportunities for new talents – the 2002 edition will focus on the relationship between dance and multimedia.

Some of France's most acclaimed contemporary dancemakers are now based in the South of France. For year-round dance, the most active scene is Marseille. Former Paris ballet star **Marie-Claude Pietragalla** has created a new repertoire at the Ballet National de Marseille. Marseille-born dancer-choreographer **Georges Appaix** and his Compagnie La Liseuse are based in the Friche la Belle de Mai. Appaix typically combines dance with text and video, and many of his works since 1985 have been working through the letters of the alphabet. Another rising contemporary star, **Michel Kelemakis**, is also Marseille-based. **Angelin Preljocaj**, the choreographer who best bridges the divide between classical ballet and contemporary dance, is based at the Centre Chorégraphique National in Aix-en-Provence (currently in the Cité du Livre, but due to move into its own high-tech building next door in 2003); he has also choreographed works for the national ballet in Paris. For new creation, also look at what's on at the **CNCDC Chateauvallon** at Ollioules, near Toulon. Preljocaj used to be here, before Toulon's council went temporarily Front National, but now a new team is in place putting on a rigorously multi-cultural Mediterranean-wide programme of contemporary dance, theatre, music and circus arts.

The highest-profile dance activity is associated with annual festivals. Dance shared the limelight with theatre at the 2001 **Festival d'Avignon** (Bill T Jones, Josef Nadj and Angelin Preljocaj). The particularity of **Les Hivernales** in Avignon in February (there's also a smaller version in summer) is its mix of performances and workshops, mainly with small but promising regionally subsidised companies. Though it is just outside the area covered by this guide, the **Montpellier Danse** festival (in June-July, 04.67.60.83.60) is one of the pillars of the dance scene in the South. The 2002 edition features Jérôme Bel, Preljocaj and the Ballet de Lorraine. **Danse à Aix**, in July-Aug, is smaller but high quality, and companies rarely overlap between the two events. Every other autumn, the **Festival International de danse de Cannes**, in the Palais des Festivals, features ballet-oriented international troupes.

Works by Douglas Gordon and Carl Andre at Avignon's **Collection Lambert**. *See p33.*

FILM

The seaboard from Marseille to Monaco – and the lavender-covered *arrière-pays* behind – is a location scout's heaven. *The French Connection* was made here, as was Luc Besson's *Taxi*. Robert Guédigian has made L'Estaque his own (*see p136*), a thousand interior design trends were launched by *Jean de Florette* and *Manon des sources*. Roger Vadim created BB and the Côte at St-Tropez, and James Bond – in his best Sean Connery incarnation – made the obligatory casino stopover in *Never Say Never Again* (for more southern films, *see p310*, **Further Reference**).

But what if you're on the audience side of the screen? Cannes Film Festival (*see p41*) lets few mere mortals up *les marches*, but France remains a passionately cinephile country and there are plenty of cinemas in all the main cities, as well as a few specialist festivals open to *tout le monde* – from deep-sea diving films at Antibes to short films at Gardanne. For art film programming and interesting retrospectives check out what's on at the **Cinémathèque de Nice**, **L'Utopia** in Avignon, the **Cité du Livre** in Aix and **Actes Sud** in Arles. For lighter fare, many seaside towns programme outdoor screenings in July and August.

MUSIC: CLASSICAL & OPERA

Classical music in the South of France benefited greatly from Mitterrand's policy of decentralisation, and both orchestras and festivals can count on a level of subsidy that most European musical directors would give their batons for. Despite this, orchestral standards can be variable. But the major opera houses make up for any shortfall: casts and stagings often rival the Bastille or the Garnier in Paris. In the best Mediterranean tradition, they tend to be at the centre of the city's music scene, and also the best places to collect information about local one-off concerts.

The region's leading temples of opera, all with full seasons, are **Opéra de Marseille**, with its vociferous Italophile public, **Opéra de Nice**, **Opéra d'Avignon**, **Opéra de Toulon** and **Opéra de Monte-Carlo**. Monte-Carlo's Palais Garnier (currently closed for restoration, with most performances now in Grimaldi Forum) is a shimmering jewel of a venue, and the principality also boasts the best orchestra in the South, the **Orchestre Philharmonique de Monte-Carlo**. The other orchestras of the region, including the 120-strong **Orchestre Philharmonique de Nice** are kept fairly busy in the opera pit, and their symphonic success is very much dependent on the quality of the visiting maestri; don't, in any case, expect the Vienna Philharmonic.

Summer festivals continue to crop up everywhere. Sometimes these are just simple marketing exercises: two or three concerts in a pretty *village perché* become the excuse for an 'International Arts Festival', without the funding or organisation to make it work. But many young and promising European musicians are to be found in chamber music events across the region; often the backdrop – whether natural or architectural – itself justifies the price of the ticket. What is disappointing for the residents of the region and for out of season tourists is that year-round culture is essentially limited to the resident opera companies, with only Menton making an effort to produce a winter musical season. Of the established major festivals, the **Festival International d'Art Lyrique** in Aix-en-Provence in July features operas, orchestral concerts and recitals by top international artists; recently, Early Music has become something of a speciality. The

The best Suite music

Mireille

Gounod's 1864 opera finds the heroine struggling across the Crau heading to Saintes-Maries-de-la-Mer. Essential listening for weary Camargue travellers.

La Dame de Monte-Carlo

Francis Poulenc's dramatic, suicidal soprano monologue with a text by Cocteau is a useful warning on the downside of the gambling paradise.

L'Arlésienne Suite

Bizet's incidental music for Alphonse Daudet's 1872 play has since become almost the official Provençal work.

La Marseillaise

The result of a lively dinner in Strasbourg in 1792, when Joseph Rouget de Lisle, a military officer, improvised a song on a tune by Lucien Grisons, using the text from a military poster. Only when the *fédérés marseillais* entered Paris in 1792 did it become known as the Marseillaise, becoming the *chant national* in 1795 and *hymne national* in 1879.

Suite Provençale

Darius Milhaud, born in Aix-en-Provence in 1892, was one of the group of composers known as Les Six and his 1937 orchestral suite pays homage to his southern origins.

Chorégies d'Orange (*see p102*) programmes international casts in a spectacular setting. At the **Festival International de Piano de la Roque d'Anthéron** the world's greatest pianists play in the park of the Château de Florans. Carpentras also has a summer festival, **Les Estivales**, but here budgetary constraints impose a more modest level of performance – unlike the rather ritzy **Musiques au Coeur** opera festival that has sprung up in Antibes.

MUSIC: ROCK, ROOTS, JAZZ & ELECTRONIC MUSIC

Until recently, homegrown southern music production largely meant Marseille rap, which seemed natural for the city's ethnic, urban melting-pot. The scene was led by groups such as **IAM** – the first to break into the big league as they blended transatlantic influences, the trans-Mediterranean input of the Maghreb and the Middle East with disco references – and **Fonky Family** and **3ème Oeil**, just to name the better-known groups, or the exuberant ragga of **Massilia Sound System**.

But recently electronic music has been making major inroads in the South of France, with emerging names like **Troublemakers** (*see right*), as well as infiltrating the poetic pop soundscape of Marseille duo **Di Maggio** (alias singer-lyricist Franck Mallauran and sound-alchemist Cyril Ximenes). If Marseille is the centre of creation and boasts the most venues in which to follow these new currents, another mover is the **Aquaplaning** festival in Hyères, created in 1999, while in Nice you can catch both DJs and electronic artists at the **Ghost House**.

Outside Marseille, it's generally visiting artists that create the most excitement. Capacity concert venues in the South include the **Zénith-Omega** in Toulon, Nice's new **Nikaia** or the Roman arena in Nîmes. Local and national rock bands can be caught in smaller venues, like the **Grenier à Sons** in Cavaillon or **Cargo de Nuit** in Arles. On the Riviera from Cannes to Nice, live music of variable genre and quality is on offer in a number of smaller dives, where there's a veritable, if hardly innovative, pub rock circuit at expat haunts, such as **Wayne's Bar** and **The Bull Dog Pub** in Nice.

Summer brings the usual logjam of festivals. Jazz fans are especially well served by the often overlapping **Nice Jazz Festival** (*see p242*) and **Jazz à Juan**. The Nice festival has a range that goes from jazz to blues, funk and world, while Juan is a more straight jazz mix of trad greats and younger, more experimental artists.

On the world music front, as well as the **Suds à Arles**, **Festival des Suds** in Marseille and **Les Nuits du Sud** in Vence, ex-gypsy king Chico organises the **Mosaïque**

Gitane flamenco festival in Arles and can be heard year round with his new group at his restaurant **El Patio de Camargue**.

THEATRE

The Mediterranean climate fuels a blaze of summer festivals of wildly varying standards. The best, though, endeavour to promote established names while showcasing new talent. Leader of the pack is the **Festival d'Avignon**, with its highbrow mix of French and international theatre and dance, and the vast fringe festival – known as **Le Off** (as in 'Off Broadway'), which fills the streets with its parading performers, frantic competition for passing trade and refreshingly anarchic spirit.

France still believes in pouring money into culture, with the result that state-supported theatres have the highest profile and attract the largest audiences, while private, independent venues have a hard time competing. Intellectually weighty productions of classics and modern classics both home-grown and international, from Molière and Shakespeare to Genet and Pinter, dominate, although contemporary French authors such as Michel Vinaver, Valère Novarina, Xavier Durringer, Véronique Olmi, Bernard Marie Koltes or Philippe Minyana also feature.

Marseille has over 20 theatres ranging from the subsidised **Théâtre national de la Criée** and municipally funded **Théâtre du Gymnase**, both of which are well attended and mix French and international contemporary and classic drama, to small fringe venues. Arles has recently seen the reopening of its **Théâtre d'Arles**, Aix has an active programme at the **Théâtre du Jeu de Paume** and **Théâtre des Ateliers**, while small towns such as Martigues, Draguignan or Cavaillon all have *scènes nationales* that see visiting companies in short (often two or three day) runs.

More rebellious, politically motivated theatre exists too: Occitan-language companies have existed in the South since the 1960s, notably André Benedetto's **Le Chêne Noir** in Avignon, the founding father of Le Off; another well-known experimental theatre is the **Théâtre de la Minoterie** in the Joliette dock area in Marseille.

The **Théâtre de Nice** is another active, state-funded institution with an interesting, largely contemporary repertoire. New director Daniel Benoin, appointed in January 2002, says 'I want to work in three domains: local, national and international.' Among his plans are the creation of a permanent troupe of actors, a policy of co-productions with other regional companies, the invitation of a foreign guest director each season and the creation of a European theatre biennial, the first of which is planned for November 2002.

Electrocity

Electronic labels, DJs and concert venues are proliferating in Marseille. Although his international career has taken pioneer DJ Jack de Marseille away from the scene, others have arisen to take his place. One such is DJ Paul, producer and manager of the Obsession label, who runs the concert-venue-cum-shop **Sweet Sofa Lounge** and organises parties under the same name. Obsession has signed acts from Marseille as well as Quebec and England. Another Marseille figure, David Carretta, created the Pornflake label. Venues like **Trolleybus** or **Café Julien** were among the first places to programme Marseille and international DJs. Since then **Fiesta des Suds** has made room in its mostly Latino and world-music programming for electronic evenings – typifying the distinctive world-edge to much Marseille electro. Similarly, Big Buddha mixes electro with Indian and other ethnic sources, while **L'Affranchi** encourages rap-electro exchanges. The crucial electronic brunch is at the **Web Bar**. And you can find electronic nights at the **Poste à Galène** and the **Two Up Australian Café** (26 cours Estienne d'Orves, 1st, 04.91.55.67.76), whose Ghost Sessions are hosted by DJs Zigz and Nasty.

At **La Friche la Belle de Mai**, AMI (Aide aux Musiques Innovatrices) has opened a workshop called Electrofriche, where DJ-producers work and compose together for a week and a half, culminating in a concert, (also broadcast on **Radio Grenouille**, a station based at La Friche). Electrofriche is above all a working laboratory, but this didn't

stop it from being the place where DJ Oil, Fred Berthet and Arnaud Taillefer hooked up to form Troublemakers. Since then they have guested at Aquaplaning and signed their first album, *Doubts & Convictions*, with Chicago's Guidance Recordings. Electrofriche is also the place to find Natarj-xt, Dupain and Alif Tree.

A clutch of record shops specialises in the new Marseille sound: **Sweet Sofa Store** (13 bd Louis Salvator, 6th, 04.96.11.22.24) for house, downtempo and funk; **Wax Records** (8 rue d'Italie, 6th, 04.91.92.09.33) for techno and teck-house; **Smart Import** (46 cours Julien, 6th, 04.91.42.62.04) for drum 'n' bass, hardcore, techno and jungle.

Troublemakers: the trio who hooked up at La Friche la Belle de Mai.

From the editors of this guide

The Festive South

In the South of France, festival fever comes out with the summer sun and lasts all year.

Festivals are everywhere in the South of France. Some have become international cultural events; others are small village affairs, riding on tradition and party spirit. Among the celebrations are fireworks, harvest parades and open-air cinema, not to mention age-old pagan rituals involving sacrificial oxen.

Cannes Festival

JG Ballard's *Super Cannes* takes the lid off a big-money, gated Riviera community. Festival goers will recognise parallels with the world's most famous film festival. At 21st-century Cannes security and pass systems are unavoidable, while the event has the air of a regimented Disney, with queues for top attractions. Rebranded as the *Festival de Cannes* for 2002, it can seem frustratingly exclusive as star paranoia grows with the demands of onlookers. 'The crowds under the

palm trees were extras… far more confident than the film actors on display… ill at ease… like celebrity animals ferried to a mass trial at the Palais,' observes Ballard. Scary.

Carefree Cannes is a legend of years. Don't expect to see Hollywood names ambling down the Croisette or a million dollar contract being signed on a napkin at the adjoining table. The only babes risking topless on the beach are porn stars evicted from the Noga Hilton.

Blue chip, as much as Palme d'Or, is the Croisette currency these days. At a media event second only to the Olympics, a slice of Cannes glamour is corporate hospitality gold dust.

And recent years have seen the emergence of London-orchestrated bashes at venues such as the Palm Beach Casino. The first was the suitably excessive all-nighter for *Trainspotting*. The French sniffed at the beer-swilling lads, then promptly staged a gala jamboree for Luc Besson's *Fifth Element*. But the parties left ripples in palmy heaven. Dave Stewart's über-fête for *Honest* in 2000 was the theatre for some ugly scenes at the door. The skirmishes made headlines, curbing the megabash trend.

The last three years have also seen an influx of roaming youth gangs on the Croisette, from Marseille, Nice and Toulon. Unable to access black-tie soirées, the unwanted lurk and festival night-revellers can receive unwelcome and sometimes violent attention. Two years ago, Cannes' most visible police presence was toy soldiers lining red carpets. Now a CRS riot police bus is stationed on the Croisette between the Palais and the luxury Carlton hotel.

55 years after its creation, everyone at Cannes stills wants a piece of Hollywood A-list action. Press conferences for obscure films can be cruelly underpopulated, but the festival does offer the chance of exposure from the assembled mass media. A four-hour epic about the trials of an unemployed Tibetan yak tamer may not have global appeal, but festival organisers receive the minority product with grace and favour; south-east Asian productions have become a major festival component. The fringe events *Un Certain Regard* and Directors' Fortnight offer international showcases to non-mainstream talents, all trying to make the second-to-none contacts within reach at Cannes.

And spare a thought for the hacks. The days of breezing into town and bagging an exclusive are long gone. Interview schedules run to stopwatch precision and gang-bang interviews quiz braces of stars simultaneously.

'Cannes has become more like a junket in the sun. Interview requests with big names are agreed in LA weeks ahead and the schedule is totally locked down by the time the festival begins,' explains a vice-president at British PR firm DDA. Power to grant access is back in the home territory and if the film has not been sold in Iceland then even the *Rekjavik Times* doesn't stand a chance. Commercial Cannes also has an absurd side. 'Every available hoarding is taken, from the billboards in front of the palace hotels to the palm trunks along the Croisette,' noted madcap US director John Waters.

While Cannes has inevitably gone down the multiplex blockbuster road, it keeps a unique mix of Hollywood and arthouse. It still creates controversy (Kusturica's 1995 Palme d'Or-winning *Underground* was attacked for being

---

▶ The annual Cannes Festival budget is €6 million. There are 30,000 accredited *festivaliers*, of whom 4,000 are journalists and 5,000 film executives. 200,000 pass through Cannes for a ringside view of the festival. The annual visitor spend on hotels, taxis, bars and restaurants is €84 million.

---

pro-Serb) and prizes throw up cerebral choices, notably the 1999 Palme d'Or to gritty *Rosetta*, awarded by jury president David Cronenberg.

The closing awards ceremony itself is a quaint affair, with none of the Oscars' polish. It even saw the audience booing Gallic babe Sophie Marceau as she flapped her way through a disastrous speech in 1999.

But all is soon forgiven. It's Ballard who pinpoints the festival's enduring allure for the *OK* magazine generation: 'For a fortnight the Croisette and its grand hotels willingly become a facade, the largest stage set in the world.'

Festival calendar

Tourist offices are good sources for concert leaflets. The useful booklet, *Terre de Festivals* (available free from main tourist offices in the region), covers summer arts festivals in the Provence-Alpes-Côtes d'Azur region; it can also be found online at **www.cr-paca.fr** and **www.festivals.laregie-paca.com**.

Festival tickets can often be bought at Offices de Tourisme or at branches of **Fnac** (www.fnac.fr) and **Virgin**, or via **France Billet** (08.92.69.26.94/ www.francebillet.com) or **Globaltickets** (01.42.81.88.98/ www.globaltickets.com).

Spring

The Rhône Delta

Féria Pascale
Les Arènes, Arles (04.90.96.03.70/ www.label-camargue.com). **Date** Easter Sat to Easter Mon.
Three spirited days of *course Camarguaise* – bull-fighting Provençal style, without blood and guts. The bill for 2002 includes international stars.

Fête des Gardians
Arènes, Arles and around town. **Information** Office de Tourisme (04.90.18.41.20). **Date** 1 May.
The Queen of Arles is crowned accompanied by *gardians* (Camarguais cattle herders) and equine bravado in the Roman arena.

Féria de Pentecôte
Les Arènes, Nîmes (04.66.02.80.80). **Date** May/June.
The biggest of Nîmes *férias* celebrates its 50th year in 2002 and will convene bullfighting stars, music and art. Smaller *férias* in September and February.

Pèlerinage de Mai
Les Stes-Maries-de-la-Mer. **Information** *(04.90.97.82.55).* **Date** 23-25 May.
Gypsies from Europe and the Middle East converge on tiny Stes-Maries-de-la-Mer for France's biggest gypsy festival, in honour of gypsy chief Black Sarah, who by legend met the three apocryphal Marys on

Flower power at the **Carnaval de Nice**.

here on their arrival from Palestine. On 23 May Sarah's relics are lowered from the church that houses them. On 24 May the relics are carried down to the sea, flanked by revelling gypsies, Arlésiennes in costume and *gardians* on horseback. The relics of Ste Marie Jacob and Ste Marie Salome follow on 25 May, to be blessed by a bishop in a fishing boat.

Avignon & the Vaucluse

Ascension Day
Cavaillon. **Information** Office de Tourisme (04.90.71.32.01). **Date** May.
A parade of bands and distinctively decorated carnival floats in the streets of Cavaillon; similar *corsos* (processions) are also held in Apt and Pertuis.

The Western Côte

Festival de la Mode
Villa Noailles, Hyères. **Information** 04.94.65.22.72/www.festival-hyeres.com. **Tickets** free, but by advance reservation only. **Date** Apr.
Young international designers showcase ideas, plus fashion photography exhibitions.

La Bravade
St-Tropez. **Information** Office de Tourisme (04.94.97.45.21). **Date** mid-May.
The colourful Bravade procession evokes the arrival of headless Christian martyr Torpes (alias Tropez) in a barge in AD68.

The Riviera

Tennis Master Series Monte-Carlo
Monte-Carlo Country Club. **Information** 04.93.41.72.00/www.mccc.mc. **Tickets** €10-€135. **Date** mid-Apr.
International men's hard-court tournament.

Cannes Film Festival
Cannes. **Date** mid-May.
Annual film-industry jamboree. *See p41.*

Grand Prix de Monaco
Monaco. **Information** 00.377.93.15.26.00/ www.acm.mc. **Tickets** €152.50-€305. **Date** June.
Formula One racing cars charge around the narrow bends of Monte-Carlo. Book in advance.

Summer

Fête de la Musique
Throughout France (www.fetedelamusique.culture.fr). **Date** 21 June.
The longest day of the year sees free concerts all over France of all types of music; from string quartets and Johnny Hallyday covers to hip hop.

Bastille Day
Throughout France. **Date** 14 July.
The French national holiday commemorates the storming of Bastille prison in Paris 1789 and the start of the French Revolution. Dances and fireworks are usually on the evening of 13 and/or 14 July.

The Rhône Delta

Festival de la Nouvelle Danse
Jardin de l'Evêché and other venues, Uzès. **Information** 04.66.22.51.51/www.danse-uzes.com. **Box office** (from mid-May) Office de Tourisme (04.66.22.68.88). **Tickets** €7.60-€18.30. **Date** June.
This festival puts the emphasis on introducing unknown dance talents. Recent visiting companies were from Switzerland, Belgium and Holland.

Rencontres Internationales de la Photographie
Espace Van Gogh, Musée Réattu, Cloître St-Trophime and other venues, Arles. **Information** 04.90.96.76.06/www.rip-arles.org. **Tickets** *exhibitions* €1.52-€5.33; *soirées* €4.47-€7.62. **Date** early July to mid-Aug.
The RIP has become a major gathering for contemporary art photography. Themed shows (based around Anonymity in 2001), retrospectives and special commissions are accompanied by debates and workshops. There's also a fringe festival, *Voies Off.*

Suds à Arles
Théâtre Antique and other venues, Arles. **Information** 04.90.96.06.27/www.suds-arles.com. **Tickets** €6.10-€21.30. **Date** July.
World music from Latin America and Africa to the

Balkans. Look out for free concerts, brass bands, dance classes, outdoor film screenings and mint tea.

Nuits Musicales d'Uzès
Uzès. **Information** Office de Tourisme (04.66.22.68.88). **Tickets** €10.70-€36.60. **Date** July.
Concerts in historic buildings by renowned Baroque ensembles such as Musica Antiqua Köln.

La Féria Provençale
St-Rémy-de-Provence. **Information** Office de Tourisme (04.90.92.74.92). **Date** mid-Aug.
Three days of bull races, parades and mounted *abrivado* (herding bulls into the ring) and *bandido* (taking them back out again).

Avignon & the Vaucluse

Festival d'Avignon
Avignon. Bureau du Festival d'Avignon, 20 rue Portail Bocquier (04.90.27.66.50/reservations 04.90.14.14.14/www.festival-avignon.com). **Date** July. **Tickets** €12-€33.
The theatre festival to end them all was established over half a century ago, cramming theatre, dance, music and visitors into buildings and courtyards across the city. The programme is balanced between classics and modern creations, from worldwide repertoires and companies. It's also a big-name draw; in 2001 Kristin Scott Thomas graced a star-cast production of Racine's *Bérénice.*

Avignon Public Off
Maison d'Off Bureau d'Accueil, Conservatoire de Musique, pl du Palais (www.avignon-off.org). **Date** July. **Tickets** €9-€13.
The Festival d'Avignon's fringe is on a very different wavelength. Anyone can perform in 'Le Off', provided they can find enough space and get through local authority red tape. Impromptu stagings range from fire-eatings to vaudevillian comedy and music.

Festival Provençal
Palais du Roure and other venues, Avignon. **Information** 04.90.86.27.76/www.nouvello.com. **Date** July.
In Avignon and nearby villages (including Cavaillon and Valréas) this festival promotes Provençal language and folklore with plays and debates.

Festival de la Correspondance
Grignan. **Information** 04.75.46.55.83/ www.festivalcorrespondance-grignan.com. **Date** early July.
Celebrate letter-writing with readings and dramatisations of epistles by noted scribblers. 2001's festival featured Colette, Madame de Sévigné and Jean Genet's prison correspondence. There are calligraphy workshops to brush up your handwriting.

Festival de la Sorgue
L'Isle-sur-la-Sorgue. **Information** Office de Tourisme (04.90.38.04.78). **Date** July.
Folklore, street theatre, exhibitions, a floating market and a *corso nautique*, in which flower-laden punts battle on the island's canals, plus concerts in L'Isle and Fontaine-de-Vaucluse.

L'Eté de Vaison
Théâtre Antique, Vaison-la-Romaine. **Information** 04.90.28.84.49/www.vaison-festival.com. **Tickets** €15.20-€38.10. **Date** July.
A dance and theatre festival; on previous line-ups were flamenco from Sara Baras, the Hamburg Ballet and modern troupes like Stomp.

Les Estivales de Carpentras
Théâtre de Plein Air, Carpentras (04.90.60.46.00). **Tickets** €25.90. **Date** July.
A multidisciplinary array of music, dance and theatre staged in an open air auditorium.

Les Chorégies d'Orange
Théâtre Antique and other venues. **Information** Bureau des Chorégies d'Orange, 18 pl Sylvain, 84107 Orange (04.90.34.24.24/ www.choregies.asso.fr). **Tickets** €2-€160. **Date** July-Aug.
Orange's Roman amphitheatre provides a sublime setting for classy lyric opera. The acoustics are miraculously good. *See p102.*

Festival International de Quatuors à Cordes
Luberon. **Information** 04.90.75.89.60. **Tickets** €7.60-€18.30. **Date** July-Sept.
Europe's best string quartets perform in the Abbaye de Silvacane, and churches at Cabrières d'Avignon, Fontaine-de-Vaucluse, Goult, L'Isle-sur-la-Sorgue and Roussillon. Tickets on the door only.

Les Musicales du Château d'Ansouis
Château d'Ansouis (04.90.09.82.70/box office 04.90.09.14.04/www.chateau-ansouis.com). **Tickets** €12.20-€19.90. **Date** Aug.
Classy vocal and chamber music on the terrace of this Renaissance château. 2001's recitals featured Bizet, Offenbach, Schumann and Gounod.

Marseille & Aix

Fête de la St-Pierre
Martigues. **Information** Office de Tourisme (04.42.42.31.10). **Date** end June.
The patron saint of fishermen's statue is carried to Martigue's port for nautical parades and blessing of boats. Also in La Ciotat, Cassis and Marseille.

Argilla, Fêtes de la Céramique Aubagne
Aubagne. **Information** Office de Tourisme (04.42.03.49.98). **Date** mid-Aug.
The biennial (the next is in 2003) ceramics market is France's biggest and emphasises art pottery.

Festival de Marseille
Various locations in Marseille. **Information** Bureau d'accueil, 6 pl Sadi Carnot (04.91.99.00.20/box office

Monster raving loony parties

The Provençals take merrymaking very seriously. Given any excuse, however bizarre, the locals in almost every town and village will gather for a *fête* or *foire* to celebrate. Provence is the party meister of France, its furious year-round revelry peaking during the summer, when you can conduct an entire holiday following the free hospitality from town to village.

The South has perfected a repertoire of ancient ceremonies, some dating back to the Middle Ages. Most enchanting are local festivities, rooted in village folklore, religion, identity and pride. *Boules* tournaments, *corsos* (parades), craft stalls, fireworks, accordion dances and *gaboulets* (traditional flutes) are standard features. Giddy with good clean fun, this is an authentic way to taste the southern *art de vivre*.

The land's flora and herbs are highly exalted. **Buis-les-Barronies**, the lime blossom capital, has held the Foire au Tilleul since 1808, venerating this 'yellow gold', popularly used for herbal tea and toothpaste, after the harvest in July. **Grasse**, the perfume bottle of

France, pumps out fragrance and jollity in Exporose in May for its centifolia rose, and the floral floats of the Jasminade in August. Lavender enjoys a huge send-off during the summer harvests (*see p107*).

Even animals are toasted, marking their importance in rural Provence. Horse festivals are held throughout the Camargue in summer, while dogs are preened, paraded and sold at the Fête du Chien in Nyons in August. Sheep get their turn during the Fête de la Transhumance (usually at Pentecost in May), when Provence comes to a standstill as flocks are led from winter to summer pastures in true pastoral style to the beat of the tambourine (even if sometimes now, as at St-Rémy-de-Provence, they arrive by lorry). **Tarascon** celebrates a more mythical creature, the Rhône-dwelling beast that once terrorised the area, defeated by St Marthe and now paraded through the village streets in June for the Fête de la Tarasque.

Easter launches the bullfighting season in **Arles** with the Féria Pascale including *abrivados*, when mounted ranchers herd the bulls, often baited by daredevil onlookers. Pentecost unites the *félibres*, disciples of Frédéric Mistral and protectors of Occitane language and culture, who meet on the feast day of their patron saint Santo Estello for a good chat that no one else can understand.

Some festivals are flagrantly weird. Vintage cars can get given their last rites at an open air mass and car blessing ceremony in **Les Baux-de-Provence** in July. In **Saintes-Maries-de-la-Mer** a catwalk of 16-year-old virgins parade the streets in July for the Fiesta Vierginenco, modelling Arles-style traditional dress and haircut. Amblers limber up in April for the *randonnée* festival in **Forcalquier**, with themed circuits and horse rides.

Certain saints' days, or *fêtes votives*, are marked throughout Provence with elaborate ceremonies. La Nuit du Petit-Saint-Jean in **Valréas** has crowned a five-year-old boy 'Petit St-Jean' every year on 24 June since 1504. The lucky lad is followed throughout town by an entourage of 400 dressed in 15th-century costumes. St Eloi, the patron saint of goldsmiths and mule drivers, is memorialised all summer around the **Alpilles** with the Char de St Eloi, a horsedrawn cart paraded through towns and villages such as St-Rémy-de-Provence, decorated in tiny mirrors and foliage. Fun and games to be had by all.

The big, hairy monster of **Tarascon**'s Fête de la Tarasque.

It's a bit early for the clubbers at **Aquaplaning**.

04.91.99.02.50/www.festivaldemarseille.com).
Tickets €9-€20. **Date** July.
An international festival of experimental dance, theatre and music. 2001's programme was typically diverse, including Choréam's hip hop choreography.

Festival International d'Art Lyrique

Aix-en-Provence. **Information** Boutique du Festival, 11 rue Gaston de Saporta (04.42.17.34.34/
www.festival-aix.com). **Tickets** €22-€182.
Date July.
One of two big opera fests in the South (the other is Les Chorégies; *see p44*). Founded in 1948, it attracts innovative directors and international divas. Mozart has always featured and the festival has recently taken in early and 20th-century repertoires. Peter Eötvös's operatic adaptation of Genet's *Le Balcon* in 2002 will mix popular song and cabaret.

Festival Danse à Aix

Aix-en-Provence. **Information** Danse à Aix, 1 pl Joan Rewald, Espace Forbin (04.42.96.05.01/box office from June 04.42.23.41.24/www.danse-a-aix.com). **Tickets** €10.70-€38.10. **Date** mid-July to mid-Aug.
Contemporary dance performances from the movers and shakers of the French scene.

Festival International de Piano

Parc du Château de Florans, La Roque d'Antheron. (04.42.50.51.15/www.festival-piano.com). **Tickets** €11.43-€60.98. **Date** mid-July to mid-Aug.
Top concert pianists perform classical repertoires in in the gardens of this Renaissance château.

Musique à l'Empéri

Château de l'Empéri, Salon-de-Provence. **Box office** (04.42.92.73.88/www.topic.fr/emperi). **Tickets** €10-€20. **Date** early Aug.
The Château de l'Empéri's courtyard is the setting for chamber music from Mozart to Dusapin.

The Western Côte

Aquaplaning

Villa Noailles and other venues, Hyères.
Information (01.40.24.02.40/www.festival-

aquaplaning.com). **Tickets** €13-€20, three days €75.
Date late June.
A three-day festival of the electronic music scene. Party people frolic in the avant-garde Villa Noailles and Antique Olbia venues, and on to Bamboo Beach. Facing crowds in previous years were Aphex Twin, Michel Houellebecq, Olaf Hund and Troublemakers.

Festival Medieval

pl de la République, Hyères. **Information** Office de Tourisme (04.94.01.84.50). **Date** July.
Jugglers, fire eaters, musicians, acrobats and story-tellers go carousing in Hyères' old streets, inspired by Louis IX's landing in 1254.

Inland Var

Draguifolies

Draguignan. **Information** Théâtres en Dracenie, bd Georges Clemenceau (04.94.50.59.50). **Date** July-Aug.
Free concerts, theatre and dance performances in numerous open-air sites around town.

Mosaïque des Suds

Théâtre du Pont d'Olive, Brignoles (04.94.72.08.27). **Tickets** €21. **Date** late July.
In a recreated amphitheatre, this festival mixes dance, art, music and theatre of 'southern' cultures around the world, from the Middle East to Spain.

The Riviera

Voiles d'Antibes

Port Vauban, Antibes (04.92.91.60.00). **Tickets** free. **Date** June.
The start of the Classic Yacht Regatta season sees four days of inshore racing between over 60 classic and modern yachts, with festivities around town.

Biennale de Céramique Contemporaine

Château-Musée Magnelli and Musée de la Céramique, Vallauris (04.93.64.16.05). **Tickets** €2-€4. **Date** end June to Sept.
This biennial potters' mecca (the next will be 2002) features contemporary ceramics from Europe.

Jazz à Juan

Juan-les-Pins. **Information** (04.92.90.53.00/ www.antibesjuanlespins.com). **Tickets** €9.14-€54.88. **Date** mid-July.
This beachside jazz festival secures legends on its line-up (Keith Jarrett, Ray Charles and Chuck Berry in 2001). There is also a fringe festival, Jazz Off.

Nice Jazz Festival

Jardins de Cimiez, Nice. **Information** Office de Tourisme (04.92.14.48.00/box office 04.92.09.75.56/ www.nicejazzfest.com). **Tickets** €6.10-€121.96. **Date** July.
Less serious than Jazz à Juan and enjoyably unpredictable – Kool and the Gang have played here, as has Gil Scott-Heron. *See p244.*

Festival International d'Art Pyrotechnique de Cannes

La Croisette, Cannes (04.92.59.41.20). **Tickets** free. **Date** July.
Fireworks from world-class pyrotechnicians, with prizes. In 2002, winners from the past three years will compete against each other for the *Vestale d'Or*.

Musiques au Coeur

Chantier Naval Opéra, Port Vauban, Antibes. **Information** (04.92.90.54.60). **Tickets** €13.70-€53.40. **Date** early July.
A small but glossy open-air opera festival, with fully staged operas, concerts and solo recitals.

Les Nuits de la Danse

Monaco. **Information** 00.377-92.16.24.20/ www.balletsdemontecarlo.com. **Tickets** €7.50-€38. **Date** mid-July.
Works from the Ballets de Monte-Carlo season are reprised on the casino terrace (undergoing repairs in 2002, when the event is held at Grimaldi Forum).

Festival de Musique

parvis St-Michel, Menton. **Information** 04.92.41.76.95/www.villedementon.com. **Tickets** €10.67-€47.26. **Date** Aug.
Founded in 1950, this festival features worthy concerts (Hélène Grimaud and Didier Lockwood in 2001) in the church square overlooking the old port.

Inland Alpes-Maritimes

Les Baroquiales

Sospel and other venues in the Roya and Bévéra valleys. **Information** 04.93.04.24.41/ www.lesbaroquiales.org. **Tickets** €7.60-€18.30. **Date** end June to early July.
Baroque musicians play in Alpine valley churches.

Autumn

Journées du Patrimoine

Throughout France (www.culture.gouv.fr). **Date** third weekend in Sept.
Architectural heritage weekend, when historic and official buildings around France open to the public.

The Rhône Delta

Fêtes des Prémices du Riz

Arles. **Information** (04.90.93.19.55). **Date** mid-Sept.
Camargue's rice harvest is marked by a *corso* (procession) of floats illustrating Provençal history, led by the *Ambassadrice du riz* on a Camargue pony.

Marseille & Aix

Fiesta des Suds

Docks des Suds, bd de Paris, Marseille (04.91.99.00.00/reservations 08.25.83.38.33/ www.dock-des-suds.org). **Tickets** €4.60-€22.90. **Date** Oct.
A musical melting pot from a collection of 'Souths', reflecting Marseille's multiracial culture. Local ragga boys Massilia Sound System usually appear; 2001 drew Greek gypsy music from Yorgos Mangas and Cheb Mami's modern Raï.

Fête du Livre

Cité du Livre, 8-10 rue des Allumettes, Aix-en-Provence (04.42.26.16.85). **Date** Oct.
Literary festival invites big-name guests and serious debates. In 2001 speaker of honour was Toni Morrison. There are also film, art and music events.

The Riviera

Art Jonction

Jardins Albert 1er, Nice. **Information** (04.97.12.12.97/www.art-jonction.com). **Tickets** €6.10. **Date** Sept.
Nice's contemporary art fair gives an overview of the European scene. Galleries (half-French, half-foreign) mainly present artists' solo shows.

Festival Mondial de l'Image Sous-Marine

Palais des Congrès, Antibes-Juan-Les-Pins (04.93.61.45.45/www.underwater-festival.com). **Tickets** €1.52-€45.73. **Date** Oct.
Divers, artists, film-makers and photographers congregate to discuss all things underwater and to battle for prizes. 2002's theme is 'Diving in Tunisia'.

Monaco Fête Nationale

Monaco (00.377-93.15.28.63). **Date** 18-19 Nov.
The Rocher's national day is celebrated with fireworks at the port on 18 November, and a Te Deum in the cathedral (by invitation), cinema and outdoor concert on the 19th, as well as a month-long fun fair.

Winter

La Pastorale

Throughout Provence. **Date** Dec-Jan.
A ritualised theatricalisation of the announcement to the shepherds of Christ's birth, interspersed with carols, performed in numerous villages.

Christmas

Date 24-25 Dec.

Christmas is celebrated with mass on Christmas Eve, followed by a dinner spread, featuring the celebrated *Treize Desserts* (*see p27*). Santons are big business, too, as individuals and churches get out their Christmas crib figures, which traditionally feature all the trades and pastimes of rural Provence.

The Rhône Delta

Salon International des Santonniers

Cloître St-Trophime, Arles. **Information** 04.90.96.47.00. **Date** Nov-Jan.
This fair, held in the cathedral cloisters, is dedicated to colourful clay *santon* figures, a traditional part of Provençal Christmas cribs. A simulataneous *santon* fair is Marseille's Foire aux Santons.

Avignon & the Vaucluse

Les Hivernales

L'Opéra, Chapelle des Pénitents Blancs and other venues in Avignon and Vaucluse. **Information** 04.90.82.33.12/reservation 04.90.82.10.66/ www.hivernales.asso.fr. **Tickets** €3-€24. **Date** Feb.
Contemporary dance performances and workshops. Daniel Larrieu sashayed into 2002 with *Le Danzón*, a sensual Cuban/Mexican tango hybrid.

Sparks fly at the **Fêtes de la Lumière**.

The Western Côte

Fêtes de la Lumière à St-Raphaël

St-Raphaël. **Information** Office de Tourisme 04.94.19.52.52/www.saint-raphael.com.
Date Dec.
For two weeks St-Raphaël is decked in lights, while France's best street theatre groups and musicians fill the town to bursting. The New Year's Eve celebration is a blaze of fireworks; there's also an open-air ice-rink.

Le Corso Fleuri

Bormes-les-Mimosas. **Information** Office de Tourisme 04.94.01.38.38. **Date** third Sun of Feb.
The advent of spring celebrated in a colourful parade of flower sculptures. Floats emerge in myriad forms, from giant fairy gowns to steam trains.

Marseille & Aix

La Chandeleur

Basilique St-Victor, Marseille. **Information** 04.96.11.22.60. **Date** 2 Feb.
A candlelit procession behind the black virgin of the Basilique St-Victor marks the end of Christmas.

The Riviera

Festival International de la Danse

Palais des Festivals and other venues, Cannes. **Information** 04.92.59.41.20/www.cannes-on-line.com. **Tickets** €16.80-€25.90. **Date** Nov.
A biennial festival (next will be held in 2003), reflecting the dynamic dance scene in Europe and the Mediterranean basin.

Rallye Automobile Monte-Carlo

Monaco. **Information** Office de Tourisme (00.377-92.16.61.16). **Date** Jan.
Since 1911, drivers have careered over snow-bound passes and down into the principality in the big date on the world rally calendar.

Festival International du Cirque de Monte-Carlo

Espace Fontvieille, Monaco. **Information** 00.377-92.05.23.45. **Tickets** €7.60-€114.
Date late Jan.
The cream of international circus artistes compete in avant-garde acrobatics and daredevil stunts.

Carnaval de Nice

Nice. **Information** 5 promenade des Anglais (04.93.92.80.73/www.nicecarnaval.com). **Tickets** €10-€20. **Date** month before Lent.
In the period of excess before Lent, carnival floats and street performers parade each weekend behind a giant carnival king and queen, with illuminated parades along the promenade des Anglais. Smaller Carnavals are in Aix-en-Provence and Marseille.

The Rhône Delta

Nîmes & Pont du Gard

Inimitable Nîmes is an intriguing concoction of southern insouciance, Roman antiquity and postmodern design.

Nîmes calls itself 'the city with an accent': it's certainly the most Spanish of the cities of the south, with its tapas bars, bullfights and late-night dining. It is also less provincial than most Midi conurbations, adeptly combining ancient and postmodern: it claims France's most important collection of Roman buildings but also makes sure the Philippe Starck bus stop gets included on the tourist map of the city. Since the TGV arrived in 2001 the railway station has been magnificently refurbished, its marble arches and arcades a knowing Roman reference. Sunny, lively, insouciant, with plenty of cafés and shady squares, Nîmes is too busy and self-absorbed to be a tourist trap. The Nîmois themselves take all that heritage stuff for granted, walking their dogs round the Roman amphitheatre and using 12th-century buildings as blank canvases for graffiti. At *féria* time, however, especially in May, the party spirit takes over the whole town, as

The symbol of Nîmes in the **place du Marché**, sculpted by Martial Raysse.

cafés open *bodegas* out onto the pavements.

Nîmes competes with Arles for the title of the Rome of France but it was a Celtic tribe that first discovered the great spring – Nemausus – that gave the city its name. Such a convenient stop on the Via Domitia between Italy and Spain was bound to attract Roman attention and by 31BC they had moved in, colonising the settlement with a legion of veterans from the Egyptian campaign. Their emblem, a crocodile chained to a palm tree, became the symbol of the city; the Nîmes football team is known as 'Les Crocos'. The Romans built roads and ramparts, a forum and a temple, the great amphitheatre, baths and fountains, as well as the Pont du Gard aqueduct, which supplied water to a busy metropolis of 25,000 people.

After the collapse of the Roman empire, Nîmes declined in importance, wracked by war and religious squabbles. It has always been non-conformist, welcoming the 12th-century Cathar heretics and becoming a major centre of Protestantism in the 16th century. It prospered in the 17th and 18th centuries from dye-making and textiles, processing the wool and silk of the region. Many of the fine mansions in the old town date from this period. Its tough local cotton of white warp and blue weft – already known as 'denim' (de Nîmes) in London by 1695 – became a contemporary icon after Levi Strauss used it to make trousers for Californian gold-diggers.

Nîmes' dusty image took a fashionable turn in the 1980s when flamboyant right-wing mayor Jean Bousquet, founder of the Cacharel fashion house, commissioned several ambitious projects, including a Jean Nouvel housing estate (cours Nemausus, av Général Leclerc) and the Carré des Arts arts complex by British architect Norman Foster, and works of art across the city.

Sightseeing

The centre of Nîmes is small enough to visit on foot, with most of the sights inside the triangle, (called 'l'Ecusson' or shield, after its shape) formed by three 19th-century boulevards: Gambetta, Victor Hugo and Amiral Courbet.

Just to the north of the city centre on Mont Cavalier, the **Tour Magne** was a key component of the pre-Roman ramparts, which

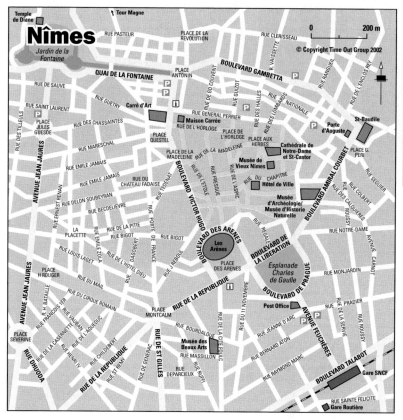

Nîmes

© Copyright Time Out Group 2002

0   200 m

were reinforced in 15BC by the Romans to become the longest city walls in Gaul at almost 7km. The tower is accessible from the **Jardin de la Fontaine**, the beautiful formal gardens laid out in the 18th century.

Also to the north of the central triangle, in rue du Fort, is the **Castellum**, a recently discovered Roman water tower that was the original distribution point for the water supply from the Pont du Gard, distributed across the city through thick lead pipes from ten holes still visible in the basin wall.

Facing each other across the north end of boulevard Victor Hugo are the glass and steel **Carré d'Art**, modern art museum and library, designed by Norman Foster, and the **Maison Carrée**, a superbly preserved Roman temple surrounded by a marble-paved open space on the site where the Roman forum stood.

To the east lies the heart of Nîmes, the pedestrianised old town, which is slowly being

refurbished. Here shops and cafés are tucked within Romanesque arches, walls are half-stripped of modern accretions to reveal the ancient stonework beneath, and many 17th- and 18th-century mansions have been beautifully restored. On rue de l'Aspic, the **Hôtel Fontfroide** has a 17th-century double spiral staircase, while there are three early Christian sarcophagi embedded in the porch of the **Hôtel Meynier de Salinelles**. On rue de Fresque look out for an intact medieval stone shopfront. There is a well-preserved Romanesque facade with elaborate carving in rue de la Madeleine. The **place du Marché**, where Nîmes' corn market used to be held, is adorned with a fountain by Martial Raysse, a modern take on the crocodile tied to a palm tree theme.

On the central place des Herbes stands the much-altered **Cathédrale de Notre-Dame et St-Castor**. Also on the *place* is the former bishop's palace, containing the **Musée de**

Satisfy your bloodlust at **Les Arènes**, Nîmes' Roman amphitheatre.

Vieux Nîmes, a collection of local curiosities. Where boulevard Gambetta joins boulevard Amiral Courbet, the **Porte d'Auguste** remains little changed since it was one of the original Roman gates of the city: the two large arches constituted a dual carriageway for carts and chariots, while the two smaller arches were for pedestrian traffic. Further down boulevard Courbet the **Muséum d'Histoire Naturelle** and **Musée d'Archéologie** are both housed in an old Jesuit college.

All roads eventually lead to the **Arènes**, the Roman amphitheatre (and, unfortunately, round it too) and it must be visited when not in use to fully appreciate its architecture. But do try and go to an event; jazz and opera concerts mean a bullfight is not obligatory.

The elegantly restored **Musée des Beaux-Arts**, with its collection of French, Dutch and Italian paintings, lies a few streets south of the rue de la République.

Les Arènes

bd des Arènes (04.66.76.72.77/féria box office 4 rue de la Violette 04.66.02.80.80). Open May-Sept 9am-6.30pm daily; Oct-Apr 9am-5.30pm daily. **Admission** €4.45; €3.20 10-16s; free under-10s. Encircled by two tiers of 60 stone arcades, this is a standard-issue Roman arena of perfect classical proportions: smaller than Arles but better preserved. The arcades surround the corridors and *vomitoria* (exits) and the great oval arena (the name comes from the *arènes*, or sands, which were spread to soak up the blood). On the exterior look out for the small carvings of Romulus and Remus, the wrestling gladiators and two bulls' heads supporting a pediment

over the main entrance on the north side. The arena is an amazing piece of engineering, constructed out of vast blocks of stone by teams of slaves; it could accommodate over 20,000 spectators. You can still sit on the original stone benches and see the podium for the president of the games and sockets for the poles that held a huge awning to shelter the crowd. For the best view of it, climb to the top tier of seats, traditionally reserved for slaves and women. The original games included gladiator fights, as well as slaves and criminals thrown to animals. Dogs were set on porcupines to get the blood flowing and the crowd excited. There were also chariot races and even mock sea battles with the arena flooded with water. After the departure of the Romans, the amphitheatre was made into a fortress. By the Middle Ages it was a huge tenement block; when it was finally cleared in the early 19th century, centuries of garbage had added six and a half metres to the original ground level. The first corrida took place in 1853. The *féria* today is a key event in the social calendar; the *Figaro* daily paper publishes a corrida special edition with a seating plan of the rich and famous in attendance.

Carré d'Art

pl de la Maison Carrée (04.66.76.35.80/library 04.66.76.35.50). Open 10am-6pm Tue-Sun. **Admission** €4.45; €3.20 10-16s; free under-10s. Opened in 1993, the Foster-designed Carré d'Art houses the Musée d'Art Contemporain and the Bibliothèque Carré d'Art, a vast library and media centre. The art gallery is constructed around a huge light-filled atrium strung with glass staircases. Its beige stone steps, glass walls and steel columns are a tribute to the ancient temple, the Maison Carrée, opposite. The museum, dubbed the 'Mediterranean Beaubourg', focuses on European art since 1960, especially avant-garde movements; see works by Martial Raysse, Christian Boltanski, Claude Viallet, Arman, Ben and Bertrand Lavier. The chic café at the top has great views and is good for a light lunch.

Cathédrale de Notre-Dame et St-Castor

pl aux Herbes (04.66.67.27.72). **Open** 9am-noon, 2-6pm Mon-Sat.

Nîmes' cathedral is not what it was. Although founded in 1096, like much of the town it was wrecked during the 16th-century Wars of Religion, and the current building is mainly a 19th-century reconstruction. The remains of a Romanesque sculpted frieze, with scenes from the Old Testament, are visible on the facade.

Jardin de la Fontaine

quai de la Fontaine (04.66.67.65.56). **Open** gardens *Apr to mid-Sept* 7.30am-10pm daily; *mid-Sept to Mar* 7.30am-6.30pm daily; viewing platform *July, Aug* 9am-9pm daily; *Sept-June* 9am-5pm daily. **Admission** *gardens* free; *viewing platform* €2.40; €1.90 10-18s; free under-10s.

The spring that bubbles up at the heart of these lovely gardens was the reason the Romans named it Nemausus after the Roman river-god. In the 18th century, around the neglected spring, formal gardens were built, designed by Jacques Philippe Mareschal, director of fortifications for Languedoc. They provided a complex system of reservoirs and distribution of the clean water that was sadly lacking after the abandoning of the Pont du Gard aqueduct. Now the canals and still green pools, with balustraded stone terraces and marble nymphs and cupids, provide a retreat from the summer heat. Amid shady chestnut trees the ruined Temple of Diana was part of the Roman sanctuary. On the edge of the garden, high up Mont Cavalier, the octagonal Tour Magne was part of Nîmes' pre-Roman ramparts. The viewing platform 140 steps up provides a good overview of the city, the garrigue landscape and Les Alpilles.

Maison Carrée

pl de la Maison Carrée (04.66.36.26.76). **Open** *Apr-Sept* 9.30am-6.30pm daily; *Oct-Mar* 9am-5pm daily. **Admission** free.

Not *carré* (square) at all but rectangular, this astonishingly well-preserved Roman temple was built in the first century BC and dedicated to Augustus' deified grandsons. With a great flight of stone steps leading up to finely fluted Corinthian columns adorned with a sculpted frieze of acanthus leaves, it has always inspired hyperbole. Arthur Young, an 18th-century British traveller, called it 'the most light, elegant and pleasing building I have ever beheld'. Thomas Jefferson, having failed to take it home, had it copied as the model for the Virginia state capital. It has remained in almost constant use, its functions ranging from legislative seat to tomb, church to stables. Today it contains drawings and photos of current archaeological work, one splendid

result of which is displayed there: a fresco, only unearthed in 1992 when the Carré d'Art was being built. Against a blood-red background sits a mythical hunter, surrounded by a border of pagan frolics, most discernibly Cassandra being dragged by her hair, and two louche-looking dwarves. Lovely as it is, the temple could do with a clean-up, and suffers from constant traffic pollution. Worst of all, the huge Roman terracotta jar that always stood outside was smashed by vandals. You can still see the pieces.

Musée d'Archéologie

13bis bd Amiral Courbet (04.66.76.74.54). **Open** *Apr-Sept* 10am-6pm Tue-Sun; *Oct-Mar* 11am-6pm Tue-Sun. **Admission** (with Muséum d'Histoire Naturelle) €4.45; €3.20 10-16s; free under-10s.

Housed in the old Jesuit college building, the archaeology museum has a magnificent collection of Roman statues, sarcophagi, entablatures, coins, mosaics and some gorgeous Roman glass. The pottery collection includes a rare pre-Roman statue, the Warrior of Grezan. Upstairs is a treasure trove of everyday items, from oil lamps to kitchen equipment, tools and cosmetic artefacts.

Musée des Beaux-Arts

rue Cité-Foulc (04.66.67.38.21). **Open** 11am-6pm Tue-Sun. **Admission** €4.45; €3.20 10-16s; free under-10s.

The imposing facade of this early 20th-century building leads straight into a beautiful restoration by architect Jean-Michel Wilmotte. It houses an eclectic collection of Italian, Flemish and Dutch works and a motley bunch of local artists, unloaded by the Louvre in the 19th century. Most notable are Jacopo Bassano's *Susanna and the Elders*, Rubens' *Portrait of a Monk* and the *Mystic Marriage of St Catherine* by Michele Giambono. The *Marriage of Admetus*, a Roman mosaic discovered in 1882, takes pride of place in the centre of the main floor.

Musée de Vieux Nîmes

pl aux Herbes (04.66.76.73.70). **Open** *Apr-Sept* 10am-6pm Tue-Sun; *Oct-Mar* 11am-6pm Tue-Sun. **Admission** €4.45; €3.20 10-16s; free under-10s.

This museum, housed in the old bishop's palace, was established in 1920 to preserve the tools of local industries and artefacts of regional life, providing an intriguing glimpse into humdrum history. The collection, much of it displayed as reconstructed interiors, comprises furniture, pottery and fabrics including some early denim, shawls and silks.

Muséum d'Histoire Naturelle

13 bd Amiral Courbet (04.66.76.73.45). **Open** *Apr-Sept* 10am-6pm Tue-Sun; *Oct-Mar* 11am-6pm Tue-Sun. **Admission** (with Musée d'Archéologie) €4.45; €3.20 10-16s; free under-10s.

In the same building as the archaeological museum, the natural history collection includes some important Iron Age menhirs, a good anthropological collection and many stuffed bears, tigers and crocodiles, as fascinating as they are politically incorrect. The lovely 17th-century chapel is used for concerts and temporary art exhibitions.

Arts & entertainment

For local entertainment listings, pick up the freebie magazine *César*.

Le Sémaphore

25 rue Porte de France (04.66.67.88.04). **Tickets** €5.20; €4.30 12-25s; €3.50 under-12s. **Credit** MC, V.

Le Sémaf, as it is affectionately known, offers an excellent programme of original-language (*version originale*) films and themed weeks showcasing a variety of foreign movies.

Théâtre de l'Armature

12 rue de l'Ancien Vélodrome (04.66.29.98.66/ www.larmature.org). **Box office** 9am-noon, 2-6pm Mon-Fri. **Shows** 9pm Thur-Sat. **Tickets** €6-€9. **No credit cards.**

Alternative theatre that acts as a showcase for touring companies, staging works by contemporary writers such as Philippe Minyana.

Théâtre de Nîmes/L'Odéon

1 pl de la Calade (04.66.36.65.00)/L'Odéon, 7 rue Pierre Semard (04.66.36.65.93). **Box office** *1 pl de la Calade (04.66.36.65.10).* **Open** 10.30am-1pm, 2.30-6pm Tue-Fri; 2.30-6pm Sat. **Shows** 8.30pm Tue, Thur-Sat; 7pm Wed; 3pm, 5pm Sun. **Tickets** €11-€30. **Credit** AmEx, DC, MC, V.

Two theatres offering an accessible programme of classic and contemporary dance, theatre and opera.

Restaurants

Le 9

9 rue de l'Etoile (04.66.21.80.77). **Open** *Apr-Oct* noon-3pm, 8pm-2.30am Tue-Sat, 8pm-midnight Sun; *Nov-Mar* by reservation only. **Menus** €20-€30. **Credit** MC, V.

Hidden behind large doors on a narrow street is a seriously fashionable establishment, with theatrically draped arches and velvet banquettes. A popular *bodega* at *féria* time, Le 9 serves southern classics like *moules gratinée*, serrano ham and *poivrons à l'anchoïade*, along with imaginative combinations like squid with artichokes and mushrooms.

Casa Bella

6 pl de la Révolution (04.66.67.64.68). **Open** 7.30-11pm Tue-Sat. **Average** €25. **Credit** MC, V.

Calling it a pizzeria in no way does justice to the sensual home cooking in this tiny restaurant close to the Maison Carrée. Gingham and candles provide a cosy setting for dishes of breathtaking, spot-on simplicity. Warm chickpeas with olive oil, fresh coriander and spices or a lasagne of morning-fresh yellow chanterelles are perfect for vegetarians, though the *carré d'agneau* is luscious and the pizzas beyond compare.

Le Chapon-Fin

3 rue du Château Fadaise (04.66.67.34.73). **Open** noon-2.30pm, 7.30-10.30pm Mon-Fri; 7.30-10.30pm Sat. Closed Aug. **Average** €22.90. **Credit** AmEx, DC, MC, V.

This Nîmois institution is a true Midi brasserie with walls hung with paintings by grateful clients. Food is generous and regional, with the *brandade* a must.

L'Enclos de la Fontaine

quai de la Fontaine (04.66.21.90.30). **Open** 12.30-2pm, 7.30-9.45pm daily. **Menus** €25.15-€51.80. **Credit** AmEx, DC, MC, V.

Overlooking a palm-shaded courtyard, the elegant restaurant of the Hôtel Imperator is much favoured by bullfighters at *féria* time. Try local specialities like *brandade*, *escabèche* (marinated fish), sea bass with fennel, mesclun of smoked duck with almonds or lacquered duck with *pêche au poivre*.

L'Esclafidou

7 rue Xavier Sigalon (04.66.21.28.49). **Open** noon-2pm, 7.30-10pm Tue-Sat. **Average** €16. **Credit** AmEx, MC, V.

This charming restaurant on a tiny square has a shady summer terrace. Provençal cuisine with lashings of olive oil, garlic and spices, generous salads, fish and omelettes – try the cep omelette in season.

La Fleur de Sel

29 rue du Grand Couvent (04.66.76.04.19). **Open** noon-2pm, 7-10pm Mon-Sat. Closed Aug. **Menus** €9-€25. **Credit** MC, V.

New owners have made the menus here a tasty hommage to fish and vegetables, serving up rare, specially cultivated varieties of the latter.

La Fontaine du Temple

22 rue de la Curaterie (04.66.21.21.13). **Open** noon-2pm, 7-11pm Mon-Sat. Closed last week Aug. **Average** €25.15. **Credit** AmEx, DC, MC, V.

This friendly, neighbourhood restaurant and bar serves local specialities like *taureau* with anchovy sauce, lamb with thyme, *brandade* with lobster sauce and snails. It also does fondues in winter.

Le Jardin d'Hadrien

11 rue de l'Enclos (04.66.21.86.65). **Open** *July, Aug* 7.30-10pm Mon, Wed; noon-2pm, 7.30-10pm Tue, Thur-Sat; *Sept-June* noon-2pm, 7.30-10pm Mon, Thur-Sat; noon-2pm Tue, Sun. **Menus** €16-€25. **Credit** AmEx, MC, V.

Sitting under the plane trees behind this dignified 19th-century house is restful after battling the throngs around the Arena. The dining room has stone walls, an open hearth and beamed ceiling. Chef Alain Vinouze does dishes with a local bent such as courgette flowers stuffed with *brandade*, aubergine charlotte, roast lamb and red mullet with *tapenade*. Inexpensive wines include a fine Costières de Nîmes.

Magister

5 rue Nationale (04.66.76.11.00). **Open** 7.30-9.30pm Mon, Sat; noon-2pm, 7.30-9.30pm Tue-Fri. Closed 20 July-20 Aug. **Menus** €22.87-€27.44. **Credit** AmEx, MC, V.

One of Nîmes' top restaurants for smooth service and perfectly judged cooking. Try the *brandade*, stuffed pigeon or lamb braised in red wine with mint. The wine list offers the best of local vintages.

The Rhône Delta

Aux Plaisirs des Halles

4 rue Littré (04.66.36.01.02). **Open** noon-2pm, 8-10pm Tue-Sat; noon-2pm Sun. Closed third week Aug. **Menus** €14.94-€44.21. **Credit** AmEx, MC, V.
Discreet, elegant little bistro near the market, serving freshly made *aïoli* with vegetables, homemade breads, sorbets and imaginative twists on regional classics, such as *brandade* with truffles and olives.

Vintage Café

7 rue de Bernis (04.66.21.04.45). **Open** noon-2pm, 8-10pm Tue-Thur; noon-2pm, 8-10.30pm Fri; 8-10pm Sat. **Menus** €12.35-€24.10. **Credit** MC, V.
This friendly place is tucked into a quiet corner of the old town. Try the oysters in anchovy *jus* or bull steak.

Wine Bar chez Michel

11 sq de la Couronne (04.66.76.19.59/ www.winebarchezmichel.com). **Open** 7pm-midnight Mon, Sat; noon-2pm, 7pm-midnight Tue-Fri. **Menus** €13-€20. **Credit** AmEx, MC, V.
Wine bars are a relatively new concept to the French hereabouts, used to drinking local wines, so this is a rare chance to eat and sample a wide variety by the glass. Despite the clichéd 60s steakhouse decor, the food – fish, shellfish and beef – is reliably fresh.

Bars, cafés & nightlife

La Bodeguita

3 bd Alphonse Daudet (04.66.58.28.27). **Open** *winter* noon-2.30pm Mon, Tue; noon-2.30pm, 7-11.30pm Wed-Fri; 7-11.30pm Sat; *summer* noon-2.30pm, 7-11.30pm Mon-Fri, 7-11.30pm Sat. **Credit** AmEx, DC, MC, V.
Spanish tapas bar with terrace, serving food (€3.05-€15.24) and wine, local and Spanish, by the glass. Themed evenings of flamenco, tango, jazz, poetry.

Le Café Olive

22 bd Victor Hugo (04.66.67.89.10). **Open** 9am-1am Mon-Sat. **Credit** MC, V.
Old stone and contemporary furniture meet in this renovated café which offers margaritas and evening concerts and revues.

Gilbert Courtois

8 pl du Marché (04.66.67.20.09). **Open** *July, Aug* 8am-midnight daily; *Sept-June* 8am-7.30pm daily. **Credit** AmEx, MC, V.
This *belle époque* café with comfortable terrace is a Nîmes institution for tea, coffee, hot chocolate and cakes. Simple meals such as omelettes, pasta and salads are also available.

Haddock Café

13 rue de l'Agau (04.66.67.86.57/ www.haddock.cafe.fr). **Open** noon-2pm, 7pm-2am Mon-Sat. **Credit** AmEx, MC, V.
This is a popular club and café with food served late, music and philosophy evenings.

Lulu Club

10 impasse de la Curaterie (04.66.36.28.20). **Open** 11pm-late Tue-Sun. **No credit cards**.
Gay bar and disco, where heteros are also welcome.

Le Mazurier

9 bd Amiral Courbet (04.66.67.27.48). **Open** 7am-1am daily. **Credit** MC, V.
Take advantage of this good old-fashioned *belle époque* brasserie for leisurely morning coffee over a newspaper on the terrace, or a *pastis* at the zinc bar.

Le Millenium Café

145 rue Michel Debré (04.66.84.07.67). **Open** 10am-midnight daily. **No credit cards**.

The astonishingly well-preserved Roman temple, the **Maison Carrée**, is still in use today. *See p53.*

This café successfully combines net surfing (€3 per hour) and computer games with billiards, bar and dance floor.

Le Pelican
54 rte de Beaucaire (04.66.29.63.28). **Open** 6.30pm-2am Tue-Sun.
Recently opened music venue offering a range of roots music from jazz to bebop and cajun; eclectic range of cuisine, too – from Languedoc to Louisiana.

Trois Maures
10 bd des Arènes (04.66.36.23.23). **Open** 7am-midnight daily. **No credit cards.**
Huge old brasserie filled with tributes to the two Nîmois preoccupations, bullfighting and *le foot*.

Shopping

Best shopping is in the old town where, despite the dispiriting spread of chain stores, you can still find splendid local stores and produce. For food, the covered market of **Les Halles** (rue des Halles, 7am-1pm daily) can't be beat (Daniel for olives, Durand for *brandade*). There is also a fleamarket Mondays on boulevard Jean Jaurès.

F **Nadal** (7 rue St Castor, 04.66.67.35.42) is a tiny shop selling olive oil from vats, handmade soaps, herbs, honey, coffee and spices. **L'Huilerie** (10 rue des Marchands, 04.66.67.37.24, closed Mon) has spices, herbs, grains, *tisanes* and beautifully packaged honeys, mustards and olive oil. **Villaret** (13 rue de la Madeleine, 04.66.67.41.79, closed Sun) is a long-established *boulangerie-pâtisserie*, with bread, tarts and the Nîmes speciality *croquants*. For local wine, visit the **Espace Costières** (19 pl Aristide Briand, 04.66.36.96.20, closed Sat, Sun). **Boutique Le Gardian** (3 rue de l'Hôtel de Ville, 04.66.21.36.45, closed Mon, Sun) has a great selection of leather waistcoats and cowboy boots; **Les Indiennes de Nîmes** (2 bd des Arènes, 04.66.36.19.75, closed Mon, Sun) turns Provençal fabric into every imaginable garment and accessory. **Marie Sara Création** (40 bis rue de la Madeleine, 04.66.21.18.40, closed Mon, Sun) is the place to buy your complete toreador outfit. Marie Sara was famous in her day as a bullfighter. **L'Oeil du Taureau** (4 rue Fresque, 04.66.21.53.28, closed Mon, Sun) is a good second-hand bookshop .

Where to stay

L'Hacienda
chemin du Mas de Brignon, Marguerittes (04.66.75.02.25). Closed Nov-Feb. **Double** €75-€140. **Credit** MC, V.
This hotel, surrounded by olive groves, is 6km outside Nîmes. It has a pool, gardens and rooms with private terraces. Food is exceptional (menus €30-€55).

Hôtel de l'Amphithéâtre
4 rue des Arènes (04.66.67.28.51). Closed Jan. **Double** €39.65-€59.45. **Credit** AmEx, MC, V.
Surprisingly smart for the price, the hotel is housed in a well-restored 18th-century building, with antique furniture and large, white-tiled bathrooms.

Hôtel Imperator
quai de la Fontaine (04.66.21.90.30/www.hotel-imperator.com). **Double** €99-€183. **Credit** AmEx, DC, MC, V.
Nîmes' top hotel is smart but unstuffy and a favourite rendezvous for toreadors and their entourage at *féria* time. It has a gourmet restaurant (L'Enclos de la Fontaine, *see p54*), a 1930s lift and luxurious rooms.

Lisita
2bis bd des Arènes (04.66.67.66.20). **Double** €33.50-€48.80. **Credit** MC, V.
The funky bullfighting-themed Lisita has balconied rooms with views over the arena. Although a bit shabby with bathrooms shoe-horned into corners, it's still a very good deal.

New Hôtel la Baume
21 rue Nationale (04.66.76.28.42/www.new-hotel.com). **Double** €91-€106. **Credit** AmEx, DC, MC, V.
A 17th-century mansion with an elegant classical interior around a beautiful stone staircase. Rooms are spacious and well decorated, and bathrooms are smart. There is also a restaurant.

L'Orangerie
755 rue de la Tour Evêque (04.66.84.50.57/ www.orangerie.fr). **Double** €60.22-€99. **Credit** AmEx, DC, MC, V.
This charming hotel just beyond the centre has a garden, small pool and good restaurant (menus €17.53-€41.16). Some rooms have private terraces.

Le Royal Hôtel
3 bd Alphonse Daudet (04.66.58.28.27). **Double** €44.21-€79.27. **Credit** AmEx, DC, MC, V.
A fashionable little hotel with a palm-filled lobby, leather club chairs and friendly proprietors. Rooms vary in size but all are sweetly decorated. Its tapas bar, La Bodeguita (*see p55*), is popular at *féria* time.

Tourist information

Office de Tourisme
6 rue Auguste, 30020 Nîmes (04.66.58 38.00/ www.ot-nimes.fr). **Open** *Apr-June, Sept, Oct* 8am-7pm Mon-Fri, 9am-7pm Sat; 10am-6pm Sun; *July, Aug* 8am-8pm Mon-Fri; 9am-7pm Sat; 10am-6pm Sun; *Nov-Mar* 8.30am-7pm Mon-Fri, 9am-7pm Sat, 10am-6pm Sun.

Accueil Information Handicap
50 bd Gambetta (08.00.20.50.88). **Open** 2-5.30pm Mon-Thur; 9am-noon Fri.

Centre Gai et Lesbien de Nîmes
11 rue Régale (06.66.53.96.81/ www.chez.com/gayzette). **Open** 7-9pm Thur.

What's the *pont*?

'As I humbled myself, suddenly something lifted up my spirits, and I cried out "Why am I not a Roman!"'. First-time visitors to the extraordinary triple-decker aqueduct of Pont du Gard – the highest the Romans ever built – are wont to come over all rhapsodic, just like Jean-Jacques Rousseau.

It is undoubtedly an astonishing sight. Frontinus, curator of Rome's aqueducts in the AD 90s, when Pont du Gard was built, labelled this piece of engineering 'the best testimony to the greatness of the Roman Empire'. What is more astonishing still is that the limestone arches, rising to a height of 49m, have resisted both the erosion of time and the interference of man.

The aqueduct originally carried drinking water from the springs at the Fontaine d'Eure in Uzès across the Gardon river to Nîmes, along a 50km route, much of it through underground channels dug out of solid rock. The bridge itself is built from gigantic blocks of stone, some weighing as much as six tons, which were hauled into place by pulleys, wheels... and huge numbers of slaves. It was built with a slight bow to enable it to withstand great water pressure; during devastating floods in 1988, the Pont du Gard stood firm while several other bridges collapsed.

At the recently opened visitors' centre, a film and exhibition on the Pont du Gard will teach you everything you ever wanted to know. A 600m^2 space is devoted to children, offering them the chance to learn about life in Roman times, archaeology, nature and water through an interactive exhibition on the history of the aqueduct.

The most atmospheric experience, though, remains the bridge itself; the architectural details of the bridge are illuminated on summer evenings by a light show designed by American artist James Turrell (10pm Fri & Sat in June & Sept, nightly in July & Aug, free). Walking across the bridge or clambering through the water channel is now forbidden: the structure is best observed from the road bridge that was built alongside in the 18th century or from either river bank. There is a little beach where you can swim, and canoes can be hired for trips along the gorge (Kayak Vert, 04.66.22.84.83, Apr-Oct).

Vistor Centre

Concession Pont du Gard, Vers-Pont-du-Gard (04.66.37.50.99). **Open** *May to mid-June* 9.30am-7pm daily; *mid-June to mid-Sept* 9am-11pm daily; *mid-Sept to Nov* 9.30am-5pm daily; *Nov-Apr* 10am-6pm daily. **Admission** €12.50, €11 6-21s, free under-6s.

North of Nîmes

Uzès & the Gardon

Uzès is a charming town, and knows it. Despite being well west of the Rhône, it seems more Provence than Languedoc, and more Italian in appearance than either. Uzès offers a variety of colourful festivals ranging from a truffle day in January and garlic fest on 24 June, via summer wine, dance and Baroque music, to the national day of the donkeys of Provence on 13 October, when 150 donkeys parade through the streets.

A major centre of Protestantism, Uzès prospered in the 17th and 18th centuries from the manufacture of linen, serge and silk. It was also an important ducal seat and still calls itself the first duchy of France. Republicanism notwithstanding, the Duke lives on, mainly in Paris, and his **Duché d'Uzès** – ducal palace – is open to visitors. The building spans several centuries, from a 12th-century tower to a Burgundian tiled chapel and Renaissance facade. A guided tour includes a visit to the dungeons, complete with hologram ghost.

By 1962, when it was designated a *ville d'art* by then-culture minister André Malraux, Uzès was sadly run down. Subsequent restoration work in the local pale, soft limestone has already taken on a time-worn look, blending in seamlessly with the historic buildings and making it a favourite location for historical films such as *Cyrano de Bergerac*.

The delightful **place aux Herbes**, with its arcaded square, sums up Uzès. The market (Wed morning, all Sat) is a great source of baskets, Provençal fabric and crockery. The 17th-century **Cathédrale St-Théodorit** (open 9am-6pm Mon-Sat) contains a superb 18th-century organ. It is dominated by the earlier **Tour Fenestrelle**, an arcaded round bell tower reminiscent of Pisa and the only part of the Romanesque cathedral to survive the Wars of Religion (it made a handy watchtower).

The late 17th-century **Palais Episcopal** (bishop's palace) houses local pottery and paintings, as well as a tribute to novelist André Gide, who was born here in 1869, returning as an adult for holidays. In impasse Port Royal, the **Jardin Medieval** contains a remarkable collection of carefully labelled local plants and medicinal and culinary herbs. At Pont des Charettes, 1km south of Uzès, is the **Musée du Bonbon**, established by manufacturer Haribo to celebrate a century of sweet-making, a nostalgia trip for adults and sheer sticky heaven for kids.

The recently excavated **Fontaine d'Eure**, the spring which originally carried water to

No, not Pisa but the Tour Fenestrelle in **Uzès**.

Nîmes via the Pont du Gard, is a short walk from Uzès town centre (take chemin André Gide out of town to the Vallée de l'Alzon). The Pont du Gard (*see p57*) itself is 14km south-east of Uzès, near Remoulins, but fragments of water channels and lost aqueduct arches still litter the area and the trail has recently been clearly signposted. The fortified Romanesque church at **St-Bonnet-du-Gard** contains stones from the aqueduct; other abandoned arches remain just outside **Vers-Pont-du-Gard**, north of the Pont.

Between Nîmes and Uzès, the **Gorges du Gardon** are the most spectacular of a series of deep river gorges cut into the limestone; they are visible from Pont St-Nicolas on the D979, where a fine seven-arched medieval bridge spans the chasm. To walk along them, detour through Poulx, taking the D135 then the D127, to pick up the GR6 footpath through the depths; at the north-east end of the gorges, the little village of **Collias** provides wonderful views.

The area is famous for its fine white clay; **St-Quentin-la-Poterie**, north of Uzès, is a must for pottery junkies. Over the centuries it churned out amphorae, roof tiles and bricks by the ton. The last large-scale factory closed down in 1974, but craft potters have returned. Their work can be seen in the Galerie Terra Viva adjoining the **Musée de la Poterie Méditerranéenne**, which has examples from Turkey, Greece, Morocco and Egypt as well as France and Spain; there are pots, bowls and bee-smoking equipment in the local green or blue glazes. The village is a delight, on the edge of gentrification, its crumbling ochre houses with loggias and carved columns festooned with washing.

Duché d'Uzès

pl de Duché, Uzès (04.66.22.18.96). **Open** 10am-noon, 2-6pm daily. **Admission** €10; €6.50 12-16s; €4 7-11s; free under-7s.

Jardin Medieval

impasse Port Royal, off rue Port Royal, Uzès (04.66.22.38.21). **Open** *Apr-June, Sept* 2-6pm Mon-Fri; 10.30am-12.30pm, 2-6pm Sat, Sun; *July, Aug* 10.30am-12.30pm, 2-6pm daily; *Oct* 2-5pm daily. Closed Nov-Mar. **Admission** €2; free under-18s.

Musée du Bonbon

Pont des Charettes (04.66.22.74.39/ www.haribo.com). **Open** *July-Sept* 10am-7pm daily; *Oct-June* 10am-1pm, 2-6pm Tue-Sun. Closed three weeks Jan. **Admission** €4; €2 5-15s; free under-5s.

Musée de la Poterie Méditerranéenne

rue de la Fontaine, St-Quentin-la-Poterie (04.66.22.74.38). **Open** *Apr-June, Oct-Dec* 2-6pm Wed-Sun; *July-Sept* 10am-1pm, 3-7pm daily. **Admission** €3.05; free under-12s.

Palais Episcopal & Musée Georges Borias

pl de l'Evêché, Uzès (04.66.22.40.23). **Open** *Mar-Oct* 3-6pm Tue-Sun; *Nov-Feb* 2-5pm Tue-Sun. Closed Jan. **Admission** €2; €1 5-15s; free under-5s.

Where to stay & eat

The **Hôtel d'Entraigues** (pl de l'Evêché, Uzès 04.66.22.32.68, double €50-€120), in a 15th-century building, is a mix of antiques and modern, and has a swimming pool unnervingly suspended over the dining room (menus €22-€49). In Arpaillargues, 4km from Uzès, **Château d'Arpaillargues** (Hôtel Marie d'Agoult, 04.66.22.14.48, closed Nov-Mar, double €76-€229) has gardens, pool, tennis courts and barbecues in summer (menus €26-€40). In Collias, the **Hostellerie le Castellas** (Grande Rue, 04.66.22.88.88, closed Jan & Feb, double €93-€198) consists of several houses converted into a hotel, with palmy garden, pool and elegant dining terrace (menus €35-€56); the simpler **Auberge de Gardon** (04.66.22.80.54, closed mid-Oct to mid-Mar, double €45-€54) is a small hotel on the riverbank with a garden and restaurant (menus €18-€27). The acclaimed **Table d'Horloge** (pl de l'Horloge, 04.66.22.07.01, closed all lunch July-Sept, Wed & Thur Sept-June and all Feb, menu €40) in

St-Quentin-la-Poterie changes its menu weekly according to what's in the market. Locals head to the **Auberge de St-Maximin** (rue des Ecoles, 04.66.22.26.41, closed all Mon & lunch Tue June & Sept, all Tue in Apr, May & Oct, all Nov-Mar, menus €23-€38) in St-Maximin, which has imaginative fare and impeccable service.

Le Vieux Castillon (rue Tureon-Sabatier, 04.66.37.61.61/www.relaischateaux.fr, closed Jan to mid-Feb, double €150-€300) in Castillon-du-Gard is the area's luxury choice, with pool and a restaurant strong on truffle dishes (closed lunch Mon & Tue, menus €45-€96).

Tourist information

Uzès market is Wednesday and Saturday.

Remoulins

Office de Tourisme, pl des Grands Jours, 30210 Remoulins (04.66.37.22.34/fax 04.66.37.22.01). **Open** *Apr-Sept* 9am-1pm, 2-6pm daily. *Oct-Mar* 9am-12.30pm, 2.30-6pm Mon-Fri.

Uzès

Office de Tourisme, Chapelle des Capucins, pl Albert 1er, 30700 Uzès (04.66.22.68.88/www.ville-uzes.fr). **Open** *June-Sept* 9am-6pm Mon-Fri; 10am-1pm, 2-5pm Sat, Sun; *Oct-May* 9am-noon, 1.30-6pm Mon-Fri; 10am-1pm Sat.

▶ Getting there & around

▶ By air

Aéroport de Nîmes-Arles-Camargue (04.66.70.49 49) is 10km SE of Nîmes. A shuttle bus links the airport to the town centre and train station (€4.30).

▶ By car

For Nîmes coming S from Lyon/Orange or NE from Montpellier, take A9 autoroute, exit no.50. West from Arles: A54 autoroute, exit no.1. For Uzès, take the D979 from Nîmes. Pont du Gard is 14km SE of Uzès on the D981, 20km NE of Nîmes on the N86; from Avignon take the N100 then the D19.

▶ By train/bus

Nîmes is on Paris-Avignon-Montpellier line, with TGV direct to Paris in around 3 hours. **STDG** (04.66.29.27.29) runs several buses a day Mon-Sat between Nîmes and Avignon and Nîmes and Uzès, fewer on Sun, plus three buses to Avignon via Remoulins for the Pont du Gard (none Sun) and three buses between Uzès and Avignon. **Cars de Camargue** (04.90.96.36.25) runs a service between Nîmes and Arles, four a day Mon-Sat, two on Sun.

The Rhône Delta

St-Rémy & the Alpilles

For all its chic boutiques and Parisian accents, St-Rémy is only a few kilometres from the improbable feudal village of Les Baux in the jagged Alpilles range.

The Rhône Delta

Caught in the inverted 'V' between the Rhône and Durance rivers south of Avignon, the fertile plain of the Petite Crau climbs to the south via chic St-Rémy-de-Provence to the craggy limestone peaks of the Chaîne des Alpilles. At the foot of the impregnable feudal stronghold of Les Baux, the Grande Crau plain stretches away south towards the Camargue.

St-Rémy-de-Provence

The St-Germain-des-Prés of the south, St-Rémy is where many of Paris' creative elite have their weekend homes. Excessively extravagant? Not really, given that the TGV now speeds from Paris to Avignon in a mere two-and-a-half hours. From there, a taxi will whisk them to St-Rémy, birthplace of Nostradamus (1503-1566) and home to Van Gogh for a year (1889-1890).

St-Rémy is a quintessential Provençal town, with its circular outer road shaded by ancient plane trees, and its centre of twisting narrow streets that lead to squares filled with fountains and *hôtels particuliers*. What gives St-Rémy irresistible allure, though, is its dramatic setting at the foot of Les Alpilles, the jagged hills whose whitewashed appearance intensifies the blue of the sky in winter and summer alike.

The circular boulevards Victor Hugo and Mirabeau, making up part of the old ramparts, are the liveliest part of town, crammed with cafés, restaurants and boutiques. At 8 boulevard Mirabeau is estate agent to the stars Emile Garcin (04.90.92.01.58). Anxious to sell only to those he feels will respect the 'soul' of the region, Garcin is capable of freezing dubious candidates out of his office. His architect partner Bruno Lafourcade (10 bd Victor Hugo, 04.90.92.10.14) can restore a house in fine Provençal style – for a superstar fee, of course.

One of St-Rémy's most pleasurable pursuits is drinking in the atmosphere at the **Café des Arts** (30 bd Victor Hugo, 04.90.92.08.50), opened in the 1950s and still a favourite with the *pastis*-swilling in-crowd. From its terrace watch the parade of soigné Parisians dressed for *la vie campagnarde*. Afterwards, head for the cluster of museums for a better appreciation of St-Rémy's ancient past.

The Hôtel de Sade, built on the site of Roman baths during the Renaissance, was once the family mansion of the Marquis de Sade; today it's the **Musée Archéologique**. On display are architectural fragments found at Glanum, the archaeological site on the outskirts of St-Rémy. Most distinctive are the pre-Roman sculptures, and a stone lintel with hollows carved to hold the severed heads of enemies.

At **Galérie Lestranger** respected art restorer Catherine Binda-Sterling holds August exhibitions in an 18th-century mansion, and sells art year-round (specialising in the period 1750-1850), along with antiques and quilts.

If it's the aromas of Provence that draw you, follow your nose to the **Musée des Arômes et des Parfums**. Here you'll find antique perfume stills and all kinds of heady potions made from essential oils.

From May 1889 to May 1890 Vincent Van Gogh was cared for by nuns in the psychiatric asylum adjoining the pretty Roman church of St-Paul-de-Mausole, just south of the town. During his stay he produced more than 150 paintings, including the celebrated *Olive Groves* and *Starry Night*. The 18th-century Hôtel Estrine inside St-Rémy is now the **Centre d'Art Présence Van Gogh** and has many reproductions of Van Gogh's work, along with letters from Vincent to his brother Théo.

About a kilometre south of the centre, just past the **Monastère St-Paul-de-Mausole** (open 9am-6pm daily), you come upon St-Rémy's impressive archaeological sites. Normally this would be an excuse for a pleasant country stroll but, given the speed of the traffic hurtling down the avenues Pasteur and Vincent Van Gogh, prepare for a dusty 15-minute sprint.

Greeks dominated the area until the first century BC, after which the Romans added to the settlement for around four centuries. The result is the fascinating mishmash of remains at **Glanum** and **Les Antiques**. Les Antiques has a magnificent Roman triumphal arch and a mausoleum, in tribute (some experts believe) to the grandsons of Emperor Augustus who ruled after Caesar. Across the road lies the entrance to Glanum, the ruins of which lay buried under river silt until 1921. What has come to light is certainly impressive but difficult to make sense of, though models and plans (and a visit to the Musée Archéologique) help, as do the facsimile temple columns, which convey a sense of scale.

The site's surprisingly good café-restaurant La Taberna Romana (open lunch May-Sept), serves tasty dishes inspired by ancient Roman food.

The south end of the site is like a corner of ancient Greece, all white limestone rocks and olive trees; you can see the sacred spring and sanctuary of the original settlers, with a deep water basin from the second century BC. The central area is the most complex, dominated by Roman temples.

Continuing south along the D5, the road twists and turns through stunning rock formations and patches of dense woodland towards Les Baux and Maussane (*see p65*).

Centre d'Art Présence Van Gogh

Hôtel Estrine, 8 rue Estrine (04.90.92.34.72). **Open** 10.30am-noon, 2.30-6.30pm Tue-Sun. Closed Jan-Mar. **Admission** €3.20; €2.30 students; free under-12s.

Galérie Lestranger

Place Jean-de-Renaud (04.90.92.57.14/06.80.25.02.62). By appointment only. **Credit** AmEx, MC, V.

Glanum

rte des Baux (04.90.92.23.79). **Open** *Apr-June, Sept* 9am-7pm daily; *July-Aug* 10am-noon, 2-7pm; *Oct-Mar* 9am-noon, 2-5pm daily. **Admission** €5.50; €3.50 18-25s; free under-18s.

Musée Archéologique

Hôtel de Sade, rue du Parage (04.90.92.64.04). **Open** *July-Aug* 10am-noon, 2-6pm daily; *Sept-Apr* 10am-noon, 2-5pm daily. **Admission** €2.50; free under-18s.

Musée des Arômes et des Parfums

34 bd Mirabeau (04.90.92.48.70). **Open** *Apr to mid-Sept* 9am-12.30pm, 2.30-7pm Mon-Sat. **Admission** free.

Where to stay & eat

Le Castelet des Alpilles (6 pl Mireille, 04.90.92.07.21, closed Nov-Mar, double €36.60-€78.50) is rustic but comfortable, with rooms looking on to a garden. Another simple but welcoming option is the **Hôtel du Cheval Blanc** (6 av Fauconnet, 04.90.92.09.28, closed 15 Nov-6 Feb, double €39.64-€45.73) in the heart of town, where Mme Maguy Ramon has been welcoming guests for 30 years. The intimate **Mas des Carassins** (1 chemin Gaulois, 04.90.92.15.48, closed 16 Nov-14 Mar, double €57.93-€86.90), has ten rooms in a converted 19th-century farmhouse with secluded gardens. Just outside St-Rémy on the road to Tarascon, the **Château de Roussan** (04.90.92.11.63, closed Nov-Feb, double €54.88-€114.34) is set in a breathtakingly romantic park. Bedrooms have antique furniture; bathrooms are a little spartan.

Tucked behind the Café des Arts' buzzing bar, the **Restaurant des Arts** (30 bd Victor-Hugo, 04.90.92.08.50, closed 10 Jan-10 Mar, average €18) is the oldest in St-Rémy and riddled with atmosphere. It specialises in rich, traditional dishes such as *daube de taureau*. There are 15 rooms upstairs (€32-€53.40, noise included). The straightforward decor of **Alain Assaud** (13 bd Marceau, 04.90.92.37.11, closed 15 Jan-15 Mar, menus €22.87-€35.06) belies the renowned chef's very sophisticated seasonal cuisine. At the good-value **La Gousse d'Ail**, (25 rue Carnot, 04.90.92.16.87, closed 10 Jan-10 Mar, menu €23.63), specialities include a sublime *soupe au pistou*.

Landseer colours of the **Alpilles** mountain range in autumn.

Shopping

St-Rémy boasts plenty of sophisticated shops. **Fabienne Villacreces** (10 rue Jaume Roux, 04.90.94.45.45) has beautifully cut, very feminine designs. **NM Déco** (9 rue Hoche, 04.90.92.57.91) offers sophisticated cashmere, silk and linen for swanning around your converted *mas*. At **Terre d'Art** (16 rue Jaume Roux, 04.90.92.41.21) you'll find no-fuss Provençal tableware. The danger at **Vent d'Autan** (49 rue Carnot, 04.32.60.06.54) is that the modern furniture and Provençal antiques will make you want to go house hunting – dream on if you're short of a few million (pounds).

Tourist information

Market day in St-Rémy is Wednesday. The Transhumance fair is on Easter Monday.

St-Rémy Office de Tourisme

pl Jean Jaurès, 13210 St-Rémy-de-Provence (04.90.92.05.22). **Open** *summer* 9am-noon, 1-7pm Mon-Sat, 9am-noon Sun; *winter* 9am-noon, 2-6pm Mon-Sat. Assorted guided tours include a night bird-watching tour of Les Alpilles to discover the largest concentration of Grand Duke owls in the world.

Châteaurenard, the Petite Crau & La Montagnette

Châteaurenard, the traffic-choked main town of the Petite Crau plain, is best known for its vast fruit and vegetable market. Two ruined towers are all that remain of the medieval castle, which came a cropper during the Revolution. More attractive by far is the hill of **La Montagnette** to the south-west, famous for its herbs. At the **Abbaye St-Michel-de-Frigolet** (*see below*) monks make a medicinal-tasting liqueur from thyme (*férigoulo* means thyme in Provençal).

At the heart of the Petite Crau, the pleasant town of **Maillane** is the birthplace of Frédéric Mistral, revered founder of the Félibrige movement (*see chapter* **History**). His house and garden – now the **Museon Mistral** – have been preserved exactly as he left them. Nearby, stop off at the sleepy village of **Graveson**, which has a Romanesque church and the **Musée Chabaud**, dedicated to the powerful landscape paintings and disturbing portraits of regional artist Auguste Chabaud (1882-1955).

Musée Auguste Chabaud

cours National, Graveson (04.90.90.53.02). **Open** *June-Sept* 10am-noon, 1.30-6.30pm daily; *Oct-May* 1.30-6.30pm daily. **Admission** €4; free under-12s.

The **Monastère St-Paul-de-Mausole** has tranquil gardens and cloisters. *See p60.*

Museon Mistral

11 av Lamartine, Maillane (mairie 04.90.95.74.06). **Open** *Apr-Sept* 9.30-11.30am, 2.30-6.30pm Tue-Sun; *Oct-Mar* 10-11.30am, 2-4pm Tue-Sun. **Admission** €3.50; €1 students; free under 11s.

Where to stay & eat

Still a monastery, the 19th-century **Abbaye St-Michel-de-Frigolet** (on D35, 04.90.95.70.07, double €28-€49, restaurant 04.90.90.52.70, closed Tue & Wed from Oct-Mar, menus €13-€16) now contains a hotel and restaurant.

Tourist information

Market day in Châteaurenard is Sunday.

Châteaurenard Office de Tourisme

11 cours Carnot, 13160 Châteaurenard (04.90.24.25.50). **Open** *July-Sept* 9am-noon, 3-7pm Mon-Sat, 10am-noon Sun; *Oct-June* 9am-noon, 2-6pm Mon-Sat.

Beaucaire & Tarascon

Beaucaire was home to one of the great medieval fairs of Europe, when thousands of merchants would sail their vessels up the Rhône to sell silks, spices, pots, skins, wines and textiles on the expanse of land between river and castle each July. Today, shabby streets

St-Rémy & the Alpilles

conceal Beaucaire's former prosperity; but closer examination reveals intricate architectural details in sculpted windows and doorways.

The **Château de Beaucaire** is now a picturesque ruin. Dominating the town and visible from almost everywhere, it's off-limits to the public except during afternoon falconry displays (daily July-Nov, daily except Wed Mar-June). The surrounding garden is a charming retreat, and contains the **Musée Auguste-Jacquet**, where odds and ends from Roman Beaucaire are beautifully displayed.

On the opposite bank of the Rhône, **Tarascon** is dominated by its great white-walled 15th-century **château**, the favourite castle of Good (as in good-living) King René. To satisfy the King's love of material comforts, the castle was lavishly decorated with spiral staircases, painted ceilings and tapestries. Snuggled around the castle is the old town. The rue des Halles has covered medieval arcades and the 15th-century **Cloître des Cordeliers**, used for exhibitions. The **Musée Souleiado** offers a history of the local textile industry.

To the French, **Tarascon** is synonymous with its fictional resident Tartarin, Alphonse Daudet's character who confirmed Parisians' preconceptions about bumbling provincials. The town is also inseparable from the Tarasque, a mythical river-dwelling beast reputedly used to devour the odd human until St Martha happened along in the ninth century. St Martha's bones are in the **Collégiale Ste-Marthe**. On the last weekend of June, a model of the dreaded beast is paraded through the streets amid fireworks and bullfights.

Four kilometres north-west of Beaucaire is the **Abbaye St-Roman**, an extraordinary fifth-century abbey with chapels, cells, altars and 150 tombs hewn out of sheer rock.

Mas des Tourelles, 4km south-west on the D38, is a copy of an ancient Roman winery, and produces wine the way the Romans did. The Centre national de la recherche scientifique (CNRS) was involved in the recreation of the recipes; we sipped and sniffed all three. They were – with the addition of ingredients such as fenugreek, honey and seawater – quite horrible. Which made their ordinary Costières de Nîmes taste like nectar, and we bought a few bottles to take away the taste. Good marketing ploy.

South of Beaucaire, **Le Vieux Mas** is a faithful reconstruction of an early 1900s Provençal farmhouse, with farm animals, original equipment and regional products.

Abbaye St-Roman
D99 (04.66.59.52.26). **Open** *Apr-Sept* 10am-6pm daily; *Oct-Mar* 2-5pm Sat, Sun & school holidays. **Admission** €4.55; free under-12s.

Château de Tarascon
bd du Roi René, Tarascon (04.90.91.01.93). **Open** 9am-noon, 2-5pm daily. **Admission** €5.50; free under-12s.

Mas des Tourelles
4294 rte de Bellegarde (04.66.59.19.72/ www.tourelles.com). **Open** *July-Aug* 10am-noon, 2-7pm daily; *Apr-June, Sept-Nov* 2-6pm daily; *Feb-Mar* 2-6pm Sat. Closed Nov-Jan. **Admission** €4.60; €1.50 under-6s.

Musée Auguste-Jacquet
In the gardens of Château de Beaucaire, Beaucaire (04.66.59.47.61). **Open** *Apr-Sept* 10am-noon, 2-6.45pm Mon, Wed-Sun; *Oct-Mar* 10.15am-noon, 2-5.15pm Mon, Wed-Sun. Closed one week Christmas. **Admission** €2.20; €0.60 under-14s.

Celebrity burials

Nostradamus
Collégiale de St-Laurent, Salon-de-Provence. *See p67.*

Albert Camus
Cimetière de Lourmarin. *See p119.*

Henri Matisse
Cimetière de Cimiez, Nice. *See p236.*

Le Corbusier
Cimetière de Roquebrune, Roquebrune-Cap Martin. *See p260.*

Roger Vadim
Cimetière Marin, St-Tropez. *See p175.*

William Webb Ellis
Cimetière de Menton. *See p262.*

Mary Magdalene
Basilique Ste-Marie Madeleine, St-Maximin-la-Ste-Baume. *See p189.*

Marc Chagall
Cimetière de St-Paul de Vence. *See p274.*

DH Lawrence (or not)
Cimetière de Vence (no body). *See p276.*

Pablo Picasso
Château de Vauvenarges (private), Montagne Ste-Victoire. *See p158.*

The Rhône Delta

Musée Souleiado
39 rue Proudhon, Tarascon (04.90.91.08.80). **Open** *May-Sept* 10am-6pm daily; *Oct-Apr* 10am-5pm Tue-Sat. **Admission** €6.10; €3.05 12-18s; free under-12s.

Le Vieux Mas
rte de Fourques (04.66.59.60.13). **Open** *Apr-Sept* 10am-7pm daily; *Oct-Mar* 10am-12.30pm, 1.30-6pm Wed, Sat, Sun & school holidays. **Admission** €5; €3.05 5-16s; free under-5s.

Where to stay & eat

The **Hôtel des Doctrinaires** (quai du Général de Gaulle, 04.66.59.23.70, double €53-€69) in Beaucaire is probably the best hotel of the two towns. Set in a 17th-century doctrinal college, dowdy but spacious guest rooms do not live up to the vaulted reception, but the trad cuisine (menus €15-€37) is popular with locals. A cheaper option is the **Hôtel Napoléon** (4 pl Frédéric Mistral, 04.66.59.05.17, double €29), in a square near the river; its restaurant offers pizzas and simple local cooking (average €12).

Across the river in Tarascon, the small **Hôtel Provençal** (12 cours Aristide Briand, 04.90.91.11.41, double €37-€43) has a restaurant serving regional specialities (menus €15-€20); not to be confused with the **Hôtel de Provence** (7 bd Victor-Hugo, 04.90.43.58.13, double €38-€50), a stylishly decorated hotel (no restaurant). Opposite the castle, **24 rue du Château** (04.90.91.09.99, double €70) is a *chambres d'hôtes* that oozes local charm.

Tourist information

Market day in Beaucaire is Thursday, in Tarascon Sunday.

Beaucaire Office de Tourisme
24 cour Gambetta, 33000 Beaucaire (04.66.59.26.57). **Open** *Apr-June, Aug, Sept* 8.45am-noon, 2-6pm Mon-Fri, 9.30am-12.30pm, 2.15-6.15pm Sat; *July* as above, plus 9am-noon Sun; *Oct-Mar* as above, closed Sat & Sun.

Tarascon Office de Tourisme
59 rue des Halles (04.90.91.03.52). **Open** *Apr-Sept* 9am-12.30pm, 2-6pm Mon-Sat, 10am-noon Sun; *Oct-Mar* 9am-noon, 2-5pm Mon-Sat.

The Alpilles, Les Baux-de-Provence & the Grande Crau

The craggy outcrop of the Alpilles is one of the more recent geological formations to be thrust up from the earth's crust, and it shows: there are no smooth, time-worn edges here, just dramatically barren rock stretching for 15km between the Rhône and the Durance. Dominating the Alpilles is the bizarre eyrie of Les Baux: not, as it seems from below, a natural phenomenon but a fortified village complete with ruined château.

The medieval Lords of Baux were an independent lot, swearing allegiance to no one and only too ready to resort to bloodshed. Their court, however, was renowned for its chivalry: only ladies of the highest birth and learning were admitted, and quibbles over questions of

Looking like a natural phenomenon, **Les Baux** nestles high in the Alpilles.

gallantry were often referred here. In 1372, the sadistic Raymond de Turenne became guardian of Alix, the last princess of Baux; dubbed 'the scourge of Provence', he terrorised the countryside for miles around, making his prisoners leap to their death from the castle walls. On Alix's death, a subdued Baux passed to Provence, then France, only to raise its head again as a Protestant stronghold in the 17th century. Cardinal Richelieu ordered the town to be dismantled and fined it into submission.

The village lay deserted for centuries, picking up again in 1822 when bauxite (named after the place) was discovered there, and subsequently when the wild and windswept became fashionable among travellers. The winding streets, cottages and noble mansions of the old town have been restored, and are visited by two million people a year. But the newer section of town has its share of interesting sights, including the **Musée Yves Brayer**, containing many of Brayer's vigorous oil paintings of the region, and the **Fondation Louis Jou**, where the presses, wood blocks and manuscripts of a typographer can be seen.

The 14th-century Tour de Brau houses the **Musée d'Histoire des Baux**, with huge models of siege engines and battering rams outside. Inside the old town, you can clamber over masonry and walk along the battlements, discovering remnants of towers and windows, a leper's hospital and breathtaking sheer drops to the plateau below.

From the edge of the escarpment, there are views across the savage, unearthly rocks of the Val d'Enfer (Hell Valley), said to have inspired Dante's *Inferno* and the backdrop for Cocteau's *Le Testament d'Orphée*. Walkers can follow Grande Randonnée 6 through the valley and along the crest of the Alpilles. The **Cathédrale d'Images** is a vast old bauxite quarry where audiovisual shows are projected on to the walls.

The lower slopes of the Alpilles are covered with vineyards producing Coteaux d'Aix-en-Provence-Les-Baux, a wine with a growing reputation. In the heart of the Alpilles (though most easily reached on the D99, then the D74 east from St-Rémy-de-Provence), the tiny village of **Eygalières** is really too pretty for its own good, now filled with overpriced interior design shops and restaurants. However, its delightful 12th-century chapel **St-Sixte**, which dominates a spartan, luminous hillside speckled with olive and almond trees, lifts the spirits. Pagan rites involving spring water from Les Alpilles were performed on the hill. Indeed, one still remains: on the day of a couple's engagement the future husband drinks spring water from his fiancé's hands. If they don't marry within a year he dies.

To the south-west, **Fontvieille** boasts one of France's great literary landmarks, the **Moulin de Daudet**. The stories in Alphonse Daudet's *Letters from my Windmill* (1860) capture the essence of life in the South, though he was accused of caricaturing the local bumpkins. He never actually lived in his windmill, preferring a friend's château nearby, but the view from the pine-scented hilltop is delightful and the little museum on milling is informative. Just outside town, on the road to Arles, are the remains of a Roman aqueduct.

Further along the same road stands the great abbey of **Montmajour**, one of the largest religious sanctuaries in medieval Provence. In the tenth century, a community of hermits under Benedictine rule was founded on a great rock surrounded by marshes. The 12th-century church and 14th-century crypt and cloisters have been painstakingly pieced together over the past century by the sensitive souls of Arles. The interior is plain, serene and cold; it's at its most human in the tiny 11th-century chapel of St Peter, with hermits' cells and an altar gouged out of a cave.

All around stretches the plain of the Grand Crau, the arid, rocky limestone 'desert' of Provence. Part of the expanse is cultivated, producing, among other things, France's only hay to be awarded an *appellation contrôlée*.

Abbaye de Montmajour

rte de Fontvieille (04.90.54.64.17). **Open** *Apr-Sept* 9am-7pm Mon, Wed-Sun; *Oct-Mar* 10am-1pm, 2-5pm Mon, Wed-Sun. **Admission** €5; free under-18s.

Cathédrale d'Images

Val d'Enfer (04.90.54.38.65). **Open** 10am-6pm daily. Closed mid-Jan to mid-Feb. **Admission** €7; €4.10 8-18s; free under-8s.

Fondation Louis Jou

Hôtel Jean de Brion, Grande Rue, Les Baux-de-Provence (04.90.54.34.17). **Open** by appointment. **Admission** €3; €1.50 7-18s; free under-7s.

Moulin de Daudet

Allée des Pins, Fontvieille (04.90.54.60.78). **Open** *Apr-Sept* 9am-7pm daily; *Oct-Mar* 10am-noon, 2-5pm daily. Closed Jan. **Admission** €2; €1 6-12s; free under-6s.

Musée d'Histoire des Baux

Hôtel de la Tour de Brau, rue de Trencart, Les Baux-de-Provence (04.90.54.55.56). **Open** *June-Aug* 9am-8pm daily; *Apr-May* 9am-6.30pm daily; *Sept-Mar* 9am-5pm daily. **Admission** €6.50; €3.50 7-17s; free under-7s.

Musée Yves Brayer

Hôtel des Porcelets, rue de l'Eglise, Les Baux-de-Provence (04.90.54.36.99). **Open** *Apr-Sept* 10am-noon, 2-6.30pm daily; *Oct-Mar* 10am-noon, 2-5pm daily. **Admission** €4; €2.50 15-18s; free under-15s.

The bauxite **Cathédrale d'Images.** *See p65.*

Where to stay & eat

In Baux, the **Mas d'Aigret** (04.90.54.20.00/ www.masdaigret.com, closed Jan, double €95-€130), situated right below the fortress on the D27A, has recently renovated rooms with balconies and a swimming pool. The **Reine Jeanne** (04.90.54.32.06, closed two weeks Nov, three weeks Jan, menus €20, €27) serves reliable regional dishes. Tucked away amid fig trees just off the main road leading up to Les Baux, **L'Oustau de Beaumanière** (Val d'Enfer, Les Baux-de-Provence, 04.90.54.33.07, closed Wed & Thur Oct-May and all Jan-Feb, menus €82-€128) is perhaps the most quietly glamorous country inn in France. Chef Jean-André Charial produces luxurious classical cooking, and there's even a seven-course vegetable *menu* from the hotel's own gardens.

L'Oustaloun (pl de l'Eglise, Mausanne-les-Alpilles, 04.90.54.32.19, closed three weeks Feb, three weeks Nov, double €55) has eight rooms in a 16th-century abbey, with a restaurant (menus €19, €29) serving regional cuisine. Deep in the Alpilles, the **Domaine de Valmouriane** (petite rte des Baux, 04.90.92.44.62, double €125-€305) is a luxurious *mas* with rooms surrounded by lawn and woods, and pool. The restaurant (menus €29.80-€64.10) offers stylish

regional cooking. The exquisitely prepared food at the **Cabro d'Or** (Mas Carita, rte d'Arles, 04.90.54.33.21, closed lunch Mon & Sun and Nov to mid-Dec, menus €45-€70) is served inside or on a serene garden terrace.

To make the most of Eygalières, stay at the **Hôtel Le Mas du Pastre** (04.90.95.92.61, closed mid-Nov to mid-Dec, double €77-€130), a charming converted farmhouse with a pool. The **Bistrot d'Eygalières** (rue de la République, 04.90.90.60.34, closed Oct-Apr) has a showbiz clientele who come for hotly tipped young Belgian chef Wout Bru. Four rooms are available (€115-€160) too.

Fontvieille has a reputation for being a fine town to eat in, with plenty of bistros. Towering above its rivals is the **Auberge La Régalido** (rue Frédéric Mistral, 04.90.54.60.22, closed Feb, double €122-€262, menus €42.70-€64), which offers old-fashioned *haute cuisine* and accommodation in an ancient *moulin à huile*.

Tourist information

Les Baux Office du Tourisme

Maison du Roi, 13520 Les Baux-de-Provence (04.90.54.34.39). **Open** *Mar-Sept* 9am-7pm daily; *Oct-Apr* 9.30am-1pm, 2-6pm daily.

Salon-de-Provence

It might sound like the drawing room of Provence to you and me, but the French associate Salon above all with the Air Force flying school, whose presence is announced by the periodic scream of jet engines overhead. The chief tourist draw of this rather characterless town on the edge of the Crau plain is the **Maison de Nostradamus**, the house where the astrologer and doctor wrote his *Centuries* and lived from 1547 until his death in 1566. A CD-guided visit talks you through some kitsch waxwork tableaux: podgy little Michel being schooled in cabalism by his uncle, his medical studies at Montpellier, the Plague (when Nostradamus became famous for his miraculous remedies, despite the fact that his first wife and two children died), and the final, consecratory visit from a busty, satin-clad Catherine de Médicis. Nostradamus' tomb is a simple tablet set into the wall of the chapel of the Virgin in the 14th-century Gothic **Collégiale de St-Laurent** (Paroisse St-Laurent, 04.90.56.06.40), beyond the city wall.

Salon's skyline is dominated by the **Château de l'Emperi**, built between the tenth and 13th centuries for the bishops of Arles. A fortified medieval outer courtyard ringed by square turrets leads through to an arcaded Renaissance inner courtyard. Within is a military museum and some Napoleonic memorabilia. The Romanesque/early Gothic church of **St-Michel** in the old town is also worth a look, as are two surviving town gateways: the **Tour de Bourg Neuf**, guarded by a black Virgin, and the **Porte de l'Horloge**, topped by a wrought-iron belfry. Modern town life centres on the tree-lined avenues surrounding the over-restored *vieille ville*, around the **Hôtel de Ville** and the shops of cours Gimon, and on place Croustillat, where cafés overlook a lumpy, mossy fountain.

Around 1900, the arrival of the railway made Salon a boomtown. Prosperous soap barons (much of what is called *savon de Marseille* is actually made here) built themselves fanciful *faux-châteaux*. Several remain, especially around the station. Installed in a 19th-century *bastide*, the **Musée de Salon et de la Crau** focuses on Salon's soap industry heyday.

East of Salon, the **Château de la Barben** was originally a fortress belonging to the Abbaye de St-Victor in Marseille, before becoming a residence of King René. Later it was home to the powerful Forbin family, who brought in André Le Nôtre of Versailles fame to redesign the gardens. The adjoining **Zoo de la Barben** is a popular family attraction.

Château & Zoo de la Barben

11km east of Salon on D572/D22 (château 04.90.55.25.41/zoo 04.90.55.19.12). **Open** *château* 10am-noon, 2-5.30pm daily; *zoo* 10am-6pm daily. **Admission** *château* €7; €4 3-13s; free under-3s; *zoo* €9.20; €4.60 3-13s; free under-3s.

Château de l'Emperi

pl des Centuries (04.90.56.22.36). **Open** 10am-noon, 2-6pm Mon, Wed-Sun. **Admission** €3.05; €2.30 7-15; free under-7s.

Maison de Nostradamus

13 rue Nostradamus (04.90.56.64.31). **Open** 9am-noon, 2-6pm Mon-Fri; 2-6pm Sat, Sun. **Admission** €3.05; €2.30 7-18s, students; free under-7s.

Musée de Salon et de la Crau

av Roger Donnadieu (04.90.56.14.65). **Open** 10am-noon, 2-6pm Mon, Wed-Fri; 2-6pm Sat, Sun. **Admission** €3; free under-17s.

Where to stay & eat

The grandest place to stay is the **Abbaye de Ste-Croix** (rte du Val de Cuech [D16], 04.90.56.24.55, closed 5 Nov-end Mar, double €137-€396), 5km out of town in the Crau. Most rooms have private gardens or roof terraces, there's a pool and a restaurant that draws local bigwigs (closed lunch Mon, menus €60-€85). Far better value is the **Hostellerie Domaine de La Reynaude** in Aurons (04.90.59.30.24, double €53-€110, menus €20-€35), a converted

coaching inn in a pretty valley. Bedrooms are modern and comfortable, but the chief draw in summer is the large pool. **Le Vincennes** (rte de Pélissanne, 04.90.42.08.67, menus €15-€27) is a popular restaurant between Salon and Pélissanne. In Salon, the **Hôtel Vendôme** (34 rue Maréchal Joffre, 04.90.56.01.96, double €40-€47) has a small garden. The best restaurant in town is **La Salle à Manger** (6 rue Maréchal Joffre, 04.90.56.28.01, average €20).

Tourist information

Market day is Wednesday.

Salon Office de Tourisme

56 cours Gimon, 13300 Salon-de-Provence (04.90.56.27.60). **Open** *15 June-15 Sept* 9am-12.30pm, 2.30-7pm Mon-Sat, 10am-4pm Sun; *16 Sept-14 June* 9am-noon, 2-6pm Mon-Sat.

▶ Getting There & Around

▶ By car

St-Rémy is on the D99 between Tarascon and Cavaillon. Or south of Avignon on the N570 and D571, via Châteaurenard. Baux-de-Provence is about 8km south of St-Rémy by D5 and D27. Tarascon and Beaucaire are reached by N570 and D970 from Avignon or D999 from Nîmes. Salon-de-Provence is at the junction of the A7 (exit no.27) and A54 (exit nos.14/15) autoroutes or by N113 from Arles.

▶ By train

Frequent TGVs serve Avignon and Nîmes. Local trains stop at Tarascon on the Avignon Centre-Arles line. Salon-de-Provence has several trains a day from Avignon; for Marseille or Arles, change at Miramas.

▶ By bus

Rapides du Sud-Est (04.90.14.59.13) runs frequent buses to Châteaurenard and St-Rémy from Avignon *gare routière*. **CEYTE** (04.90.93.74.90) runs one afternoon bus from Arles to Tarascon Mon-Fri, and two or three buses a day from Arles to Les Baux, Mon-Sat. **Les Cars de Camargue** (04.90.96.94.78/www.lepilote.com) buses between Aix and Arles stop at Salon-de-Provence, St-Martin-de-Crau and Mouriès. **STD Gard** (04.66.29.27.29) runs roughly six buses a day betwee Nîmes and Avignon stopping at Beaucaire and Tarascon. **Cévennes** (04.66.84.96.86) runs six buses a day between St-Rémy and Tarascon Mon-Fri, plus Sat during school terms.

Arles

Arles is fiercely proud of its Provençal heritage but its appetite for culture extends from Roman antiquities to contemporary photography and literature.

Straddling the river Rhône, Arles wears its history with ease; the town's ancient monuments are not museum pieces but part of the urban fabric. The great Roman arena is encircled by the old town like a snail in its shell, while newer buildings snuggle up to the walls of the cathedral of St-Trophime. Arles and its surrounding region are littered with antiquities, so much so that a recent state ruling proposing archaeological research before undertaking any new construction was held off with difficulty by the mayor of Arles.

The medieval centre of Arles was built over the Roman ruins and happily incorporates earlier vestiges, such as the column embedded in the Grand Hôtel Nord Pinus on the site of the original forum. It has an intimate feel; narrow streets providing protection from the chilly blasts of the mistral, cobbled alleys and hidden courtyards concealing centuries of history.

Arles was a Greek trading port as early as the sixth century BC, but its importance grew by leaps and bounds in 104 BC when the Romans constructed a canal to facilitate river navigation between the city and the sea. In 49 BC, the city backed Julius Caesar in his victorious bid to break Marseille's stranglehold on not only sea trade but the Domitian Way land route from Rome to Spain. Arles' moment of glory had arrived, and it began to acquire its rich heritage of no-expense-spared monuments. The city was home to a roaring trade in everything the Orient produced, as well as its own flourishing output of textiles and silverware.

Dark Ages battles took a relatively minor toll on the town and, by the Middle Ages, Arles had regained its clout, becoming a major centre of religious and temporal power. At its height, the kingdom of Arles included Burgundy and part of Provence. The kingdom was so influential that in 1178 Holy Roman Emperor Frederick Barbarossa pitched up and was crowned King of Arles in the newly finished cathedral.

Gradually, however, the sea retreated, Marseille took over as the most important Rhône port and railway traffic replaced river traffic. And though Frédéric Mistral and his Félibrige freedom fighters (*see chapter* **History**) fought tooth and nail in the 19th century to restore the area's prestige, Arles never really regained its former glory.

This fact has failed to dent the Arlésian attachment to local traditions. Athough long-running festivals, especially the exciting climax of the bullfight *férias* in April and July, prompt the most colourful displays of local pride when everyone from middle-aged matrons to teenagers appears in full Arlésienne fig (lace *fichus*, shawls, bonnets and all), just about any event will bring Arles' citizens out en masse: the **Rencontres Internationales de la Photographie**, which sees photo exhibitions all over town; **Les Suds à Arles** world music festival, and **Mosaïque Gitane**, a flamenco festival, in July and August; the **Fêtes des Prémices du Riz** rice harvest in September (*see chapter* **The Festive South**).

Arles is irrevocably linked with **Van Gogh**, who arrived here in February 1888 in search of southern light and colour, only to discover the city covered in thick snow. Undaunted, he rented the 'Yellow House' and began working furiously. In the space of 15 months, punctuated by the occasional stay in the town asylum and the lopping off of his own ear, he produced some 300 canvases of startling colours and contours. In truth the good citizens of Arles, like everybody else, rejected the unbalanced Dutchman, who in April 1889, terrified that he was losing his artistic grip, checked himself into the asylum at nearby St-Rémy-de-Provence. Somewhat embarrassed by not owning a single one of the 300 works that the artist churned out while in Arles, the city makes do with a mock-up of one of his most famous subjects, the **Café de la Nuit**, and the **Espace Van Gogh** bookshop and arts centre. The **Fondation Van Gogh**, however, pays the right sort of homage to the misunderstood genius. Its superb collection of works by contemporary masters would have pleased Van Gogh, who so much wanted to establish a community of artists here.

Sightseeing

The best view of Arles is from the top tier of the **Arènes** (Roman amphitheatre), looking across terracotta roofs and ochre walls to the River Rhône. Adjacent to the Arènes are the crumbling remains of the **Théâtre Antique** (Roman theatre), described by Henry James as 'the most touching ruins I had ever beheld'.

Les Alyscamps: the place to be buried BC.

Today they provide an atmospheric backdrop for a summer theatre season in June and July. Further down the hill on place de la République stands the great Romanesque **Cathédrale St-Trophime**. The magnificent 12th-century sculpture around the doorway on the newly scrubbed façade is equalled only by the superb cloisters next door. At the centre of the square is a fountain and an Egyptian granite obelisk, moved here from the Roman circus in the 17th century, and the **Hôtel de Ville** with its Versailles-inspired facade and celebrated vestibule vaulting. Accessible from the vestibule is the Plan de la Cour, a small square of medieval buildings with several historic municipal buildings, the 13th-century Palais des Podestats with its Romanesque doorway and windows and, next to it, a lovely 15th-century *maison commune*. Beneath the Hôtel de Ville are the **Cryptoportiques**, an underground gallery built by the Romans to support the forum (accessible from rue Balze.)

A block away is Frédéric Mistral's pet project, the **Museon Arlaten**, with its vast collection devoted to Provençal folklore, crafts and particularly costumes, all housed in a 16th-century mansion with a courtyard built round the columns of the original Roman forum. At every turn is intriguing evidence of Arles' many layers, such as the Corinthian columns (themselves a reference to the Romans) of a 12th-century cloister door on rue de Cloître, the antique bas-reliefs on the Hôtel des Amazones in rue des Arènes, or the 18th-century bulls' heads sculpted on the façade of the Grande Boucherie in rue du 4 Septembre.

The **place du Forum**, adjacent to the original forum site, is the centre of Arles life today, buzzing with cafés and restaurants, notably the Van Gogh-pastiche **Café de la Nuit**, and the **Grand Hôtel Nord Pinus**, where bullfighters and their acolytes congregate. All is watched over by a statue of Frédéric Mistral, leaning on his stick and looking, as he himself complained, as if he's waiting for a train. From here it is a short stroll to the banks of the Rhône, where you can walk along the quais, visit the partly excavated **Thermes de Constantin** baths complex or browse through the collections of Picasso and other modern masters in the **Musée Réattu**, housed in a lovely old priory with a facade that was once part of the city walls.

At the southern end of rue de l'Hôtel de Ville and the Jardin d'Eté, the shady, café-lined **boulevard des Lices** is the best place to observe *le tout Arles*, especially on Saturday mornings, when the market held there offers southern colours and smells. Local cheeses, olives, hams and sausages – donkey is the local speciality – are generally good buys, as are the pottery and olive-wood bowls.

Further south, the necropolis of **Les Alyscamps** lies on the ancient Aurelian Way from Rome. The avenue of marble sarcophagi is a wonderfully melancholy place to stroll, especially at dusk when the owls start to hoot. The best of the tombs and sculptures, however, have been transferred to the **Musée de l'Arles Antique**, west of the old centre. Spanking new and purpose-built for the city's collection of old marbles, the museum lies on the banks of the Rhône by the site of the Roman circus, itself under excavation.

Before leaving Les Alyscamps, spare a thought for ancient monuments of another kind: the Jeanne Calment retirement home is named after the woman who held the title of world's oldest person (able to remember Van Gogh in her mother's *boulangerie*) before she died aged 120 in 1997.

Les Alyscamps

av des Alyscamps (04.90.49.36.87). **Open** *Apr-Sept* 9am-7pm daily; *Oct-Mar* 10am-4.30pm daily. **Admission** €3.50; €2.06 12-18s; free under-12s. **No credit cards**.

From its beginnings as a pre-Christian necropolis until well into the Middle Ages, Les Alyscamps (the name means the Elysian Fields) was one of the most fashionable places in Europe to spend eternity. Corpses from up-country were parcelled up and floated down the Rhône with the burial fee in their mouths, to be fished out by gravediggers' assistants on the Trinquetaille bridge. By the Renaissance, many of the magnificent stone sarcophagi had been stolen or presented to distinguished visitors; in the 19th century the railway cut through one end of the cemetery. But it remains as wonderfully atmospheric as when Van Gogh painted the avenue of remaining tombs. You can still see the tiny ruined church of St-Honorat, with its Romanesque tower, and the marks where St Trophime is said to have kneeled to bless the spot.

Les Arènes

rond-point des Arènes (04.90.49.36.86/box office 04.90.96.03.70/www.label-camargue.com). **Open** *Mar* 9am-5.30pm daily; *Apr-May* 9am-noon, 2-7pm daily; *June-Sept* 9am-6.30pm daily; *Oct-Feb* 10am-4.30pm daily. Closed during events. **Admission** €4; €3 12-18s; free under-12s.

This Roman amphitheatre is one of the oldest in the Roman world, built in the first century AD to accommodate 21,000 spectators, with tunnels at the bottom through which wild beasts were released into the arena. Like Nîmes, it had three storeys of 60 arcades each, but the top floor here was plundered for building stone in the Middle Ages. The rest is in remarkably good shape because it was fortified for defensive purposes in the Middle Ages. The rabble that constructed a slum town within its walls a couple of centuries later was not cleared out until 1825, when restorations began.

For a true taste of Roman-style bloodlust, come for a bullfight, when the arena echoes to the sound of the spectators and the persecuted animal. The arena is used for both classic Spanish-style bullfighting and the more humorous, less bloodthirsty local variant, *course Camarguaise*. The bullfighting season gets underway with the April *féria* and the *gardian* festival on 1 May, when the Queen of Arles is crowned; it culminates at the beginning of July when

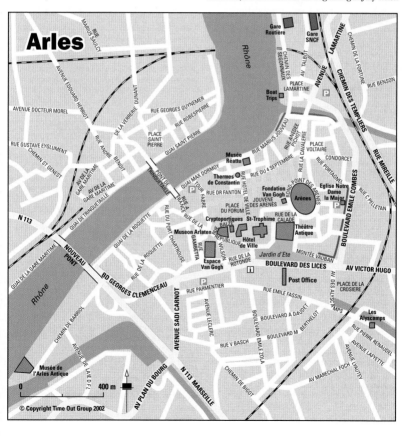

Getting in on the Actes

The cultural heart of Arles is a publishing house. Actes Sud was established just over 20 years ago – a rare exception in France where publishing has long been heavily centralised in Paris. Today, its lively complex on the banks of the Rhône includes a large, well-stocked bookshop, a cinema, a comfortable bar and a Moroccan restaurant, **l'Entrevue**, that is favoured by the fashionable *jeunesse* of Arles. There is even the **Hammam Chiffa**, a gorgeous Turkish bath, where you can order lamb couscous to follow the steam room. Actes Sud also sponsors concerts and art and photography exhibitions in the nearby Chapelle St-Martin du Méjan.

Actes Sud was set up in 1978 by Belgian writer Hubert Nyssen and his wife, translator Christine Le Boeuf, in Le Paradou, a small village in the Alpilles not far from where Mistral had kick-started the Provençal literary renaissance a century before. They moved to the present location in 1983 and subsequently opened a Paris office. Early success came with Nyssen's discovery of the unpublished work of Russian exile Nina Berberova. Her novel, *L'accompagnatrice*, was published in 1985, followed by many other works, including her autobiography, *C'est moi qui souligne*. Translation is key and the main list includes many foreign authors, from Don DeLillo and Paul Auster to WG Sebald and Joyce Carol Oates. There are children's, travel, art, cinema and food books, too, all bearing the distinctive, elegant Actes Sud typography. The Sinbad imprint covers a huge range of Arabic works from history and classics to contemporary writers, thus bridging the cultural gap not just between Paris and the south but the north and south of the Mediterranean.

Actes Sud

23 quai Marx Dormoy. **Librairie** 9am-7pm Mon-Fri; **Cinéma** *(04.90.93.33.56) films* 6.30pm, 9pm Mon-Sat, 3pm, 6pm Sun; **L'Entrevue** *(04.90.93.37.28)* 11am-2pm, 7.30-10.30pm Mon-Sat; 11am-2pm Sun; **Hammam Chiffa** (04.90.96.10.32) *men* 5.30-10pm Mon, Wed, Thur; *women* 9am-5pm Mon, Sat, Sun; 9am-10pm Tue-Fri.

the coveted Cocarde d'Or prize is awarded. Tickets are usually available on the gate, but must be booked ahead for the *féria* and Cocarde d'Or events. During summer, the arena also hosts concerts and films. There's a superb view of Arles from the top.

Cathédrale St-Trophime

pl de la République (04.90.96.07.38). **Open** *church* 8.30am-6.30pm daily; *cloister* 10am-5.30pm daily. **Admission** *church* free; *cloister* €3.50; €2.06 12-18s; free under-12s.

A church has stood on this site since the fifth century. The current, stunning Romanesque cathedral was built in the 12th century to house the relics of St Trophimus, a third-century bishop of Arles. Its austere nave is impressively tall, hung with Aubusson tapestries and dotted with Roman sarcophagi and 17th-century Dutch paintings. It is the portal, however, that really takes your breath away. Recently restored, its vivid carving is clearly visible: the tympanum shows Christ in glory, with life-size apostles accommodated in the columns below. The frieze – its style perhaps inspired by Roman sarcophagi – depicts the Last Judgement, with souls being dragged off to hell in chains or handed over to saints in heaven. The cloister sculptures are Romanesque in the north and east arcades and 14th-century Gothic in the south and west; the two styles form a surprisingly harmonic whole. The carved columns and capitals feature a rich profusion of characters and stories from the Bible. Above the cloister, a walkway offers good views of the bell tower and the town.

Cryptoportiques

rue Baize. **Open** *Apr-Sept* 9am-7pm daily; *Oct-Mar* 10am-6.30pm daily. **Admission** €3.50; €2.06 12-18s; free under-12s.

These mysterious, horseshoe-shaped Roman underground galleries were originally constructed to support the hillside foundations of the forum and may also have been used as a religious sanctuary or for grain storage. During World War II they provided refuge for Resistance members and still exude a chill and sinister atmosphere.

Fondation Van Gogh

Palais de Luppé, 24bis rond-point des Arènes (04.90.49.55.49). **Open** *Apr to mid-Oct* 10am-7pm Tue-Sun; *mid-Oct to mid-Mar* 9.30am-noon, 2-5.30pm Tue-Sun. Closed one week Mar. **Admission** €5; €3.50 8-18s; students, free under-8s.

Work by contemporary artists in tribute to Van Gogh include a Hockney chair, a Rauschenberg sunflower in acrylic yellow and blue on steel, plus works by Bacon, Rosenquist, Lichtenstein and Viallat, and photos by Doisneau and Cartier-Bresson. The excellent catalogue explains how Vincent inspired each artist. *July-Sept 2002.* Francis Bacon's series *Self-Portraits of Van Gogh Walking on the Road to Tarascon* will be shown in France for the first time.

Musée de l'Arles Antique

presqu'île du Cirque Romain (04.90.18.88.88/ www.arles-antique.org). **Open** *Mar-Oct* 9am-7pm

Les Arènes: gladiatorial heart of the city.

daily; *Nov-Feb* 10am-6pm daily. **Admission** €5.35; €3.80 12-18s; under-12s free.

On the fringes of the Roman circus, which is currently being excavated, this modern blue triangle (designed by Henri Ciriani) houses the many antiquities once scattered throughout Arles' museums and archeological sites. The well-displayed collection includes statues, capitals, carved friezes, pottery, jewellery, glass and villa mosaics along with maps, models and town plans. Best of all are the beautifully carved sarcophagi from the necropolis of Les Alyscamps, many of which date from the fourth century AD or earlier.

Musée Réattu

10 rue du Grand Prieuré (04.90.49.36.74). **Open** *Mar-Apr* 10am-12.30pm, 2-5.30pm daily; *May-Sept* 10am-12.30pm, 2-7pm. *Oct-Feb* 1-5.30pm daily. **Admission** €4; €3 12-18s; free under-12s.

Housed in a fine 15th-century priory, this museum contains works by its founder, Provençal artist Jacques Réattu, along with a collection of more modern work by Léger, Dufy, Gauguin and others. Most notable are the 57 drawings made by Picasso in 1971 and donated to the museum by the artist a year later to thank Arles for amusing him with its bullfights. Also by Picasso is a delicious rendering of Lee Miller as an Arlésienne painted in Mougins in 1937.

Museon Arlaten

29 rue de la République (04.90.93.58.11). **Open** *Apr, May* 9.30am-12.30pm, 2-6pm *July-Aug* 9am-1pm, 2-6.30pm daily; *Oct* 9am-noon, 2-5.30pm Tue-Sun; *Nov-Mar* 9am-noon, 2-5pm Tue-Sun; *Apr-May* 9am-noon, 2-6pm Tue-Sun; *June* 9am-1pm, 2-6.30pm Tue-Sun. **Admission** €4; €3 12-18s; free under-12s.

Frédéric Mistral used the money from his Nobel Prize for Literature in 1896 to set up this museum to preserve the traditions of Provence, thus establishing an enduring fashion for collections of regional memorabilia. Attendants wear Arlésien costume and captions come in French and Provençal only. Despite the stuffiness, this is a worthwhile and authentic collection of humble domestic and rural objects: furniture, tools, kitchen equipment, shoes and clothing. Best of all is a bizarre haul of traditional talismans: a fig branch burned to encourage maternal milk, a ring fashioned from the third nail of a horseshoe to ward off haemorrhoids and large quantities of toothache-prevention equipment. There are large tableaux, too: a home birth; a Christmas scene with the traditional 13 desserts of Provence; and a Camargue *gardian's* cabin.

Le Pont Van Gogh

route de Port-St-Louis.

Van Gogh's famous Pont du Langlois has recently been restored (it was damaged by bombing during World War II) and moved to the southern outskirts of Arles. Follow direction Port-St-Louis-du-Rhône out of Arles and look out for a sign to the left.

Théâtre Antique

rue de la Calade (04.90.49.36.25). **Open** *Dec, Jan* 10-11.30am, 2-4.30pm daily; *Feb* 10-11am, 2-4.30pm daily; *Mar* 9am-noon, 2-4.30pm daily; *Apr to mid-June, last two weeks Sept* 9am-noon, 2-6.30pm daily; *mid-June to mid-Sept* 9am-6.30pm daily; *Oct, Nov* 10am-noon, 2-5.30pm daily. **Admission** €3; €2.05 12-18s; students, free under-12s.

The Roman theatre, dating from the first century BC and ransacked for building stone from the fifth

century, is today a mess of tumbledown columns and fragments of carved stones. Its forlorn glory makes it a particularly romantic setting for summer theatre and music performances. Vestiges of the original tiers of stone benches remain, along with two great sections of the stage wall, once used as a gallows. It was here in 1651 that the Venus of Arles, now in the Louvre, was dug up.

Thermes de Constantin

rue du Grand Prieuré. **Open** *Apr-Sept* 9am-7pm daily; *Oct-Mar* 10am-6.30pm daily. **Admission** €3; €2.06 12-18s; free under-12s
At the fourth-century Roman baths, once part of a complex of baths on the banks of the Rhône, you can still see the vaulted pool and the bricks of the caldarium, the underfloor heating system.

Arts & entertainment

See also Les Arènes, above. For entertainment listings, pick up fortnightly freebie *César* (www.cesar.fr) in shops and the tourist office.

Espace Van Gogh

pl du Docteur Félix Rey (04.90.49.37.53). **Open** 1-5pm daily. **Admission** free.
A library, bookshop and exhibition space set around a garden courtyard in the hospital where the painter was treated, restored to look as it did in his time.

Théâtre d'Arles

bd Georges Clemenceau (04.90.52.51.51). **Box office** 1-6.30pm Tue-Fri, 10am-12.30pm, 2.30-6pm and one hour before performance Sat. **Tickets** €20.
Finally restored and re-opened in 2001, this splendid old theatre offers a variety of performances – plays, music, storytelling and lectures.

Théâtre de la Calade

Le Grenier à Sel, 49 quai de la Roquette (04.90.93.05.23/www.theatredelacalade.voici.org). **Box office** 10am-12.30pm, 2-6pm Mon-Fri. **Tickets** €4.60-€16.80.
Based in a former salt warehouse, this theatre company offers its own performances, opera, visiting companies and workshops.

Restaurants

L'Affenage

4 rue Molière (04.90.96.07.67). **Open** noon-2pm, 7-9.30pm Mon-Sat. Closed two weeks Aug. **Menus** €16-€160. **Credit** MC, V.
An old coach house, with a rustic atmosphere and a large fireplace, serving a buffet of Provençal starters (grilled veg, *tapenade, anchoïade*) and dishes, such as duck *confit* and calf's liver with balsamic vinegar.

Au Bryn du Thym

22 rue du Dr Fanton (04.90.49.95.96). **Open** noon-2pm, 7-10pm daily. Closed Tue Nov-Mar. **Menu** €15. **Credit** AmEx, MC, V.
Tucked behind place du Forum, this intimate new

restaurant – all white beams, white tablecloths, tiled floor and bunches of lavender – serves Provençal-based cuisine with a rich touch: *gambas a la crème de whisky*, pumpkin soup with scallops, duck with figs, *taureau* steak with *mirabelles*. Good tarts, cheese and fresh verbena tea from *madame*'s garden.

Brasserie Nord Pinus

14 pl du Forum (04.90.93.02.32). **Open** *June-Aug* noon-2.30pm, 7-10.30pm daily; *Sept-May* noon-2.30pm, 7-10.30pm Mon, Tue, Thur-Sun. Closed mid-Jan to mid-Mar. **Menus** €15-€29. **Credit** MC, V.
A classic grand brasserie with elegant table settings and immaculate service. The menu features stylish French regional cooking, with dishes such as cold tomato soup with croûtons and goat's cheese, red tuna with *pipérade* and *soupe de figues* with liquorice ice-cream for dessert.

La Gueule de Loup

39 rue des Arènes (04.90.96.96.69). **Open** 7.45-9.45pm Mon; 12.30-1.30pm, 7.45-9.45pm Tue-Sat. **Average** €34. **Credit** MC, V.
You get to this first-floor, wood-beamed restaurant through the deliciously scented kitchen where *madame* busily chops shallots in her big white apron. Try the *charlotte d'agneau* with aubergines and red pepper coulis, a *tarte Tatin* of deliciously sweet turnips with foie gras, scallop and sorrel terrine and chestnut mousse with almond milk. Book.

Lou Caleu

27 rue Porte de Laure (04.90.49.71.77). **Open** noon-2pm, 7-10pm Tue-Sat. Closed 15 Jan-15 Feb. **Menus** €15-€25. **Credit** AmEx, DC, MC, V.
The best of several little restaurants on a street near the Roman theatre gives a light touch to Provençal cooking in dishes such as chicken with herbs and honey, tomato stuffed with aubergine, roast suckling pig or pork *daube*. Desserts are uninspired.

La Mule Blanche

9 rue du Président Wilson (04.90.93.98.54). **Open** noon-3pm, 8pm-11.30pm Mon-Sat. Closed Jan. **Average** €17. **Credit** MC, V.
Be prepared to wait for a seat on the palm-shaded terrace to sample the fresh Mediterranean cuisine of olive oil, grilled fish and meat, salads and pasta. Chicken with olives is a speciality.

La Péniche

Halte Fluviale, quai St-Pierre de Trinquetaille (06.08.45.91.66). **Open** 7.30-11pm Mon, Sat; noon-2pm, 7.30-11pm Tue-Fri. Closed Jan. **Menus** €22, €13.50 lunch only. **No credit cards**.
Cross the Trinquetaille bridge to this barge restaurant for a romantic moonlit dinner on the Rhône. Good dishes include salmon carpaccio with grapefruit and *taureau* steak with anchovy sauce, to be consumed with Côtes du Rhone, *bien sûr*.

Le Pistou

30bis rond-point des Arènes (04.90.18.20.92). **Open** noon-2.30pm, 7-10.30pm Mon, Wed-Sun. **Menus** €14.94-€16.46. **Credit** MC, V.

A small, friendly restaurant in stone vaults opposite the amphitheatre. Try favourites like salad with chicken livers, *tellines* (tiny clams) with creamy garlic sauce and fresh basil, mignon of pork with Beaumes de Venise or banon cheese with peppered oil.

Bars & cafés

Andalucia Café
14 bd des Lices (04.90.96.40.72). **Open** *summer* 9am-2am daily; *winter* 9am-12.30am daily. **Credit** AmEx, DC, MC, V.
The old Grande Brasserie of Arles has metamorphosed into a celebration of southern Spain, with fountains, columns and the inevitable bullfighting theme. Good for coffee, *tapas* or a cooling gaspacho on the terrace at the height of summer.

Café de la Nuit
pl du Forum (04.90.96.44.56). **Open** 9.30pm-midnight daily. **Credit** MC, V.
Good people-watching terrace on a sociable town square, with a lofty interior painted in vibrant Van Gogh colours and a bar decorated to look like his painting of the same name. Try the very good tagliatelle or bull *daube* with an inexpensive carafe of regional wine. Great fun.

Toast Vin et Compagnie
2 rue du Dr Fanton (04.90.96.22.26). **Open** 6pm-midnight Mon-Sat. **Credit** AmEx, MC, V.
Charming café with big windows and comfortable banquettes where you can get *tartines* (Poilâne bread with cheese, pâté or foie gras, perhaps) and salads, with a selection of wine by the glass.

Clubs & music venues

Cargo de Nuit
7 av Sadi Carnot (04.90.49.55.99/ www.cargodenuit.com). **Open** 8pm-5am Thur-Sat, some Sun. Closed July-Aug. **Admission** from €6.10 (free on Thur). **Credit** MC, V.
Listen to world music, rock, electronic and jazz (live and canned). Food available.

El Patio de Camargue
chemin de Barriol (04.90.49.51.76/www.chico.fr). **Open** 8pm-late Sat, by reservation only. **Average** €38. **Credit** AmEx, MC, V.
This Spanish restaurant on the banks of the Rhône serves tapas and paella, accompanied by gypsy guitar, songs and dancing from Chico et les Gypsies, led by the founder member of the Gypsy Kings.

Shopping

Arles' market takes place on boulevard des Lices on Saturdays and on boulevard Emile Combes on Wednesdays. Both offer local fruit, vegetables and fish, and a vast array of nuts, spices, herbs, *charcuterie* and bric-a-brac. More bric-a-brac can be found on the boulevard des

Cathédrale St-Trophime: crisply carved.

Lices on the first Wednesday of the month.
The streets of the old town, west of the Arena from rue de la République to the river, are pleasant for shopping (all open Mon-Sat unless stated). Best buys are local products such as perfumes, incense, soaps and candles with a good range at **L'Occitane** (58 rue de la République, 04.90.96.93.62) and **Fragrances** (53 rue de la République, 04.90.18.20.64). At **Santons Chauve** (14 rond-point des Arènes, 04.90.96.15.22), you can buy Provençal crèche figures and see them being made.
L'Arlésienne (12 rue de la République, 04.90.93.28.05) is the place to buy Provençal fabrics, waistcoats, frilly skirts, *gardian* cowboy shirts and even a complete Arlésienne costume by the designer who dresses the assistants in the Museon Arlaten. **Souleiado** (4 bd des Lices, 04.90.96.37.55), the Tarascon-based Provençal fabric producer, has a huge range of colourful patterns for clothing and furnishing, as well as ready-to-wear garments.
Christian Lacroix (52 rue de la République, 04.90.96.11.16) is a native of Arles, and his exuberant style screams South of France; gorgeous clothes and jewellery, plus kidswear, porcelain and tablelinen, fill this, his first shop.
Food, too, is worth seeking out. **Boitel** (4 rue de la Liberté, 04.90.96.03.72, closed three weeks Feb) sells regional delicacies, from handmade chocolates to cakes, biscuits and nougat, and also has a small tea room.
Charcuterie Bouchon Lyonnais (51 rue des Arènes, 04.90.96.56.96, closed Sun & Mon.) supplies the cognoscenti with sausages, *charcuterie* and a good choice of wine.
La Maison des Gourmands (28 rond-point des Arènes, 04.90.93.19.38) is the place for Provençal nougat, biscuits, olive oil and honey.

The best bookshop is **Actes Sud** (*see p72*, **Getting in on the Actes**), with a branch and children's bookshop in the Espace Van Gogh. **Forum Harmonia Mundi** (3 rue du Président Wilson, 04.90.93.38.00) is another institution. Now a chain all over France, the classical, jazz and regional music specialist started here in 1958.

Near the Musée Reattu and the banks of the Rhône is a small antiques enclave with, notably, **Antiquités Maurin** (4 rue de Grille, 04.90.96.51.57, closed am Mon & all Sun), a large shop crammed with Provençal furniture, paintings and *objets d'art*. **Les Pénitents Bleus** (3 rue des Pénitents-Bleus, 04.90.93.72.04) is a bookshop stuffed full of antiquarian books, maps, photos and postcards, wonderful for browsing for original gifts.

Where to stay

Hôtel d'Amphithéâtre
5 rue Diderot (04.90.96.10.30/ www.hoteldamphitheatre.fr). **Double** €53. **Credit** AmEx, MC, V.
This is a gem of a hotel in tiny street, in a restored 17th-century building, with warm old tiles, yellow walls and original wrought-iron banisters. Rooms are small but charmingly decorated, and bathrooms well designed with big mirrors. Garage available.

L'Arlatan
26 rue du Sauvage (04.90.93.56.66/www.hotel-arlatan.fr). Closed two weeks Jan. **Double** €77-€137. **Credit** AmEx, DC, V.
This Provençal mansion is built over part of the Roman basilica (you can see the excavations under glass) and has many period details, carved ceilings and antiques. There is an elegant *salon* with vast fireplace, an enclosed garden courtyard and a pool.

Le Calendal
5 rue Porte de Laure (04.90.96.11.89/ www.lecalendal.com). **Double** €60-€75. **Credit** AmEx, DC, MC, V.
This romantic hotel occupies several cleverly linked old buildings around a large, shady garden with tables and palm trees. Rooms, each different, have sunny colours and look over either the Théâtre Antique or the garden. The *salon de thé* serves light meals. Internet access available.

Le Cloître
16 rue du Cloître (04.90.96.29.50). Closed Nov to mid-Mar. **Double** €43-€62.50. **Credit** AmEx, MC, V.
Good-value hotel in a narrow street near the Roman theatre, with a Romanesque vaulted dining room and exposed stone walls in the bedrooms.

Grand Hôtel Nord Pinus
14 pl du Forum (04.90.93.44.44/www.nord-pinus.com). Closed Nov-Jan. **Double** €143-€166. **Credit** AmEx, DC, MC, V.

The bullfighters' favourite haunt, opened in the 19th century, is a fashionable place to stay and dramatically decorated with heavy carved furniture, Peter Beard's giant black-and-white photos, *féria* posters and mounted bulls' heads. Book well ahead in *féria* time. It has an elegant bar and restaurant, the Brasserie Nord Pinus (*see p75*).

Hôtel du Musée
11 rue du Grand Prieuré (04.90.93.88.88). Closed Dec-Jan. **Double** €45-€64. **Credit** AmEx, DC, MC, V.
The rooms of this small hotel in a 16th-century mansion have been recently restored and elegantly decorated with Provençal antiques. Breakfast is served in a leafy inner courtyard.

Hôtel St-Trophime
16 rue de la Calade (04.90.96.88.38). Closed mid-Nov to Feb. **Double** €45-€55. **Credit** AmEx, MC, V.
Housed in an atmospheric old building in the centre of Arles, this hotel boasts a stone-arched lobby, carved ceilings and a courtyard.

Essentials

Getting there

By air
Arles is only half an hour from Nîmes airport. A taxi costs about €30.

By car
The A54 passes right through Arles; exit 5 is the closest to the centre, or take the N570 from Avignon.

By train
Arles is on the main coastal rail route, and connects with Avignon for the TGV to Paris.

By bus
Cars de Camargue (04.90.96.36.25) runs buses between Nîmes and Arles three times daily Mon-Fri, twice on Sat (none on Sun) and four buses a day, Mon-Fri, between Arles and Stes-Maries-de-la-Mer. There are three or four buses daily (Mon-Sat) from Avignon; for details call the bus station on 04.90.49.38.01.

Tourist information
It's best to walk around the town centre, but STAR runs a free bus 'Starlette', which starts at the Musée d'Arles and stops at most museums and monuments. The Pass Monument and Circuit Arles Antique passes are available at the tourist office, museums and sights.

Office de Tourisme
bd des Lices, 13200 Arles (04.90.18.41.20/www.ville-arles.fr). **Open** *Apr-Sept* 9am-7pm daily; *Oct-Mar* 9am-5.45pm Mon-Sat; 10am-noon Sun.

The Camargue

Swaying grasses, pink tamarisk bushes and sun-bleached blue lagoons are the landscape of this marshy region peopled by its own breed of cowboy.

The great flat region of marsh, pasture, salt-water *étangs* (lakes) and sand dunes that nestles in the delta between the Grand and Petit Rhône is one of Europe's major wetlands, a vast protected area of 140,000 hectares. Eerily beautiful, it is a wonderland of flora and fauna: purple herons and pink flamingos; black bulls and grey ponies, wild boar; the beavers that thrive again here after reaching the verge of extinction; eagles and kites; bulrushes and samphire; not to mention dense clouds of France's most bloodthirsty mosquitoes.

It was not until the Middle Ages that the marshes were settled by Cistercians and Templars. Salt was harvested as a commodity, as it still is, in vast quantities, today. With the decline of religious establishments in the 16th century, the Camargue passed into the hands of cattle- and horse-raising *gardians*, descendants of whom, dressed in black hats, high leather boots and velvet jackets, still herd small black

The **Etang de Vaccarès** provides 6,500 hectares of quiet backwaters.

fighting bulls on horseback. The area is still dotted with white, thatched *gardians'* cabins, with their characteristic semi-circular end, set against the mistral.

In 1970, 85,000 hectares of the Camargue, including the town of **Stes-Maries-de-la-Mer** (*see p80*), became a regional nature reserve, protecting the area from rapacious developers. The reserve centres on the Etang de Vaccarès, a body of water covering 6,500 hectares.

The **Musée Camarguais**, in a converted sheep ranch on the D570 between Arles and Stes-Maries-de-la-Mer, explains the history of the region, its produce and its people, and provides information on nature trails. Further along the same road, by the small Etang de Ginès, the **Centre d'Information du Parc** gives information on riding and local ecology and has a good view of avian antics from its upstairs windows. For a closer brush with the bird life, visit the **Parc Ornithologique de Pont de Gau**, which replenishes stock in its aviaries and gives access to birdwatching trails along the Ginès lagoon.

The 20km walk from Stes-Maries-de-la-Mer to the salt-processing town of **Salin-de-Giraud** along the dyke built in 1857 to protect the wetlands from the sea allows extensive views across the reserve. The dyke is off limits to cars, though mountain bikes are tolerated. If you don't wish to part with your vehicle, various points on the D37 and C134 roads allow glimpses of herring gulls and blackheaded gulls, herons, avocets and egrets as well as the slender-billed gull and the red-crested pochard, which breed nowhere else in France.

East of the Etang de Vaccarès, the hamlet of **Le Sambuc** is home to the **Musée de Riz**, dedicated to the vital role played by rice in the agriculture of the Camargue; not only is it an important cash crop, but it also absorbs the salt in the soil, enabling other cereals to grow. For solitude strike out along the sea wall walk at the Pointe de Beauduc or the vast empty beach of Piémanson at the mouth of the Grand Rhône.

Across the salt lagoons, west of Arles, **St-Gilles-du-Gard** was an important medieval port left high and dry by the receding coastline and forced to turn to agriculture for its livelihood. The tiny village is dominated by its 12th-century abbey church, founded by Cistercian monks as a resting place on the pilgrimage route to Santiago de Compostela. All that remains of the original Romanesque building after Huguenot forces wreaked havoc during the Wars of Religion is the facade and the rib vaulting of the crypt; the rebuilt 17th-century version was half the size. The church remains one of Provence's greatest artistic treasures, with carving on the three portals that rivals St-Trophime in Arles. Opposite, the Maison Romane is a superb 12th-century house with finely carved arches and elaborate mouldings. Now home to the **Musée de St-Gilles**, it has a varied collection of medieval sculpture and local memorabilia. St-Gilles is relatively tourist free and has a pleasantly thriving Camarguais atmosphere.

Centre d'Information du Parc naturel et régionel de Camargue

Pont de Gau, rte d'Arles, Stes-Maries-de-la-Mer (04.90.97.86.32). **Open** *Apr-Sept* 10am-5.30pm daily; *Oct-Mar* 9.30am-5pm Mon-Thur, Sat, Sun.

Musée Camarguais

Mas du Pont de Rousty, D570, Stes-Maries-de-la-Mer (04.90.97.10.82). **Open** *Oct-Mar* 10.15am-4.45pm Mon, Wed-Sun; *Apr-Sept* 9.15am-5.45pm daily (July-Aug until 6.45pm). **Admission** €4.60; €2.30 10-18s; free under-10s.

Musée du Riz

rte de Salin-de-Giraud, Le Sambuc (04.90.97.20.29). **Open** 8.30am-noon, 1.30-5.30pm Mon-Fri; Sat, Sun by appointment. **Admission** €3.80; €2.30 children.

A load of bull

One of the most arresting sights in the Camargue are the little black cattle that graze its marshlands, roaming intermingled with grey Camargue ponies in semi-wild herds and rounded up by mounted *gardians*. Small and sturdy with lyre-shaped horns, the black bulls of the Camargue have been raised here specifically for bullfights – as well as for the region's tables – since the 19th century. And if you think tauromania is restricted to Spain you only have to see the Camarguais enthusiasm for the *féria* that take place not only in the spectacular Roman arenas of Arles and Nîmes, but also in Stes-Maries-de-la-Mer, St-Martin-de-Crau and St-Rémy-de-Provence.

Provençal bullfighting is a smaller, gentler and wittier form than the fight to the death of Spanish *corridas* (although these also feature at Arles and Nîmes). The *Course Camarguaise* or *Course à la cocarde* began as a game with lions, dogs, bears and men chasing and baiting a bull. By the end of the 19th century, it had evolved into a battle in which human wits and dexterity were pitched against taurine speed and weight. The *raseteurs*, decked out in white, try to snatch the *cocarde* (rosette) and *ficelles* (tassels) attached to the head of the bull, using a metal comb or *crochet*. The bull does not, as a rule, relish the indignity, and chases his rival round the arena, often forcing him to leap the barrier. Bravery and skill earn points and prize money for the *raseteur*; the bull has to make do with applause and a burst of *Carmen* over the PA system as he is led out of the ring. The real competition nowadays is between the *manades* (bull breeders); bulls can become as famous as the *raseteurs* against whom they do battle.

Musée de St-Gilles

La Maison Romane, St-Gilles-du-Gard (04.66.87.40.42).
Open *June, Sept* 9am-noon, 2-6pm Mon-Sat; *July-Aug*
9am-noon, 3-7pm Mon-Sat; *Oct-May* 9am-noon,
2-5pm Mon-Sat. Closed Jan. **Admission** free.

Parc Ornithologique de Pont de Gau

rte d'Arles, 4km from Stes-Maries-de-la-Mer
(04.90.97.82.62/www.parc-ornitho.com). **Open** *Apr-*
Sept 9am-8pm daily; *Oct-Mar* 10am-5pm daily.
Admission €6; €3 4-10s; free under-4s.

Where to stay & eat

Just outside Stes-Maries-de-la-Mer begins a long
succession of ranch-style hotels, all of which are
pleased to organise horse riding or 4WD trips.
Pride of place goes to the luxurious **Mas de la
Fouque** (rte du Bac du Sauvage, 04.90.97.81.02,
closed Nov-Apr, double €275), whose large,
stylish rooms have wooden balconies overlooking
a lagoon. Even the ornothologically challenged
will be impressed, and the boss cooks a mean
leg of local lamb to enjoy after swimming in the
big pool. **Le Pont des Bannes** (rte d'Arles,
04.90.97.81.09/www.pontdesbannes.com, closed
Nov, double €216; demi-pension July, Aug and
Easter, €150) is a converted hunting lodge with
a certain rustic chic. **Mangio Fango**
(04.90.97.80.56, closed Jan, double €72-€116) is
a friendly hotel with a luxuriant garden,
swimming pool, large rooms and a good
restaurant (closed Wed, menus €26-€32). If you
are looking for a particularly nice pool the **Mas
du Tadorne** (rte d'Arles, 04.90.97.93.11/
www.masdutadorne.camargue.fr, closed Jan-
Feb, double €135-€160) is a good choice. Lower
down the scale, **Le Boumian** (rte d'Arles,
04.90.97.81.15/www.leboumian.camargue.fr,
double €84, menu €20-€32) is a friendly ranch
hotel with pools and horseriding. The
restaurant at **Hostellerie du Pont de Gau**
(rte d'Arles, 5km NW of Stes-Maries-de-la-Mer,
04.90.97.81.53, closed Wed from mid-Nov to
Easter, closed Jan to mid-Feb, menus €17-€44)
has serious Provençal cookery and good
service. The **Lou Mas Dou Juge** (rte du Bac
du Sauvage, Pin Fourcat, 04.66.73.51.45,
weekend €76-€91) is a *chambres d'hôtes* with
seven rooms in a working farm on the Petit
Rhône, with horse-riding (€15/hour) and a
restaurant (reservation essential, menus €53-
€63). East of the Etang de Vaccarès, **Le Mas
de Peint** (Le Sambuc, 04.90.97.20.62, closed 20
Nov-20 Dec and mid-Jan to mid-Mar, double
€197-€246, restaurant closed Wed, menus €30-
€43) is the last word in Camargue chic: stone
floors, linen sheets, beams and log fires,
presided over by an owner happy to show you
his bulls and let you ride his horses. The
Authentiques Cabanes de Gardian de la

Grand Mar (04.90.97.00.64,closed two weeks
Nov, three weeks Feb, minimum two days stay,
maximum six people €144-€175) are real (or
well-faked) self-catering *gardian* cabins with a
restaurant and horse-riding. In St-Gilles, **Le
Cours** (av François Griffeuille, 04.66.87.31.93/
www.hotel-le-cours.com, closed mid-Dec to mid-
Mar, double €43-€62, menus €10.60-€26) is a
friendly and simple Logis de France; its
restuarant is a local favourite.

Tourist information

St-Gilles market is Thursday and Saturday.
4WD trips are run by **Destination Camargue**
(rue de la Calade, Arles, 04.90.96.94.44).

Office de Tourisme

1 pl Frédéric Mistral. 13800 St-Gilles-du-Gard
(04.66.87.33.75/www.ot-saint-gilles.fr). **Open** *May,*
June, Sept 9am-noon, 2.30-6pm Mon-Sat; *July-Aug*
9am-12.30pm, 3-7pm Mon-Sat; 10am-noon Sun;
Oct-Apr 8.30am-noon, 1.30-5.30pm Mon-Sat.

Stes-Maries-de-la-Mer

Each May gypsies from all over Europe and the
Middle East converge on Stes-Maries-de-la-Mer
for an exuberant three-day pilgrimage (*see p42*),
during which the streets throb with flamenco,
horse races and bullfights. Soon after the death
of Christ, the legend goes, Mary Magdalene (*see
p189*), Mary Salome (mother of James and John)
and Jesus' aunt Mary Jacob fled Palestine by
sea and washed up on the shores of Provence,
where they were met by Black Sarah the gypsy
chief (who may, according to another version,
have travelled from the Holy Land with the
three Marys as their maid). The local populace
converted *en masse* and Sarah was adopted by
the gypsies as their patron saint. The Church
came up with some convenient relics in 1448:
three sets of bones that may indeed be those of
Middle Eastern women of the first century AD.
The vast, fortified 12th-century church still
dominates the present town, its blackened
interior the only memory of the all-night
candlelit vigil, which was banned recently to
prevent further damage to the building.

But Stes-Maries is primarily a seaside resort,
with a long, sandy beach, cheap cafés and too
many shops for picking up that essential
Provençal cowboy shirt. The low-rise hacienda-
style second homes mean that you will not need
to linger long, but it's a good place to take a
boat trip, hire a bike or go on photo safari. The
Musée Baroncelli has exhibits on
bullfighting and other traditions, plus the odd
stuffed flamingo donated by the Marquis Folco
de Baroncelli, a 19th-century aristocrat who
become a Camargue cowboy.

Musée Baroncelli

rue Victor Hugo (04.90.97.87.60). **Open** *May-mid-Nov* 10am-noon, 2-6pm Wed-Mon. Closed mid-Nov to Apr. **Admission** €1.50; €1.30 6-12s; free under-6s.

Where to eat

For the seaside resort atmosphere head for **Brasserie de la Plage** (1 av de la République, 04.90.97.84.77, menu €16). The **Brûleur de Loups** (av Gilbert Leroy, 04.90.97.83.31, closed Tue and two weeks Jan, menus €23-€36), has a sea view and specialities including bull *carpaccio* and *bourride*. In the village centre, **L'Impérial** (1 pl des Impériaux, 04.90.97.81.84), closed Tue and Jan, menus €20-€27) serves imaginative dishes on a shady terrace.

Tourist Information

Market is Mon and Fri morning. Boat trips can be taken on the sea and the Rhône delta on *Tiki III* (04.90.97.81.68, Le Grau d'Orgon, closed mid-Nov to mid-Mar). Bike hire: **Le Vélo Saintois** (19 av de la République, 04.90.97.74.56).

Office de Tourisme

5 av Van Gogh, 13700 Stes-Maries-de-la-Mer (04.90.97.82.55/www.saintesmariesdelamer.com). **Open** *Apr-June, Sept* 9am-7pm daily; *July-Aug* 9am-8pm daily; *Oct* 9am-6pm daily; *Nov-Feb* 9am-5pm daily.

Howdy cowboy: *gardians* ride proudly through the streets of **Stes-Maries-de-la-Mer**.

Aigues-Mortes

On the western edge of the Camargue, the walled medieval city of Aigues-Mortes (from the Latin for 'dead waters') rises up from the rather gloomy salt marshes and acres given over to the cultivation of Listel Gris wine. This would surely be nobody's first choice for urban development but Louis IX wanted to set out on crusade from his own port rather than using then-Provençal Marseille. Realising that the take-up for his new town would be low, he offered generous tax and commercial incentives. The resulting town thrived through the Hundred Years War, when the Burgundians seized it, only to have it snatched back by the Armagnacs, who after slaughtering their enemies stored the salted corpses in the **Tour des Bourguignons**. Receding sea and the silting up of the surrounding canals led to the town's decline in the 15th century.

The monumental splendour of the ramparts, punctuated by massive towers, is particularly striking and makes for a great walk. The most spectacular tower is the **Tour de Constance**. Built 1240-49, and containing a small chapel, it doubled as cells for celebrity political or religious prisoners. Once within the ramparts, the town has more than its share of tacky souvenir shops and in summer becomes overrun with day-trippers from the nearby beach developments of Le Grau-du-Roi and Port Camargue. The church of **Notre-Dame-des-Sablons** has suffered from too many refits, but

Boats trips weave through the canals.

its wood-framed nave has a certain austere charm. The **Chapelle des Pénitents Blancs** and **Chapelle des Pénitents Gris** are interesting Baroque buildings that would benefit from more regular opening (ask at the tourist office). Place St-Louis, the main square, is a lively hub, with some interesting exhibitions in the town hall during the holidays. Summer (June in 2002) also brings the Festival des Nuits d'Encens (04.66.73.91.23), celebrating the traditional music of the Mediterranean.

Aigues-Mortes is the starting point for boat trips (Aventure en Camargue, 04.66.73.74.74) around the canals of the Camargue. You can also visit the **Caves de Listel** to swig some of the flinty *rosé* or learn all about commercially culled salt at the **Salins du Midi**. Northeast of Aigues-Mortes, the **Château de Teillan** was the former priory of the Abbaye de Psalmody, who sold the land for Aigues-Mortes to Louis IX.

Caves de Listel

domaine de Jarris (04.66.51.17.00). **Open** *Apr-Sept* 10am-6.30pm daily; *Oct-Mar* 10am-noon, 2-5pm Mon-Fri. **Admission** free.

Château de Teillan

(04.66.88.02.38). **Guided tours** *mid-June to mid-Sept* 2-6pm Tue-Sun. Admission €4.60; €3 12-15s; free under-12s.

Salins du Midi

(04.66.51.12.44). **Open** *Mar-Oct* 9am-6.45pm daily (mini-train/bus runs from Aigues-Mortes). Closed Nov-Feb. **Admission** €6; €4 4-12s; free under-4s.

Tour de Constance & Ramparts

(04.66.53.61.55). **Open** *May* 9.30am-1pm, 2-6pm daily; *June-Aug* 9.30am-8pm daily; *Sept* 9.30am-7pm; *Oct* 10am-6pm; *Nov-Apr* 10am-1pm, 2-5pm daily. **Admission** €5.49; free under-18s.

Where to stay & eat

Most entertaining restaurant within the city walls is **Café de Bouzigues** (7 rue Pasteur, 04.66.53.93.95, closed Mov-Mar, average €34), which has an atmospheric terrace and serves modern European food. Restaurants on the main square are fun for an apéritif, though locals prefer the frantically decorated bistro-pizzeria **Coco** (19 rue Jean Jaurès, 04.66.53.91.83, menu €12). **Hôtel Les Templiers** (23 rue de la République, 04.66.53.66.56, doubles €90-€125) has been restored with just the right dose of distressed elegance. The courtyard is a welcome oasis, and produces some tempting roast lamb cooked over an open fire. A more old-fashioned atmosphere reigns at **Hôtel Restaurant St-Louis** (10 rue Amiral Courbet, 04.66.53.72.68/www.lesaintlouis.fr, closed Nov-Mar, doubles €69-€91), but the garden terrace is very attractive. Just outside the city walls the **Hôtel Tour de Constance** (1 bd Diderot, 04.66.53.83.50. closed mid-Nov to Feb, double €24-€53) is clean and practical.

Tourist Information

Market is Wednesday and Saturday morning.

Office de tourisme

porte de la Gardette, 30220 Aigues-Mortes (04.66.53.73.00/www.ot-aiguesmortes.fr). **Open** *June, Sept* 9am-6pm daily; *July, Aug* 9am-8pm daily; *Oct-May* 9am-noon, 1-6pm Mon-Fri; 10am-noon, 2-6pm Sat, Sun.

▶ Getting There & Around

▶ By car

Leave the A54 at exit no.4 and take the D570 to Stes-Maries-de-la-Mer. For Aigues-Mortes take the D570 from Arles or Stes-Maries and then the D58, or autoroute A9, exit 26 and D979.

▶ By train/bus

The nearest SNCF station is Arles, from which buses run to Stes-Maries-de-la-Mer, with other stops around the reserve (**Cars de Camargue**, 04.90.96.36.25, five buses a day July-Aug, two a day out of season). From Nîmes TGV station, you can get to Aigues-Mortes by train or by bus (**STDG**, 04.66.29.52.00, five to seven buses a day).

The Rhône Delta

Avignon &
the Vaucluse

Features

Truly Optimistic

Agent Provocateur

TimeOut

**LONDON'S
LIVING GUIDE**
EVERY WEEK

timeout.com

PHOTOGRAPHY JONATHON FOSTER WILLIAMS

Avignon

There may never have been dancing on the bridge, but the walled city of Avignon has a thriving arts scene and a year-round sense of theatre.

Avignon is still contained within its 14th-century city walls – 4km of beautifully preserved ramparts with 39 towers and nine gates, crenellated in the 19th century by ubiquitous 'improver' Viollet-le-Duc, who filled in the moat. Looming from within is the fairytale centrepiece of the Palais des Papes and the golden Virgin gleaming at the top of the cathedral of Notre-Dame-des-Doms.

For three weeks each summer, Avignon becomes France's performing arts capital, its **Festival d'Avignon** drawing throngs of visitors from around the world. Recently the city has re-styled itself in response to the crowds, and the new arrivals from the TGV train station opened in 2001. A surge of new bars, cafés, restaurants, hotels and shops have opened, with students and the thriving gay community leading the way in hip hang-outs. The city also recently acquired its first contemporary art collection, the **Collection Lambert**.

Yet beyond the grandeur is another Avignon, best captured by Lawrence Durrell's *Avignon Quintet*: a town of gloomy, twilit streets, chill with autumn river damps or blasted by a howling mistral. Huge parts of Avignon remain shabby and unrestored and although the city is lively and cultured during the festival season, it has a tendency to rest on its laurels: theatre companies struggle to remain open all year, the publishing trade has moved to Arles and the famous Roumanille bookshop closed in 1996.

Outside the ramparts, the contrast is even starker. The suburbs are a cultural backwater, turning increasingly into gangsterland. Montclar and La Croix-des-Oiseaux in particular are no-go-zones for the avignonnais intra-muros, and regularly feature in the crime columns of local paper *La Provence*.

HISTORY

Avignon started life as a neolithic settlement on the **Rocher des Doms**. Under the Romans, the town flourished as a river port, but it was not until the 12th century, when Avignon's clergy became a power to be reckoned with, that the village started to think big, building towers and churches, the Romanesque cathedral and the bridge of St-Bénézet.

In 1306, French Pope Clement V brought his court from turmoil-wracked Rome to the safety of the independent Vatican-owned Comtat Venaissin. Clement always professed Avignon to be a temporary sanctuary, but after his death in 1314 six further French popes saw no reason to relocate to Rome. Their 68-year 'Babylonian captivity' – as furious Italians branded it – utterly transformed the quiet provincial backwater. The population soared and artists, scholars, architects, weavers and jewellers flocked to find patronage. The virtue industry fostered vice in equal measure: 'a sewer,' sniffed Petrarch, 'the filthiest of cities'. A lively demi-monde of prostitutes, heretics, refugees and criminals flourished in Avignon's streets, as did the plague, halving the population in 1348.

Gregory XI, elected in 1370, was badgered by the very persuasive St Catherine of Siena into returning to the Holy See. He took her advice, went back, and promptly died in 1378. The Italians elected a Roman pope, but the French were loath to lose their hold on the reins of power and swiftly elected Clement VII in Avignon. The rival popes excommunicated each other, sparking the Great Schism, a 40-year period when Christendom found itself with two heirs of St Peter, finally ending when all sides agreed on the election of Martin V in 1417.

Even after the popes returned to Italy, Avignon remained papal territory. Without French censorship, and far enough from Rome to escape heavy-handed Vatican checks, the town flourished as an artistic, religious and publishing centre, a tradition that continued after the French Revolution when the town was returned to France in 1791: it was to Avignon that the Félibrige turned in the 19th century to get its Provençal revival works into print.

Sightseeing

The terraced gardens of the **Rocher des Doms**, perched on a cliff above the Rhône, is where Avignon started, and it's also a good place to begin a visit, although if you arrive by train the Centre Ville station is at the opposite side of the old town. From the Rocher, the view ranges over the whole city, 'its closely knitted roofs of weathered tile like a pie crust fresh from the oven', as Lawrence Durrell wrote. It also takes in a great sweep of the Rhône and Villeneuve-lès-Avignon on the opposite bank.

Jutting into the river below the Rocher des Doms stand the four remaining arches of the **Pont St-Bénézet**. It can be reached by walking along the only section of the city walls open to the public, providing a short historic walk and a scenic entrance onto the bridge. Between the Dom and the bridge, the **Musée du Petit Palais**, a former cardinal's palace, has a superb collection of early Italian paintings, and sculptures rescued from the churches of Avignon.

The massive bulk of the **Palais des Papes**, more like an ogre's castle than pontiff's palace, dominates the square it shares with **Cathédrale Notre-Dame-des-Doms** and the elaborately swagged and furbelowed former Hôtel des Monnaies (mint), now the Conservatoire de Musique. Before entering the Palais, get a real grasp of the solidity of the place by walking along rue de la Peyrollerie to see its great towers, which are embedded in sheer rock.

A little further south, **place de l'Horloge** is the centre of town life, with its cafés, **Théâtre Municipal** and grand 19th-century Hôtel de Ville. A Gothic clock tower gives the square its name. At festival time the square is home to a whirling carousel of musicians and minstrels; *murals* on the surrounding streets are a reminder of the jollity for the rest of the year.

West of here lies the smart part of town, its streets packed with fashionable restaurants and beautifully restored mansions. On rue St-Agricol, the **Eglise St-Agricol** (open 10-11.30am Wed, 3-6pm Sat, 9-10.30am Sun), with its 15th-century carved doorway, is at last being restored. An alley off rue Agricol leads to the 15th-century **Palais du Roure**, where the aristocratic *gardian* (Camargue cowboy) poet Folco Baroncelli was born, and where Frédéric Mistral edited *Aïoli*, his journal in Provençal.

Rue Joseph Vernet, which curves round to join the main thoroughfare rue de la République, is a shopholic's dream of designer stores and handmade chocolates in a parade of 17th- and 18th-century *hôtels particuliers*. Off its northern end, the **Hôtel d'Europe** on rue Baroncelli has long been a favourite with visiting foreign lovers, among them the eloping Brownings. John Stuart Mill and Mrs Taylor (Harriet Hardy) also checked in; when Harriet died there, Mill was so distraught that he stayed on, buying a house overlooking the cemetery where she was buried and furnishing it with the contents of their last hotel room.

Further south on rue Victor Hugo, the **Musée Vouland** is a lavishly decorated private house, full of 18th-century French furniture and faïence. Back on rue Joseph Vernet, the **Musée Calvet** displays an eclectic collection of sculptures and paintings in the elegant colonnaded galleries of an 18th-century palace. In another wing is the **Muséum Requien**, an old-fashioned natural

history museum. Nearby, another renovated 18th-century *hôtel* now contains the cutting-edge contemporary art of the **Collection Lambert**.

On the other side of rue de la République, the lovely church of **St-Didier** was built in the simple, single-aisled Provençal Gothic style. Close by the church, the **Médiatheque Ceccano**, a 14th-century cardinal's residence, is now the town library and multimedia centre, surrounded by a shady garden. Around the corner in rue Laboureur is the **Fondation Angladon-Dubrujeaud**, a worthwhile private art museum; the **Musée Lapidaire** collection of ancient sculpture is housed nearby in a former Jesuit chapel. Across rue des Lices, not far from the tourist office, shady place des Corps-Saints in front of the 14th-century **Chapelle de St-Michel et tous les saints** becomes a sea of café chairs in summer.

Heading east out of place St-Didier, rue du Roi René has several fine 17th- and 18th-century mansions; at No.22 a plaque records that this was where the 14th-century Italian poet Petrarch first set eyes on Laure, the woman he was to idolise for the rest of his life (*see chapter* **History**). At the far end, the boho **rue des Teinturiers** is one of Avignon's most atmospheric streets, winding along beside the river Sorgue, where the water wheels of the dye works that gave the street its name are still visible. Production of the patterned calico fabrics known as *indiennes* thrived here until the end of the 19th century. Now the street is home to cafés under spreading plane trees, second-hand bookshops and art galleries.

The winding, partly pedestrianised streets to the north of place St-Didier are the heart of the medieval town. Most of this district is surprisingly shabby, dimly lit at night, with empty statue niches and pigeon-daubed churches. At the Hôtel de Rascas on rue des Fourbisseurs, note the corbels of a projecting upper storey, evidence of a cardinal's demands for extra airspace. Place Pie to the east is home to the **fruit and flower market** (7am-1pm Tue-Sun). In place St-Pierre to the north stands the Gothic church of **St-Pierre** (open for services only), which has finely carved walnut doors and a handsome belfry.

The winding streets behind the Palais des Papes lead to rue Banasterie (basketmakers' street) and the **Chapelle des Pénitents Noirs**, which has a sumptuous Baroque interior but is rarely open. Round the corner on rue des Escaliers Ste-Anne, the **Utopia** arts cinema is one of Avignon's liveliest cultural centres. Further east on place des Carmes, the **Eglise St-Symphorien** (04.90.82.10.56, open 8.30-9.30am Tue, Thur, 6.30-8pm Mon, Fri, 8.45am-noon Sat-Sun) has a 15th-century Gothic facade and some lovely polychrome wooden statues inside. Its

14th-century cloisters now house one of Avignon's oldest theatre companies, **Théâtre des Carmes**. This is the university district, packed with bars, cafés and second-hand bookstores. Past the porte St-Lazare, avenue Stuart Mill leads to the **Cimetière St-Véran**

(04.90.80.79.95, open 8.30am until sunset daily) where Harriet Hardy and Mill are buried.

Cathédrale Notre-Dame-des-Doms
pl du Palais (04.90.82.12.24). Open Feb-Oct 7.30am-6pm daily; *Nov-Jan* 7.30am-5pm daily; *treasury Apr-Nov* 9am-noon, 2-7pm daily; *Dec-Mar* by appointment.

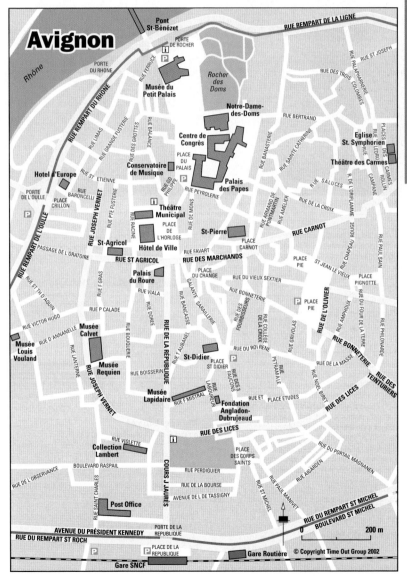

Avignon

Rhône

Pont St-Bénézet

RUE REMPART DE LA LIGNE

PORTE DE ROCHER

PORTE DU RHONE

RUE FERRUCE

Musée du Petit Palais

Rocher des Doms

RUE DES TROIS COLOMBES

RUE ST JOSEPH

RUE PALAPHARNERIE

RUE REMPART DU RHONE

RUE LIMAS

RUE GRANDE FUSTERIE

RUE DES GROTTES

RUE BALANCE

Notre-Dame-des-Doms

RUE BERTRAND

Centre de Congrès

Conservatoire de Musique

PLACE DU PALAIS

RUE SAINTE CATHERINE

RUE BANASTERIE

Eglise St. Symphorien

Théâtre des Carmes

Hotel d'Europe

RUE ST ETIENNE

RUE JOSEPH VERNET

RUE PTE FUSTERIE

RUE GD PHILIPPE

RUE PEYROLERIE

Palais des Papes

RUE ARMAND DE PONTMARTIN

RUE AMELIER

RUE DE LA CROIX

RUE SALUCES

R. DE L'ORIFLAMME

PLACE DES CARMES

CAMPANE

ROLLIN

PORTE DE L'OULLE

RUE BARONCELLI

PLACE CRILLON

RUE RACINE

Théâtre Municipal

PLACE DE L'HORLOGE

St-Pierre

RUE CARNOT

RUE CHAPEAU ROUGE

RUE PAUL SAIN

RUE REMPART DE L'OULLE

PASSAGE DE L'ORATOIRE

St-Agricol

Hôtel de Ville

RUE ST AGRICOL

RUE FAVART

RUE DES MARCHANDS

PLACE CARNOT

PLACE PIE

ST JEAN LE VIEUX

PLACE PIGNOTTE

RUE ST TH D'AQUIN

RUE F GRAS

Palais du Roure

RUE VIALA

PLACE DU CHANGE

RUE DU VIEUX SEXTIER

RUE DE L'OLIVIER

RUE DU FOUR DE LA TERRE

RUE AMPHOUX

RUE VICTOR HUGO

RUE DORÉE

RUE P CALADE

GALANTE

SARRALLERIE

RUE BANCASSE

RUE DES FOURBISSEURS

RUE COLLEGE DE LA CROIX

RUE BONNETERIE

RUE GRIVOLAS

RUE BONNETERIE

RUE PHILONARDE

Musée Louis Vouland

RUE D'ANNANELLE

Musée Calvet

RUE LANTERNE

RUE BOUQUERIE

RUE DE LA RÉPUBLIQUE

RUE AUBANEL

St-Didier

RUE DU ROI RENE

RUE PETRAMALE

RUE DE LA MASSE

RUE DES TEINTURIERS

RUE JOSEPH VERNET

Musée Requien

RUE BOISSERIN

PLACE ST DIDIER

RUE DES 3 FALCONS

RUE NOEL BIRET

Musée Lapidaire

RUE F MISTRAL

RUE LABOUREUR

Fondation Angladon-Dubrujeaud

RUE ET PLACE ETUDES

RUE DES LICES

RUE DES LICES

Collection Lambert

RUE VIOLETTE

COURS J JAURÈS

PLACE DES CORPS SAINTS

RUE DU PORTAIL MAGNANEN

RUE DE L'OBSERVANCE

BOULEVARD RASPAIL

RUE PERDIGUIER

RUE AIGARDEN

RUE SAINT CHARLES

Post Office

RUE DE LA BOURSE

AVENUE DE L DE TASSIGNY

RUE ST MICHEL

RUE PAUL MANIVET

RUE DU REMPART ST MICHEL

BOULEVARD ST MICHEL

0   200 m

AVENUE DU PRÉSIDENT KENNEDY

PORTE DE LA RÉPUBLIQUE

RUE DU REMPART ST ROCH

PLACE DE LA RÉPUBLIQUE

Gare Routière

© Copyright Time Out Group 2002

Gare SNCF

In July, the whole town gets set for the Festival d'Avignon.

A surprisingly unspiritual church. Apart from the Romanesque porch and a fine marble throne, any vestiges of its 12th-century origins have been almost obliterated by subsequent destruction or additions: a Baroque gallery, a rebuilt tower and a tacky golden statue of the Virgin perched on the pinnacle of the tower. Even the Simone Martini frescoes have been removed to the Palais des Papes.

Collection Lambert

Hôtel de Caumont, 5 rue Violette (04.90.16.56.20/ www.collectionlambert.com). **Open** 11am-7pm Tue-Sun. **Admission** €5.50; €4 under-12s.

Parisian art dealer Yvon Lambert has loaned his formidable contemporary art collection to Avignon for 20 years. Housed in an 18th-century *hôtel particulier*, the 850 pieces, spanning the late 1950s to the present, are interwoven with temporary exhibitions and new commissions. Particularly strong on conceptual and minimalist art, the collection takes in painting, sculpture, installation, video and photography by names such as Nan Goldin, Douglas Gordon, Thomas Hirschhorn, Barbara Kruger, Jean-Michel Basquiat, Robert Ryman and Cy Twombly. The Jenny Holzer work in the entrance with its message 'Thinking too much only causes problems' sets the tone of the museum, which is deliberately low on explanatory texts, and high on encouraging the public to view the artwork on its own merits. There is a bookshop and courtyard café.

Eglise St-Didier

pl St-Didier (04.90.86.20.17). **Open** 8am-noon, 2-4.30pm Mon; 8am-noon, 2-6pm Tue-Sun.

This pretty example of a Provençal Gothic church

has delicate 14th-century Italian frescoes in the north chapel. In the Chapelle St-Bénézet are relics of the bridge-building saint himself, or his skull at least; an expert who examined it in 1984 established that he was only 25 at his death.

Fondation Angladon-Dubrujeaud

5 rue Laboureur (04.90.82.29.03/www.angladon.com). **Open** *mid-June to Sept* 1-6pm Tue-Sun; *Oct to mid-June* 1-6pm Wed-Sun. **Admission** €5; €1.5 7-14s; free under-7s.

In an 18th-century mansion, gems from the collection of Jacques Doucet are hung with an eye to the right setting – thus, Dutch oils, including a charming baby Jesus eating cherries, are complemented by oak chests, *armoires* and faïence, while 18th-century French portraits occupy a lavish gilt and brocade salon. There are later paintings by Degas, Picasso and Modigliani, and the only Van Gogh in Provence.

Musée Calvet

65 rue Joseph Vernet (04.90.86.33.84/ www.fondation-calvet.org). **Open** 10am-1pm, 2-6pm Mon, Wed-Sun. **Admission** €6; €3 12-18s; free under-12s.

The beautifully restored fine art museum displays its collection in elegant, colonnaded rooms around a courtyard. The ground floor has Gobelins tapestries and medieval sculpture. 18th- and 19th-century French paintings include works by the Avignon-based Vernet family and David's *La Mort du jeune Bara*. There is a good modern section with works by Soutine, Sisley, Manet, Utrillo and Dufy, and Camille Claudel's head of her brother, Paul Claudel, who had his sister carted off to a mental asylum near

Avignon when her relationship with Rodin became too scandalous. The newly opened Salle de la Méridienne is a restored 18th-century bathroom with exquistite plaster mouldings.

Musée Lapidaire

27 rue de la République (04.90.85.75.38/ www.fondation-calvet.org). **Open** 10am-1pm, 2-6pm, Wed-Mon. **Admission** €2; €1 12-18s; free under-12s. Avignon's archaeological collection, part of the Esprit Calvet donation, is superbly displayed in a 17th-century Jesuit chapel. As well as Greek, Gallo-Roman and Etruscan sculpture, mosaics and glass, it is rich in Egyptian sculpture, stele and shabti, most notably the funeral inscription of the High Priest Ptahmose. Among the Gallo-Roman selection is a depiction of the *Tarasque of Noves*, the man-eating monster that used to terrorise these parts.

Musée Louis Vouland

17 rue Victor Hugo (04.90.86.03.79/ www.vouland.com). **Open** *May-Oct* 10am-noon, 2-6pm Tue-Sun; *Nov-Apr* 2-6pm Tue-Sun. **Admission** €4; €2.5 12-18s; free under-12s. A 19th-century *hôtel particulier* with *trompe l'oeil* ceilings houses the largely 18th-century decorative arts collection of former resident Louis Vouland. A preserved meat salesman, Vouland spent 50 years building up his collection of furniture and porcelain which includes decorated faïence from the Moustiers, Montpellier and Marseille factories, Ming porcelain and intricate inlaid writing-desks. Temporary modern art exhibitions are held upstairs.

Musée du Petit Palais

pl du Palais-des-Papes (04.90.86.44.58). **Open** *June-Sept* 10am-1pm, 2-6pm Mon, Wed-Sun; *Oct-May* 9.30am-1pm, 2-5.30pm Mon, Wed-Sun. **Admission** €6; €3 12-18s; free under-12s. First constructed in 1308 for a cardinal, the Petit Palais was altered to house the local bishop in 1335, only to undergo another transformation in the late 15th century for Cardinal Giuliano della Rovere, the future Pope Julius II, who added its Renaissance facade and decorative tower. Today, the Petit Palais houses magnificent medieval paintings, frescoes and sculpture, many rescued from churches destroyed in the Revolution. Note the sarcophagus of Cardinal Jean de Lagrange, with its anatomically realistic depiction of a decaying corpse, and his brutally mutilated tomb effigy. The bulk of the paintings were assembled by Gian Pietro Campana di Cavelli, a 19th-century Italian collector with such an insatiable appetite for art that he went bankrupt, allowing Napoléon III to snap up his entire estate. It provides a fine introduction to the International Gothic style brought to Avignon by the mostly Sienese artists patronised by the popes, and clung to long after it had gone out of fashion elsewhere. To get an idea of the local development of the style, take a look at the *Virgin and Child with an Apple* by Enguerrand Quarton. Other highlights include Taddeo Gaddi's *Virgin and Child*, Barna's exquisite *Ste*

Festival hotspots

The **Festival d'Avignon** (www.festival-avignon.com), held for three weeks every July, was founded by actor Jean Vilar and his Théâtre Nationale Populaire in 1947 to bring the performing arts to the masses. If the masses that throng Avignon are now numerical rather than sociological, the spirit of Vilar's venture still permeates the city. The streets are littered with live acts, tourists reading maps and plays and theatre posters flapping from every building and lamppost. The excitement is stifling as over half a million people devour the official 'In' and fringe 'Off' performances.

Churches, chapels, convents, cloisters and palaces are requisitioned for stagings of anything from Beckett to Molière, Homer and Shakespeare to new playwrights, as well as big-name contemporary dance (2001 featured Bill T Jones, Angelin Preljocaj and Josef Nadj) and classical concerts. The most prestigious productions are held in the imposing Cour d'Honneur in the Palais des Papes.

Like Edinburgh, with which Avignon Festival is most-often compared, the official 'In' festival has been joined – and dwarfed – by the entertaining and anarchic **Le Off** (www.avignon-off.org), as the fringe is known. Unlike Edinburgh, the weather can usually be guaranteed and it is largely Le Off that fills the streets and any odd corner with minstrels, fire-eaters, stiltwalkers and oddball comedians as some 400 rival ventures vie to find their bit of space (there is no selection procedure, any one can stage a production if they can find a space and deal with the ticketing bureaucracy). Although the official festival soon sells out, there is no advance booking for Off productions, so you're sure to be able to find a place for something. The **Café In et Off** (*5 pl du Palais, 04.90.85.48.95, open May-June, Sept-Oct 7am-8pm daily; July-Aug 7am-midnight daily*) and gay bar **L'Esclave** (*12 rue du Limas, 04.90.85.14.51/www.esclavebar.com, open 11pm-4am Mon-Thur, Sun; 11pm-5am Fri-Sat*) are well-known known festival rendez-vous, but, so then, is virtually every *terrasse* in town as the cafés and brasseries of place de l'Horloge, place Pie and place des Corps-Saints become a hotchpotch of theatrical headgear.

Madeleine, Allegretto Nuzi's *Virgin in Majesty* and Botticelli's *Madonna and Child*.

Muséum Requien d'Histoire Naturelle

67 rue Joseph Vernet (04.90.82.43.51). **Open** 9am-noon, 2-6pm Tue-Sat. **Admission** free.

An old-fashioned natural history museum, packed with rocks, minerals, stuffed animals, fossils. Buried in the archives, a botanical section includes John Stuart Mill's collection of dried flowers and herbs.

Palais des Papes

pl du Palais (04.90.27.50.74/www.palais-des-papes.com). **Open** *Apr-July* 9am-7pm daily; *Aug-Sept* 9am-8pm; *Nov-Mar* 9.30am-5.45pm daily. **Admission** €9.50; €4 students; free under-8s.

More of a fortress than the palace of God's representative on earth, the Palais des Papes is a brutal power statement. The interior is strangely empty after the devastation wreaked during the Revolution, when 60 pro-papal prisoners were flung into the Tour des Latrines. During the palace's subsequent use as a prison and barracks soldiers chipped off bits of fresco to sell but many exquisite fragments remain. The Palais is a complicated labyrinth with two interlocking parts: the forbidding Palais Vieux, built in the 1330s for the austere Cistercian monk Pope Benedict XII (who razed the original palace enlarged by John XXII), and the more showy Palais Neuf, tacked on a decade later by Clement VI in fashionable new Gothic style.

You can wander at will (an audio guide is included in the entry fee), or join one of the regular guided tours (some in English). Across the main courtyard from the entrance and ticket office is the Salle de Jésus, the antechamber of the papal council room or Consistoire, where frescoes by Simone Martini have been displayed since they were detached from the cathedral in 1960. In the Chapelle St-Jean next door are some delightful frescoes (c1346) by Matteo Giovannetti, Clement VI's court painter. Upstairs, the ceiling of the Grand Tinel banqueting hall was once coloured blue and dotted with gold stars to resemble the sky. Next door, the kitchens with their huge pyramid-shaped chimney could feed 3,000 guests. There are more Giovannetti frescoes, lavish with lapis lazuli and gold, in the Chapelle St-Martial off the side of the Grand Tinel. Beyond the Salle de Parement (robing room), Benedict XII's tiled study was only discovered in 1963. The papal bedchamber is followed by the Chambre du Cerf, Clement VI's study, with some delightful frescoes, which exude the spirit of courtly love. Vast as it is, the Chapelle Clementine, which you come to next, was barely large enough to hold the college of cardinals when it gathered in conclave to elect a new pope. Through the Chamberlain's Room, whose raised stone slabs mark the spot where papal treasure was discovered, stairs lead up to the battlements, with a dramatic view over the city and Villeneuve-lès-Avignon. Back on the ground floor, the Grande Audience hall has a bevy of Biblical prophets frescoed by Giovannetti. A new guided tour, Palais Secret (€21.50, including Provençal brunch) has been introduced at weekends to reveal palace rooms, terraces and gardens as yet unseen by the public, including the steamrooms, storerooms and the garden of Benoit XII.

Palais du Roure

3 rue du Collège du Roure (04.90.80.80.88). **Open** *guided tour* 3pm Tue or by appointment. **Admission** €4.60; free under-16s.

The birthplace of Marquis Folco de Baroncelli-Javon, protector of the Camargue *gardians*, who devoted his life to writing poetry, breeding bulls and preserving Camargue traditions, has a charming courtyard with fragments of frescoes and a splendid carved doorway. It is now a literary archive and library, and headquarters of the Festival Provençal (*see chapter* **The Festive South**).

Pont St-Bénézet

rue Ferruce (04.90.82.74.02). **Open** *mid-Mar to June, Oct* 9am-7pm; *July-Sept* 9am-8pm; *Nov to mid-Mar* 9.30am-5.45pm. **Admission** €3; free under-8s.

The original bridge was begun in 1185, by a divinely inspired shepherd boy from the Ardèche who became St Bénézet. He lifted the first massive stone, convincing the sceptical populace that construction was possible. When completed, the bridge was 22 arches and nearly a kilometre long, and contributed greatly to the development of Avignon, although in 1660, after a huge flood, the avignonnais gave up the unequal maintenance struggle. Today, only four arches and a tiny Romanesque fisherman's chapel remain. Despite the old song *Sur le pont d'Avignon*, it seems unlikely that anyone ever danced on the narrow, traffic-packed structure. It is more likely that people danced '*sous le pont*' (under the bridge): the Ile de la Barthelasse, which the bridge used to cross, was a favourite R&R spot in the Middle Ages.

Arts & entertainment

Le Chêne Noir

8bis rue Ste-Catherine (04.90.82.40.57). **Box office** open one hour before show. **Tickets** €19.82; €7.62 under-12s. **Credit** AmEx, MC, V.

Innovative theatre specialising in performances for and involving children.

Espace St-Louis

20 rue Portail Boquier (mairie 04.90.80.80.00). **Open** during exhibitions and festival.

Adjoining Hôtel Cloître St-Louis, this gallery hosts contemporary art exhibitions organised by the town hall, becoming a box office during the festival.

Galerie JE Bernard

13 rue de la Grande Fusterie (04.90.80.04.04/ www.galeriejebernard.com). **Open** 11am-1pm,

The brutal mass of the **Palais des Papes** showed who was boss in the 14th century.

3-7.30pm Tue-Sat. Closed Jan.
This gallery specialises in young artists, and also runs a programme of music and dance.

L'Hélicon

23 rue Bancasse (04.90.16.03.99). **Open** *May-Aug* Mon-Sat; *Sept-Apr* Thur-Sat. **Menus** €17.53-€19.82. **Credit** MC, V.
Chanson is performed by guest stars or the owner himself, with the young clientele begging for traditional favourites as they munch good hearty fare.

Maison Jean Vilar

8 rue de Mons (04.90.86.59.64). **Open** *library* 1.30-5.30pm Tue-Fri; 10am-5pm Sat; *videothèque* 9am-noon, 1.30-5.30pm Tue-Fri; 10am-5pm Sat. Closed Aug.
A library of theatre, music, dance and film. Screenings can be reserved from the catalogue in the lobby.

Piscine de la Barthelasse

Ile de la Barthelasse (04 90 82 54 25). **Open** *May-Aug* 10am-7pm daily. **Admission** €5; €2 2-5s.
Olympic-sized open-air pool for when the city gets too hot to bear. Cross the Pont Edouard Daladier and the pool is on your right.

Théâtre des Carmes

6 pl des Carmes (04.90.82.20.47). **Box office** 9am-4pm Mon-Fri. **Tickets** €12.96. **Credit** MC, V.
Avignon's oldest theatre company, based in the restored Gothic cloister of Eglise des Carmes, is still firmly committed to radical theatre.

Théâtre du Chien qui fume

75 rue des Teinturiers (04.90.85.25.87/www.chien-qui-fume.com). Closed Aug. **Box office** open one hour before show. **Shows** 8.30pm Fri, Sat. **Tickets** €3-€20. **No credit cards.**
Director Gérard Vantaggioli adamantly refuses to allow this to become a festival-only theatre. He stages new productions regularly, with a *soirée* for fresh talent on the last Friday of the month.

Théâtre Municipal

20 pl de l'Horloge (04.90.82.81.40). **Box office** 11am-6pm Mon-Sat; 11am-12.30pm Sun. **Tickets** €2.75-€56.41. **Credit** MC, V.
The main permanent house in Avignon stages official festival productions in July and opera, ballet, comedy, chamber and symphony music year round.

Utopia

4 rue des Escaliers Ste-Anne (04.90.82.65.36). **Box office** 11am-11pm Mon-Sat. **Tickets** €5; €40 ten-show pass. **No credit cards.**
Avignon's main *version originale* (original language) cinema has a nice bistro attached. Pick up the free information sheet, *La Gazette*.

Restaurants

Le Caveau du Théâtre

16 rue des Trois Faucons (04.90.82.60.91). **Open** noon-2pm, 7-10pm Mon-Fri; 7-10.30pm Sat. **Menus** €10.55-€18. **Credit** V.

Pub Z: stripey boho student haunt. *See p95.*

Keeping up the festival theatrics throughout the year, this popular bistro is decorated as a wine cellar in one room, and a theatre backstage in the other. Sensible theatre going couples come here for good-value dishes such as *moules cassoulet* with mushrooms and raspberry crème brûlée. Friendly staff, and jazz trotting in the background.

La Compagnie des Comptoirs

83 rue Joseph Vernet (04.90.85.99.04/www.jardin-des-sens.com). **Open** noon-2pm, 7-10.30pm daily. **Average** €38.11. **Credit** AmEx, MC, V.
The celebrated Porcel twins of Montpellier have opened another offshoot in the former Cuisine de Reine, with a southern cuisine that brings in influences from India, Italy and Morocco. The interior is by Imaad Rahmouni, who also redid the Maison Blanche in Paris, with the 15th-century cloister draped in Indian fabrics in summer.

L'Epicerie

10 pl St-Pierre (04.90.82.74.22). **Open** 12.30-2.30pm, 7-10pm Mon-Sat. Closed Dec-Apr. **Average** €20. **Credit** MC, V.
Fashionable, picture-perfect L'Epicerie hides alone in a tiny cobbled square, its terrace tables and green awning rolling out at the foot of Eglise St-Pierre. Relaxed staff serve a vegetable-strong Mediterranean menu to local families and bright young things. Try the beef and aubergine tarte in a tomato coulis or the assortment of Provençal starters.

La Ferme

chemin des Bois, Ile de la Barthelasse (04.90.82.57.53/www.hotel-laferme.com). **Open** noon-1.15pm, 7-9pm Tue, Thur-Sun. Closed Nov-Mar. **Menus** €20-€41.15. **Rates** €66-€76. **Credit** AmEx, MC, V.

This rustic *auberge* on an island in the Rhône (five minutes by car or bus from the city centre) serves fresh food that changes according to season. It also has accommodation (double €66-€76) and a pool.

Le Grand Café

La Manutention, 4 rue des Escaliers Ste-Anne (04.90.86.86.77). **Open** 11am-midnight Tue-Sat (meals noon-2pm, 7.30-11pm). Closed Jan. **Menus** €15.24-€24.39 **Credit** AmEx, DC, MC, V.

Avignon goes all 'designer dining room' in this converted army supplies depot. There's a small lunch menu and afternoon tea, while in the evenings the acoustics swell with well-to-do conversation as waiters glide between the long tables, serving inventive if overpriced Mediterranean cuisine. It all feels a bit too urban-chic for the south, before you emerge at the foot of the Palais de Papes, a soberingly magnificent sight. Reserve at weekends.

Maison Nani

29 rue Théodore Aubanel (04.90.82.60.90). **Open** 11.30am-2.30pm Mon-Thur; 11.30am-2.30pm, 7-11pm Fri, Sat. **Average** €15. **No credit cards.**

Charming, casual wood-panelled café with newspapers and magazines to peruse. Select from imaginative salads to accompany carpaccio of salmon, *brochette de boeuf, foie gras* or a variety of cheeses.

Le Mesclun

48 rue de la Balance (04.90.86.14.60). **Open** *Sept-June* noon-2.15pm Tue-Sat; *July* noon-2.15pm, 7.30-10.30pm Mon-Sat; *Aug* noon-2.15pm, 7.30-10.30pm Tue-Sat. **Menu** €17.53. **No credit cards.**

Great for a quick lunch, with brisk service and fresh dishes; try the *anchoïade* with raw vegetables or the potato tart. Father restaurant Brunel next door lets you enjoy the same lunch menu seated in Philippe Starck chairs, with more sophisticated fare at night.

La Mirande

4 pl de la Mirande (04.90.85.93.93/www.la-mirande.fr). **Open** 12.30-2pm, 7.30-10pm daily. Closed Jan. **Menus** €28-€47. **Credit** AmEx, DC, MC, V.

Since the arrival of Ducasse-trained chef Daniel Hébet in 1997, the restaurant of Hôtel de la Mirande has become *the* place to eat in Avignon. In good weather, meals are served in the garden; the rest of the year in the sumptuous dining room. Hébet's exciting desserts include a delicious pistachio and morello cherry macaroon with tarragon salad.

Numéro 75

75 rue Guillaume Puy (04.90.27.16.00). **Open** *June-Aug* noon-2pm, 7.30-10pm daily; *Sept-May* noon-2pm, 7.30-10pm Tue-Sat. **Average** €38 **Credit** MC, V.

The former *hôtel particulier* of the Pernod family has been converted into a stylish new restaurant. Fantasy chandeliers and vibrant colours set the postmodern tone with square-plated, modern European cookery to match the style-conscious crowd.

L'Opéra Café

24 pl de l'Horloge (04.90.86.17.43). **Open** 9am-1am daily. **Meals served** noon-2.15pm, 7-11.30pm. **Menu** €27.44 **Credit** DC, MC, V.

This vampish purple makeover of the République bar is the latest amethyst in the crown of place de l'Horloge. Café, bar and restaurant, with DJ at night, it serves classics like rabbit pâté in truffle vinaigrette and cod with sesame seeds. The puffy terrace chairs are full all day with a mixed crowd.

Rose au Petit Bedon

70 rue Joseph Vernet (04.90.82.33.98). **Open** noon-1.30pm, 7.30-9.30pm Tue-Sat. Closed two weeks Aug. **Menus** €16.77-€25.92. **Credit** AmEx, MC, V.

This small, cosy restaurant with velvet banquettes serves Provençal home cooking such as fish pâté and timbale of lamb with *tapenade*.

Woolloomooloo

16 bis rue des Teinturiers (04.90.85.28.44). **Open** 7-11.30pm Tue-Sun. **Menus** €10-€22. **Credit** MC, V.

This funky candlelit restaurant in an old printing works, complete with exotic furniture, cushions and Indian fabrics, serves a variety of oriental and African dishes. It is permanently buzzing with Avignon's boho crowd and university students.

Bars & cafés

Le Cid Café

11 pl de l'Horloge (04.90.82.30.38). **Open** 7am-1am daily. **Credit** MC, V.

The Queen of the café parade on place de l'Horloge is run by the same crew as the new L'Opéra Café. The terrace tables are ceaselessly packed with tourists and pretty boys. The crowd is pleasantly mixed by day, gay by night, when it becomes a lively bar, with DJs at weekends.

Caves Breysse

41 rue des Teinturiers (04.32.74.25.86). **Open** 10am-3pm, 5-10pm Tue-Sat. Closed 1-15 Jan. **Credit** AmEx, DC, MC, V.

Young, new, with wine on tap, here is where to start the evening with a *ballon de rouge* and make life-long friends with Avignon's arty crowd. Selling fine Côtes du Rhône since 1927, the *caves* have recently been uncorked for apéritifs by Thomas Sylvestre, whose mother makes soups and *plats du jour* at noon and his friends provide the art exhibits on the walls.

Le Café de la Comédie

15 pl Crillon (04.90.85.74.85). **Open** *Oct-July* 7am-1am Mon-Sat; *festival* 7am-3am Mon-Sat. Closed one week in Feb and Aug. **Credit** DC, MC,V.

Its terrace dripping with fairy lights, Café de la Comédie attracts late-twentysomethings who huddle under a plane tree looking out onto the Renaissance facade of Avignon's first theatre.

Simple Simon Tea Lunch

26 rue Petite Fusterie (04.90.86.62.70). **Open** noon-7pm Mon-Sat. Closed Aug. **Average**

€9.50. **Credit** MC, V.

A slice of Britain complete with beams, English china and swirly carpets, this tea room has a permanent stream of sweet-toothed visitors. The spotlit cake table is piled with bakewell tart and scones; savoury staples are served all day.

Clubs & live music

The Red Zone

25 rue Carnot (04.90.27.02.44). **Open** 7pm-3am, Mon-Sat; 9pm-3am first Sun of month. **Credit** AmEx, DC, MC, V.

Recently overhauled to look even redder, this popular bar/club near the university is where Avignon youth comes after a night's drinking on place Pie. Varied dance nights include funk, house and salsa, with student nights on Thursday.

Le Bokao's

9 bis quai St-Lazare (04.90.82.47.95). **Open** 7pm-3am Mon-Sat. **Admission** free. **Credit** AmEx, DC, MC, V.

In an old wood-panelled bar, this club has a large dancefloor and plays an eclectic selection of music. You only get in if the staff like the look of you.

Rhône, Rhône, Rhône the boat

The panorama of Avignon and Villeneuve-lès-Avignon can be enjoyed by boat, with river trips ranging from A-B transport to gourmet cruising. Excursions leave from the Allée de l'Oulle, just outside the ramparts between Porte de l'Oulle and Porte St-Dominique.

The **Bateau Bus** is the most scenic way to get from Avignon over to Villeneuve and replaces the terrifying hike across the traffic thundering Pont Daladier. Leaving six times a day in July and August (and once a day June and Sept), it makes its way over an hour and a half up to the Pont St-Bénézet, passing the Rocher des Doms and the Palais des Papes, looping back round the tip of Ile Piot and on to Villeneuve-lès-Avignon. Between the two the view is mostly vegetation and people's back gardens. Sun-worshippers can bask on deck, while the ray-shy have shade at the stern or inside in the café-bar. Tickets cost €7 (€3.50 2-12s), and include a free mini-train ride from the landing stage to Villeneuve's town centre and back again. At night, the boat offers a dinner cruise €43-€55 (€28.20 2-12s), leaving at 8.30pm and returning at 11pm.

The more sophisticated cruise option is the **Mireio**, a restaurant boat that operates year round and offers excursions along the Rhône, the Durance and the canals of the Rhône delta. Arles, the Camargue, the vineyards of Châteauneuf-du-Pape, Roquemaure, Beaucaire, Tarascon and Villeneuve-lès-Avignon can all be visited with the added temptation of a gourmet lunch or dinner followed by dancing and cabaret (€16.77-€54.12). For information on all three options call 04.90.85.62.25 or visit website www.avignon-et-provence.com/mireio.

Pub Z

58 rue Bonneterie (04.90.85.42.84). **Open** 11am-1am
Mon-Sat. Closed last week Aug. **No credit cards.**
A lifesize zebra welcomes you into the black and
white striped bar popular with rockers and students.
Bobos – the zebra enthusiast and barman with an
impossibly gravelly voice – oversees proceedings,
and there is a DJ at weekends.

The Red Lion

21, 23 rue St Jean les Vieux (04.90.86.40.25).
Open 8am-1am daily. **Credit** AmEx, MC, V.
This butch British pub recently joined the throng
near place Pie, and is one of the many 'foreign'
venues popular with students from the nearby university. Guinness, Stella and Becks are available on
tap and the solid pub-grub includes steak, mushrooms and chips. There is live rock and blues (10pm-
12.30am) on Wednesday and Sunday.

Shopping

The indoor **Les Halles** market in place Pie is
open from 7am to 1pm Tuesday to Sunday
selling fruit and flowers. The **place des
Carmes** holds a flower market on Saturday
morning, and a fleamarket on Sunday morning.
All shops open Mon-Sat unless stated.

Rue de la République is the commercial
centre, with high-street names such as **Zara**
(No.25, 04.90.80.64.42), **H&M** (No.22,
04.32.76.74.50) and **Fnac** (No.19, 04.90.14.35.35).
Peeling off down the pedestrian rue des
Marchands is a maze of clothes shops and
boutiques; **Les Olivades** (No.22,
04.90.86.13.42) sells Provençal fabrics by the
metre and clothes, **Mouret** (No.22,
04.90.85.39.38), listed an historic monument, is
an enchanting hatter fossilised in the 1860s,
where you can try on hats in long Louis XVI
style mirrored walls.

Rue St Agricole acts as a slip-road to chic,
coming west off place de l'Horloge, with
Parisian designers such as **Christian Lacroix**
(No 10, 04.90.27.13.21) and **Hermès** (No.7,
04.90.82.61.94). **La Tropézienne** (No.22,
04.90.86.24.72.) is a Provençal food paradise,
selling wine, *marrons glacés* and the local
speciality, *papaline*, a pink, spiky-coated
oregano liqueur chocolate. Opposite, ice-cream
shop **Deldon** (No.35, 04.90.85.59.41) is a good
heat buster in the summer.

Rue Joseph Vernet is the city's elegance
capital, with **Cacharel** (No.8, 04.90.86.19.19)
and **Comptoir des Cotonniers** (No.27,
04.90.14.63.84). Chocolatier **Puyricard** has an
outpost at No.33 (04.90.85.96.33). Parallel rue
des Petites Fusterie has recently turned into a
home decoration hotbed with **Galerie 5, 6, 7**
(No.17, 06.10.25.76.69) selling 50s-70s furniture,
Papa Est Dans Le Déco (No.15,

04.90.82.30.63) selling quirky Indian-inspired
lighting and cushions, while more traditional
antiques and garden furniture are found at
Hervé Baume (No.19, 04.90.86.37.66).

International newspapers can be bought at
Khedive (6 pl de l'Horloge, 04.90.82.96.73). A
wide selection of second-hand novels and travel
books in English, French and German can be
found at **Shakespeare** (155 rue Carreterie,
04.90.27.38.50, closed Mon, Sun), situated near
the university and doubling as a tearoom.

Where to stay

See also p92, **La Ferme.**

Auberge de Chassagne

*450 allée de Chassagne, Le Pontet (04.90.31.04.18/
www.hotelprestige-provence.com).* Closed Jan-Feb.
Double €100-€480. **Menus** €50-€80. **Credit**
AmEx, DC, MC, V.
If you want to avoid the bustle of the town centre,
this is Provençal-style accommodation of exceptional quality, set around a peaceful garden and
small swimming pool. The gastronomic restaurant
is filled with serious local foodies.

La Banasterie

11 rue de la Banasterie (tel/fax 04.32.76.30.78.).
Double €90-€140. **No credit cards.**
Ex-media couple Françoise and Jean-Michel Brochet
recently opened this elegant 18th-century *maison
d'hôtes* in the centre of town. Three guest rooms and
a suite each have private use of a roof garden, balcony or fountain courtyard.

Camping Municipal

*Île de la Barthelasse (04.90.80.63.50/www.camping-
avignon.com).* Closed Nov-Mar. **Rates** two-person
tent €9.50-€19.65; four-person bungalow €310-€400
per week. **Credit** MC, V.
A campsite on an island in the Rhône – take Pont
Edouard Daladier to reach it.

Hôtel de Blauvac

*11 rue de la Bancasse (04.90.86.34.11/
www.hotel-blauvac.com).* Closed Jan. **Double** €47-
€65. **Credit** AmEx, DC, MC, V.
A 17th-century building overlooking a quiet, winding street. The de Blauvac is very reasonably priced,
with large, well-designed rooms and friendly service.

Hôtel Colbert

*7 rue Agricol Perdiguier (04.90.86.20.20/
www.lecolbert-hotel.com).* Closed Nov-Feb. **Double**
€45-€53. **Credit** DC, MC, V.
Part of a cluster of budget hotels on a tiny street
bang in the middle of town, Le Colbert has newly
redecorated clean rooms and air-conditioning. You
can breakfast in the courtyard.

Hôtel Cloître St-Louis

*20 rue Portail Boquier (04.90.27.55.55/
www.cloitre-saint-louis.com).* **Double** €84-€214.

Credit AmEx, DC, MC, V.

A clever combination of ancient and modern: a 16th-century cloister and chapel wing has been complemented by a steel and glass extension by Jean Nouvel, with a walled garden and rooftop pool.

Hôtel d'Europe

12 pl Crillon (04.90.14.76.76/www.hotel-d-europe.fr). **Double** €120-€385. **Credit** AmEx, DC, MC, V.

Napoléon, Victor Hugo, John Stuart Mill and Jackie Onassis are just some of the past guests at this Avignon legend set in a 16th-century mansion. The elegant salons are hung with tapestries and paintings; the rooms and suites are spacious and tastefully decorated and the gardens surround the hotel.

Hôtel Innova

6 rue Joseph Vernet (04.90.82.54.10). **Double** €23-€36.50. **Credit** MC, V.

Cheap for its elegant setting in a *hôtel particulier* in the rue Joseph Vernet, this homely hotel with an abundance of potted plants is popular with young travellers. Rooms are basic and clean and the upper floors are due for renovation in time for spring 2002.

Hôtel de la Mirande

4 pl de la Mirande (04.90.85.93.93/ www.la-mirande.com). **Double** €260-€430. **Credit** AmEx, DC, MC, V.

This 18th-century cardinals' palace between the Palais des Papes and place de l'Horloge combines exquisitely styled period panelling, tapestries, fine

The ramparts of **Fort St-André**, Villeneuve.

linen and antique furniture with 21st-century luxury and service. It has just added a new apartment suite in a *hôtel particulier* next door, and also has one of Avignon's best restaurants (*see p93*).

Hôtel Mignon

12 rue Joseph Vernet (04.90.82.17.30/ www.hotel-mignon.com). **Double** €35-€39. **Credit** AmEx, MC, V.

A sweet little hotel with small but good-value rooms and pretty Provençal furnishings. The enchanting breakfast room is hung with a trellis of plastic flowers and the management is extremely welcoming.

Hôtel de Mons

5 rue de Mons (04.90.82.57.16). **Double** €45-€58. **Credit** AmEx, MC, V.

A budget choice right off place de l'Horloge, this is a quaintly converted medieval chapel, with winding stairs and rooms squeezed into nooks and crannies – some are a little too squeezed for comfort, so insist on seeing them first.

Hôtel du Parc

18 rue Agricol Perdiguier (04.90.82.71.55). **Rates** €26.70-€41.15. **Credit** AmEx, MC, V.

Opposite the Splendid with views on to the park, the Parc's balconies cascade with greenery, and the newly decorated interior with Provençal fabrics. Exposed beams and stone walls remain intact.

Hôtel Le Splendid

17 rue Agricol Perdiguier (04.90.86.14.46/ www.avignon-splendid-hotel.com). **Rates** €39-€49. **Credit** AmEx, MC, V.

Simple and neat, with several rooms looking out onto the flower-filled square Agricol Perdiguier. New owners the Lemoines plan to redecorate in winter 2002 to give all rooms *en suite* facilities.

Essentials

Getting there

By air

Avignon's airport, Caumont-Avignon (04.90.81.51.51), is 8km south of town. You can catch a bus to the centre from the Lycée Agricole, 500m from the airport (about 20 buses a day, 15 mins). More information on 04.90.82.07.35.

By car

From the A7 autoroute, exits nos.23 (Avignon Nord) and 24 (Avignon Sud) link with the outer ring road.

By train

Avignon is at the junction of the Paris-Marseille and Paris-Montpellier lines. The Gare Centre Ville has frequent links to Arles, Nîmes, Orange, Toulon and Carcassonne. The new Gare TGV is 4km south of Avignon. A bus service leaves from the station at the arrival of each train, taking passengers to the Gare Centre Ville and leaves from the centre for the Gare TGV every 15 mins (08.92.35.35.35, www.tgv.com).

By bus

Daily buses connect Avignon with Carpentras,
Cavaillon, St-Rémy, Orange, Nîmes, Arles, Aix,
Marseille, Nice and Cannes. The bus station
(04.90.82.07.35) is on av Montclar, just next to the
Centre Ville train station.

Tourist information

The **Pass Avignon-Villeneuve Discovery
Passport** gives 20-30% reductions (after the
first ticket) on most museums and sights. Pick
it up at the first museum you visit or the tourist
office. It's valid for a fortnight and covers up to
four people. Two mini tourist trains (**STTG
Eisenreich**, 04.90.82.64.44) make circuits of
Avignon (Mar-Oct 10am-7pm daily) from place
du Palais. One gives a 30 minute tour of the
main sites (€6), the other runs to the Rocher des
Doms (€2). Town buses are run by **TCRA**
(04.32.74.18.32). Bikes can be hired from
Aymard (80 rue Guillaume Puy, 04.90.86.32.49,
closed Mon, one week Aug). Mopeds and
motorbikes can be hired from **Holiday Bikes**
(52 bd St Roch, 04.90.27.92.61/ www.motovelo.com,
open daily Apr-Oct, by appointment Nov-Mar).

The cheapest and most comfortable Internet
café, **Arobase** (14, 16 rue de Limas,
04.90.16.02.18, open 10am-10pm Mon-Sat; 4-
10pm Sun, €4 per hour) is run by the Esclave
club next door and has a webcam, loud blues
music and non-alcoholic bar. **Cyberdrome** (68
rue Guillaume Puy, 04.90.16.05.15, open *May-
Aug* 8am-midnight Mon-Sat, 2pm-midnight
Sun, *Sept-Apr* 8am-9pm, €4.60) has 26
terminals and an alcohol-free bar with music.

Avignon Office de Tourisme

*41 cours Jean Jaurès, 84008 Avignon
(04.32.74.32.74/www.ot-avignon.fr).* **Open** *Apr-Sept*
10am-8pm Mon-Sat, 10am-5pm Sun; *Oct-Mar* 9am-
6pm Mon-Fri, 9am-1pm, 2-5pm Sat, 10am-noon Sun.
Branch: Espace St-Bénézet, esplanade St-Bénazet.
Open *Apr-Oct* 10am-7pm daily.

Police & lost property

*Police municipale, pl Pie (04.90.80.80.00/Lost
property 04.32.76.01.73).* **Open** 24 hours daily; lost
property 9am-noon, 1-5pm Mon-Fri.

Post office

cours Président Kennedy (04.90.27.54.00). **Open**
8am-7pm Mon-Fri; 8am-noon Sat.

Villeneuve-lès-Avignon

The historic skyline and gentle tourism of
Avignon spills over across the Ile de la
Barthelasse into Villeneuve-lès-Avignon, the

Quarton's **Coronation of the Virgin**. *See p98.*

eastern point of Languedoc Roussillon (reached
from Avignon by Pont Edouard Daladier, bus
11 from Porte l'Oulle or the **Bateau Bus**, *see
p94*). This small settlement centred on the
tenth-century Abbaye St-André came into its
own in 1307, when King Philippe le Bel decided
it was a prime location for keeping an eye on
Papal goings-on across the Rhône. A heavily
fortified 'new town' (*villeneuve*) sprang up, plus
a watchtower – the **Tour Philippe le Bel** –
which grew higher as Avignon became more
powerful. Unjustifiably overshadowed by its
brasher neighbour, Villeneuve offers some
stunning architecture, a superb view and one
matchless work of art.

For the view, head for the west tower of the
Fort St-André, the fortress built in the 14th
century around the abbey, and climb along the
massive ramparts. Inside are the remains of the
Abbaye St-André: bewitching terraced
gardens, with paths of roses, lavender and
wisteria, leading to a tiny restored Romanesque
chapel, the ruins of the 13th-century church and
a graveyard with sarcophagi laid out like little
beds – more moving by far than all of
Avignon's great palaces.

Below the fort, the **Chartreuse du Val de
Bénédiction** was once the largest Carthusian
monastery in France. The charterhouse has

been painstakingly restored, removing all signs of the depredations suffered during the Revolution, when to add insult to injury the tomb of Pope Innocent VI, who founded the monastery in 1352, was converted into a white marble rabbit hutch. There are monks' cells resembling little rows of terraced cottages off two pale stone cloisters, as well as a laundry, kitchen, prisons and a herb garden funded by beauty company Yves Rocher. A small chapel off the Cloître du Cimetière has exquisite frescoes by Matteo Giovanetti, while Innocent VI's tomb, now fully restored, can be seen in the church. The Chartreuse now acts as a state-funded centre for playwrights.

The **Musée Pierre de Luxembourg** contains four floors of art, including a superb, delicately carved ivory *Virgin and Child* and 16th- and 17th-century religious paintings by Mignard and de Champaigne. The collection's masterpiece is the extraordinary *Coronation of the Virgin* (1453-54) by Enguerrand Quarton, a leading light in the Avignon school. The entire medieval world view is represented in detailed landscape and human activity: the terrestrial world divides the devils and the damned in hell from the clerics, saints and martyrs among the elect in heaven. The Virgin wears a stunning blue cloak, flanked by Jesus and God as the heavenly twins.

Just south of the museum, the 14th-century **Eglise Notre-Dame** has works by Mignard and Levieux, a lavish 18th-century altarpiece, a copy of Enguerrand Quarton's *Pietà* (the original is in the Louvre) and a cloister.

Chartreuse du Val de Bénédiction

rue de la République (04.90.15.24.24/ www.chartreuse.org). **Open** *Apr-Sept* 9.30am-5.30pm daily; *Oct-Mar* 9am-6.30pm daily. **Admission** €5.50; under-18s free.

Eglise Notre-Dame

pl du Chapitre. **Open** *Apr-Sept* 10am-12.30pm, 3-7pm daily; *Oct-Mar* 10am-noon, 2-6.30pm daily; Closed Feb. **Admission** free.

Fort St-André & Abbaye St-André

montée du Fort (fort 04.90.25.45.35/ abbey 04.90.25. 55.95). **Open** *fort Apr-Sept* 10am-1pm, 2-6pm daily; *Oct-Mar* 10am-1pm, 2-5pm daily; *gardens Apr-Sept* 10am-12.30pm, 2-6pm Tue-Sun; *Oct-Mar* 10am-12.30pm, 2-5pm Tue-Sun; *abbey* by appointment. **Admission** *fort* free (*tower* €3.96; free under-18s); *abbey and gardens* €6; €3 16-18s; free under 16s.

Musée Pierre de Luxembourg

rue de la République (04.90.27.49.66). **Open** *mid-Apr to mid-June* 10am-12.30pm, 3-7pm Tue-Sun; *mid-June to mid-Sept* 10am-12.30pm, 3-7pm daily; *mid-Sept to mid-Apr,* 10am-noon, 2-5.30pm Tue-Sun. Closed Feb. **Admission** €3; €1.20 students; free under-18s.

Tour Philippe le Bel

rue Montée de la Tour (04.32.70.08.57). **Open** *Apr to mid-June* 10am-12.30pm, 3-7pm Tue-Sat, *mid-June to mid-Sept* 10am-12.30pm, 3-7pm daily; *mid-Sept to Mar* 10am-noon, 2-5.30pm Tue-Sat. Closed Feb. **Admission** €1.60; free under-18s.

Where to stay & eat

Villeneuve's hotels absorb the overflow when Avignon is booked out during the festival, but are also worth considering in their own right. The luxury option is **Le Prieuré** (7 pl du Chapitre, 04.90.15.90.15, closed Nov to mid-Mar, double €151-€290), an exquisitely restored, if slightly retro, 14th-century archbishop's palace with a library, garden and pool. A dreamier option is the 17th-century **Hôtel de l'Atelier** (5 rue de la Foire, 04.90.25.01.84, closed Nov-Dec, double €44-€99), recently redecorated by set designer Dominique Baroush as an airy modern-rustic guest house. The new owner has bought the former Gelateria Notre-Dame opposite (its owner mysteriously disappeared to join a sect) and is turning it into a *salon de thé*.

Villeneuve's trendiest restaurant, **Mon Mari Etait Pâtissier** (3 bd Pasteur, 04.90.25.52.79, closed Mon, menus €17-€25) serves original dishes such as swordfish tartare, and exquisite desserts. **Aubertin** (1 rue de l'Hôpital, 04.90.25.94.84, closed Sun, Mon and two weeks Aug, menus €23-€45) has just been redecorated in a minimalist yet Provençal style, and offers inventive cuisine by chef Jean-Claude Aubertin; potatoes stuffed with *petits gris* (little snails) or mullet *aïoli*. In next door village Les Angles, **C'est la Lune** (270 montée du Valadas, 04.90.25.40.55, mid-Sept to mid-May closed Mon-Wed & Sun and lunch Thur-Sat, average €27) is a North African fusion bar-restaurant, where hip Avignon and Villeneuve congregate to eat prune *tajine*, and dance it off with the help of the house ti'ponch. The two salons are redecorated virtually every week by globetrotting owner Georges, also the brainchild between Woolloomooloo in Avignon.

Tourist Information

A €6.86 pass gives free entrance to Villeneuve's five main monuments. In July and August a **tourist train** makes a circuit of the historic centre five times a day (€1.52) and also greets travellers from the **Bateau Bus** (*see p94*).

Villeneuve Office du Tourisme

1 pl Charles David, 30400 Villeneuve-lès-Avignon (04.90.25.61.33/www.villeneuve-lez-avignon.com). **Open** *Mar-June, Sept* 9am-12.30pm, 2-6pm Mon-Sat; *Oct-Feb* 9am-12.30pm, 2-5pm Mon-Sat; *July* 10am-7pm daily; *Aug* 9am-12.30pm, 2-6pm daily.

Orange & Around

With Roman theatres, holy bridges, rare daubs and stupendous red wines, the Orange area provides enough grand opera for everyone.

Around about Orange, the Rhône starts to get big and bloated. Its meanderings over the centuries have made for a flat, agricultural landscape, rising into low hills here and there – as around the wine citadel of Châteauneuf-du-Pape. On this eastern bank the evidence of Roman occupation is everywhere. The western bank belonged to Languedoc and the king, while the east was Popish and imperial.

Orange

The Roman city of Arausio was founded in 35 BC as a golden handshake for retiring soldiers of the Gallic second legion. During its Roman golden age, the colony was four times as large as today's town. Orange declined sharply in the Dark Ages, but picked up in the 12th century, as an enclave governed by troubadour-prince Raimbaut d'Orange. In 1530 the town passed to a cadet branch of the German house of Nassau, and gave its name to the branch's Dutch principality 14 years later. Thereafter, Orange became a sort of Protestant buzzword (finding its way into Ulster's Orange Order and the Orange Free State) and the town itself attracted Protestant refugees from all over Provence.

The Dutch Nassaus managed to hold on to their little piece of France against the odds, and in 1622 Maurice de Nassau built an impressive château and fortifications around the town. Unfortunately he used stones from the remaining Roman monuments not previously destroyed by the Barbarians, and only the Arc de Triomphe and the Théâtre Antique survived the pillaging. In 1673, as he was embarking on another war with Protestant Holland, Louis XIV ordered the destruction of the château. The Treaty of Utrecht in 1713 finally gave the principality to France, but the proudly independent town has not forgotten its roots, and Queen Juliana of the Netherlands was back in 1952 planting an oak tree on the site of the château. Tourism apart, the town is home to the cavalry regiment of the French Foreign Legion, who stroll around the town in full uniform, an ironic reminder that this is one of only a handful of French towns with a National Front-led local council (*see box*, **Black or Orange?**).

Geographically and emotionally, the **Théâtre Antique** dominates the town. Quite simply, this is the best-preserved Roman theatre anywhere. What sets itself apart from similar theatres is the unrivalled state of preservation of the stage wall, a massive, sculpted sandstone screen 36m high which Louis XIV referred to as 'the finest wall in my kingdom'. The amphitheatre was a multifunctional space, like the *salles*

Black or Orange?

A visit to Orange can bring on a crisis of political conscience. Is it really possible that the National Front mayor, the popular Jacques Bompard, was re-elected at the local election in 2001 with a massive 59.87 per cent vote? How could the citizens of this sleepy town have voted predominantly for a party associated with racial discrimination of the nastiest sort? The extreme right pedal the idea that a fatal dilution of the French way of life is underway, led by North African immigrants in cahoots with Zionists – an interesting notion in a town which, until the 18th century, was a foreign enclave. Visitors will see few outward signs of the ruling junta's politics, although an annual comics and graphic book festival was wound up in 1996, and there has been pressure on the organisers of the Chorégies (*see box p102*) to programme more authentic 'Gallic' works to match the traditional costumes worn by staff on performance evenings. This is a seemingly charming idea but in Orange even an exhibition charting the history of olive oil may not be as innocent as it seems, if the aim behind it is to ferment and channel regional pride. Libraries are apparently put under pressure to remove provocative, supposedly left-wing propaganda, which includes such unlikely titles as daily newspaper *Libération*. The tourist information pack has no entry for North African restaurants, but there is an excellent Arabic pâtisserie just beside the Roman theatre; buy some sticky cakes as a tourist act of solidarity.

polyvalentes that litter municipal France; it would have hosted everything from political meetings to concerts, sporting events and plays. In the fourth century the theatre was abandoned and makeshift houses were built within the auditorium. It was not until the 19th century that restoration began and the famous opera festival, the **Chorégies d'Orange**, was born. The Roman statue of Augustus, which presides over the stage from his niche in the wall, was placed here in 1951.

On top of the hill of **St-Eutrope**, into which the curve of the seats was excavated, is a pleasant park with the ruins of Maurice de Nassau's château and the Piscine des Cèdres (04.90.34.09.68, open end June-end Aug), an open-air swimming pool which is a temptation in a town that can get very hot and dusty in summer. It is also the scene of important recent archaeological excavations. Opposite the main entrance to the theatre, the **Musée Municipal**, houses an interesting collection of Roman artefacts, including a unique series of cadastres. These engraved marble tablets map the streets, administrative divisions and geographical features of the Orange region in Roman times in the course of three successive surveys (the earliest dates from 77AD). On the top floor is an unsuspected curiosity: a selection of post-Impressionist paintings by Welsh artist Frank Brangwyn. The curators also have a bafflingly large collection of his drawings, which can be seen by appointment. The local tradition of the printed cotton cloth known as *indiennes* is celebrated in another series of paintings by 18th-century artist GM Rossetti. Modern-day *indiennes* can be tracked down next door at **La Provençale** (5 pl Sylvain, 04.90.51.58.86, closed Mon, Sun and Jan, Feb, Nov).

The old town, in front of the theatre, is a tight knot of twisting streets that liven up at festival time, but provide little architectural competition for the towering classical monuments, although they abound in attractive shady squares, ideal for a pre-dinner *pastis*. The best and liveliest cafés and the majority of the town's eating places are in front of the Roman theatre.

Out of the centre, on the northern edge of the town, the **Arc de Triomphe** is Orange's other great Roman monument. The triumphal arch spanning the former Via Agrippa, which linked Lyon to Arles, was built in 20BC, is the third largest of its kind in the world; the north side is a riot of well-preserved carving, with military paraphernalia arranged in abstract patterns.

Musée Municipal

rue Madeleine Roch (04.90.51.18.24). **Open** *Oct-Apr* 9.30am-noon, 1.30-5.30pm daily; *May-Sept* 9.30am-7pm daily. **Admission** (incl Théâtre) €5; €4 10-16s; free under-10s.

Théâtre Antique

pl des Frères-Mounet (04.90.51.17.60). **Open** *Apr-Sept* 9.30am-6pm daily; *Oct-Mar* 9.30am-noon, 1.30-5pm daily. **Admission** (incl museum) €5; €4 10-16s; free under-10s.

Where to stay & eat

The most comfortable hotel in the town centre is the recently renovated **Arènes** (pl de Langes, 04.90.11.40.40, double €67-€91.50). The basic but attractive **Arcotel** (8 pl aux Herbes, 04.90.34.09.23, double €33.54-€38.11) is on a charming small square in the old town, while the **Glacier** (46 cours Aristide Briand, 04.90.34.02.01/www.le-glacier.com, closed Sat, Sun Nov-Feb and 23 Dec-10 Jan, double €44.21-€57.93) has outstandingly helpful staff.

Authentic local cuisine can be had at **Le Forum** (3 rue Mazeau, 04.90.34.01.09, closed Mon, Sat lunch & 15-31 Aug, two weeks in Feb, menus €14.94-€49), including a fine *lièvre à la royale* for game lovers. On a hectic performance evening we were impressed by the **Brasserie**

The **Théâtre Antique**'s mighty stage wall: a backdrop to splendid performances.

du **Théâtre** (pl des Frères Mounet, 04.90.34.12.39), who came up in record-breaking speed with an excellent *steak-frites* and crunchy *salade niçoise* with a bottle of local wine for under €30. If you have overdosed on the indigenous cuisine, **Le Saigon** (20 pl Sylvain, 04.90.34.18.19, average €25) is a decent Chinese restaurant just beside the Théâtre Antique.

Tourist information

Market day is Thursday morning.

Office de Tourisme

5 cours Aristide Briand, 88100 Orange (04.90.34.70.88/www.provence-orange.com). **Open** *Apr-Sept* 9am-7pm Mon-Sat, 9am-6pm Sun; *Oct-Mar* 10am-1pm, 2-5pm Mon-Sat.

Châteauneuf-du-Pape

Châteauneuf-du-Pape – like Sancerre or Roquefort – is one of those places that says exactly what it does. Just to reinforce the point, the road south from Orange has vines growing right down to the edge of the tarmac, their grapes destined not only for the princely red that takes its name from the village, but also Côtes du Rhône and the Côtes du Rhône Villages. As every second farm is a wine estate, invitations to taste and visit are thick on the ground. The local tourist office offers a comprehensive list of vineyard visits. A strong nerve is required to resist buying when you have sniffed, sipped and slurped every vintage for the last ten years, but the local winemakers are a philosophical crowd and won't kill or curse your firstborn if you don't buy a case.

The original vineyards were planted at the instigation of the popes from Avignon (commemorated in the village's name) who summered here in the castle built by wine-lover John XXII in 1316. The tight rules regarding yield and grape varieties laid down in 1923 were far-sighted blueprints for France's *appellation d'origine contrôlée* regulations, and sealed the reputation of the local red, which is a blend of at least eight varieties, dominated by grenache. The alluvial soil, sprinkled with heat-

Avignon & the Vaucluse

Les Chorégies d'Orange

This spectacular festival has the muscle to attract the greatest names in opera, who relish the challenge of singing in the Roman theatre, without amplification, to over 9,000 spectators. Providing the mistral doesn't get up, the acoustics are miraculously good. There used to be no more than two performances a year, but recently these have been extended to seven or more amid pressure to create more of a season. Other venues are being brought into use, such as the intimate Cour St-Louis for vocal recitals and the nearby Château Malijay-Jonquières for opera productions with rising young singers. The 2001 Verdi centenary was celebrated in handsome style with fine performances of *Aida*, *Rigoletto* and *Don Carlos*. The 2002 festival (6 July-3 Aug) promises Mozart's *Magic Flute* and *Requiem*, and a stellar production of Gounod's *Roméo et Juliette* with opera's controversial hot couple of the moment, Angela Gheorghiu and Roberto Alagna. Good tickets should be booked well ahead, but last-minute arrivals usually find somewhere to sit. In a new initiative, it should be possible to log on to performances on the net, something the Romans would no doubt have approved.

Bureau des Chorégies d'Orange

18 pl Sylvain, 84107 Orange Cedex (04.90.34.24.24/www.choregies.asso.fr). **Tickets** €15-€160.

absorbing pebbles, the widely spaced vines and the cloud-dispersing mistral all contribute to the muscular alcoholic content (12.5 per cent) and complex nose of the wine. Recently, white Châteauneuf-du-Pape (a minimum five-grape blend) has made a name for itself, too.

All that wine money has at least been put to good use. **Châteauneuf-du-Pape** is an outstandingly beautiful village, tastefully restored, with a characterful town centre and a good central *cave* (**Le Domaine du Père Caboche**, 1 rue Joseph Ducos, 04.90.83.50.66) from which to embark on a glass-by-glass tour of the local vintages. One of the winemakers, le Père Anselme, has had the clever idea of opening a museum to celebrate the area's winemaking tradition: the **Musée des Outils de Vignerons**. The exhibition of baskets, pruners and suchlike is interesting enough, but the shop and tasting-room at the end is what this is all about. If you need a sugar rush to get out of here, there is a good chocolate factory, **Castelain** (rte d'Avignon, 04.90.83.54.71).

To work off that hangover, climb up to the ruins of the **Château des Papes**, destroyed in the Wars of Religion. Little remains of the building, but the views are exceptional.

Musée des Outils de Vignerons

Le Clos (04.90.83.70.07/www.brotte.com). **Open** *July-Sept* 9am-1pm, 2-7pm daily; *Oct-June* 9am-noon, 2-6pm daily. **Admission** free.

Where to stay & eat

Châteauneuf is a good base if you want to avoid drinking and driving. **La Garbure** (3 rue Joseph Ducos, 04.90.83.75.08/www.la-garbure.com, closed Sun & one week in Jan, double €53.36-€62.50) in the main street is an attractive choice, both for local cuisine (average €27.44) and its comfortable rooms. For something more elaborate, the **Hôtellerie Château des Fines Roches** (rte de Sorgues, 04.90.83.70.23/fax 04.90.83.78.42, double €145-€183), a 19th-century *faux château* set in a vineyard, with a good though pricey restaurant (menus €29-€69). At Courthezon, 7km NE, **Lou Pequelet** (pl Edouard Daladier, 04.90.70.28.96, closed Sun & two weeks in Sept) offers home-cooking (average €21.34) in an unspoilt village.

Tourist information

Market day is Friday morning.

Office de Tourisme

pl Portail, 84103 Châteauneuf-du-Pape (04.90.83.71.08). **Open** *July-Aug* 9am-7pm Mon-Sat, 10am-5pm Sun; *Sept-June* 9am-12.30pm, 2-6pm Mon-Sat.

Wine not sample the local speciality at **Châteauneuf-du-Pape**?

Pont-St-Esprit & Bagnols-sur-Cèze

The Bridge of the Holy Spirit spans the Rhône just where it enters Provence. Built 1265-1319 by a brotherhood inspired by one Jéhan de Thianges, who was 'led by divine inspiration', the bridge was originally a more elaborate affair with bastions and towers. It remains an impressive curved structure, with 19 of the 25 arches still in their original state. **Pont-St-Esprit** was badly bombed in World War II and was at the centre of a scandal in 1951, when the town's bread became mysteriously poisoned. In the town itself, pretty rue St-Jacques is named after the pilgrims who stayed here on their way to Santiago de Compostella. The religious paintings and artefacts in the **Musée d'Art Sacré du Gard** may not set your pulse on fire, but the building is a well-preserved medieval merchant's house that was inhabited by the same family for six centuries. More odds and ends, including 220 18th-century pharmacy jars, are displayed in the **Musée Paul Raymond**.

Bagnols-sur-Cèze, 11km south, has one of the best markets in the region, and one of the most satisfying small museums. If you are a fan of nuclear processing plants, it also offers the **Centre atomique de Marcoule**, which has quadrupled the town's working population and which has a well-conceived visitors' centre. The old town is full of character, particularly on

Wednesday market day, when most of the centre of town is given over to produce of all sorts. This is the place to stock up on local gastronomic products or good-quality Provençal fabrics. Rue Crémieux, which runs up to the place Mallet, is filled with fine townhouses dating from the 16th to the 18th centuries. Look up at the riotous gargoyles of number 15, and browse in the organic food shop housed in the courtyard. On the second floor of the town hall, a 17th-century mansion in place Mallet, is the town's big cultural draw, the **Musée Albert André**. In 1923, a fire destroyed the museum's patchy and parochial collection of daubs. Painter Albert André, who was standing in as curator, launched an appeal – with the help of his friend Renoir – to the artists of France, to help him fill the empty walls. They responded in force, and today the museum provides a frozen snapshot of early 20th-century figurative art, with works by Renoir, Signac, Bonnard, Matisse, Gauguin and others. Memories of the rich archaeological past of the town, both Celtic-Ligurian and Gallo-Roman, are housed in the **Musée d'Archéologie Léon Alègre**.

Perched above the river Cèze, 10km west of Bagnols, **La Roque-sur-Cèze** is a picture-postcard village with a fine Romanesque church, approached by an ancient single-track bridge. Just downstream, the Cèze cuts through the limestone to form the spectacular **Cascade de Sautadet**. Bathers should beware for this stretch of the river is a frequent scene of tragic drownings. North of La Roque, in the midst of an oak forest that would not be out of place in a medieval romance, is the 13th-century **Chartreuse de Valbonne** monastery, now a hospital for tropical diseases, which produces its own Côtes du Rhône wine.

Centre atomique de Marcoule

Cogema-Marcoule, Bagnols-sur-Cèze (04.66.79.51.55). **Open** *July-Aug* 10am-noon, 3.30-7.30pm Wed, Sat, Sun; *Sept-June* 2.30-5pm Wed, Sat, Sun; *guided visits July-Aug* coaches leave Bagnols tourist office 1.30pm Wed, 8.30am Fri (04.66.89.54.61). **Admission** free.

Chartreuse de Valbonne

St-Paulet-de-Caisson (04.66.90.41.24/vineyard 04.66.90.41.00). **Open** *May-Aug* 9am-12.30pm, 2-7.30pm daily; *Sept-Apr* 9am-noon, 1.30-5.30pm daily. **Admission** €3.05; €1.05 10-16s; free under 10s.

Musée Albert André

pl Mallet, Bagnols (04.66.50.50.56). **Open** *July-Aug* 10am-12.30pm, 2-6.30pm Tue-Sun; *Sept-Jan, Mar-June* 10am-noon, 2-6pm Tue-Sun. **Closed** Feb. **Admission** €3.05; €1.52 10-16s; free under-10s.

Musée d'Archéologie Léon Alègre

24 av Paul Langevin, Bagnols (04.66.89.74.00). **Open** 10am-12.30pm, 2-6pm Tue, Thur, Fri. **Admission** €3; €1.05 12-16s; free under-12s.

Musée d'Art Sacré du Gard

2 rue St-Jacques, Pont-St-Esprit (04.66.39.17.61). **Open** *July-Aug* 10am-7pm Tue-Sun; *Sept-June* 10am-noon, 2-6pm Tue-Sun. Closed Feb. **Admission** €3.05; €1.83 10-16s; free under-10s.

Musée Paul Raymond

pl de l'Hôtel de Ville, Pont-St-Esprit (04.66.39.09.98). **Open** *July-Aug* 10am-7pm Tue-Sun; *Sept-June* 10am-noon, 2-6pm Tue-Sun. Closed Feb. **Admission** €1.83; €1.37 12-16s; free under-12s.

Where to stay & eat

In Pont-St-Esprit, the **Auberge Provençale** (rte de Nîmes, 04.66.39.08.79, closed 24 Dec-2 Jan & Sun Oct-Mar, double €24.39-€30.49) has simple accommodation and a popular restaurant (menus €9.91-€19.06). Typical Provençal fare is served at **Lou Recati** (6 rue Jean Jacques, 04.66.90.73.01, closed Mon, Tue lunch & two weeks in Oct, menus €11.45-€21).

Between Pont-Esprit and Bagnols, the **Hôtel Valaurie** (St-Nazare, 04.66.89.66.22, double €49) lacks a pool, but is a comfortable enough stop, though it changed management in Jan 2002. The luxurious **Château de Montcaud** (5km W of Bagnols, rte d'Alès Combe, Sabran, 04.66.89.60.60, closed mid-Oct to mid-Mar, double €175-€555) is a 19th-century pile with shady wooded grounds, a nice pool and a Turkish bath. Special breaks

are available with tickets for Les Chorégies and *demi-pension*. Its restaurant, **Les Jardins de Montcaud** (closed Sat, average €61) offers fine country cooking in a stone *mas* with tables on the patio in summer. For a quick snack in Bagnols, **Crêperie/Saladerie Clementine** (12 pl Mallet, 04.66.89.42.26, closed Sat, Sun, average €12) has a terrace overlooking a pretty square. At La Roque-sur-Cèze, **Le Mas du Belier** (04.66.82.78.73, closed Mon and Nov & Jan, average €18) is a romantic waterside inn. At the entrance to the village, **La Tonnelle** (pl des Marronniers, 04.66.82.79.37, closed Nov-Mar, double €54) is a good-value *chambres d'hôtes*.

Tourist Information

Market day is Saturday in Pont-St-Esprit and Wednesday in Bagnols-sur-Cèze.

Bagnols-sur-Cèze

Espace St-Gilles, av Léon Blum, 30200 Bagnols-sur-Cèze (04.66.89.54.61/www.ot-bagnols-sur-ceze.com). **Open** *July-Aug* 9am-7pm Mon-Fri, 9am-6pm Sat, 10am-1pm Sun; *Sept-June* 9am-noon, 2-6pm Mon-Fri, 9am-noon Sat.

Pont-St-Esprit

Résidence Welcome, 30130 Pont-St-Esprit (04.66.39.44.45). **Open** *June-Aug* 9am-12.30pm, 1.30-6.30pm Mon-Fri, 9am-12.30pm, 3-6pm Sat, 9am-noon Sun; *Sept-May* 8am-noon, 2-5.30pm Mon-Fri, 9am-noon Sat.

▶ Getting There & Around

▶ By car

From A7 motorway take exit 21 for Orange or exit 19 and N86 to Pont-St-Esprit and Bagnols-sur-Cèze. For Châteauneuf-du-Pape take the D68 from Orange or N7 and D17 from Avignon.

▶ By train

Orange station (av Frédéric Mistral, 04.90.11.88.00) is on the main Paris-Avignon-Marseille line, but only a few TGVs stop here, so a change is often inevitable.

▶ By bus

Rapides du Sud-Est (04.90.34.15.59) runs six buses a day, Mon-Sat, between Avignon and Orange. **Cars Auran** (04.66.39.10.40) runs buses Mon-Sat between Avignon, Pont-St-Esprit and Bagnols-sur-Cèze. **Sotra Ginaux** (04.75.39.40.22) runs daily buses, Mon-Fri (less in school holidays), between Orange and Pont-St-Esprit, Avignon to Aubernas via Pont-St-Esprit, and Aubunars to Bagnols.

Carpentras & Mont Ventoux

An independent spirit and tolerable tourist levels characterise this fertile enclave renowned for its fruit, veg and truffles.

The area around Carpentras, including Mont Ventoux, Vaison-La Romaine, Avignon and Cavaillon, is known as the Comtat Venaissin. For more than 500 years this was a papal enclave inside French territory, a sort of huge, rural Vatican City. Ceded to the Holy See in 1274, the Comtat remained in papal hands until 1791, when it was reunited with France.

Carpentras

Carpentras, a bustling town with a population of 30,000, is a good provincial antidote to tourist fatigue. Though there are no must-see monuments, the place is full of character, with an independent spirit, a great market and a few surprises that make it worth a detour. The name comes from the Gallic word for a two-wheeled chariot, whose construction was, in ancient times, the local speciality. Of the city walls only the 14th-century Porte d'Orange remains, but the congested town centre still follows a walled city plan and it is virtually compulsory to leave your car and explore the town centre on foot.

The **Musée Comtadin** and the **Musée Duplessis** are in the same building; the first concentrates on the customs and history of the region, while the Duplessis floor is dedicated to local primitive painting. More charming is the **Musée Sobirats**, a well-preserved pre-Revolutionary nobleman's house in a typical 18th-century street, evocatively furnished.

The **Cathédrale St-Siffrein** (pl St-Siffrein, open 8.30am-noon, 2-6pm daily) is an extraordinary mish-mash of styles and epochs, ranging from 15th-century Provençal Gothic to an early 20th-century bell-tower. The 15th-century door on the south side is known as the Porte des Juifs. When Philippe le Bel expelled the Jews from France, many of them fled to the papal-controlled Comtat Venaissin, only to be blackmailed or bullied into a Catholic baptism. The chained Jews passed through this door on their way to conversion. Note the carved rats gnawing on a globe above the door; explanations are as numerous as they are unconvincing. The cathedral's interior is rather gloomy but the Treasury (admission €0.30) is worth a look for its wonderful 14th-century wooden statues, and an important relic, the St-Mors, made from two nails taken from the cross. This symbol appears in the crest of the town from the 13th century onwards.

Just behind the cathedral is an unobtrusive Roman triumphal arch. It lacks the grandeur and state of preservation of its big brother in Orange, but features some good carving, notably the chained prisoners on the east side. Next door, the 17th-century **Palais de Justice** has frescoes from the 17th and 18th centuries (the tourist office can arrange a visit). This is the spiritual hub of the old town and it is here,

Cathédrale St-Siffrein's **Porte des Juifs**.

on a specially erected outdoor scaffold, that the intermittently interesting arts festival takes place in the second fortnight of July. From here one can explore the smart shops of the **Passage Boyer**, the result of a mid-18th-century job creation scheme and based on the Parisian covered passages.

Opposite the Hôtel de Ville is France's oldest **Synagogue**, dating from the 14th century, though largely rebuilt in the 18th. The lower floor, where there are ovens for baking unleavened bread and a piscina for women's purification rites, is currently closed for restoration but you can visit the sanctuary (men must wear a copal). Today, the Jewish community numbers just 122, but the culture remains strong. The Jewish cemetery just outside town was desecrated some years ago, an event which gained widespread national attention, although the true identity of the perpetrators is still uncertain.

South of the centre, the **Hôtel Dieu** is a splendid 18th-century hospital (visits through tourist office), with a rich collection of earthenware pharmacy jars, exemplifying the French dedication to all things medical, and a Baroque chapel containing the tomb of Bishop d'Inguimbert, the hospital's founder.

The lively Friday market held on the town's spacious tree-lined avenues is a great place to stock up on olive oil and tresses of garlic. For huntin', shootin' and fishin' types, the town is also famous for its decoys. If you're visiting between December and February, look out for black truffles, while the sticky, brightly coloured, locally made humbugs, *berlingots*, are available all year. Marquis de Sade devotees will be disappointed – or amused – to know that his château in the nearby village of Mazan is now an old people's home.

Musées Comtadin & Duplessis

234 bd Albin Durand (04.90.63.04.92). **Open** *Apr-Oct* 10am-noon, 2-6pm Mon, Wed-Sun; *Nov-Mar* 10am-noon, 2-4pm Mon, Wed-Sun. **Admission** €0.30, free under-12s.

Musée Sobirats

rue du Collège (04.60.63.04.92). **Open** *Apr-Oct* 10am-noon, 2-6pm Mon, Wed-Sun; *Nov-Mar* 10am-noon, 2-4pm Mon, Wed-Sun. **Admission** €0.30, free under-12s.

Synagogue

pl de l'Hôtel de Ville (04.90.63.39.97). **Open** 10am-6pm Mon-Fri. Closed Jewish holidays. **Admission** free but small donation welcome.

Where to stay & eat

L'Atelier de Pierre (30 pl de l'Horloge, 04.90.60.75.00, closed Sun & Mon and 2-17 Jan;

menus €21.34-€57.93), set in a delightful courtyard in the shadow of an ancient belfry, is the only upmarket gastronomic choice in Carpentras. The food is inventive and sophisticated. The centrally located **Le Vert Galant** (12 rue de Clapiès, 04.90.67.15.50, closed lunch Mon, dinner Sun Oct-Mar and all Sun Apr-Sept, menus €24.60-€41) offers a special truffle option (€70) in season, but service can be stretched. Tucked behind the tourist office, the **La Garrigue** pizzeria (90 rue Cottier, 04.90.63.21.24, closed Sun, menus €12.20-€21.34) offers good value for money and a few regional dishes alongside pizza. Be aware that Carpentras tends to shut down early and eating after 8.30pm condemns you to late-night pizzerias.

For a real gastronomic treat head off on the D942 towards Avignon and you will come to **Le Saule Pleureur** (145 chemin de Beauregard, Monteux, 04.90.62.01.35, closed all Mon, lunch Sat, dinner Sun and 1-15 Nov & three weeks in Mar, menus €30-€44), where classical French cuisine is prepared to the highest standard by Michel Philibert. There's a winter truffle menu (€114) and in February he and his wife run a series of truffle 'galas'.

Le Fiacre (153 rue Vigne, 04.90.63.03.15, double €46-€107), set in a characterful old townhouse, is the best hotel in the centre. **La Bastide Ste-Agnès** (1043 chemin de la Fourtrousse, 04.90.60.03.01, closed mid-Nov to mid-Mar, double €70-€81) is a luxurious *chambres d'hôtes* with pool. Between Pernes and Carpentras, **L'Hermitage** (04.90.66.51.41/ www.ifrance.com/lhermitage, closed Nov-Mar, double €61-€75) is an unpretentious country-house hotel with garden and pool.

Tourist information

Carpentras Office de Tourisme

170 av Jean Jaurès, 84200 Carpentras (04.90.63.00.78/www.tourisme.fr/carpentras). **Open** *June-Sept* 9am-7pm Mon-Sat; 9.30am-1pm Sun; *Oct-May* 9am-12.30pm, 2-6.30pm Mon-Sat.

Pernes-les-Fontaines

The 37 fountains that give Pernes its name and fame date from the mid-18th century. Pernes is a good place to while away an afternoon, with its fine old houses, chapels and towers. The 16th-century **Porte Notre-Dame** town gate – a remnant of the city walls – incorporates the chapel of **Notre-Dame-des-Grâces**. Nearby is the most striking of Pernes' fountains, the **fontaine du Cormoran**, crowned by an open-winged cormorant and featuring the town's emblem of a pearl and the sun.
The **Eglise Notre-Dame-de-Nazareth**

Blue highways

Lavender – described by Giono as 'the soul of Haute Provence' – has coloured the high plains and brought prosperity, strife and strong smells to village life since the wild *baïassières* plantations of the Middle Ages.

The lavender route forms a thick blue band connecting 2,000 producers across the Drôme, the plateau du Vaucluse and Alpes-de-Haute-Provence. Two variants of the *lavandula* genus grow naturally in the dry, limestone soils: high up, the AOC *lavande vraie* or *fine*, whose subtle essential oil is found in perfumes by Dior, Gaultier and Annick Goutal and, lower down, the *lavande aspic*. *Lavandin* is the less-refined hybrid, mass-produced since the 1920s and accounting for 90 per cent of the world lavender market; this is the stuff that finds its way into washing powders and household products.

Today, this tiny flower powers a substantial tourist machine. **L'Association des Routes de la Lavande**, (04.75.26.65.91/ www.routes-lavande.com) publishes a brochure with themed itineraries. In June 2001, place des Vosges in Paris was transformed into a lavender field of 6,000 pert blue shrubs to tempt noses and eyes down south to the real thing.

The trend for natural remedies has given lavender a make-over, helped by the stylish Provençal bodycare branding of L'Occitane (*see p118*). Its disinfectant qualities (the Latin root *lavanda* means 'that which washes') are now widely recognised alongside its healing properties. It acts as a calmative against stress, migraines and sunburn, and is used to treat rheumatism and vertigo.

The lavender season lasts from spring to autumn, with the harvest from July to mid-August. Arranged in long nodding rows, the plants stripe the landscape in a haze of bees, their colour maturing from baby blue to deep mauve before being shaved down to their silver stalks. The smell is overwhelming. The harvest cuts open the flowers' scent, and the distilleries suck out the unmistakable, throat-catching odour of the essential oil.

The most generous patches are found around the plateau d'Albion and Sault on the edge of Mont Ventoux, the pays de Buëch, Digne-les-Bains and the plateau de Valensole. A walk or bicycle ride here in summer is just as glorious as the postcards make out.

The **Musée de la Lavande** (rte de Gordes, Coustellet, 04.90.76.91.23/ www.museedelalavande.com), in the Luberon, provides a bilingual film on the history of lavender production, a gleaming collection of 16th-century copper stills and a smelling machine demonstrating the difference between *lavande vraie* and *lavandin*.

Françoise Richez, of the **Moulin de Savoirs** (04.75.28.15.94) is one of many *guides de pays*, full of natural and historic local knowledge. She organises themed walks through the lavender fields of Ferrassières

and Mévouillon in the Drôme Provençale and runs workshops to make essential oils and vinegars from 'grandmother's recipes'. **Château de la Gabelle** in Ferrassières (04.75.28.80.54), a *chambres d'hôtes* on a lavender farm, and the **Jardin des Lavandes** in Sault (04.90.64.14.97), also offer floral and perfume workshops. Fans of the honeybee can learn about lavender pollination on an 'entomology outing' with guide Evelyne Antoine at **St-Michel-l'Observatoire** (04.92.76.68.40). The giant lavender vats are open for visits, generally free, in most villages; **Distillerie Bleu Provence** in Nyons (04.75.26.10.42) and the **Distillerie des Agnels** in Apt (04.90.74.22.72) give tours year round. If you want to sleep in lavender, **La Forge Ste-Marie** (04.75.28.42.77) in reomote Eygalayes is one of many themed resting places. The guest house has a 'lavender relaxation room' offering spa, jacuzzi, massage and sauna.

At lavender fêtes – at Ferrasières and Valensole in early July, Digne-les-Bains and Valréas on the first weekend in August, and Sault and Esparron-de-Verdon on 15 August – you can indulge in beauty pageants, scythe tournaments, majorettes' competitions and helicopter rides over the landscape till you are blue in the face.

nearby has sections dating from the 11th century. Pernes' artistic jewels are the 13th-century frescoes that decorate the upper floors of the **Tour Ferrande** (contact the tourist office to arrange a visit), which depict lively Biblical stories and scenes from the life of Charles of Anjou. The tower overlooks the **fontaine Guillaumin** or *du gigot*, so called because of its resemblance to a leg of lamb.

The town's other tower, the **Tour de l'Horloge** (rue du Donjon, open 9am-7pm in summer, 9am-5pm in winter), is all that remains of the château of the counts of Toulouse, who ruled over Pernes from 1125 to 1320, when it was the capital of the Comtat Venaissin.

Locals will tell you that if you drink the water from the **fontaine de la Lune** at the base of the 14th-century Porte St-Gilles, you'll go quite mad. Should the water have no effect, celebrate with pastries from the excellent *boulangerie* in place Aristide Briand.

Where to stay & eat

The **Au Fil du Temps** (73 pl Louis Giraud, 04.90.66.48.61, closed Tue & Wed, menus €16-€45) is presided over by young chef Frédéric Robert, offering affordable market-fresh dishes and delicious desserts. Nearby Le Beaucet, which holds an annual pilgrimage in honour of the patron saint of Provençal farmers, St Gentius, is also home to one of the best restaurants in the region, the **Auberge du Beaucet** (04.90.66.10.82, closed Mon & Sun and all Dec & Jan, menu €29), which offers local wines and cuisine, goat's cheeses all produced in the village and a spectacular country view.

Tourist information

Market day in Pernes-les-Fontaines is Saturday.

Pernes Office de Tourisme

pl Gabriel Moutte, 84210 Pernes-les-Fontaines (04.90.61.31.04). **Open** *mid-June to mid-Sept* 9am-noon, 2.30-7.30pm Mon-Sat; 10am-noon Sun; *mid-Sept to mid-June* 9am-noon, 2-5pm Mon-Sat.

Mont Ventoux

When the Italian poet Petrarch reached the summit of Mont Ventoux in 1336, he 'remained immobile, stupefied by the strange lightness of the air and the immensity of the spectacle'. He has been credited with inventing the sport of mountain climbing – it had never occurred to anybody before to do such a thing just for the hell of it. Nowadays, the summit is easily reached by a hairpin, graffiti-daubed road built in the 1930s, though in summer crowds of cyclists make the job as difficult as possible for themselves by panting up to the Air Force radar station and television masts which scar the otherwise bare summit. In 1994 UNESCO designated Mont Ventoux a biosphere reserve.

The mass of the mountain dominates the entire Rhône Valley. As you climb, the vegetation changes noticeably, as does the

Pernes-les-Fontaines is full of stately stone and fine old chapels and towers.

temperature. Winds can howl across Mont Ventoux ('windy mountain') at up to 250km per hour. At 1,909m, the barren summit is snow-capped in winter and often shrouded in mist in summer. On a clear day the view is spectacular.

The main D974 summit route forks off from the Vaison-Carpentras road at **Malaucène**. Just beyond Malaucène the **source du Groseau** spring may have been venerated by ancient Celtic inhabitants; the Romans certainly thought highly of it, channelling its waters down to quench thirst in Vaison (*see p110*). The unusual octagonal chapel of **Notre-Dame-de-Groseau** was part of an 11th-century monastery, all other traces of which have disappeared. Just below the summit is the small ski resort of **Mont Serein**, a riot of shell suits and four-wheel-drives in winter.

An alternative approach to the summit is to take the quieter and prettier D19, which runs past the remains of a 17th-century aqueduct to the **Belvedere du Paty** above **Crillon-le-Brave**, with fine views towards Carpentras. To the east, **Bédoin** with its fine church is the last village of any size before the long haul to the top. It's also the starting point for a direct four-hour hike to the summit; information and maps can be picked up at the tourist office.

Mont Ventoux is famous for *épeautre*, or wild barley. Previously known as the poor man's wheat, it has been revived as a local gastronomic treat, to be washed down with the local red wine, Côtes du Ventoux.

Where to stay & eat

The centuries-old buildings of the **Hostellerie de Crillon-le-Brave** (pl de l'Eglise, 04.90.65.61.61/www.crillonlebrave.com, closed Jan to mid-Mar, double €150-€400, menus €24-€70) in the southern lee of Ventoux have been tastefully restored using natural fabrics and tiles. The atmosphere is welcoming and the cooking is sophisticated with a Provençal twist.

East of Bédoin is **Le Mas des Vignes** (04.90.65.63.91; closed Mon, lunch Tue, lunch July & Aug, and mid-Oct to mid-Mar, menus €28-€40) with fine food and spectacular views over the Dentelles de Montmirail. The **Hôtel Pins** (1km out of Bédoin on chemin des Crans, 04.90.65.92.92, closed Nov-Mar, double €51-€58) in a beautiful position and with the bonus of a pool, is a good place to rest up.

Tourist information

Market day in Bédoin is Monday. For skiing information contact either the *mairie* in Beaumont-du-Ventoux (04.90.65.21.13) or the *chalet d'accueil* at Mont Serein (04.90.63.42.02).

Bédoin Office de Tourisme

Espace Marie-Louis-Gravier, pl du Marché, 84410 Bédoin (04.90.65.63.95). **Open** *June-Aug* 9am-12.30pm, 2-6pm Mon-Fri; 9am-noon, 2-6pm Sat; 9am-noon Sun; *Sept-May* 9am-12.30pm, 2-6pm Mon-Fri; 9am-noon Sat.

Les Dentelles de Montmirail

Dentelle is lace, and the curious limestone formations of these peaks certainly present an intricate and arresting pattern on the skyline. Jurassic limestone strata pushed upwards then eroded by the elements, the Dentelles draw walkers, rock-climbers and landscape artists and are surrounded by some pretty villages which turn out eminently quaffable wines.

Circling the Dentelles from the market-garden flatlands below, the skyscape is in constant flux. **Malaucène**, on the road separating the Dentelles from Mont Ventoux, is the jumping-off point for both. The village perches on a hill and is dominated by the 14th-century fortified church of **St-Michel-et-Pierre**. At **Le Barroux**, south of here, are the ruins of a 12th-century castle (04.90.62.35.21; ring for opening times), worth a visit for the views over the Dentelles.

On the road to **Beaumes-de-Venise** is the pretty Romanesque chapel of **Notre-Dame-d'Aubune**. Terraced Beaumes-de-Venise is famous for its sweet dessert wine, made from the muscat grape, which was a marketing phenomenon in Britain in the 1980s. You can see Beaumes' olive oil pressed in the *moulin à huile* at **La Balméenne**.

On the western flank of the Dentelles, the tiny village of **Gigondas** gives its name to the famous grenache-based red wine. Above Gigondas is the **Col du Cayronis** pass, a challenge for rock-climbers. A little to the north, an excellent Côtes du Rhône Villages wine is produced around the hill village of **Séguret**. Car-free and oozing charm, Séguret gets more tourist attention than is good for it, with its 12th-century church, old houses and great views. Above Séguret is **Le Crestet** with a pretty arcaded square and 14th-century church. Climb up to the 12th-century castle and enjoy the view. Outside the village, the **Crestet Centre d'Art** is a stunning Modernist artists' studio. Its exhibitions follow the worthy French contemporary tradition, but the centre's mission is to increase appreciation of all branches of modern art, including dance, music and cinema.

Moulin à huile La Balméenne

bd Jules Ferry (04.90.62.94.15), Beaumes-de-Venise. **Open** *Sept-Nov, Jan-Apr* 8am-noon, 2-6.30pm Mon-Sat; *May-Aug, Dec* 8am-noon, 2-6.30pm Mon-Sat; 2.30-6.30pm Sun. **Admission** free.

Avignon & the Vaucluse

Crestet Centre d'Art
chemin de la Verrière, between Vaison-la-Romaine and Malaucène (04.90.36.35.00). **Open** 11am-6pm daily (during exhibitions). Closed mid-Dec to Mar. **Admission** free; €3 July, Aug.

Where to stay & eat

The restaurant-hotel **Les Florets** (04.90.65.85.01, closed Jan to mid-Mar, double €80-€85, menus €22-€32) is in a vineyard 2km outside Gigondas; outstanding local dishes are served and if you liked the wine you drank with your meal you can load up at the family's own *cave,* **Domaine la Garrigue,** A Bernard et fils (Vacqueyras, 04.90.65.84.60). In Montmirail, the **Montmirail Hôtel** (6km south by D7 and D8, 04.90.65.84.01/www.hotelmontmirail.com, closed mid-Oct to mid-Mar; double €60-€84) has a pool and garden. A sporty alternative is the basic **Gîte d'Etape des Dentelles** in Gigondas (04.90.65.80.85, closed mid-Dec to Mar, dormitory €14), which provides courses and expert information on climbing holidays, mountain biking and walking in the mountains.

At Le Crestet, **Le Mas de Magali** (quartier Chante Coucou, 04.90.36.39.91, closed mid-Oct to Apr, double €57-€72 including dinner) is a luxuriously converted farm with swimming pool. For elegant living among the vines try the **Domaine de Cabasse** (between Séguret and Sablet, 04.90.46.91.12/www.domaine-de-cabasse.fr, closed Nov-Apr, double €82-€120), which provides cosseting, a good-sized swimming pool and its own wine.

Tourist information

Market day in Malaucène is Wednesday. The Club Alpin Français de Provence in Marseille (04.91.54.36.94) organises accompanied climbing trips.

Gigondas Office de Tourisme
pl du Portail, 84190 Gigondas (04.90.65.85.46/ www.beyond.fr/villages/gigondas.html). **Open** *Apr-Nov* 10am-noon, 2-6pm daily; *Dec-Mar* 10am-noon, 2-5pm Mon-Sat.

Malaucène Office de Tourisme
Syndicat d'Initiative, pl de la Mairie, 88340 Malaucène (04.90.65.22.59). **Open** *Apr* 10am-noon, 3-5pm Mon-Sat; *July-Aug* 9am-12.30pm, 3-6pm Mon-Sat; *Oct-Mar* 10am-noon Mon-Sat.

Vaison-la-Romaine

A proudly independent, prosperous town since Roman times, when it was federated to the empire rather than colonised, Vaison-la-Romaine's pale, red-roofed houses sprawl over both banks of the Ouvèze river. On 22 September

Vaison's **Hostellerie le Beffroi**. *See p111.*

1992, swollen by heavy rains, the Ouvèze turned into a raging torrent, sweeping away houses and an entire industrial estate, and killing 37 people. Incredibly, of the town's two bridges, it was the modern road bridge that was destroyed; the 2,000-year-old **Pont Romain** lost its parapet – since rebuilt – but otherwise held up.

Vaison has picked itself up and gone back to being a neat and discreet small town, qualities appreciated by the Parisians who converge here in summer. The old town, perched on a cliff and dominated by the 12th-century château of the Contes de Toulouse, is a web of twisting medieval streets. It is some distance from the modern town, north of the river across the Pont Romain, built up from the 18th century on, when the old town was virtually abandoned. But it is this modern town which covers the original Roman nucleus of Vaison. Beneath the houses, banks and cafés are the forum and associated temples. By the time excavations began in earnest in 1907, only the suburbs of the Roman town were left to explore. Two slices of ancient life were exposed – the Quartier de Puymin and the Quartier de la Villasse. The ticket to the site gives admission to both *quartiers,* the museum and the cloisters of the cathedral, Notre-Dame-de-Nazareth.

Start at the museum in the **Quartier de**

Puymin. Admirably organised, the collection features statues, mosaics and domestic objects found in and around Vaison. Especially striking is a marble family group, dating from AD121, showing a stark-naked Emperor Hadrian standing proudly next to his elaborately dressed wife Sabina, who is clearly trying to humour her husband. Pride of place, though, goes to a third-century AD silver bust, and charming floor mosaics from the Peacock villa. Behind the museum is the Roman amphitheatre, which hosts a music and theatre festival, L'Eté de Vaison, from mid-July to mid-August.

Head out and past the tourist office to the **Quartier de la Villasse**. The colonnaded main street, with its huge paving stones and monumental scale, evokes the prosperity of Roman Vaison better than any other single sight. On either side of this street are the remains of shops, baths and villas, including the one where the silver bust in the museum was found. Whoever owned this property was in the money; the 5,000m² *domus* had its own private baths and an extensive hanging garden.

The **cathedral** is a ten-minute walk away on avenue Jules Ferry. It is an unusual example of Provençal Romanesque architecture, with fine carving and pure lines. Recent excavations have revealed that the cathedral proper was built on the ruins of an important Roman building. Inside, the most notable feature is the 11th-century high altar on four delicate marble columns.

Up the hill north of the cathedral is the curious **Chapelle de St-Quenin**, a Romanesque building with a unique triangular apse, based on an earlier Roman temple – for centuries the good citizens of Vaison thought it *was* Roman. Check for opening times at the tourist office as it is now closed for restoration.

Quartiers de Puymin & de la Villasse

Open *Feb, Oct* 10am-12.30pm, 2-5.30pm daily; *Mar-May* 10am-12.30pm, 2-6pm daily; *June-Sept* 9.30am-12.30pm, 2.30-6.15pm; *July-Aug* 9.30am-12.30pm, 2-6.45pm. **Admission** €6, €3 12-18s from tourist office (incl entry to cathedral cloisters).

Where to stay & eat

The **Hostellerie le Beffroi** (rue de l'Evêché, 04.90.36.04.71/www.le-beffroi.com, closed Feb-Mar, double €80-€110) has fine views from its charming 16th-century building; the restaurant (closed all Tue, lunch Mon-Fri and dinner Sat & Sun, menus €25.50-€41) offers good value for high-class fare. The **Vieux Vaison** (8 pl du Poids, 04.90.36.19.45, closed Wed and Jan, average €15) is simpler, with a pleasant terrace. The **Logis du Château** (Les Hauts de Vaison, 04.90.36.09.98, closed Oct-Mar, double €46-€76,

restaurant closed lunch Mon-Fri, menus €17.50-€30.80) offers simple modern rooms and a traditional restaurant, plus pool and tennis court.

Near the Roman ruins the **Brin d'Olivier** (4 rue du Ventoux, 04.90.28.74.79, closed two weeks in Mar, June & Oct, double €61-€68, restaurant closed all Wed, lunch Sat & Thur, menus €23-€32) is an attractive small hotel with interesting Provençal food. The **Hôtel Burrhus** (1 pl de Montfort, 04.90.36.00.11, closed Dec-Jan, double €44-€58) is on the liveliest square in town and has some original art in the public rooms and bedrooms, while **Le Bateleur** (1 pl Théodore Aubanel, 04.90.36.28.04, closed all Mon & dinner Sun, menus €15-€28) is a serious family restaurant. The place for a treat, though, is **Le Moulin à Huile** (quai Maréchal Foch, 04.90.36.20.67, closed all Mon, dinner Sun, menus €38-€68). Robert Bardot is a true master chef and his magical menu served in a garden just by the Pont Romain is a heavenly feast.

Tourist information

Market day in Vaison-la-Romaine is Tuesday, plus Thursday and Saturday June to September.

Vaison Office de Tourisme

pl Chanoine Sautel, 84110 Vaison-la-Romaine (04.90.36.02.11/www.vaison-la-romaine.com). **Open** *July-Aug* 9am-noon, 2-7pm daily; *Sept-June* 9am-noon, 2-6pm Mon-Sat.

▶ Getting There & Around

▶ By car

Take autoroute A7 (exit 21) and then the D950 to Carpentras. The D938 goes south to Pernes and north to the Mont Ventoux area and Vaison-la-Romaine. The D7 goes to Beaumes-de-Venise and Gigondas.

▶ By train

The TGV runs to Avignon, with some services stopping at Orange.

▶ By bus

Cars Arnaud (04.90.63.01.82) runs two buses a day from Marseille to Carpentras, via Pernes-les-Fontaines, four buses a day from Orange to Carpentras and four a day from Avignon to Carpentras. **Cars Comtadins** (04.90.67.20.25) operates services between Carpentras and Vaison-la-Romaine (also serving Malaucène) and Bédoin. Orange to Vaison via Sablet, north of Gigondas, is served by **Cars Lieutaud** (04.90.36.05.22).

The Drôme Provençale

The Drôme Provençale gives the south of France a grand entrance: vivid green terrain, olives, herbs and sculpted peaks.

Punned as being 'Midi moins le quart', with a varied Mediterranean landscape of mountain pastures, hills and plains, the Drôme Provençale still feels like a great discovery. The land teems with natural produce: Côtes du Rhône bordering the west, gnarled black truffles (known locally as *rabasses*) embedded in the **Tricastin** plain, the black *tanche* olive around **Nyons** and apricots in the **Baronnies** mountains. France's leading aromatic and medicinal herb garden, it cultivates vast swathes of lavender and lime-blossom. History left a trail of Roman bridges, Romanesque churches, and medieval to Renaissance châteaux. A more recent and alarming eyesore is the nuclear power plant at **Pierrelatte**, which has nonetheless helped buttress the local economy.

The Tricastin & Grignan

The Gaul tribe of the Tricastanii baptised this Rhône-side plain of vineyards, lavender and cyprus trees. **St-Paul-Les-Trois-Châteaux** remains its ancient capital, boasting a grand total of zero châteaux. More worth a visit are the *villages perchés* – medieval hilltop villages – that pepper the area, notably **Grignan** and **Suze-la-Rousse**. Tiny **Richerenches** comes into its own in winter when truffles are sold out of car boots at the Saturday truffle market.

The **Château de Grignan** poses amid rose gardens on a hillock, above a train of winding medieval streets. Facing south, its view scans the Baronnies, Les Dentelles de Montmirail, and the bald head of Mont Ventoux – inspiration to local French writer Philippe Jaccottet.

The 12th-century feudal fort built by the Adhémar de Monteil dynasty was retouched from the 15th to 17th centuries into one of the finest examples of Renaissance architecture in south-east France, with Aubusson tapestries hanging in well-preserved furnished apartments, today providing an elegant venue for exhibitions and jazz and classical concerts. Madame (or Marquise) de Sévigné immortalised the château through her gushy letters from the court of Versailles to her daughter, Comtesse de Grignan, wife of the legendarily unattractive François de Grignan. Buried in front of the 16th-century **Collégiale St-Sauveur** in 1696, the Marquise is lauded as one of France's

wittiest and most insightful letter-writers and the village is now exhaustingly themed in her name – her statue stands quill-poised in front of the town hall, the Festival de la Correspondence is a celebration of letter writing in July, and the **Musée de Typographie** houses old printing presses. Visit the 19th-century columned *lavoir* in place du Mail – the Tuesday marketplace – ignoring the empty beer bottles inside.

10km south of Grignan on the west bank of the river Lez, the village of **Suze-la-Rousse** is named after the Celt 'uz', meaning high place and, allegedly, the auburn mane of one of the ladies of **Château de Suze** – Marguerite de Baux. An architectural hybrid, the fortified château began as a 12th-century hunting lodge for the Princes of Orange (who ruled the Tricastin in the Middle Ages), before being grafted with an Italianate *cour d'honneur*. Pillaged during the Revolution, it now displays wine gadgets and dubious art exhibitions and houses the **Université du Vin**. A world first when created in 1978, this bastion of higher education and research has its own vineyard, with 70 different European grape varieties. The **Caves Coopératives** (04.75.04.80.04) is a good filling station for Coteaux de Tricastin.

St-Restitut and **Le Garde-Adhémar** are picturesque hilltop stop-offs, each containing fine examples of Romanesque architecture.

The Drôme: still waiting to be discovered.

Château de Grignan

Grignan (04.75.46.51.56). **Open** *July-Aug* 9.30-
11.30am, 2-6pm daily; *Sept-June* 9.30-11.30am,
2-5.30pm daily (closed Tue Nov-Mar). **Admission**
guided visits €5; €3 11-18s; *free under-10s; gardens*
€1.50; free under-10s.

Château de Suze-la-Rousse

Suze-la-Rousse (04.75.04.81.44). **Open** *July-Aug*
9.30-11.30am, 2-6pm daily; *Sept-June* 9.30-11.30am,
2-5.30pm daily (closed Tue Nov-Mar). **Admission**
€3; €2 11-18s; €1 under-10s.

Musée de la Typographie

Maison du Bailli, Grignan (04.75.46.57.16). **Open**
June-Sept 10am-7pm daily; *Oct-May* 10am-12.30pm,
2-6pm Tue-Sun. **Admission** €2.30; €1.30 8-16s; free
under-8s.

Université du Vin

*Suze-la-Rousse (04.75.97.21.30./www.universite-du-
vin.com).* **Open** *Sept-July* 9am-noon, 2-6pm Mon-Fri.

Where to stay & eat

In Grignan, **Café de Sévigné** (pl Sévigné,
04.75.46.51.82) in front of the town hall is good
for a scenic beer. **Le Clair de la Plume** (pl du
Mail, 04.75.91.81.30, closed Feb, double €85-
€150) has elegant guest rooms and an English
tea room in its trellised garden. A few doors up,
at recently opened **Le Poème** (montée du
Tricot, 04.75.91.10.90, closed lunch Mon, all Tue
and Feb, menu €25), Hervé Dondane prepares
smart dishes, such as scallops with truffle
butter. Monique at **L'Eau à la Bouche** (rue
St-Louis, 04.75.46.57.37, closed Mon & Tue in
winter, and Jan & Oct, average €15.50) serves
homely *plats* in a dining room crammed with
flowers and cat memorabilia. 18th-century
L'Autre Maison (rue du Grand Faubourg,
04.75.46.58.65/www.lautremaison.com, closed
Nov-mid Dec & Jan, Feb, double €54-€77) is a
modern-rustic guesthouse, with homemade jam
for breakfast. 3 km west towards Valaurie, **La
Maison du Moulin** (quartier petit Cordy,
04.75.46.56.94/www.maisondumoulin.com,
closed Feb, double €75-€120), an old water
mill, has a pool, library and rooms faithfully
decorated in glossy magazine style. At the foot
of Château de Grignan, roses adorn the gardens
and curtains of the 19th-century **Manoir de la
Roserie** (rte de Valreas, 04.75.46.58.15/
www.chateauhotels.com/roserie, closed beg Jan-
mid Feb & beg Dec, double €141-€297, menus
€30.49-€54.12). Despite a pool, tennis court and
impeccable lawns, its luxuriance just misses
good taste, but chef Régis Douysset is a rising
star. In humble contrast, **Hôtel Sévigné** (28 pl
Castellane, 04.75.46.50.97, double €38.11-
€53.40) has reassuring 70s carpeted walls.
Campsite **Les Truffières** (lieu-dit-Nachony,
04.75.46.93.62/www.lestruffieres.com, closed
Oct-Mar) has an outdoor swimming pool.

South of Suze-la-Rousse, the luxury option is
the **Château de Rochegude** (Rochegude,
04.75.97.21.10/www.chateauderochegude.com,
double €114-€335, restaurant closed Mon
dinner & Sun mid Nov-mid Mar, menus €38-
€99), which occupies a grandiose castle, dating
back to the 12th century. The atmosphere is
formal but welcoming, with a park, swimming
pool and tennis courts. Deer gambol in the
grounds, touchingly unaware of the propensity
of chef Thierry Frebout for a little venison. At
La Garde Adhémar, cosy, stone **Le Prédaïou**
(rue de la Fontaine, 04.75.04.40.08, closed dinner
Sept-June except Sat, menus €18-€25) offers a
contemporary take on regional cuisine.

Avignon & the Vaucluse

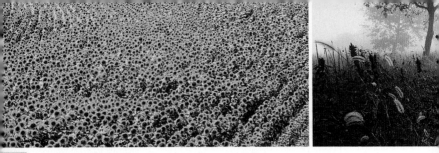

Sun-packed meadows in France's leading herb garden.

Tourist Information

Market day in Grignan is Tuesday, Suze-la-Rousse is on Friday.

Grignan Office de Tourisme

Grande Rue, 26230 Grignan (04.75.46.56.75/ www.guideweb.com/grignan). **Open** *Apr-Sept* 10am-12.30pm, 2-7pm daily; *Sept-Mar* 10am-noon, 2-6pm Mon-Sat.

Suze-la-Rousse Office de Tourisme

av des Côtes-du-Rhône, 26790 Suze-la-Rousse (tel/fax 04.75.04.81.41). **Open** 3-6pm Mon, 9am-noon, 2.30-6pm Tue-Fri, 9am-noon Sat.

Nyons

Dubbed Petite Nice, Nyons crouches from the mistral in a microclimate at the opening of the Eygues valley. With its own regenerative wind, the *pontias*, perennial sun and a halo of olive groves, Giono called it 'paradise on earth'. The retired seem to agree. Claiming to be France's olive capital (celebrated in Les Olivades in July and Alcicoque in February), Nyons is the most northerly olive growing area in Europe, and its emblematic black *tanche* – giving a mild, fruity oil – was the first variety in France to be awarded an *appellation d'origine controlée*. **L'Institut du Monde de l'Olivier** (04.75.26.90.90) promotes the olive's comeback through lectures and exhibitions. The family-run **Les Vieux Moulins** on the banks of the Eygues, and the **Musée de l'Olivier** give interesting olive-pressing history tours. Olive-related products and local wines are available all year at the **Moulin Autrand-Dozol** and the **Coopérative du Nyonsais**. **La Scourtinerie** is the last artisanal workshop in France to make natural fibre, olive pressing mats, now sold as doormats. The medieval town is built on a hill, providing a labyrinth of historic walks. Visit the place des Arcades, the vaulted rue des Grands Forts, the remains of the feudal château and the 13th-century **Tour Randonné**. Once a prison and now a chapel, its wedding-cake neo-Gothic crest dominates the town. The 'Roman' donkey bridge, an elegant single arch actually built in the 13th and 14th

centuries, is enveloped in summer by the scent of lavender distilling downstream at the **Distillerie Bleu Provence**.

Coopérative du Nyonsais

pl Olivier de Serres (04.75.26.12.12/www.coop-du-nyonsais.fr). **Open** *Apr-Oct* 8.45am-12.30pm, 2-7pm Mon-Sat, 10am-12.30pm, 2.30-6pm Sun; *Nov-Mar* 8.45am-12.15pm, 2-6.30pm Mon-Sat, 10am-12.30pm, 2.30-6pm Sun. **Admission** free.

Distillerie Bleu Provence

58 promenade de la Digue (04.75.26.10.42/ www.adelys.com/distilleriebleuprovence). **Open** 2.30-6.30pm Mon; 9.30am-12.30pm, 2.30-6.30pm Tue-Sun. **Admission** free.

Musée de l'Olivier

allée des Tilleuls (04.75.26.12.12/ www.guideweb.com/ musee/olivier). **Open** 10-11am, 2.30-6pm daily. **Admission** €1.83; €0.91 7-18s; free under-7s.

La Scourtinerie

36 rue de la Maladrerie (04.75.26.33.52). **Open** 9.30am-noon, 2.30-6.30pm Mon-Sat. **Admission** €1.52; free under-8s.

Les Vieux Moulins

4 promenade de la Digue (04.75.26.11.00). **Open** *July-Aug* 10am-noon, 2-6pm Mon-Sat, 10am-noon Sun; *Sept-June* 10am-noon, 2-6pm Tue-Sat. **Admission** €4; free under-12s.

Where to stay & eat

The restaurant bonanza includes **Resto des Arts** (13 rue des Déportés, 04.75.26.31.49, closed Tue & Wed and 24 Dec-10 Jan, menus €12.20-€22.87) dangling with local artwork. **Le Petit Caveau** (9 rue Victor Hugo, 04.75.26.20.21, closed Mon & dinner Sun, menus €26-€39) serves good local cuisine and wine – Mme Cormont trained at l'Université du Vin. **Hôtel au Petit Nice** (av Paul Laurens, 04.75.26.09.46, closed Nov & beg July, double €26-€81.20) is the cheap, central, retro option. **La Picholine** (promenade de la Perrière, 04.75.26.06.21, closed Mon, Tue & Feb) offers hillside views and a pool shaded by olive trees (€47.26-€59.46). **Une Autre Maison** (pl de la République, 04.75.26.43.09, closed first two weeks Nov, double €100-€140) is the

comfortable design choice, with Provençal touches, walled garden, pool and lithe guests mooching around in hotel dressing-gowns.

Tourist information

Market day is Thursday, plus Sunday from June-September. Mountain bikes can be hired from **VTT Loisirs** (31 hameau des Tuilieres (04.75.26.27.98/www.vttloisirsnyons.fr.fm).

Nyons Office de Tourisme

pl de la Libération, 26110 Nyons (04.75.26.10.35/ www.nyonstourisme.com). **Open** *July, Aug* 9am-12.30pm, 2.30-7pm Mon-Sat, 10am-1pm Sun; *Sept-June* 9am-12pm, 2.30-5.45pm Mon-Sat.

Buis-les-Baronnies

The Baronnies mountains swell southeast from Nyons: precipitous limestone peaks coated with vineyards, pines and apricot orchards, interrupted only by medieval villages and grey-blue hills, popular for rock-climbing and riding.

Buis-les-Baronnies was the medieval capital of the Barons de Mévouillon and a Catholic stronghold, sheltered beside the river Ouvèze under the Rocher St-Julien. Decorated by the Renaissance facade of the Ursuline convent chapel, its calm is interrupted only by the constant thud of *pétanque* under the plane trees. Since the 19th century, Buis has produced almost all of France's world-class lime-blossom, harvested for Europe's largest *tilleul* fair in July. Aromatic and medicinal herbs are available at the Wednesday market in place des Arcades, or at herborist **Bernard Laget** (pl des Herbes, 04.75.28.12.01). The Institut des Plantes Aromatiques et Médicinales, due to open in spring 2002, will give the history of aromatic plants and visits to a herb garden.

For the best views, climb north to the Gorges Ubrieux, and descend towards St-Jalle, or follow the foot of Mont Ventoux east towards charming **Montbrun-les-Bains** village.

Where to stay & eat

The terrace of **La Fourchette** (pl des Arcades, 04.75.28.03.31, closed Mon, dinner Sun & all Nov, menus €19.80-€29) is good for classic fare while watching *grand-mères* nattering under the arches. **Hôtel les Arcades** (pl des Arcades, 04.75.28.11.31, double €38-€55) is homely and rambling with a garden, and gentle wake-up calls from the fountain in the square. **Bar des Passions** (allée des Platanes, 04.75.28.12.32, double €30.50) is a shrine to the Renault Alpine and Johnny Hallyday – owner Michel has his own Johnny museum; rooms are basic but welcoming. At Mérindol-les-Oliviers, **Auberge de la Gloriette** (04.75.28.71.08, closed Jan to mid-Feb, double €38.11-€53.36, menus €15-€21) is famous for *miche d'agneau* cooked in the adjacent bakery; rooms are pleasant.

Tourist information

Buis-les-Baronnies Office de Tourisme

pl des Quinconces, 26170 Buis-les-Baronnies (04.75.28.04.59/www.buislesbaronnies.com). **Open** *July-Aug* 9.15am-noon, 3-7pm Mon-Sat, 9.30-noon Sun; *Sept-June* 9.15am-noon, 2-5pm Mon-Sat, 9.30-noon Sun.

► Getting There & Around

► By car
Leave the A7 autoroute at exit 18 and take D541 for Grignan, or exit 19 and D994 for Suze-la-Rousse. Nyons is 20km from Grignan by D538 and D46.

► By bus/train
Nearest train stations are Avignon, Orange and Montélimar. **Cars Lieutaud** (04.90.36.05.22/www.cars-lieutaud.fr) runs one bus a day, Mon-Sat, between Nyons and Avignon and twice daily buses between Avignon and Buis-les-Baronnies via Vaison-la-Romaine. **Cars Dunevon** (04.75.28.41.54) runs three buses a day, Mon-Fri, between Nyons and Buis, fewer during school holidays. **Cars Teste** (04.75.00.27.90) runs three buses a day between Montélimar and Nyons via Grignan, plus buses between Grignan and Nyons via Valréas. **Autocars Petit Nice** (04.75.26.35.58) runs three buses a day, Mon-Sat, between Nyons and Vaison.

The Luberon

There's more to the Luberon than hill villages, vines and Renaissance châteaux; it also hides France's own Colorado.

The Luberon is classic inland Provence: perched hill villages, stone farmhouses, old fortresses and the Renaissance châteaux of a proudly unconventional land that was heavily embroiled in the 16th-century Wars of Religion. The area was declared a Parc Régional in 1977 and, despite the arrival of French caviar socialists and Brits eager to grab a slice of the lifestyle described by former ad man Peter Mayle in *A Year in Provence*, it remains – mostly – unspoiled. Incomers can be relied on to renovate village houses and decrepit *bastides*, and there is a limit on new construction; but some villagers fear that high property prices are pricing locals out. The Luberon remains a major producer of fruit and veg, from melons, apples and cherries to asparagus, while dedicated producers are working hard to keep alive olive oil and lavender production and to improve the quality of the regional wines (the Parc includes three *appellations contrôlées*: Côtes du Luberon, Côtes du Ventoux and Coteaux de Pierrevert.

At the heart of the Parc Régional is the rocky limestone massif of the Montagne du Luberon, cut in two by the Aiguebrun valley. This divides what is known as the Petit Luberon to the west, and the Grand Luberon, rising to the 1,125m Mourre Nègre, to the east. Luxuriant with oak, pines, vines and fruit trees, the Luberon remains pleasantly green even in high summer and offers plenty of opportunities for walking, riding and cycling. Footpaths include the *grandes randonnées* GR6, 9, 92 and 97.

'Le Luberon en vélo' is a 100km bike route chosen for the beauty its of sites (including Oppède-le-Vieux and Lacoste) and running partially along disused railway tracks; arrows with a pin man on a bike are in green and white in the direction Cavaillon-Apt-Forcalquier and green and orange in the opposite direction. In 2002, a new southern route completes the loop.

North Luberon: from Taillades to Saignon

Once important for stone quarrying, the rugged northern flank of the Montagne du Luberon is punctuated by a string of picturesque perched hill villages. At the western edge of the ridge, **Taillades** is the village that best recalls the

history of stone quarrying. Houses seem to sit on blocks of cut rock and the remains of two châteaux – one fortified, one Renaissance – face each other across a ravine. A path climbs to a chapel perched over one former quarry, now an outdoor theatre that provides one of the most atmospheric venues during the Avignon Festival.

In a grandiose setting, **Oppède-le-Vieux** perfectly symbolises the rebirth of the Luberon. The old village was abandoned during the 19th century and gradually fell into ruin until resettled since the 1960s by artists, potters and writers; it still remains romantically overgrown. At the top are the recently restored Romanesque **Collégiale Notre Dame d'Alidon**, which has a gargoyle-adorned belltower, and the ruined castle of notorious baron Jean de Meynier. The **Sentier Vigneron** follows footpaths and quiet lanes amid vineyards, with discreet panels signposting different grape varieties and the stages of wine production.

Just east of here you enter Peter Mayle country – literally – at **Ménerbes**, which, despite featuring in *A Year in Provence*, remains a clock-stopped stone village with traces of a more prosperous past. At the top, the turreted former château was once a stronghold of the Waldensians (*see chapter* **History**). On the plain below the village, you can visit the impressive cellars of the **Domaine de la Citadelle**, a vineyard created since 1989 out of a mass of tiny parcels of land by Yves Rousset-Rouard, producer of the *Emmanuelle* films. The visit also takes in the corkscrew collection of the **Musée du Tire-Bouchon**. On the scenic D109 between Ménerbes and Lacoste, a bumpy track leads to the isolated **Abbaye St Hilaire**, the remains of a 13th-century Carmelite priory.

With its medieval gateways and cobbled streets, the tiny, semi-deserted village of **Lacoste** should not be missed. The ruined castle at the top belonged to the Sade family; the scandalous Marquis lived here on and off for 30 years until his imprisonment in 1786 (*see chapter* **History**), and it has recently been acquired by designer and global fashion magnate Pierre Cardin. From here the road curves and zigzags up the ramparts of **Bonnieux**. Inhabited since Neolithic times,

The Luberon is a hit-parade of Provence at its most achingly picturesque.

Bonnieux became a Templar commanderie and later a papal outpost. A 12th-century church on the hilltop is reached up cobbled steps from rue de la République, past the Mairie; the newer parish church in the lower village contains four 15th-century panel paintings from the old church.

In the less-known eastern half of the Luberon above Apt, the remarkably unspoiled village of **Saignon** stretches along a craggy escarpment between a square-towered Romanesque church and cemetery and a rocky belvedere, where a ruined chapel and several houses are built into the rock. Its remote location and mountain site made the nearby hamlet of **Buoux** an important refuge during the Wars of Religion: on the hillside are ruins of the fortress demolished by Louis XIV to deter Huguenots

from taking refuge here. At the end of the secluded Aiguebrun valley, assorted footpaths lead to Sivergues and the Mourré Nègre; the overhanging crags are popular with climbers.

Abbaye St-Hilaire

Menerbes (04.90.75.88.83). **Open** *summer* 9am-6pm daily; *winter* 10am-5pm daily. **Admission** free.

Collégiale Notre Dame d'Alidon

Oppède-le-Vieux (Mairie 04.90.76.90.06). **Open** *May, June* 9am-6pm Sat, Sun or by appointment; *July, Aug* 10am-6.30pm daily.

Musée du Tire-Bouchon

Domaine de la Citadelle, Le Chataignier, chemin de Cavaillon, Ménerbes (04.90.72.41.58). **Open** *Apr-Sept* 9am-noon, 2-7pm daily; *Oct-Mar* 9am-noon, 2-6pm Mon-Fri. **Admission** €4; free under-15s.

Provençal People: Olivier Baussan

L'Occitane is the high-street ambassador of Provence. This body and beauty product chain is 25 years old and has 200 shops worldwide, pumping the essence of Provence from its headquarters in Manosque as far afield as Buenos Aires, Seoul and Dusseldorf.

Olivier Baussan, its founder and philosopher, was brought up in the village of Ganagobie, just east of Forcalquier. A disciple of the 1970s ecology movement, he lugged an old still behind his 2CV through the Lure mountains, collecting and distilling plants in riverside fields. He soon put his money where his nose was, and in 1976 began a market stall selling essential oils: 'I tried out everything that I thought was simple to do around the subject of beauty,' he explains. The formula worked immediately.

In 1997 Baussan also founded sister chain Olivier & Co, an upmarket showcase for Mediterranean olive oil, and luxury nibbles.

L'Occitane's products are based on natural ingredients grown by farmers predominately from the south of France, including olive oil, lavender, myrtle, lemon and sunflower, though incorporating foreign extracts such as vanilla and the best-selling shea butter. 'I like products with a story – products with real authenticity and respect,' says Baussan.

In common with The Body Shop's Anita Roddick, Baussan passionately believes in respect for the environment and preserving local heritage and humanity, both at home and abroad: L'Occitane works with some 40 producers in France, 100 overseas, and the factory in Manosque now employs 200. His

main argument against synthetic products is that they require a minimal labour force: 'If I put lavender in a product, I need to know that farmers will live off that lavender.'

Worthiness aside, one of L'Occitane's most striking achievments is its branding, a modern-rustic exception to the florid twee of much Provençal merchandising. Blending earthy creams, khakis and apricots, the globally inspired palette expresses L'Occitane's inclusive vision: 'Provence is a land of tolerance, so I welcome new colours and forms to create a totality, which gives a hot, Mediterranean atmosphere... I want people to come into my shops and feel warmth and conviviality, expressed in every detail.'

Where to stay & eat

At Robion, **Lou Luberon** (av Aristide Briand, 04.90.76.65.04, closed Sun, menus €11.23-€23.63) looks like a simple roadside bar but serves delicious salads and carefully prepared regional dishes like stuffed rabbit. At Coustellet, **Maison Gouin** (04.90.76.90.18, closed Wed & Sun and 15 Nov-5 Dec & Feb, menus €10.70-€27.45) combines butcher, upmarket deli and a very good bistro.

In Bonnieux, the semi-troglodyte **Le Fournil** (5 pl Carnot, 04.90.75.83.62, closed Mon & Tue and Dec-Jan, menus €15-€29) in an old bakery – John Malkovich's favourite – is the very definition of low-key Provençal style, with great service and a menu using local produce. The 18th-century **Hostellerie de la Prieuré** (rue Jean-Baptiste Auvard, 04.90.75.80.78, closed Nov-Mar, restaurant also closed lunch Tue-Fri, double €53-€98, menus €19-€33.50), on the descent to Lacoste, has a chapel and vast fireplaces as reminders of its past; bedrooms overlook a walled garden or ramparts. On the garrigue-covered plateau above the village, the upmarket **La Bastide de Capelongue** (1.5km east on D232, 04.90.75.89.78, closed mid-Nov to mid-Dec, mid-Jan to mid-Mar, double €183-€259 incl dinner, menus €46-€69) is a tastefully decorated modern *bastide* with a pool. Off the D194 **Les Trois Sources** (St Victor, 04.90.75.95.58) is a lovely *chambres d'hôtes* (double €55-€95) in an ancient building that was probably a priory before becoming a silkworm farm (hence all the mulberry trees).

The remote **Auberge des Seguins** (Buoux, 04.90.74.16.37, double €55-€76), under the crags at the end of a valley, is a popular choice with walkers and rock climbers. In Saignon, the **Auberge du Presbytère** (pl de la Fontaine, 04.90.74.11.50, closed 15 Nov-15 Dec, double €50-€110; restaurant closed Wed & lunch Thur, menus €13-€28) has individually decorated rooms in an ancient presbytery overlooking the village square. **Chambre de Séjour avec Vue** (04.90.04.85.01/www.chambreavecvue.com, double €68) is an old village house that has been transformed with a remarkable eye for colour and design by Kamila Regent; she invites artists in residence to work and exhibit in the house, while also letting out three bedrooms and an apartment.

Tourist Information

Bonnieux Office de Tourisme

7 pl Carnot, 04480 Bonnieux (04.90.75.91.90). **Open** 2-6.30pm Mon; 9.30am-12.30pm, 2-6.30pm Tue-Sat.

South Luberon Châteaux

The southern edge of the range is known for its trio of Renaissance châteaux. One of the largest and liveliest Luberon villages, **Lourmarin**, with its cluster of grey-shuttered stone houses and medieval church, is the *de facto* gastronomic capital of the area. Despite all the antiques shops, gift shops and estate agents, tourism here remains civilised, with action centred on the main street, where Café Gaby and Café de l'Ormeau enjoy a friendly rivalry. Rue du Temple leads to the mainly 16th-century **Château de Lourmarin**, with its square tower and large Renaissance windows. The château narrowly escaped destruction in the Revolution; it was restored in the early 1900s and since 1925 has received artists and writers in residence. It is also used for chamber music in summer. Don't miss the cantilever staircase and an extraordinary Renaissance fireplace which combines classical Corinthian capitals with native Indian figures from the newly discovered Americas. Albert Camus lived on the edge of the village and is buried in the cemetery alongside his wife.

West of Lourmarin, **Mérindol** is worth a visit not so much for its second homes of today as the moving evocation of what used to be. Climb the route des Valdois to Vieux Mérindol, the still partly ruined village that is witness to the brutal massacre of 1545. Follow signs up steps to the Memorial set into a fragment of wall from the feudal fortress. Only one large villa spoils the sense of abandon and there are hilltop views as far as the Alpilles, Montagne Sainte Victoire and the Sainte Baume massif.

West of Mérindol, the **Gorges de Regalon** (parking €2.29), where the river has sculpted out a narrow gorge (dry in summer, but apt to flood after heavy rain), provide a welcome breath of cool air: pleasant for a stroll amid luxuriant vegetation or the start of a more ambitious walk to Oppède across the range.

More workaday than chic Lourmarin, **Cadenet** has some charming stepped streets and ancient houses, as well as the small **Musée de la Vannerie**, devoted to basketmaking, once one of the town's principal activities. The main square features a statue of the drummer boy of Arcole, born in the village, who saved French troops in the war against Austria in 1796.

East of Lourmarin on the D27, the still partly walled village of **Cucuron** is less touristy than many Luberon villages, although its olive press (open Nov-Jan) is a favourite with some super-chefs. On place de l'Horloge, a fortified bell-tower gateway leads to a ruined keep. The **Eglise Notre-Dame-de-Beaulieu** contains a Baroque altarpiece and Gothic side chapels.

Beyond the square where the market is held on Tuesday morning, footpaths lead from Cucuron and Cabrières d'Aigues up the **Mourre Nègre**, the Luberon's highest point.

Ansouis is dominated by its Renaissance château, still inhabited by the Sabran-Pontevès family – who sometimes give the tours. The visit takes in baronial halls and massive kitchens, but the highlight is the terraced gardens. The church, entered via a semi-circular flight of stairs, is built into the edge of the ramparts.

Further east at **La Tour-d'Aigues**, amid rolling vineyards, are the remains of what was once the finest of the Renaissance châteaux, destroyed by fire in 1792. The pedimented entrance and part of the wings survive. Two museums, **Musée des Faïences** and **Musée de l'Histoire du Pays d'Aigues**, are housed in the cellars; the first contains a collection of ceramics from a local 18th-century factory.

In an area of vineyards, oak and pine forests are the fortified village of **Grambois** (where part of *La Gloire de mon père* was filmed) and **La Bastide de Jourdans**, founded in the 13th century but now much smaller than when it was a centre of silk production.

Château d'Ansouis

rue Cartel, Ansouis (04.90.09.82.70). **Open** *May-Sept* 2.30-5.30pm daily; *Oct to mid-Nov & mid-Feb to Apr* 2.30-5.30pm Mon, Wed-Sun; *mid-Nov to mid-Feb* 2.30-4.30pm Sat, Sun. **Admission** €6; €3 6-18s; free under-6s.

Château de Lourmarin

Lourmarin (04.90.68.15.23). **Guided tours** Feb-Dec 11am, 2.30pm, 3.30pm, 4.30pm, 5.30pm daily; Jan 11am, 2.30pm, 4pm Sat, Sun. **Admission** €5; €2 10-16s; free under-10s.

Musée des Faïences

Château de la Tour-d'Aigues (04.90.07.50.33/ www.chateau-latourdigues.com). **Open** *July, Aug* 10am-1pm, 2.30-5.30pm daily; *Sept-June* 9.30am-noon, 2-5pm Mon, Wed-Fri; 10am-noon Tue; 2-5pm Sat, Sun. **Admission** €4.57; €1.52 8-12s; free under-8s.

Musée de la Vannerie

La Glaneuse, av Philippe de Girard, Cadenet (04.90.68.24.44). **Open** 10am-noon, 2.30-6.30pm Mon, Thur-Sat; 2.30-6.30pm Wed, Sun. Closed Nov-Mar. **Admission** €3; €1.50 12-18s; free under-12s.

Where to stay & eat

Lourmarin has become the gourmet capital of the Luberon thanks in part to Reine Sammut at **La Fenière** (on D945 rte de Cadenet, 04.90.68.11.79, closed lunch Mon & all Tue and mid-Jan to mid-Feb & end Nov, menus €35-€83.85). Housed in a stylish modern *mas*, she's particularly good at starters, often using produce from her vegetable garden. There are

also some attractive rooms upstairs (double €91). Sammut is rivalled by young Edouard Loubet at **Le Moulin de Lourmarin** (rue du Temple, 04.90.68.06.69, closed Mon lunch, Tue and mid-Jan to mid-Feb, menus €65-€140, double €155-€280) in a controversially converted but very comfortable water mill at the edge of Lourmarin. He concocts sublime dishes with herbs and wild plants, although can come unstuck when he gets too complicated. **Maison Ollier** (pl de la Fontaine, 04.90.68.02.03, closed dinner Tue & all Wed except in July & Aug, closed mid-Nov to mid-Dec, menus €18-€46), in a restored village house with garden, has a Mediterranean-inspired menu ranging from tagliatelle to tagines. Amid vineyards 2km east of Lourmarin, the **Hôtel de Guilles** (rte de Vaugines, 04.90.68.30.55/www.guilles.com, closed 15 Dec-31 Jan, double €74-€138, restaurant dinner only, menu €38) is a cleverly converted *mas* with vaulted entrance hall, bedrooms with attractive *armoires* and patchwork spreads, swimming pool and tennis courts. It is coming under new management in 2002, and prices may go up. The **Hostellerie du Paradou** (rte d'Apt, 04.90.68.04.05, closed mid-Nov to Jan, double €50-€93), a short walk from the village, is a stone *mas* with spacious lawns and nine simple rooms; the restaurant serves regional fare accompanied by well-chosen local wines (closed all Thur & lunch Fri, menus €18-€22)). Adorable staff.

In ungentrified Lauris, **La Table des Mamées** (rue Murier, Lauris, 04.90.08.34.66, closed Mon & dinner Sun, average €30) serves dishes often adapted from historic recipes in three vaulted rooms; live musical entertainment Thur-Sat evenings. **La Tuilière** (04.90.68.24.45/www.latuiliere.com, double €61-€76) in Cadenet offers five rooms in a big old house, with ramshackle terraced garden, small pool, ping pong and billiard table. The **Camping Val de Durance** (Les Routes, Cadenet, 04.90.68.37.75/www.homer-vacances.fr, closed Oct-Mar, €4.50-€6.50 per person) offers well-spaced pitches, screened by trees. You may want to cool off in the small lake which has been arranged for swimming with grassy enclosure, small sandy beach and scenic views (open May-Sept 9am-8pm daily).

In scenic Cucuron, good-value **L'Horloge** (55 rue Léonce Brieugne, 04.90.77.12.74, closed Wed and Feb school holidays, €14.50-€21) is housed in vaulted cellars, a cool retreat for some quietly creative Provençal cooking. **L'Arbre de Mai** (rue de l'Eglise, 04.90.77.25.10, closed mid-Jan to Feb, double €53-€62) is a basic, comfortable hotel and restaurant (closed Mon & Tue, menus €15 and €23) serving traditional food.

Nearby at Vaugines, the **Hostellerie de Luberon** (cours St Louis, 04.90.77.27.19/ www.hostelleriedeluberon.com, closed Nov-Feb, restaurant closed lunch Wed, double €105 incl dinner, menus €15-€25) is a modern *mas* with tables inside and out overlooking swimming pool and vineyards. Specialities include *caillettes*, fish and local lamb.

There are fewer options on the eastern slopes of the Luberon, but the regional fare at **Restaurant de la Fontaine** (pl de la Fontaine, 04.90.07.72.16, closed Mon-Wed and 10 Dec-10 Jan, two weeks in Feb, menu €26) at St-Martin-de-la-Brasque is popular. In La Bastide de Jourdans, the **Auberge du Cheval-Blanc** (04.90.77.81.08, closed Feb, double €66-€76) is an old coaching inn with four spacious rooms and restaurant (closed Thur, menus €24-€33).

Tourist information

Market day is Thur and Sat in Ansouis, Tue in Curcuron and La Tour d'Aigues, Fri in Lourmarin and Wed in Mérindol,

Ansouis Office de Tourisme
pl du Château, 84240 Ansouis (04.90.09.86.98/ www.ansouis.fr). **Open** *Apr-Sept* 10am-noon, 2-6pm daily; *Oct-Mar* 10am-noon, 2-5pm.

Cucuron Office de Tourisme
rue Léonce Brieugne, 84160 Cucuron (04.90.77.28.37). **Open** *May-Sept* 9am-noon, 3-7pm daily. *Oct-Apr* 9am-noon Mon-Sat.

Lourmarin Office de Tourisme
17 av Philippe de Girard, 84160 Lourmarin (04.90.68.10.77/www.lourmarin.com). **Open** 9.30am-1pm, 3-7pm Mon-Sat; 9.30am-noon Sun.

Mérindol Office de Tourisme
rue du Four, 84360 Mérindol (04.90.72.88.50). **Open** *June-Sept* 8.30am-12.30pm, 2-6pm daily; *Oct-May* 9am-12.30pm, 2-5pm Mon-Sat; 9.30am-12.30pm daily.

L'Isle-sur-la-Sorgue & Fontaine-de-Vaucluse

L'Isle-sur-la-Sorgue is known as the 'Venise Comtadin' for its ring of canals. Dripping wheels recall a past when water powered a silk industry and later paper mills. What makes the town tick today is France's largest concentration of antiques dealers outside Paris. Star sight is the **Collégiale Notre-Dame-des-Anges**, an extraordinary Baroque church with heavens full of cherubim. Gilded virtues fly over the arches along the nave, while the sanctuary boasts a gleaming carved altarpiece. The side chapels reveal frescoes, faux marble, wood carving and painted altarpieces. The square outside contains the pretty **Café de France**, galleried houses and the tourist office. The **Musée Donadeï de Campredon** puts on exhibitions of modern and contemporary art.

Upstream (7km by D25), surrounded by a bowl of mountains, **Fontaine-de-Vaucluse** clusters around the source of the Sorgue river:

Avignon & the Vaucluse

The ruins of **La Tour d'Aigues** sit atop cellars now housing two museums. *See p120.*

water mysteriously gushes out of a sheer cliff face into a jade-green pool, giving the name Vallis Clausa (closed valley) or Vaucluse to the whole *département*. Numerous divers, including the late Jacques Cousteau, have attempted without success to find the source; their exploits, and the geological wonders of the area, are explained in the underground museum **Le Monde souterrain de Norbert Casteret**.

Above the village is a ruined castle, originally built by monks to protect pilgrims to the tomb of St-Véran, who saved the village from a dragon in the sixth century and evangelised the region. Abandoned factories hint at Fontaine's more industrial past. The pretty Romanesque church has a painting of St Véran and an 11th-century open altar table. Across the river, the **Musée Pétrarque** stands on the site where

On the antiques trail

Antiques dealers began settling in L'Isle-sur-la-Sorgue after the first *foire à la brocante* in 1962 and there are now an estimated 300, concentrated along avenue de la Libération, avenue des Quatre Otages and around the station, some of them in picturesque canalside locations. On Sunday, the antiques shops and arcades (open 10am-7pm Mon, Sat, Sun) are joined by squadrons of junkier *brocanteurs* along avenue des Quatre Otages, with major antiques fairs that flow into additional fields at Easter and on 15 August. Merchandise ranges from high-quality antiques to quirky collectibles, including many Provençal items, such as gilt mirrors, carved buffets, printed fabrics and Moustiers and Marseille faïence. There are also architectural salvage specialists offering old zinc bars, bistro fittings and hotel reception booths. Le Rendezvous des Marchands (91 av de la Libération, 04.90.20.84.60, closed dinner Mon & Tue) is a café-cum-antiques shop

where you can stop for a drink among a clutter of items for sale, or a canal-side meal.

Even if there are few true bargains (some shops seem to pack up entire crates of furniture for shipping direct to stores in the US, and it's not uncommon to hear prices being discussed in dollars), prices are noticeably lower than in Paris, where a fair number of the goods end up. Needless to say, the usual bargaining rules apply.

Hôtel Dongier
9 pl Gambetta (04.90.38.63.63).

L'Isle aux Brocantes
7 av des Quatre Otages (04.90.20.69.93).

Village des Antiquaires de la Gare
2 bis av de l'Egalité (04.90.38.04.57).

Le Quai de la Gare
4 av Julien Guigue (04.90.20.73.42).

Italian Renaissance scholar Petrarch (1304-74) wrote his famous *Canzoniere*.

Between April and December, the Sorgue can be navigated by canoe between Fontaine-de-Vaucluse and Partage des Eaux. Canoes can be hired at **Canoë Evasion** (on D24 at Pont de Galas, 04.90.38.26.22, closed Jan-Mar).

Collégiale Notre-Dame-des-Anges

pl de la Liberté, L'Isle-sur-la-Sorgue **Open** *May-Oct* 9am-noon, 3-6pm daily; *Nov-Apr* 10am-noon, 3-5pm Tue-Sat.

Le Monde souterrain de Norbert Casteret

chemin de la Fontaine, Fontaine-de-Vaucluse (04.90.20.34.13).

Musée Donadeï de Campredon

20 rue du Docteur Taillet, L'Isle-sur-la-Sorgue (04.90.38.17.41). **Open** 9.30am-noon, 2-6pm Tue-Sun (closed for renovation until Oct 2002).

Musée Pétrarque

quai du Château Vieux, Fontaine-de-Vaucluse (04.90.20.37.20). **Open** *Apr to 15 Oct* 10am-noon, 2-6pm Mon, Wed-Sun (15-30 Oct until 5pm). Closed Nov-Mar. **Admission** €3.50; €1.50 12-18s; free under-12s.

Where to stay & eat

Hungry antiques browsers are served by a rash of restaurants along the canals and within the markets of L'Isle-sur-la-Sorgue. One of the best is stylish bistro **Le Carré des Herbes** (13 av des Quatres Otages, 04.90.38.62.95, closed Tue & Jan or Feb, meuns €12-€24), now under the wing of fêted Paris chef Bernaud Pacaud. By the riverside, **Le Pescador** (04.90.38.09.69, closed Wed & Jan to mid-Feb, double €44-€53) is an affordable place to kip, with a reliable restaurant (menus €16-€22).

Fontaine-de-Vaucluse is strong on snacks and ice cream; the **Hostellerie Le Château** (quai du Château Vieux, 04.90.20.31.54, closed Dec-Mar, double €35) offers budget lodgings in a waterside setting, with a veranda restaurant open year round (menus €18-€29).

Tourist information

Isle-sur-la-Sorgue market days are Thur and Sun.

L'Isle-sur-la-Sorgue

Office de Tourisme, pl de l'Eglise, 84800 L'Isle-sur-la-Sorgue (04.90.38.04.78/www.ot-islesurlasorgue.fr). **Open** 9.30am-12.30pm, 2.30-6pm Mon-Sat; 9am-12.30pm Sun.

Fontaine-de-Vaucluse

Office de Tourisme, chemin de la Fontaine, 84800 Fontaine-de-Vaucluse (04.90.20.32.22/fax 04.90.20.21.37). **Open** 10am-6pm Mon-Sat.

Cavaillon is the melon capital of France: the juicy globes are celebrated in a festival in July, and crop up in everything from jam to chocolates. Cavaillon injects a dose of real life into the Luberon – housing estates, lounging youths and an absurd number of roundabouts – but compensates with an all-year arts scene thanks to a Scène Nationale theatre and the **Grenier à Sons** (157 av du Général de Gaulle/ 04.90.06.44.20) weekly music venue. In recent years the town has been more associated with militant farmers dumping produce than with sightseeing, but past the anonymous periphery is an old town with relics from what was once an important medieval diocese.

The earliest visible reminder of Cavaillon's past is the spindly first-century **Arc Romain** (pl du Clos), bearing traces of sculpted flowers and winged victories. A footpath zigzags up the cliff to the medieval **Chapelle St-Jacques** offering panoramic views over the town and the Durance valley. At the foot of the Arc, peer into the time-capsule **Fin de Siècle** café.

The raggedy old town is presided over by the Romanesque **Cathédrale Notre-Dame et St-Véran** (closed Mon & Sun), with its cloister (badly damaged during the Wars of Religion), octagonal tower and a sundial with a winged angel. Tree-shaded **place Philippe de Cabassole** has a couple of fine 18th-century houses. The Baroque facade of the Grand Couvent reflects church power during the Comtat Venaissan; in the **Musée de l'Hôtel Dieu**, archaeological finds from a neolithic settlement on St-Jacques hill are displayed in the former hospital and its 18th-century chapel.

Like nearby **Carpentras**, Cavaillon had a sizeable Jewish community, and its light-filled **synagogue** (built 1772-4) is one of the finest in France. The pink and blue upper level, with bronze chandeliers, baroque tabernacle and delicate ironwork, was reserved for the men. The lower level doubled as a bakery. It now contains the **Musée Juif Comtadin**, housing the tabernacle doors from the earlier synagogue on the site, prayer books and other possessions that had belonged to the community.

Musée de l'Hôtel Dieu

Grand-Rue (04.90.76.00.34). **Open** *June-Sept* 9.30am-12.30pm, 2.30-6.30pm Mon, Wed-Sun; *Oct-May* by appointment. **Admission** €3; €1.05 12-18s; free under-12s.

Synagogue/Musée Juif Comtadin

rue Hébraïque (04.90.76.00.34). **Open** *Apr-Sept* 9am-12.30pm, 3-6.30pm Mon, Wed-Sun; *Oct-Mar* 9am-noon, 2-5pm Mon-Fri. **Admission** €3; €1.05 12-18s; free under-12s.

Where to stay & eat

Cavaillon's hotels leave quite a lot to be desired,
but culinary prospects are more promising.
Upmarket, old-fashioned **Prévot** (353 av de
Verdun, 04.90.71.32.43, closed dinner Sun, all
Mon, menus €20.50-€49) is famed for its
inventive summer melon menu. **Le Pantagruel**
(5 pl Philippe de Cabassole, 04.90.76.11.30, closed
lunch Mon & Tue, all Sun, menus €20.50-€30)
has a striking high-ceilinged dining room with a
huge open fire on which meat is grilled in winter.
In summer, start with the gigantic anchoïade
before roast lamb with herbs and honey. **Côté
Jardin** (49 rue Lamartine, 04.90.71.33.58, closed
dinner Sun, all Mon, three weeks Jan, menus
€13-€23) has tables around a courtyard fountain
and good-value Provençal cooking, especially
fish. The *belle époque* café **Le Fin de Siècle**
(46 pl du Clos, 04.90.71.12.27, closed dinner Tue,
all Wed and Aug to mid-Sept, menus €10-€33.50)
has kept its mosaic frontage, mouldings and
large mirrors; upstairs is a restaurant. Baker
Auzet (61 cours Bournissac, 04.90.78.06.54,
closed Tue) serves light meals and will even
organise bakery courses for groups.

Outside town, the lovely **Mas du Souléou**
(5 chemin St Pierre des Essieux, 04.90.71.43.22/
www.souleou.com, doubles €73) is a *chambres
d'hôtes* in a 19th-century mas restored with
enormous taste, where Mr Lepaul concocts
dinner (€20) served in the family kitchen.

Tourist information

Market day is Monday.

Office de Tourisme

*pl François Tourel, 84300 Cavaillon (04.90.71.32.01/
www.cavaillon-luberon.com).* **Open** 9am-12.30pm,
2-6.30pm Mon-Sat (plus 9.30am-12.30pm Sun July, Aug).

Apt

At first sight there is not much going on in Apt,
with its industrial outskirts, plane trees and
sleepy squares along the Calavon river. But it
comes alive on Saturday morning with the
largest market for miles around.

Place de la Bouquerie is the main access
point for the old town, via the narrow main street,
rue des Marchands. The **Ancienne Cathédrale
Ste-Anne** throws an arch across the street; now
demoted to the status of parish church, it is a
curious mix of Gothic and Baroque. The church's
two crypts reveal the ancient origins of the
building: the upper one dates from the 11th
century, the lower from the fourth. A Roman
sarcophagus harks back to the town's foundation
as a staging post on the Via Domitia.

Cherubic **Notre-Dame-des-Anges**. *See p121.*

Nearby, the **Maison du Parc** has
information about the flora, fauna and geology
of the Parc Régional du Luberon, plus the small,
child-oriented **Musée de la Paléontologie**.
The **Musée d'Apt** displays Apt's typical
cream or marbled faience and archaeological
finds, old pharmacy jars and ex-votos from the
cathedral over three floors of an 18th-century
hôtel particulier. Today although plenty of
pottery can be picked up at market, only
Faïence d'Apt (286 av de la Libération,
04.90.74.15.31, closed am Mon, all Sun)
continues the traditional marbleware, using
different coloured clays. A new museum
devoted to Apt's industrial past opens in a
former candied fruit factory in autumn 2002. If
all this mind-candy whets your appetite for the
real thing, head for **Aptunion**, the town's
biggest manufacturer of candied fruits.

Ancienne Cathédrale Ste-Anne

rue de la Cathédrale (04.90.74.36.60). **Open** *Oct-
June* 10am-noon, 2-4pm Tue-Fri; 10am-noon Sat, Sun;
July-Sept 10am-noon, 3-6pm Tue-Fri; 10am-noon Sat,
Sun. **Treasury open** *July-Sept* guided tours only
11am, 5pm Mon-Sat, 11am Sun. **Admission** free.

Aptunion

on N100, quartier Salignan (04.90.76.31.43).
Open *factory* by appointment; *shop* 9am-noon,
2-6pm Mon-Sat.

Maison du Parc & Musée de la Paléontologie
60 pl Jean Jaurès (04.90.04.42.00). **Open** 8.30am-noon, 1.30-6pm Mon-Sat. **Admission** €1.50; free under-18s.

Musée d'Apt
27 rue de l'Amphithéâtre (04.90.74.78.45). **Open** *Oct-May* 2-5.30pm Mon, Wed-Fri; 10am-noon, 2-5.30pm Sat; *June-Sept* 10am-noon, 2-5.30pm Mon, Wed-Sat; 2-6pm Sun. **Admission** €2; €1 12-18s; free under-12s.

Where to stay & eat

At the **Auberge du Luberon** (8 pl du Fbg Ballet, 04.90.74.12.50, closed dinner Sun, all Mon and Christmas & New Year, menus €37-€64), chef Serge Peuzin offers a special *menu aux fruits confits* in which Apt's speciality, candied fruit, features in every course; there are also 14 bedrooms (€45-€76).

Tourist information

Office de Tourisme
20 av Philippe de Girard, 84400 Apt (04.90.74.03.18/fax 04.90.74.03.18). **Open** *mid-June to mid-Sept* 9am-7.30pm Mon-Sat; 9am-12.30pm Sun; *mid-Sept to mid-June* 9am-noon, 2-6pm Mon-Sat.

Gordes & the Plateau de Vaucluse

Fiefdom of the *gauche caviar*, France's champagne socialists – or the *gauche tapenade* as some dub them here – **Gordes** is almost too pretty for its own good, with a spectacular hilltop setting, dominated by the turrets of its château, drystone walls and steep, stepped alleys weaving down the hill. Renovation and wealth have given Gordes a rather chi-chi sheen, but it is this combination of historic stones and worldly buzz that draws the well-dressed people-watchers who loll at its café tables. Tasteful shops sell the usual Provençal crafts and produce, while the château, which long displayed kinetic art by Vasarely, now has a semi-permanent exhibition by the Belgian painter Pol Mara.

West of Gordes, the **Village des Bories** is a group of restored drystone, beehive-shaped huts, inhabited between the 16th and 19th centuries; they may have been built over – or on the model of – much earlier dwellings. An attempt has been made to reconstruct the rural lifestyle of the Borie dwellers, and a photo exhibition shows similar drystone structures in other countries.

North of Gordes, at the base of a wooded valley, the **Abbaye Notre-Dame-de-Sénanque**, founded in 1148, is one of the great

triumvirate of Provençal Cistercian monasteries (with Silvacane and Thoronet). Set amid lavender fields, the beautifully preserved Romanesque ensemble – church, cloister, dormitory, chapter house – still houses a monastic community.

Surrounded by strangely eroded outcrops of ochre-red rocks, **Roussillon** is among the most picturesque of all the Luberon villages, although it can get suffocatingly full of tourists. The houses are painted in an orange wash, which makes the entire village glow. Walk past the belfry-sundial of the **Eglise St-Michel** to an orientation table, and note the 18th-century facades on place de la Mairie. To the left of the village cemetery, above car park 2, the **Sentier des Ocres** (closed Nov-Mar, €2, free under-10s), a footpath with information panels, offers spectacular views amid peculiar rock formations, the result of centuries of ochre quarrying. On the D104 towards Apt, the former ochre works have reopened as the **Conservatoire des Ocres et Pigments Appliqués**. Guided tours show how the rock was purified and made into pigment.

Reached by small lanes south of the D22 towards Rustrel from Apt, the **Colorado de Rustrel** is less-touristed and more extensive than Roussillon. The undulating green countryside suddenly gives way to a valley littered with rocks long exploited for ochre pigment which has resulted in a dramatic landscape of canyons and chimneys, half man-made, half by natural erosion in colours that vary from pale cream via yellows and orange to deep, russet red. Near the car park, a path descends to a picnic site and *buvette* and relics of disused ochre works. Wear decent shoes and do stick to the *sentiers* – colour-coded waymarked paths of varying lengths – which lead you round some of the most spectacular turrets and banks.

Abbaye Notre-Dame-de-Sénanque
3km N of Gordes on D177 (04.90.72.05.72/ www.senanque.fr). **Open** *Feb-Oct* 10am-noon, 2-6pm Mon-Sat; 2-6pm Sun; *Nov-Jan* 2-5pm Mon-Fri; 2-6pm Sat, Sun. **Admission** €5; €2 6-18s; free under-6s.

Château de Gordes
Gordes (04.90.72.02.89). **Open** 10am-noon, 2-6pm daily. **Admission** €4; €3 10-17s; free under-10s.

Conservatoire des Ocres et Pigments appliqués
Usine Mathieu, D104, Roussillon (04.90.05.66.69). **Tours** 11am, 3pm, 4pm; plus noon, 5pm in July, Aug. **Admission** €5; free under-11s.

Village des Bories
Les Savournins, Gordes (04.90.72.03.48). **Open** *June-Sept* 9am-8pm daily; *Nov-May* 9am-5pm daily. **Admission** €5.50; €3 10-17s; free under-10s.

Where to stay & eat

In Gordes, **La Bastide de Gordes** (rte de Combe, 04.90.72.12.12, closed Nov to mid-Dec, Jan to mid-Feb, double €79-€206) is an upmarket hotel on the ramparts, with spectacular views. The **Domaine de l'Enclose** (rte de Sénanque, 04.90.72.71.00, closed mid-Nov to mid-Dec, double €88-€150) offers all mod cons in a garden setting; ground-floor rooms have private gardens, the restaurant (menus €36; closed lunch to non-residents) serves creative seasonal cooking. Adjoining the château, **Café-Restaurant La Renaissance** (pl du Château, 04.09.72.02.02, menus €11.50-€30) has tables on the square and very hip waitresses. In Roussillon, **David** (pl de la Poste, 04.90.05.60.13, closed Mon, 20 Nov-20 Mar, menus €19.50-€46) is the most reliable of several bistros and snack bars. On the edge of the village, the ochre-washed **Sables d'Ocre** (on D104, Roussillon, 04.90.05.55.55, double €49-€67, closed 15 Jan-1 Mar & 15 Nov-15 Dec) is a friendly family-oriented modern hotel with pool.

In Goult, just north of the N100 Avignon-Apt road, the **Café de la Poste** (pl de la Libération, 04.90.72.23.23, lunch only, closed Mon and Nov to Feb, menu €10) gained fame in Mayle's *A Year in Provence* and Jean Becker's film *L'Eté meurtrier*. Join locals and chic second-homers for gossip and home cooking at this café which doubles as bar, *tabac*, newsagent and restaurant.

Tourist information

Market is Tuesday morning in Gordes, Thursday am in Roussillon.

Gordes Office de Tourisme

Le Château, 84220 Gordes (04.90.72.02.75/ www.gordes-village.com). **Open** *July, Aug* 9am-12.30pm, 2-6.30pm Mon-Sat; *Sept-June* 9am-noon, 2-6pm Mon-Sat.

Roussillon Office de Tourisme

pl de la Poste, 84220 Roussillon (04.90.05.60.25/www.roussillon-provence.com). **Open** *July, Aug* 10am-noon, 2-6pm Mon-Sat; *Sept-June* 1.30-5.30pm Mon-Fri.

Manosque

Though it nestles at the eastern edge of the Luberon range, Manosque is very much a Durance Valley town – the largest in the sparsely populated *département* of Alpes de Haute Provence. Housing and industrial parks now sprawl over the hillside, but for a long time the town remained within the city walls, where the not-yet-tarted-up network of narrow streets, squares and covered passageways gives an interesting perspective on what the rest of the Luberon must have been like before it became so hip. Manosque is positively moribund on a Sunday out of season and liveliest on a Saturday, when a market takes over the whole centre.

Porte Saunerie leads into **rue Grande**, Manosque's main shopping street. At No.14, a plaque marks the house where novelist Jean Giono (1895-1970), son of a shoemaker, was born. At No.21 is a branch of **Occitane**, the phenomenally successful Manosque-based cosmetics company that is now one of the town's main employers *(see p118)*. Note also the fine 18th-century balcony at No.23. There are two historic churches, **St-Sauveur**, which features in Giono's swashbuckler *Le Hussard sur le Toit*, and **Notre-Dame-de-Romigier** on place de l'Hôtel de Ville, which has a fine Renaissance doorway and a black Virgin inside. From here rue des Marchands leads into rue Soubeyron and out to a gateway-belfry, the Porte Soubeyron.

The Giono link is exploited to the full with literary competitions and walks on the theme of 'Jean Giono, poet of the olive tree' (Haute-Provence olive oil gained an *appellation contrôlée* in 1999). The **Centre Jean Giono**, in an 18th-century *hôtel particulier*, has temporary exhibitions and a permanent display about the writer's life and work. His own house, **Lou Paraïs** (montée des Vraies Richesses, 04.92.87.73.03), north of the old town, is open for guided visits on Friday afternoons (ring ahead).

Centre Jean Giono

1 bd Elémir Bourges (04.92.70.54.54). **Open** *Apr-Sept* 9.30am-12.30pm, 2-6pm Tue-Sat; *Oct-Mar* 2-6pm Tue-Sat. **Admission** €4; €2 12-18s; free under-12s.

Where to stay & eat

Within town, the best-placed hotel is the **Grand Hôtel de Versailles** (17 av Jean Giono, 04.92.72.12.00; double €26-€61), a former coaching inn. A smarter option is the **Hostellerie de la Fuste** (rte Oraison, Valensole, 04.92.72.05.95, double €117-€151), 4km away across the Durance. Manosque's top chef is **Dominique Bucaille**, whose same-name restaurant in the modern town (43 bd des Tilleuls, 04.92.72.32.28, closed dinner Wed, all Sun and mid-July to mid-Aug, menus €15-€61) offers refined classical cooking and seasonal dishes, including a special vegetable menu. Within the old town, try the regional cooking at **Le Luberon** (21*bis* pl du Terreau, 04.92.72.03.09, closed Mon, Sun dinner and three weeks in Oct, menus €11.43-€39.70).

The **Colorado de Rustrel**: ochre mountain high. *See p125.*

Tourist information

Market day in Manosque is Saturday.

Office du Tourisme

pl du Dr Joubert, 04100 Manosque (04.92.72.16.00/ www.ville-manosque.fr). **Open** *Sept-June* 9am-12.15pm, 1.30-6pm Mon-Sat; *July, Aug* 9am-7pm Mon-Sat; 10am-noon Sun.

Pays de Forcalquier

In the early Middle Ages, the counts of Forcalquier rivalled those of Provence. The two were united in 1195 when Gersande, Comtesse de Forcalquier, married Alphonse, Count of Provence; their son Raymond Bérenger V succeeded in marrying all four daughters to future kings. Today Forcalquier is light years from its illustrious past but still a lively local centre, with a big market every Monday morning.

The sober Romano-Gothic **Cathédrale Notre Dame du Bourguet** is almost as wide as it is long, with triple nave and impressive organ loft. The former Couvent des Visitandines now contains the **Cinématographe** cinema, the Mairie, and the **Musée Municipal** where local archaeological finds include a fine Roman head from nearby Lurs. Niched under the ramparts, the **Couvent des Cordeliers** was heavily damaged in the Wars of Religion but visits take in the cloister and monastic buildings.

Narrow streets next to the cathedral lead into the old town, where there are some particularly fine houses on rue Béranger and a fancy Gothic fountain on place St-Michel. Climb up the wooded mound of the former citadel, topped by the octagonal **Chapel Notre-Dame de Provence**, built in 1875 with romantic neo-Gothic figures of musician angels. Forcalquier's other main sight is its **cemetery**, north-east of the centre, visited not so much for who is buried here as for its striking landscaping, where funerary monuments stand out against towering, geometric walls of tightly clipped yew.

At **Mane**, once a market halt on the Via Domitia, houses climb up from the main square in a series of concentric curtain walls around the well-preserved feudal castle (private). At the exit of the village, the former Benedictine monastery of **Notre Dame de Salagon** combines fascinating botanical gardens with an ethnographical museum. The 12th-century Romanesque chapel has traces of medieval frescoes and modern red stained-glass by abstract painter Aurélie Nemours. Around the priory buildings, exhibits relate to sage growing, lavender production and the art of beekeeping, and the reconstructed forge from one of the Luberon's last blacksmiths, but it is the themed gardens that best capture the relationship between village life and nature. A medieval garden planted with herbs, turnips, parsnips and pulses seems closer to our image of northern staples than of Provençal cuisine, but most of what seems quintessentially Provençal didn't then exist in Europe. Other gardens are planted with herbs and aromatic plants, ancient varieties of cultivated plants and flowers used in popular remedies.

A colony of white domes erupting out of the hillside above St-Michel-l'Observatoire belong to the **Observatoire de Haute-Provence**, a site chosen for the national astronomical research laboratory for the purity of its air and clear skies. The **Centre d'Astronomie** tries to make astronomy accessible to the public and runs observation evenings in July and August.

Centre d'Astronomie

plateau du Moulin à Vent, St-Michel-l'Observatoire (04.92.76.69.69/www.astrosurf.com/centre.astro). **Open** July, Aug observation nights 9.30pm-12.30am Tue-Fri; Sept-June 2-4.30pm Wed. Closed 25 Nov-1 Jan. **Admission** €4.57-€7.62; €3.05-€6.10 6-12s; free under-6s.

Couvent des Cordeliers

bd des Martyrs de la Résistance, Forcalquier (04.92.75.02.38). **Guided visits** *mid-June to mid-Sept* 11am, 2.30pm, 4.30pm daily; *mid-Sept to mid-June* by appointment. **Admission** €3.80; €2.30 under-13s.

Prieuré Notre Dame de Salagon

Musée-Conservatoire ethnologique de Haute-Provence, Mane (04.92.75.70.50). **Open** *May-Sept* 10am-noon, 2-7pm daily. *Oct* 2-6pm daily. *Nov-Apr* 2-6pm Sat, Sun and school holidays. **Admission** €4.60; €2.40 12-18s; free under-12s.

Musée Municipal

pl du Bourguet, Forcalquier (04.92.75.91.19). **Open** *Apr-Sept* 3-6pm Wed-Sat. Closed Oct-Mar. **Admission** €2; free under-18s

Observatoire de Haute Provence

St-Michel l'Observatoire (04.92.70.64.00/www.obs-hp.fr). **Open** *Apr-Sept* 2-4pm Wed; *Oct-Mar* 3pm sharp Wed. **Admission** €2.30; €1.50 10-18s; free under-10s.

Where to stay & eat

Hotels are low-key and unflashy in Forcalquier. On the main street, not far from the cathedral, the no-longer-so-grand **Grand Hôtel** (18 bd Latourette, 04.92.75.00.35, double €25-€40) offers dubious wallpaper, but spacious, clean rooms; those on the main street are double glazed. Old-fashioned **Hostellerie des Deux-Lions** (11 pl du Bourguet, 04.92.75.25.30, restaurant closed dinner Tue & all Wed, double €48-€58, menus €16-€24) serves classical cooking in a resolutely provincial setting to local worthies. There are several café-brasseries on place du Bourguet and around place St Michel in the old town. **Oliviers & Co** (3 rue des Cordeliers, 04.92.75.05.70, closed Tue from Nov-Mar) has a café attached serving gratins and salads.

Tourist Information

Market in Forcalquier is Monday morning. Internet access is available at the Royal Tabac (2 bd Latourette, 04.92.75.15.81).

Office de Tourisme

13 pl du Bourguet, 04300 Forcalquier (04.92.75.10.02/www.forcalquier.com). **Open** *June-Sept* 9am-12.30pm, 2-7pm Mon-Sat; 10am-1pm Sun. *Oct-May* 9am-noon, 2-6pm Mon-Sat.

► Getting There & Around

► By car

From A7, exit No 25 for Cavaillon. D2 runs from Cavaillon to Taillades and joins the N100, the Avignon-Apt-Forcalquier road, which rings the Montagne de Luberon to the north. L'Isle-sur-la-Sorgue is on the N100 or by D938 from Cavaillon. To the south, the D973 runs along the Durance from Cavaillon via Mérindol and Lauris to Cadenet and Pertuis. The range is crossed by the D943 from Cadenet via Lourmarin, which then forks to Apt (D943) and Bonnieux (D36). Manosque can be reached by D973 and N96 or A51 autoroute from Aix-en-Provence. For Cadenet from Aix, take the N7 and D543/D943 via Rognes.

► By train

TGV to Avignon. Local trains run from Avignon Centre Ville to Cavaillon. Manosque is on the branch line from Marseille to Gap via Aix, though the station Manosque-Gréoux-les-Bains is 1.5km S of the centre, with hourly buses to town Mon-Sat.

► By bus

Buses are limited, although the main towns are reasonably connected. **Cars Sumian** (04.91.49.44.25) runs two buses daily between Marseille and Apt, via Cadenet, Lourmarin and Bonnieux, and two buses daily between Aix and Apt, via Cadenet and Lourmarin. **Cars Arnaud** (04.90.38.15.98/www.voyages-arnaud.fr) runs between L'Isle-sur-la-Sorgue and Fontaine de Vaucluse and L'Isle-sur-la-Sorgue and Avignon, none on Sun. **Barlatier** (04.32.76.00.40) runs eight buses a day between Avignon and Apt, three a day between Cavaillon and Avignon and once daily between Cavaillon and Apt and Cavaillon and Forcalquier, all Mon-Sat, none on Sun. **Express de la Durance** (04.90.71.03.00) runs two buses a day between Cavaillon and Gordes. There are no bus services to Roussillon.

Marseille & Aix

Features

Marseille

Combining a stunning rocky coastline and a magnificient cultural heritage, feisty, oft-maligned Marseille is up for reappraisal.

Marseille & Aix

In June 2001 a new stretch of TGV brought Marseille to a mere three hours from Paris. Property prices have been rising and there is increasing talk of Parisians snapping up *pieds-à-terres* by the sea. Is Marseille, with its fishy reputation, destined to become a weekend resort for stressed-out executives? Or will the Euroméditérannée dockland redevelopment project bring a much-awaited economic boom?

As is so often the case here, there is no simple answer: the oldest city in France is one of fascinating contradictions. The sun almost always shines but the ferocious mistral chills the bones for 100 days each year. The rocky coastline is one of the most breathtaking in France but the best beaches call for a map and hiking boots. The architecture can be stunning but many historic buildings are crumbling and Marseille has its share of modern eyesores. It doesn't have the cultural facilities of Paris but the arts scene thrives all year round. The neighbourhoods nearest the Vieux Port remain relatively poor while the Corniche, the coastal road to the east, is lined with extravagant mansions. A dangerous reputation lingers but the crime rate is no higher than in other major French cities. The Marseillais seem down on their city but will vigorously defend it.

All of this, in the end, provides compelling reasons to do more than spend a few hours in Marseille clutching your valuables on your way to somewhere else. *Bouillabaisse* might illustrate the ethnic mix here but France's second-largest city is more than a bowl of bony fish stew – its Paris-meets-Tangiers-meets-fishing-village atmosphere is unique. The Marseillais warn that their city does not give easily of itself – you'll get back what you put in. Which, after all, is remarkably like fish stew.

HISTORY

Life in Marseille has revolved around the Vieux Port ever since a band of Phocaean Greeks sailed into this well-placed natural harbour in 600BC. On that very day a local chieftain's daughter, Gyptus, was to choose a husband and

the Greeks' dashing commander Protis clearly fitted the bill. The bride came with a donation of land, a hill near the mouth of the Rhône, where the Greeks founded a trading post named Massalia, a name that still crops up in modern Marseille – one of the city's best-known bands has dubbed itself Massilia Sound System.

Legend aside, the history of Marseille is irrevocably linked to its development as a port. By 500BC, Massalia's Greeks were trading throughout Mediterranean Europe and from Cornwall to the Baltic. Caesar besieged the city in 49BC, seizing almost all its colonies, and Massalia's Greeks were left with little more than their famous university and their much-vaunted independence, which they were to lose and regain several times over the years.

After a harsh buffetting from Saracens and marauding latter-day Greeks, Marseille swiftly reactivated its port in the 12th century and made a killing from embarking, and maintaining, supply lines to Crusaders. The city was seized by Charles d'Anjou in 1214 and was annexed to France by Henri IV in 1481, but kept up its time-honoured tradition of fighting every battle available… often on the losing side.

Louis XIV ushered in the first great transformation since the arrival of the Greeks; he pulled down the city walls in 1666 and expanded the port to the Rive Neuve. The city was devastated by plague in 1720, losing more than half its population of 90,000. By the Revolution, however, its industries of soap manufacture, oil processing and faïence were flourishing. The demand for labour sparked a wave of immigration from Provence and Italy.

Marseille supported the Revolution enthusiastically, only to turn monarchist under the First Empire and republican under the Second. By the time of Napoléon III, Algeria had become a French *département*, leading to a huge increase in trans-Mediterranean shipping. The emperor initiated the construction of an entirely new port, La Joliette, which was completed in 1853. In 1869, the Suez Canal opened and Marseille became the greatest boom town in 19th-century Europe. Between 1851 and 1911, the population rose by 360,000. As immigrants arrived from all over southern Europe, it acquired the astonishingly cosmopolitan population that it maintains to

> ► For information on visiting the gorgeous **Calanques** that stud the coast between Marseille and Cassis, *see p162*.

this day. In 1915, the city received some 20,000 Armenians fleeing Turkish genocide.

But Marseille's heyday was soon to come to an abrupt halt. In 1934, King Alexander of Yugoslavia and Louis Barthou, the French foreign minister, were assassinated on La Canebière. In 1939, the city was placed under national guardianship when widespread corruption in local government was revealed.

Following the independence of Tunisia in 1956 and Algeria in 1962, Marseille received a mass exodus of French colonials, North African Jews and North Africans who had been involved in colonial administration. At the same time, the loss of these colonies hit Marseille's shipping trade. From 1954 to 1964, the population grew by 50%, creating a severe housing shortage. New neighbourhoods were rapidly constructed to cope with the influx. Areas of high unemployment throughout the 1970s and 80s, these neighbourhoods were infamously home to drug dealing and crime.

Significantly, however, while Jean-Marie Le Pen and his 'France for the French' brand of extreme-right politics gained ground in neighbouring towns like Vitrolles, Marseille is one place where the melting pot seems to work. The city continued to elect a socialist council from 1953 to 1995. Jean-Claude Gaudin, the conservative (but not extremist) mayor of Marseille since 1995, easily won the 2001 municipal elections; the socialists led by René Olmeta now seem divided and aimless. Olmeta made himself unpopular by addressing the question of Marseille's 17% unemployment rate (the national rate is under 10%) – Gaudin prefers to keep an upbeat tone. After centuries in which brawn was what counted, the city is repositioning itself as a service and research centre, and is learning to capitalise on its spectacular setting and cultural facilities.

Sightseeing

Marseille takes in 37km of seafront from L'Estaque in the west to the Calanques in the east and is laid out in 16 *arrondissements* moving clockwise from the Vieux Port, then anticlockwise in an outer semi-circle.

Vieux Port & La Canebière

If you think of Marseille as a gritty city, you'll be surprised by the beauty of the **Vieux Port**. Fashionable bars and avant-garde theatres rub shoulders with ships' chandlers. Luxury yachts bob alongside fishing trawlers, which glide up to the quai des Belges every morning to deliver the day's catch at one of France's most photogenic markets. Here, you don't need to ask if the fish is fresh: the octopus are still slithering while sea bream try valiantly to hop out of the tub. This eastern quay is the departure point for ferries to Château d'If, the Iles de Frioul and the Côte Bleue.

From this vantage point the two forts guarding the entrance to the port come into view: **Fort St-Jean** (only open for special exhibitions) on the north bank and **Fort St-Nicolas** (closed to the public) on the south. The

Notre Dame de la Garde still keeps watch over **Vieux Port** sailors.

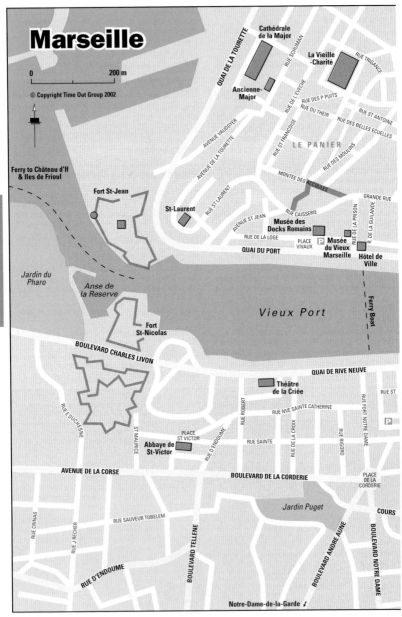

Marseille

0   200 m

© Copyright Time Out Group 2002

QUAI DE LA TOURETTE

Cathédrale
de la Major

RUE SCHUMAN

La Vieille
-Charité

RUE TRIGANCE

Ancienne-
Major

RUE DE L'EVECHE

RUE DES P PUITS

RUE ST ANTOINE

RUE DU THEIR

RUE DES BELLES ECUELLES

AVENUE VAUDOYER

RUE ST FRANCOISE

LE PANIER

AVENUE DE LA TOURETTE

RUE DES MOULINS

Ferry to Château d'If
& Iles de Frioul

MONTEE DES ACCOULES

Fort St-Jean

RUE ST LAURENT

GRANDE RUE

St-Laurent

AVENUE ST JEAN

RUE CAISSERIE

RUE DE LA PRISON

R. DE LA GUILANDE

Musée des
Docks Romains

RUE DE LA LOGE

PLACE
VIVAUX

P

Musée
du Vieux
Marseille

QUAI DU PORT

Hôtel de
Ville

Jardin du
Pharo

Anse de
la Reserve

Vieux Port

Ferry Boat

Fort
St-Nicolas

BOULEVARD CHARLES LIVON

QUAI DE RIVE NEUVE

Théâtre
de la Criée

RUE ST

RUE ROBERT

RUE NVE SAINTE CATHERINE

RUE FORT NOTRE DAME

P

RUE E DUCHESNE

RUE DE LA CROIX

RUE RIGORD

ST MAURICE

PLACE
ST VICTOR

RUE SAINTE

RUE D'ENDOUME

Abbaye de
St-Victor

AVENUE DE LA CORSE

BOULEVARD DE LA CORDERIE

PLACE
DE LA
CORDERIE

Jardin Puget

COURS

RUE CRINAS

RUE J RECHER

RUE SAUVEUR TOBELEM

BOULEVARD TELLENE

BOULEVARD ANDRE AUNE

BOULEVARD NOTRE DAME

RUE D'ENDOUME

Notre-Dame-de-la-Garde ✓

Marseille & Aix

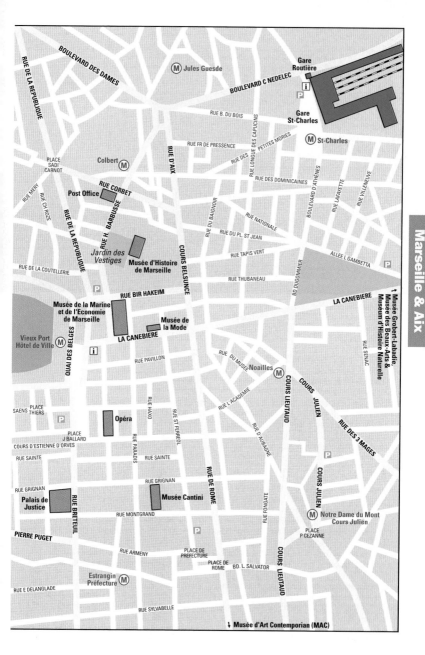

Heading out to sea past **Fort St-Jean**.

former was built in the 12th century and the latter under Louis XIV. Tellingly, their guns faced towards, rather than away from, the city: the Marseillais, whose local identity has always been at least as strong as their national one, are still proud of this display of the king's (quite justified) doubts about their allegiance.

The quai du Port, to the north, is the quieter side – the Nazis razed many of its ancient buildings in 1943, having thoughtfully given the residents 24 hours to evacuate, but the 1950s apartment blocks that replaced them, designed by architect Fernand Pouillon, look quite proud and elegant in their way. They are offset by the fine 17th-century **Hôtel de Ville**. Remains of much earlier shipping activity can be seen just near here in the **Musée des Docks Romains**, while the **Maison Diamantée** hints at the prosperous merchants' houses that stood here in the 16th century. Behind this, a staircase leads up to the ancient Le Panier district.

The quai de Rive Neuve on the opposite bank contains some of the city's hippest bars and clubs, though its busy road leading past the **Palais du Pharo**, a fancy residence built for Napoléon III, to La Corniche is faster-paced and less pedestrian-friendly. The **Théâtre de la Criée** was created from the city's old fish market in the 1970s. Behind the *quai* a thriving restaurant and café district has sprung up on place Thiers and rue d'Estienne d'Orves, around the former arsenal buildings constructed by Colbert for Louis XIV. Climb up behind to the ancient **Abbaye de St-Victor**, a

fascinating double-decker church and once one of the most powerful abbeys in the south.

A small ferry runs from Hôtel de Ville on the north side of the port to place aux Huiles on the south side from 8am to 6.30pm and costs €0.50 – don't count on it in the winter, when 'maintenance' can take months.

Running east from the Vieux Port, La Canebière (from *canèbe*, hemp in Provençal, after a rope factory once located here), the city's main drag long served as the dividing line between the 'poor' north and the 'rich' south of Marseille. Though it lost much of its glory with the decline of the French empire and is now dominated by chainstores, it still makes for an interesting walk with its 19th-century wedding-cake facades. At the Vieux Port end, across the street from the main tourist office, the Vieux Bourse with ship carvings that allude to the importance of the port now contains the **Musée de la Marine**. Nearby a modern cubic building houses the dynamic **Musée de la Mode** and a fashion-industry trade centre.

To the west of La Canebière stretches the North African neighbourhood of **Belsunce**, known for its handsome 18th-century *hôtels particuliers* (and, to wary locals, as the best place to be mugged). At the end of the Cours, the Porte d'Aix is a triumphal arch built 1825-33. The souk-like rue d'Aubagne and surrounding streets offer a vibrant experience of Marseille today, with corner-shop mosques, boutiques selling cheap fabrics and gadgets, and sweetmeats of every kind. It's minutes from the Vieux Port but so different is the mood, you might have spent the past 24 hours on a ferry.

Abbaye de St-Victor

3 rue de l'Abbaye, 7th (04.96.11.22.60). M° Vieux-Port. **Open** 9.30am-7pm daily. **Admission** €2; free under-6s.

This spectacular, fortified medieval church was built on the remains of an antique necropolis. The earlier church, founded in the fifth century by St Jean Cassian, was the city's first basilica and heart of a powerful abbey complex. Destroyed by Saracens in the 11th century, it was rebuilt and fortified in the 14th century, but chunks of the earlier church remain in a convoluted series of crypts, where ancient sarcophagi include the tomb of St Victor, ground to death between two millstones by the Romans.

Jardins des Vestiges

Centre Bourse, 1 sq Belsunce, 1st (04.91.90.42.22). M° Vieux-Port. **Open** noon-7pm Mon-Sat. **Admission** €2; €1 10-16s; free under-10s.

While the foundations for the Centre Bourse shopping centre were being dug in the 1970s, remains of Marseille's original Greek walls and a corner of the Roman port were unearthed. They're conserved here in a roofed shelter. The star feature of the adjoining Musée d'Histoire de Marseille is a remarkably well-preserved ship dating from the third century and hauled from the seabed in 1974.

Musée Cantini

19 rue Grignan, 6th (04.91.54.77.75). M° Estrangin-Préfecture. **Open** *June-Sept* 11am-6pm Tue-Sun; *Oct-May* 10am-5pm Tue-Sun. **Admission** €3; €1.50 12-18s; free under-12s.

Reopened in January 2002, this 17th-century mansion houses one of the foremost Fauvist and Surrealist art collections together with some fine post-war works. Artists include Bacon, Derain, Dubuffet, Ernst, Léger, Matisse, Picabia and Picasso.

Musée des Docks Romains

pl du Vivaux, 2nd (04.91.91.24.62). M° Vieux-Port. **Open** *June-Sept* 11am-6pm Tue-Sun; *Oct-May* 10am-5pm Tue-Sun. **Admission** €2; €1 10-18s; free under-10s.

During post-war reconstruction in 1947, the remains of a first-century Roman shipping warehouse on the edge of the Vieux Port were uncovered. This museum preserves the site intact, and documents the equipment and techniques used in maritime trade with exhibits of terracotta jars, amphorae and coins.

Musée de la Marine et de l'Economie de Marseille

Palais de la Bourse, 9 La Canebière, 1st (04.91.39.33.33). M° Vieux-Port. **Open** 8.30am-6.30pm Mon-Fri. **Admission** €2; €1 12-18s; free under-12s.

This grandiose building housing the city's Chamber of Commerce was inaugurated by Napoléon III in 1860. Medallions in the hall celebrate the ports of the world, from Liverpool to Montevideo, with which

the city was trading at the time. The museum charts the maritime history of Marseille from the 17th century with paintings, models and engravings.

Musée de la Mode de Marseille

11 La Canebière, 1st (04.91.56.59.57/ www.espacemodemediterranee.com). M° Vieux-Port. **Open** 10am-5pm Tue-Sun. **Admission** €2.74; €1.37 10-16s; free under-10s.

Marseille's fashion museum adjoining the Espace Mode Méditérranée has more than 4,000 pieces of clothing and accessories, dating mainly from 1945 onwards, displayed in original changing exhibits.

Musée du Vieux Marseille (Maison Diamantée)

rue de la Prison, 2nd (04.91.55.28.68). M° Vieux-Port. **Open** 10am-5pm Tue-Sun. **Admission** €3; €1.50 10-18s; free under-10s.

The Maison Diamantée, so named because of its diamond-faceted Renaissance façade, was built in 1570 by Pierre Gardiolle, a rich merchant. It is currently closed for renovation, but a small part remains open for an exhibition of old photographs.

Le Panier & La Joliette

Le Panier, the oldest part of the city, rising between quai du Port and grimy rue de la République, has been the traditional first stop for successive waves of immigrants and today is at the top of the tourist's itinerary. It's hard to resist the charm of its narrow, hilly streets, steep stairways and ancient, pastel-coloured houses – this could easily be Italy – but locals still think of the Panier as a dodgy area, even a bit sinister at night. Its population is gradually changing as teachers, students and arty professionals renovate flats, and chic boutiques selling pottery and soap attest to its aspirations – it remains to be seen whether Le Panier will become the Marais of Marseille. At the top is the stunning **Vieille-Charité**, built as a poorhouse but now home to two museums and a pleasant café. West of the Vieille-Charité, with an unimpeded line to God and sea were it not for the flyover roaring alongside, is the kitsch 19th-century **Cathédrale de la Major** and its predecessor **l'Ancienne Major**.

Behind Le Panier is another up-and-coming area, La Joliette. This is not so much a tourist destination as centre of the Euroméditerranée project, which intends to stimulate the city's economy. Cargo ships and a frenetic motorway make it a distinctly unpleasant place to visit, but this is supposed to change with the construction of a tunnel that will allow the motorway to be replaced with gardens.

Cathédrale de la Major

pl de Major, 2nd (04.91.90.53.57). M° Joliette. **Open** 10am-noon, 2-5.30pm daily.

Provençal People: Robert Guédiguian

Robert Guédiguian has become the cinematic biographer of working-class Marseille. Fiercely committed to his roots, this *cinéaste du quartier* has spent over 20 years making populist films about the life and strife of the small fry in the dockland suburb of L'Estaque, where he was born in 1953. Guédiguian's choice of locations is political rather than nostalgic – he was bred on the Communist and anarcho-syndicalist ancestry of the industrial labourforce. 'My films are set in Marseille, not about Marseille,' he says. Yet he returns home every time, choosing to archive the city's social evolution and use its particular cinematic 'language': 'the colour, light, matter and sea'. His universal scenarios of doom, gloom and glory, can, he claims, all be found *chez lui* – especially concerning issues of mixed race. Half-German, half-Armenian, Guédiguian confronts the issue of racial tension in films such as *À la Place du Coeur* (1998), exploring the ethnic hotchpotch that constitutes modern Massilia.

The award-winning 1997 film *Marius et Jeanette* is defiantly utopic: Jeanette, a single mother and disgruntled supermarket attendant, sacked for inappropriate use of the Tannoy, and Marius a security guard, fall in love in the abandoned cement works. It celebrates solidarity, generosity and humour.

By contrast, his latest release *La Ville est Tranquille* (2000) stirs a singularly bleak cocktail of drug abuse, prostitution, murder and the Front National to depict modern society on the point of collapse. Guédiguian's characters, though, are a feisty bunch of capitalist-bashers: 'I generally show people on the edge of an abyss, who are obviously victims but don't let themselves be victims.' Every film features the same loyal group of actors-cum-friends, including his wife, Ariane Ascaride, and childhood buddy Gérard Meylan. Often compared to Ken Loach, Guédiguian recognises his brand of realism is more stylised than documentary, as swirling classical scores, flashbacks, and voices-off soften the edge with romance: 'Things to do with the Mediterranean are generally more poetic, more allegorical and therefore less realist. I try to talk about the reality that surrounds me, but I communicate it through things that are excessive and theatricalised.'

The largest cathedral built in France since the Middle Ages, the neo-Byzantine Nouvelle Major was started in 1852 and completed in 1893 with Oriental-style cupolas and a lustrous mosaic. The 11th-century Ancienne Major, parts of which go back to Roman times, was severely hacked about to make room for its larger neighbour and is now in a bad state of disrepair so cannot be visited.

Docks de la Joliette
10 pl de la Joliette, 2nd (04.91.14.45.00). M° Joliette. **Open** 9am-7pm Mon-Sat.
This 19th-century industrial port was built to accommodate the steamships that were replacing schooners. The handsome stone warehouses that run along the waterfront for almost a mile were modelled on St Katharine's Dock in London and were state of the art when they opened in 1866. As traffic declined and cargo shifted to containers, the buildings fell into disuse and there were plans to raze them. However, they have been brilliantly renovated into office space by architect Eric Castaldi and form the centrepiece of the Euroméditerranée redevelopment project.

La Vieille-Charité
2 rue de la Charité, 2nd (04.91.14.58.80). M° Vieux-Port. **Open** *June-Sept* 11am-6pm Tue-Sun; *Oct-May* 10am-5pm Tue-Sun. **Admission** €2; €1 10-18s; free under-10s.
Built 1671-1749, as a poorhouse, this ensemble designed by Pierre and Jean Puget has beautiful open loggias on three storeys around a courtyard, which is dominated by a magnificent chapel with an

oval-shaped dome. It was renovated and reopened as a cultural complex in 1986. The former chapel houses temporary exhibitions. Around the sides are the Musée d'Archéologie Méditerranéenne and the Musée d'Arts Africains, Océaniens and Amerindiens (MAAOA). The former has a superb collection of archaeological finds from Provence and the Mediterranean, including statues and ceramics from ancient Greece, Roman glassware and bronzes, and the most important Egyptian collection in France outside Paris. The MAAOA has tribal art and artefacts from Africa, the Pacific and the Americas, including some tastefully engraved human skulls.

Longchamp & Gare St-Charles

Northwest of Belsunce is the main railway station, the **Gare St-Charles**, with its majestic staircase. In a working-class district behind the station, a former squat in a disused tobacco factory has become the **Friche de la Belle de Mai**, a thriving cultural centre.

At the far end of boulevard de Longchamp is the Palais Longchamp, a grandiose 19th-century monument with horseshoe-shaped colonnade and cascading fountains, which now holds the **Musée des Beaux-Arts** and **Muséum d'Histoire Naturelle**.

Further out in the 13th *arrondissement*, heading past the bright blue Hôtel du Département designed by British architect Will Alsopp, the Château-Gombert district is home to a 'technopole' but also to a charming little village of winding roads where property is now sought-after, as well as the delightful **Musée de Château-Gombert**.

Musée des Beaux-Arts & Muséum d'Histoire Naturelle

Palais Longchamp, bd de Longchamp, 4th.
M° Longchamp-Cinq Avenues. **Open** Musée des Beaux-Arts (04.91.14.59.30): *June-Sept* 11am-6pm Tue-Sun; *Oct-May* 10am-5pm Tue-Sun; Muséum d'Histoire Naturelle (04.91.14.59.50): 10am-5pm Tue-Sun. **Admission** Musée des Beaux-Arts €2; €1 10-18s; free under-10s; Muséum d'Histoire Naturelle €3; €1.50 10-16s; free under-10s.
No other monument expresses the ebullience of 19th-century Marseille better than the Palais Longchamp. This grandiose complex, inaugurated in 1869, was built to celebrate the completion of an 84km aqueduct bringing the diverted waters of the Durance river to the drought-prone port. A massive horseshoe-shaped classical colonnade, with a triumphal arch at its centre and museums in either wing, crowns a hill landscaped into a massive series of fountains. On the ground floor of the fine art museum are works by Marseille sculptor and architect Pierre Puget (1620-94); on the first floor is a fine collection of 16th- and 17th-century French, Italian and Flemish paintings; the second floor is devoted to French 18th- and 19th-century works, such as

Courbet's *Le Cerf à l'eau*, and old master drawings. The natural history museum has zoological and prehistoric artefacts, plus a tankful of exotic fish.

Musée de Château-Gombert

5 pl des Héros, 13th (04.91.68.14.38). M° La Rose, then no.5 bus. **Open** 9am-noon, 2-6.30pm, Mon, Wed-Fri; 2.30-6.30pm Sat, Sun. **Admission** €3.10; €1.60 6-14s; free under-6s.
Founded in 1928, the museum offers a charming insight into Provençal culture, with hand-painted 18th-century dressers, faïence, dolls and ancient kitchen gadgets such as a fig-drier.

Musée Grobert-Labadie

140 bd de Longchamp, 1st (04.91.62.21.82). M° Longchamp-Cinq-Avenues. **Open** *June-Sept* 11am-6pm Tue-Sun; *Oct-May* 10am-5pm Tue-Sun. **Admission** €2; €1 10-16s; free under-10s.
The intimate Musée Grobert-Labadie houses the private art collection of a wealthy 19th-century couple. Their 1873 mansion, scrupulously renovated, offers an intriguing glimpse of the cultivated tastes of the time, ranging from 15th- and 16th-century Italian and Flemish paintings to Fragonard and Millet, medieval tapestries and sculpture, and 17th- and 18th-century Provençal furniture and faïence.

Cours Julien, Le Prado, La Corniche & south

Stretching south of the Vieux Port, the 6th, 7th and 8th *arrondissements* are considered the chic districts of Marseille and you'll notice less of an ethnic mix among its bourgeois 19th-century residences. The city's most famous landmark, the stripy, neo-Byzantine basilica of **Notre-Dame-de-la-Garde**, rises on a peak to the south of the Vieux Port (a pleasant sign-posted climb) and offers a panoramic view of Marseille.

Perched on a hill east of the Canebière, surrounded by narrow streets, is the bohemian **Cours Julien** on the site of the former central food market (it still has a local flower market Wed and Sat morning, and organic food Fri morning). 'Cours Ju' is home to an eclectic collection of fashion boutiques, bookshops, French and ethnic restaurants (you can eat your way from Albi to Alsace, Lebanon to Lahore), cafés with broad terraces for soaking up the sun, and a number of theatres including the concert venue **Espace Julien**.

It's very different in mood to the fine 19th-century apartment blocks, strung with fine wrought iron balconies, that line rue de Rome in the area around the Préfecture. East of here, **place Castellane** with its elegant Cantini fountain (1911-13) marks the beginning of the broad avenue du Prado, which has the grace of the Champs-Elysées without the megastores or the overpriced cafés.

Past the Rond-Point du Prado is the **Stade Vélodrome**, proud home to Marseille's football team, the Olympique de Marseille. On this boulevard you can also stop in for a drink in Le Corbusier's landmark **Cité Radieuse**. Further along, on avenue de l'Haïfa, just before a gigantic bronze version of César's *Pouce* (thumb), the **Musée d'Art Contemporain** contains one of France's most important public collections of contemporary art.

The avenue du Prado ends at the **Plage du Prado** before a bold marble copy of Michelangelo's *David*. Along this broad, recreational stretch of beach, you'll see David-like windsurfers being tossed about on the waves as they brave Marseille's fearsome mistral. Facing the Plage du Prado, the 17-hectare **Parc Borély**, with its racetrack, botanical garden, lake and château, is a haven for families, joggers and *pétanque* players. The Corniche Président Kennedy, known as La Corniche, offers stunning views of the rocky coastline and the spooky Château d'If. This stretch of coast, with its series of sand and shingle beaches, shows Marseille at its most sporty and Californian, but the picturesque ports of **Pointe-Rouge** – where the **Musée de la Faïence** is housed in a fine example of the sort of château put up by wealthy burghers – **Madrague** and the tiny **Vallon des Auffes** remain typically Marseillais. 1.7km after Madrague in an apparently remote village surrounded by barren, rather forbidding outcrops, is **Les Goudes**, which actually belongs to Marseille's 8th *arrondissement*. With its small stone houses which blend into the orangy rock it attracts fishing enthusiasts, divers, hikers and holidaymakers. Seemingly far from the urban sprawl, this is a great place to feast on fresh fish or wood-fired pizza.

La Cité Radieuse

280 bd Michelet, 8th (hotel 04.91.16.78.00)
M° Rond-Point du Prado + bus 21 or 22. **Guided tours** 11am, 2.30pm daily. **Admission** €4.57 for a minimum of three people.
La Maison de Fada, or the House of the Madman, as the Marseillais once scornfully but now affectionately call Le Corbusier's 1952 reinforced-concrete apartment block, is where the architect tried out his prototype for mass housing. The vertical garden city became the model for countless urban developments. Perched on stilts, creating an impression of lightness, the complex contains 340 balconied flats that house 1,600 people, plus a floor that functions as a 'village street', with a hotel, post office, restaurant and shops. On the roof are an open-air theatre, a gym and a nursery school. The flats are mostly duplexes in which the architect designed everything down to the knobs on the kitchen cupboards. *See also p145,* **Where to Stay.**

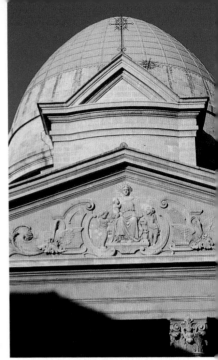

Puget's **La Vieille Charité.** *See p136.*

Musée d'Art Contemporain (MAC)

69 av d'Haïfa, 8th (04.91.25.01.07). Bus 23 or 45.
Open *June-Sept* 11am-6pm Tue-Sun; *Oct-May* 10am-5pm Tue-Sun. **Admission** €3; free under-10s.
Marseille's specialist contemporary art museum is located in a hangar-like space that opened in 1994. Its wide-ranging international collection includes Rauschenberg, César, Roth, Balkenhol, Absalon and Laffont, as well as temporary shows.

Musée de la Faïence

157 av de Montredon, 8th (04.91.72.43.47).
M° Prado + bus 19. **Open** *June-Sept* 11am-6pm Tue-Sun; *Oct-May* 10am-5pm Tue-Sun. **Admission** €2; €1 10-16s; free under-10s.
Surrounded by a magnificent park, the Château Pastre was built in the 18th century by a family that had grown rich trading with Egypt. Today it houses the Musée de la Faïence, recalling one of Marseille's main industries. However low pottery comes on your list of priorities, the beauty of these pieces may grip you, and the château itself is well worth a visit.

Notre-Dame-de-la-Garde

rue Fort du Sanctuaire, 7th (04.91.13.40.80).
Bus 60 from Vieux Port or Petit Train de la Bonne Mère. **Open** *July, Aug* 7am-8pm daily; *Sept-June* 7am-7pm daily.
Perched on a 162m-high peak, 'La Bonne Mère', topped by a massive gilded statue of the Virgin and child, is the emblem of Marseille. Building began in 1853 and was completed in 1870, while the interior

decoration continued until 1899. Deeply loved by the Marseillais, its Byzantine-style interior is filled with remarkable *ex votos*, including one for Olympique de Marseille. The mosaic floors were made in Venice, and alternating red and white marble pillars add to the richness of the surprisingly intimate chapel. Outside, the esplanade offers spectacular views.

Stade Vélodrome (Olympique de Marseille)

3 bd Michelet, 8th. M° Rond-Point du Prado. Club office 25 rue Negresco, 8th (04.91.76.56.09/ www.olympiquedemarseille.com).

Olympique de Marseille football team commands the sort of fervour that separatist movements might elsewhere. OM needed plenty of fighting spirit in 1993, when shiny saviour-president Bernard Tapie, a former socialist minister, was found to have set up OM's victory over Valenciennes using money that had been buried in a player's garden. The club has clawed its way back from disgrace with determination, thanks to a crop of new talent and French internationals such as Christophe Dugarry and Robert Pires – and Tapie has bounced back since April 2001 as 'sporting director', though in early 2002 OM was again under investigation for dodgy transfer deals. The Stade Vélodrome is the largest stadium in France after the Stade de France, with 60,000 seats. The best (€30) are in the Jean-Bouin stand. For a cheaper (€15-€23) but still relatively peaceful viewpoint, head for the Ganay stand. Tickets can be bought from the stadium on match day or in advance from L'OM Café, 3 quai des Belges, Vieux Port.

L'Estaque

The faded industrial district of L'Estaque, hugging the coast on the west of the city, looks like an unlikely place to have swayed the history of modern art, but it did. When Paul Cézanne first visited it in 1870, the little fishing village was already evolving into a working-class suburb living off its tile factories and cement works. The transition clearly intrigued him, because his most famous painting of the town, *Le Golfe de Marseille vu de L'Estaque* (now in the Art Institute of Chicago), has a factory chimney smoking in one corner. The main attraction for Cézanne (and Derain, Braque, Dufy and the others who came in their wake) – the remarkable light and profusion of different forms on the landscape – survives today. It's not easy to pick out the locations the painters immortalised, but you can take a Circuit des Peintres walking tour organised by the Marseille tourist office.

Arts & entertainment

For information on what's on, pick up weekly *L'Hebdo* (inside *La Provence*) and *Le Pavé* from kiosks, or freebies *In Situ*, *Vox* and *Ventilo*.

Cité de la Musique

4 rue Bernard Dubois, 1st (04.91.39.28.28/ www.citemusique-marseille.com). M° Colbert. **Box office** 8.30am-7pm Mon-Fri. **Shows** 8.30pm Mon-Fri. **Tickets** €9-€14. **No credit cards.**

This well-equipped, city-sponsored conservatory offers modestly priced music lessons and concerts that reflect the city's ethnic diversity.

Frac Provence-Alpes-Côtes d'Azur

1 pl Francis Chirat, 2nd (04.91.91.27.55). M° Joliette. **Open** 10am-12.30pm, 2-6pm Mon-Sat. **Admission** free.

Marseille & Aix

Top ten Little-known museums

Collection Lambert
Cutting-edge contemporary art, installations and video in Avignon. *See p88.*

Donation Suzy Solidor
Paintings by all those artists who knew Suzy in the Château Grimaldi. *See p228.*

Musée de l'Annonciade
Signac and pals in St-Tropez. *See p175.*

Musée du Fort St-Roch
The mysteries of the Maginot line in Sospel. *See p281.*

Musée de la Mode
Fabulous frocks and 20th-century fashion hits in Marseille. *See p135.*

Museon Arlaten
Arcane regional memorabilia and bizarre talismen in Arles. *See p73.*

Musée Pierre de Luxembourg
Leading lights of Papal Avignon in Villeneuve-lès-Avignon. *See p98.*

Musée de la Préhistoire
A brand new building to take you back a million years. *See chapter* **Les Gorges du Verdon.**

Palais Lascaris
Genoese palace in Nice. *See p234.*

Prieuré Notre Dame de Salagon
Ethnology and ancient plants in a lonely priory at Mane. *See p128.*

The Fonds régional d'art contemporain has a wide-ranging collection of contemporary art, from international names to young artists, exhibited, along with special commissions, here and in schools, museums and cultural centres across the PACA region.

La Friche la Belle de Mai

41 rue Jobin, 3rd (04.95.04.95.04/www.lafriche.org). Mᵒ Gare St-Charles. **Open** 2-6pm Mon-Fri. **Admission** free.

A disused tobacco factory in the scruffy Belle de Mai quarter north of the centre, La Friche started life as an artists' squat but is now home to numerous artistic, musical and theatrical groups, including the Association des Musiques Innovatrices, Massalia Théâtre des Marionnettes, and Georges Appeix's La Liseuse dance company. Its gallery is used for exhibitions put on by its resident artists and associations such as Astérides and Vidéochroniques.

Galérie Roger Pailhas

20 quai Rive Neuve, 7th (04.91.54.02.22/ www.rogerpailhas.com). Mᵒ Vieux-Port. **Open** 11am-1pm, 2-6pm Tue-Sat.

Among Marseille's commercial galleries, Pailhas has long set the agenda. Over the years Pailhas has collaborated with major international artists including Dan Graham and Daniel Buren, but he also picks out young talents such as Corinne Marchetti.

Gyptis Théâtre

136 rue Loubon, 3rd (04.91.11.00.91). Bus 31, 32, 33 or 34 from Centre Bourse. **Box office** 1-6.30pm Mon-Fri. **Tickets** €8-€19. **Credit** MC, V.

Run by two directors and actors, the Gyptis' varied programme is dedicated to giving young directors, writers and artists their first break.

Opéra Municipal

2 rue Molière, 1st (04.91.55.11.10). Mᵒ Vieux-Port. **Box office** 10am-7pm Tue-Sun. **Tickets** €8-€54. **No credit cards**.

The original Marseille opera was one of the city's great 18th-century buildings. Partially burnt down in 1919, it was rebuilt in art deco style, conserving only the original facade. Today, it is used for for both opera and the Ballet National de Marseille, directed since 1999 by Marie-Claude Pietragalla. The ballet headquarters, which also houses a Centre Chorégraphique National, is at 20 bd Gabès (04.91.32.73.27).

Théâtre National de la Criée

30 quai Rive Neuve, 7th (04.91.54.70.54). Mᵒ Vieux-Port. **Box office** 10am-6pm (in person 1-6pm) Tue-Sat. **Tickets** €10-€25. **Credit** MC, V.

This celebrated theatre was created from the former fish market in 1981. New director Jean-Louis Benoit took over the reins in January 2002 in partnership with Frédéric Bélier-Garcia.

Théâtre du Gymnase

4 rue du Théâtre-Français, 1st (04.91.24.35.35). Mᵒ Noailles. **Box office** noon-6pm Mon-Sat. **Tickets** €12-€28. **Credit** MC, V.

This beloved candy-box of a theatre dates from 1834 and was restored in 1986 with a grant from the late oil tycoon Armand Hammer, whose parents landed in Marseille after fleeing the pogroms. Directed by Dominique Bluzet, it's one of the best-attended, most innovative theatres in France, staging its own take on everything from classics to contemporary drama.

Théâtre de la Minoterie

9-11 rue d'Hozier, 2nd (04.91.90.07.94/ www.minoterie.org). Mᵒ Joliette. **Box office** 9am-1pm,

La Cité Radieuse: Le Corbusier's carefully conceived plan for urban living. *See p138.*

2-6pm Tue-Sun. **Shows** 9.02pm Tue, Fri, Sat; 7.23pm Wed, Thur. **Tickets** €1.50-€10. **No credit cards.** The experimental nature of this theatre extends to its location in an industrial zone flanking the port, and its unconventional show times. It is used by regional theatre companies and also for dance.

The quality of Marseille's restaurants has been steadily improving over the past ten years. *Bouillabaisse* – which Marseillais say can only be made authentically here – is a must for any visitor. Seek out a well-reputed restaurant such as **Le Miramar** for this dish and be prepared to pay at least €30 per person. Pizza is another speciality, thanks to immigration from Naples.

Les Arcenaulx
25 cours d'Estienne d'Orves, 1st (04.91.59.80.30). *M° Vieux-Port.* **Open** noon-2.30pm, 8-10.30pm Mon-Sat. Closed one week in Aug. **Menus** €24-€45. **Credit** AmEx, DC, MC, V.
In a restored 18th-century arsenal building that also contains a bookshop and print gallery, this charming, book-lined restaurant serves delicious and quite refined Provençal dishes, such as aubergine purée with fresh tomato and *brousse* and sea bream with a grapefruit and pistachio salsa.

Chez Michel
6 rue des Catalans, 7th (04.91.52.64.22). Bus 83. **Open** noon-2pm, 7.30-10pm. **Average** €35. **Credit** AmEx, MC, V.
A Marseille institution, Chez Michel looks out across the Anse des Catalans where the Vieux Port opens out into the Mediterranean, and is a failsafe choice for *bouillabaisse*. The fish are expertly deboned by sea-weathered waiters and served with a garlicky *rouille*. The fried squid is excellent, too, though desserts can be a let-down. The good value white Cassis (€20) is a fine fish accompaniment.

Chez Vincent
25 rue Glandèves, 1st (04.91.33.96.78). M° Vieux-Port. **Open** noon-2pm, 8-11pm Tue-Sat; 8-11pm Sun. **Average** €20. **No credit cards.**
In the mini red-light district near the Vieux Port, this old-fashioned Italian place has a clubby crowd of regulars and is popular with night owls, including singers from the nearby Opéra. Try the spaghetti with tiny clams, lasagne or one of the pizzas.

Country Life
14 rue Venture, 1st (04.96.11.28.00). M° Estrangin-Préfecture. **Open** restaurant 11.30am-2.30pm Mon-Fri; food shop 9am-6.30pm Mon-Thur, 9am-3pm Fri. **Average** €5. **Credit** AmEx, MC, V.
Formerly based in Paris, Country Life uprooted itself to open in Marseille. Though the locals have been slow to catch on to vegetarian ways, the food shop features fresh-looking produce and the cook turns out a tempting array of vegetable tarts and quiches.

L'Epuisette
Anse du Vallon des Auffes, 7th (04.91.52.17.82). *Bus 83.* **Open** noon-2pm, 7.30-10pm Tue-Fri; 7.30-10pm Sat; noon-2pm Sun. **Menus** €32-€61. **Credit** AmEx, DC, MC, V.
Dramatically located on a craggy stone finger surrounded by the Med, this excellent seafood restaurant has gorgeous views. Young Marseille native Guillaume Sourrieu is thriving here after stints with Bernard Loiseau and the Fermes de Marie in Megève. Try shellfish ravioli in a sea urchin sauce and sea bass baked in a salt crust. Excellent wine list and desserts, notably the runny chocolate tart.

L'Escale
2 bd Alexandre Delabre, Les Goudes, 13th (04.91.73.16.78). Bus 19 or 20. **Open** noon-2pm, 8-10pm daily. Closed Jan. **Menus** €20-€22. **Credit** AmEx, MC, V.
It's hard to believe that the sleepy fishing village of Les Goudes is actually part of Marseille, but it's only 20 minutes from the centre. Come to the seaside terrace for a catch of the day that doesn't get much fresher. Former fishmonger Serge Zaroukian does a delicious sauté of baby squid and perfectly cooked monkfish served with ratatouille and onion gratin. Ideal for Sunday lunch, when almost everything in town is closed – but it's very popular, so book ahead.

Des Mets de Provence Chez Maurice Brun
18 quai de Rive-Neuve, 7th (04.91.33.35.38). *M° Vieux-Port.* **Open** 8-10.30pm Mon; noon-2pm, 8-10.30pm Tue-Fri; 8-10.30pm Sat. Closed first two weeks Aug. **Menus** €49. **Credit** MC, V.
Founded in 1936, this place proudly perpetuates the traditional cuisine of Provence. There's a big *rotisserie* in the fireplace, and pretty mix-and-match table settings. There's no printed menu: the proprietor recites the daily offerings, part of a substantial, delicious prix-fixe that might include *galinette*, boned and stuffed with vegetables, or a *daube* of wild boar.

Le Miramar
12 quai du Port, 1st (04.91.91.10.40). M° Vieux-Port. **Open** noon-2pm, 7-10pm Tue-Sat. Closed two weeks Jan and three weeks Aug. **Average** €60. **Credit** AmEx, DC.
This appealing 1950s-vintage restaurant is one of the best places to sample the city's fabled *bouillabaisse*. Since *bouillabaisse* is always a two-course meal – first, the soup, and then the fish – don't order a first course. Dessert should be a palate cleanser; perhaps the fantastic raspberry and basil soufflé.

Orient Extreme
9 rue De Jean, 6th (04.91.33.54.15). M° Estrangin-Préfecture. **Open** 11.30am-2pm, 7-11pm Mon-Fri; 7-11pm Sat. Closed Aug. **Menu** €14. **No credit cards.**
The neo-Egyptian wall paintings aren't terribly alluring, but the cooking – a variety of Egyptian and Middle Eastern dishes – is authentic and copiously served. Lounge on leather pillows around the brass tray tables upstairs and try the couscous or kefta.

Le Peron

*56 Corniche JF Kennedy, 7th (04.91.52.15.22). Bus
83.* Open *noon-2.30pm, 8-10.30pm Mon-Sun.* Menus
€35-€50. Credit *AmEx, MC, V.*
Le Peron reopened in 2001 under new ownership and
has been Marseille's latest fashionable address ever
since. The dark-wood decor is sleek and modern, and
the sea view one of the very best in town. Go for original dishes such as raw oysters in a hot mushroom
soup, scallops with a purée of purple potatoes and a
peppered fig tart with ginger ice cream. Book.

Au Petit Naples

14 plage de l'Estaque, 16th (04.91.46.05.11). Bus 35.
Open *noon-2pm, 7.30-10pm Tue-Fri, Sun; 7.30-10pm
Sat. Closed Sept.* Menus €9.50-€15. No credit cards.
Some say the pizza at this beachfront restaurant is
even better than Etienne's (*see below*); fried squid is
another speciality. Portions are huge.

Pizzaria Etienne

43 rue Lorette, 2nd (no phone). M° Vieux-Port. Open
7.30-11pm Mon-Sat. Average €22. No credit cards.
A legendary Panier personality, Stéphane Cassaro
used to be known for having no menu and announc-
ing the price at the end, based on his assessment of
you. A menu is now posted outside but otherwise
little has changed and the pizzas from the wood-fired
oven are still up to Neapolitan standards. Be warned,
pizza is considered a starter here and main courses
are enormous. Pasta can be disappointingly mushy,
so go for meat, or fried squid with garlic.

Une Table au Sud

2 quai du Port, 2nd (04.91.90.63.53). M° Vieux-Port.
Open *noon-2pm, 7.30-20.30pm Tue-Sat.* Menus
€29.73-€45. Credit *AmEx, MC, V.*
After working for Alain Ducasse in Paris for eight
years, chef Lionel Lévy opened this relaxed, contemporary restaurant and has quickly won a reputation for his modern French cooking. Try dishes
such as a fricassée of squid, country ham and confit tomatoes with Espelette peppers and sesame, and
a pear with rosemary-scented *crème anglaise*.

Toinou Dégustation

*5 Cours St-Louis, 1st (04.91.33.14.94). M° Vieux-
Port.* Open *11.30am-2.30pm, 6.30-10.30pm Sun-Thur;
11.30am-2.30pm, 6.30pm-midnight Fri, Sat. Closed
Aug.* Menus €10.90-€39. Credit *MC, V.*
The best place in Marseille for raw seafood (though
the oysters are not local due to toxic seaweed). Its
shuckers have won prizes for speed, if not necessarily for precision – still, a meal here is fun, festive
and fast, and the good-value *plateau pirate* (oysters,
mussels, clams and prawns) costs just €10.

Via Mermoz

*4 rue Jean Mermoz, 8th (04.91.37.88.33).
M° Castellane.* Open *noon-2.30pm, 8-10pm Mon-Fri;
8-10pm Sat. Closed Aug.* Average €10.
Credit *AmEx, MC, V.*
Off the chic avenue du Prado, this spacious, com-
fortable restaurant boasts a convincing *trompe l'oeil*

of a Provençal facade. The friendly owner expounds
his menu with enthusiasm – the giant *steak marseillais* comes with stuffed courgette, aubergine with
tomato and a baked potato – and recommends tasty
wines, such as a La Verrerie Côtes du Luberon.

Cafés & bars

Le Bar de la Marine

*15 quai Rive Neuve, 7th (04.91.73.46.90). M° Vieux-
Port.* Open *7am-2am daily.* Credit *AmEx, V.*
Formerly frequented by sailors and fishermen, this
tiny waterfront bar has a fading but slightly raffish
air and attracts a diverse crowd. It functions as a
café by day and a bar at night, when it's popular for
a drink before heading to the nearby clubs.

La Boutique du Glacier

*1 pl Général de Gaulle, 1st (04.91.33.76.93).
M° Vieux-Port.* Open *7.45am-7.15pm Mon-Sat; 7.45
am-1pm, 3.30-7pm Sun.* Credit *MC, V.*
Enjoy the vintage 1960s turquoise tiles, frosted glass
and rattan chairs while they last – or, better yet, try
to talk the owner out of the ruthless renovation
planned for June 2002. The cakes are decadent and
ice cream and sorbets are made on the premises.

Café Parisien

1 pl Sadi Carnot, 2nd (04.91.90.05.77). M° Colbert.
Open *4.30am-11pm Mon-Wed, Sat; 4.30am-1.30am
Thur, Fri; 4.30am-1pm Sun.* Credit *MC, V.*
A beautifully renovated 1901 café with handsome
belle époque stucco mouldings and green-washed
walls. This is where the night people come when the
clubs close, for quiet breakfasts, light lunches or dinners. There are also first-rate tapas (€6.86 for a large
plate) on Thursday and Friday from 6.30 to 9pm.

La Caravelle

*34 quai du Port, 2nd (04.91.90.36.64). M° Vieux-
Port.* Open *9am-2am daily.* Credit *AmEx, MC, V.*
Hidden away up a flight of stars, La Caravelle serves
breakfast and lunch but is above all a boho (though
not cheap) cocktail bar with a piano player some
nights. A handful of tables on the narrow balcony
offer an idyllic view of the Vieux Port.

Le Crystal

*148 quai du Port, 2nd (04.91.91.57.96). M° Vieux-
Port.* Open *Apr-Aug 9am-2am daily; Sept-Mar 9am-
6pm Mon, Sun; 9am-2am Tue-Sat.* Credit *AmEx, DC,
MC, V.*
Recently renovated, this café has a 1950s-diner
appeal with red leatherette banquettes and Formica
bar, but in sunny weather the terrace will lure you
outside. Brunch is served at weekends.

M P Bar

*10 rue Beauvau, 1st (04.91.33.64.79). M° Vieux-
Port.* Open *5.30pm-dawn nighly.* Credit *DC, MC, V.*
Though its just behind the Vieux Port don't expect
rum-toting sailors at the bar. The regulars here are
young, gay scene Marseillais; midweek is quiet. The
owner also runs a sauna at 82 La Canebière.

Chez Michel: a fabled destination for fish soup. *See p141.*

O' Cours Ju

67 cours Julien, 6th (04.91.48.48.58). M° Notre-Dame-du-Mont-Cours-Julien. **Open** 6.30am-7pm Mon-Sat. **No credit cards**.

This is one of the more bohemian cafés along the Cours Julien and its small, plastic-furnished terrace attracts the biggest crowd for coffee, beer and 'Brunoschettas', toast with various toppings.

La Part des Anges

33 rue Sainte, 1st (04.91.33.55.70). M° Vieux-Port. **Open** 9am-2am Mon-Sat; 9am-1pm, 6pm-2am Sun. **Credit** AmEx, MC, V.

Georges hunts down wines from all over France and sells them by the glass or bottle. Food includes cheese, charcuterie and a few hot dishes. La Part des Anges attracts an eclectic crowd, from young trendies and arty types to ladies taking a break from plying their trade on the nearby pavement.

Plauchut

168 La Canebière, 1st (04.91.48.06.67). M° Réformés-Canebière. **Open** 7am-8pm Tue-Sun. Closed July or Aug. **Credit** MC, V.

The perfect place for Sunday breakfast, this famed yet down-to-earth pâtisserie/tea room has an art nouveau interior by Rafaël Ponson whose swirls and flourishes rival those of the towering cakes.

Web Bar

114 rue de la République, 2nd (04.96.11.65.11/ www.webbar.fr). M° Joliette. **Open** 10am-2am daily. €5 hour. **Credit** MC, V.

Nearly a carbon copy of the Paris original, this vast restaurant, concert and exhibition space has computers upstairs for surfing and a shop selling funky designer creations. A cool spot, but some Marseillais consider it 'too Parisian'.

Clubs & music venues

Most venues don't have box offices and tickets are on sale through ticket agencies. *See also* **Electrocity** *in chapter* **Arts & Entertainment**.

L'Affranchi

212 bd St Marcel, 1st (04.91.35.09.19/ www.l-affranchi.com). Bus 40. **Admission** €8. **No credit cards.**

L'Affranchi, a showcase for Marseille rap, also encourages exchanges between rap and electro.

Dock des Suds

bd de Paris, 2nd (04.91.99.00.00/08.25.83.38.33/ www.dock-des-suds.org). M° National. **Admission** €8-€22.

The 5,000m² dock hosting the Fiesta des Suds each autumn is now programming music with a world and Latin bias, all year round.

Dôme-Zénith

48 av St-Just, 4th (04.91.12.21.21/www.le-dome.com). M° St-Just-Hôtel du Département. **Admission** varies.

A big modern venue for international rock acts and stars of French *variété*.

Espace Julien

39 cours Julien, 6th (04.91.24.34.10/www.espace-julien.com). M° Notre-Dame-du-Mont-Cours-Julien. **Admission** varies.

Long standing, very active venue on the boho Cours Ju goes from international pop and blues to local electro; smaller bands and DJs play in the Café Julien.

L'Intermédiaire

63 pl Jean Jaurès, 6th (04.91.47.01.25). M° Notre-Dame-du-Mont-Cours-Julien. **Open** 7pm-2am Mon-Sat. **Admission** free. **No credit cards.**

The hippest venue in town for jazz, blues and rock (concerts 10.30pm Wed-Sat; jam session Tue) is crowded but friendly. It also has a pool table. Watch out for Gachempega, a local group that has a contemporary take on southern French music.

Le Moulin
47 bd Perrin, 13th (04.91.06.33.94). M° St Juste. **Box office** 7.30pm on day or through agencies. **Admission** €12-€21. **No credit cards**. This converted cinema has become one of Marseille's main venues for visiting French and international rock, reggae and world music bands.

The New Cancan
3 rue Senac-de-Meilhan, 1st (04.91.48.59.76). M° Réformés-Canebière. **Open** *July, Aug* 11pm-6am nighly; *Sept-June* 11pm-6am Wed-Sun. **Admission** €10.60-€13.70. **Credit** AmEx, MC, V.

Marseille's largest gay club has changed little since the 70s. Stage shows enliven the atmosphere as does the backroom. Friendly, mixed, uninhibited crowd.

La Poste à Galène
103 rue Ferrari, 5th (04.91.47.57.99). M° Notre-Dame-du-Mont-Cours-Julien. **Box office** 8.30-9.30pm on day or from agencies. **No credit cards**. Varied theme club nights and music showcases for everything from punk and reggae to electronic.

Le Trolleybus
24 quai Rive Neuve, 7th (04.91.54.30.45). M° Vieux-Port. **Open** 11pm-dawn Wed-Sat. **Admission** free Wed-Fri, Sun; €9.15 Sat. **Credit** MC, V. This sprawling club is the ground zero of Marseille nightlife. Different zones offer techno, salsa, funk… and *pétanque*. An equally heterogeneous crowd goes from young bankers to rappers in tracksuits.

In search of Monte Cristo

The **Ile d'If**, a tiny islet of sun-bleached white stone minutes from the Vieux Port, is today inhabited by salamanders and seagulls. Its two most famous residents – Edmond Dantès and Abbé Faria, the main characters of Alexandre Dumas' *The Count of Monte Cristo* – never existed. To keep Marseille under control, François 1er had a fortress built here in 1524 so formidable that it never saw combat and was eventually converted into a prison. Thousands of Protestants met grisly ends here after the Edict of Nantes was revoked in 1685. But it was Dumas who put If on the map by making it the prison from which Dantès escaped: wily administrators soon caught on and kept tourists happy by hacking out the very hole through which Edmond slid to freedom in the story.

The Château is quickly visited: there's little there aside from a few posters about its history and Alexander Dumas. So bring a picnic and enjoy the clean sea water. Off-season, the one café is likely to be closed, making for a long, cold wait between ferries.

It's easy to combine a visit to Château d'If with the **Iles de Frioul**, a collection of small islands, two of which – Ile Ratonneau and Ile Pomègues – were joined by the *digue de Berry* in the 18th century. Aside from a few holiday flats by the marina, they consist largely of windswept rock and fragrant clumps of thyme and rosemary. The islands can seem desolate in winter and wonderfully isolated in the summer, when they have beautiful beaches.

Château d'If
7 quai des Belges, 1st (04.91.59.02.30).

Open *May-Aug* 9.30am-6.30pm daily; *Sept-Apr* 9.30am-5.30pm Tue-Sun. **Admission** €4; €2.50 18-25s; free under-18s.

Ferries
GACM (04.91.55.50.09/www.answeb.net/gacm) runs five crossings a day, most of which stop at If and the Iles de Frioul. Return tickets costs €8; €4 3-6s; free under-3s for one island; €13 and €6.50 for both.

Shopping

The rue St-Ferréol in the 1st *arrondissement* is lined with shops, including **Galeries Lafayette** (No 40, 04.96.11.35.00) department store and high-fashion boutiques such as Prada. For a quirkier selection, head to the Cours St-Julien area or check out **La Thuberie**. The Centre Bourse near the Vieux Port is the main shopping centre, with a **Fnac** record shop on the second floor. The flea market on avenue du Cap-Pinède in the 15th *arrondissement* (bus 35) is well worth a visit, with antiques on Sunday (plus some Fridays and Saturdays). Marseille offers some 30 markets, the most famous of which are the fish market on quai des Belges (daily), Cours Julien (flowers Saturday and Wednesday morning, organic food Friday morning) and avenue du Prado (every morning, flowers Friday).

Ad Hoc Books
8 rue Pisançon, 1st (04.91.33.51.92). Mº Vieux-Port. **Open** 10am-7pm Mon-Sat. **Credit** MC, V.
New English-language bookshop opened in 2001 by Adrian Simmonds, who used to work at Foyles.

Arax
24 rue d'Aubagne, 1st (04.91.54.11.50). Mº Noailles. **Open** 8am-12.30pm, 3.15-7pm Mon-Sat. Closed Aug. **No credit cards**.
This fragrant cavern of a shop is an edible reflection of the city's astonishing ethnic diversity, selling everything from Black Sea anchovies and Armenian dried beef to stuffed vine leaves.

Arterra
3 rue du Petit Puits, 2nd (04.91.91.03.31). Mº Colbert. **Open** 9am-1pm, 2-6pm Mon-Sat. Closed two weeks Aug. **No credit cards**.
Santons (Christmas crib figures) can be cloying, but a visit to this workshop in the Le Panier district shows how charming they can be when dosed with a bit of artful talent. In addition to the Holy Family, there are lots of secular Provençal figurines.

Bataille
25 pl Notre-Dame-du-Mont, 6th (04.91.47.06.23/ www.g-bataille.com). Mº Notre-Dame-du-Mont-Cours-Julien. **Open** 8am-8pm Mon-Sat. **Credit** AmEx, MC, V.
The most venerable *traiteur* (deli) in Marseille is the perfect place to shop for a picnic: there's an excellent cheese counter and delectable prepared salads and cold cuts. The olive oils are wonderful, too.

Chocolatière du Panier
4 pl des 13 Cantons, 2nd (04.91.91.67.66). Mº Joliette. **Open** 9.30am-1pm, 2.30-7.30pm Tue-Sat. **No credit cards**.
The rotund Michèle Leray proudly displays a photo of Jacques Chirac's visit to her shop. Her reputation is based on high-quality dark chocolate studded with fruits which are candied on the premises.

Compagnie de Provence
1 rue Caisserie, 2nd (04.91.56.20.94). Mº Vieux-Port. **Open** 10am-1pm, 2-7pm Mon-Sat. **Credit** MC, V.
This is the place to come for cubes of *savon de Marseille*. The classic is non-perfumed olive-oil green, but vanilla, jasmine and honey are also available.

Daniel Antoine
91 rue d'Aubagne, 1st (04.91.55.50.80). Mº Notre-Dame-du-Mont-Cours-Julien. **Open** 10am-7pm Tue-Sat. **Credit** AmEx, DC, MC, V.
Showcasing local designers, this shop sells furniture, lamps, mirrors and clocks that range from whimsical to downright kitsch.

Four des Navettes
136 rue Sainte, 7th (04.91.33.32.12). Mº Vieux-Port. **Open** 7am-8pm Mon-Sat; 9am-1pm, 3-5.30pm Sun. **Credit** MC, V.
Founded in 1781, this bakery is famous for its boat-shaped *navettes*, orange-scented biscuits that are modelled on the tiny boat in which Mary Magdalene and Lazarus supposedly arrived on French shores.

Madame Zaza de Marseille
74 cours Julien, 6th (04.91.48.05.57). Mº Notre-Dame-du-Mont-Cours-Julien. **Open** 10am-1pm, 2-7pm Mon-Fri; 10am-7pm Sat. **Credit** AmEx, MC, V.
Fashion and costume jewellery with a baroque, boho edge. Expect flowing velvet coats and rich colours.

Manon Martin
10 rue de la Tour, 1st (04.91.55.60.95). Mº Vieux-Port. **Open** 10am-7pm Mon-Sat . **Credit** MC, V.
This pedestrianised street near the Vieux Port has become something of a focus for local creators, led by the flamboyant hat stylist Manon Martin.

Pâtisserie d'Aix
2 rue d'Aix/1 rue Nationale, 1st (04.91.90.12.50). Mº Colbert. **Open** 5am-8pm daily. **No credit cards**.
This famous Tunisian pastry shop in the Belsunce district is stacked high with pyramids of honey-drenched delights, as well as traditional breads.

La Thuberie
14-16 rue Thubaneau, 1st (04.91.90.84.55). Mº Colbert. **Open** 10.30am-7pm Tue-Sat. Closed Aug. **No credit cards**.
This hip boutique is a sign of the reviving fortunes of the Belsunce area. Run by designer Linda Cohen, it's a showcase for local fashion talent – look for Tectus and Benoît Missolin designs – plus housewares.

Where to stay

Bonneveine Youth Hostel
impasse du Dr Bonfils, 8th (04.91.17.63.30/ www.multimania.com/ajmb). Mº Rond-Pont-du-Prado + bus 44. Closed mid-Dec to Feb. **Rates** €11.10-€13.60 per person. **Credit** Dc, MC, V.
Just 200m from the sea and very near the Calanques, this comfortable youth hostel is a good bet if you're looking for a holiday in nature.

Hôtel Alizé

35 quai des Belges, 1st (04.91.33 66 97). M° Vieux-Port. **Double** €58 (without view)-€71 (with view). **Credit** AmEx, DC, MC, V.
Ignore the charmless decor and admire the view from one of the 16 rooms (of 39) that face the Vieux Port. A good choice for business travel on a budget.

Etap Hôtel Vieux Port

46 rue Sainte, 1st (04.91.54.73.73). M° Vieux-Port. **Double** €41.25. **Credit** AmEx, MC, V.
The facade of this old arsenal building is gorgeous, even if the rooms feel a bit like prison cells. Still, you can't beat the location or the price.

Hôtel Hermès

2 rue Bonnetière, 2nd (04.96.11.63.63/ www.hotelmarseille.com). M° Vieux-Port. **Double** €60-€71. **Credit** MC, V.
Though its rooms are small, this simple hotel just steps from the Vieux Port is good value. Several rooms on the top floor have small terraces with superb views of the harbour and Notre-Dame-de-la-Garde. There's a top-floor sundeck, too.

Hôtel Le Corbusier

280 bd Michelet, 8th (04.91.16.78.00). M° Rond-Point du Prado + bus 21 or 22. **Double** €45. **Credit** MC, V.
Though rooms veer more towards the cheap than the cheerful, Le Corbusier fans won't want to pass up the opportunity to spend a night at this hotel in the Modernist architect's famous Cité Radieuse.

Mercure Beauvau Vieux Port

4 rue Beauvau, 1st (04.91.54.91.00/ www.mercure.com). M° Vieux-Port. **Double** €101-€120. **Credit** AmEx, DC, MC, V.
This historic hotel, where Chopin and George Sand once stayed, overlooks the Vieux Port. Public rooms have Louis Philippe and Napoléon III-style furniture; bedrooms are done up in Provençal prints.

Mercure Prado

11 av de Mazargues, 8th (04.96.20.27.37/ www.mercure.com). M° Rond-Pont-du-Prado. **Double** €84-€102. **Credit** AmEx, DC, MC, V.
Opened in 2000, the Mercure Prado has a vibrant postmodern design with furniture by Marc Newson, Ingo Maurer and Philippe Starck. The rooms have all swish comforts, including Internet access on request. A good choice for business travel, yet within walking distance of the beach and Parc Borély.

Mersea Yachts

21 rue de la Loge, 2nd (04.91.90.10.81/www.mersea-yacht.com). M° Vieux-Port. **Rates** from €76. **Credit** AmEx, MC, V.
For a unique view of Marseille, ask Gilles Olivier to reserve a cabin for you in one of the boats moored on the Vieux Port. A spacious 14-metre yacht with kitchen, bathroom and sun deck costs €114 per night in high season. You will need a little time to understand the workings of your temporary home – including what to do if it starts to sink.

Hôtel Péron

119 Corniche JF Kennedy, 7th (04.91.31.01.41). Bus 83. **Double** €47-€53. **Credit** AmEx, MC, V.
This eccentric family-run hotel is a study in kitsch – Moorish, Oriental, Dutch and Breton rooms were decorated in the 1960s when it was the first hotel in Marseille to install baths – which are tiny yet charming. Most rooms have stunning sea views.

Le Petit Nice

anse de Maldormé, Corniche JF Kennedy, 7th (04.91.59.25.92/www.petitnice-passedat.com). Bus 83. Closed three weeks in Nov. **Double** €177-€420. **Credit** AmEx, DC, MC, V.
A luxurious villa with 13 rooms and a swimming pool, the Petit Nice is the address of choice for visiting stars. Though the marine setting is splendid, the restaurant has its ups and downs.

Hôtel Résidence du Vieux Port

18 quai du Port, 2nd (04.91.91.91.22/ www.hotelmarseille.com). M° Vieux-Port. **Double** €100-€115. **Credit** AmEx, DC, MC, V.
This 1950s building features antique furniture, balconies (except on the second floor, which is to be avoided) and unbeatable views from every room across the Vieux Port to Notre-Dame-de-la-Garde. Unless you have a penchant for floral wallpaper, the Provençal rooms are not worth the extra money.

Hôtel Le Rhul

269 Corniche JF Kennedy, 7th (04.91.52.01.77/ www.bouillabaissemarseille.com). Bus 83. **Double** €76.30. **Credit** AmEx, MC, V.
Though it doesn't have the character of Le Peron, the slightly pricier Le Rhul has the advantage of spacious terraces with jaw-dropping sea views (ask for one when you book), and a restaurant renowned for its *bouillabaisse*. It has its share of history, too – the Rolling Stones stayed here in their early days.

Essentials

Getting there

From the airport

Aéroport CCI Marseille-Provence (04.42.14.14.14) is 25km north-west of the city in Marignane. GTRPA (04.42.14.31.27) runs buses every 20 mins 6.30am-9.50pm to the Gare St-Charles; from the station to the airport 6.30am- 8.50pm. The trip takes 25 mins and costs €8. A taxi to the Vieux Port costs around €37.

By car

Marseille is served by three major autoroutes: A51-A7 heads north to the airport, Aix and Lyon. The A55 runs west to the airport. The A50 runs east to Toulon and Nice. The Prado-Carenage tunnel (€1.40 toll) links the A55 to A50 avoiding city streets.

By train

The main station is the Gare St-Charles on the TGV line, with frequent trains from Paris, and main coast route east to Nice and Menton, and west via Miramas and Arles, as well as branch lines to Miramas via Martigues and the Côte Bleu, and to Aix and Gap. In the station, SOS Voyageurs (04.93.82.62.13, open 9am-noon, 3-6pm Mon-Fri) helps with stolen or lost luggage, missed trains, children and the elderly.

By bus
The *gare routière* is on 3 pl Victor Hugo, 3rd, Mᵒ St-Charles, 04.91.08.16.40). **Cartreize** (08.00.19.94.13/www.lepilote.com) is the umbrella organisation for all bus services in the Bouches du Rhône. **Phocéens Cars** (04.91.50.57.68) operates long-distance buses between Marseille and Avignon, Nice via Aix-en-Provence and daily coaches to Venice, Milan and Rome, Barcelona and Valencia.

By boat
SNCM (61 bd des Dames, 2nd, Mᵒ Joliette) is the primary passenger line from the Gare Maritime de la Joliette; call 08.36.67.95.00 for Sardinia, Corsica or Italy; 08.36.67.21.00 for Algeria, Tunisia or Morocco.

Getting around

By bus & Métro
RTM (04.91.19.55.55 or infoline 04.91.91.92.10) runs a comprehensive system of 81 bus lines, as well as the city's two Métro lines (5am-9pm) and a tram. The same tickets are used on all three and can be bought in Métro stations, on the bus, at *tabacs* and newsagents. An individual ticket costs €1.37 and entitles the user to one hour's travel. A one-day ticket is €3.81, weekly pass €8.84, monthly pass €42.69.

By taxi
There are cab ranks on most main squares or you can call a cab: Eurotaxi (04.91.97.12.12), Marseille Taxi (04.91.02.20.20), Radio Taxi (04.91.05.80.80),

Taxi Plus (04.91.03.60.03) or Taxi Radio Tupp (04.91.05.80.80). The pick-up fare is €1.70, then €1.48/km during the day, €1.55/km at night.

Tourist information

For **Internet access** try the Info-Café (1 quai Rive-Neuve, 1st, 04.91.33.74.98/www.info-cafe.com) or the **Web Bar** (*see p143*).

Marseille Office du Tourisme
4 La Canebière, 1st (04.91.13.89.00/www.destination-marseille.com). Mᵒ Vieux-Port.
Open *July-Sept* 9am-7.30pm Mon-Sat; 10am-6pm Sun; *Oct-June* 9am-7pm Mon-Sat; 10am-5pm Sun. **Branch:** Gare St-Charles, 1st (04.91.50.59.18). **Open** *June-Sept* 9am-6pm Mon-Sat; *Oct-May* 10am-1pm, 1.30-5pm Mon-Fri.

Post office
rue Henri Barbusse, 1st (04.91.15.47.00). Mᵒ Colbert. **Open** 8am-6.30pm Mon-Fri, 8-11.30am Sat.

Around Marseille

Martigues & the Côte Bleue

Beyond L'Estaque towards Carro is the rather neglected Côte Bleue, much loved by Marseillais at weekends with its share of impressive cliffs, small fishing ports and beaches. For once this is an area as easy to reach by train as by car: while the D5 meanders between inlets and over the red hills of the Chaine de l'Estaque, still

Canal-side **Martigues** still looks more fishing village than petrochemicals.

scarred from recent fires, the railway chugs scenically over a series of viaducts along the coast between Marseille and Martigues. Tiny coves like **Niolon** and **La Madrague de Lignac** give stunning views of the Marseille cityscape across the bay. The main resorts are **Sausset-les-Pins** and **Carry-le-Rouet**, with its crowded beach. **Carro** has a picturesque fishing port and is a favourite with windsurfers.

Inland, **Martigues** is a pretty little town of pastel houses built along canals, on the edge of the heavily industrialised – and polluted – Etang de Berre, a lagoon that is surrounded by one of the largest petrochemical and oil refining complexes in Europe. Martigues is the result of a fusion of three villages: Jonquières, Ferrières and the Ile Brescon, linked by a series of spectacular bridges. In Jonquières, the chief sight is the small but wildly colourful Baroque **Chapelle de l'Annociation**, built 1664-71, which adjoins the church of St-Genies. On the Ile Brescon, the **Eglise de la Madeleine** is another fine Baroque edifice with ornately carved facade. Over in Ferrières, the modern **Théâtre des Salins** contrasts with colour-washed fishermen's cottages, while the **Musée Ziem**, housed in a former customs house, contains works by artists who painted in the region, including Félix Ziem, Manguin and Dufy, as well as the statue of St-Pierre, patron saint of fishermen, which is paraded from here to the port for the Fête de St-Pierre every June.

Musée Ziem

bd du 14 Juillet (04.42.41.39.60). **Open** *July, Aug* 10am-12.30pm, 2.30-6.30pm Wed-Mon; *Sept-June* 2.30-6.30pm Wed-Sun. **Admission** free.

Where to eat

In Sausset-les-Pins, locals delight in the imaginative cooking – red mullet salad with mint, monkfish with mangoes – of Joëlle Boudara at **Les Girelles** (rue Fréderic Mistral, 04.42.45.26.16, closed Mon dinner in July & Aug, all Mon & dinner Sun Sept-June and all Jan, menus €21-€50). In Carro, friendly, family-oriented **Le Chalut** (port de Carro, 04.42.80.70.61, closed dinner Mon, all Tue, menus €15-€25) specialises in fish and seafood. In Martigues, try the *poutargue*, a delicacy of dried, pressed and salted fish eggs, at **Le Miroir** (4 rue Marcel Galdy, 04.42.80.50.45, closed Mon, lunch Sat, dinner Sun, two weeks Dec, two weeks Apr, menus €13.42-€28.20). Sausset is an easy excursion from Aix or Marseille, but if you want to stay over the **Hôtel Cigalon** (35 bd du 14 juillet, 04.42.80.49.16/ www.lecigalon.fr, double €34-€54) is a cheerfully painted, simple hotel.

Tourist information

Martigues Office du Tourisme

2 quai Pierre Doumer, 13500 Martigues (04.42.42.31.10). **Open** *Easter to mid-Sept* 9am-7pm Mon-Sat; 10am-noon Sun; *mid-Sept to Easter* 8.45am-6.30pm Mon-Sat.

Aubagne

Aubagne, 17km east of Marseille, is a busy commercial centre, but its *vieille ville* is pleasant and dotted with tree-lined squares with a market on Tuesday and Sunday. Writer and filmmaker Marcel Pagnol was born here in 1895 and the shop facades have retained (or recreated) a nostalgic, Pagnol-like feel. Aubagne tourist office organises a day-long 9km hiking tour (one donkey for every five people), which covers Pagnol's 'childhood memories' (in French). It can also provide directions for the Circuit Pagnol, for which you'll need your own wheels to reach sites such as the village of La Treille, which appears in *Jean de Florette* and *Manon des Sources*, and is where the writer is buried. Aubagne is renowned for its ceramics industry, with a dozen *santon* workshops in town and the biennial **Argilla** ceramics fair and pottery market (next in 2003). Aubagne's other claim to fame is as the home of the French Foreign Legion. The **Musée de la Légion Etrangère** pays homage to this legendary military fraternity with displays of medals, weaponry, uniforms and photographs.

Musée de la Légion Etrangère

Caserme Vienot, west of Aubagne on D44 (04.42.18.82.41). **Open** *June-Sept* 10am-noon, 3-7pm Tue-Sun (closed Fri pm); *Oct-May* 10am-noon, 2-6pm Wed, Sat, Sun. **Admission** free.

Where to eat

La Farandole (6 rue Martino, 04.42.03.26.36, closed dinner Mon, all Sun and two weeks in Feb, menus €14.50-€22.50) serves delicious Provençal cooking. With its warm decor and blue-and-white painted bowls, the Tunisian restaurant **La Goulette** (8 bd Jean Jaurès, 01.42.03.44.59, closed Mon, Tue and dinner Wed & Sun, menu €10) is a local favourite. The meatballs served with couscous are especially succulent. Step into the snack shop next door for a crunchy, honey-soaked pastry.

Tourist information

Aubagne Maison du Tourisme

av Antide Boyer, 13400 Aubagne (04.42.03.49.98/ www.aubagne.com). **Open** 9am-12.30pm, 2.30-6pm daily.

Aix-en-Provence

The Romans established it, the 18th-century embellished it. As elegant as ever, Aix is the apotheosis of southern café society.

Aix, the intellectual and elegant, is the eternal rival of rough diamond Marseille. It's not that it doesn't have its share of housing estates around the edges, but the overall impression is one of golden stone buildings, sophisticated cafés and tinkling fountains: for Aix's origins as a restful place to take the waters go back to Roman times. Aquae Sextiae was founded in 122BC by Roman consul Sextius after he had defeated the Celto-Ligurian *oppidium* at Entremont, the remains of which lie just outside the city. Aix declined with the Roman empire but remained important enough to see its first cathedral in the fifth century.

In the 12th and 13th centuries, the independent Counts of Provence held court in Aix, but it was in the 15th century that the city saw a true resurgence. In 1409, the university was founded by Louis II of Anjou, and under Good King René (1409-80), poet and patron of the arts, the city flourished and the court drew artists like Nicolas Froment and Barthélémy

van Eyck. After its absorption into France in 1486, Aix became the capital of the *parlement* of Provence – the southern arm of the country's strongly centralised administration. Aix boomed again in the 1600s, when the newly prosperous political and merchant class began building elegant townhouses in the Quartier Mazarin, to the south of the *vieille ville*, virtually doubling the city's size. A ring of boulevards, the *cours*, came to replace the ramparts.

Aix elected the radical, and hypnotically ugly, Comte de Mirabeau as *député* to the *Etats généraux* in 1789. A brilliant orator, he played an important role in the early days of the Revolution. In the 19th century, bypassed by the main railway line, Aix lost out in terms of trade to Marseille, but remained an important university and legal city.

Aix has expanded even more rapidly in the past 20 years, as new housing, business and university districts have swallowed up rural villages and the grandiose agricultural *bastides* built by the nobility outside the city. Aix is home to France's biggest appeal court outside Paris, numerous research institutes and a high-tech industry pole that rivals Sophia Antipolis.

Despite a reputation as the haughty bastion of the bourgeoisie, and its highbrow Festival International d'Art Lyrique every summer, Aix is a surprisingly young city, with some 40,000 students and a thriving café society.

The heart of Aix in every sense is the busy, café-filled **Cours Mirabeau**.

Sightseeing

Vieil Aix

At the heart of the city is the **cours Mirabeau**, laid out in 1649 as a broad carriageway on the trace of the old ramparts and a favoured spot for local nobility to construct their mansions. Nowadays it is mainly cafés down the sunny side (odd numbers), banks and businesses in the shade (even) but, at No 53, the legendary Deux Garçons still plays out its role as artistic and intellectual meeting place. There are three fountains on the Cours itself: the *Fontaine des neufs canons*, the *Fontaine d'eau chaude*, a mossy lump bubbling out water at 34°C, and the *Fontaine du Roi René*, with a statue of the wine-loving king holding a bunch of grapes. At one end is place Charles de Gaulle, better

known as **La Rotonde**, marked by a grandiose
19th-century fountain in black and white
marble. North of cours Mirabeau lies Vieil Aix,
a remarkably well-preserved maze where
elegant squares and smart mansions alternate
with more secretive, winding *ruelles*. Fountains
splash in almost every square, statues peer out
of niches on street corners and the whole place
is buzzing with small bistros, cafés and shops.

Parallel to cours Mirabeau runs rue Espariat,
where the Baroque church of **St-Esprit** and the
bell tower of a former Augustinian monastery
nestle amid cafés and shops. Take a detour up
the narrow rue Bédarrides to the bistros on
place Ramus or continue north along rue
Espariat into rue Fabrot, home to the smartest
designer clothes boutiques in Aix. To get there

you cross the glorious, cobbled **place
d'Albertas**, a U-shape of uniform classical
facades with Corinthian pilasters. Almost
opposite is the elegant 1672 Hôtel Boyer
d'Eguilles, now part pharmacy, part school and
part **Muséum d'Histoire Naturelle**.

Busy shopping streets rue Aude and rue
Maréchal Foch lead to **place Richelme**, which
has a daily fruit and vegetable market. The
door of the late 17th-century Hôtel Arbaud (7
rue Maréchal Foch) is framed by two muscular
male slaves. In beautiful **place de l'Hôtel de
Ville**, the Gothic belfry with astrological clock
and rotating figures of the seasons was a
former town gateway. The **post office** next
door to the Hôtel de Ville occupies a
magnificent 18th-century former grain market,

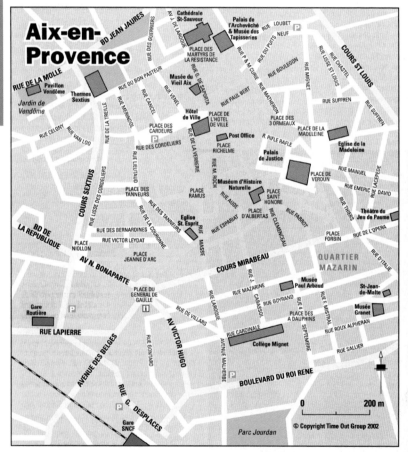

whose pediment, an allegory of the Durance and Rhône rivers, is given a wonderful spark of life by a leg dangling lasciviously out of the frame.

Running north from Hôtel de Ville, rue Gaston de Saporta contains some of Aix's finest *hôtels particuliers*: Hôtel Etienne de St-Jean (No.17) contains the **Musée du Vieil Aix**; Hôtel de Châteaurenard (No.19) has a staircase painted with *trompe l'oeil* by Daret (it houses the city's social services, but you can visit the entrance hall); Hôtel Maynier d'Oppedé (No.23), with a fine 1757 facade, belongs to the university. The street leads into the historic core of the university with the former law faculty, now the Institut des Etudes Politiques. Opposite is the **Cathédrale St-Sauveur**, with its sculpted portals and fortified towers. Next door, the Baroque Palais de l'Archevêché contains the **Musée des Tapisseries** and hosts Festival productions in the courtyard.

West of the town hall, long place des Cardeurs is lined with ethnic restaurants. Underground car park aside, it looks as ancient as any of the other squares in Aix but, in fact, was created only in the 1960s, when the old Jewish quarter was demolished. From here, narrow streets lead to the **Thermes Sextius** (the thermal baths), a last surviving fortified tower and, on rue des Etuves, some fragments of medieval city wall as well as the last surviving tower on boulevard Jean Jaurès. Just west of the baths, the **Pavillon Vendôme** still stands in its formal gardens.

South-east of the town hall, the colonnaded mass of the **Palais de Justice** was built in the 1820s on the site of the former Comtal palace. In front, place de Verdun fills with bric-a-brac and book stalls on Tuesday, Thursday and Saturday mornings. Place des Prêcheurs, the first square in Aix, and place de la Madeleine resound to the city's main food market on the same days, with a flower market on other days, in the shadow of the neo-classical **Eglise de la Madeleine**. Further east from the Palais de Justice lies the Villeneuve *quartier*, which replaced the royal gardens in the late 16th century. Several ornate *hôtels particuliers* remain on rue Emeric David and rue de l'Opéra. Cézanne was born at No.25; at No.17 is the **Jeu du Paume**, a real tennis court built in 1660 and transformed into a theatre a century later.

Cathédrale St-Sauveur

pl de l'Université (04.42.21.10.51). **Open** 7.30am-noon, 2-6pm daily (except during services); *cloister* 9.30-11am, 2.30-4.30pm Mon-Sat. **Admission** free.

Aix cathedral is a hotchpotch of Romanesque, Gothic, Renaissance and Baroque, reflecting its long on-off construction from the fifth to 18th centuries. At first sight the interior looks unremarkable, but it has two jewels. The first is off the right-hand

nave: a polygonal, fifth-century Merovingian baptistry, with crisply carved capitals and traces of frescoes (the hole in the ground is a throwback to the days of total immersion baptism). The second is in the central nave: Nicolas Froment's symbolically loaded 15th-century triptych of *Mary in the Burning Bus*h, with King René and Queen Jeanne praying in the wings. At the end of the left nave, the 17th-century Corpus Domini chapel has a fine wrought-iron grille and a painting by Jean Daret.

Eglise de la Madeleine

pl des Prêcheurs (04.42.38.02.81). **Open** 8-11.30am, 3-5.30pm daily. **Admission** free.

This former Dominican convent was rebuilt in the 1690s in the Baroque style. A neo-classical facade, busy with swags and garlands, was added in the 19th century. Inside there are several Baroque altarpieces by Carlos Van Loo and an *Annunciation* (1444) attributed to Flemish painter Barthélémy van Eyck. Regularly used for classical concerts.

Hôtel de Ville

pl de l'Hôtel de Ville (04.42.91.90.00). **Open** *Salle des Etats de Provences* 10am-noon, 3-4.30pm Mon-Fri. **Admission** free.

The town hall was built between 1655 and 1678 by Pierre Pavillon. A wrought-iron gateway leads into an elegant cobbled courtyard. At the back, a double stairway leads up to the Salle des Etats de Provences, the regional assembly room where taxes were voted, hung with portraits and mythological subjects.

Muséum d'Histoire Naturelle

6 rue Espariat (04.42.26.23.67). **Open** 10am-noon, 1-5pm daily. **Admission** €2; free under-15s.

Mineralogy and palaeontology collections, including hundreds of dinosaur eggs discovered on the Montagne Ste-Victoire, in a fine 17th-century *hôtel*.

Musée des Tapisseries

pl des Martyrs de la Résistance (04.42.23.09.91). **Open** 10am-noon, 2-5.30pm Mon, Wed-Sun. **Admission** €2; free under-25s.

On the first floor of the former bishop's palace, the tapestry museum houses a collection of 17th- and 18th-century tapestries discovered here in the 19th century. There's a particularly lively series of scenes from *Don Quixote*, made at Beauvais 1735-44, and costumes and sets from opera productions. Temporary exhibitions feature contemporary textiles.

Musée du Vieil Aix

17 rue Gaston de Saporta (04.42.21.43.55). **Open** *Apr-Sept* 10am-noon, 2.30-6pm Tue-Sun; *Oct-Mar* 10am-noon, 2.30-5pm Tue-Sun. **Admission** €4; free under-14s.

This small but worthwhile collection focuses on folk art, with *santons* (Christmas crib figures), some fine lacquered furniture and faïence. Two folding wooden screens and a fragile line of mechanical puppets depict the *Fête-Dieu* (Corpus Christi) procession that was a feature of Aix life every June until the beginning of the 20th century.

Pavillon Vendôme

32 rue Célony (04.42.21.05.78). **Open** 10am-noon, 2-5.30pm Mon, Wed-Sun. **Admission** €2; free under-25s.
This perfect pleasure dome was built by the aptly named Pierre Pavillon for the Duc de Vendôme in 1665, following Doric, Ionic and Corinthian orders. Giant fruit-laden Atlantes hold up the balcony and the interior is adorned with 18th-century furniture.

Thermes Sextius

55 cours Sextius (08.00.63.96.99/www.thermes-sextius.com). **Open** 8.30am-7.30pm Mon-Fri; 8.30am-1.30pm, 2.30-6.30pm Sat.
Behind a wrought-iron grille and classical facade, the Thermes now house the glass and marble pyramids of an ultra-modern health spa. You can wander in and look at the small fountain, which still marks the original warm spring of the 18th-century establishment. To the right of the entrance are the remains of first-century BC Roman baths.

Quartier Mazarin

Laid out on a strict grid plan in 1646, the Quartier Mazarin was conceived as a speculative venture and sold off in lots masterminded by Mazarin, Archbishop of Aix and brother of Cardinal Mazarin. It gradually became the aristocratic district. There are few shops or restaurants, other than some classy *antiquaires* and select designer fashion names, but plenty of fine doorways, balustrades and wrought-iron balconies. The fitfully interesting **Musée Paul Arbaud** lies on rue du 4 Septembre, the area's main thoroughfare, which leads into **place des Quatre Dauphins**, with a Baroque fountain. On the square, at the rear of an arcaded courtyard, is the beautiful 1650 Hôtel de Boisgelin, while nearby, on rue Cardinale, is the **Collège Mignet** (formerly Bourbon), where Cézanne and Zola went to school. At the far end of rue Cardinale stands the **Eglise St-Jean-de-Malte**, built by the Knights of Malta (note the Maltese cross on the fountain in front) at the end of the 13th century, one of the earliest Gothic structures in Provence and once the burial place of the Counts of Provence. Beside the church, the **Musée Granet** in the Commanderie of the Knights of Malta houses the city's fine art and archaeology collections.

Musée Granet

pl St Jean de Malte (04.42.38.14.70). **Open** 10am-noon, 2-6pm Mon, Wed-Sun. **Admission** €2; free under-25s.
An ambitious expansion project should eventually quadruple the exhibition area here. At the time of writing, though, there was disappointingly little to see; an important collection of 17th-century Provençal painters and Flemish masters is not on show. Upstairs, there is a room with several small Cézannes and works by the museum's founder, the

now obscure François Granet. Granet's donations also include Ingres' huge *Jupiter et Thétis*. The archaeological collection is in the basement.

Musée Paul Arbaud

2a rue du 4 Septembre (04.42.38.38.95). **Open** 2-5pm Mon-Sat. **Admission** €2.50; free under-10s.
Old masters from the Mirabeau family hang amid fine pieces of Marseille and Moustiers faïence and manuscripts collected by scholar Paul Arbaud.

Further out

Circling the old town, the busy peripheral boulevards follow the former ramparts. Beyond here lies 'new Aix', a post-war sprawl, which includes the Quartier Sextius Mirabeau, home to the dynamic **Cité du Livre**. It is still dotted with former country villas and *bastides*, such as the Pavillon Lenfant (now part of the University of Aix), **Château de la Pioline**, now a hotel (*see p157*), and Jas de Bouffon, a country residence bought by Cézanne's father in 1859. The latter has given its name to a redevelopment zone that incorporates the 70s **Fondation Vasarely** (2km west of centre by the A8/A51). Nearby at **Les Milles** is the brick factory that was used as a prison camp and is now a memorial to its victims (*see p154*, **The Writing on the Wall**). Further south, beneath the perched village of Bouc-Bel-Air, the **Jardins d'Albertas**, terraced, 18th-century formal gardens with extravagant fountains, are a testimony to the power of the Albertas family.

North of Vieil Aix, past the pyramidal Mausoleum of Joseph Sec – a rare example of Revolutionary architecture dating from 1792 – a steep hill climbs to the Lauves where Cézanne built his last studio, the **Atelier Cézanne**. The remains of the Celto-Ligurian Oppidium d'Entremont, site of Sextius' victory in the second century AD, are just north-west of the city.

Atelier Cézanne

9 av Paul Cézanne (04.42.21.06.53). **Open** *Apr, May* 10am-noon, 2.30-6pm daily; *June-Sept* 10am-6pm daily; *Oct-Mar* 10am-noon, 2.30-5pm daily. **Admission** €5.50; free under-16s.
Cézanne built this studio in 1902, and worked here until his death in 1906. Then outside the town with views of the rocky ravines of the Montagne Ste-Victoire, it now overlooks post-war housing developments. The first-floor studio is a masterpiece of artistic clutter, with Cézanne's easels and palettes and many of the props – fruit, vases, a broken cherub statue – that are familiar from his still lifes. To reach the Atelier, take bus no.1 from La Rotonde.

Atlantes hold up the balcony of the 17th-century pleasure dome **Pavillon Vendôme.**

Fondation Vasarely

1 av Marcel Pagnol, Jas de Bouffan (04.42.20.01.09).
Open 10am-1pm, 2-6pm Mon-Fri; 10am-6pm Sat,
Sun. **Admission** €6.10; €3.90 7-18s; free under-7s.
Here, Hungarian-born abstract artist Victor Vasarely (1906-97), put his theories of geometrical abstraction and kinetic art into practice on an architectural scale. The building itself is composed of hexagonal structures of black and white squares and circles that reflect off water. Within the building, the hexagonal volumes are hung with large-scale paintings, tapestries and reliefs reflecting different periods of his work. Even if Vasarely's kinetic art seems strangely out of sync with contemporary art concerns, it remains an interesting 70s timewarp.

Jardins d'Albertas

N8, Bouc-Bel-Air (04.42.22.29.77). **Open** *May, Sept,
Oct* 2-6pm Sat, Sun; *June-Aug* 3-7pm daily.
Admission €3.50; €2.50 7-16s; free under-7s.
Jean-Baptiste Albertas, president of the Cour des Comptes, dreamed of constructing a lavish rural retreat, but he was assassinated on 14 July 1790, the château was never built and only the gardens, laid out with terraces and pools containing water-gushing sea beasts, were ever completed.

Oppidium d'Entremont

*2km north-west of centre via av Solari (D14)
(04.42.21.97.33). Bus 21.* **Open** 9am-noon, 2-6pm
Mon, Wed-Sun. **Admission** free.
This Celto-Ligurian hilltop settlement developed around the second century BC and was destroyed by Romans in the second century AD at the request of the land-hungry Marseillais. Excavated sections of wall reveal a residential zone, plus traces of shops, warehouses and workshops. Archaeological finds from the site are in the **Musée Granet**.

Arts & entertainment

Pick up *Le Mois à Aix*, a monthly listings magazine published by the tourist office (also on **www.aix-en-provence.com**), and regional freebie weekly *César*, distributed in hotels and some restaurants.

3BisF

*Hôpital Montperrin, 109 av du Petit Barthélémy
(04.42.16.17.75).* **Open** 9am-6pm Mon-Fri.
Admission *exhibitions* free; *theatre/dance* €9; €4.50
under-15s.
Artists' studios, exhibition space, contemporary dance, theatre productions and workshops within a hospital complex not far from the Cité du Livre.

Cité du Livre

8-10 rue des Allumettes (04.42.91.98.65). **Open**
noon-6pm Tue, Thur, Fri; 10am-6pm Wed, Sat.
Admission free.
The name and the gigantic book that marks the entrance are slightly misleading. As well as hosting an annual literary festival in October and housing the historic Bibliothèque Méjanes library, this con-

The writing on the wall

The tall chimneys, the long red-brick building, stacked crates of bricks, the railway siding... today the tuileries of Les Milles on the outskirts of Aix-en-Provence has every air of what it is – a brick factory. But between 1939 and 1943, it also had a quite different role – a role which for a long time lay, if not actively concealed, ignored and forgotten.

Requisitioned as early as 1939 (before the German occupation), in a period of growing xenophobia and nationalism, Les Milles was used to round up 'enemy subjects' in France. These included both refugees from the Spanish Civil War and German and Austrian intellectuals, many of them Jewish, who had fled the Nazi regime. Among them were two Nobel prizewinners and the Surrealist painters Max Ernst and Hans Bellmer. After June 1940 (although Provence at this point was part of Free France administered by Vichy), it became a transit camp; nearly 2,000 Jews were deported from here towards Auschwitz via the transit camp of Drancy on the edge of Paris and Les Milles became the most important camp in the south, administering other smaller camps at Manosque, Lambesc and Le Ciotat.

It was only in 1982, when the refectory was up for demolition, that associations of resistants, deportees and Jews campaigned to preserve the site. Since 1997, the building has become the Mémorial National des Milles. In the entrance hall, documents and archive photographs relate the history of Les Milles and other internment camps. But it is the refectory that is the most telling witness, decorated with murals painted by prisoners that seem to take a subtly satirical slant with a caricatural row of warders and a parody on Leonardo's *Last Supper*.

Across the road, at the former Gare des Milles, a railway wagon recalls those who were transported to Auschwitz via Drancy.

Site Mémorial des Milles

(04.42.24.34.68). **Open** 9am-noon, 12.45-5pm Mon-Thur; 9am-noon, 12.45-4pm Fri.
Admission free.

Marseille & Aix

verted match factory is also home to the Institut de l'Image (rep cinema, library of opera on video, short film festival in Dec) and the Fondation St-John Perse exhibition space. Angelin Preljocaj's Centre National Chorégraphique (04.42.93.48.00) is due to move to a new high-tech dance centre next door in 2003.

Espace Musical Ste Catherine

20 rue Mignet (04.42.23.42.79). **Concerts** 7pm Tue. **Tickets** €3; free under-12s.
Former church used for classical concerts, essentially chamber music with a festival in March.

Galerie d'Art du Conseil Général

21bis cours Mirabeau (04.42.93.03.67). **Open** 10.30am-6pm daily. **Admission** free.
Run by the Conseil Général des Bouches du Rhône, Espace 13 puts on exhibitions of contemporary art and photography.

Théâtre des Ateliers

29 pl Miollis (04.42.38.10.45). **Box office** performance nights only. **Tickets** €7.50-€11.50. **No credit cards**.
A smallish theatre that works on co-productions of new work with other subsidised theatre venues.

Théâtre du Jeu de Paume

17 rue de l'Opéra (04.42.99.12.00/box office 04.42.99.12.12). **Box office** 10am-5pm Mon-Sat. **Tickets** €20-€28. **Credit** MC, V.
This beautiful vintage theatre reopened in 2000 after major renovation. Director Dominique Bluzet (of the Théâtre du Gymnase in Marseille) brings in successful Paris plays and visiting companies; it is also one of the venues for the Festival d'Art Lyrique.

Restaurants & brasseries

L'Aixquis

22 rue Victor Leydet (04.42.27.76.16). **Open** 7-10pm Mon; noon-2pm, 7-10pm Tue-Sat. Closed Aug. **Menus** €15-€58. **Credit** AmEx, MC, V.
In a dressy little dining room in a street of elegant mansions, young chef Benoît Strom modernises the classics, using fresh market produce.

Antoine Côté Court

19 cours Mirabeau (04.42.93.12.51). **Open** 7.30pm-midnight Mon; noon-2.30pm, 7.30pm-midnight Tue-Sat. **Average** €23. **Credit** DC, MC, V.
The fashionable folk of Aix come to this stylish, lively Italianate restaurant, which serves veal dishes, gnocchi and pasta.

Brasserie des Deux Garçons

53 cours Mirabeau (04.42.26.00.51/ www.les2garcons.com). **Open** noon-3pm, 7-11.30pm daily. **Menu** €20. **Credit** AmEx, MC, V.
Alias 'les 2 G', the Deux Garçons café, founded in 1792 and named after the two waiters who bought it in 1840, still has its original canopied entrance and *consulaire* interior. It serves proficient brasserie fare but it's the café buzz that counts.

Chez Féraud

8 rue du Puits Juif (04.42.63.07.27). **Open** 7.30-9.30pm Mon; noon-1.30pm, 7.30-9.30pm Tue-Sat. Closed Aug. **Menus** €18.29-€23.63. **Credit** AmEx, MC, V.
Provençal cooking is served amid summery decor. Specialities include *soupe au pistou*, peppers stuffed with salt cod, and rabbit with basil; good desserts.

Chez Maxime

12 pl Ramus (04.42.26.28.51). **Open** 7-10pm Mon; noon-2pm, 7-10.30pm Tue-Sat. **Menus** €21-€41. **Credit** DC, MC, V.
The *raison d'être* of Chez Maxime is meat, which Maxime himself saws up in full view of guests. Big hunks of good-quality beef and lamb grilled on charcoal are a treat, especially if you opt for the *côte de boeuf* for two rather than one of the *menus*, though starters and veg are rather lacklustre.

Clos de la Violette

10 av de la Violette (04.42.23.30.71/ www.closdelaviolette.fr). **Open** 7-9.30pm Mon, Tue; noon-2pm, 7-9.30pm Wed-Sat. Closed two weeks Aug. **Menus** €45-€99. **Credit** AmEx, MC, V.
In a spacious garden under ancient chestnut trees, chef Jean-Marc Banzo produces food that is at once light and unmistakeably Provençal. The service can be erratic, and the welcome cool.

Le Grillon

49 cours Mirabeau (04.42.27.58.81). **Open** noon-3pm, 7pm-1am daily (café 6am-2am). **Menus** €11.50-€30.50. **Credit** MC, V.
Sit on the terrace or in the pretty upstairs dining room. Plenty of Aixois eat here as well as tourists. Roast lamb with herbs and daily fish dishes are simple but proficient; the pasta is best forgotten.

La Vieille Auberge

63 rue Espariat (04.42.27.17.41). **Open** 7-10pm Mon; noon-2pm, 7-10pm Tue-Sun. Closed Jan. **Menus** €15-€38. **Credit** MC, V.
A beamed, pink washed dining room is the setting for chef Jean-Marie Merly's sophisticated cooking, seen in dishes like red mullet stuffed with aubergine and parmesan on a red pepper *pain perdu*.

Yamato

4 rue Lieutaud (04.42.38.00.20). **Open** noon-2.30pm, 7-10.30pm Tue-Thur, Sat, Sun; 7-10.30pm Fri. **Menus** €27-€43. **Credit** AmEx, DC, MC, V.
Female waiting staff glide around in kimonos at this Japanese restaurant adorned with No masks. As well as excellent sushi and sashimi and crisp, light tempura you'll find good grilled fish and sukiyaki.

Bars, clubs & music venues

Le Bistrot Aixois

37 cours Sextius (04.42.27.50.10). **Open** 7am-6pm Mon; 7am-4am Tue-Sat. **Credit** AmEx, MC, V.
This Aixois institution has the BCBG student set queuing to get in. Once inside, there are drinks, billiards and a small dance floor.

Marseille & Aix

La Fonderie

14 cours St-Louis (04.42.63.10.11). **Open** 8pm-1am
Thur-Sat. Closed Jan-Apr, Sept. **Admission** €7.50-
€11. **No credit cards**.
Eclectic live venue in a former metal foundry where
the roster ranges from jazz to local hard rock and
garage outfits.

Hot Brass

rte d'Eguilles (04.42.21.05.57). **Open** 10.30pm-dawn
Fri, Sat. **Admission** €16-€19. **Credit** MC, V.
5km out of town, the Hot Brass offers live funk, soul,
rock, blues and Latin bands, mainly local outfits.
Reserve on the answerphone.

Mediterranean Boy

6 rue de la Paix (04.42.27.21.47). **Open** 7pm-2am
nightly. **Credit** AmEx, DC, MC, V.
Upstairs is a classic gay bar tended by the avuncu-
lar fiftysomething *patron*. Downstairs is a large cellar area with tables and the opportunity for heavy
petting. More twilight zone than dark room.

Le Mistral

3 rue Frédéric Mistral (04.42.38.16.49). **Open**
10.30pm-dawn Tue-Sat. **Admission** €11-€15.
Credit MC, V.
Behind a discreet entrance is this long-established
student haunt with a selective door policy. Attracts
name DJs such as DJ Abdel.

Le Richelm

*24 rue de la Verrerie (04.42.23.49.29/
www.euronight.com/richelm).* **Open** 11.30pm-dawn
Mon-Sat. **Admission** €9-€15. **Credit** MC, V.
Popular bar/club in the heart of Vieil Aix with a
small dance floor, varied nights and a restaurant.

Unplugged Pub

25 rue du Bon Pasteur (04.42.23.40.84). **Open** 8pm-
2am Tue-Sat. Closed Aug. **Credit** AmEx, MC, V.
A sociable studenty corner bar with vaulted cellar.
There's beer and sangria, and sometimes live music.

Le Verdun

20 pl de Verdun (04.42.27.03.24). **Open** 6am-2am
daily. **Credit** MC, V.
Young staff, eclectic clientele and a classic decor of
zinc bar and banquettes are the appeal of this café
near the Palais de Justice. Steaks and salads served
all day and tables on the square in summer.

Shopping

Aix offers some of the most sophisticated
shopping in Provence (all open Mon afternoon-
Sat unless stated). Leader of the fashion brigade
is **Gago** (18, 20, 21 rue Fabrot, 04.42.27.60.19)
with up-to-the-minute men's and women's
designer wear, but you'll also find **Yohji
Yamamoto** (No.3, 04.42.27.79.15) and **Max
Mara** (No.12, 04.42.38.44.87) on this street. For
simpler, casual wear **Sugar** (4 rue Maréchal
Foch, 04.42.27.48.33) is worth a look. **Agnès b**

(2 rue Fernand Dol, 04.42.38.44.87) is across the
Cours Mirabeau. A clutch of good children's
wear shops include **Catimini** (9 pl des
Chapeliers, 04.42.27.51.14), **Marese** (4 rue
Aude, 04.42.26.67.00), and **Du Pareil au
Même** (14 rue Maréchal Foch, 04.42.26.48.49).

Aix's culinary speciality is the *calisson d'Aix*,
diamond-shaped sweets made out of almonds,
sugar and preserved melon; some of the best
come from **Leonard Parli** (35 av Victor Hugo,
04.42.26.05.71). Aix's most celebrated *santon*
(terracotta figurines) maker is **Santons
Fouque** (65 cours Gambetta, 04.42.26.33.38,
closed Sun), on the road to Avignon.

There are numerous antique and interior
design shops on place des Trois Ormeaux and
rue Jaubert. **La Maison Montigny** (19 rue
Lucas de Montigny, 04.42.27.74.56, closed Mon)
has two floors of high-tech kitchen equipment
and stained, restored furniture; **Scènes de Vie**
(3 rue Jaubert, 04.42.21.13.90) stocks
sophisticated Provençal pottery, while **Galerie
du Lézard** (2 rue Jaubert, 04.42.99.06.00) goes
for contemporary lamps, vases and glassware.

Of Aix's bookshops, the **Librairie de
Provence** (31 cours Mirabeau, 04.42.26.07.23)
has a good fine art section, while **Librairie
Paradox** (15 rue du 4 Septembre,
04.42.26.47.99) stocks books, videos and CD-
Roms in English. **La Bulle Noire** (36-38 pl des
Tanneurs, 04.42.26.82.89) caters for the French
addiction for *bandes-dessinées*.

Where to stay

Château de la Pioline

*260 rue Gauillaume du Vair, La Pioline
(04.42.52.27.27/www.chateauxhotels.com/pioline).*
Double €136-€290. **Credit** AmEx, DC, MC, V.
5km out of the centre, this 16th-century château has
a graceful stairhall, elegant dining room (closed Feb)
and formal garden, but sadly it's bang next to a commercial centre and you can hear the motorway.

Grand Hôtel Nègre Coste

33 cours Mirabeau (04.42.27.74.22). **Double**
€68.60-€122. **Credit** AmEx, MC, V.
The hospitable Hôtel Nègre Coste has a prime location and plenty of old-fashioned style, with period
furniture and chandeliers. Rooms at the front look
over cours Mirabeau, quieter ones at the back have
a view over rooftops to the cathedral.

Hôtel Aquabella

2 rue des Etuves (04.42.99.15.00/www.aquabella.fr).
Double €118-€136. **Credit** AmEx, DC, MC, V.
This modern, 110-room hotel adjoining the Thermes
Sextius may lack the character of Aix's older hotels
but compensates with spacious, comfortable rooms,
helpful staff and a good location for exploring Vieil
Aix. Special spa treatment packages are available.

Beautiful **place d'Albertas** was built in 1745 by the powerful Albertas family. *See p150.*

Hôtel des Augustins

3 rue de la Masse (04.42.27.28.59). **Double** €92-€229. **Credit** AmEx, DC, MC, V.
On a sidestreet off the cours Mirabeau, this appealing hotel was part of an Augustine convent until the Revolution. The reception is in a spectacular vaulted space and rooms are comfortable with Provençal-style furnishings.

Hôtel Cardinal

24 rue Cardinale (04.42.38.32.30). **Double** €58. **Credit** MC, V.
Much loved by writers and musicians here for the festival, this little hotel in the Quartier Mazarin has bags of charm. Several rooms have stucco mouldings and a couple have original 18th-century painted overdoor panels. Suites in the annexe by Musée Granet have a small kitchenette.

Hôtel des Quatre Dauphins

54 rue Roux Alphéran (04.42.38.16.39). Closed three weeks Feb. **Double** €55-€70. **Credit** MC, V.
A simple but tastefully decorated 17th-century building on a corner of one of the most pleasant streets of the Quartier Mazarin. The 12 rooms are hardly enormous, and there's no air-conditioning, but most guests are returnees, so book well ahead.

Villa Gallici

10 av de la Violette (04.42.23.29.23/ www.villagallici.com). **Double** €245-€500. **Credit** AmEx, DC, MC, V.
Slightly out of the centre in an elegantly renovated *bastide*, luxurious Villa Gallici offers plush comfort, with Italianate trimmings. Some rooms have private gardens, and there's a swimming pool.

Essentials

Getting there

By car

Leave the A8 autoroute at exit nos.29-31. Take the N7 from Avignon or St-Maximin-la-Ste-Baume. From Marseille, take the A51.

By train

Aix is now served by the TGV Méditerranée, but note that the new station is 10km west of the city, served by regular shuttle buses. The old Aix station is on the slow Marseille-Sisteron line, with trains roughly every hour from Marseille-St-Charles.

By bus

For information on services to Avignon (six to ten daily) and the hourly shuttle to Marseille airport, ring the *gare routière* on 04.42.91.26.80. Aix is also one of the stops on the Marseille airport to Nice airport service (three to four daily in each direction) operated by Phocéen Cars (04.93.85.66.61).

Tourist information

Pick up the English-language *Aix Bienvenue* guide at the tourist office. Cybercafés now abound in student Aix, the largest is **Pl@net Web** (20 rue Victor-Leydat, 04.42.26.83.01). **Cycles Zammit** (27 rue Mignet, 04.42.23.19.53, closed Mon, Sun) offers bikes for hire. The centre of Aix is best explored by foot. Local buses for outlying areas leave from La Rotonde in front of the Office de Tourisme, where there is an information/ticket desk (04.42.26.37.28). Take No.4 for the Fondation Vasarely, No.1 to Atelier Cézanne, No.20 for the Oppidium d'Entremont, No.16 for La Pioline and Les Milles.

Aix office de Tourisme
2 pl du Général de Gaulle (04.42.16.11.61/ www.aixenprovencetourism.com, hotel reservations 04.42.16.11.84/ www.aixenprovencetourism.com). **Open** *June, Sept* 8.30am-8pm Mon-Sat; 10am-1pm, 2-6pm Sun; *July-Aug* 8.30am-10pm Mon-Sat; 10am-1pm, 2-6pm Sun; *Oct-Mar* 8.30am-7pm Mon-Sat; 10am-1pm, 2-6pm Sun. **Ticket office** (04.42.16.11.70) 9am-noon, 2-6pm Mon-Sat.

Around Aix

Montagne Ste-Victoire

The Montagne Ste-Victoire is inextricably linked with Cézanne, who explored its geometric structure and changing colours in over 60 canvases and countless watercolours. The Montagne also offers rugged villages and wild landscapes for walking.

Cézanne was born into a wealthy Aix family in 1839 (his father had a hat business on the Cours Mirabeau before founding the Banque Cézanne et Cabassol) and while at school would go for long walks on the mountain with his friend Emile Zola (curiously Cézanne is said to

The Cistercian **Abbaye de Silvacane**, built on marshy land north-west of Aix.

have excelled at literature and Zola at drawing). Their friendship came to an end in 1886 when Cézanne perceived the character of Claude Lantier in Zola's *L'Oeuvre* as a portrait of him.

The best way to approach the Montagne Ste-Victoire is in a loop, taking a detour on the way out of Aix to the **Pont des Trois Sautets** (also painted by Cézanne). At Le Tholonet, the **Moulin Cézanne** has an exhibition on local history, the *barrage Zola* (built by Emile's dad) and the friendship between Cézanne and Zola. The D17 follows the southern edge of mountain, from where a footpath leads to the hermit's chapel of St-Ser, and through the village of **Puyloubier**, although the easiest access for walkers is from the north off the D10. Picasso is buried in the grounds of the Château de Vauvenarges (private), which he had bought in 1958. It's easiest to travel by car, but Aix tourist office organises weekly bus tours to the main Cézannian sites (Apr-Nov 2-7pm Thur, €24.39).

Moulin Cézanne
rte Cézanne, Le Tholonet (04.42.66.90.41). **Open** *May-Oct* 3-6pm Tue-Sun. **Admission** free.

West & north of Aix

Overlooking the lush plain west of Aix, sleepy **Lambesc** boasts a neo-classical church, an old *lavoir* and some fine houses dating from 1646-1786, when it was the seat of the regional assembly. Across the rolling countryside of the Chaîne de la Trévaresse, the D15 (or N7 and D543 from Aix) leads to the **Abbaye de Silvacane**, the third of Provence's great Cistercian Romanesque abbeys (with Sénanque and Thoronet). It has a sober church, vaulted chapter house and a refectory with contemporary stained glass by artist Sarkis. Just to the west, the small town of **La Roque-d'Anthéron** is known for its international summer piano festival.

North of Aix, the fortified **Château de Meyrargues** is now an upmarket hotel and restaurant (04.42.63.49.90). This area lacks the cachet of the Luberon, which means fewer tourists – so you might well arrive at **Peyrolles** and find the cafés shut and the streets deserted. A pity, because Peyrolles was once a residence of good king René. A grand gateway leads into the courtyard of the former royal château, now the *mairie* (town hall). On the other side of the village is the beautifully austere Chapelle de la St-Sépulcre (*mairie* 04.42.57.80.05, open by appointment Mon-Fri).

Abbaye de Silvacane
La Roque-d'Anthéron (04.42.50.41.69). **Open** *Apr-Sept* 10am-6.30pm daily; *Oct-Mar* 10am-1pm, 2-5pm Mon, Wed-Sun. **Admission** €5.50; free under-17s.

The Western Côte

Cassis to Toulon

The stretch of coast between Cassis and the gritty port of Toulon offers a succession of quiet resorts and plenty of wine-tasting.

Cassis

A quiet fishing village out of season, awash with *flaneurs* and sun-worshippers in summer, Cassis is best known for its delicate white wines and dazzling *calanques* (*see p162*). Though the Académie Francaise considers the final 's' to be silent, locals consider that to be for Parisians and snobs, and pronounce it anyway. The pretty smattering of fishing boats and colourful houses along the port attracted early 20th-century artists including Dufy, Matisse and Vlaminck, though sadly none of their works have made it into the tiny **Musée Municipal**, a meagre display of town history and bad southern art housed in a 1703 rectory. Besides two pleasant beaches – Plage de la Grande Mer on the sea side of the breakwater, and sheltered Plage du Bestouan at the western end of the port – Cassis offers a variety of watersports and some of southern France's best rock-climbing with numerous sports shops to provide equipment and guides. Cassis wines can be tasted at **La Ferme Blanche** (rte de Marseille, 04.42.01.00.74) and at **Clos Ste-Magdeleine** (chemin du Revestel, 04.42.01.70.28, closed Sat, Sun). Heading east out of Cassis, the route des Cretes (D141) climbs up Cap Canaille, the highest coastal cliffs (416m) in Europe.

Musée Municipal

rue Xavier d'Authier (04.42.01.88.66).
Open *Apr-Oct* 10.30am-12.30pm, 3.15.-6.30pm Wed-Sat; *Nov-Mar* 10.30am-12.30pm, 2.30-5.30pm Wed-Sat. **Admission** free.

Where to stay & eat

On the Plage du Bestouan, the pink **Hôtel-Restaurant Le Jardin d'Emile** (23 av Amiral Ganteaume, 04.42.01.80.55, closed mid-Nov to mid-Dec & Jan, double €61-€100) stands in a tropical garden against the old city walls. The restaurant (closed Wed, average €45) serves the best Provençal cuisine in town. Winston Churchill learned to paint while staying at **Les Roches Blanches** (rte des Calanques, 04.42.01.09.30/www.roches-blanches-cassis.com, closed Nov-Mar, double €103-€229, restaurant closed Mon, dinner Sun, menu €35) perched above the sea facing Cap Canaille. On the port, pleasant **Hôtel du Golfe**

(3 pl Grand Carnot, 04.42.01.00.21, closed Nov-Mar, double €58-€74) has a palmy brasserie that serves lunch (average €9), and drinks and giant ice creams morning to night. Fish shop **La Poissonnerie Laurent** (6 quai Barthélémy, 04.42.01.71.56, closed all Mon, dinner Thur, menu €20) was opened 65 years ago by fisherman Laurent Cinque and his wife Marie, now 82. She joins her grandsons Laurent and Eric at their new restaurant, where catch-of-the-morning fresh fish lie on icy counters.

Tourist information

Market is Wed and Fri morning. **Buroprim'** (7 av de la Viguerie, 04.42.01.98.28) offers Internet.

Cassis Office du Tourisme

promenade Aristide Briand, 13260 Cassis (04.42.01.71.17/ www.visitprovence.com). **Open** *Oct-May* 9.30am-6pm Mon-Fri; 10am-noon, 2-5pm Sat; 10am-noon Sun; *June-Sept* 9am-7pm Mon-Fri; 9am-1pm, 3-7pm Sat, Sun.

La Ciotat & St-Cyr-sur-Mer

When the Krupp dockyard with its tall seaside crane closed down in 1989, 10,000 people in a town with a population of 30,000 lost their jobs. Yet the tiny medieval port still manages to put on a lively face, with café tables spilling onto the streets and fishermen selling their catch in the harbour. Since the mid-19th century, La Ciotat has doubled as a genteel summer residence. Among illustrious guests were Auguste and Louis Lumière, who filmed and showed the first movie in the world here. Their short film of the Toulon-Marseille train pulling into La Ciotat station was a thriller for the Parisians invited to the first Champagne projection in September 1895 at the Eden Théâtre, still standing on the seafront boulevard Anatole France. The train station survives too, adorned with movie posters to celebrate its place in cinema history. The **Espace Lumière** continues the theme with a display of photos, posters and a film archive. Overlooking the old port, the **Musée Ciotaden** presents the town's maritime history.

At the eastern end of the Baie de la Ciotat, **St-Cyr-sur-Mer** boasts cafés and a market under a golden replica of the *Statue of Liberty*,

A shady, shoreside setting at Cassis' Hôtel-Restaurant Le Jardin d'Emile.

€128; restaurant closed Tue & Wed from Dec to Apr, average €30) are in a large coastal nature reserve. On the port, hungry fishermen head for **La Mamma** (Vieux Port, 04.42.08.30.08, closed Oct to mid-Nov, two weeks Feb, menus €15-€20) where La Mamma herself, Mme Dessolis, cooks up lasagne and ravioli to serve with the freshest possible seafood. **Riviera del Fiori** on the new port of Les Lecques (04.94.32.18.20, closed dinner Tue, all Wed & Feb, menus €15-€20) grills fish hand-caught by local divers and simmers local catch in its *bouillabaisse*. The **Grand Hôtel des Lecques** (24 av du Port, 04.94.26.23.01, closed Oct to mid-Mar, double €120-€230 incl dinner) has old-world charm, an exotic garden, plus a pool and a slightly boring restaurant, **Le Parc** (menus €22.87-€54). **Hôtel Petit Nice** (11 allée du Dr Seillon, 04.94.32.00.64, closed mid-Oct to mid-Mar, rates €45-€55) has a shady pool near the beach. On the coast path past La Madrague to Bandol (or by car D559, C6) the beach restaurant of **Calanque Port d'Alon** (04.94.26.20.08, open May-Sept, lunch only Oct-Apr, closed Nov-Jan; menus €25-€30) grills fish on an open fire. For sports enthusiasts, **Hôtel-Golf le Fregate** (04.94.29.39.39/www.dolce.com, closed 10-27 Dec, double €170-€280) has an 18-hole course within the Domaine de Fregate vineyards.

Tourist information

La Ciotat Office de Tourisme
bd Anatole France, 13600 La Ciotat (04.42.08.61.32/www.laciotat.com). **Open** *June-Sept* 9am-8pm Mon-Sat; *Oct-May* 9am-noon, 2.30-6pm Mon-Sat.

Les Lecques Office de Tourisme
pl de l'Appel du 18 Juin, 83270 Les Lecques (04.94.26.73.73/www.saintcyrsurmer.com). **Open** *July-Aug* 9am-7pm Mon-Fri, 9am-noon, 2-7pm Sat; *Sept-Apr* 9am-5pm Mon-Fri, 9am-noon, 2-5pm Sat; *May-June* 9am-6pm Mon-Fri; 9am-noon, 2-6pm Sat.

Bandol is a curate's egg of a town. Its old port is today a massive grey parking lot. But the old town that fronts the quays is lined with palm trees and cafés and the *ruelles* around the 18th-century Eglise St-François-de-Sales buzz with shops and restaurants. Westwards towards the Baie de Renecros are some of the *belle époque* houses that once made Bandol famous.

Ferries sail hourly from the Embarcadéro (Paul Ricard Boats, 06.11.05.91.52, €6) to the **Ile de Bendo**r, 2km out to sea, which was just a rock in the Mediterranean until the 1950s, when it was bought by *pastis* magnate Paul Ricard.

donated by sculptor Bartholdi. St-Cyr's seaward extension, **Les Lecques**, is a clutter of fashion shops and holiday eateries. The long beach promenade is family-friendly, with sand brought in by barge each June. Les Lecques claims to have been the Greek trading post of Taureontum, and to prove it, the **Musée de Taureontum** displays Greek and Roman artefacts from two first-century Roman villas. Past the museum, a 9km footpath (waymarked in yellow) clings to the coastline through pine and oak forests from La Madrague to Bandol.

Espace Lumière
20 rue Maréchal Foch, La Ciotat (04.42.08.94.56). **Open** 3-6pm daily. **Admission** free.

Musée Ciotaden
Ancien Hôtel de Ville, 1 quai Ganteaume, La Ciotat (04.42.71.40.99). **Open** *June-Sept* 4-7pm Mon, Wed-Sat; *Oct-May* 3-6pm Mon, Wed-Sat. **Admission** €3.20; €1.60 12-18s; free under-12s.

Musée de Taureontum
7 rte de la Madrague, St-Cyr (04.94.26.30.46). **Open** *June-Sept* 3-7pm Mon, Wed-Sun; *Oct-May* 2-5pm Sat, Sun. **Admission** €3.20; €1.60 12-18s; free under-12s.

Where to stay, eat & drink

For wild beauty, La Ciotat offers its Calanque de Figuerolles, where the rustic bungalows and restaurant of **Chez Tania** (04.42.08.41.71, www.figuerolles.com, closed Nov, double €37-

The Western Côte

Today, the island has mostly been cemented over and the main attraction, the Exposition Universelle des Vins et Spiritueux, was closed in 2001 by the Ricard family. At its western tip, Daddy & Milou restaurant (04.94.32.30.46) provides sunbeds and umbrellas: plunge off the rocks or slink down a ladder for a swim. The Fun Plage behind the port has pedalos for hire.

Wine was first produced around Bandol by the Greeks in 2500BC and was exported as far as Egypt by the Romans. Terraced vineyards slope down to the sea, protecting the grapes from winds and ensuring a long growing season. An *appellation contrôlée* since 1941,

Bandol wines owe their character to mourvèdre, a rare black grape variety, making for spicy, rich reds and full, fresh *rosés*. On the first Sunday in December, for the Fête du Millésime, the 52 vintners of the region bring kegs of three-month-old wine to the portside for a public tasting, before putting them to bed in wooden casks for 18 months. Stock up at the **Maison des Vins de Bandol** (29 allée Vivien, 04.94.29.45.03, closed Wed, Sun & Feb).

In a sweep of Bandol winetasting up-country, there are 20 vineyards along the D559 road between Bandol and the medieval village of **La Cadière-d'Azur**, where wines can be tasted

Les Calanques

The spectacular gashes in the limestone cliffs between Marseille and Cassis offer stunning natural beauty and tiny boho fishing ports. The Mediterranean equivalent of fjords and lochs, the Calanques were formed during the Ice Age when rivers cut deep valleys that were flooded when the sea level rose, leaving deep inlets and curious rock formations. In the dry limestone landscape, bushes, rare flowers, ferns and occasional trees cling on to the rocks. The Calanques forge the rugged seaboard of a 5,000-hectare national reserve, with trails to explore underwater, up cliffs and across mountain passes. Eagles and falcons fly the skies with ever-present seagulls and cliff colonies of puffins and stormy petrels.

For hiking in the Calanques, the IGN map 3615 is a must. The *grande randonnée* GR98, the 'balcony of the Mediterranean', twists high above the sea, stretching for 28km from La Madrague de Montredon (bus 19 or 20 from Prado Castellane) in Marseille to Cassis (approx a 12-hour hike). You can also reach the Calanques by a shorter walk from Université de Luminy in the east of Marseille (bus 21 or 21s from Canebière-Bourse). From Luminy, footpath 6a leads directly to the **Calanque de Morgiou** or joins the GR98. The fire risk is enormous: there are no refuges in the national park, no tents and no campfires allowed at any time, although hikers can pitch sleeping bags under the stars Oct-May. Be sure to bring food and water if you are exploring the interior. The GR98 remains open all year, but smaller inland paths are closed from mid-June to mid-September. For ecologically minded guided nature walks, rock climbing lessons, diving, kayaking or sailing along the Calanques, contact **NaturoScope** (10 rue St-Clair, Cassis, 04.42.01.20.91).

Of the eight Calanques from the Cassis side, only the first, **Port-Miou**, is fully accessible by car. Boats sail the other inlets. The best rock-climbing is the 'finger of God' rockspur in **En-Vau**, which has a nice secluded beach, or, for hardened professionals, the cliffs of **Devenson**. The Marseille side is flatter, with wider Calanques. **Sormiou** and **Morgiou** are dotted with *cabanons*: run-down, century-old holiday cabins so cherished by Marseille families that they are passed down from generation to generation and are now listed buildings. They are built by recycling what lies around – salt-dried plywood, rusty tin, driftwood and shells – to be one with nature.

and purchased at the **Cave Cooperative La Cadièrenne** (by A50 motorway exit, 04.94.90.11.06, closed Sun). More wineries line the D626, which meanders via Brulat to **Le Castellet**, a fortified village once owned by King René of Provence, with ramparts, a stern 15th-century château and a sprinkling of artsy shops. Towards **Le Beausset**, where an olive-press millstone serves as an altar in the church, more wines can be sampled at the **Cave Cooperative Les Maîtres Vignerons du Beausset** (on N8, 04.94.98.70.17, closed Sun). Above Le Beausset, Formula One drivers test out their wheels at the Circuit Paul Ricard at

Castellet. The N8 continues east to the grey stone village of **Ste-Anne-d'Evenos**, above which perches the ruined village of **Evenos**, built on ancient lava with crazy upside-down rock-climbing and sweeping coastal views.

Where to stay, eat & drink

In Bandol, escape holiday crowds on the private beach of the **Golf Hôtel**, once the casino (plage Renécros, end of bd Lumière, 04.94.29.45.83/ www.golfhotel.fr, closed Nov-Easter, double €44-€84). **Hôtel L'Oasis** (15 rue des Ecoles, 04.94.29.41.69/www.oasisbandol.com, closed

A meal at the spectacularly located **Le Lunch** in Sormiou (04.91.25.05.37, closed Nov to mid-Mar, average €32) is as close as you're likely to get to enjoying the stylish but casual lifestyle of the locals. *Bouillabaisse* has to be ordered in advance. Otherwise, go with the excellent grilled fish and a bottle of Cassis white. **Le Nautic** (04.91.40.06.37, average €21), is a decent bar-restaurant on the tiny port at Morgiou. In Callelongue, **La Grotte** (1 av des Pebrons, 04.91.73.17.79, average €30) draws a young crowd including hikers for pizzas and grilled fish. Boats from Cassis will drop you off at Morgiou; there are no boats to Sorgiou. If you plan to arrive by

car, the single-track fire-roads to Sormiou and Morgiou are closed from Easter to 15 Sept, 7am-8pm, but both let in a limited number of cars to those with lunch reservations. For dinner, drive down after 8pm. The only place to stay within the Calanques is **La Fontasse** hostel (04.42.01.02.72, closed Jan-Feb, dormitory €8) roughly an hour's walk from Cassis; bring your own food and drinking water (there's a tank for washing).

Under the sea
Human presence in the Calanques goes way back into pre-history. In 1991, Henri Cosquer, a diver from Cassis, swam into a long, narrow tunnel 37 metres below sea level between Sormiou and Morgiou, eventually emerging into a huge grotto. On the walls, he found the world's oldest-known cave paintings – bison, horses, handprints and penguin-like creatures dating back 27,000 years. The cave has since been sealed, but Cosquer can still be found on his boat **Cro-Magnon** in the port of Cassis or at his shop (3 rue Michel Arnaud, 04.42.01.89.16/www.cassis-services-plongee.fr, closed mid-Nov to mid-Mar) and accompanies divers into less artistic grottos.

Boat trips
Small craft leave for the Calanques from Cassis (04.42.01.03.31) at around 10am each morning. Tickets are sold at the booth at the eastern end of the port and cost €9-€14.50 depending on how many Calanques you see. You can be dropped-off or picked-up (be prepared to jump on to rocks while the ship tosses in waves) at En-Vau or Morgiou. In July & Aug, glass-bottomed boats leave Cassis at 10.30pm to view the sealife (€10).

From Marseille, boats leave from quai des Belges on the Vieux Port (**GACM** 04.91.55.50.09) daily July-Aug and Wed, Sat, Sun the rest of the year.

The Western Côte

Dec, double €52), an old parsonage, is near the old town and port. Near the church, **L'Oulivo** (19 rue des Tonneliers, 04.94.29.81.79, closed lunch Wed, Sat, Sun May-Sept, Wed Oct-Apr, and two weeks in Feb, menus €11.50-€18) offers fine Provençal cooking by the daughter of Lulu, of the Tempier Bandol Vineyard, who taught celebrated Californian chef Alice Waters.

In La Cadière, **Le Bérard** (av Gabriel Péri, 04.94.90.11.43/www.hotel-berard.com, closed Jan, double €71-€141) has rooms in an old convent and a gourmet restaurant (closed lunch Mon & Sat, menus €40-€99) where snazzy Provençal fare is served by sometimes sullen staff. In Ste-Anne-d'Evenos, the Marquise Dutheil de La Rochère (04.94.90.35.40, double €69) offers *chambres d'hôtes* at the **Château-Ste-Anne** vineyard. There's a pool under the olive trees and tastings of the château's exquisite reds. The **Hôtel du Castellet** (3001 rte des Hauts du Camp, Le Beausset, 04.94.98.38.88, double €335-€535) at the Circuit Paul Ricard is a luxury pit-stop for racing teams and fans, where you can park your private jet at the adjoining aerodrome.

Tourist information

Bandol's **Bibliothèque Mediathèque** (34 rue Pons, 04.94.29.37.55, closed Mon, Thur, Sun) offers Internet services. Bikes can be hired at **Holiday Bikes** (127 rte de Marseille, 04.94.32.21.89/www.holiday-bikes.com).

Bandol Maison du Tourisme
Bandol port, allée Vivien, 83150 Bandol (04.94.29.41.35/www.bandol.org). **Open** *July-Aug* 9am-1pm, 2-7pm daily; *Sept-June* 9am-noon, 2-6pm Mon-Fri; 9am-noon Sat.

Ollioules, Sanary-sur-Mer & the Iles d'Embiez

From Ste-Anne-d'Evenos, the N8 winds gently south along the river Reppe through the Gorges d'Ollioules where steep cliffs are riddled with caves that once hid Gespard, the bandit-hero of local folk tales. **Ollioules** is set amid terraced hills where locals tend olives, vines, citrus fruits and, most importantly, flowers, which end up in the town's wholesale cut flower market. Medieval streets climb from the massive 11th-century Romanesque church (open 9am-noon daily) on the main square up to a ruined 13th-century château. In the eastern pine forests, the **CNCDC Chateauvallon** cultural centre was known for its summer dance festival until a run-in with Toulon's rightwing politicos in the mid-90s, but a new regime now presents a varied multicultural programme of theatre,

dance and music in its open-air arena (June-Aug) or on its indoor stage, all year round.

The palm-lined port of **Sanary-sur-Mer** has daily fish and vegetable markets. In the 1930s, it became the refuge of anti-Nazi German writers, including Thomas Mann; Aldous Huxley and a young Sybille Bedford, who records the period in *Jigsaw*, were other visitors. The 13th-century tower at the edge of the port houses **Musée Frédéric-Dumas** diving museum.

On the wind-battered Sicie peninsula, **Six-Fours-les-Plages** is a string of modern beach bars and restaurants. When the mistral is blowing, angry waves pound the aptly named Plage Brutal, making it a surfer's paradise. On a hill to the north, the 11th-century **Collégiale-St-Pierre-aux-Lions** is all that remains of the old village of Six-Fours. 3km further north, the fifth-century chapel **Notre-Dame-de-Pepiole** (open 3-6pm daily) is one of France's oldest Christian churches, with three unusual naves.

Most visitors to **Le Brusc** stay only long enough to get a ferry to the **Iles des Embiez** (Paul Ricard Ferries 04.94.10.65.21, €7.50, €5.50 3-12s), former salt-panning islands bought by Paul Ricard in 1958. The main island houses the **Institut Océanographique Paul Ricard** and offers miles of footpaths and cycle tracks. Bikes can be hired by the ferry quay.

CNCDC Chateauvallon
794 chemin Chateauvallon, Ollioules (04.94.22.74.00). **Box office** 10am-7pm Mon-Fri. **Tickets** €18; €11 under-25s.

Collégiale-St-Pierre-aux-Lions
montée du Fort Militaire, Six-Fours-les-Plages (04.94.34.24.75). **Open** *June-Sept* 3-7pm Mon, Wed-Sat, 9am-noon, 3-7pm Sun; *Oct-May* 2-6pm Mon, Wed-Sat, 10am-noon, 2-6pm Sun. **Admission** free.

Institut Océanographique Ricard
Iles des Embiez (04.94.34.02.49/www.institut-paul-ricard.org). **Open** *July-Oct* 10am-12.30pm, 1.30-5.30pm daily. *Apr-June* closed am Wed & Sat, pm Sun; *Nov-Mar* closed am Wed, Sat, Sun. **Admission** €4; €2 4-11s; free under-4s.

Musée Frédéric-Dumas
Sanary-sur-Mer (04.94.74.80.23). **Open** *July-Aug* 10am-noon, 3-7pm daily; *Sept-June* 10am-noon, 3-7pm Sat, Sun. **Admission** free.

Where to stay, eat & drink

2km outside Ollioules, the Domaine de Terrebrune offers tastings of its Bandol wines and serves good Provençal lunches at its terrace restaurant, **La Table du Vigneron** (124 chemin de la Tourelle, 04.94.88.36.19, closed Mon, Tue and mid-Dec to mid-Jan, menu €30-€38), reservation essential. On the port in Sanary, **Hôtel-Restaurant de la Tour** (24

quai Général de Gaulle, 04.94.74.10.10, double
€53-€76) serves fabulously fresh seafood
(closed Tue & Wed, menus €19-€43) and has
pleasant rooms. For an aperitif try **Le
Baroudeur** (32bis rue Siat Marcelin,
04.94.88.32.55, open 7pm nightly) where
yachtsman Alain serves tapas Bandol-style,
with 38 local wines by the glass.

In Le Brusc, the **Restaurant Le St-Pierre**
(47 rue de la Citadelle, 04.94.34.02.52, closed
Mon, dinner Sun & Jan; menus €15-€30) serves
grilled fish and good *bouillabaisse* in a garden
above the port. **Jardin de la Ferme** (688
chemin des Faisses, 04.94.34.01.07) has cabins
(€470-€564 /week) and rooms (€50-€55) or
you can pitch your tent (€12 for two).

Tourist information

Ollioules Office de Tourisme

*116 av Philippe de Hautecloque, 83190 Ollioules
(04.94.63.11.74).* **Open** 2-6pm Mon; 9am-noon,
2-6pm Tue-Fri; 9am-noon Sat.

Sanary-sur-Mer Maison du Tourisme

*Les Jardins de la Ville, 83110 Sanary-sur-Mer
(04.94.74.01.04/www.sanarysurmer.com).* **Open**
June-Sept 9am-noon, 2-7pm Mon-Sat; 9am-noon Sun;
Oct-May 9am-noon, 2-5.30pm Mon-Sat.

Six-Fours Office du Tourisme

*promenade Charles de Gaulle, 83140 Six-Fours-les-
Plages (04.94.07.02.21/www.six-fours-les-
plages.com).* **Open** *July-Aug* 9am-7pm Mon-Sat,
10am-1pm Sun; *Apr-June, Sept* 9am-noon, 2-6.30pm
Mon-Sat; *Oct-Mar* 8.30am-noon, 1.30-5.30pm Mon-
Fri, 9am-noon, 1.30-5.30pm Sat.

Toulon

Even Toulon's tough reputation has blown into
the port like flotsam, from prisoners working
their terms as galley slaves to sex-hungry
sailors. Toulon is a city of contrasts: ugly with
postwar high-rises and beautiful in its medieval
streets; a place with some frankly dodgy
nightlife and a colourful café scene by day, a
place where the political right presides over a
huge North African community.

The Greeks and Romans knew about the
impressive natural harbour, and exploited the
local deposits of murex shells to make purple
dye. But only since 1481, when Provence became
part of France, did the port become strategically
important. A major shipyard was constructed in
the 16th century, and the town fortified with
star-shaped bastions by Louis XIV's military
architect Vauban in the late 17th century.

In 1789 Toulon chose the royal camp and was
delivered to British rule, until it fell to an
unknown young Revolutionary officer called
Napoléon Bonaparte in 1793 and narrowly
escaped being razed to the ground. The
royalists scuppered their ships and blew up the
shipyards to stop the Revolutionaries getting
their hands on them. In a remarkable rerun, the
French scuttled their Mediterranean fleet in the
harbour in 1942 as German forces advanced, and
much of the old town was destroyed in 1944 by
air-raiding Allies and retreating Germans.

Toulon is still France's leading naval port
and home to the trouble-plagued aircraft carrier
Charles de Gaulle, but the city is moving into

The Western Côte

Tranquil **Sanary-sur-Mer** was once a safe harbour for German intellectuals.

Toulon shows its pretty face at the ornate Second Empire **Opéra de Toulon**.

the present with dynamism: the sleek **Zénith Oméga**, near the station, is venue for all manner of rock groups from Vanessa Paradis to weirdly named local outfits; cool new venture **Rolling Town** (04.94.92.46.80) attracts hundreds of Toulonnais the first Friday of every month for a city-wide rollerblade rally.

On quai Cronstadt, two 1657 atlantes sculpted by Pierre Puget survive from the old town hall, embodying the labour of early dock-workers. The **Musée de la Marine** juts out into the westerly Darse Neuve, the 'new dock' built in 1680, and houses figureheads, ship models and marine paintings. The ornate 18th-century doorway was once the dockyard entrance. Nearby are the heavily guarded gates of the military port. A wall is all that remains of the gruesome La Bagne penal colony, described vividly by Victor Hugo in *Les Misérables*, when, from 1748 to 1873, the shipyards often used labour from galley slaves imprisoned on prison hulks moored in the port.

Back from the port lies the gritty red-light district, where sex shops and 'American bars' (read fleshpots) line avenue Micholet. The neighbourhood, known locally as **Le Petit Chicago** (and getting smaller) is currently undergoing the biggest civic restoration in France, but the few remaining slums in rue Auban exude infinitely more character than the pristine heritage now being projected

elsewhere. Where the sex industry doesn't have a stranglehold, the maze of streets is packed with designer shops and crafts workshops. On place Vezzani, a six-metre head of Neptune by Pierre Puget sticks out of a tenement wall.

In the heart of the *vieille ville*, café-filled place Puget was the site of a grain market in the 17th century; Victor Hugo lived at No.5 while researching *Les Misérables*. Several streets to the south-east, the atrociously lit **Cathédrale Ste-Marie** (closed noon-3pm) was built and rebuilt between the 11th and 17th centuries, escaping destruction during the Revolution only because it was used as an arms depot. One block east, the **cours Lafayette** becomes a vast and colourful market (open morning Tue-Sun). Halfway along the street, the **Musée du Vieux Toulon** documents Toulon's history.

Behind the *vieille ville* and the port lies the new town. At place Victor Hugo, the **Opéra de Toulon** curtain-calls theatre productions, as well as opera and dance. Further west, the lovely 19th-century former Var assembly building is now the **Hôtel des Arts**, putting on exhibitions of contemporary Mediterranean art. The often-overlooked **Musée des Beaux-Arts** runs from Fragonard and marine paintings by Vernet up to postwar abstract art and the cartoon-influenced *nouvelle figuration* of Combas and the Di Rosa brothers.

Rising above the town, **Mont Faron** can be reached by funicular (04.94.92.68.25, closed Mon, Dec-Jan and windy days). As well as offering spectacular views, it is the site of a small zoo and the **Musée du Débarquement** commemorating the 1944 liberation of Provence.

Along the western shore in depressing, industrial **La Seyne-sur-Mer** (best access by ferry from Toulon to avoid the shopping-strip traffic), Fort Balaguier is where Napoléon captured Toulon in 1793, honoured in the Fort's **Musée Naval**. Or stop by to see an exhibition in the 1890s **Villa Tamaris Pacha**.

East of the city, the prosperous suburb of **Le Mourillon** has parks, nightlife, a good beach and a fort dating back to 1514. At garden-filled **Le Pradet**, a coast path leads to the sandy Plage du Monaco, accessible only to hikers and boaters; Plage des Bonnettes, where the east wind blows up a serious surf; Plage de la Garonne; and Plage des Oursinières, with a small port. The path continues into the woods of Le Bau Rouge and the **Musée de la Mine du Cap Garonne**, where you can descend a shaft to experience conditions in the mine where copper was extracted between 1862 and 1917.

Hôtel des Arts

236 bd Leclerc (04.94.91.69.18). **Open** (during exhibitions) 11am-6pm Tue-Sun. **Admission** free.

Musée des Beaux-Arts
113 bd Maréchal Leclerc (04.94.36.81.00). **Open** *1-6pm daily.* **Admission** free.

Musée de la Marine
pl Monsenergue (04.94.02.02.01/www.musee-marine.fr). **Open** *Apr-Sept* 10am-6.30pm daily; *Oct-Mar* 10am-noon, 2-6pm Mon, Wed-Sun. **Admission** €4.60; €2.30 6-10s; free under-6s.

Musée-mémorial du Débarquement
Tour Beaumont, rte du Faron (04.94.88.08.09). **Open** *July-Aug* 9.45-11.45am, 13.45-5.30pm daily; *Sept-June* 9.45-11.45am, 13.45-4.30pm Tue-Sun. **Admission** €3.80; €1.55 8-16s; free under-8s.

Musée de la Mine de Cap Garonne
chemin du Bau Rouge, Le Pradet (04.94.08.32.46/ www.mcg.fr.fm). **Open** *July-Aug* 2-5.30pm daily; *Sept-June* 2-5pm Wed, Sat, Sun. **Admission** €6.20; €3.80 12-18s; €3.10 under-12s

Musée Naval du Fort Balaguier
924 corniche Bonaparte (04.94.94.84.72). **Open** *mid-June to mid-Sept* 10am-noon, 3-7pm Tue-Sun; *mid-Sept to mid-June* 10am-noon, 2-6pm Tue-Sun. Closed Jan & Feb. **Admission** €2; €1 5-12s; free under-5s.

Musée du Vieux Toulon
69 cours Lafayette (04.94.62.11.07). **Open** 2-6pm Mon-Sat. **Admission** free.

Opéra de Toulon
pl Victor Hugo (04.94.92.70.78/ www.operadetoulon.fr). **Box office** 10am-12.30pm, 2.30-5.30pm Mon-Fri. **Tickets** price varies.

Villa Tamaris Pacha
av de la Grande Maison, La-Seyne-sur-Mer (04.94.06.84.00). **Open** 2-6.30pm Tue-Sun. **Admission** free.

Where to stay, eat & drink

In the *vieille ville*, the pleasant **Hôtel les 3 Dauphins** (9 pl des 3 Dauphins, 04.94.92.65.79, double 170F-250F) has sunny renovated rooms (and new beds). Try **La Chamade** (25 rue de la Comedie, 04.94.92.28.58, closed lunch Sat & all Sun, closed Aug, menu €30) for cheery but formal dining and slightly exotic cuisine, or **Chez Odette Le Cellier** (52 rue Jean-Jaures, 04.94.92.64.35, closed Sat, Sun and two weeks Aug, menus €14-€24) for homelier local specialities. For couscous and North African wines, **Sidi Bou Said** (43 bis rue Jean Jaurès, 04.94.91.21.23, closed Sun & lunch Mon, average €16) is a hangout of Toulon's large North African community and can barely handle the crowds in its cheerful new locale. At Le Pradet, gourmet Provençal cuisine is served at **Chanterelle** (50 rue de la Tartane, port des Oursinières, 04.94.08.52.60, closed Wed from Oct to Easter and Jan & Feb, menus €30-€38).

For after-hour drinks, studenty **Bar à Thym** in Le Mourillon (32 bd Cuneo, 04.94.41.90.11) has tapas and live music. The **113 Café** (113 av Infanterie de Marine, 04.94.03.42.41, menus €8-€23) is a happening bar-restaurant in an old warehouse, with billiards, live jazz and salsa and DJs on Fri & Sat nights.

Tourist information

Net access at **Bureau Information Jeunesse** (pl Raimu, 04.94.09.09.79, closed pm Sat & Sun).

Toulon Office de Tourisme
pl Raimu, 83000 Toulon (04.94.18.53.00/ www.toulontourisme.com). **Open** *June-Sept* 9am-6pm Mon-Sat; 10am-noon Sun; *Oct-May* 9.30am-5.30pm Mon-Sat; 10am-noon Sun.

▶ Getting There & Around

▶ By air
Toulon-Hyères airport is in fact in Hyères, 35km east of Toulon; but most airlines use Marseille-Provence airport.

▶ By car
Leave the A50 autoroute at exit no.8 for Cassis, nos.9 and 10 for La Ciotat and St-Cyr, no.12 for Bandol, no.13 to Six-Fours, Sanary-sur-Mer and Ollioules. The A50 from the west and A57 from the east dump straight into Toulon (construction on a cross-city expressway has been in progress for 20 years). Or for Cassis from eastern Marseille, take the D559 over the chaîne de St-Cyr. The D141 route des Crêtes climbs from Cassis to La Ciotat; the D559 goes direct and continues to Toulon via Les Lecques, Bandol and Sanary-sur-Mer.

▶ By train
Toulon is on the main TGV line from Paris. Hourly local trains between Marseille and Toulon stop at Cassis, La Ciotat, St-Cyr (each about 3km from the centre), Bandol and Sanary-Ollioules, and hourly trains between Toulon and Nice.

▶ By bus
Cartreize (04.42.08.41.05) runs buses between Cassis and La Ciotat and La Ciotat and Les Lecques. **Littoral Cars** (04.94.74.01.35) runs buses daily between Bandol and Sanary, Le Brusc, Six-Fours, La Seyne and Toulon. **Orlandi** (04.94.63.42.73) runs buses between Ollioules and La Seyne and Toulon-Ollioules. **Sodétrav** (04.94.12.55.12) runs buses between Toulon and Hyères.

The Western Côte

Hyères to the Maures

Hyères lives on past glories, but beyond lie some of the least spoiled beaches in the South and an interior of dense cork and chestnut forests.

Hyères & Giens

In the 19th century, when its mild climate was recommended for the consumptive, Hyères rivalled Nice as a seaside resort. A new town of broad avenues lined with palm trees and stucco villas grew up around the medieval centre and spread southwards towards the sea. It was particularly favoured by the British: Queen Victoria paid a one-off visit in 1892, introducing the locals to Irish stew, and Robert Louis Stevenson supposedly found inspiration for *Treasure Island* on the Ile de Porquerolles. But

when the fashionable season changed from winter to summer Hyères, perched up on a hill 5km from the sea, was left high and dry. Today the grand hotels have all gone, holidaymakers remain firmly on the seaside strip and the busy, multiracial town lives by salt, cut flowers and date palm rearing as much as tourism.

Hyères' medieval *vieille ville* clusters beneath the ruins of the 13th-century castle and is approached through the medieval Porte Massillon. From there rue Massillon leads to café-filled place Massillon, where the much-restored **Tour St-Blaise** is all that remains of a Templar monastery. From here follow rue Ste-Catherine to the **Collégiale St-Paul**, with its medieval belltower and Renaissance doorway. On place de la République, the 13th-century church of **St-Louis** (open 8am-7pm daily) was once a Franciscan monastery where King Louis IX prayed in 1254 on his return from crusading.

Above, **Parc Ste-Claire** (open 8am-7pm summer, 8am-5pm winter), which surrounds the 19th-century castle that was home to novelist Edith Wharton, is packed with exotic plants. Up rue du Paradis, **Parc St-Bernard** (open 8am-7pm summer, 8am-5pm winter) is equally lush. On its edge, the **Villa Noailles** recalls Hyères avant-garde heyday. Designed in 1924 by Modernist architect Robert Mallet-Stevens for aristocratic patrons Charles and Marie-Laure de Noailles, in its day, it was the scene of trysts and parties frequented by A-list bohemians including Picasso, Stravinsky, Luis Buñuel and Man Ray, who shot part of his film *Les Mystères du Château de Dé* here. Long left to abandon, the house was restored by the municipality in the 1990s and is now used for exhibitions and the Aquaplanning music fest.

The charms of the *belle époque* town are now distinctly faded and marred by an appalling one-way system, though the Villa Tunisienne on avenue de Beauregard points to the 1880s taste for the exotic and the **Casino des Palmiers** still supplies a touch of glamour. Further south on avenue Thomas, the pseudo-Moorish **Villa Olbius Riquier** is surrounded by subtropical gardens, complete with hothouse and mini-zoo. In place Lefebvre, the **Musée**

Villa Noailles: perfect geometrical adaptation to the jet-set lifestyle.

Municipal contains archaeological finds,
furniture and local paintings.

The beach, below the town, is a long stretch
of sand reaching around the Rade d'Hyères bay
and down a narow strip of land calle **La
Capte**, which joins what used to be the Ile de
Giens to the mainland. The esplanade by the
marina is a fiesta of activity in high season,
with a fleamarket on Sunday morning.

In the Almanarre district to the west, set
against a luscious maritime backdrop, the **Site
Archéologique d'Olbia** bears fragmentary
traces of Hyères' earliest forbears in the Greek
trading post of Olbia, along with Roman homes
and baths and part of a medieval abbey. The
Almanarre beach is home each year to heats
for the world windsurfing championships.
Between here and La Capte stretch the Étang
des Pesquiers salt pans.

The bulge at the end of the isthmus is the
pretty though built-up **Giens** peninsula, with
its namesake hilltop village. The main square,
place Belvédère, affords fantastic views and
hosts a market on Tuesday morning. Boats
leave for the islands at **La Tour Fondue**, a
squat fortress built by Richelieu.

Casino des Palmiers

1 av Ambroise Thomas, Hyères (04.94.12.80.80).
Open *casino* 10am-4am daily; *restaurant* 8-10.30pm
daily. **Average** €35. **Credit** AmEx, V, MC.

Collégiale St-Paul

pl St Paul, Hyères (no phone). **Open** *Apr-Oct* 3-6pm
Mon; 10am-noon, 3-6.30pm Wed-Sat; 10am-12.30pm
Sun; *Nov-Mar* 3-6pm Mon, Wed-Sun.

Musée Municipal

*Cité Administratif, pl Théodore Lefebvre, Hyères
(04.94.00.78.42).* **Open** 10am-noon, 2.30-5.30pm
Wed-Sun. **Admission** free.

Parc Olbius Riquier

av Ambroise Thomas, Hyères (04.94.00.78.65).
Open *May-Sept* 8am-8pm daily; *Oct-Apr* 7.30am-5pm
daily. **Admission** free.

Site Archéologique d'Olbia

*quartier de l'Almanarre, Hyères (04.94.57.98.28/
www.monum.fr).* **Open** *Apr-Sept* 9.30am-noon, 3-
8pm daily. Closed Oct-Mar. **Admission** €3.80;
€2.30 12-18s; free under-12s.

Villa Noailles

montée de Noailles, Hyères (04.94.12.70.63). **Open**
mid-June to mid-Sept 10am-noon, 4-7pm Wed-Sun,
guided tours 4pm Fri; *mid-Sept to mid-June* during
exhibitions only 2-5.30pm. **Admission** free.

Where to stay & eat

Hyères is short of decent accommodation.
Overlooking La Gavine pleasure port, the
Potinière (27 av de la Méditerranée,

Medieval **Hyères** keeps quietly aloof
from the antics of the seashore below.

04.94.00.51.60, closed Jan, double €49-€75) has
large rooms and a private beach. La Capte is
dotted with campsites and mostly downmarket
hotels. Best choice is the **Hôtel Ibis Thalassa**
(allée de la Mer, La Capte, 04.94.58.00.94/
www.thalassa.com), a low-slung modern
building with 96 rooms which zigzag around
gardens, a restaurant offering traditional and
health menus, direct access to the
thalassotherapy spa and a private beach.

Deep in the *vieille ville*, **Bistrot de Marius**
(1 pl Massillon, 04.94.35.88.38, closed lunch Tue
& Wed and mid-Nov to mid-Dec, mid-Jan to
mid-Feb, menus €14.48-€30.34) serves
authentic Provençal cuisine, including
bouillabaisse. In the modern town, **Les
Jardins de Bacchus** (32 av Gambetta,
04.94.65.77.63/www.les-jardins-de-
bacchus.com, closed lunch Sat,dinner Sun, all
Mon, 2nd and 3rd weeks of Jan, June to mid-
July, menus €30.18-€47.25) does good
contemporary Provençal fare.

In Giens, the **Provençal** (pl St Pierre,
04.98.04.54.54, closed Nov-Mar, double €60-
€107), a pleasant 1950s building, has a pool and
terraced gardens that descend right to the sea.
The **Tire Bouchon** (1 pl St-Pierre,
04.94.58.24.61, closed all Tue & Wed, 2 weeks
in Oct and mid-Dec to mid-Jan, menus €23-
€29) does an excellent octopus *fricassée*. In the
tiny cove of Port du Niel, **L'Eau Salée**
(04.94.58.92.33, closed all Sun, Mon and Jan,
menus €25.61-€34.76) serves fish (and clients)
straight off the boat.

Tourist information

Office de Tourisme

*3 av Ambroise Thomas, 83400 Hyères
(04.94.01.84.50/www.ot-hyeres.fr).* **Open** *July-Aug*
8am-8pm daily; *Sept-June* 9am-6pm Mon-Fri; 10am-
4pm Sat.

The Western Côte

Bormes les Mimosas: simply luscious.

Bormes-les-Mimosas

Set above the coast in the hills, **Bormes-les-Mimosas** is a picturesque clutter of colour-washed houses, where sun terraces point to contemporary preoccupations, but covered passages (*cuberts*) and vaulted interiors betray their medieval origins. The floral handle was added to the name in 1968, to emphasise the point that Bormes had the highest density of these scented, yellow-puffball bearing trees on the Riviera. (Mimosa, assorted species of acacia native to Australia and other tropical and sub-tropical regions, were introduced to France in the early 19th century.) Mimosa blooms Jan to Mar; the rest of the year, houses and terraces drip with creepers and purple bougainvillea. Place Gambetta, with its cafés and restaurants, makes a good starting point for wandering down streets like ruelle du Moulin, venelle des Amoureux and rue Rompi Cuou or up to the remains of the medieval castle of the Lords of Fos. The 18th-century **Eglise St-Trophime** contains some curious polychrome wood saints reliquaries as well as *trompe l'oeil* frescoes round the choir. On the edge of the old village, the **Chapel St François** was built in 1560 in thanks to St François de Paule, who delivered the village from the Plague in 1481.

Further down the hill, the **Musée d'Art et d'Histoire** has some Rodin sketches and a gripping historical section dedicated to illustrious 18th-century natives Ippolite Bouchard (who set up the Argentinian navy) and Ippolite Mourdeille (who was killed while chasing the Spaniards from Montevideo).

Apart from the small hamlet of Cabasson and the heavily guarded 16th-century Fort de Brégançon (the French president's official summer retreat), **Cap Bénat**, which juts out south-west of Bormes, is one of the least built-up stretches of coast in the Midi. Here there's no urban sprawl, nor even any luxury villas, just the solid square **Château de Brégançon** (639 rte de la Léoube, 04.94.64.80.73, open Mon-Sat) source of a robust Côtes de Provence wine – woodland and vineyards and a number of unspoiled beaches: you pay for the car parks, but otherwise entrance is free. West of Brégançon, the **Plage de l'Estagnol** (parking €6.10-€7.62 Apr-Oct) is a lovely sandy strip shaded by pine trees, with shallow water that makes it a good for children and, set back from the sea, a good fish restaurant (04.94.64.71.11) and cheerful café Chez Richard. The Sentier du Littoral coastal path winds round the peninsula (waymarked in yellow).

Bormes' beach suburb of **La Favière** is a modern but inoffensive low-rise development with modern port, watersports, diving (*see p217*), a large, family-oriented sandy public beach, and plenty of shops for beach gear and picnic fare.

Musée d'Art et d'Histoire de Bormes

103 rue Carnot (04.94.71.56.60). **Open** 9-10am, 2.30-5.30pm Mon, Wed-Fri; 9-10am, 2.30-5pm Sat; 10am-noon Sun. **Admission** free.

Where to stay & eat

In Bormes village, the **Bellevue** (14 pl Gambetta, 04.94.71.15.15, closed Oct-Mar, double €46-€99) offers a *belle* view and lots of boho allure, with homemade jam and fresh fruit at breakfast on the terrace. Its simple café-restaurant serves great ice creams. Near the sea, **Hôtel de la Plage** (rond point de la Bienvenüe, La Favière, 04.94.71.02.74, closed Oct-Mar, double €48-€59 incl dinner) has been run by the same matronly management since the 1960s (average age of staff about 70). Rooms are spotless and have balconies or terraces.

Bormes Village offers the best gastronomic choices in the area. **Restaurant La Tonnelle** (23 pl Gambetta, 04.94.71.34.84, closed Wed & Thur and 20 Nov-20 Dec, menus €17-€35) is a true discovery thanks to the inventive modern cooking of chef Gilles Renard. Atmospheric

Lou Portaou (rue Cubert des Poètes, 04.94.64.86.37, closed Tue and mid-Nov to mid-Dec, menus €28.20) in a medieval tower has a short but original choice of Provençal dishes. **L'Escoundado** (2 ruelle du Moulin, 04.94.71.15.53, closed Oct-Jan and Mon, Tue Feb-May, menu €18-€26.68) is friendly but the trad fare is perhaps resting on its laurels.

In Cabasson, comfortable **Les Palmiers** (240 chemin du Petit Fort, 04.94.64.81.94, closed mid-Nov to mid-Feb, doubles €70-€185, half-pension obligatory July-Sept, menus €25-€46) is resolutely provincial. It has steps down to the beach and a reliable classic restaurant.

Tourist information

Office de Tourisme
1 pl Gambetta, 83230 Bormes-les-Mimosas (04.94.01.38.38/www.bormeslesmimosas.com). **Open** *Apr-Sept* 9am-12.30pm, 2.30-6.30pm daily; *Oct-Mar* 9am-12.30pm, 2-6pm Mon-Sat.

Le Lavandou to Cavalaire

Le Lavandou hugs the coast east of Bormes. A concretey promenade and a couple of unfortunate tower blocks hide a pretty old town, behind what was once a major fishing

Treasure islands

Strung across the entrance to Hyères bay are the islands of Levant, Port-Cros and Porquerolles, known as the Iles d'Hyères or Iles d'Or. Colonised in the fifth century by the monks of Lérins, the islands were seized by the Saracens in 1160 before the latter were turfed out by François 1er, who fortified **Porquerolles**, with the Fort du Petit-Langoustier and the Fort Ste-Agathe, which looms over the yacht marina. Up the hill from the port, Porquerolles village was built as a retirement colony for Napoleonic officers and still resembles a colonial outpost, centred on place d'Armes, with its pungent eucalyptus trees. Here there are plenty of cafés as well as stalls for picnic supplies. For 60 years from 1911, the village was the private property of Belgian engineer Joseph Fournier, who introduced the exotic flora. Full of well-dressed French *BCBGs* cycling *en famille*, Porquerolles still feels privileged today. There are numerous bike hire outlets in both port and village. You don't need two wheels to get to the white sand and lush backdrop of the Plage d'Argent (west) or Plage de la Courtade (east), each an easy 10-15 minute walk through pine woods. Forest tracks lead to the more mountainous southern half of the island and the lighthouse of the Cap d'Arme; note that these may be closed during high winds in summer due to fire risk.

The hilly, lush **Ile de Port-Cros** is a nature reserve with no cars, no smoking (!) and nature paths that extend under the sea for swimmers and divers to look at marine flora.

Eight per cent of the **Ile du Levant** is still military property, though no longer a shooting range. The remaining area, Héliopolis, is a nudist colony where participating visitors, as opposed to voyeurs, are welcome.

Where to stay & eat
On Porquerolles, **Le Mas du Langoustier** (04.94.58.30.09, closed Nov-Apr, double 1,200F-1,500F, menus 330F-500F), 3km west of the port, has luxurious rooms and a fabulous fish restaurant, though it can be off-puttingly snobbish. Guests are met at the ferries by electric buggy. If simpler is more your style, **Les Glycines** (22 pl d'Armes, 04.94.58.30.36, double €74.70-€271.36, menus €15.09-€25.76) has lovely rooms in Provençal hues. Hipper bar-restaurant **L'Oustaou** (pl d'Armes, 04.94.58.30.13, double €76-€130, average 23) serves pasta or *plats du jour* like squid cooked in its ink and also has six rooms, some with sea view. On Port-Cros, **Le Manoir** (04.94.05.90.52, closed Oct-Apr, rates €125-€165 incl dinner) is the only hotel; its restaurant (menus €40-€45) serves Provençal classics. Levant is better served for hotels and campsites, though most are clothes-free zones. Mimosa-swathed **La Villa Delphes** (chemin du Couvent, 04.94.05.90.63, closed Oct-Mar, double €53-€69) has a pool and private beach.

Ferry services
There are frequent ferries in July and August; more limited services the rest of the year. **TLV** (www.tlv-tvm.com) runs ferries from La Tour Fondue in Giens (04.94.58.21.81) to Porquerolles (takes 20 mins, €14 return, free under-4s) and from Hyères to Port-Cros and Le Levant (€19.06-€22.11 return, free under-4s). **Vedettes Iles d'Or** (04.94.71.01.02) runs boats from Le Lavandou to Port-Cros (takes 35-60 mins, €20 return, children €15) and Levant (takes 35-60 mins, €20 return, children €15). There are daily services to Porquerolles and Port-Cros from Cavalaire and La Croix-Valmer.

Spiritual seclusion

Looming like a fortress halfway up a remote hillside, the Chartreuse de la Verne has a powerful sense of isolation even today. How much more so when a group of Carthusian monks settled here in 1170 and where better to live out their chosen life of silence? Soon the monastery owned more than 3,000 acres of forest, pasture and salt works. Although the Romanesque chapel has survived, the monastery was burned on several occasions in the 12th century and in the Wars of Religion and rebuilt on each occasion in a mix of brown-grey schist with local dark-green serpentine facing around doorways and vaults. After the Revolution the lands were confiscated, the monks fled to Nice by boat from the Plage de St-Clair and the monastery become state property. Restoration began in the 1970s and since 1983 the monastery, although still partly ruined, has been occupied by a community of nuns.

The visit takes in the massive gatehouse, once a vegetable store, the granary and bakery, a restored monk's cell with its private courtyard where the monk lived and meditated in solitude except for two daily religious services, the cloister and cemetery, the Romanesque church and later 17th-century chapel, the oil press and the crypt.

Chartreuse de La Verne

(04.94.43.45.41). **Open** *Apr-Sept* 11am-6pm Mon, Wed-Sun; *Oct-Mar* 11am-5pm Mon, Wed-Sun. Closed Jan. **Admission** €5; €3 10-16s; free under-10s.

port, now a pleasure marina. Its rather glitzy seafront is particularly animated at night, though the quieter Plage St-Clair further east in a bay surrounded by mountains is more attractive for bathing. From here to Cavalaire-sur-Mer, the **Corniche des Maures** follows some of the coast's most unspoiled scenery. Villas are tree-swamped on the whole, and the view uphill from silver-sand beaches is unimpeded by development. Pramousquier was one of the beaches of the 1944 landings, while the Plage de Cavalière offers watersports.

The village of Le Rayol-Canadel is home to the **Domaine du Rayol** gardens, created in 1910 by Paris banker Alfred Courmes, who packed the grounds with exotic plants from Chile, South Africa and Australia before losing all his money in the crash of 1929. Since 1989, gardening wizard Gilles Clément has added New Zealand and Asiatic gardens and a 'Garden in Motion'. Gullies, bowers and secret paths are dotted about this jungle of green and dramatic vistas. Outdoor concerts are held in July and August. Above Le Rayol-Canadel, spectacular sea views can be had from the Col du Canadel pass. The idyll comes to a halt at **Cavalaire-sur-Mer**, a built-up sprawl with a long beach frequented by unglamorous families.

Where to stay & eat

In Le Lavandou, Hispano-Moresque **Auberge de la Calanque** (62 av du Général de Gaulle, 04.94.71.05.96, closed Nov-Easter, double €91.47-€183) has a pool and garden; some rooms have sea views; its restaurant (menu €36.59, closed lunch Wed, Thur and Oct-Easter) serves good Provençal fare with an Italian twist. Pick of the fish restaurants overlooking the port is **Restaurant du Vieux-Port** (quai Gabriel Péri, 04.94.71.00.21, closed Tue & Wed and mid-Dec to Jan, menus €18-€30). One street back from the seafront, **Auberge Provençale** (11 rue Patron Ravello, 04.94.71.00.44, closed lunch Mon-Wed and 15-30 Nov & Jan, menus €20-€29) serves carefully prepared southern dishes, both land and sea, and has some simple, spacious rooms (doubles €30-€46). Glitzy bar **Bora Bora** (3 rue Charles Cazin, 04.94.71.05.54) is joyfully kitsch with cocktails served in conch shells and variable live music in summer. On the edge of the beach in St-Clair, the **Auberge de la Falaise** (34 bd de la Baleine, 04.94.71.01.35, double €106-€138 incl dinner) offers pleasant rooms and seafood (menu €26). **Les Tamaris** (chez Raymond, Plage de St-Clair, 04.94.71.07.22, closed Nov to mid-Feb except Christmas, and Tue in Oct, Mar, Apr, average €30) is excellent for fish. Further east, the luxurious **Les Roches** (1 av des Trois Dauphins, Aiguebelle Plage, 04.94.71.05.07/

www.hotellesroches.com, closed Nov-Mar, double €186-€564) plunges down the cliff to the sea, and has chic bar, pricey restaurant (menus €50-€65), spacious antiques-furnished rooms and a half-seawater pool. In Pramousquier, **Le Mas** (9 av du Capitaine Ducourneau, 04.94.05.80.43, closed Nov-Jan, doubles €39.64-€65.55) has lovely views and a pool.

In Le Rayol-Canadel, **Le Maurin des Maures** (04.94.05.60.11, closed dinner mid-Nov to mid-Dec, menus €10.67-€22.71) is celebrated for seafood and consistently packed – so book.

Tourist information

Market day in Le Lavandou is Thursday morning, in Cavalaire Wednesday morning.

Cavalaire-sur-Mer

Office de Tourisme, Maison de la Mer, 83240 Cavalaire-sur-Mer (04.94.01.92.10/ www.franceplus.com/cavalaire). **Open** *June-Sept* 9am-7pm daily; *Oct-May* 9am-12.30pm, 2-6pm Mon-Fri; 9am-12.30pm Sat.

Le Lavandou

Office de Tourisme, quai Gabriel Péri, 83980 Le Lavandou (04.94.00.40.50/www.lelavandou.com). **Open** *Apr-Sept* 9am-noon, 2.30-7pm daily; *Oct-Mar* 9am-noon, 2.30-6pm Mon-Sat.

The Massif des Maures

Taking the D41 out of Bormes to Collobrières, you are at once in a surprisingly wild, remote mountain area with near precipitous wooded slopes, schist outcrops and a hair-raisingly winding road that zigzags up to the Col du Babaou.

Surrounded by cultivated chestnut trees and the massive, gnarled oak trees from which cork is hewn, **Collobrières** is France's *marron glacé* capital – and celebrates the chestnut in a festival each October. Around 1850, it was an important logging centre, and 19th-century wood barons' houses contrast with higgledy-piggledy medieval streets and severe stone houses perched over the Réal Collobrière river. Off the D14 to Cogolin, 12km east of here, stands the brooding **Chartreuse de La Verne** (*see p172*).

On the northern side of the Massif, near Gonfaron, the **Village des Tortues** is a conservation centre for Hermann's tortoise, found only in the Maures and in Corsica. Further east, **La Garde-Freinet** fort was the last bastion of the Moors before their retreat from France in the tenth century.

The heart of the Massif, with its peaks, remote chapels and neolithic menhirs can only be reached on foot. The Massif is crossed east-west by the GR9 and GR51 footpaths and north-south by the GR90. For the less ambitious, two short waymarked discovery footpaths part from near the Office de Tourisme in Collobrières.

Village des Tortues

Gonfaron (04.94.78.26.41). **Open** *Mar-Nov* 9am-7pm daily. **Admission** €8; €5 3-16s; free under-3s.

Where to stay & eat

In Collobrières, **La Petite Fontaine** (1 pl de la République, 04.94.48.00.12, closed dinner Sun, all Mon, two weeks in Sept & Feb, menus €21-€25) serves good local fare. **Hôtel-Restaurant Notre Dame** (15 av de la Libération, 04.94.48.07.13, closed Dec-15 Feb, double €26-€31, menus €15-€23) is a simple Logis de France overhanging a stream. For a truly rustic experience, sample the home-made delights at the **Ferme de Peigros** (Col de Babaou, 04.94.48.03.83, closed dinner Sept-June, menu €20) near the Col du Babaou mountain pass, which produces its own goat's cheese.

Tourist information

Collobrières market is Sunday morning.

Collobrières

Office de Tourisme, bd Caminat, 83610 Collobrières (04.94.48.08.00/www.collotour.com). **Open** *July, Aug* 10am-12.30pm, 3-6.30pm Mon-Sat; *Sept-June* 10am-noon, 2-6pm Tue-Sat.

▶ Getting There & Around

▶ By air

Toulon/Hyères airport (04.94.00.83.83) is near to Hyères port.

▶ By car

The A570, an offshoot of the A57, runs right into Hyères before merging with the N98 coast road which continues to Bormes and then cuts along the south of the Massif des Maures. The D559 at Bormes follows the coast to Le Lavandou and Cavalaire-sur-Mer.

▶ By train

Hyères station is on a branch line that separates from the main coast line just east of Toulon, with several trains a day between Toulon and Hyères.

▶ By bus

Phocéens Cars (04.93.85.66.61) runs two buses a day (Mon-Sat) between Nice airport and Hyères. **Sodétrav** (04.94.12.55.12) operates several bus lines between Toulon and Hyères and from Hyères to St-Tropez, stopping at Bormes, Le Levandou, Le Rayol-Canadol and Cavalaire-sur-Mer, note there are few buses on Sunday. From June-Aug, a local bus connects Bormes Village and the beaches of La Favière and Le Lavandou.

St-Tropez

They still play *pétanque* and go fishing in the ultimate playboy playground, but if you want to make it with the smart set you can never try *trop* hard.

So inconspicuous and unimportant was the rocky headland on which St-Tropez stands that no one thought to supply it with roads until early last century. Today, the approaches to St-Tropez are a purgatory of slow-moving traffic during the summer season. Up on the vine-covered headland, however, all you'll find are luxury homes and badly lost beach babes.

St-Tropez

Given the hedonistic reputation of St-Tropez, it's fitting that the arch-hedonist Nero should have put the place on the map. In the first century AD, the emperor had a Christian centurion by the name of Torpes beheaded in Pisa. Torpes' headless trunk was loaded aboard a boat and set adrift with a rooster and a dog. When the boat washed up on the beach now named after the hapless centurion, the starving dog hadn't taken so much as a nibble of the corpse, a sure sign of sainthood.

In the Middle Ages, the small fishing community at St-Tropez was harried by Saracens until the 15th century, when tough Genoese settlers were imported to show the pirates who was who. The place was still a tiny backwater in 1880 when Guy de Maupassant sailed his boat in briefly to give the locals their first taste of bohemian eccentricity. A decade later, post-Impressionist Paul Signac, driven into port by a storm, liked the place so much that he bought a house, La Hune (on what is now avenue Paul Signac), inviting his friends – including Matisse, Derain, Vlaminck, Marquet and Dufy – and converting their palettes from dark northern tones to brilliant St-Tropez hues. Colette lived here, too: her only complaint about the place was that in order to concentrate on writing, she had to turn her back on the attention-monopolising view.

Another wave of personalities washed up in 1956 after Roger Vadim, his young protégée Brigitte Bardot and a film crew descended on the town to make *Et Dieu créa la femme* (*And God Created Woman*). It was no time before St-Tropez became the world's most famous playboy playground.

The millionaires and superstars are still there (including Bardot, who alternates between her

The spikier nosed the better on the **Vieux Port** at St-Tropez.

house up in the hills and her near-legendary seafront home at La Madrague, now officially the headquarters for her animal rights group). Nowadays, however, they're locked in a bitter love-hate relationship with the Instamatic hordes who come to gawp, only exacerbated in 2001 by the descent of the Lofters (*see p178*).

You'll inevitably find yourself drawn to the Vieux Port, where the yacht-and-Champagne scenario is oddly compelling. Multimillion-pound yachts back up to the quayside to give café terraces a ringside view of their owners' antics. The port was badly bombed in World War II and reconstructed pretty much as it was, with multi-coloured houses that line the quays.

St-Tropez has other attractions, too, beginning with the **Musée de l'Annonciade**, in a 16th-century chapel situated between the old and new port areas. Signac had long wanted to set up a permanent exhibit of his friends' works here, but it was not until 1937 that it came to pass, thanks to the donation by Georges Grammont. In this superb collection of early 20th-century art, the brilliant effects of St-Tropez light can be seen. Pointillists like Signac, Fauves, Nabis, Expressionists and Cubists are all represented in this extraordinary – and extraordinarily under-visited – gallery, including a lovely Vuillard interior and Fauve canvases by Derain, Braque and Vlaminck.

East of the Vieux Port, the **Château de Suffren**, where the occasional art show is staged, dates back to 980. Back from the quai Jean Jaurès, heading towards the Port de Pêche (yes, even in glitzy St-Tropez there are real, working fishermen), the place aux Herbes and rue de Ponce are quieter, less-sanitised, distinctly more lived-in areas of town. The former is home to a lively daily fish market.

Still further around the seafront, the 16th-century citadel contains the fairly bland **Musée Naval**, and allows access on to ramparts with a fantastic view over town and coast. The lovely **Cimetière Marin**, where Roger Vadim is buried, is right on the coast itself. Behind the port, St-Tropez's *pétanque*-playing fraternity hangs out on plane tree-lined place des Lices. It's also home to a market on Tuesday and Saturday. Fruit, vegetables, *charcuterie*, honey and wine fill the stalls but traders are really there to catch up on the local gossip and see friends. Bardot is a regular. On the hill, 1km out of town, the pretty **Chapelle Ste-Anne** (closed to the public) commands spectacular views over the bay, and hosts flash weddings.

The most accessible beaches from town are the built-up **Bouillabaisse** to the west, **Les Graniers** in Baie des Canebiers just past the Citadel, and the horribly crowded **Les Salins** (a 5km drive – there's a 5,000-capacity car park

It's a fair cop

Forget BB, Vadim and Godard. Could St-Tropez's coolest moment in cinema history actually be when a flying saucer lands on the St-Tropez peninsula? *Les Gendarmes et les extraterrestres* (1978), in which the invading aliens have the ability to take on the appearance of human beings – sunbathers and gendarmes included – as long as they take regular drinks of motor oil, was the fifth and silliest film in a series that began with *Le Gendarme de St-Tropez* (1964) and ended with *Le Gendarme et les gendarmettes* (1982). A French equivalent of the Carry On movies, and proof that the French perhaps don't take St-Trop so seriously after all, the films all star anxious-looking Louis de Funès; recurring characters include his wife and a 2CV-driving nun, with cameos by Café Le Senequier, the Vieux Port of St-Tropez and bikini-clad beach babes.

– or 12km hike round the headland), though from here you can also reach the less-peopled **Plage de la Mouette**. But it is the **Baie de Pampelonne** that made St-Trop's reputation, a 5km stretch of white sand (technically in Ramatuelle, *see p179*, **St-Tropez Peninsula**) and its legendary beach clubs **Tahiti** (04.94.97.18.02) and **Club 55** (04.94.55.55.55).

Musée de l'Annonciade

pl Gramont (04.94.97.04.01). **Open** *June-Sept* 10am-noon, 3-7pm Mon, Wed-Sun; *Oct-May* 10am-noon, 2-6pm Mon, Wed-Sun. **Admission** €4.60 (€5.30 during exhibitions); €2.30 (€3.10) 12-18s; free under-12s.

Musée Naval

Mont de la Citadelle (04.94.97.59.43). **Open** *Apr-Nov* 11am-5.30pm Mon, Wed-Sun; *Dec-Mar* 10am-noon, 1-4pm Mon, Wed-Sun. **Admission** €4; €2.50 8-25s; free under-8s.

Restaurants

La Bouillabaisse

plage de la Bouillabaisse (04.94.97.54.00). **Open** *Mar-Apr, June to mid-Nov* 12.30-2.45pm, 7.45-10.30pm daily; *May* 12.30-2.45pm, 7.45-10.30pm Mon, Thur-Sun; 12.30-2.45pm Tue. Closed mid-Nov to Feb. **Average** €34. **Credit** AmEx, MC, V.
In contrast to many restaurants in St-Tropez, both the service and food here are excellent. While away the afternoon on the terrace, enjoying simple, well-prepared dishes such as tagliatelle with freshly made *pistou* and toasted pine nuts. Or indulge yourself by ordering the *bouillabaisse* a day in advance.

The Western Côte

La Brasserie des Arts

pl des Lices (04.94.97.68.26). **Open** lunch and dinner daily. **Average** €38. **Credit** AmEx, DC, MC, V.

At night dance music ups the tempo at this beautiful-people haunt, with its brightly coloured interior and eclectic paintings. There's a range of meat and fish; the speciality is sea bass in a truffle vinegar sauce. Pricey but worth it for the people-watching.

Le Café

pl des Lices (04.94.97.44.69). **Open** daily; hours vary with season. **Menus** €24-€31. **Credit** AmEx, MC, V.

This place is on the site of the Café des Arts, the legendary watering hole for the place des Lices *boules* players. Take a drink at the bar with the locals and cast an eye over the wooden *boules* lockers by the front door. The restaurant at the rear is a hideout for summertime celebs hoping to avoid the hordes. In winter a fire blazes in the grate. The grilled sea bass is a treat, as is the home-made apple tart.

Le Frégate

52 rue Allard (04.94.97.07.08). **Open** noon-2pm, 7-11pm daily. Closed mid-Jan to Feb. **Menus** €17-€24. **Credit** MC, V.

This unassuming restaurant, which seats just 25, serves unpretentious Provençal cuisine, including fish soups and grills, plus *aïoli* every Friday.

Leï Mouscardins

Tour du Portalet (04.94.97.29.00). **Open** *July-Aug* 7-11pm daily; *Sept-June* noon-2pm, 7-10pm Mon, Thur-Sun. Closed mid-Jan to mid-Feb. **Menu** €60. **Credit** AmEx, DC, MC, V.

Laurent Tarridec's quayside restaurant is easily the best and chicest table in this hotbed of hedonism, where people tend to be more concerned about their figures than their gastronomic pleasures. The menu changes seasonally, but may include baby squid and vegetables in a balsamic vinegar and squid-ink dressing and stuffed *capon de mer.*

La Table du Marché

38 rue Georges Clemenceau (04.94.97.85.20). **Open** *Apr-Oct* 7am-midnight daily; Nov-Mar 7am-7pm Mon, Tue, Fri; 7.30am-midnight Sat, Sun. **Menu** €18-€30. **Credit** AmEx, MC, V.

A mouthwatering spread of regional specialities and superb wines in a cosy bistro/deli with an afternoon tea room and a sushi bar (summer only), masterminded by celebrity chef Christophe Leroy. Try for the upstairs dining room, set up like a stage with antique bookshelves and overstuffed armchairs.

Bars & cafés

Bar du Port

7 quai Suffren (04.94.97.00.54). **Open** *July-Aug* 7am-3am daily; *Sept-June* 7am-11pm daily. **No credit cards.**

St-Trop's bar of the moment has a prime portside position, *tabac* and affordable bistro food.

Café de Paris

15 quai Suffren (04.94.97.00.56). **Open** *Apr-Oct* 7am-4am daily; *Nov-Mar* 7am-1am daily. **Menus** €14-€18. **Credit** AmEx, MC, V.

Philippe Starck gave this old bar a makeover and it now has a long counter, red velvet banquettes, chandeliers and a sushi menu. In summer it's packed, and the terrace is a prime position for people-spotting.

Café Le Senequier

quai Jean Jaurès (04.94.97.00.90). **Open** *July-Aug* 8am-3am daily; *mid-Sept to June* 8am-6.30pm daily. Closed mid-Nov to mid-Dec. **No credit cards.**

This vast terrace filled with scarlet chairs may no longer attract the glamorous, but it remains a thoroughly entertaining place for apéritifs, people-watching and yacht-gazing at sunset.

Chez Fuchs

7 rue des Commerçants (04.94.97.01.25). **Open** *June-Sept* 7am-2am Mon, Wed-Sun; *Oct-May* 7am-11pm Mon, Wed-Sun. Closed mid-Jan to end Feb. **Credit** MC, V.

This tiny *bar-tabac* doubles as a moderately priced bistro, with tasty regional beef stew, stuffed vegetables and a friendly atmosphere (lunch all year, dinner only June-Sept). It's a legendary hangout for the local thirtysomething crowd.

Le Gorille

1 quai Suffren (04.94.97.03.93). **Open** *July-Aug* 24 hours daily; *Sept-June* 6am-8pm daily. Closed Jan. **No credit cards.**

A corner caff, Le Gorille is open 24 hours a day in summer, when its menu is honed down to burgers or steak served with the house *frites.*

Nightlife

Caves du Roy

Hôtel Byblos, av Paul-Signac (04.94.97.16.02). **Open** *June-Sept* 11pm-dawn daily; *Oct-May* 11pm-dawn Fri, Sat. **Admission** €23 (incl 1st drink). **Credit** AmEx, DC, MC, V.

Though VIP has made a splash, the cavernous basement club of the Hôtel Byblos has not faltered. Swingers *d'un certain âge* – rocker Johnny Hallyday, music impresario Eddie Barclay – party until dawn. Big, but getting in ain't always easy.

Octave Café

pl de la Garonne (04.94.97.22.56). **Open** *Mar-Oct* 10pm-5am daily; *Nov-Dec* 6pm-1am Tue-Sat. Closed Jan-Feb. **Admission** €11-€14 (incl 1st drink). **Credit** AmEx, MC, V.

A stylish piano bar with soft music, squishy cushioned chairs, low black tables and a chic clientèle. Liza Minnelli and the inimitable Johnny have been known to pop in and croon a few tunes just for fun.

Le Papagayo

résidences du Nouveau Port (04.94.97.07.56). **Open** *Apr-June, Sept to mid-Oct* 11.30pm-5am Fri-Sun; *July-Aug* 11.30pm-5am daily. Closed mid-Oct-Mar.

Admission €23. **Credit** AmEx, MC, V.
Ever since the 60s, this legendary club has attracted the showbiz crowd; it's still one of the nocturnal
hotspots. El Bodega du Papagayo (04.94.97.76.70) is
a favourite early-evening rendez-vous.

Le VIP Room

résidences du Nouveau Port (04.94.97.14.70).
Open from May 2002 7pm-dawn daily. Ring to check
in winter. **Admission** €18 (incl 1st drink). **Credit**
AmEx, MC, V.
The southern outpost of Jean Roch's Champs-
Elysées club has just been revamped as a two-level
complex integrating the fashionable Madrague
restaurant (menu €29). The decor has been alternatively described as 'baroque' and 'minimalist', so
take your pick, and the music is modern and edgy.

Shopping

Since long before the onslaught of designer
boutiques, **Claire l'Insolite** (1 rue Sibille,
04.94.97.10.74, closed two weeks in Nov & Jan),
has offered a little bit of everything from the
world of trendy designer fashions and glamour
bikinis, along with friendly service. For old-
fashioned home linens, sweet-smelling soaps,
Provençal pottery and unusual *objets d'art*, try
La Maison des Lices (2 & 18 bd Louis Blanc,
04.94.97.64.64. closed Mon & Sun Dec-May, and
Nov). **La Tarte Tropézienne** (36 rue Georges
Clemenceau, 04.94.97.71.42) is the place to
discover the local speciality, *la tropézienne*, a
light sponge cake filled with custard cream.

Where to stay

If you're planning to stay in St-Tropez in high
season, book months ahead.

Château de la Messardière

rte de Tahiti (04.94.56.76.00/www.messardiere.com).
Closed Dec-Mar. **Double** €180-€580. **Credit** AmEx,
DC, MC, V.
Perched on a hilltop of parasol pines, this restored
19th-century castle, complete with turrets and
canopy beds, once belonged to an aristocratic family whose spirit lives on in the tarot-inspired art
adorning the arches of the elegant lobby, designed
by the current Countess de la Messardière.

Hôtel Byblos

av Paul Signac (04.94.56.68.00/www.byblos.com).
Closed mid-Oct to Easter. **Double** €350-€680.
Credit AmEx, DC, V.
An eclectic mix of Byzantine kitsch and Provençal
neo-rustic, the perennially trendy Byblos has 52
rooms and 42 suites spread over twee chalets amid
palm- and fountain-filled gardens, right in the centre of town. Food is taken very seriously by chef
Georges Pélissier at Le Byblos restaurant and he
also oversees the new Spoon Byblos. There's a pool
with counter-current, sauna and beauty treatments.

Yacht etiquette

If you don't have a boat in St-Tropez, then
you shouldn't be there at all. Or that is
how you are made to feel by the hulking
gin palaces that cruise the Cap.
  The high-speed offshore days of the 80s
cigarette boat have now been overtaken by
slower pursuits: lounging along the coast
on open-deck vessels, with full viewing
capacity. Little navigation is needed –
reverse manoeuvre into the Vieux Port
(where a slot on the *quai d'honneur* in
front of Café Le Senequier at the Cap
is worth over €800 a day) assures the
riffraff on land a fabulously smug spectacle
that has taken all day to prepare.
  The millionaire eurotrash, oil royalty and
international liggers at the helm spend the
day scouting the talent along Baie de
Pampelonne for trophy totty to lure on
board. Implausibly pretty girls barely in
bikinis audition for the invitation by
dancing on tables at La Voile Rouge. The
prize: an afternoon – or whole summer – of
free hedonism and being mauled on deck,
tactically moored off Club 55. The drunken
circus returns to the quay at sunset, where
ostentatious Champagne and lobster
banquets are laid on to dazzle the crowd.
  You, too, could be one of them. A large
pleasure boat can be bought or hired from
brokers in St-Tropez. The Rodriguez
dynasty has an office at **SNP Boat
Services** (rue du Cepoun San Martin,
04.94.97.06.90), with exclusive sale of
the Mangusta brand. The 33m Mangusta
108, the largest open cruiser in the world,
costs €9 million and up; the smaller
Mangusta 80 is for hire at around €5,335
a day, crew included. For classic style, the
mahogany Riva is available second-hand
from **Sportmer** (rtes des Salins,
04.94.97.32.33): €229,000 for a
retouched Riva Aquarama. **MSC Yachting
Ltd** (rue Portalet, 04.94.97.73.86) will rent
you a Riva: three hours for €600.
  It is an expensive business, and that's
without filling up at the harbour petrol
station (04.94.54.86.63) or your boating
licence – a five-day €381 ticket to glamour
with instructor Joël Griffon
(04.94.54.46.51). If all else fails, take a
short, commented cruise with **Taxi Bateau
Vasse** (04.94.54.40.61) or **MMG**
(04.94.96.51.00), or just act as vulgar as
possible – someone might just spot you…

Hôtel La Maison Blanche

pl des Lices (04.94.97.52.66/
www.hotellamaisonblanche.com). **Double** €167.69-
€747. **Credit** AmEx, DC, MC, V.
Recently given a stylish facelift by minimalist interior designer Fabienne Villacrèces, La Maison
Blanche is an oasis of calm, yet only a stroll from the
port. In the evening laze on wicker loungers on the
terrace and enjoy a cool cocktail. With only five bedrooms and four suites La Maison Blanche is exclusive while retaining its village hotel charm.

Hôtel La Mistralée

1 av du Général Leclerc (04.98.12.91.12/
www.mistralee.fr). **Double** €200-€380.
Credit AmEx, MC, V.
This is a good-value intimate hotel in a romantic
white stucco villa near the Vieux Port.

Les Palmiers

24-26 bd Vasserot (04.94.97.01.61/
www.hotel-les-palmiers.com). **Double** €69-€168.
Credit AmEx, MC, V.
A verdant path leads to reception and in season the
branches are loaded with limes, mandarins and
grapefruits. Rooms giving on to the courtyard each
have a mini-patio. Service is friendly and the bar
large enough to invite friends for a pre-club apéritif.

Le Pré de la Mer

rte des Salins (04.94.97.12.23/
www.lepredelamer.com). Closed Oct-Easter. **Double**
€86-€139. **Credit** AmEx, V.
Three conventional bedrooms and eight self-contained studio apartments in a pretty Provençal
setting slightly outside town.

Résidence de la Pinède

plage de la Bouillabaisse (04.94.55.91.00/
www.residencepinede.com). Closed Oct to Easter.
Double €235-€805. Credit AmEx, DC, MC, V.
Only a stone's throw from the mad summer hordes
of downtown St-Trop, this tranquil oasis of luxury
has its own private beach, a spillover pool, an
unbeatable view of the bay and one of the best
restaurants around (meals served noon-2.30pm, 7.30-
10pm daily, menus €75-€104). Try Belgian chef
Alois Vanlangeenaeker's delectable *menu Provence*.

Loft conversion

In summer 2001, a blonde bombshell hit the
elite resort: Loana Petrucciani. The brassy
babe had won through as the female half of
the winning couple in *Loft Story*, the French
version of *Big Brother*. To get their hands on
the 1.5 million franc prize money the pair had
to stay – together – 45 days in a villa in St-
Tropez under telesurveillance. But when
Loana and consort Christophe ventured out
under the telephoto lenses of the paparazzi,
the townfolk got distinctly sniffy. Holding court
on Vieux Port terraces, the 23-year-old ex-
gogo dancer held up traffic and worse, much
worse… hogged the limelight. God famously
created woman in St-Tropez in the shapely
form of Brigitte Bardot under the guidance of
director Roger Vadim. This parvenue, single
mother created herself, and celebs winced at
the grating imposition of a popularly elected
bimbo. The Loana episode is just the most
public manifestation of a downmarket
takeover. Left Bank on Sea considers the
buzzing port its fief where acceptance is in its
gift. The Hôtel Byblos and its club Les Caves
du Roy made it clear that Les Lofters were
not welcome. 'Up until now it has been a cosy
closed circle of media professionals and their
Parisian friends. Shows like *Loft Story* and
the French version of *Survivor* have upset
these people,' says Alain Grasset, showbiz
editor on popular daily *Le Parisien*. While

mega-buck yachts still hold sway, there are
powerful new forces swirling in the azure
waters of the jet-set playground. While the
resort relies on mass exposure, it doesn't
relish exposure to the masses.

Le Sube
15 quai Suffren (04.94.97.30.04). Closed three weeks Jan. **Double** €150-€250. **Credit** AmEx, DC, MC, V.

Plum in the centre of the old port, the Sube is woody and cosy, and a favourite with yachting enthusiasts. The unusually large bar has a view on to the port, with a balcony so popular it can be difficult to squeeze on to in high season. Don't worry, just ease back into a leather armchair and admire the nautical artefacts that deck the mantlepiece and tables.

Tourist information

St-Tropez Office de Tourisme
quai Jean Jaurès, 06390 St-Tropez (04.94.97.45.21/ www.ot-saint-tropez.com). **Open** 9am-noon, 2-6pm daily.

St-Tropez Peninsula

When the truly chic or truly rich talk about summering in St-Trop, often as not they actually mean hiding out in the hills in Garbo-esque seclusion well away from the wannabes who frequent the old port. Here amid Côtes de Provence vineyards and overlooking pristine blue coves, the hill villages of Ramatuelle and Gassin retain a sense of exclusivity. **Ramatuelle** began as a Saracen stronghold; it was razed in 1592 during the Religious Wars, then rebuilt in 1620, as many inscriptions above doors testify. **Gassin** sits at the end of some frightening hairpin bends, and is a delightful place to stroll around picturesque alleyways when it's too hot to breathe down on the coast. Mick and Bianca Jagger honeymooned here after an action-packed wedding in St-Tropez's Chapelle Ste-Anne in the early 1970s.

On route Ramatuelle (D61 towards Gassin), **Château Minuty** (04.94.56.12.09, closed Sat & Sun) produces a highly rated rosé and fine reds. The cellars, grounds and 18th-century chapel can be visited. Further along the D61 is the equally charming **Château de Barbeyrolles** (04.94.56.33.58, closed Sun Oct-Apr). Local co-operative **Les Maîtres Vignerons de St-Tropez** (04.94.56.32.04, closed Sun) is by the La Foux junction on the N98, where there's a farmers' market on Sunday morning in summer.

Slightly back from the coast, **La Croix-Valmer** is a residential town with fine views across cliffs dotted with the holiday villas of discreetly well-heeled French families. Though the *croix* (cross) in its name refers to an airborne one allegedly seen around here by the co-Emperor Constantine, the town was only built in 1934. From here, there is easy access to the stunning coastal conservation area on the Cap Lardier and the lovely Plage de Gigaro.

The relics of St Torpes with his head back on.

Where to stay & eat

Below Ramatuelle, **Les Moulins** (rte des Plages, 04.94.97.17.22, closed mid-Nov to Apr, double €222-€252) has six pretty rooms and an excellent restaurant (menus €34-€88), run by Christophe Leroy of St-Trop's La Table du Marché. Opposite Tahiti Beach, **Hôtel Les Bouis** (rte des Plages-Pampelonne, 04.94.79.87.61, closed end Oct-Easter, double €125-€186) offers all creature comforts in the wilds of St-Tropez beachland. **Chez Camille** (plage de Bonne Terrasse, 04.94.79.80.38, closed Oct-Easter) is great for fish dinner on the beach. In Ramatuelle, **Terrasse-Hostellerie Le Baou** (av Gustave Etienne, 04.98.12.94.20, closed mid-Oct to Easter, double €120-€620), has spectacular views across the vine-clad peninsula, pleasant rooms, a pool and a restaurant (menus €37-€60) serving reliable Provençal faves. At **La Forge** (rue Victor Léon, 04.94.79.25.56, closed Nov to mid-Mar, menu €28.20) chef Pierre Fazio and wife serve up good Provençal cuisine in a cleverly converted smithy. **Café de l'Ormeau** (pl de l'Ormeau, 04.94.79.20.20, closed Wed and mid-Feb to mid-Mar) is pure central casting, with creeper-covered terrace and long wooden bar. In Gassin, **Le Micocoulier** (pl des Barrys, 04.94.56.14.01,

The Western Côte

Pretend you're a humble Veneto fisherman at **Port Grimaud.**

closed Mon & mid-Oct to Apr, menus €27-€40)
serves Provençal food, with an Italian twist.

South-east of the Croix-Valmer, the 19th-
century **Château de Valmer** (rte de Gigaro,
04.94.79.60.10/www.chateau-valmer.com, closed
Nov-Apr, double €162-€355) has a pool amid
vines, palms and fruit trees, soothing salons
and Laura Ashley/Pierre Frey fabrics. Under
the same ownership, **La Pinède Plage** (plage
de Gigaro, 04.94.54.31.23/www.pinede-
plage.com, double €162-€310, menu €45) has
spacious, comfortable rooms and a restaurant
and pool overlooking the *grand bleu*. The two
share La Pinède's beach with windsurfing,
kayaks and pedalos. Soberly elegant **Souleias**
(plage de Gigaro, 04.94.55.10.55/www.hotel-
souleias.com, closed mid-Oct to end Mar, double
€147-€325), sits on the clifftop; its restaurant
(menus €29-€50) serves classic Provençal food.

Tourist information

La Croix-Valmer Office de Tourisme

*Les Jardins de la Gare, 83400 La Croix-Valmer
(04.94.55.12.12/fax 04.94.55.12.10).* **Open** *mid-June
to mid-Sept* 9.15am-12.30pm, 2.30-7pm Mon-Sat;
9.15am-1.30pm Sun; *mid-Sept to mid-June* 9.15am-
noon, 2-6pm Mon-Fri; 9.15am-noon Sat, Sun.

Ramatuelle Office de Tourisme

*pl de l'Ormeau, 83350 Ramatuelle (04.98.12.64.00/
www.nova.fr/ramatuelle).* **Open** *Apr-mid Oct* 8.30am-
12.30pm, 3-7pm Mon-Sat; *mid-Oct to Mar* 8.30am-
12.30pm, 2-6pm Mon-Fri.

Cogolin, Grimaud & Ste-Maxime

West of St-Tropez, **Cogolin** wins no prizes for
beauty, but it does qualify as a real town with
an economy based around the manufacture of
corks, briar pipes, bamboo furniture and carpet-
making, a trade imported by Armenian
immigrants in the 1920s. The 11th-century
church of St-Sauveur (open 8am-7pm daily) has
a lovely altarpiece by Hurlupin. The **Espace
Raimu** has a collection of memorabilia of the
actor Jules Muraire, alias Raimu.

Further north, picture-perfect *village perché*
Grimaud was a Saracen stronghold before
falling to the Templars. Nowadays, the quaint
shops brigade is firmly in command. Up top are
the ruins of an 11th-century castle. Rue des
Templiers has basalt arcades and imposing
doorways, and there's a pretty Romanesque
church, St-Michel (open 9am-6pm daily).

Back down on the coast, Port Grimaud was
built in the late 1960s on reclaimed land,
designed by architect François Spoerry to look
like a perfect miniature Murano, complete with
canals instead of streets. Kitschily pretty, this is
real estate for the seriously rich, but the owners
magnanimously let visitors wander along the
brasserie-lined canals to admire the yachts
parked at the bottoms of gardens.

Ste-Maxime comes in sharp contrast to the
rarefied glamour of St-Tropez across the gulf,

and the residents are proud of the small-town welcome they offer. They're also happy to take up the slack of big-spending holiday-makers who found no room at the inn in St-Tropez. The esplanade is crowded with family restaurants facing on to the pines and the port.

Espace Raimu

18 av Clemenceau, Cogolin (04.94.54.18.00/ www.musee-raimu.com). **Open** 10am-noon, 3-6pm Mon-Sat, 3-6pm Sun. **Admission** €3.50; €1.65 11-18s; free under-11s.

Where to stay, eat & drink

A lovely new addition to accommodation in Cogolin is **La Maison du Monde** (63 rue Carnot, 04.94.54.77.54, double €80-€145), with 12 stylishly decorated rooms, pool and garden. Simple **Hôtel Clemenceau** (pl de la République, 04.94.54.15.17, double €35-€49) has an English-speaking host. On the road to St-Tropez, **Relais de Font-Mourier** (domaine Bellevue, 04.94.56.60.61, closed Oct-Mar, double €80-€125) has a pool and tennis courts.

Grimaud's only hotel is the **Côteau Flori** (pl des Pénitentas, 04.94.43.20.17/ www.coteaufleuri.fr, closed Nov-Dec, double €42-€84), a gem with views over the Massif des Maures. **Restaurant Le Murier** (quartier La Boal, D14, 0494.43.34.94, menus €32-€75) was taken over by chef Jean-Philippe Dubourg (formerly at Souleias) in 2001. Among revisited classics and original inventions are an incredible dessert of green asparagus ice cream with confit vegetables and sweet, morel-flavoured sauce. On the D558 out of Grimaud, **Les Santons** (04.94.43.21.02, closed Nov-Mar, menu €33-€42) is a little stiff but dishes such as *blanquette d'agneau* or chicken with a ginger and citrus sauce are excellent. Down in Port Grimaud, the luxurious **Giraglia** (pl du 14 Juin, 04.94.56.31.33/www.hotelgiraglia.com, closed Oct-May, double €250-€350) has a pool and garden and is perfect for watching boat traffic.

In Ste-Maxime, the **Belle Aurore** (4 bd Jean Moulin, 04.94.96.02.45/www.belleaurore.com, closed mid-Oct to mid-Mar, double €130-€488) has white-jacketed staff, a view of the sea across the golf course, a swimming pool and a good restaurant (closed Wed Sept-June, menus €32-€46). The **Mas des Oliviers** (quartier de la Croisette, 04.94.96.13.31, double €46-€130), 1km west of the centre, has 20 rooms, some with balconies and sea views, plus a pool and tennis courts. **La Marine** (6 rue Fernard Bessy, 04.94.96.53.93, closed Nov-Feb, menus €23-€30) serves reliable seafood and **La Maison Bleue** (48 rue Bert, 04.94.96.71.69, closed Tue and Nov-end Dec, Jan-Feb, menus €16-€22) serves pasta and fish alfresco. Of Ste-Maxime's

bars, the **Café de France** (pl Victor Hugo, 04.94.96.18.16) and **Le Wafu** (pl Victor Hugo, 04.94.96.15.74), both with sun-kissed terraces, are institutions that open late in summer.

Tourist information

Market is Wednesday and Saturday at Cogolin, Thursday at Grimaud, Friday at Ste-Maxime.

Cogolin Office de Tourisme

pl de la République, 83310 Cogolin (04.94.55.01.10). **Open** *July-Aug* 9am-1pm, 2-3pm Mon-Sat; 9.30am-12.30pm Sun; *Sept-June* 9am-12.30pm, 2-6.30pm Mon-Fri; 9.30am-12.30pm Sat.

Grimaud Office de Tourisme

1 bd des Aliziers, 83310 Grimaud (04.94.43.26.98). **Open** *Apr-June, Sept* 9am-12.30pm, 2.30-6.30pm Mon-Sat; *July-Aug* 9am-12.30pm, 3-7pm Mon-Sat; *Oct-Mar* 9am-12.30pm, 2.15-5.30pm Mon-Sat.

Port Grimaud Office de Tourisme

83310 Port Grimaud (04.94.56.02.01). **Open** *June, Sept* 9am-12.30pm, 2.30-6.30pm Mon-Sat; *July-Aug* 9am-12.30pm, 3-7pm Mon-Sat; 10am-1pm Sun.

Ste-Maxime Office de Tourisme

promenade Simon Lorière, 83120 Ste-Maxime (04.94.55.75.55). **Open** *June, Sept* 9am-12.30pm, 2-7pm Mon-Sat; *July-Aug* 9am-8pm Mon-Sat; *Oct-May* 9am-noon, 2-6pm Mon-Sat.

▶ Getting There & Around

▶ The right sort arrive in St-Tropez by yacht or helicopter. There is no train station.

▶ By car

Sweat it out on the notoriously busy N98 coast road. There are plans for an expressway in 2005. Ramatuelle is on the D61 south of St-Tropez; for Gassin take one of the signposted roads off the D61 or D559. Ste-Maxime is on the D98 coast road; alternatively, leave the A8 at exit no.36 and take the D25.

▶ By bus

Sodetrav (04.94.12.55.12) runs daily buses between St-Tropez and Toulon via Hyères. There is one morning service a day between St-Tropez, Ramatuelle and Gassin in July and Aug and on Tue, Wed, Fri and Sat in Sept-June, and daily services between St-Tropez and St-Raphaël, via Grimaud, Cogolin and Ste-Maxime.

▶ By boat

Les Bateaux Verts (04.94.49.29.39) runs hourly boat services from Ste-Maxime to St-Tropez Apr to Oct.

The Western Côte

St-Raphaël & the Estérel

It is one of the least flashy towns on the Côte d'Azur, but you can't go anywhere in the surrounding area without being gob-smacked by ever-more dazzling views.

All-season resort St-Raphaël is known for its sheltered beach and its double marina. Along with its once Roman sister Fréjus, it stands at the western end of the Corniche de l'Estérel, where the red volcanic rocks of the Massif de l'Estérel loom over the deep blue sea, providing the most striking colour contrasts on the Côte d'Azur.

St-Raphaël

Alphonse Karr (1808-90), a journalist opposed to Napoléon III and exiled in Nice, settled in St-Raphaël in 1864. Writing to a Parisian friend, he said 'Leave Paris and plant your stick in my garden: next morning, when you wake, you will see it has grown roses.' Writers and artists heeded his invitation: Dumas, Maupassant and Berlioz all found inspiration here.

Following their lead, Félix Martin, local mayor and civil engineer, transformed the village into a smart getaway. Further illustrious guests began to mark their stay in St-Raphaël with works of art: Gounod composed *Romeo and Juliet* here in 1869, Scott Fitzgerald wrote *Tender is the Night* and Félix Ziem painted some of his pictures.

Today, the 'village' is a maze of cafés, restaurants and shops with all the multicoloured paraphernalia of sea sports, from windsurfing boards to the latest fluorescent garb. Although the old harbour is crowded with mountain-bikers and Rollerbladers, promenade René Coty offers a view worth stopping for of the sea and the twin rocks known as the Land Lion and the Sea Lion.

St-Raphaël still has the feel of an unflashy, family- and pensioner-oriented destination, as it was for the wealthy Romans who came down from Fréjus to take the sea air in the Gallo-Roman resort that once stood on the site now occupied by the casino. On 9 October 1799, Napoléon rescued it from oblivion by landing here after taking a beating at the hands of the British in Egypt. His arrival is commemorated by a pyramid on avenue Commandant Guilbaud.

St-Raphaël's medieval and *belle époque* centre was largely destroyed by wartime bombing. From the west, the skyline is dominated by the neo-Byzantine **Notre-Dame-de-la-Victoire-de-Lépante** (bd Félix Martin), built in 1883 with remarkably modern stained-glass

windows. This truly beautiful church is sadly surrounded by apartments with all the allure of office blocks. Far more picturesquely situated in the old town is the church of **St-Pierre-des-Templiers** (follow rue des Remparts), built in the 12th century in Provençal Romanesque style, which doubled as a fortress at times of attack by pirates. It is home to a gilded wooden bust of St Peter that is still carried by fishermen in procession to the Sea Lion in August. Next door, beside the remains of the Roman aqueduct, the **Musée Archéologique** contains ancient artefacts from the harbour, plus a display on underwater archaeology. In the **Quartier de Valescure** there is a park laid out following the advice of Paris Opera House architect Charles Garnier, with ornaments from the Palais des Tuileries in Paris. Beneath the railway arches on rue Victor Hugo, the daily market is a rare patch of noisy local character.

Musée Archéologique

pl de la Vieille Eglise (04.94.19.25.75). **Open** 10am-noon, 2-5.30pm Tue-Sat. **Admission** (including entry to St-Pierre-des-Templiers) €1.50; €0.80 10-18s; free under-10s.

Where to stay & eat

The family-run **Excelsior** (193 bd Félix Martin, 04.94.95.02.42/www.excelsior-hotel.com, double €100-€150) is a *belle époque* hotel on the sea front with 40 rooms and an English pub. **Le Méditerranée** (1 av Paul Doumer, 04.94.82.10.99/www.lemediterranee.fr) has airy apartments (double €273-€540 per week) and friendly staff. **La Potinière** (169 av de la Gare de Boulouris, 04.94.19.81.71/www.la-potiniere.com, double €62-€132) is a villa by the sea surrounded by eucalyptus trees, 5km east of town. In the city centre, Philippe Troncy at **L'Arbousier** (6 av de Valescure, 04.94.95.25.00, closed Mon, dinner Wed & Sun, one week in Nov, two weeks in Dec, menus €30-€51) is one of St-Raphaël's most innovative chefs. Behind the *vieux port*, **La Gargoulette** (29 rue Pierre Aublé, 04.94.95.48.18, closed Mon, dinner Sun and July, menus €30-€50) offers Mediterranean classics. St-Raphaël institution **Pastorel** (54 rue de la Liberté, 04.94.95.02.36, closed Mon, dinner Sun, two weeks in Mar &

The Western Côte

Fréjus' **Pagode bouddhique** was built by Vietnamese soldiers. *See p184.*

Nov, one week in May, menus €26-€32) has been serving local specialities for 70 years. **La Bouillabaisse** (50 pl Victor Hugo, 04.94.95.03.57, closed Mon and Dec, average €35) serves nothing but its namesake dish. The **Loch Ness Pub** (15 av de Valescure, 04.94.95.99.49) offers beer (€5 a pint), live music and sandwiches. The **Hôtel San Pedro** (890 av du Colonel Brooke, 04.94.19.90.20/ www.hotel-sanpedro.com, closed Nov, double €75-€136, menus €28-€45) has a good Provençal-style restaurant.

Tourist information

Market daily in St-Raphaël.

St-Raphaël Office de Tourisme

210 rue Waldeck Rousseau, 83702 St-Raphaël (04.94.19.52.52/www.saint-raphael.com). **Open** *July-Aug* 9am-8pm daily; *Sept-June* 9am-12.30pm, 2-6.30pm Mon-Sat.

Fréjus & Roquebrune-sur-Argens

Inland from St-Raphaël, **Fréjus** attracts fans of ancient civilisations, as well as offering the more childlike attractions of the **Parc Zoölogique** and **Aquatica** water park. Its Roman ruins include the most extensive naval base of the Roman world alongside that of Ostia

in Italy. Fréjus was founded – as Forum Julii – by Julius Caesar in 49BC and became a naval post for Augustus' swift-sailing galleys, which defeated Antony and Cleopatra at Actium in 31BC. The harbour was guarded by two large towers; one, the **Lanterne d'Auguste**, still rises high at the end of the south quai. During the long years of Roman peace, the once-crucial port became a tiny backwater. Today Fréjus is still smaller than it was in its heyday.

It takes the best part of a day to see Fréjus' scattered Roman remains. Most impressive is the amphitheatre, which can still seat 10,000 and is used for bullfights and plays. The two Roman columns were discovered on a wreck in the Gulf of St Tropez. Near the railway station, the half-moon-shaped **Porte des Gaules** was part of the Roman ramparts. On the other side of the station around the port, the Butte St-Antoine mound formed a western citadel and has a tower which was probably a lighthouse. The **Platforme**, its counterpart on the east, served as military headquarters. Inland from here stretches of the Roman aqueduct are visible from avenue du XV Corps d'Armée. Further north, the Roman theatre has had new modern seats installed for summer concerts.

Facing on to place Formigé, the **Cathédrale St-Léonce** is at the heart of the unusual fortified Cité Episcopale (cathedral close). The carved 16th-century cathedral doors show Mary and Saints Peter and Paul amid scenes of

Saracen butchery. Opposite, the octagonal baptistry dates to the fifth century. Excavations have uncovered the original white marble pavement and the pool. The two-tier, 13th-century cloisters have twin columns of white marble and disturbing 15th-century paintings of characters from the Apocalypse on the ceiling. Upstairs, the **Musée Archéologique** has some outstanding Gallo-Roman antiquities recovered from the Fréjus excavations.

North of town, two surprising constructions evoke France's colonial past. On the N7, the **Pagode bouddhique Hông Hiên** (Buddhist pagoda) was built by Vietnamese soldiers who fought in France in 1917, and has an exotic garden with a collection of sacred animals and guardian spirits. Nearby, a war memorial rises above the graves of over 24,000 soldiers and civilians who died in Indochina. Jutting out amid pine woods stands the **Mosquée de Missiri**, a replica of the celebrated Missiri de Djenné mosque in Mali, built for Sudanese troops in the 1920s. Two false termite mounds have been added to create the impression of Africa.

North-west of Fréjus, the small town of **Roquebrune-sur-Argens** is perched on a rocky peak at the foot of the Rocher de Roquebrune. Originally a stronghold, the *castrum*, located near the church, was once surrounded by a curtain wall destroyed during the Wars of Religion in 1592. Traces of the wall are still visible, particularly in boulevard de la Liberté. The church of St-Pierre-St-Paul is a 16th-century late Gothic structure with fine altarpieces in the two chapels. Some houses in picturesque rue des Portiques date back to the 16th century.

The first left fork on the D7 north of town leads to the red sandstone **Rocher de Roquebrune**. At the summit, stand three crosses by sculptor Bernar Vernet, in memory of three famous crucifixions painted by Giotto, Grunewald and El Greco, using the summit to symbolise Golgotha. Take the trail marked with yellow paint, and prepare yourself for breathtaking views.

Aquatica

RN98, Quartier Le Capou (04.94.51.82.51/ www.parc-aquatica.com). **Open** *June, 1-15 Sept* (weather allowing) 10am-6pm daily; *July-Aug* 10am-7pm daily. **Admission** €22; €18 under-11s. **Credit** MC, V.

Les Arènes

rue Henri Vadon (04.94.51.34.31). **Open** *Apr-Oct* 10am-1pm, 2.30-6.30pm Mon, Wed-Sun; *Nov-Mar* 10am-noon Mon, Wed-Sun. **Admission** free.

Cité Episcopale

48 rue de Fleury (04.94.51.26.30). **Open** *Apr-Sept* 9am-7pm daily; *Oct-Mar* 9am-noon, 2-5pm Tue-Sun. **Admission** €3.96; €2.44 18-25s; free under-18s.

Musée Archéologique

pl Calvini (04.94.52.15.78). **Open** *Apr-Oct* 10am-1pm, 2.30-6.30pm Mon, Wed-Sat; *Nov-Mar* 10am-noon, 1.30-5.30pm Mon, Wed-Sat. **Admission** free.

Pagode bouddhique Hông Hiên

13 rue Henri Giraud (04.94.53.25.29). **Open** 9am-noon, 2-5pm daily. **Admission** €1.

Parc Zoölogique de Fréjus

D4 (04.98.11.37.37/www.zoo-frejus.com). **Open** *June-Sept* 9.30am-6pm daily; *Oct-May* 10am-5.30pm daily. **Admission** €10; €6 3-10s; free under-3s. **Credit** MC, V.

Where to stay & eat

Most people stay in St-Raphaël rather than Fréjus, but there are some charming options. The **Aréna** (145 rue Général de Gaulle, 04.94.17.09.40/www.arena-hotel.com, closed mid-Dec to mid-Jan, double €73-€144, restaurant closed lunch Mon & Sat, menus €23-€43) in the old town offers a warm welcome, garden and pool, while its restaurant serves the best Provençal cuisine in town. The **Bellevue** (pl Paul Vernet, 04.94.17.27.05, double €38-€45) is cheaper with smallish rooms but good views. Down on the beach, the modern **Sable et Soleil** (158 rue Paul Arène, 04.94.51.08.70, closed mid-Nov to mid-Dec, double €30-€59) is bright and friendly.

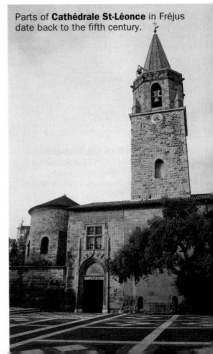

Parts of **Cathédrale St-Léonce** in Fréjus date back to the fifth century.

La Cave Romaine (114 rue Camelin, 04.94.51.52.03, open dinner only, closed Tue, average €30) serves Italian pasta and pizzas, and grilled meat and fish. Hidden down a tiny backstreet, **Les Potiers** (135 rue des Potiers, 04.94.51.33.74, closed Tue, lunch Wed, and one week in Jan & Feb, menus €21-€28) serves reliable classics. The **Bar du Marché** (5 pl de la Liberté, 04.94.51.29.09), with tables outside under spreading boughs, offers a filling *plat du jour* for €7. In Fréjus port, **El Salmon** (pl des Galoubets, 04.94.51.05.07, closed Wed, lunch Fri, dinner Sun in Dec, Feb & Mar and all Jan & Nov, menus €12-€27) has a good seafood selection and specialises in… salmon.

In Roquebrune-sur-Argens try **Le Gaspacho** (21 av Général de Gaulle, 04.94.45.49.59, closed Wed from Oct to Mar and 2 weeks in Nov, menus €11-€18.50). Food is trad French and the chocolate mousse worth every guilty calorie. **Le Sainte Candie** (pl Germain Ollie, 04.94.45.71.01, closed Mon and last two weeks in Feb) serves typical Provençal cuisine in an intimate, candlelit setting.

Tourist information

Market days are Wednesday, Saturday and Sunday in Fréjus and Tuesday and Friday in Roquebrune-sur-Argens.

Fréjus Office de Tourisme

325 rue Jean Jaurès, 83160 Fréjus (04.94.51.83.83/ www.ville-frejus.fr). **Open** *Sept-Mar* 9am-noon, 2-6pm Mon-Sat; *Apr-Aug* 9am-12.30pm, 2-7pm daily.

Roquebrune Office de Tourisme

rue Jean Aicard, 83520 Roquebrune-sur-Argens (04.94.45.72.70/www.ville-roquebrune-argens.fr). **Open** *Apr-Sept* 9am-noon, 2-6pm Mon-Sat, 9-noon Sun; *Oct-Mar* 9-noon, 2-6pm Mon-Fri.

The Corniche de l'Estérel

If the hairpin turns and imposing red rocks of the dramatic clifftop road don't steal your breath away, the coastal views certainly will. Among these spectacular vistas, the **Pointe du Dramont**, 10km east of St-Raphaël, stands out. Auguste Lutaud was duly impressed and, in 1897, he bought tiny **Ile d'Or** just off the point. After building a four-storey mock-medieval tower from the red stone of the Estérel, he proclaimed himself King Auguste I of the Ile d'Or and, as the darling of fashionable society, threw some of the wildest parties on the Côte. Hergé's Black Island in his Tintin adventures was inspired by Lutard's bit of rock.

Enjoy the **Plage du Dramont**, famous for being the bit of sand where the 36th division of the US Army landed on 15 August 1944.

Alternatively, for a spectacular view, take the paved, signposted, one-hour walk up to the **Sémaphore du Dramont** from the N98. Another path descends to the port of Agay.

Discovered by the ancient Greeks, **Agay** is one of the Côte's more relaxed resorts. It is shadowed by the Rastel d'Agay, whose red slopes are lined by a large and sunny beach. Its outcrops of blue porphyry were prized by the Romans for columns. Daredevil author of *Le Petit Prince* Antoine de St-Exupéry crashed his plane just around the bay in World War II.

The beach of **Anthéor** is dominated by the **Plateau d'Anthéor**, from where a path leads up to the Rocher de St-Barthélemy and a beautiful view over the Pic du Cap Roux. Climbing to the Cap Roux peak takes about two hours return. Further along the coast road is the **Pointe de l'Observatoire**, offering views over the crags.

Le Trayas has a pleasant, modest beach. The bay of **La Figueirette**, reached from the harbour of **Miramar**, was a tuna-fishing centre in the 17th century and has ruins of a lookout tower for guarding the nets. The coast road then leads into **La Galère** at the western limit of La Napoule Bay. Below the road is a controversial seaside housing development designed in the 1970s by architect Jacques Couelle. There are also three small, as yet untouristy beaches at **Théoule-sur-Mer**, where an 18th-century soap factory has been transformed into an impressive-looking private property.

The chief curiosity at **La Napoule** is the **Fondation Henry Clews**, a pseudo-medieval folly conjured out of the ruins of a Saracen castle in 1917. Mr and Mrs Clews – he a failed Wall Street banker turned sculptor, she an American society heiress – and their servants dressed in costume, gave medieval banquets and crusaded against galloping modernity. Henry's works, visible in the garden, tend towards the gargoyle. Today the foundation has a programme of artists' residencies, conferences, exhibitions and children's workshops.

Set amid cypress trees and oak woods further along the coast is the **Ermitage de St Cassien** (first right off the road to Cannes-Mandelieu airport from the N7), a 14th-century chapel built over a Roman temple.

When you tire of the coast, the **Massif de l'Estérel** can be traversed by car along the N7. A well-marked path climbs **Mont Vinaigre**, the cork-tree-clad highest point of the range, offering stunning views.

Fondation Henry Clews

Château de la Napoule, av Henry Clews (04.93.49.95.05/www.lnaf.org). **Open** *Mar-June, Sept, Oct* 2.30-5.30pm Mon, Wed-Sun; *July-Aug* 2.30-6.30pm Mon, Wed-Sun. Closed Nov-Feb. **Admission** €4.60; €3.05 3-18s; free under-3s.

Where to stay & eat

Overlooking the Ile d'Or, the isolated **Sol et Mar** (rte Corniche d'Or, 04.94.95.25.60/www.francehotelevasion.com, closed mid-Oct to early Feb, double €61-€120, menus €23-€33) has large rooms, saltwater pool and Provençal restaurant. In Agay, the **Hôtel L'Estérella** (197 bd de la Plage, 04.94.82.00.58, closed Nov-Jan, double €50-€70) is a quiet option on the beach, with smallish rooms. Try the *coquilles St Jacques* at its restaurant (closed Mon from Oct to June, menu €23). **Hôtel Restaurant Le Lido** (bd de la Plage, 04.94.82.01.59, closed end Oct to Feb, double €90) has private beach, friendly service and a fish restaurant (average €20).

The **Relais des Calanques** (rte des Escales, 04.94.44.14.06, closed Oct-Mar, double €45.70-€88.40) near Le Trayas is a private nature's paradise, with a good restaurant (*plat du jour* €15). **Auberge Blanche** (1061 rte des Calanques, 04.94.44.14.04, closed Oct-Mar, double €49-€65) at the Le Trayas bus stop has rooms with a view. Youth hostel **Le Trayas** (9 av de la Véronèse, 04.93.75.40.23/www.fuaj.org, closed Jan to mid-Feb, rates €11.50 per person) is 2km up the hill with rooms for four to eight; book ahead to avoid a long, pointless walk if you don't have a car.

In Théoule is the friendly **Pizzeria Nino** (6 promenade Prayderol, 04.92.97.61.11, closed end Sept to Mar, average €12), with tables jutting out to sea. Théoule is also home to the **Etoile des Mers** at the **Miramar Beach Hôtel** (47 av de Miramar, 04.93.75.05.05/www.mbhriviera.com, double €115-€305, restaurant closed lunch Mon-Fri in July, Aug, menus €37-€69), where chef Laurent Mouret does wonderful mod-Med things. In Mandelieu-la-Napoule, the **Ermitage du Riou** (av Henry Clews, 04.93.49.95.56/www.ermitage-du-riou.fr, double €112-€274, menus €36.60-€74.70) has delightful rooms, private beach and a pool; the restaurant offers simple, exquisite dishes. At pricey **L'Oasis** (rue Jean-Honoré Carle, 04.93.49.95.52/www.oasis-raimbault.com, closed Mon & dinner Sun from mid-Oct to Jan and two weeks in Feb, menus €58-€115), Stéphane Raimbault produces fine classical cooking and sumptuous desserts. **La Pomme d'Amour** (209 av du 23 Août, 04.93.49.95.19, closed Tue, lunch Wed and Nov, menus €21-€32) has a beautiful patio, and a varied menu. **La Calanque** (bd Henry Clews, 04.93.49.95.11, closed Nov-Mar, double €29.70-€45.70) has views over the Clews' folly, but very small rooms. **Le Coelacanthe** (pl du Château, 04.93.49.95.15, closed dinner Mon & Sun, menus €22.60-€33.23) serves excellent modern Provençal fare and has a *fumoir* (smoking room).

Tourist information

Market is Wed at Agay, Fri at Théoule-sur-Mer, Thur at Mandelieu, Thur & Sat at La Napoule.

Agay Office de Tourisme

pl Giannetti, 83530 Agay (04.94.82.01.85/www.esd-fr.com/agay). **Open** *Apr to mid-June* 9am-noon, 2-6pm Mon-Sat; *mid-June to Sept* 9am-8pm Mon-Sat; *Oct-Mar* 9am-noon, 2-5pm Mon-Fri.

Mandelieu-la-Napoule Office de Tourisme

av Henry Clews, 06210 Mandelieu-la-Napoule (04.93.49.95.31/www.ot-mandelieu.fr). **Open** *July, Aug* 10am-12.30pm, 2-7pm daily; *Sept-June* 10am-12.30pm, 2-6pm Mon-Fri.

Théoule-sur-Mer Office de Tourisme

1 Corniche d'Or, 06590 Théoule-sur-Mer (04.93.49.28.28/www.theoule-sur-mer.org). **Open** *May-Sept* 9am-7pm Mon-Sat, 10am-1pm Sun; *Oct-Mar* 9am-noon, 2-6.30pm Mon-Sat.

▶ Getting There & Around

▶ By car

Leave the A8 at exit nos.37 or 38. St-Raphaël is on the N98 coast road. For Fréjus leave the A8 at exit 37 or 38. The D2098 follows the coast. For Mandelieu-la-Napoule, leave the A8 at exit no.40.

By train

St-Raphaël is on the main coastal line with TGV links from Paris, Nice and Marseille. Frequent trains from Nice and Marseille also stop at Fréjus and Mandelieu. Local trains on the St-Raphaël-Cannes line stop at Agay and Théoule-sur-Mer.

By bus

Cars Phocéens (04.93.85.61.81) runs a daily service from Nice to St-Raphaël. From Marseille **Cars Phocéens** (04.91.50.57.68) go to St-Raphaël (one per day, Mon-Sat), with a change at Aix-en-Provence. From Hyères airport there are (four daily) buses to Hyères bus station, where buses (eight daily) go to St-Raphael, with a change at La Foux. **Estérel Bus** (04.94.52.00.50) runs a regular service (12 per day Mon-Sat, five on Sun) between St-Raphaël and Draguignan, via Fréjus and Roquebrune. Between Mandelieu and Cannes **Bus Azur** (04.92.99.20.05) runs nine daily. **Estérel Bus** runs between St-Raphael and Agay (15 per day Mon-Sat, ten per day Sun) and from Le Trayas to Cannes, via Miramar and Théoule-sur-Mer (eight per day Mon-Sat, five on Sun).

Inland Var

Brignoles & the Sainte Baume

A sense of religion permeates this region, with its pilgrimage sites and sacred crypts, but it's also a centre of sporting life.

Brignoles & the Green Var

Brignoles is the busy commercial centre of the western villages, with a steady stream of traffic. Once famous for its 'sugar plums' (now mysteriously extinct) that were sent for 1,000 years to the royal courts of Europe, it later became prosperous through bauxite mining. The old town around place Carami bustles with café life and the tourist office can provide a walking-tour map of towers and ramparts (built 2m thick in the 15th century against the plague). Stroll up the covered stairway of rue du Grand Escalier past the church of St-Sauveur to the 13th-century Palace of the Counts of Provence, now the **Musée du Pays Brignolais** housing Provençal curiosities including *santons*, religious paintings by the local Parrocel family, a concrete canoe and a play-it-safe half-pagan, half-Christian second-century sarcophagus. A tiny plum tree has been planted in the courtyard in an attempt to revive the Brignoles delicacy. There's a packed fleamarket on the promenade along the Carami

The streets of **Brignoles**' old town are ideal for a walking tour: place Carami is the hub.

river every second Sunday of the month. Brignoles is also a springboard to the outdoor life of La Provence Verte, or the Green Var. The **Vallon Sourn** (D554 north from Brignoles, then D45 east at Châteauvert), the steep upper valley of the Argens river, is a favourite for rock-climbing, kayaking and biking. **Correns**, capital of the Argens, is the number one organic village of France with 95% of its wines and farm-produce grown organically.

Barjols, 22km north of Brignoles, lies in a valley fed by springs. Twelve wash basins and 30 fountains have earned it the hopeful nickname of 'the Tivoli of Provence'. In Réal, the old part of town north of the Romanesque-Gothic Eglise-Notre-Dame-des-Epines, former tanning factories now house galleries and artists' studios. Sombre Barjols comes alive every 16 January for the decidedly pagan Fête de St-Marcel, when the saint's bust is paraded through town with a garlanded ox that is later sacrificed, roasted and eaten. Atop a hill in rolling countryside east of Barjols is the village of **Pontevès**, whose ruined château makes a good picnic spot.

On the southern outskirts of Brignoles by D405, the tiny village of **La Celle** once

attracted those seeking religious solace at the
12th-century royal abbey; today's visitors have
more venal aims, as the abbey is now a luxury
hôtel/restaurant under the sway of super-chef
Alain Ducasse. **La Roquebrussanne**, 15km
south, is reached through woods beneath the
odd-shaped rock formations of La Loube
(830m). The village sits squat on a plain of
Coteaux Varois vineyards and serves as the
central wine pressing co-operative for the
region. The D64 leads east of here past two
lakes (a couple of spooky holes in the earth with
no visible water source) to the British-owned
Château des Chaberts (04.94.04.92.05)
vineyard, a reliable wine producer of *rosés* and
reds, which offers tastings. South of La
Roquebrussanne, the D5 winds through
vineyards (try Domaine des Laou and Domaine
la Rose des Vents) to the sleepy village of
Méounes-les-Montrieux, a cool stop with its
fountains, stream, ancient houses and
meandering streets.

Musée du Pays Brignolais

pl des Comtes de Provence, Brignoles (04.94.69.45.18).
Open 10am-noon, 2.30-5pm Wed-Sun. **Admission**
€3.05; €1.52 students; free under-8s.

Where to stay & eat

Hôtel de Provence (pl du Palais de Justice,
04.94.69.01.18, closed two weeks Dec, double
€37) is the only hotel in old Brignoles, and
convenient if you like cigarette smoke and the
roar of passing scooters. **Café le Central** (pl
Carami, 04.94.69.11.10, closed Mon & Sun)
serves a strong breakfast coffee and a good
lunchtime *plat du jour* (€7.62). *Maison d'hôte*
La Cordeline (14 rue des Cordeliers,
04.94.59.18.66, closed Nov-Feb, double €61-
€91.50) has six artsy rooms in a 17th-century
residence and serves intimate family dinners
(€23, Wed, Sat only). Checking into a posh
room at the **Hostellerie de l'Abbaye de la
Celle** (pl du Général de Gaulle, La Celle,
04.98.05.14.14/www.abbaye-celle.com, double
€175-€290) is the only way to go after a candlelit
Alain Ducasse dinner in the adjoining Gothic
convent (menus €45-€65). **Club Barbaroux**
at the Golfe de Barbouroux (5km east of
Brignoles on D79, rte de Cabasse, 04.94.69.63.63/
www.barbaroux.com, double €61) has hotel
and restaurant on an 18-hole golf course.

At Méounes, the **Hôtel de France** (pl de
l'Eglise, 04.94.33.95.92, doubles €38.11) has five
rooms and a terrace restaurant (menus €15-
€18) under ancient plane trees; it is changing
hands in 2002 and prices may change. At
Restaurant L'Olivier (11 rue Neuve,
04.94.33.96.01, closed Sat dinner & July, menus

€11-€20), Gilbert Giraud serves one of the
oldest recorded delicacies in Provence:
tiny snails called *sucarelles* that you suck out of
their shells (call to confirm availablity: both
hunters and snails are nearing extinction).
Archaeologists have found shells from the
creatures dating back 2,000 years in local caves.

In Correns, the **Camping Municipal le
Grand Jardin** is for sports lovers (enquiries to
the *mairie* 04.94.37.21.95, closed Nov-Mar, tent
€3, adult €2.29). The *chambres d'hôtes* **Val**

Something about Mary

Her tomb is the third most important in
Christendom and was a holy site by the
fifth century; yet today, it is as incognito as
during the Dark Ages. Despite this
omission in Christian history, legend claims
that after the crucifixion, the disciples were
chased out of Palestine by the Romans (as
was Herod, who ended up in the Pyrenean
village of St-Bertrand-de-Comminges). The
family of Bethany sailed the Mediterranean
in a little boat, landing in Saintes-Maries-de-
la-Mer in the Camargue. Mary Magdalene
and her brother Lazarus evangelised in
Marseille, while fellow traveller Maximin
went to Aix-en-Provence. But Mary felt a
need for reflection and sought out the
mountain retreat, where God bade her
spend 33 years of penitence. After this,
close to death, she tried to return to her
friend Maximin in St-Maximin (then called
Villalata), but she was too old to walk
down, so six angels appeared to transport
her. She was buried in town by St Maximin.
Her body was discovered in 1280 in a
fourth-century crypt, with a sprig of fennel
on her tongue and a patch of skin on her
forehead, where Christ had blessed her
during his resurrection, saying 'Touch me
not'. The crypt remains under the basilica
edified on the spot by Charles II, with the
addition of a reliquary for Mary's skull and
a crystal tube containing the *noli me
tangere* skin.

The Feast of Mary Magdalene takes
place in St-Maximin on the fourth Sunday
of July with a procession of her relics
through town. At Easter, a procession led
by Dominican monks climbs the mountain
to the Grotte-de-la-Ste-Baume, for mass
inside the cave.

Inland Var

The **Basilique Ste-Marie-Madeleine** at St-Maximin-la-Ste-Baume, a Gothic pilgrimage site.

d'Argens (pl Arenien, 04.94.59.57.02, www.canoe-kayak-provence.com, closed Nov-Feb, double €58, menus €15-€20) by the river has rooms and a lovely garden restaurant – no mosquitos, they say – with boat rentals available (ask about the four-day guided trip down to Fréjus). The Bruno (think expensive truffle lunches) extravaganza in Correns is the **Auberge du Parc** (pl Général de Gaulle, 04.94.59.53.52, double €89-€175; breakfast with truffles €9.15, restaurant closed dinner Sun & all Mon-Wed from Jan-Mar, menu €32), a temple of pale blue cupid murals, with a fumoir by the entry.

Near Pontevès, **Domaine-de-St-Ferréol** (1km from Pontevès across D560, 04.94.77.10.42, closed Nov-Feb, double €49-€58) offers upmarket *chambres d'hôtes* in an 18th-century farm set in vineyards and has a superb pool.

Tourist information

Market in Brignoles and Barjols is Sat morning. Internet is available at **IMF Informatique**, just behind the Maison de Tourisme in Brignoles (04.94.69.18.83, closed Sat, Sun).

Barjols Office de Tourisme
bd Grisolle, 83670 Barjols (04.94.77.20.01/www.ville-barjols.fr). Open 9am-noon, 3-6pm Mon-Sat.

Brignoles Office du Tourisme
Hôtel de Clavier, rue des Palais, 83170 Brignoles (04.94.69.27.51). Open 9am-noon, 1.30-5.30pm Mon-Fri.

La Provence Verte
Maison du Tourisme, La Provence Verte, carrefour de l'Europe, 83170 Brignoles (04.94.72.04.21/ www.la-provence-verte.org). Open June-Sept 9am-12.30pm, 2-7pm daily; Oct-May 9am-12.30pm, 2-6.30pm Mon-Sat.

St-Maximin-la-Ste-Baume & La Sainte Baume Massif

In the farming country between Brignoles and Aix, the **Basilique Ste-Marie-Madeleine** at St-Maximin-la-Ste-Baume soars above miles of vineyards: once a divine beacon to caravans of pilgrims, today an excellent marker for anyone travelling the A8 motorway. The basilica is the finest Gothic edifice in Provence – and one of the very few outposts of this style in the largely Romanesque South – and pilgrimage site for the tomb of Mary Magdalene. It was founded in 1295 by Charles II, King of Sicily and Count of Provence, who hoped to improve his standing by building a resplendent shrine for the relics of Mary (*see p189*) above the fourth-century crypt where her sarcophagus had been found. The interior of the basilica contains much fascinating decoration by Dominican monks, such as the 94 choir stalls carved in walnut by Brother Vincent Funel. The altarpiece of the Passion by Antoine Ronzen was painted in 1520. Over the altar is a gilded plaster sunburst of cherubs and saints (1678-82) by Lieautaud. The monumental 18th-century organ was saved from destruction during the Revolution by Lucien Bonaparte, Napoléon's youngest brother, who used it for performances of *La Marseillaise*.

Adjoining the basilica is the **Couvent Royal**, a royal foundation begun at the same time as the church, now a hotel (*see below*). You can visit the chapel, the refectory and the Gothic cloister; the capitular room, originally the monks' assembly room, is now a restaurant. Just south of the basilica, the rue Colbert runs through the 13th-century medieval quarter and along the sombre arcades of the Jewish district established in 1303 in this passionately Catholic town. Street life revolves around place Malherbe, where the Wednesday market creates a turmoil of shoppers and traffic, and **Café La Renaissance** (04.94.78.00.27) tries to keep up with the demand for *pastis* at its terrace tables.

The town is a good starting point for exploring the limestone hills of the **Massif-de-la-Ste-Baume**, which stretches south-west of the town, and the villages of **Rougiers**, with its ruined castle, and **Mazaugues** with its ice factory, which for centuries sent ice (to preserve fresh fish) to Toulon and Marseille.

Nans-les-Pins is a hiking centre (the GR9, GR9A trails run nearby) and is on the original *chemin des rois*, the holy road leading from the basilica of St-Maximin through the sacred forest to the **Grotte Ste-Marie-Madeleine**, where legend claims Mary Magdalene lived out her life in solitude. Hidden in the cliffs at 950m, it is reached by climbing a 1km footpath from the **Hôtellerie de la Baume** (on D95 6km south of Nans-les-Pins, plan d'Aups, 04.42.04.54.84), a Dominican monastery, which still offers accommodation for pilgrims (dormitory €9, double €22). Another path climbs to the holy site of St-Pilon, from where the GR9 leads across the massif to **Signes**.

Basilique Ste-Marie-Madeleine

pl de Precheurs, St-Maximin (04.42.38.01.78). **Open** 8am-11.30am, 3-6pm Mon-Sat; mass 9am Mon-Sat; 8am, 11am Sun.

Grotte Ste-Marie-Madeleine

(04.42.62.57.57). **Open** reopens Apr 2002.

Where to stay & eat

Hôtellerie du Couvent Royal (pl Jean Salusse, 04.94.86.55.66, double €44-€73). The royal convent adjoining the basilica is the only place worth staying in at St-Maximin. Rooms in former monks' cells – inhabited from 1316 to 1957 – have been converted with taste and keep a sense of monastic calm; those in the 'modernised' wing offer more mod cons. The **Maison des Vins du Var** (04.94.78.09.50, closed dinner Sun & Mon, menus €26-€37) runs

a restaurant and wine bar in the capitular room. At Nans-les-Pins, the 18-hole **Golf Club La Sainte Baume** lies under the Ste-Baume cliffs (04.94.78.60.12/www.opengolfclub.com, golf fees €37-€46). In the middle, the ancient **Hôtel Domaine de Châteauneuf** (Nans-les-Pins, 04.94.78.90.06, closed Nov-Mar, double €138, restaurant closed dinner Mon-Fri, menus €43-€70) was once a stopping point for Crusaders heading to the Holy Land and later hosted Napoléon. Across the N560, the 18th-century **Château de Nans** (04.94.78.92.06/ www.chateau-de-nans.fr, closed mid-Nov to mid-Dec, two weeks in Jan, double €91.47-€152.45, restaurant closed Mon & Tue, menus €35-€49) dishes up divine delicacies such as wild rabbit and deer with juniper berries. Hikers can throw down their backpacks at the 18th-century **La Vieille Bastide** (300 chemin du plan de Chebron, Signes, 04.94.90.81.45 closed Jan & Feb, double €70-€95), a charming *chambres d'hôtes* just west of Signes.

Tourist information

St-Maximin market is Wed morning. Internet at **SMI St-Maximin Informatique** (9 rue de la République, 04.98.05.92.70, closed Mon & Sun).

St-Maximin Office de Tourisme

Hôtel de Ville, 83470 St-Maximin-la-Ste-Baume (04.94.59.84.59). **Open** *June-Sept* 9.30am-12.30pm, 2.30-6.30 daily; *Oct-Mar* 9am-12:30pm, 2-6pm daily.

Nans-les-Pins Office de Tourisme

2 cours Général de Gaulle, 83860 Nans-les-Pins (04.94.78.95.91/www.multimania.com/nanslespins). **Open** *July, Aug* 9am-noon, 3-6pm Mon-Sat, 9am-noon Sun; *Sept-June* 9am-noon, 2-5pm Mon-Sat, 9am-noon Sun.

▶ Getting There & Around

▶ By car

A8 autoroute Brignoles exit (no.35); St-Maximin-la-Ste-Baume is on the N7 between Aix-en-Provence and Brignoles or exit no.34 from A8.

▶ By bus

Autocars Blanc (04.94.69.08.28) in Brignoles serves most towns in the Var, with six buses daily between Brignoles and St-Maximin and St-Maximin and Aix, and daily services between Brignoles and Barjols; call for details on Nans-Les-Pins, Correns and Signes routes. **Phocéen Voyages** (04.93.85.66.61) runs buses twice daily from Nice, and once a day from Marseille, to both Brignoles and St-Maximin.

The Var Heartland

From rolling vineyards to craggy wooded mountains, the central Var provides all the requisite perched villages, plus a dragon or two.

The central Var area that rolls out from the busy commercial centre of Draguignan has all the classic ingredients of cream-coloured churches, *pétanque* pitches and Côtes de Provence vineyards. But even if the Var has been discovered by the British, many of these villages remain pleasantly untrafficked.

Draguignan & the Gorges de Châteaudouble

The *Year in Provence* brigade has a real downer on **Draguignan**, mainly because, with its military barracks (the town hosts the French army artillery school) and Parisian-style boulevards, it doesn't conform to all those *boules*, lavender and village fountain clichés. As far as the outskirts go, they have a point: the approach roads are lined with shopping malls, discount stores and fast food joints, but the town centre is a surprisingly pleasant place to while away a couple of hours. In the 19th century, Baron Haussmann used Draguignan as a mini-pilot for his geometrical reorganisation of Paris. At that time the town was the capital of the Var (a privilege it lost only in 1974), having replaced Toulon, disgraced during the French Revolution for its royalist sympathies. During the day at least, Draguignan (whose name derived from the dragon-slaying exploits of fifth-century St Hermentine) tries to emulate its prestigious past, especially on the boulevard Georges Clemenceau, with its big-name boutiques. But to appreciate the town's real charm head up to the place du Marché – filled with elegantly dilapidated townhouses, adorned with blue shutters and hanging plants. If you can face the crowds in the summer heat come on market days (Wednesday and Saturday) when the *place* and surrounding alleys are perfumed with the scent of roasting chickens, thyme, goats' cheese and *pastis*. There are two worthwhile rainy-day museums in the old town: the **Musée Municipal**, housed in the summer palace of the Bishop of Fréjus, with a patchy collection of paintings, antiques and archeology; and the **Musée des Traditions Provençales**, recreating traditional life in Provence through displays of agricultural tools, furnishings, glassworks and tiles, plus a collection of *santons*. American visitors might be interested to know there's a US war cemetery in the town: 861 soldiers who arrived on the Riviera in 1944 are buried here and a wall commemorates 3,000 men who disappeared.

As for the dragon, apparently it hung out in the **Gorges de Châteaudouble** north of town, reached via the scenic D955. First stop on this road is the **Pierre de la Fée** (fairy stone), a giant dolmen from 2400 BC. Further along, a dirt road on the right takes you through the beautiful vineyard of the **Domaine du Dragon** (04.98.10.23.00), once the 12th-century fortified Castrum de Dragone of the Draguignan family, where archeologists have recently discovered a medieval chapel on first-century foundations. The D955 winds along the gorge floor passing **Rebouillon**, a hamlet built like a horseshoe around a large central meadow on the banks of the Nartuby. From the gorge road, **Châteaudouble** (also reached direct by D45) suddenly appears high on spectacular cliffs, as the scenery changes dramatically to a far more Alpine landscape with jagged rock formations. Châteaudouble was originally called the Devil's Gap. In winter the village is full of huntsmen, buying arms for tracking wild boar.

West of Draguignan is a flatter landscape, ripe with vineyards and fruit trees. The D557 heads into **Flayosc**, a fortified village centred around its timeworn fountain and a church with the characteristic wrought-iron belfry of these parts. In a bucolic hamlet 1km north of Flayosc, the 13th-century **Moulin de Flayosquet** is the oldest operating olive mill in the Var. Fifth-generation owner Max Doleatto offers guided visits and tastings of olive oil.

Moulin du Flayosquet
1km north of Flayosc (04.94.70.41.45). **Open** *Jan, Dec* 9am-12.30pm, 2.30-7.30pm daily; *Feb-June, Sept-Nov* 9am-noon, 2-6.30pm Tue-Sat; *July-Aug* 9am-12.30pm, 2.30-7.30pm Mon-Sat.

Musée Municipal
9 rue de la République, Draguignan (04.94.47.28.80). **Open** 9am-noon, 2-6pm Mon-Sat. **Admission** free.

Musée des Traditions Provençales
15 rue Roumanille, Draguignan (04.94.47.05.72). **Open** 9am-noon, 2-6pm Tue-Sat; 2-6pm Sun. **Admission** €3.50; €1.50 6-18s; free under-6s.

The cliffs of **Villecroze** have long been beloved of cave-dwellers. *See p194.*

Where to stay & eat

In Draguignan, **Hôtel-Restaurant La Pergola** (6 av du 4 Septembre, 04.94.67.01.12, double €38.11, menus €10-€30) is a pretty yellow townhouse a short stroll from the main square. The rooms are functional but quiet and the welcome friendly. More to the point, the cuisine, served in the front garden, is so good that locals come here for an evening treat (try the starter of fresh mussels in saffron sauce, followed by roast pigeon). **Les Milles Colonnes** (2 pl aux Herbes, 04.94.68.52.58, closed Sun and last two weeks Aug, menu €15.10) is a lively brasserie in the old town serving up fresh market dishes.

In Châteaudouble, the view's the thing at the **Restaurant de la Tour** (pl Beausoleil, 04.94.70.93.08, closed Wed and two weeks in Jan, menus €15-€25) but the food comes a close second – do try the excellent *brouillade* truffle omelette if you're around between November and February. **Château** (04.94.70.90.05, closed Tue & Wed from Oct to Mar, menus €28-€40) offers a modern take on local cuisine plus views over the Nartuby gorge. In Flayosc, **L'Oustaou** (5 pl Brémond, 04.94.70.42.69, closed Mon, dinner Thur & Sun, and mid-Nov to mid-Dec, menus €19.90-€43.50) is a well-regarded regional restaurant with tables on the village square, where you can sample Provençal specialities such as *pieds et paquets*.

Tourist information

Market days Fri in Châteaudouble, Wed & Sat Draguignan; Mon in Flayosc; Tue in Lorgues.

Châteaudouble Office de Tourisme

Hôtel de Ville, pl de la Fontaine, 83300 Châteaudouble (04.98.10.51.35/fax 04.98.10.51.36). **Open** 9-11.30am Mon-Fri.

Draguignan Office de Tourisme

2 av Lazare Carnot, 83300 Draguignan (04.98.10.51.05/www.ot-draguignan.fr). **Open** *July, Aug* 9am-6pm Mon-Sat; *Sept-June* 9am-12.30pm, 2-6pm Mon-Sat.

Flayosc Office de Tourisme

pl Pied-Barri, 83780 Flayosc (04.94.70.41.31/ www.ville-flayosc.fr). **Open** *July-Aug* 9am-noon, 3-6pm Mon-Sat; 10am-noon Sun; *Sept-June* 9am-noon, 3-6pm Mon-Fri; 9am-noon Sat.

Salernes, Aups & around

Salernes was made for market days, thanks to its large central square, cours Théodore Bouge, shaded by centuries-old plane trees. On Wednesday and Sunday market mornings, parking places and café seats are rare finds, especially at the bustling Café de la Bresque. When not crammed with stalls selling fresh local produce and Salernes' famous enamelled tiles (*see p195* **Tile file**), the village is surprisingly quiet, even at the height of

Inland Var

summer. This is the moment to explore its pretty backstreets and squares, especially the handsome place de la Révolution which has a superb Roman fountain dribbling spring water. Down by the river Bresque, which flows along the southern side of the town, **La Muie** is an exceptionally pretty bathing site, with crystal-clear water and sandy banks that are the local inhabitants' secret pleasure ground.

A short drive north on the D31 brings you to the tightly knit town of **Aups**. If Salernes is the capital of *tommettes*, Aups is the truffle centre of the Var. Every Thursday morning at 10am between the end of November and the end of February there is a high-stakes truffle auction in the main square, where the precious commodity – all the more valuable as it is exempt from taxes – is sold right out of the trunks of Citroën station wagons. Sadly, due to bad weather conditions, the 2001 harvest yielded only 15kg of truffles: bad news for the local gastronomic trade, where the luxurious **Chênes Verts** near Tourtour, **Fontaine d'Ampus** in Ampus and **Chez Bruno** in Lorgues all specialise in the black fungus.

Aups life revolves around the cafés on tiny place Girard which leads into rue Maréchal Foch, filled with Provençal artefacts and the antique shop Le Déniche which sells beautiful old Provençal linen. A little further up on avenue Albert Premier, don't miss the **Musée Simon Segal**, housed in a former Ursuline convent, and containing the work of Russian-born artist Simon Segal and other lesser-known but impressive artists of the Ecole de Paris.

The 7km drive from Aups to the newly fashionable village of **Villecroze** on the D557 offers breathtaking views of the Var's wooded landscape as far as the Maures mountain range. Villecroze is set against a stunning cliff face riddled with caves known as the **Grottes Troglodytes**, which a local lord turned into dwellings in the 16th century. A waterfall cascades down the cliff into a stream in the picturesque garden beneath.

The village of **Tourtour** is situated just above Villecroze, reached by a twisting switchback road that gives credence to its title 'the village in the sky'. St Trinian illustrator Ronald Searle had the good taste to settle here in the mid-70s and hasn't moved his drawing board since. Luckily, the place is too small to house many souvenir shops, while **Florence** (pl des Ormeaux, 04.94.70.56.90), the only clothes boutique, is as sophisticated as a Paris equivalent. The *boules* pitch below the town hall has a 180-degree view of the Var and is particularly picturesque on market days (Wednesday and Saturday). Further up, the 11th-century church is surrounded by cypress

trees. The village also has a still-operative 17th-century olive press and the medieval **Tour Grimaldi** watchtower.

Take the quiet D51 out of Tourtour to reach the sleepy hamlet of **Ampus**, which harbours an 11th-century Romanesque church and the pretty chapel Notre-Dame-de-Spéluque, which has a beautifully sculpted altar.

Grottes Troglodytes

Villecroze. **Guided visits** (reserve at tourist office) *May-June* 2-6pm daily; *July-Sept* 10am-noon, 2.30-7pm daily. **Admission** €2; €1 under-16s.

Musée Simon Segal

av Albert 1er (04.94.70.01.95). **Open** *15 June-15 Sept* 10am-noon, 4-7pm daily. **Admission** €2.29; €1.52 10-18s; free under 10s.

Where to stay & eat

Aups comes alive in January for the Fête des Truffes. The rest of the year, Catherine at **Le Yucca** (3 rue Foch, 04.94.70.12.11, closed dinner Mon & all Tue and Oct, menus €12.20-€23) prepares divine ravioli with truffles; weekly jazz concerts in summer. Best by far of the cafés and restaurants in Tourtour's square is **Farigoulette** (pl des Ormeaux, 04.94.70.57.37, menu €17), where the olive oil is divinely perfumed, the *daube provençale* one of the best in the region and the service relaxed and

In **Aups** pigs do the detective work and the locals reap the truffly rewards.

welcoming. Just outside Tourtour, **Le Mas l'Acacia** (rte d'Aups, 04.94.70.53.84, double €54) offers *chambres d'hôtes* with spectacular views and a pool. **La Bastide de Tourtour** (04.98.10.54.20, double €115-€281, restaurant dinner only except July & Aug, menus €24-€49) invariably has an array of Bentleys and Jaguars in its carpark. However, despite its sumptuous views and large park, this château hotel has never managed to shake off its antiseptic atmosphere. Perched on a hill below Tourtour is the **Mas des Collines** (camp Fournier, 04.94.70.5930, double €125-€116) with magnificent views from the balconies of its albeit rather charmless rooms, and a pool. 2km out towards Villecroze, **Les Chênes Verts** (04.94.70.55.06, closed Tue & Wed and June, menu €43) is a gourmet restaurant where chef Paul Bagade does great things with truffles (when they're available); it also has three charming rooms (closed June, double €92).

Hidden in the countryside 3km from Villecroze, the **Hôtel au Bien-Etre** (04.94.70.67.57, closed Nov & Feb, double €44-€49, restaurant closed lunch Mon-Wed, menus €28.20-€59) has motel-style rooms with little terraces (your neighbours can be a little too close for comfort) in a small garden, but locals come for the sophisticated cuisine of proprietor/chef Michel Audier. It would be a sacrilege not to pay a visit to the **Fontaine d'Ampus** (04.94.70.98.08, closed Oct, Feb, all Mon & Tue except dinner Tue July-Aug, menu €30). As well as local truffles, other specialities on the seasonal menus are pigeon served with chestnuts and fried aubergines and tomatoes.

Tourist information

Market day is Wed and Sun in Salernes, Wed and Sat in Aups and Tourtour. Truffle market in Aups Thur mornings end-Nov to end-Feb.

Ampus Office de Tourisme

Hôtel de Ville, 83111 Ampus (04.94.70.97.11/ www.mairie-ampus.fr). **Open** 9.30am-12.30pm Mon-Fri.

Aups Office de Tourisme

pl Mistral, 83630 Aups (04.94.84.00.69). **Open** *July-Aug* 9am-7pm Mon-Sat; 9am-noon Sun; *Sept-June* 9am-noon, 2-5.30pm Mon-Sat.

Salernes Office de Tourisme

pl Gabriel Péri, 83690 Salernes (04.94.70.69.02/fax 04.94.70.73.34). **Open** *July-Aug* 9am-7pm Mon-Sat; *Sept-June* 9.30am-12.30pm, 3-6.45pm Mon-Sat.

Villecroze Office de Tourisme

rue Ambroise Croizat, 83690 Villecroze (tel/fax 04.94.67.50.00). **Open** *June-Sept* 8.30am-12.30pm, 1.30-6.30pm daily; *Oct-May* 9am-noon, 1.30-4.30pm Mon-Fri; 2-5pm Sat, Sun.

Tile file

The mere word Provence conjures up fields of lavender, wild thyme and rosemary and the pungent aroma of virgin olive oil. Once indoors, however, there is nothing more redolent of the Midi than the hexagonal-shaped terracotta tiles known as *tommettes* that cover the floors of traditional Provençal homes. Salernes is the tile-producing capital of the Var, thanks to its pure clay, abundance of spring water and the wood from nearby forests that fuels its furnaces. Indeed, Salernes is believed to be Europe's most ancient terracotta site with production dating back to 6000 BC. Today there are 16 tiling workshops, all with their particular speciality. For *tommettes* in their purest, most natural form, **Sismondini** (rte de Sillans, 04.94.04.63.06, closed Sun) is king. The workshop follows a meticulous process of filtering spring water through the clay, shaping the pieces with a hammer following ancient practice, then firing them using local wood. **Les Terres Cuites des Launes** (quartier des Launes, 04.94.70.62.72, closed Sun) is equally faithful to its roots with its wood-fired tiles that are very resistant to time. Founded in 1718, **Jacques Brest Céramiques** (quartier des Arnauds, 04.94.70.60.65, closed Sun) is one of Salernes' oldest existing tile manufacturers, producing hand-moulded pieces in traditional formats. Over the past few decades, like certain of his peers, Brest has perfected the enamel work on his tiles. However, it was **Carrelages Pierre Boutal** (rte de Draguignan, 04.94.70.62.12, closed Sun) who first introduced painted Salernes tiles in the 1960s. Boutal is passionate about preserving Provençal culture, hence his extensive range of designs incorporating such motifs as lavender fields, olive groves and locals in traditional costume. One of the most prolific ceramics designers is the **Atelier Pierre Basset** (quartier des Arnauds, 04.94.70.70.70, closed Sat, Sun), which offers over 2,000 hand-painted patterns, while **Alain Vagh** (rte Entrecasteaux, 04.94.70.61.85, closed Sun) is perhaps the most imaginative: his creative mosaic work includes a pink-tiled Harley Davidson and a grand piano with green-tiled keys.

Inland Var

Cotignac & around

Framed by an 80m-high and 400m-wide rock face pierced with caves and topped with the ruins of a 15th-century castle, the lively village of **Cotignac** takes its name from quince (*coing*), as for centuries the community has made jelly from the fruit. The British have been buzzing around its numerous estate agents for years, seduced by the town's position and charm. Locals and would-be locals lounge on the café terraces under the huge old plane trees that line the cours Gambetta – don't be surprised to spot Cotignac aficionado Robbie Williams among the crowd. The medieval rue Clastre has the oldest houses, while the place de la Mairie has an exquisite bell tower dating from 1496. On and around the Grande Rue there are many elegant Varois townhouses dating from the 16th and 17th centuries, while place de la Liberté boasts particularly pretty fountains – there are a total of 18 in Cotignac. The magnificent waterfall (La Trompine) that issues from the river Cassole and cascades down the cliff face has provided hydroelectric power for decades. Just outside Cotignac the **Théâtre de Gassière**, an amphitheatre surrounded by vineyards and olive groves, is used for outdoor concerts in July and August.

To witness Provençal Romanesque architecture in its purest form it's worth visiting the 12th-century **Eglise St-Pierre** in the town centre; while **Notre-Dame de Grâces**, situated at the southern entrance, holds a special place in French history. A Paris monk had a dream that the only way Louis XIII could have children was for Anne of Austria to carry out three novenas, including one at Cotignac. Lo and behold, Louis XIV was born after the Queen left the town. To be on the safe side, Louis XIV paid his respects here in 1660 on his journey to marry the infanta Marie-Thérèse in St-Jean-de-Luz.

About 3km outside of Cotignac on the D13 lies the impressive **Monastère St-Joseph-du-Bressillon**. The monastery's cloister and dormitories have been lovingly restored by its 16 resident Benedictine nuns. To hear the nuns singing in Gregorian and reciting mass in Latin is a rare, moving experience. Mass is held daily at 11am, vespers at 5pm.

Continue north on the D13 to the village of **Fox-Amphoux**, originally a Roman encampment and the last staging post of the Knights Templar. Locals still pronounce its name 'foks-amfooks' in true Provençal style. There are precious few locals in the village itself, though, which has been turned into a northern European vision of what a Provençal village should look like. In ruins only 20 years

ago, it is now a soulless place full of over-restored second homes and slow-moving hire-cars. Still, the 12th-century Romanesque church is still intact on place de l'Eglise.

Between Fox-Amphoux and Salernes, **Sillans-la-Cascade** is a pretty, refreshingly unrestored village with a sunny square and two restaurants facing the river Bresque. Just in front of the old chapel, a hand-painted wooden sign marks the start of the 30-minute hike to *la cascade* itself, a waterfall that crashes down into a refreshingly cool pool.

East of Cotignac on the remote D50, the delightful village of **Entrecasteaux**, is dominated by a magnificent 17th-century **château**. Narrowly saved from destruction during the Revolution, the château was in ruins when Scottish painter Ian McGarvie-Munn – whose chequered life included a stint as commander of the Guatemalan navy – purchased it and began repairs in the 1970s. Although very long, the structure is only one room deep, tempting one to classify it more as a folly than a proper castle. Its surrounding formal garden designed by Le Nôtre is far more satisfying to amble around. East of here on a road with beautiful views back over Entrecasteaux is the hamlet of **St-Antonin-du-Var**, a farming community that is about as far as you can get from the glitz of the coast.

Château d'Entrecasteaux

Entrecasteaux (04.94.04.43.95). **Guided tours** *Apr-June* 4pm Mon-Fri, Sun; *July-Sept* 11am, 3.30pm, 4.30pm Mon-Fri, Sun. **Admission** €5.50; €3.50 12-16s; free under-12s.

Where to stay & eat

Olives grow in abundance around the friendly *chambres d'hôtes* **La Radassière**, 1km east of Cotignac (rte d'Entrecasteaux, 04.94.04.63.33, closed Jan, double €61), where Maryse Artaud serves local quince jelly for breakfast; nice garden and pool. In Cotignac, the **Modern Bar** (12 cours Gambetta, 04.94.04.65.92, closed Mon) is the best place for a drink on the town's main drag. **La Fontaine** (27 cours Gambetta, 04.94.04.79.13, closed Mon & dinner Sun between Nov and Apr, menus €15-€38.50) is good for lively terrace lunches, especially on market Tuesdays. In Fox-Amphoux take a room at the 11th-century **Auberge du Vieux Fox** (pl de l'Eglise, 04.94.80.71.69, closed Nov-Jan, double €68-€86) for the views down the hillside. For an antidote to this prettiness, phone ahead to book a table for lunch at **Chez**

Potters are even controlling the breathtaking views from **Fayence**.

Jean, at the roundabout of La Bréguière north of the village (04.94.80.70.76, closed dinner and two weeks Nov, menu €9.91). Under the vigilant gaze of a stuffed owl and boar, Jean and Chantal Serre serve abundant, wholesome fare, with wine charged according to how much of the bottle you drink. In Sillans-la-Cascade, **Hôtel-Restaurant Les Pins** (04.94.04.63.26, rates around €36.59, menus €12.20-€27.44) offers pleasant rooms and meals in a countrified dining room. Opt for the fish stew with *pistou* in summer and game in winter.

Tourist information

Market day is Tuesday in Cotignac, Friday in Entrecasteaux.

Cotignac Office de Tourisme

rue Bonaventure, 83570 Cotignac (04.94.04.61.87). **Open** times vary; usually 10am-noon, 2-4.30pm daily.

Entrecasteaux Office de Tourisme

cours Gabriel Péri, 83570 Entrecasteaux (04.98.05.22.05). **Open** *June-Sept* 10am-noon, 4-6.30pm Mon-Sat; *Oct-May* call ahead.

Sillans-la-Cascade Office de Tourisme

Le Château, Grande Rue, 83690 Sillans-la-Cascade (04.94.04.78.05/fax 04.94.04.71.96). **Open** call for details. Closed winter.

The Argens Valley & Thoronet

South of Draguignan, the Côtes-de-Provence appellation moves into top gear, with vineyards lining the gentle slopes on either side of the Argens river. The most popular activity sport here is the estate crawl – something best done by bicycle, with a solemn promise that you'll

Provençal People: Bruno

The centre of the Provençal truffle universe lies around Lorgues. Here, Bruno Clément, alias Bruno de Lorgues, is the emperor, his legendary kitchen the depot for local rifle-toting truffle hunters (be warned, they'll shoot at poachers on their terrain). Helicopters from Monaco park alongside sleek black Mercedes in the vineyards in front of the restaurant, bringing wealthy gourmets to Sunday lunch. Truffles are, after all, one of the most expensive foods in the world, selling at around €4,420/kg for white alba magnatum, €915/kg for black melanosporum.

Bruno, a white giant in his chef's apron, packs truffles generously into his cuisine: whole pungent black truffles soaked in port and baked in flaky pastry; a *parmesan de truffes* grated on to lobster and tagliatelle; rich truffle sauce heaped over pheasant and chestnuts; caramelised truffle ice-cream to top apple pie. Or if none of that suits, how about a truffle-and-egg breakfast at Bruno's **Auberge du Parc** (*see p190*) in Correns?

Since opening Chez Bruno at Lorgues in 1983, Bruno has been busy spreading the truffle word. He's opened a flurry of new spots in the most luxurious corners of the South of France, from the **Café de Paris** (*see p176*) in St-Tropez to the **Bruno Restaurant** (00.377-93.50.20.03) in Monaco, sometimes jointly with his pal Alain Ducasse, as at the 12th-century convent **Hostellerie l'Abbaye de**

la Celle (*see p189*). 'I want to bring truffles to people around the world,' he said in globalisation-lingo at the opening of his bistro in Nice, **Terres de Truffes** (*see p240*), where you can even order take-away truffle sarnies. 'Not many people know about them.'

Chez Bruno

rue des Arcs, Campagne Mariette, Lorgues (04.94.85.93.93/www.restaurantbruno.com). Closed lunch Sun, all Mon in winter. Menu €45.

come back later with the car to pick up the 15 cases of rosé. Most French visitors think of **Le Muy** as the A8 motorway exit for St-Tropez. But this small, flat, militantly working-class town (one of the few in the Côte d'Azur region to have had a Communist mayor) has been caught in the crossfire of history a couple of times: once when the locals tried to assassinate the Holy Roman Emperor Charles V (they failed, nailing a stand-in instead, and were promptly nailed themselves); and again when Le Muy was the parachute bridgehead for Operation Dragon, the August 1944 Allied liberation of Provence. The **Musée de la Libération**, where memorabilia includes cockpits, jeeps, parachutes and documents, complements a visit to the American War Cemetery in Draguignan.

Betwen Le Muy and Les Arcs lie the vineyards and medieval chapel of the **Château Ste-Roseline**. Saintly noble lass Roseline de Villeneuve (1263-1329) used to feed starving peasants during Saracen invasions; after her death, her corpse refused to decompose and has since reclined in a glass casket in the chapel. The chapel is mainly Baroque, but there are some unexpected works including music stands by Diego Giacometti, brother of the more celebrated Alberto, and a mosaic by Chagall.

Les Arcs itself has pretty cream-coloured buildings and a medieval centre that twists up steeply to the keep of the 11th-century **Villeneuve** castle, that now offers dining and accommodation. The **Maison des Vins** on the N7 road south of town, is an excellent one-stop shop for those who don't have the time, or the patience, to tour the vineyards; though it also has route maps and brochures for those who do. The quiet villages of Vidauban and Taradeau offer plenty of excuses for estate hopping. Just outside Taradeau, the **Château St-Martin** gives a *son et lumière* show (in French or English) in the 15th-century wine cellar portraying the history of Provençal wines.

The D48 north to Lorgues crosses the Argens river and winds between giant plane trees to the magnificent **Château d'Astros** (04.94.73.00.25), which featured in Yves Robert's film of Pagnol's *Le Château de ma mère*. **Lorgues** has a pleasant main street lined with peeling plane trees, fountains and cafés; it also has one of the Var's top foodie destinations. Park at the massive 18th-century **Collégiale St-Martin** and look in at the multi-coloured marble altar. The *ruelles* of the old town, full of medieval houses, run up behind the main square.

The **Abbaye du Thoronet**, a 12th-century Cistercian abbey nestling in the middle of the Darboussière forest, is a silent and imposing place. The beauty of the building lies in its sparse, geometric lines: pure and stripped of

Silent and brooding in the forest of Darboussière, the **Abbaye du Thoronet**.

ornaments, they reflect the austere lifestyle of this back-to-basics order. Man-made reinforcements are shunned: the blocks of warm pinkish stone are glued together by the force of gravity alone. The first of the three great Cistercian foundations of Provence (along with Silvacane and Sénanque), Thoronet stays faithful to the Romanesque, though by 1160, when work began, northern France was already under the sway of Gothic. Stairs lead up to the monks' dormitories, which look very much as they must have done in the Middle Ages, apart from the glass in the windows. The cloister, built on different levels to accommodate the slope of the ground, has a charming fountain house. This extraordinary haven is, however, under threat. The hills south-west of the abbey are riddled with bauxite mines and every day lorries loaded with the product shudder past, putting enormous pressure on the building. Sadly, experts are now advocating that concrete columns be used to reinforce the site.

Abbaye du Thoronet

(04.94.60.43.90). **Open** *Apr-May* 10am-6pm daily; *June-Sept* 9am-7pm daily; *Oct-Mar* 10am-1pm, 2-5pm daily. Closed for visits during Sun mass (noon-2pm). **Admission** €5.50; free under-18s.

Chapelle & Château Ste-Roseline

D91 4km east of Les Arcs (04.94.99.50.30/ tours 04.94.47.56.10/www.sainte-roseline.com).

A vertiginous view from medieval **Montauroux**, now prouder of its link with Dior. *See p202.*

Open *chapel May-Sept* 2-6pm Tue-Sun; *Oct-Apr* 2-5pm Tue-Sun; *wine tasting* 9am-noon, 2-6.30pm Mon-Fri; 10am-noon, 2-6pm Sat, Sun. **Admission** *chapel* free; *guided tours* €11.50 (incl wine); €3 under-16s.

Château St-Martin
(04.94.73.02.01). **Open** *Apr to mid-Oct* 9am-6pm daily; *mid-Oct to Mar* 9am-1pm, 3-7pm Mon-Sat. **Admission** free; *son et lumière* €4.50; *tastings* €3.05-€10.67.

Maison des Vins Côtes de Provence
Les Arcs (04.94.99.50.20/www.caveaucp.fr). **Open** *June, Sept* 10am-1pm, 3.30-7pm daily; *July-Aug* 10am-1pm, 1.30-8pm daily; *Oct-May* 10am-1pm, 1.30-6pm daily.

Musée de la Libération
Tour Charles-Quint, Le Muy (info & tours Office du Tourisme 04.94.45.12.79). **Open** *Apr-June, Sept* 10am-noon Sun; *July-Aug* 10am-noon Thur, Sun; *Oct-Mar* by appointment. **Admission** free.

Where to stay & eat

In Les Arcs, reserve well ahead for the hotel-restaurant **Le Logis du Guetteur** (04.94.99.51.10/www.logisduguetteur.com, closed 18 Jan-8 Mar, double €103.67, menus €27.29-€73.18), which occupies the remains of the Villeneuve château, looking out over red-tiled roofs and vineyards; it has 13 charming rooms and dining in vaulted stone chambers. The jovial Boeuf brothers have the gourmet

eating scene in Vidauban sewn up. Alain runs the hearty **La Concorde** on the pleasant central square (pl de la Mairie, 04.94.73.01.19, closed dinner Tue from Sept to June, all Wed, two weeks Nov & two weeks Feb, menus €24-€41), while brother Christian recently opened the more designer-elegant **Bastide des Magnans** (D48, rte de La Garde-Freinet, 04.94.99.43.91, closed all Mon & dinner Sun, and dinner Wed Oct-June, menus €22-€14); both offer solid but elegant *cuisine de terroir*.

Tourist information

Market is Thursday and Sunday at Le Muy; Tuesday at Lorgues.

Les Arcs Office de Tourisme
pl Général de Gaulle, 83460 Les Arcs (tel/fax 04.94.47.56.10). **Open** *July-Aug* 9am-noon, 2-6pm Mon-Fri; 9am-noon Sat; 10am-noon Sun; *Sept-June* 9am-noon, 2-5.30pm Mon-Fri; 9am-noon Sat.

Le Muy Office du Tourisme
rte de la Bourgade, 83490 Le Muy (04.94.45.12.79/www.lemuy-tourisme.com). **Open** *July to mid-Sept* 9.30am-noon, 4-7pm Mon-Sat; 10am-noon Sun; *Sept-June* 9.30am-noon, 3-5pm Mon-Fri; 9.30am-noon Sat.

Lorgues Office de Tourisme
pl d'Entrechaux, 83510 Lorgues (04.94.73.92.37). **Open** *July to mid-Sept* 9am-12.30pm, 3.30-7pm Mon-Sat; 9am-noon Sun; *mid-Sept to June* 9am-12.30pm, 3-6pm Mon-Fri; 9am-12.30pm Sat.

Bargemon & Bargème

The stone houses of **Callas** cluster around a Romanesque church and a ruined castle with spectacular views southwards towards the Maures and Estérel massifs. North of town, the D25 crosses the Boussague Pass towards Bargemon. It's worth detouring through the ravine that flanks the D425 to **Claviers**, a quaint village with a fiercely patriotic church clock on the main square.

Bargemon was the last link in a chain of six Roman fortifications stretching from here to Montauroux via Fayence. The chapel of **Notre-Dame-de-Montaigu** houses a hidden, miracle-working statue of the Virgin, which is brought out once a year on Easter Monday. In the 14th-century church of **St-Etienne** – built into the town wall next to a so-called 'Roman' but, in fact, 12th-century gate – is a fascinating collection of votive offerings.

To the north, there's a distinct change of climate and vegetation as the D25 loops ever upwards in steep hairpin bends to the **Col de Bel Homme** look-out. The road flattens out across the mountain plateau and military training grounds of Camp Canjuers. At the fork of La Colle, head left on the D37 for **Bargème**, a windswept village, which blends into the rocky limestone terrain. At 1,097m it is the highest village in the Var, with a population of just 115. The tourist information office in the town hall runs guided tours to the fortified gateways, the 12th-century **Eglise St-Nicholas** and the Pontevès family château, which was destroyed during the Wars of Religion in the 16th century.

Where to stay & eat

At the southern entrance to Callas on the D225, **Camping Les Blimouses** (04.94.47.83.41, closed Dec-Mar, two people €11.50) offers mid-range campsite facilities. Far more imposing is the hospitality on offer at the **Hostellerie Les Gorges de Pennafort** (04.94.76.66.51/ www.hostellerie-pennafort.com, closed 15 Jan-15 Mar, double €95-€168, restaurant closed Wed lunch from Oct to May, menus €30.50-€99), an elegant *bastide* in a rocky gorge 7km south of Callas on the D25. Host Phillippe da Silva does excellent regional dishes in classic cordon bleu mode and succulent desserts. Twelve rooms and four suites are on hand for those who want to get far, far away from it all. In Claviers, the **Auberge le Provençal** (2 pl du 8 Mai 1945, 04.94.47.80.62, closed Mon and Jan, menus €10.37-€15) is good for a cheap meal, with lots of salads and fish, and tables in the square in summer. **Hôtel-Restaurant**

Auberge des Arcades (2 av Pasteur, 04.94.76.60.36, double €45-€75, restaurant closed Tue, menus €16.77-€29) in Bargemon is an old Provençal inn with a huge shady terrace. In tiny Bargème, Annie Noel provides *chambre d'hôte* rooms and good home cooking at **Les Roses Trémières** (Le Village, 83840 Bargème, 04.94.84.20.86, closed Nov-Easter, double €52), in the ruins of the château.

Tourist information

Market is Thur in Bargemon; Sat & Tue in Callas.

Bargème Mairie

83840 Bargème (04.94.50.21.94). **Open** July-Aug 2-6pm daily; Sept-June 2-5pm Mon, Tue, Thur, Fri.

Bargemon Syndicat d'Initiative

av Pasteur, 83830 Bargemon (04.94.47.81.73). **Open** 9am-noon daily.

Callas Syndicat d'Initiative

pl du 18 Juin 1940, 83830 Callas (04.94.39.06.77). **Open** July-Aug 9am-12.30pm, 4-7pm Mon-Sat; Sept-June 10am-12.30pm Tue, Thur.

Fayence & around

Halfway between Draguignan and Grasse, **Fayence** is a hotbed of British subversives plotting to make Provence drive on the left. Pottery and antiques are big around here. On **place St-Jean-Baptiste**, with its glorious view over the mountains to the south, the 18th-century church of **Notre-Dame** has a marble altarpiece by Provençal mason Dominique Fossatti. Cobbled streets lead into the village and the **Four du Mitan**, an old bakery with a *tableau vivant* breadmaking display.

West of Fayence, the D19 passes the Romanesque chapel of **Notre-Dame-de-l'Ormeau**, with a fine 16th-century altarpiece. Beyond here cream-coloured **Seillans**, the oldest of six fortified Roman villages in the eastern Var, appears cut out of the forest like a cubist sculpture. Three Roman gates lead into town, where steep cobbled streets ascend to a château and tower. A reminder of troubled times, the name Seillans is derived from the Provençal word *seilhanso* – the pot of boiling oil that villagers dumped over the ramparts on to the heads of Saracen attackers. Less bellicose now, the inhabitants concentrate their energies on honey, perfume and flower cultivation. The village was home to Surrealist painter Max Ernst during the last years of his life.

A stone's throw from Fayence, **Tourrettes** is named after the two square towers of its château, home of the powerful Villeneuve family. **Callian**, 4km east of Tourrettes, is

Inland Var

tiny and pedestrian, its lanes spiralling up to an impressive feudal château. In summer, chill your feet in the fountain on place Bourguignon, courtesy of the same Roman aqueduct that once supplied water to Fréjus. From Callian, it's 2km along the D37 to **Montauroux**. The main square opens on to a fine view and *boules* players congregate for *pastis* at the corner bar. Montauroux has lately taken to selling itself as 'the village of Christian Dior'. The Dior family once owned the 12th-century **Chapelle St-Barthélémy** above the village, bequeathing it to the community when the couturier died. Montauroux is handy for watersports on the **Lac St-Cassien**, 6km south-east on the D37.

Where to stay & eat

The old-fashioned charm and Provençal cooking of the **Hôtel des Deux Rocs** (pl Font d'Amont, 04.94.76.87.32, restaurant closed Dec-Mar, rates €46-€91, menus €14-€32) in Seillans makes it a favourite with the back-country brigade. In Fayence, **Hôtel La Sousto** (4 pl du Paty, 04.94.76.02.16, double €43-€49) offers a taste of village life with its cheerful rooms. Just around the corner, the tiny **Restaurant Patin Couffin** (pl de l'Olivier, 04.94.76.29.96, closed Mon & Dec-Mar, menus €15-€22) is a *très* rustic experience with dishes such as lamb or rabbit in sage, garlic and olives. Back 4km along the Seillans road, **Le Castellaras** (04.94.76.13.80, closed dinner Mon,

all Tue, and end Mar, end June and mid-Nov to mid-Dec, menus €28.25-€45.75) is the area's gourmet pull, offering excellent Provençal food (including a vegetarian menu) in a lovely garden with a swimming pool. In Montauroux, the **Auberge des Fontaines d'Aragon** (04.94.47.71.65, closed Wed & Thur and 10-30 Nov, 20-30 Jan, menu €34-€45), serves smart Mediterranean fare; the **Hôtel-Restaurant Le Marina** (2 rue Droite, 04.94.76.43.33, closed Jan, double €30, restaurant closed lunch Sat, menus €13-€22.90) moves outside in summer.

Tourist information

Market days in Fayence are Tue, Thur and Sat; Tue in Montauroux; Wed in Seillans.

Fayence Office de Tourisme

pl Léon Roux, 83440 Fayence (04.94.76.20.08/ www.mairiedefayence.com). **Open** *May-Sept* 8.30am-noon, 2-6pm daily; *Oct-Apr* 9am-noon, 2-6pm Mon-Sat.

Montauroux Office de Tourisme

pl du Clos, 83440 Montauroux (04.94.47.75.90/ http://tourisme.montauroux.com). **Open** 9am-12.30pm, 2.30-6pm Mon-Sat.

Seillans Office de Tourisme

pl du Valat, 83440 Seillans (04.94.76.85.91/ www.seillans-var.com). **Open** *Apr-Sept* 9.30am-12.30pm, 2.30-6.30pm Mon-Sat (plus *July-Aug* 10am-1pm, 3-6pm Sun); *Oct-Mar* 9.30am-12.30pm, 2.30-6pm Tue-Sat.

▶ Getting There & Around

▶ By car

The A8 autoroute runs along the Argens valley. Take exit no.36 (Le Muy) and then N555 for 12km for Draguignan; same exit and N7 for Les Arcs and Lorgues. Salernes is west of Draguignan on the D557 and D560. Cotignac is south-west of Salernes on the D22. Bargemon is about 25km northeast of Draguignan on the D562, D225 and D25. Fayence lies halfway between Draguignan and Grasse; from either, take the D562 (signed as the D2562 from Grasse), then the D563 3km north.

▶ By train or bus

The station at Les Arcs-Draguignan is on the main Paris-Nice line served by TGVs and slower trains between Nice and Marseille. **Les Rapides Varois** (04.94.50.21.50) runs hourly buses into Draguignan (fewer at weekends) from Les Arcs station, and also runs two to five buses a day (Mon-Sat) between Draguignan and Aups, stopping at Tourtour and Ampus, and buses from Les Arcs station

to Lorgues and Le Thoronet (Mon-Sat, none Wed in school holidays). **Cars Blanc** (04.94.69.08.28) runs roughly two buses a day (more in school term) between Draguignan and Marseille via Les Arcs, Vidauban, Brignoles, St-Maximin and Aix-en-Provence, as well as a few buses between Brignoles and Aups, Sillans, Villecroze, Salernes, Entrecasteaux, Cotignac and Lorgues. **Estérel Cars** (04.94.52.00.50) runs regular bus services from Draguignan to St-Raphaël and Le Muy. **Transvar** (04.94.28.93.28) runs roughly five buses a day (three on Sun) between Draguignan and Toulon, also stopping at Les Arcs and Vidauban (three on Sun). **Gagnard** (04.94.76.02.29) runs three buses a day Mon-Sat from Draguignan to Callas, Bargemon and Claviers, continuing to Seillans, Fayence, Callian, Montauroux and Grasse. There are only two daily buses in the other direction. It also runs a service between Fayence and St-Raphaël. For local bus times contact Draguignan *gare routière* (04.94.68.15.34).

Les Gorges du Verdon

The river Verdon has carved out Europe's largest canyon through the high limestone plateau: perfect for rock-climbers, canoes and cavemen.

Dizzying cliffs line the Verdon gorge, which ranges between 215m and 1,650m wide in the eastern Upper Gorge and narrows claustrophobically in the lower section to between six and 108m. The Grand Canyon proper runs for 21km from just south of Rougon to the reservoir at the **Lac de Ste-Croix**. The high fluorine content of the water in the upper sector makes it an unnaturally vibrant green; it also makes it undrinkable. West of the lake, the cliffs of the lower gorge climb no higher than 500m. It is, however, a pleasant enough place to splash about on a pedalo.

Few people, save locals, even knew about the existence of this natural wonder until its depths were fully explored in 1905. Even then, some avid Parisian nature-lover suggested that the best thing to do with such a large, unproductive gash would be to wall it up and make a dam. In the event, the dams were built downstream at the Lac de Ste-Croix and below the Basses Gorges. The whole spectacular, sparsely populated but much-visited area was made into a Parc Naturel Régional in 1977.

The Grand Canyon

Though fraught with hairpin bends and heavy traffic in high season, the 130km circuit on the perilous roads perched either side of the canyon is an experience not to be missed. The route is best tackled from **Castellane**, a small town situated on the Route Napoléon. The great man himself stopped off here for a bite in March 1815, at what is now the **Conservatoire des Arts et Traditions Populaires** museum. The 12th-century **Eglise St-Victor** was an offshoot of Abbaye St-Victor in Marseille. The town nestles beneath a massive rocky outcrop topped by the **Notre-Dame-du-Roc** chapel (kept locked), a 20-minute ascent from the centre, giving a majestic view of the entrance to the Gorges, the town and its ramparts.

12km out of Castellane, the D952 Gorges road forks. Turn left along the D955 to Trigance and then the narrow D90 for access to the *Corniche Sublime* (D71), which runs along the canyon's southern flank. For a more immediate scenic fix, continue to the aptly named **Point Sublime**

The **Corniche Sublime** road: the ultimate challenge for Sunday cyclists. *See p204.*

viewpoint at the head of the canyon. A sequence of death-defying bends follows, above cliffs that plunge a sheer 800m to the ribbon of river below. Further on, the small town of **La Palud-sur-Verdon** has plenty of accommodation.

Just before La Palud, the D23 branches off to the left, offering an airy circular route that climbs more than 500m before plunging halfway down the side of the canyon to the **Chalet de la Maline**, departure point for a walk along the valley floor (*see below*).

On the D71 southern route, the canyon is first glimpsed from the Balcon de la Mescla lookout. Shortly beyond, **Pont d'Artuby** is Europe's highest bridge, suspended 650m above the Artuby torrent. If a simple crossing does not set your pulse racing sufficiently, tourist offices in the area will direct you to sports clubs that organise bungee-jumping over the edge. Further along at the Etroit des Cavaliers, the Corniche

Walking deep

You can hike along most of the Grand Canyon, though it's no easy task, and all but the most experienced walkers should consider hiring a guide on more demanding routes. If you're determined to go it alone, the full two-day Sentier Martel canyon trail from Rougon to Maireste is explained in a walker's guide that can be picked up from tourist offices in Castellane and Moustiers-Ste-Marie. Remember to check the latest weather forecast before setting out, and ask about the water level, too: the EDF electricity generating company controls the flow artificially, and opens the floodgates at intervals (recorded information 04.92.83.62.68).

For the less adventurous, there are a host of less demanding hikes. The walk through the 670m Couloir Samson (Samson corridor) is a two-hour round trip from the Point Sublime lookout. The trail, which is clearly signposted from the car park, takes you down to a footbridge spanning the river Baou and through a series of tunnels through the rock (take a torch and a sweater), from which you emerge to a fantastic panorama of the Chaos de Tréscaïre rock formations. From Point Sublime you can also take the much more strenuous waymarked six- to eight-hour hike to Chalet de la Maline on the Route des Crêtes. There's an easier path to the Chalet de la Maline from the Etroit des Cavaliers, a two-hour descent.

Sublime road, an engineering feat completed only in 1947, winds above the gorge towards the splendidly perched town of Aiguines.

Wild and windy **Aiguines** has the western entrance to the canyon to one side and the Lac Ste-Croix to the other. The fairytale castle – a faux-Renaissance pile with multicoloured towers – is not open to the public. Once famous for wood-turning, and boules-making in particular (using boxwood gathered by intrepid climbers from trees at the base of the gorge), Aiguines' crafts are commemorated in the **Musée des Tourneurs sur Bois**. In **Les Salles-sur-Verdon**, below Aiguine, all kinds of watersports equipment can be hired. The lake is great for swimming unless the water level is low, when it becomes muddy.

The northern and southern routes meet in **Moustiers-Ste-Marie** to the north of the Lac de Ste-Croix. Built like an amphitheatre on the edge of a precipice, Moustiers enjoys a Mediterranean climate despite its altitude. On a rock above town is the medieval **Notre-Dame-de-Beauvoir** chapel, with a stunning view over the canyon. Suspended from a chain between two rocks above the chapel is a star said to have been hung there by a grateful knight, relieved at having returned from the Crusades unscathed.

Moustiers was renowned in the 17th and 18th centuries for its faïence pottery. After 200 years of production it was dethroned by the fashion for porcelain and English bone china, and the last oven went cold in 1874. Recently, attempts have been made to resuscitate the craft, and there are now 19 workshops in operation, the output of which is given a very hard sell in the town's all too numerous crafts and souvenir shops.

Conservatoire des Arts et Traditions Populaires
34 rue Nationale, Castellane (04.92.83.71.80). **Open** *May, June, Oct* 9am-noon, 2-6pm Tue-Sat; *July-Sept* 10am-1pm, 2.30-6.30pm Tue-Sun. Closed Nov-Apr. **Admission** €2; €1 7-18s; free under-7s.

Musée des Tourneurs sur Bois
Aiguines (04.94.70.20.89). **Open** *mid-June to mid-Sept* 10.30am-1pm, 3-7pm Mon, Wed-Sun; *mid-Sept to mid-June* by appointment. **Admission** €2; free under-14s.

Where to stay & eat

In Aiguines, the **Auberge Altitude 823** (04.98.10.22.17, closed Nov-Mar, double €151-€165 including dinner) is a good budget option. East of town, the **Hôtel du Grand Canyon** (D71, Falaise des Cavaliers, 04.94.76.91.31, closed Oct-Mar, double €45.70-€70.10) is a little more upmarket, and has a restaurant; prices reflect the spectacular view more than the service offered.

Castellane abounds with mid-range hotels, *gîtes*, campsites and B&Bs. The **Hôtel de Commerce** (pl Marcel Sauvaire, 04.92.83.61.00, closed Nov-Feb, double €51-€63) has an excellent restaurant (closed Tue & lunch Wed from mid-Sept to mid-June, menus €19.90-€40), run by a pupil of Alain Ducasse, while the **Canyons du Verdon** (bd St-Michel/rte de Digne, 04.92.83.76.47, closed Nov-Apr, rates €518 per week) rents studio appartments for up to four people and has a pool. Rooms at the **Auberge du Teillon** in the nearby hamlet of Garde (rte Napoléon, 04.92.83.60.88, closed mid-Dec to mid-Mar, double €39-€49) are nothing special but the restaurant is so book well ahead (closed Mon from Sept-June, dinner Sun from Oct to Apr, menus €18-€38). The grandest option is the medieval **Château de Trigance**, in the delightful hilltop village of the same name (04.94.76.91.18/www.chateau-de-trigance.fr, closed Nov-Mar, double €107-€150), with its baronial halls, four-poster beds and a vaulted restaurant (closed lunch Tue & Wed in Apr-June, Sept, Oct, menus €34-€60). **Grand-Hôtel-Bain** in Comps-sur-Artuby (2 av de Fayet, 04.94.76.90.06/www.grand-hotel-bain.fr, closed mid-Nov to Dec, double €42.70-€45.70) has been run by the same family for eight generations.

There are several acceptable mid-range hotels at Moustiers: **La Bonne Auberge** (04.92.74.66.18/www.labonneauberge.com, closed Nov-Mar, double €54.90-€64), **Le Belvédère** (rue d'Orville, 04.92.74.66.04, closed Dec-Jan, double €42.70) and **Le Relais** (pl du Couvert, 04.92.74.66.10, closed Jan-Feb, double €38-€49). **Les Santons** restaurant (pl de l'Eglise, 04.92.74.66.48, closed dinner Mon, all Tue and Jan & Dec, average €65) is pricey but well worth a visit (booking advised). For a true gourmet experience, head for super-chef Alain Ducasse's **La Bastide de Moustiers** (04.92.70.47.47/www.bastide-moustiers.com, double €145-€280, menu €49), in nearby La Grisolière, which also has 11 delightful rooms.

At La Palud-sur-Verdon, **Le Provence** hotel (rte de la Maline, 04.92.77.38.88, closed Nov-Mar, double €43-€53) has stunning views, a terrace, and a restaurant (average €18.30).

Tourist information

Market day is Friday in Aiguines, Wednesday and Saturday in Castellane, Friday in Moustiers.

Aiguines Office de Tourisme

Les Buis, 83630 Aiguines (04.94.70.21.64/ www.verdonaccueil.com). **Open** *July-Aug* 9am-12.30pm, 3-7pm Mon-Sat; *Sept-June* 9-noon, 1.30-5pm Mon-Fri.

Castellane Office de Tourisme

rue National, 04120 Castellane (04.92.83.61.14/

Pont d'Artuby: a favourite with bungee-jumpers. *See p204.*

www.castellane.org). **Open** *July, Aug* 9am-12.30pm, 1.30-7pm Mon-Sat, 10am-1pm Sun; *Sept-June* 9am-noon, 2-6pm Mon-Fri.

Moustiers-Ste-Marie Office de Tourisme

Hôtel Dieu, 04360 Moustiers-Ste-Marie (04.92.74.67.84/www.ville-moustiers-sainte-marie.fr). **Open** *July-Aug* 9am-8pm daily; *Sept-June* 2-5pm daily.

La Palud-sur-Verdon Syndicat d'Initiative

Le Château, 04120 La Palud-sur-Verdon (04.92.77.32.02). **Open** *Apr-Oct* call for details.

Riez & the Basses Gorges du Verdon

Only half as sheer as the Grand Canyon, the Basses Gorges are still pretty dramatic. Though part of the Parc Naturel, this area is more given over to agriculture. Lavender is the main crop on the Plateau de Valensole, which separates the Basses Gorges from the town of Riez; it colours and perfumes the whole area in summer.

West of the Lac de Ste-Croix, sleepy **Riez** is a pretty, unspoiled little place whose impressive main street suggests it has seen better days. Four seven-metre columns in a field on the western outskirts bear witness to the town's Roman past. On the opposite bank of the river stands a rare early Christian monument: a sixth-century Merovingian baptistry with more plundered Roman columns inside. Ramparts surround the old town, which is dominated by a 16th-century clocktower. The western gate, the **Porte Saint-Sols**, opens onto the Grande Rue where flamboyant Renaissance constructions include the Hôtel de Mazan at No.12, which has a beautiful 16th-century staircase with Gothic flourishes. The market, on Wednesday and Saturday, is a good place to pick up local truffles, honey, lavender and faïence.

The best approach to the Basses Gorges themselves is from **Quinson**, 21km south-west of Riez. This tiny village is the site of the ambitious **Musée de Préhistoire**, in a partially buried, elliptical building designed by Sir Norman Foster, which opened in April 2001. The route through a million years of prehistory is accessibly presented using reconstructions, including a mock-up cave complete with paintings, dioramas of Stone Age life and archaeological finds, indicative of the thriving cave life in the pock-marked Verdon. South of the village, a path descends to a broad, partially dammed stretch of the river; there's a swimming area, and pedalos for hire. On the southern flank, paths lead to the end of the abyss, but no further.

A twisty but scenic route winds over the mountain past **Esparron-de-Verdon**, dominated by its fortified château (*see below*, **Where to stay & eat**) beside a lake popular for sailing, windsurfing and pedalos. The ancient spa town of **Gréoux-les-Bains**, shortly before the Verdon flows into the Durance, offers a large choice of hotels, an old town crowded around a severe Templar castle, and the **Thermes de Gréoux-les-Bains**, a troglodyte spa (so as not to lose the therapeutic qualities of the calcium-, sodium-, suphate- and magnesium-rich water through exposure to daylight).

Musée de Préhistoire des Gorges du Verdon

rte de Montmeyan, Quinson (04.92.74.09.59/ www.museeprehistoire.com). **Open** *Feb to mid-June, mid-Sept to mid-Dec* 10am-6pm Mon, Wed-Sun; *mid-June to mid-Sept* 10am-8pm daily. **Admission** €5.80; €3.10 6-18s; free under-6s.

Thermes de Gréoux-les-Bains

av des Thermes, Gréoux-les-Bains (04.92.70.40.01). **Open** *Mar-Dec* 6am-4.30pm daily. Closed Jan, Feb. **Admission** €41 one-day pass, €216 six-day pass.

Where to stay & eat

In Riez, the ugly **Carina** hotel (Quartier St-Jean, 04.92.77.85.43, closed Nov-Mar, double €45.70-€53.40) is more acceptable when looking out.

Quinson's bars are strong on hunting dogs and low on gourmet facilities, but the museum

happily has a café. At Esparron get a feel for the aristocratic lifestyle at *chambres d'hôtes* at the **Château d'Esparron** (Esparron de Verdon, 04.92.77.12.05/www.esparron.com, closed Nov to mid-Apr, double €110), still in the hands of the Castellane family who built it in the 12th century. Bedrooms in the 18th-century wing are colossal and high-ceilinged. Although it has something of a geriatric feel as curists come to take the waters, Gréoux-les-Bains offers numerous hotels and restaurants. Try **Villa La Castellane** (av des Thermes, 04.92.78.00.31, closed Nov-Mar, double €44-€63), a former hunting lodge set in an attractive garden.

Tourist information

Market is Thursday in Gréoux-les-Bains, Wednesday and Saturday in Riez.

Gréoux-les-Bains Office de Tourisme

5 av des Maronniers, 04800 Gréoux-les-Bains (04.92.78.01.08/www.greoux-les-bains.com). **Open** 9am-noon, 2-6pm Mon-Sat, 9am-noon Sun.

Riez Office de Tourisme

4 allée Louis Gardiol, 04500 Riez (04.92.77.99.09). **Open** *June-Sept* 8am-12.30pm, 1.30-6.30pm daily; *Oct-May* 8am-noon, 1.30-5.30pm Mon-Sat.

► Getting There & Around

► By car

For the Grand Canyon, leave the A8 autoroute at exit no.42 and take the N85 to Castellane via Grasse, or exit no.36 for Draguignan and then D955. For Quinson, leave the A8 at exit no.34 at St-Maximin and take the D560/D13. From Aix-en-Provence, take the A51 or D952 to Gréoux-les-Bains; the latter continues to Moustiers.

► By bus

Public transport is very limited. **Sumian** (04.42.67.60.34) runs buses from Marseille to Castellane via Aix-en-Provence, La Palud-sur-Verdon and Moustiers-Ste-Marie (July to mid-Sept one a day Mon, Wed, Sat; mid-Sept to July on Sat only). **VFD** (04.93.85.24.56) runs a daily service between Nice and Grenoble stopping at Grasse, Castellane and Digne-les-Bains. **Guichard** (04.92.83.64.47) runs buses around the canyon (Apr-June Sat, Sun only; July, Aug daily) linking Castellane with Point Sublime, La Palud and La Maline. Otherwise the best option for the car-less might be a day trip; try **Santa Azur** in Nice (04.97.03.60.00) who operate day trips to the Gorges du Verdon every Sun, Apr-Oct.

The Riviera

Cannes

And you thought tanning was a thing of the past... Not in Cannes, where the upmarket beach culture is as important as the film-star glam of La Croisette.

Cannes already attracted the high fashion crowd long before its film festival. In 1834, the British Lord Chancellor Lord Brougham settled in the fishing village of Cannes after an outbreak of cholera made it impossible to continue on to Nice. He built himself a house, convinced King Louis-Philippe to spend two million francs on a harbour wall and for the next 34 years spent the summers here. Before long the English aristocracy had invaded *en masse* and art and literature celebs followed.

In 1939 Cannes was selected to host a Festival International de Cinéma in order to break the Italian Fascists' monopoly on cinematic prize-giving, but World War II disrupted the preparations. The first festival took place in 1946 at the old Palais des Festivals (where the Noga Hilton now stands). Local legend has it that the architects forgot to put a window in the projection booth – only after several embarrassed minutes of hammering and chiselling was a glamorous audience able to enjoy its first festival movie.

Capitalising on the film festival, Cannes has launched itself as the European media festival hub. The **Palais des Festivals** swarms at various times of the year with advertisers (MIPCOM), music-makers (MIDEM), TV producers (MIP-TV) and a range of other conference-goers who keep the hotels full.

Cannes has also embraced an upmarket beach culture. In the summer every available inch of sand is covered by bronzing, often topless bodies. Public beaches are mostly found along boulevard du Midi (plus straight and gay nude beach La Batterie out on the N7 towards Antibes). If there is a row of beach chairs don't sit – unless you want to pay to swim in the same water as everyone else.

Lounging with a cocktail is also an important pastime. Le boulevard du Midi and La Croisette – the two main sea-front drags – are a late-afternoon must, lined with bars, restaurants and luxury hotels. On **La Croisette** sits the Palais des Festivals with its film star hand-prints in the pavement, and the trinity of palace hotels: the Majestic, the Martinez and the Carlton. From **Pointe de la Croisette**, there's a glorious view across the bay of La Napoule. Modern art and photography exhibitions are held at **La Malmaison**, a 19th-century

mansion that was part of the old Grand Hôtel.

To the west is the port and, perched on a hill above, the old town of **Le Suquet** with one of the best food markets in the Midi. The **Musée de la Castre** occupies what's left of the town's 12th-century fortifications and has spectacular views of the bay, as well as an eclectic collection ranging from a painting by Pasteur to musical instruments. Easily overlooked amid the colourful shops around rue Meynadier is **Le Musée de l'Enfance**, where passionate collector Mme Nicod gives an intimate version of 19th-century French history through the display of antique dolls and accessories.

West of the centre **Cannes-La Bocca** is a less-expensive residential area, with a nice stretch of public beach and cheaper stores and restaurants on avenue Francis Tonner. On the other side of Cannes is the **Quartier de la Californie** which has the **Chapelle Bellini** (allée de la Villa-Florentina) designed in elaborate baroque style, as well as **l'Eglise orthodoxe St-Michel Archange** (30 bd Alexandre III), whose choral group is renowned for its interpretations of the Russian liturgy. Further north, the hilltop suburb of Le Cannet has been popular with many artists, from Renoir and Bonnard to the playwright Victorien Sardou. The chemin des Collines winds through the hills above Cannes. On avenue Victorien sits an Oriental-style villa (private property) given to Yvette Labrousse by her husband, the Aga Khan. **Le Cannet** is also home to **La Palestre**, a large concert venue that has seen stars like Vanessa Paradis rock the night away.

La Malmaison

47 La Croisette (04.93.99.04.04). **Open** *July-Aug* 10.30am-12.30pm, 2-7.30pm Mon, Wed-Sun; *Sept-June* 10.30am-12.30pm, 2-6.30pm Mon, Wed-Sun. **Admission** €3.05; free under-18s.

Musée de la Castre

Château de la Castre, pl de la Castre (04.93.38.55.26). **Open** *Apr-June* 10am-noon, 2-6pm Mon, Wed-Sun; *July-Sept* 10am-noon, 3-7pm Mon, Wed-Sun; *Oct-Mar* 10am-noon, 2-5pm Mon, Wed-Sun. **Admission** €1.50; free under-18s.

▶ For more on Cannes film festival turn to The Festive South, starting on page 41.

The Riviera

Le Musée de L'Enfance

2 rue Venizelos (04.93.68.29.28). **Open** 2-6pm daily during school holidays; at other times by appointment. **Admission** €5.50; €4 13-18s; €3 under-13s.

Palais des Festivals

1 La Croisette (04.93.39.01.01/
www.cannes-on-line.com). **Admission** varies.

La Palestre

730 av Georges Pompidou, Le Cannet
(04.93.46.48.88/www.lapalestre.com).
Admission €20-€40.

Restaurants

Astoux et Brun

27 rue Félix Faure (04.93.39.21.87). **Open** noon-3pm, 7-11.30pm daily. Closed July. **Average** €45.73. **Credit** AmEx, MC, V.
This is simply the best place for *fruits de mer* of impeccable freshness. A swarthy sailor-type shucks oysters to order and specials include fish casserole and the ultimate seafood platter, *l'assortement royale.*

Athènes

18 rue des Frères Pradignac (04.93.38.96.11). **Open** noon-2pm, 7-10.30pm Mon, Tue, Thur-Sat. **Menus** €25.15-€29.73. **Credit** AmEx, MC, V.
A Greek restaurant with a nice mixture of vegetarian and meat options. The decor favours Greek columns and statues of goddesses. Book in winter.

La Cave

9 bd de la République (04.93.99.79.87). **Open** noon-2pm, 8-10pm Mon-Fri; 8-10pm Sat. **Menus** €27.14. **Credit** AmEx, MC, V.
A small but stylish restaurant with consistently good food (try the fabulous *soupe au pistou*), usually packed with a mixture of tourists and locals. Book.

L'Echiquier

14 rue St Antoine, Le Suquet (04.93.39.77.79). **Open** 7-11pm Mon-Sat. **Average** €38.11. **Credit** AmEx, MC, V.
The candlelit dimness sometimes helps disguise more famous movie-industry visitors, and big-wigs from Paramount and MGM have been known to stop by when in town. The tomato and bocconcini salad on fresh greens is excellent. Booking advised.

Le Farfalla

1 La Croisette (04.93.68.93.00). **Open** 11am-2am daily. **Average** €39.64. **Credit** AmEx, MC, V.
This steak house with milk bar decor is *the* rendezvous for bright young things. There's a full menu, or lighter salads and snacks. The terrace is for grade-A people watching; alternatively, seek refuge in an intimate booth on the mezzanine.

Le Marais

9 rue du Suquet, Le Suquet (04.93.38.39.19). **Open** 7.30-11pm Tue-Sun. Closed mid-Nov to Dec. **Menus** €21.34-€28.97. **Credit** MC, V.

This busy locals' favourite is friendly and informal with a menu that makes the most of Provençal ingredients, along with homemade ravioli and foie gras.

Neat

11 sq Mérimée (04.93.99.29.19). **Open** noon-2pm, 7-10pm Tue-Sat. **Average** €15-€70. **Credit** AmEx, DC, MC, V.
Richard Neat trained at Pied à Terre in London and set up his own restaurant in Cannes in 1999. Modern French cooking is the house style, and the top dish is snails with dried mushrooms and garlic.

Le Relais des Semailles

9 rue St Antoine (04.93.39.22.32). **Open** 10am-10.30pm Tue-Sun. **Menus** €15-€50. **Credit** AmEx, MC, V.
An intriguing place to eat, filled with 19th-century trinkets, old paintings and mirrors. It serves dishes made from fresh market produce such as truffle risotto. Reservations recommended.

Le Restaurant Arménien

82 La Croisette (04.93.94.00.58/
www.lerestaurantmenien.com). **Open** noon-1.30pm, 7-10.30pm Tue-Sun. Closed one week in Dec. **Menu** €40. **Credit** DC, MC, V.
At the eastern end of La Croisette, this restaurant offers superb eating in a calm setting. 16 different

Cannes' old town, **Le Suquet**. *See p209.*

meze make up the first course. Mains include stuffed mussels and barley pasta with pistachios.

Le Siam

50 bd Lorraine (04.93.99.77.46). **Open** 7pm-2.30am Mon,Tue, Thur-Sun. **Average** €15-€31. **Credit** AmEx, MC, V.

This gem of a Thai restaurant is tucked down a side-street off rue d'Antibes. Try the pineapple, red onion and cilantro salad, and fabulous ginger chicken.

Villa de Lys

Hôtel Majestic, 14 La Croisette (04.92.98.77.00). **Open** noon-2pm, 7.30-10pm Tue-Sat. Closed mid-Nov to mid-Dec. **Menus** €39.64-€118.91. **Credit** AmEx, DC, MC, V.

Chef Bruno Oger is one of the rising young turks on the Riviera. He worked at the Oriental in Bangkok, and the Thai influence is clear in dishes like lobster in a broth spiked with lemongrass, lime leaves and coriander. More traditional dishes are available too.

Bars, cafés & snacks

Le Blue Café

corner rue des Fréres Pradignac and Victor Cousin (04.92.59.12.37). **Open** 11am-3pm, 6pm-2.30am Mon-Sat. **Menu** €19. **Credit** MC, V.

A newly opened Cannoise secret. In the daytime, stop by for a quick sandwich or plate of fries; in the evening order from a menu selected from five different restaurants around the café. Great for those who can't decide if they want sushi, or Greek, or both.

Grand Café

2 les Allées de la Liberté (04.93.99.93.10). **Open** 9am-1am daily; *karaoke* Fri-Sun. **Credit** AmEx, DC, MC, V.

A bar, café and karaoke place all wrapped up in one. Don't be mislead by ideas of wannabe stars warbling out of tune, they take karaoke seriously here. A great place to start out the night with a cocktail.

La Pizza

3 quai St Pierre (04.93.39.22.56). **Open** noon-1.30am daily. **Average** €9.15.

This is a veritable institution in Cannes: constantly busy, great pizza, quick service, reasonable prices.

Le 72 Croisette

71 La Croisette (04.93.94.18.30). **Open** *May-Oct* 24hrs daily; *Nov-Apr* 6am-8pm daily. **Credit** AmEx, MC, V.

Of all the Croisette bars this remains the most feistily French. You'll have to battle hordes of locals to get a ringside seat from which to watch the rich and famous enter the Martinez next door.

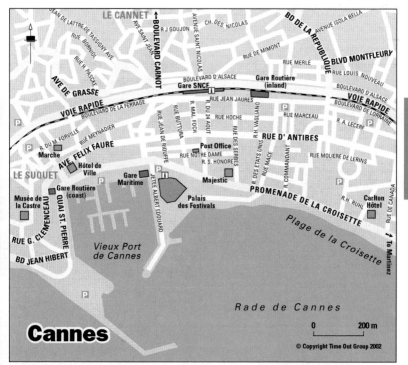

The Riviera

© Copyright Time Out Group 2002

Nightlife

Caliente

84 La Croisette (04.93.94.49.59). **Open** 10pm-dawn nightly. **Admission** free, reservation recommended. **Credit** AmEx, MC, V.

This very hip Latino bar is jam-packed nightly with salsa-dancing-Corona-drinking regulars. Thursday-Saturday there is a live Brazilian band.

Les Coulisses

29 rue de Commandant André (04.92.99.17.17). **Open** 6pm-2.30am daily. **Credit** AmEx, V.

The stylish and the beautiful flock to this club. During the film festival Parisian media folk move in and in summer the action spills out on the street.

Disco 7

7 rue Rouguière (04.93.39.10.36). **Open** 11.30pm-8am daily. **Admission** €15.24. **Credit** DC, MC, V.

This hole in the wall gay club happily jams in all sorts from yuppie to alternative. Local drag queens belt out the classics, both French and English.

Le Loft

13 rue du Dr Monod (06.21.02.37.49). **Open** 10.30am-2.30am (restaurant 5pm-2am) Mon-Sat. **Credit** AmEx, MC , V.

This trendy, upmarket bar has been part of the scene for several years and continues to attract the well-dressed and beautiful. Downstairs, in an aquarium-like interior, Tantra restaurant serves a good selection of sushi (average €53).

Midnight Blues

10 rue Georges Clemenceau (04.93.39.66.26). **Open** 8pm-2.30am Tue-Sat. **Credit** MC, AmEx, V.

One of the oldest bars in Cannes, with live rock every Wednesday night. With a nice mix of student men-tality and ageing boomers, it is a great place to start (or finish) the night.

Morrison's Irish Pub

10 rue Teisseire (04.92.98.16.17). **Open** 5pm-2.30am Mon-Sat; 6pm-2.30am Sun. **Credit** AmEx, DC, MC, V.

An excellent Irish pub with live music every Wednesday and Thursday at 10pm and big-screen TV tuned to English and Irish news and football.

Zanzi Bar

85 rue Félix Faure (04.93.39.30.75). **Open** 6pm-4am daily. **Credit** AmEx, MC, V.

The tunnel-like Zanzi Bar claims to be the oldest gay bar in France but has recently got the boystown make-over. Attracts the international gay jet set.

Shopping

La Croisette, rue d'Antibes and the streets that link the two are the luxury shopper's paradise. **Cartier** (57 La Croisette, 04.92.59.28.20, closed Sun) will be happy to help you choose between platinum or solid gold for that trinket to accompany your **Chanel** (5 La Croisette, 04.93.38.55.05, closed Sun) outfit up *les marches*. The essential accessory for any Croisette stroll is best picked up at **Sunglass Hut** (37 rue d'Antibes, 04.93.39.78.88, closed Sun).

For typical Provençal articles make for rue Meynadier which runs parallel to the port. The

Riviera princess **The Carlton**. *See right.*

The controversial new **Palais des Festivals** puts on the red carpet treatment. *See p209.*

winding streets of Le Suquet are also a good bet for souvenirs and trinkets. In **allée de la Liberté**, a Saturday morning market offers regional crafts. **Forville produce market** on rue Forville behind the old port is a magnificent covered market (Tue-Sun mornings). On Monday it turns into a *brocante*. There is also a *brocante* every Saturday (and first Sun of the month) '*sur les allées*' opposite the old port. **Place Gambetta**, a block north of rue d'Antibes east of the train station, is a smaller but still sizeable market (closed Mon).

Ceneri (22 rue Neynadier, 04.93.39.63.68, closed Sun, Mon) is the place for cheese and gourmet goodies. For sweet treats, the new **Lenôtre** outlet (63 rue d'Antibes, 04.97.06.67.67, closed Sun) tempts with delicious sweets, cakes and pâtisseries. **Schies** (125 rue d'Antibes, 04.93.39.01.03) offers a vast range of handmade chocolates made with local products. **Star Glaces** (71 rue Félix Faure, 04.93.39.79.78) has the best ice cream and sorbets, and great service.

The Cannes branch of **Fnac**, selling CDs, books, videos and electrical goods, is at 83 rue d'Antibes (04.97.06.29.29, closed Sun). **Cannes English Book Shop** (11 rue Bivouac Napoléon, 04.93.99.40.08, closed Sun) can provide English-language material for festival bluffing or beach reading. British and US dailies can be found at **Le Temps de Vivre** (7 La Croisette, 04.93.39.14.51, open daily) but they tend to run out early.

Where to stay

Palace hotels

Carlton Hôtel

58 La Croisette (04.93.06.40.06/
www.interconti.com). **Double** €370-€750. **Credit** AmEx, DC, MC, V.
Built in 1911, the Carlton is a trademark of Riviera glamour and an enduring symbol of the film festival. Its two coupoles were inspired, it's said, by the breasts of the gypsy courtesan, *la belle otéro*. Though some top stars have shipped camp to the super-swank Hôtel du Cap Eden-Roc in Cap d'Antibes, the Carlton remains the first choice for festival purists, and its terrace is a prime location for people-spotting. The Carlton Casino Club on the 7th floor is as elegant as the hotel and more upmarket than the Vegas-style Jimmy Z at the Martinez.

Majestic

10 La Croisette (04.92.98.77.00/
www.lucienbarriere.com). Closed mid-Nov to Dec.
Double €215-€785. **Credit** AmEx, DC, MC, V.
During the film, music or advertising festivals the Majestic throbs as industry folk loudly renew acquaintances. The hotel's Villa des Lys restaurant (*see p211*) offers one of Cannes' best dining experiences and Paris brasserie Fouquet's recently opened an offshoot here, too, while the fumoir has all the havanas and coronas any self-respecting mogul could want. The Majestic bar is mythical, the Cecil B DeMille decor paying homage to the Pharaonic ambitions of the film types who frequent the place.

The Riviera

Martinez

*73 La Croisette (04.92.98.73.00/www.hotel-
martinez.com).* **Double** €240-€1000. **Credit** AmEx,
DC, MC, V.

Constructed at the end of the Roaring Twenties, the
Martinez prides itself on its art deco appeal, which
is lovingly preserved by the bubbly Taittinger family. This is the most relaxed of Cannes' big three; the
discreet rich can be found of an evening snacking at
the hotel's Palm d'Or restaurant. The other notable
feature of the Martinez is Jimmy at the piano in the
bar. Jimmy hires (and fills) Carnegie Hall in New
York for an annual one-nighter: you can hear him
play here for the price of a dry martini.

Budget & moderate hotels

Hôtel des Allées

*6 rue Emile Négrin (04.93.39.53.90/www.hotel-des-
allees.com).* Closed mid-Nov to Dec. **Double** €64-
€175. **Credit** AmEx, MC, V.

A happy family atmosphere compensates for the
lack of a lift and the cramped rooms.

Hôtel Beverly

14 rue Hoche (04.93.39.10.66/www.hotel-beverly.com).
Double €54-€66. **Credit** AmEx, DC, MC, V.

Situated centrally on a shopping street parallel to La
Croisette, all 19 rooms have recently been redecorated. It's cosy but a little noisy so book ahead to
secure a room with a balcony at the rear.

Hôtel Savoy

*5 rue François Einsey (04.92.99.72.00/www.hotel-
savoy-cannes.com).* **Double** €106-€261. **Credit**
AmEx, DC, MC, V.

The rooftop terrace-with-pool of this designer hotel
is considered Cannes' best: a restful crow's nest with
a magnificent view over the city, it's a magnet for
high-density sunbathers.

La Madrilène

*15 bd Alexandre III (04.97.06.37.37/fax
04.93.94.38.78).* **Double** €51.83-€91.47. **Credit**
AmEx, DC, MC, V.

Situated in beautiful La Californie, the hotel is within walking distance of Cannes. It has a great family
atmosphere and is bright and clean. Ask for a room
in the back with a lovely view of the garden.

Le Mistral Croisette

*13 rue des Belges (04.93.39.91.46/fax
04.93.38.35.17).* Closed two weeks in Dec. **Double**
€45-€54. **Credit** MC, V.

In the centre of Cannes, Le Mistral has friendly staff
and the brightly painted rooms are welcoming.

Le Mondial

1 rue Teisseire (04.93.68.70.00/fax 04.93.99.39.11).
Double €98-€134. **Credit** AmEx, DC, MC, V.

This 1930s edifice dominates rue Teisseire – only a
short walk from La Croisette – and looks southwards to the sea. It's newly renovated, with sound-
proofed, modern rooms, many with tiny balconies.

Splendid

*4 rue Félix Faure (04.97.06.22.22/www.splendid-hotel-
cannes.fr).* **Double** €107-€218. **Credit** AmEx, DC,
MC, V.

The original Cannes palace, the Splendid stands
wedding-cake proud with flags fluttering across
from the festival HQ. Its picture-postcard charms
lure a loyal, mostly American clientele. New restaurant Palm Square has replaced the Planet Hollywood, offering a mix of Thai, French and Italian
cuisine (menus €50-€75, closed Wed).

Self-catering

Résideal

*11 rue Bertrand Lepine (tel/fax 04.93.05.50.00/
www.resideal.com).* Closed mid-Nov to mid-Dec.
Rates two-person studio per week €189-€714.
Credit AmEx, DC, MC, V.

Tall trees shade this secluded modern apartment
block (all with balcony), providing privacy poolside
where top talent greets the world's media during the
festival. Breakfast in the grounds is a real treat.

Tourist information

Mondego Café (15 sq Merimée, 04.93.68.19.21,
open 11am-9pm daily, €6.85 per hour) is a
reasonably priced **Internet café** right outside
the Palais des Festivals, and offers anything
from chocolate brownies to whisky while you
wait to plug in.

Cannes Office de Tourisme

*Palais des Festivals, 1 bd de la Croisette
(04.93.39.24.53/www.cannes-on-line.com).* **Open**
July-Aug 9am-8pm daily; *Sept-June* 9am-6.30pm daily.
Branch: *Gare SNCF rue Jean-Jaurès
(04.93.99.19.77/fax 04.93.39.40.19).* **Open** 9am-
noon, 2-6pm Mon-Fri.

Iles de Lérins

A 15-minute boat ride from the old port of
Cannes, the Iles de Lérins are a dramatic
contrast to the glitz of La Croisette. Known to
the ancients as Lero and Lerina, these two
oases, where secluded paths criss-cross thick
forests of aleppo pine and eucalyptus, now go
by the names of **St-Honorat** and **Ste-
Marguerite**, after the religious siblings who
formed monastic communities here in the fourth
century. By the seventh century, Lérins was one
of Europe's key monastic institutions. Today
it's a religious backwater where a handful of
Cistercian monks make a liqueur called Lerina.
Planaria (04.92.98.71.38) runs daily boats (8am-
4.30pm) to St-Honorat; Compagnie Esterel
Chantelclair (04.93.39.11.82) runs daily boats
(9am-noon) to Ste-Marguerite.

Honoratus, credited with being one of the
founders of monasticism, had the usual early

Reflective mood in the **harbour**.

Monastère Fortifié

St-Honorat (04.92.99.54.00). **Open** *mid-Sept to mid-June* 10.30am-12.30pm, 2.15-5pm daily; *mid-June to mid-Sept* 9am-5pm daily. Closed during Sun mass. **Admission** free.

Musée de la Mer

Fort Ste-Marguerite (04.93.43.18.17). **Open** *Oct-Mar* 10.30am-1.15pm, 2.15-4.45pm Tue-Sun; *Apr-Sept* 10.30am-1.15pm, 2.15-5.45pm Tue-Sun. Closed three weeks in Jan. **Admission** €3; free under-16s. **No credit cards**.

Mougins

A satellite of Cannes and yet still charmingly rural, Mougins is the place where film people come to get away from the crush on La Croisette. Old Mougins is an extraordinary hilltop site carpeted in flowers and bushes with narrow lanes and restored houses built on the line of earlier ramparts. The walls date from the Middle Ages when Mougins was bigger than Cannes and rich from its luxury harvest: olives, wine, jasmine and roses.

In the interwar period, Mougins was discovered by the Surrealists, among them Cocteau, Picabia (who built the fanciful Château de Mai) and Picasso, who discovered Mougins in the company of Dora Maar and Man Ray. Local lore has it that cash-strapped Picasso covered his room and the outside walls with art to pay for his board and lodging; the enraged owner made the still obscure artist whitewash over them the next day. Undaunted, he settled here in 1961 with his wife Jaqueline, and spent much of his time here until his death in 1973.

Today Mougins bristles with galleries and painters and offers second homes for the better sort of resident, noticeable by all the closed-circuit cameras peeping out from behind the bougainvillea. The worst sort of residents are welcome, too, as long as they are discreet: Haitian dictator Baby Doc Duvalier used to have a pied-à-terre here.

Views from the medieval centre are spectacular; for the best panorama, climb up to the terrace of the bell tower of **St-Jacques-le-Majeur** in rue des Orfèvres. The **Musée Municipal** is located on the first floor of the town hall, which was built on the foundations of an old chapel dedicated to St Bernardin. It contains an interesting retrospective of the history of Mougins using period literature. **Le Lavoir**, once the village laundry, is now an exhibition centre that showcases local artists. Next to the 12th-century Porte Sarassin, the **Musée de la Photographie** includes old cameras and an engaging series of photos of Picasso by André Villers, as well as photos by Doisneau and Lartigue.

Christian attributes of extreme asceticism and a way with snakes: it was he who did away with the smaller island's venomous inhabitants, and it was here that St Patrick trained in the same art before setting out for Ireland – or so the story goes. The little that remains on St-Honorat of the earlier monastery buildings was incorporated into the current Abbaye de Lérins in the 19th century. The nearby keep – the **Monastère Fortifié** – built by the monks in 1073 to protect themselves when Saracens attacked, still has a decidedly impregnable air.

Ste-Marguerite is more touristy. The **Musée de la Mer** in the Fort Ste-Marguerite is visited not so much for its collection of underwater archaeological finds as for its reputation as the prison of the Man in the Iron Mask. Made lastingly famous by novelist Alexandre Dumas and by countless cinematic tall tales, the Man may have been Louis XIV's twin brother. Many hapless Huguenots were confined here during Louis XIV's religious crackdown, and the place was re-fortified in 1712 by royal architect Vauban, though why – seeing as it faces landwards and is fairly useless for defensive purposes – is difficult to imagine. The port is awash with rather overpriced fish restaurants, but the sea around the islands is cleaner than over on the mainland.

Five km south-east of Mougins on the A8 motorway (access from Aire de Bréguières service station) is the **Musée de l'Automobiliste**. Adrien Maeght, son of Aimé and Marguerite Maeght (*see page 274*), set up this state-of-the-art glass and concrete tribute to cars and motorbikes with around a hundred sleek racing cars on rotating display.

Le Lavoir

av Charles Mallet (04.92.92.50.42). **Open** *Mar-Oct* 10am-7pm daily. **Admission** free.

Musée de l'Automobiliste

772 chemin de Font-de-Currault (04.93.69.27.80/ www.weblane.fr/musee-auto-mougins). **Open** *Apr-Sept* 10am-7pm daily; *Oct to mid-Nov, mid-Dec to Mar* 10am-6pm daily. Closed mid-Nov to mid-Dec. **Admission** €7; €4 12-18s; under-12s free. **Credit** AmEx, MC, V.

Musée Municipal

2 pl Commdt Lamy (04.92.92.50.42). **Open** 9am-5pm Mon-Fri; 2-6pm Sat, Sun. Closed mid-Oct to mid-Dec. **Admission** free.

Musée de la Photographie

67 rue de l'Eglise (04.93.75.85.67). **Open** *July-Sept* 10am-8pm daily; *Oct-June* 10am-noon, 2-6pm Wed-Sat; 2-6pm Sun. Closed Nov. **Admission** €0.76. **No credit cards.**

St-Jacques-le-Majeur

rue des Orfèvres (04.93.75.85.67). **Open** *July-Sept* 10am-8pm daily; *Oct-June* 10am-noon, 2-6pm Wed-Sat; 2-6pm Sun. Closed Nov. **Admission** free. Key from Musée de la Photographie.

Where to stay & eat

Mougins may be small, but it packs a gastronomic punch. Consistent as the star player is Roger Vergé's **Le Moulin de Mougins** (424 chemin du Moulin, av Notre-Dame-de-Vie, 04.93.75.78.24, closed Mon and 10 Dec-10 Jan, menus €90-€118) a temple of modern Provençal cuisine that also hosts works and installations by artists such as César, Arman and Folon. It also has three rooms (€137-€183) and four suites (€297-€320). Chefs from the restaurant also run cookery courses at the **Ecole de Cuisine de Soleil** in Mougins village (04.93.75.35.70, €46 for a two-hour lesson); each multilingual session is organised around a menu or seasonal theme. **Restaurant aux Trois Etages** (10 pl du Village, 04.93.90.01.46, closed Nov, average €30) serves Provençal-style cuisine in a lovely three-storey setting beside the town hall. At **Le Feu Follet** (pl de la Mairie, 04.93.90.15.78, closed Mon & dinner Sun, menus €23-€43), Jean-Paul Battaglia heads a battalion of young chefs in an open-plan kitchen. Dishes like Salade-Feu Follet

The wet set

If lying on a beach is just too tame for you, the Riviera offers plenty of more active alternatives and a mushrooming of rental agencies. The more daring have taken up ski-surfing (which requires controlling a large kite-like parachute and launching yourself in the air with a water-ski attached to your feet). The less adventurous are satisfied with the more traditional jet-ski. Prices range from around €54 to €61/half hour for a jet ski, €9.15/hour for a windsurfer. In Cannes, check out **Cannes Jeunesse** (Port du Mourre Rouge, 04.92.18.88.88), **Ski Nautique/Motonautisme** (04.93.38.64.85) or **Centre Nautique Municipal** (9 rue Esprit Violet, 04.93.47.40.55), which organises sailing, water-skiing, surfing and diving activities.

There are diving schools for all levels all along the coast. For beginner-level courses try **Nice Diving** (26 bd Stalingrad, Nice, 04.93.89.42.44) or **Golfe Plongée Club** (Port de Golfe-Juan, 04.93.64.22.67). For experienced and PADI instructor courses try the **IT College** (95 av Dr Picaud 04.93.47.04.82). Further west, **Bormes Plongée** (La Favière, Bormes-les-Mimosas, 06.75.33.27.52/www.nautica-dive.com) runs diving expeditions around the Var coast, Iles de Hyères and shipwrecks; at Cassis, renowned diver **Henri Cosquier** (*see p171*) leads expeditions into the cave-pocked Calanques.

For more information contact the **Fédération Française d'Etudes et de Sports Sous-Marins** in Marseille (04.91.33.99.31).

The Riviera

with smoked salmon and foie gras make every mouthful a pleasure. **Les Muscadins** (18 bd Courteline, 04.92.28.28.28, closed Tue Dec-Apr and Nov, menus €30.49-€48.78, double €160-€375), where Picasso fell in love with Mougins in 1936, has recently been taken over by St-Trop's celebrity chef Christophe Leroy. **La Terrasse à Mougins** (31 bd Courteline, 04.92.28.36.20/www.la-terrasse-a-mougins, closed 10 Dec-10 Jan, double €137-€228, menus €27.44-€48.78) is a hotel and restaurant with super-chic decor, good vegetarian options and panoramic views over the Alps, Cannes and the islands. **Chez Cyriaque** (24 rue Honoré Henry, 04.93.90.05.36, closed Mon, average €18) is very cosy, with welcoming staff and dishes such as goat's cheese and red pepper bruschetta. For country calm, head for **Le Manoir de l'Etang** (bois de Fontmerle, allée du Manoir, 04.93.90.01.07/www.manoir-de-letang.com, closed Nov-Feb, double €92-€153), a *bastide* hotel/restaurant with swimming pool in a peaceful setting, or camp at **L'Eau Vive** (713 chemin des Cabrières, 04.93.75.36.35, two-person tent €13.72).

Tourist information

Mougins Office de Tourisme

15 av Jean-Charles Mallet, 06250 Mougins (04.93.75.87.67/www.mougins-coteazur.org). **Open** *mid-June to mid-Sept 10am-8pm daily; mid-Sept to mid-June 2.30-5.30pm Mon; 10am-5.30pm Tue-Sat.*

Everything's gone to pot in **Vallauris** since Picasso left town.

Vallauris & Golfe-Juan

Vallauris would have little to offer but beautiful scenery were it not for Picasso. Georges and Suzanne Ramié, who owned the Madoura pottery workshop in Vallauris, introduced the painter to the joys of clay and he single-handedly rekindled the town's dying ceramics industry. A mixed blessing, in view of some of the crimes committed in the name of *céramique artistique* in Vallauris' main drag, avenue Georges Clemenceau.

There are a few serious workshops lurking behind the hordes of souvenir driven shops. **Galerie Madoura** (rue Suzanne Georges Ramié, 04.93.64.66.39, closed Sat, Sun and Nov), is now run by the son of the original owners and still has the rights to reproducing Picasso's designs in signed, limited editions. Prices start at around €1,200 for the smallest model.

By 1949 Picasso's passion for clay was waning; perhaps worried that such a prestigious resident was about to desert them, the good people of Vallauris gave him *carte blanche* to decorate the tiny, medieval chapel in the courtyard of the village castle – now the **Musée National Picasso**. The speed-painted essay on the theme of war and peace is breathtaking in its visual power. The ticket also gives admission to the **Musée Magnelli/ Musée de la Céramique** on the second floor of the castle, with more Picasso ceramics. The bronze statue of a man and sheep in the main place de la Libération is also a Picasso creation, presented to his adopted town in 1949 on the condition that children always be allowed to climb all over it.

Vallauris' seaward extension, Golfe-Juan, has a fine kilometre-long sandy beach, sheltered from the worst of the mistral. This is where Napoléon landed on 1 March 1815, at the beginning of the Hundred Days that would see his triumphant return to Paris, rapid popular disaffection, Waterloo and a second, permanent exile on St Helena. A story relates that one of the first people he met after setting foot on dry land was the Prince of Monaco, who told Napoléon that he was on his way back to reclaim his realm, now that the Revolution had blown over. 'Then, sir, we are in the same business,' replied the Corsican. Those who wish to retrace his route as far as Grenoble can do so on the Route Napoléon, which begins in Golfe-Juan.

Musée National Picasso, Musée Magnelli, Musée de la Céramique

Château de Vallauris, pl de la Libération (04.93.64.16.05). **Open** *mid-June to mid-Sept* 10am-12.15pm, 2-6pm Mon, Wed-Sun; *mid-Sept to mid-June* 10am-12.15pm, 2-5pm Mon, Wed-Sun. **Admission** €3; free under-16s. **No credit cards**.

Where to stay, eat & drink

In Vallauris, **Le Manuscrit** (224 chemin Lintur, 04.93.64.56.56, closed Mon and mid-Nov to 6 Dec, mid-Jan-6 Fev) is a rare surprise with its beautiful terrace and fantastic set menus (€16-€28): try the beef roquefort and mouth-watering snails with garlic cream. Old-fashioned style (shorts are frowned on) is the hallmark of **La Gousse d'Ail** (11 rte de Grasse, 04.93.64.10.71, closed dinner Tue & Sun, all Mon, all Nov and last two weeks in June), just behind the church (menus €20.50-€30). It's the *bouillabaisse* that's the draw at the excellent, upmarket **Bijou Plage** (bd Littoral, 04.93.61.39.07, menus €18.50-€45).

Good hotels are limited in Vallauris. Try **Auberge Siou Aou Miou** (105 chemin des Fumades, 04.93.64.39.89, double €47-€58) with old manor-house charm. It's better to stay down at Golfe-Juan, where the selection includes the upmarket **Résidence Hotelière Open** (av Georges Pompidou, 04.93.63.33.00/www.resorts-open.com, double €68-€116) and the **Mas Samarcande** *chambres d'hôtes* (138 Grande bd de Super Cannes, tel/fax 04.93.63.97.73, double €110) where Mr and Mme Diot lay on all home comforts. Gastronomic pickings are varied in Golfe-Juan: **L'Abri Côterie** (port Camille Rayon, 04.93.63.06.13, closed Dec) offers a nice

lunch menu (€15) and doubles as a piano bar in summer. A must for seafood is **Nounou** (bd des Frères Roustan, plages des Soleil, 04.93.63.71.73, closed Mon, Tue and Nov) with great decor (menus €29.70-€53). **Restaurant Tetou** (bd des frères Roustan, plages des Soleil, 04.93.63.71.16, closed Wed and Nov to mid-Mar) is a beautiful New York-style restaurant with a price-tag to match (average €92). For a convivial drink, head for **Le Café Bleu** (port Camille Rayon, 04.93.63.48.02, closed Mon mid-Sept to mid-June and Nov), which has live jazz on Fridays.

Tourist information

The market is daily (except Mon) in Vallauris and on Fridays in Golfe-Juan.

Vallauris Office de Tourisme

sq du 8 Mai 1945, 06220 Vallauris (04.93.63.82.58/www.vallauris-golfe-juan.com). **Open** *July-Aug* 9am-7pm daily; *Sept-June* 9am-noon, 2-6pm Mon-Sat.

▶ Getting There & Around

▶ By air

The nearest airport to Cannes is Nice.

▶ By car

For Cannes, leave the A8 at exit no.41 or no.42, or take the RN7 direction Cannes. Mougins is 3.5km north of Cannes on N85. For Vallauris, leave the A8 at exit Antibes and follow signs to Vallauris on the D435. The N7/N98 coast road runs through Golfe-Juan.

▶ By train

Cannes is served by the TGV from Paris. The journey takes 5h 10 mins. There are regular trains along the coast to Juan-les-Pins, Antibes and Nice.

▶ By bus

Cannes' main bus station by the port serves coastal destinations: **RCA** (04.93.39.11.39/ www.rca.tm.fr) goes to Nice via the villages along the coast and to Nice airport (every 30 mins, Mon-Sat). From the SNCF bus station **RCA** goes to Grasse (every 30 mins Mon-Sat, every hr Sun) via Mougins. **Phocéens** (04.93.85.66.61) runs 3 services per day (Mon-Sat) to Marseille airport and one to Avignon via Aix-en-Provence.

From Vallauris bus station (rte de Grasse) **STGA** (04.93.64.18.37) goes to Golfe-Juan SNCF station (every 20 mins, Mon-Sat, every 40 mins Sun) and to Cannes SNCF (every hr, Mon-Sat, every 2 hrs Sun).

The Riviera

Antibes to Cagnes

The stretch of coast around Cap d'Antibes is the playground for the rich and famous, so get your hiking boots on and go estate spotting.

St-Tropez may become Paris-by-the-sea in summer, but Antibes – with its beachside satellite of Juan-les-Pins – attracts the rich and famous all year round. The seaward extensions of the next towns east, Villeneuve-Loubet and Cagnes-sur-Mer, are more downmarket, but both have attractive medieval citadels, set well back from the coastal horrors.

Antibes Juan-les-Pins

The Greeks set up their trading post of Antipolis in the fifth century BC. Ligurian tribes fought hard to get their hands on the town over the following centuries, forcing Antibes' residents to turn to Rome for protection in 154 BC. But the fall of Rome left Antibes prey to attacks from every passing marauder, from Barbarians to Vandals, Visigoths, Burgundians, Ostrogoths and Franks. In the tenth century, Antibes fell into the hands of the Lords of Grasse before passing to the bishops of Antibes and, at the end of the 14th century, to the Grimaldi family of Monaco. It remained theirs until 1608, when Henri IV of France purchased Antibes for his kingdom, turning it into the front line of defence against the Savoy kingdom across the bay in Nice.

To host the initial trickle of Europe's titled and wealthy who came seeking winter sunshine, a local entrepreneur had opened the Grand Hôtel du Cap in 1870. But it was Coco Chanel and US tycoon Frank Jay Gould who turned Antibes Juan-les-Pins into a year-round playground, and artists, writers and alcohol-fuelled socialites such as F Scott and Zelda Fitzgerald hightailed it down to what was the Riviera's first chic society resort.

The conurbation of Antibes Juan-les-Pins is a mainly unappealing, sprawling mass wedged between the sea and the A8 motorway. The old districts are best approached from the **Fort Carré**, which stands on the point separating the St-Roch inlet from Baie des Anges. The original fort was constructed in the 16th century to counter the Savoy threat to the east; in the 17th century, Louis XIV's military architect Vauban gave it its eight-pointed star shape. Just to the south of the fort, the marina of **Port Vauban** is Europe's largest yacht harbour, harbouring some of Europe's largest

pleasure craft and plenty of glitzy boutiques, where you can hire – sorry, charter – your own craft and join the yachterati. Yachties should visit in early June to catch the **Voiles d'Antibes**, a major boating event which fills the bay with splendid sailing vessels and motor yachts for five days. For those preferring dry land, hidden behind the sheltered ancient walls of the quay is **Plage de la Gravette**, a free sandy beach with gently shelving waters, in the heart of town. South of the marina, at the other end of the ramparts, is the **Musée d'Histoire et d'Archéologie**, containing reminders of the town's multi-faceted past, including Greek and Etruscan amphorae. Also squeezed within the ramparts is the **Eglise de l'Immaculée-Conception** (open 8.30am-noon, 3-6pm daily) Antibes' former cathedral, built on the site of a Roman temple to Diana.

The **Château Grimaldi** next door still follows the plan of the earlier Roman fort, despite rebuilding in the 16th century by the Grimaldis. In 1946, when Picasso rented a cold, damp room on the second floor, it belonged to a certain Romuald Dor, and already contained a small archaeological collection. Dor had ulterior motives in his offer of such prime Riviera studio space; the works Picasso left behind in lieu of rent enabled him to upgrade his lacklustre collection and re-baptise it the **Musée Picasso**. This was a fertile period for the bald Spaniard with the stripy vest. As proper artists' materials were almost impossible to get hold of in 1946, Picasso used ships' paint slapped on to some odd-looking bits of wood, and discovered the joys of pottery (*see p216,* **Vallauris**). Disappointingly, Picasso's treasures here are limited, occupying only one in three floors of the collection, though the Germaine Richier sculptures around the castle walls and the Nicholas de Staël paintings compensate somewhat. Just inland from the castle, the **Cours Masséna**, the Greek town's main drag, plays host to one of the region's liveliest and best-supplied produce markets, open every morning (except Mon in winter). Look out for **Balade en Provence** (25bis cours Massena, 04.93.34.93.00, open daily), which sells 50 sorts of olive oil, pistou, honey, hams and *absinthe*. This area of the old town is a hive of Anglo-Frenchness, home to **Heidi's English**

Palmy pleasures in **Antibes'** cosmopolitan old town.

Bookshop (24 rue Aubernon, 04.93.34.74.11, open daily) and the **Antibéa Theatre**, which stages plays in English by the Red Pear group. Just beyond the theatre, in place Nationale, comic artist Raymond Peynet pokes fun at all nationalities in the **Musée Peynet**, a charming museum dedicated to cartoon art.

Heading south out of Antibes, the scenery changes dramatically from built-up citadel to leafy lap of luxury. **Cap d'Antibes** peninsula is a playground for the very, very wealthy, and makes no bones about it. To appreciate the prosperity to the full, rent a bike from one of the many outlets along boulevard Wilson and take in the views as you wend your way up to **Parc Thuret**, a botanical testing site established in 1856 with the aim of introducing more varied flora to the Riviera. There are today around 3,000 plant species laid out in families, while 200 new species are introduced each year and their acclimatisation carefully studied. If that walk sounds like too much exertion, take advantage of the Cap's surprisingly long stretches of public beach, Plage de la Salis and Plage de la Garoupe. Between the two, and a fair hike uphill, the **Sanctuaire de la Garoupe** has a great collection of unlikely *ex-votos*. At the southern tip of the peninsula, the **Musée Naval et Napoléonien** has model ships and charts and mementos of the great man, who parked his mother in Antibes on one occasion. Next to the museum is another historical landmark where most people would opt to park themselves, rather than their mothers: the **Hôtel du Cap**.

To the west of the peninsula, **Juan-les-Pins** has no pretensions to history: a sandy, forested, deserted headland until the 1920s, it was conceived as, and still is, a magnet for the Riviera's hedonists. The centre is a seething mass of boutiques and restaurants – but if it seems frantic during the day, you should see it at night: Juan-les-Pins isn't in the habit of wasting good partying time on sleep. The beautiful beach has public and private sections; on the latter, a patch of sand with deck chair will set you back around €9.15 a day (or €45.73 on the Hôtel du Cap's private strip).

If playing at sardines on the strand is not your thing, there are watersports galore; it was in Juan-les-Pins, they say, that water-skiing was invented in the 1930s. You'll find everything from jet skiing to big game fishing at **Watersports Services** (15-17 bd Baudouin, La Pinède, 04.92.93.57.57, closed Nov-Mar).

If a cruise is your idea of nirvana, **Yachtbrokers International** (21 rue Aubernon, 04.93.34.04.75, closed Sun) can provide a six-berth, 29-knot motoryacht with two crew from €1,525 a day, plus fuel, port fees, food and drink. A week on a yacht sleeping 20-22 with palatial staterooms, studies, dining rooms and a one-to-one guest to crew ratio, will set you back considerably more. East of Antibes (4km by N7) is **Marineland** marine theme park (*see p225*), the most visited (paid-for) attraction in the South of France.

Antibéa Théâtre

15 pl Clemenceau (04.93.34.24.30).
Tickets €14-€23.

Fort Carré

rte du Bord de Mer, N98 (06.14.89.17.45). **Open**
June-Sept 10am-6pm; *Oct-May* 10am-4pm. Closed
Mon. **Admission** €3; free under-18s.

Musée d'Histoire et
d'Archéologie

Bastion St-André, Antibes (04.92.90.54.37). **Open**
June-Sept 10am-6pm Tue, Wed, Thur, Sat, Sun,
10am-10pm Fri; *Oct-May* 10am-noon, 2-6pm Tue-Sun.
Admission €3; free under-18s.

Musée Naval et Napoléonien

av Kennedy (04.93.61.45.32). **Open** 9.30-11.45am,
2-6pm Mon-Fri; 9.30-11.45am Sat. Closed Oct.
Admission €3.05; free under-15s.

Musée Peynet et du Dessin
Humoristique

pl Nationale (04.92.90.54.30). **Open** *June-Sept* 10am-
6pm Tue-Sun; *Oct-May* 10am-noon, 2-6pm Tue-Sun.
Admission €3.05; free under-18s.

Musée Picasso

*Château Grimaldi, pl Mariejol, Antibes
(04.92.90.54.20)*. **Open** *June-Sept* 10am-6pm
Tue-Sun; *Oct-May* 10am-noon, 2-6pm Tue-Sun.
Admission €4.57; free under-18s.

Parc Thuret

62 bd du Cap, Cap d'Antibes (04.93.67.88.00).
Open *summer* 8am-6pm Mon-Fri; *winter* 8.30am-
5.30pm Mon-Fri. **Admission** free.

Where to eat

Antibes' cosmopolitan old town is best for cafés
and bistros rather than swanky restaurants.
Newly opened is **Le Broc'en Bouche** (rue des
Palmiers, 04.93.34.75.60, closed Mon & Sun in
winter, average €8.38), where fresh Provençal
produce makes up fare such as duck tarts and
salads; there are scrumptious puddings too, all
eaten to Latino music in a pseudo-antique shop.

Walks on the wild side

Five famous capes jut out into the
Mediterranean from the spectacularly beautiful
Riviera coastline. Each has a walkway leading
to secluded beaches and bays. These ancient
maritime trails, the *sentiers des douaniers*,
were used by customs officials to patrol the
coast, from Napoleonic times until
the 20th century. Now it is
nature-lovers and joggers
who do the rounds. The
only thing smuggled
today might be a kiss
on the rocks or a little
skinny-dipping in a
secluded cove…

Cap d'Antibes

The Cap d'Antibes
was once a wild,
rocky headland: the
rich and talented
residents who built
estates here had to
import their own dirt and
trees. The trail, which takes
about 90 minutes, starts at the
beach of La Garoupe, which faces north to
snow-crested Alps. There is plenty of parking
here and the **Plage Keller** (04.93.61.33.74,
menu €29.73) beach-restaurant serves lunch
and refreshments. Garoupe was the famous
1920s playground of the so-called Lost
Generation, where Picasso, Rudolph
Valentino and Ernest Hemingway passionately

pursued the crazy new fad of 'sun-tanning'
and where pal Scott Fitzgerald set his book
Tender is the Night. Past the rocky shore, the
Château de la Garoupe, rented out in 1922
by Cole Porter, stares out to sea, while just
beyond, the sumptuous **Château de la Croé**
is where Wallis Simpson listened to
the abdication speech of her new
husband Edward VII on the
radio and where he later
arrived in exile from
England. The trail ends
at **Villa Eilenroc**
(04.93.67.74.33, villa
open Wed 9am-noon &
1:30-5pm, gardens
open 9am-5pm Tue,
Wed, closed July &
Aug) designed by
architect Charles
Garnier of Paris and
Monte Carlo opera-house
fame. Its name is
purposefully echoed by the Hôtel
du Cap Eden-Roc (where the terrace
of Madonna's suite is so big that she can
rehearse her European tour on it). Eilenroc
houses one of Renoir's first paintings, inspired
by his 1869 hike across the Riviera.

Getting there *By car, park at La Garoupe or
on av Mrs LD Beaumont by Eilenroc. By bus,
no. 2A stops at the Office de Tourisme,
La Garoupe & Eilenroc.*

L'Ancre de Chine, (26 bd d'Aiguillon, 04.93.34.27.70, closed Sat lunch and last two weeks in Jan, menus €12.96-€20.58) is justifiably busy, as it's the best Chinese in town. **L'Eléphant Bleu** (28 bd d'Aiguillon, 04.93.34.28.80, menus €9.15-€38.87), next door, serves up good Thai and Vietnamese, while **Le Brulot** (3 rue Frédéric Isnard, 04.93.34.17.76, www.brulot.com, closed Aug, menus €12.96-€33.54) specialises in dramatic wood-fired grills. **Xtrême Café** (6 rue Aubernon, 04.93.34.03.90) is a fashionable bar for cocktails, aperitifs and nibbles.

Stylish foodies make straight for Cap d'Antibes. For fish to die for, including a knockout *bouillabaisse*, check out venerable **Bacon** (bd de Bacon, 04.93.61.50.02, closed Nov-Jan and Tue lunch, *menus* €42.70-€68.60, except evenings in Jul, Aug). This luxury fish house is all about studied casual elegance:

overlooking the Baie des Anges, the almost all-white dining room has a tented ceiling that is rolled back in good weather. For the full-on local experience, try **La Taverne du Safranier** (pl du Safranier, 04.93.34.80.50, closed mid-Dec to mid-Jan, menu €10).

At Juan-les-Pins there are plenty of beach establishments. The painfully romantic **Plage de la Jetée** (av Guy de Maupassant, 04.93.61.16.74, closed Oct-Mar) specialises in fresh fish grilled in salt. The lively **La Bodega** (av Docteur Dautheville, 04.93.61.07.52, menu €12.96) stays open until all hours in summer to feed revellers from local nightlife haunts, while the **Bijou Plage** (bd du Littoral, 04.93.61.39.07, menus €18.50-€45) serves reliable seafood on the seafront. Elegant **La Terrasse** (Hôtel Juana, La Pinède, av Gallice, 04.93.61.08.70, closed Nov-Mar, menus €52-€114) attracts a clientele more likely to spend the day in white

Cap de Nice

On this walk, take care: the wind blows up a gale of salty crust that will stick to new Italian sunglasses as you step around the steep, hot sea-rocks, only two metres above the waves. From the Basse Corniche, head down the very steep staircase of av du Cap de Nice (do not attempt to climb back up) to the sea and walk towards Nice, marvelling at the châteaux: **Palais Maeterlinck**, built by Nobel prize-winning novelist Maurice Maeterlinck, now a luxury hotel frequented by celebrities (Prince Albert of Monaco and Miss France have been sighted). The **Pink Palace** is a *belle époque* folly built by a British colonel returning from India. Elton John hoped to buy it, but settled instead on top of Mont Boron, just up the hill, not far from where the Spice Girls have an abode. Sean Connery's white Villa Roc hangs over the emerald water, while the Renaissance-style towers of Villa Beau-Site and Villa La Tour grace the hills. The panoramas are stunning: to the east you have the **Bay of Villefranche**, one of the deepest ports in the world, and to the west, the **Vieux Port** of Nice.

The trail is also accessible heading east

from the Corsica ferry port in Nice and down the stairs of the **Belvedere Coco Beach**. Magnificent sunsets seen from here drip the colour of rosé wine into the Bay of Angels. At the old La Réserve hotel, **Restaurant Le Sextant** (60 bd Franck Pilatte, 04.93.55.82.77, closed dinner daily and closed mid-Dec to mid-Jan, menus €12.96-€15.24) is balanced above the sea horizon. Next door at **Le Plongeoir Bar-Restaurant** (60 bd Franck Pilatte, 04.93.89.27.97, average €15) daredevils dive into the iridescent bay from a ten-metre tower, all that remains of the pier destroyed in World War II. The walk takes about half an hour each way.

Getting there *By car, park at the Vieux Port in Nice or on the Basse Corniche at bd du Mont Boron. By bus, nos.30 and 32 stop at the port and av de Nice.*

Cap Ferrat

Three distinct walks border the coast of Cap Ferrat, which juts into the sea between Villefranche and Beaulieu. All are easily accessible from the village of **St-Jean-Cap-Ferrat** at the tip of the peninsula, where colourful fishing boats still dock alongside smooth white yachts. The **Sentier du Bord de Mer of the Pointe St-Hospice** (a 45-minute ▶

linen than in bathing suits. It was here that Alain Ducasse won the second star that propelled him to fame; chef Christian Morisset, who's been at the helm since 1986, continues the tradition of wonderful food. For an affordable gourmet experience from former Maximin chef, Frédéric Ramos, try the €17.53 lunch menu on the seafront terrace of **Le Grill** at **Eden Casino** (15 bd Baudoin, 04.92.93.71.71).

Nightlife

Juan-les-Pins' annual jazz festival earns the most international attention but, as a more affordable club scene than St-Tropez or Monaco, Juan attracts the young end of the market, creating some of the liveliest nightlife on the Côte. Without doubt, the best club is **Le Village** (1 bd de la Pinède, Juan-les-Pins, 04.92.93.90.00, open Fri & Sat only, except daily July & Aug, admission €16) with arches and vast monastic interior. DJs play a mix of pop and house and the club oozes atmosphere, enhanced by the pumped-up, topless barmen in bow-ties who dance and mingle with the fashionable, mixed (straight/ gay) crowd. Just behind that, **La Fourmi Rouge** (5 bd de la Pinède, open Fri & Sat Sept-June only, admission €10) serves up thumping techno in a dark neon-lit room. Nearby, Juan icon **Whisky à Go Go** (5 av Jacques Léonetti, La Pinède, 04.93.61.26.40, open Fri & Sat only, except daily June-Sept, closed Feb, admission €16) is showing its age with a kitsch 70s disco feel. Apart from the jazz festival, fans of smoke and sax are eminently catered for in the cavernous **Au Bar en Biais** (600 1ère Avenue, Antibes, 04.93.74.10.98, closed July & Aug, admission €8-€16), a jazz school and bar holding evening jam sessions (1st & 3rd Fri of month) and

> ## Walks on the wild side (continued)

walk) juts out to the east past the pine-scented **Paloma Beach** (04.93.01.64.71; open daily May-Sept), good for light lunches. In the sixth century, the monk Hospice lived as a hermit on the windswept point. Today, the **Chapel Saint-Hospice** (open daily 10am-6pm), a Saracen tower and an 11-metre-tall bronze statue of the Virgin Mary and Christ child (pilgrims rub her golden toes) dominate the central hill, which offers spectacular views.

The eastern walk, from **Beaulieu** to **St-Jean** (entry by the Royal Riviera Hôtel) is an easy 30-minute stroll on a civilised, polite trail – quite like the gentlemanly qualities of St-Jean's most beloved resident, David Niven. It's best walked in the morning when the sun is to the east and coffee is brewing in St-Jean's portside cafés.

The **Chemin de la Carrière** or Quarry Trail (a 90-minute walk) runs south to the tip of the peninsula into a barren landscape of reef-like rocks. The Grand Hôtel du Cap Ferrat – summer residence of Victorian royalty and where the Beatles learned to swim with salad bowls over their heads (it's all in the breathing exercises) – stands atop the cliffs, its swimming pool an oasis amid the heaps of rocks. The trail mounts the western promontory at the lighthouse, winding above tiny beaches in the Baie de Villefranche with views of Nice across the sea, ending at the Plage Passable and Belgian King Leopold II's **Villa La Radiana**.

Getting there By car, park at the port of St-Jean or at Plage Passable. By bus, no.111 runs Nice to St-Jean to Beaulieu.

Cap d'Ail

In winter, Cap d'Ail is awash in yellow jasmin. Its seaside promenade is positively the sweetest of the cape walks. To reach it, twist down the narrow roads of Cap d'Ail, situated between Eze and Monaco, to the restaurant **La Pinède**, where stairs descend to the rocky path. From here, the trail can be divided into two distinct walks: dramatic to the west (30 minutes), gentler to the east (an hour). West takes you past Greta Garbo's old neighbourhood of elegant *belle époque* villas where palm branches brush against pastel-toned shutters. Head around the western point, where the trail becomes a shelf on the sheer sea wall. A series of cliffside stairs lead concerts (2nd & 4th Fri & all Sat) in the middle of industrial Antibes. A superb club and casino on the seafront east of Antibes is **La Siesta** (rte du Bord de Mer, 04.93.33.31.31, open daily June-Sept only, admission €15-€18), where in summer you can dance to pop and house in the open air and people-watch on terrace loungers. It's less special in winter, when dancing moves indoors to a small piano bar.

Where to stay

Of all the hotels on the French Riviera, the **Hôtel du Cap Eden-Roc** (bd Kennedy, Cap d'Antibes, 04.93.61.39.01/www.edenroc-hotel.fr, closed mid Oct-end Mar, double €360-€1100) is probably the most exclusive, certainly the most expensive. The gleaming white building nestles back from the coast in 25 acres of woodland. It was here that the cult of the suntan was born,

when a poor winter season persuaded Antoine Sella, Italian owner of the Hôtel du Cap, to keep his doors open through the summer of 1923. American society hosts Gerald and Sara Murphy (immortalised as Dick and Nicole Diver in F Scott Fitzgerald's *Tender is the Night)* came down from Paris and told all their friends. The hotel is pretentious enough not to accept credit cards, and can be annoyingly overrun by celebrities and their bodyguards. A comparitively cheap alternative nearby is the **Hôtel Beau Site** (141 bd Kennedy, 04.93.61.53.43/www.hotelbeausite.net, closed Nov-Feb, double €51.83-€106.71), offering clean, simple accommodation and a pool. Serious budget travellers can find a bed just a stone's throw from the beach at the **Relais International de la Jeunesse** (25 av de l'Antiquité, Cap d'Antibes, 04.93.61.34.40/ www.riviera-on-line.com/caravelle, closed

into a clear blue bay and the lovely **Plage Mala** where its little beach houses and cafés have a feel of the South Seas. **Eden Beach** (04.93.78.17.06, closed Oct-Easter, menu €20.58) serves lunch and dinner. The sentier can also be reached here by a long, steep stairway down (or up) the cliff. If you go east from La Pinède, you'll discover pretty bays basking in the sun. In certain spots, the trail tunnels through stone, arching open to a watery blue horizon. This walk ends by swinging into a sandy beach near **Fontvieille**, the most recently built up district of Monaco.
Getting there *By car, park on av Gramaglia by La Pinède or on allée Mala above the beach. By train, stop at Cap d'Ail station just above La Pinède.*

Cap Martin

On any sunny day – in other words, for much of the year – billows of red silk hang in the sky above Cap Martin. Dozens of paragliders swoop down an aerial slalom trail at 40km/hr from the heights of Mont Agel above Monaco, to land on the small pebbly beach of **La Plage du Golfe Bleu**, which has a restaurant with picnic tables in the sand (don't be fooled, weekend lunch reservations are a must at this popular Italian hang-out; 04.93.35.10.59). The coastal trail that hugs Cap Martin can be

started here, just below the **Cabbe** train station. Walk east along the **Promenade Le Corbusier**, named after the Modernist architect who hid away here in a tiny wood cabin squeezed between the railway tracks and the sea – in which he later drowned (reserve through Roquebrune Cap-Martin tourist office to visit). You may also get a glimpse of Eileen Gray's E-1027 villa. The trail crooks out to the open sea, softening with Mediterranean pines into a tumble of stairs and idyllically calm coves. Rocky fingers disappear into the waves and the views from the tip of Cap Martin – upwards through tropical flora to glimpses of millionnaires' hideaways, east to the mountains of the Italian Riviera and west to the sleek skyline of Monaco – make your head spin. It takes about 75 minutes to circle Cap Martin, but once past this exclusive enclave, the walk can be continued along the much less exclusive urban seafront of Carnoles, the whole way into Menton (about two and half hours from Monaco).
Getting there *By car, park at the Cabbe train station or on the av de Winston Churchill at Cap Martin. Trains on the hourly Nice-Ventimiglia line stop at Cabbe or Carnoles.*

The Riviera

Nov-Mar, dormitory €11.40). Staff at the **Auberge Provençale** (61 pl Nationale, 04.93.34.13.24, double €53.36-€76.22) in Antibes' old town are friendly enough to make up for the hotel's lack of finesse, and it's attached to an excellent restaurant (menus €25.90-€41.10). In a central but more peaceful location, former coaching inn **Le Relais du Postillon** (8 rue Championnet, Antibes, 04.93.34.20.77/www.relais-postillon.com, double €43-€78) has cheery rooms overlooking the park or courtyard. The **Hôtel Le Passy** (15 av Louis Gallet, Juan-les-Pins, 04.93.61.11.09, closed Jan-Mar, rates €64.46-€98.46) is in a great location, while the **Hôtel Juan Beach** (5 rue de l'Oratoire, Juan-les-Pins, 04.93.61.02.89, closed Nov-Mar, rates €70-€105) is a ten minute walk from nightlife action. The **Hôtel Castel Mistral** (43 rue Bricka, Juan-les-Pins, 04.93.61.21.04, closed Oct-Mar, rates €48.80-€106) is a charmingly dilapidated place, and handy for the beaches. To do Juan in style stay at the **Hôtel Juana** (La Pinède-Avenue Gallice, Juan-les-Pins, 04.93.61.08.70/www.hotel-juana.com, closed Nov-Mar, double €185-€460), an art deco jewel behind the La Terrasse restaurant (*see p224*).

For spa treatments, the rather clinical but well-priced **Thalazur** (770 chemin des Moyennes Bréguières, Antibes, 04.92.91.82.00, double €80-€165) offers thalassotherapy, using waters pumped up from the sea. A two-treatment package with use of spa facilities costs from €44.21. Dietary menus and medical advice are available.

Tourist information

Antibes Office de Tourisme

11 pl de Gaulle, 06160 Antibes (04.92.90.53.00/www.antibes-juanlespins.com). **Open** July-Aug 9am-7pm daily; Sept-June 9am-12.30pm, 1.30-6pm Mon-Fri; 9am-noon, 2-6pm Sat.

Juan-les-Pins Office de Tourisme

51 bd Guillaumont, 06160 Juan-les-Pins (04.92.90.53.05/www.antibes-juanlespins.com). **Open** July-Aug 9am-7pm daily; Sept-June 9am-noon; 2-6pm Mon-Fri; 9am-noon Sat.

Biot

Once, long ago, a clever PR company was sent into the hinterland of the Côte d'Azur to give its villages instant brand recognition. That, at least, is how it sometimes appears. Grasse is perfume, St-Paul-de-Vence is art, Vallauris is pottery (and Picasso), and **Biot** (pronounced Bee-ot) is glass (and Léger). But it was not always so. In fact, until as late as the 1950s, the name of this picturesque old village, perched on

Art museum **Château Grimaldi**. *See p228.*

a volcanic outcrop above the River Brague, was linked to pottery. One of Fernand Léger's protégés set up a ceramic workshop in Biot dedicated to reproducing the master's designs, and Léger himself spent his last few years here.

Fifteen days before he died, in 1956, the artist acquired a piece of land in Biot, intending to build a house. His widow, Nadia, used the site to build a fitting tribute to her husband's long and varied career, the **Musée National Fernand Léger**. The low-slung building – its facade dominated by a huge ceramic mosaic commissioned for Hanover Stadium – is set back from the road in undulating sculpture gardens. It traces the work of this restless, politically committed artist from his first Impressionist stirrings in 1905, through the boldly coloured, strongly outlined 'machine art' canvases of the 1920s and 30s to his later work in other media, including murals, stained glass, ceramics and tapestries. Nine, mostly early, canvases are on long-term loan from the Centre Pompidou in Paris can be seen on the first floor, including a wonderful Cubist collage of Charlie Chaplin.

Glass came to Biot only at the end of the 1950s, when the **Verrerie de Biot** fired up its furnaces. Half working factory and half gallery-cum-showroom, the Verrerie lies just off the main D4 road, below the town walls. One can watch the unique Biot 'bubble glassware' (*verre bullé*) being blown, and there are plenty of chances to buy the end result both here and in the village itself, where **rue St-Sébastien**, the main street, is lined with glass workshops. At No.9 the **Musée d'Histoire et de Céramique Biotoises** has a patchy but charming collection of local costumes and artefacts, including the domestic ceramics that the town was once renowned for. Past the boutiques and bars is the pretty **place des Arcades**, surrounded by Italianate loggias – a home-from-home touch brought by Genoese settlers who moved in to repopulate Biot after the Black Death. The village church, which overlooks the square, has two good altarpieces by those stalwarts of 15th-century Niçois religious art, Louis Bréa and Giovanni Canavesio. Classical concerts and recitals are held in the square on summer evenings.

On the way out of Biot, miniaturist fans can pick up tips and buy plants at the **Bonsai Arboretum**, a permanent collection of over 1,000 Bonsai in a Japanese garden, worked on for two generations by the family Okonek.

Bonsai Arboretum

229 chemin du Val de Pôme (04.93.65.63.99). **Open** *Apr-Sept* 10am-noon, 3-6.30pm; *Oct-Mar* 10-noon, 2-5.30pm. Closed Tue. **Admission** €4; €2 6-18s.

Musée d'Histoire et de Céramique Biotoises

9 rue St-Sébastien (04.93.65.54.54). **Open** *July-Sept* 10am-6pm Wed-Sun; *Oct-June* 2-6pm Wed-Sun. Closed Nov. **Admission** €1.52; free under-16s.

Musée National Fernand Léger

chemin du Val de Pôme (04.92.91.50.30). **Open** *July-Sept* 11am-6pm Mon, Wed-Sun; *Oct-June* 10am-12.30pm, 2-5.30pm Mon, Wed-Sun. Closing for renovation from Oct/Nov 2002 until summer 2003. **Admission** €4; free under-18s.

La Verrerie de Biot

chemin des Combes (04.93.65.03.00/ www.verreriebiot.com). **Open** *July-Aug* 9.30am-7pm Mon-Sat, 10am-1pm, 3-7.30pm Sun; *Sept-June* 9.30am-7pm Mon-Sat, 10.30am-1pm, 2.30-6.30pm Sun. **Admission** free. **Guided tours** €4.60; €2.30 7-14s, free under-7s.

Where to stay & eat

Biot's hotel of choice is the delightful **Hôtel des Arcades** (16 pl des Arcades, 04.93.65.01.04, rates €46-€76). The decor of this 15th-century mansion mixes ancient (huge fireplaces, four-poster beds) and modern. The owner is a collector, and the gallery/restaurant – a good, reasonably priced alternative to the town's more serious eating options (menus €24-

A whale of a time

Marineland, a must for any child visiting the Côte d'Azur, contains five parks, the best of which is Marineland itself, offering the sort of view of marine life you can only otherwise get in a cage at sea. Through the glass-surround whale tank, you can watch killer whales interact with their trainer in a relationship that is less one of master and subject than one of best friends. The dolphins occupy one of the biggest dolphin pools in Europe. There's a walk-through, underwater shark tunnel and the ray touch-pool lets children stroke the rays as they swim by.

Launched in 1970, Marineland is the baby of Roland de la Popye, whose passion for marine mammals encouraged him to set up a research centre for marine life. As if in testament, three out of the nine whales in the world born in captivity were born here.

Then there are the other four parks. The **Little Provençal Farm**, best for under-5s, has domestic animals, pony rides, an enchanted river boat ride and bouncy inflatables. The **Jungle of Butterflies** harbours butterflies, iguanas, parrots, snakes and bats. **Aqua-Splash** (mid-June to mid-Sept, 10am-7pm) features seawater wave pools, a lazy river, 13 giant toboggans and a toddlers' pool. **Adventure Golf** boasts three tricky mini-golf courses.

Arrive early: it's difficult to fit more than two parks in one day, and agony to decide what to leave out.

Marineland

306 av Mozart (04.93.33.49.49). **Open** *Apr-June, Sept* 10am-8pm daily; *July-Aug* 10am-midnight daily; *Oct-Mar* 10am-6pm daily. **Admission** €22.70; €15.10 3-12s, free under-3s; two park combination €24.40; €18.15 3-12s, free under-3s.

The Riviera

€27.50) – displays works by artists including Vasarely, Léger and Folon. Brigitte Guignery is chef at the **Auberge du Jarrier** (30 passage Bourgade, 04.93.65.11.68, closed Mon & Tue Sept-June, menus €36-€54), a relaxed restaurant in a converted jar factory at the end of a laundry-festooned passageway, serving Mediterranean dishes. Tucked away in what was a 16th-century potter's workshop, stylish **Les Teraillers** (11 rue du Chemin Neuf, Biot (04.93.65.01.59, closed Wed & lunch Thur June-Aug and Wed & Thur from Sept-May, menus €29-€60) has an atmosphere almost as delicious as its take on Provençal dishes such as courgette flowers stuffed with veal in truffle butter, and sea bass cooked in a crust of salt.

Tourist information

Market days are Tuesday and Friday mornings.

Office du Tourisme

46 rue St-Sébastien, Biot 06410 (04.93.65.78.00/ www.biot-coteazur.fr). **Open** *July-Aug* 10am-7pm Mon-Fri; 2.30-7pm Sat, Sun; *Sept-June* 9am-noon, 2-6pm Mon-Fri; 2-6pm Sat, Sun.

Villeneuve-Loubet & Cagnes

The coast road between Antibes and Nice passes through a sprawl of increasingly downmarket resorts. The interest lies inland, in the medieval centres of Villeneuve-Loubet and Cagnes – towns that also give their names to their beachside offshoots.

Villeneuve-Loubet Plage stretches around the Marina Baie des Anges, a huge pyramid-shaped apartment complex that was arguably the low-water mark of 1970s Riviera architecture. Ignore it if you can and head instead to **Villeneuve-Loubet** proper, where the 12th-century castle in which François 1er signed a decidedly shaky peace treaty with Charles V of Spain in 1538 is intact (not open to the public). The **Musée de l'Art Culinaire** celebrates one of Villeneuve's most famous sons, Auguste Escoffier, who was taken under the wing of Britain's King Edward VII after transforming cooking from a trade to an art. Escoffier later became head chef of the Savoy in London. A photograph of opera star Nellie Melba – after whom the peachy sundae was named – just about sums up the modest charms of this collection, whose highlights are the menus and cuttings elaborating tales of Escoffier's life as chef to political leaders and kings.

Obscured by the traffic system that thunders through the sprawl of suburbs south-west of Nice, **Cagnes** is in fact three separate entities: unalluring Cros-de-Cagnes on the seafront, misleadingly named Cagnes-sur-Mer, which is in fact inland, and medieval Haut-de-Cagnes, perched on high and home to the UNESCO-sponsored Festival International de la Peinture (International Painting Festival) each summer. This labyrinth of zones is impossible to navigate without a local map, so follow signs for the nearest tourist office on arrival.

Cros-de-Cagnes was once a fishing village but today offers little more than crowded beaches, oversubscribed watersports facilities and a string of restaurants and hotels of varying qualities along the beachfront.

On the other side of the busy A8 lies **Cagnes-sur-Mer**, best known for Auguste Renoir's estate, **Les Collettes**. The artist had the house built in 1908 after his doctor prescribed a drier, warmer seaside climate for his rheumatoid arthritis. Renoir spent the last years of his life here, working right up until his death in 1919, and battling against the growing paralysis in his hands. The house is preserved pretty much as he left it, and his olive tree-filled garden is worth visiting, particularly on the evening in summer when professional storytellers visit. There's also a collection of paintings of the artist by his friends, as well as a few of the works he made here.

Rising above its noisy, polluted neighbours is **Haut-de-Cagnes**, a favourite spot for contemporary artists of all persuasions, drawn not only by the annual arts festival but by the **Musée Mediterranéen d'Art Moderne** and the **Donation Suzy Solidor**, both of which are housed (along with the **Musée de l'Olivier**, a tribute to that local mainstay, the olive tree) in the dramatic 14th-century **Château Grimaldi**. The 40 portraits from the collection of popular *chanteuse* and lesbian icon, Suzy Solidor, after whom the song 'If you knew Suzy like I know Suzy' was written, include works by Cocteau, Dufy, Lempicka and others, many of whom also feature in the modern art museum. The Renaissance interior of the château is worth a look in itself.

Chateau-Musée Grimaldi

pl Grimaldi, Cagnes-sur-Mer (04.92.02.47.30). **Open** *May-Sept* 10am-noon, 2-6pm Mon, Wed-Sun; *Oct-Apr* 10am-noon, 2-5pm Mon, Wed-Sun. Closed three weeks Nov. **Admission** €3.05 (€4.57 with Musée Renoir); free under-18s

Musée de l'Art Culinaire

3 rue Escoffier, Villeneuve-Loubet (04.93.20.80.51/www.fondation-escoffier.org). **Open** 2-6pm Tue-Sun. Closed Nov. **Admission** €4.50; €2.50 11-16s; free under-11s.

Musée Renoir, Les Collettes

chemin des Collettes, Cagnes-sur-Mer (04.93.20.61.07). **Open** *May-Sept* 10am-noon, 2-6pm Wed-Mon; *Oct-Apr* 10am-noon, 2-5pm Wed-Mon.

Closed Nov. **Admission** €3.05 (€4.57 with Château-Musée Grimaldi; free under-18s. Storytelling evening annually in late June (04.93.73.93.04, admission free).

Where to stay, eat & drink

The area's most luxurious accommodation option is **Le Cagnard** (rue Sous-Barri, 04.93.20.73.21/www.le-cagnard.com, double €167.69-€182.94) in Haut-de-Cagnes. Its many modern comforts have failed to disturb the 12th-century magic of the building, which offers spectacular views. There is an excellent restaurant (closed Nov to mid-Dec, menus from €48.78). A recent luxury addition is the **Villa Estelle** (5 montée de la Bourgade, Haut-de-Cagnes, 04.92.02.89.83/www.villa-estelle.com, double €145-€230), a medieval coaching inn converted into a top-notch bed & breakfast. **Le Grimaldi** (6 pl du Château, Haut-de-Cagnes, 04.93.20.60.24, closed Feb & Tue, double €33.54-€45.73) is a cheaper option. In Cros-de-Cagnes, the **Hôtel Beaurivage** (39 bd de la Plage, 04.93.20.16.09/www.beaurivage.org, closed Dec & first week in Jan, double €47.26-€70.13) has rooms with balcony and sea view. For those who want to sample the effects of the local waters, **Biovimer Spa** (Marina Baie des Anges, 04.93.22.71.71/www.biovimer.fr, double €49-€117), tucked between the port and the architectural monster at Villeneuve-Loubet, is a modern thalassotherapy spa with rooms and apartments. Weekend thalassotherapy packages start at €343; one-day use of heated outdoor infinity pool, indoor pool, sauna, jacuzzi, hammam and gym from €53.

Haut-de-Cagnes' leading eating place, after Le Cagnard is the **Restaurant des Peintres** (71 montée de la Bourgade, 04.93.20.83.08, closed Mon and two weeks in Nov, two weeks in Jan, menus €24.39-€28.20), offering simple Provençal elegance with views over Cap d'Antibes. But **Entre Cour et Jardin**, with its cosy vaulted cellar (102 montée de la Bourgade, 04.93.20.72.27, closed Tue and two weeks in Jan, menus €24.39-€39.64) is a reliable alternative.

Good seafood can be found at the port in Cros-de-Cagnes at **La Bourride** (04.93.31.07.75, closed dinner Sun, all Wed, Feb school holidays, menus €28.66-€60.22) while **La Réserve** aka **Lou Lou** (91 bd de la Plage, 04.93.31.00.17, closed 13 July-1 Aug, menu €25) is a chic, snooty but justifiably acclaimed restaurant.

Tourist information

Cagnes-sur-Mer has a market every day but Monday; Villeneuve-Loubet on Tuesday and Friday mornings.

Cagnes-sur-Mer Office de Tourisme

6 bd Maréchal Juin, 06800 Cagnes-sur-Mer (04.93.20.61.64/www.cagnes.com). **Open** *July-Aug* 9am-7pm daily; *Sept-June* 9am-noon, 2-6pm Mon-Sat.

Villeneuve-Loubet Office de Tourisme

pl de l'Hôtel de Ville, 06270 Villeneuve-Loubet (04.93.20.16.49/www.ot-villeneuveloubet.org). **Open** *June-Sept* 9am-noon, 1.30-5.30pm Mon-Fri; 9.30am-12.30pm, 2-6pm Sat; 10am-1pm Sun; *Oct-May* 9am-noon, 2-6pm Mon-Fri; 9.30am-12.30pm Sat. **Branch:** Villeneuve-Loubet Plage, *16 av de la Mer, 06270 Villeneuve-Loubet (04.92.02.66.16).* **Open** *July-Aug* 9am-7pm Mon-Fri; 9am-noon, 2-5pm Sat; 10am-1pm Sun; *Sept-June* 9am-noon, 2-6pm Mon-Fri; 9am-noon, 2.30-5.30 Sat.

▶ Getting There & Around

▶ By car

For Antibes Juan-les-Pins, leave the A8 at exit no.44, or drive along the N98 coastal road, easier and prettier. Juan-les-Pins is west of the Cap d'Antibes, Villeneuve-Loubet and Cagnes are east of Antibes. Avoid the N7 Antibes to Nice at the Biot junction in summer, which becomes one long car park, especially when Marineland is emptying out. For Biot, take the N7 and then D4 Biot-Valbonne road, 3km after Antibes.

▶ By train

Antibes is on the main south coast route, served both by high-speed TGV trains from Paris and more frequent local trains, which also stop at Juan-les-Pins, Biot, Cagnes-sur-Mer, Cros-de-Cagnes and Villeneuve-Loubet-Plage. Shuttle buses conect Cagnes-sur-Mer and Haut-de-Cagnes and Villeneuve-Loubet-Plage and the old town. It's worth taking the train for the view, as it runs parallel to the sea for the best part of the journey from Nice.

▶ By bus

RCA (Rapides Côte d'Azur 04.93.39.11.39) bus no.200 between Cannes and Nice runs every 20 minutes Mon-Sat, 30 mins Sun, stopping at Antibes, Biot, Villeneuve and Cagnes. Shuttle bus 10A runs hourly between Antibes station and Biot. More information at Antibes bus station (04.93.34.37.60). Regular **TAM** (04.93.85.61.81) buses run between Cagnes and Nice, also serving Biot, Antibes, Cannes, Vence and St Paul. **CFTI** (04.92.96.88.88) buses run from Cagnes via Nice Airport to Grasse.

Musées nationaux

chagall

du XX⁰ siècle

F.LEGER

Picasso

des Alpes-Maritimes

Musée national
Message Biblique
Marc Chagall

Avenue Dr Ménard
06000 Nice
t. (33) 04 93 53 87 20
f. (33) 04 93 53 87 39

Musée national
Message Biblique
Marc Chagall
Nice

Musée national
Fernand Léger

Chemin du Val de Pome
06410 Biot
t. (33) 04 92 91 50 30
f. (33) 04 92 91 50 31

Musée national
Fernand Léger
Biot

Musée national
Picasso
La Guerre et la Paix

Place de la Libération
06220 Vallauris
t. (33) 04 93 64 16 05 et
  (33) 04 93 64 98 05

Musée national
Picasso
La Guerre et la Paix
Vallauris

Liberté · Égalité · Fraternité
RÉPUBLIQUE FRANÇAISE

Culture
Communication

ASIAN ARTS MUSEUM
MUSEUM OF THE GENERAL COUNCIL OF THE ALPES-MARITIMES

405, PROMENADE DES ANGLAIS
ARÉNAS - 06200 NICE, FRANCE

TEL : +33 (0)4 92 29 37 00
FAX : +33 (0)4 92 29 37 01
www.arts-asiatiques.com

OPEN EVERY DAY EXCEPT TUESDAY
2 MAY TO 15 OCTOBER: 10AM TO 6PM
16 OCTOBER TO 30 APRIL: 10AM TO 5PM
CLOSED MAY 1 AND ON CHRISTMAS AND NEW YEAR'S DAY

CONSEIL GÉNÉRAL DES ALPES-MARITIMES

Nice

Rollerbladers may have replaced English lords on the promenade des Anglais, but the historic seaside resort still has an undeniable buzz.

Some 400,000 years ago, prehistoric man set up camp at the site known as Terra Amata at the foot of Mont Boron, not far from where Sir Elton John's hilltop mansion now sprawls. In the fourth century BC, Phocaean Greeks from Marseille sailed into the harbour and founded a trading post around another prominent hill – now the Colline du Château – and named their city Nikaïa (after Nike, goddess of victory).

The Romans arrived in 100BC and built an entire, no-expense-spared city on a third hill that they called Cemenelum (today's Cimiez). Cimiez's prime location made it an obvious target in the Dark Ages for invading Saracens and Barbarians, who left it in ruins; it was to take many centuries – and a bunch of wintering Brits – before it regained its exclusive status.

By the 14th century, the once-Greek part of the city – including the port – was thriving again, and the population was determined to stay that way. After sizing up the local balance of power, they opted to shun Louis d'Anjou and ally themselves with the Counts of Savoy, thus opening up huge new Italian markets for their commerce. The Savoys fortified this key outpost against France. An artistic school flourished around Louis Bréa in the late 15th and early 16th centuries. By the 17th century, the city was spreading beyond its walls.

But so rich a prize was Nice that France laid hands on it several times during the 17th and 18th centuries; on one occasion Louis XIV took advantage of temporary control to have the medieval fortifications blown up. The city finally passed to France under the Treaty of Turin in 1860, which was ratified later in a plebiscite (the final result of some 25,000 pro-French to 160 anti-French votes had a strong smell of election-rigging about it), though the Italian past is still evident in Niçois cuisine.

Over a century before that, however, this sunny and conveniently non-French spot had been discovered by British travellers seeking winter warmth. So fond were they of the place that they raised a subscription in 1822 for the building of a seafront esplanade, still called the promenade des Anglais in their honour. By the time Queen Victoria visited later that century, the hilly Cimiez district, filled with luxury villas, was the place to stay. The queen pitched camp in the Régina palace-hotel, as did Henri

Matisse in the 1940s. The Musée Matisse now stands just across the road.

Now France's fifth-largest city, 20th-century Nice was beset by high crime levels and tainted (not to mention financially damaged) by the shenanigans of its long-time mayor, Jacques Médecin. The reputation for corruption has lasted into the 21st century with an investigation of the city's legal favours and a vice scene fuelled by Eastern European prostitution rings.

Nice's golden era of seaside palaces, casinos, red Bugattis and unmitigated glamour has receded. Some essential things, however, really haven't changed: city residents, never tired of the beauty of the place, get up early to buy baskets of vine tomatoes, perfect peaches and wild mushrooms at the daily market. On Sundays, families roam the promenade des Anglais en masse on bicycles or Rollerblades or pushing strollers. Young trendies are moving back into Vieux Nice and the distinctive local dialect Nissart is enjoying a revival, with bilingual street names, bi-monthly magazine *Lou Sourgentin* and local band Nux Vomica. Unlike 20 years ago, Nice has a surge of cultural attractions, boosted by the new Palais Nikaia and redynamised summer jazz festival, and a youthful nightlife: if you're up until dawn, check out the early-opening bars by the market, where you'll find sun-wizened farmers about to set up their wares quietly sipping espresso beside bleary-eyed twentysomething clubbers.

Sightseeing

Vieux Nice & Colline du Château

Vieux Nice is Nice's most colourful neighbourhood – tiny serpentine alleys where countless shops, galleries and restaurants nestle among the stacked medieval buildings with laundry hanging outside the windows like pastel banners. Once shunned as crime-plagued and poverty-stricken, it is fast becoming the city's trendiest district. The main square, place Rosetti, is home to two places of pilgrimage: the **Cathédrale de Ste-Réparate**, Nice's patron saint, and the **Fennocchio** ice-cream parlour. Another favourite with the locals is the nearby Baroque **Chapelle de l'Annonciation**. A few blocks north-east, through bustling streets of little shops, the **Palais Lascaris** is a fascinating museum in a lavishly decorated 17th-century home, a reminder that this was once the aristocratic quarter. Further up, rue Droite goes into rue St-François, busy with local food shops along with tourist trinkets and some curious ecological clothing. Place St-François is the site of the fish market (daily, except Tue), the city's 17th-century former town hall and the campanile from a former Franciscan monastery (entrance rue de la Tour).

But the heart of the *vieille ville* lies to the south, along **cours Saleya**, where cut flowers perfume the air and stalls piled high with lush fruit and vegetables, olives and candied fruit operate from dawn to lunch, Tuesday to Sunday; Niçois institution Chez Thérèse

cheerfully touts her chickpea *socca* – the cheap but filling snack that is to Nice what the hotdog is to New York – from a stand every morning. On Monday there are antiques, junk and second-hand clothes. All around, shoppers and onlookers crowd bars and eateries. There's another fancy Baroque edifice on the cours itself, the **Chapelle de la Miséricorde**, but it is only open in visits organised by the Palais Lascaris. On neighbouring place du Palais de Justice there's a book and print market on Saturdays. Towards the seafront, the **Opéra de Nice** is grandly *belle époque*.

Rising up the eastern side of Vieux Nice is the **Colline du Château**, a grassy park with an impressive waterfall but no château: this was destroyed in the 18th century. If you don't

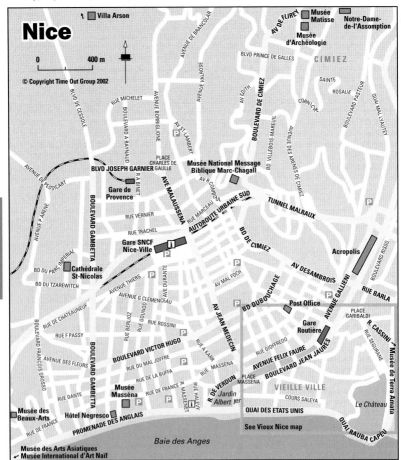

The Riviera

The angelic **Baie des Anges,** colonised – and tamed – by *anglais* in the 19th century.

fancy the long slog up (steps climb from rue du Château or rue Ste Claire in the old town) to the magnificent view from the top, interpreted by a radial map, there's a lift (open 8am-6pm daily) by the **Tour Bellanda**, home of the Musée Naval, on the quai des Etats-Unis.

Continuing round the *quai*, or reached from place Garibaldi, you arrive at the attractive **Vieux Port**, which is lined with tall, colour-washed houses, the neo-classical church known as Notre-Dame-du-Port and plenty of simple cafés where you can snack on a *pan-bagnat* and watch the comings and goings of ferries to Corsica. The possible extension of the Old Port has recently been the subject of heated political debate between the Chamber of Commerce, the City of Nice, the State and the citizens. Nice's right-wing officials praise the economic benefits that luxury liners would create, opponents fear not only that the char of this landmark would be ruined, but the environmental effects of pollution on the beaches and marinelife.

East of the Colline du Château, the **Parc Forestier le Mont Boron** is an idyllic spot for a picnic, with winding paths through acres of aleppo pines and breathtaking views of the coast. Between the two hills, in an area still dotted with fanciful late 19th-century villas and mock castles, the **Musée Terra Amata** documents the area's earliest settlement.

Cathédrale de Ste-Réparate
pl Rossetti (04.93.62.34.40). **Open** 7.30am-noon, 2-6pm daily. **Admission** free.

Located on Vieux Nice's most charming square, this 17th-century church, replete with stucco, marble and a colourfully tiled dome, is named after a 15-year-old virgin martyred in the Holy Land, who was towed here in a flowery boat by angels (landing, naturally, in what is now the Baie des Anges) in the fourth century. It's an important venue for Baroque music concerts and other musical events.

Chapelle de l'Annonciation
1 rue de la Poissonnerie (04.93.62.13.62). **Open** 7.30-noon, 2.30-6.30pm daily. **Admission** free.
Join a steady trickle of locals in this lovely little gilded Baroque gem and light a candle for St Rita – the patron saint of miserable middle-aged women – to whom the chapel is dedicated.

Musée Naval (Tour Bellanda)
Parc du Château (04.93.80.47.61). **Open** June-Sept 10am-noon, 2-7pm Wed-Sun; *Oct-May* 10am-noon, 2-5pm Wed-Sun. **Admission** €2.30; free under-18s.
On the western flank of Nice's grassy Colline du Château park, this circular 19th-century tower, once the home of Hector Berlioz, offers an exhibition of model boats, arms and navigation instruments. A lift or stairs take you up to the park above.

Musée de Terra Amata
25 bd Carnot (04.93.55.59.93). **Open** 9am-noon, 2-6pm Tue-Sun. Closed 1-15 Sept. **Admission** €3.80; free under-18s.
Find out what life was like on the Riviera 400,000 years ago. The highlights of this museum, built on an excavation site, include a reconstituted prehistoric cave, a human footprint in limestone, traces of fire and records of ancient elephant hunters.

Palais Lascaris

15 rue Droite (04.93.62.05.54). **Open** 10am-noon,
2-6pm Tue-Sun. **Admission** free.

Ornate Baroque furniture, 17th-century paintings
and Flemish tapestries are displayed in a miniature
Genoese-style palace with vaulted frescoed ceilings
of tempestuous mythological scenes and a dramatic balustraded staircase adorned with busts and
grotesques. French and Italian maiolica from the
Musée Masena is currently on display on the first
floor until the latter reopens in 2004.

The new town

The new town, laid out in the 18th and 19th
centuries with palm trees, squares and stucco
villas, is divided from the old town by the river
Paillon, though you'd never know it as it is
covered over for most of its length. The pink
facades of **place Masséna** and the Jardins
Albert 1er, which run down the river's course to
the promenade des Anglais, form the
centrepiece of the area. Among the 20th-century
buildings in variable taste north of place
Masséna are the **Théâtre de Nice** and the
striking **Musée d'Art Moderne et d'Art
Contemporain** (MAMAC). Northeast of here,
bordering the old town is the elegantly arcaded,
though traffic-infested, **place Garibaldi**. It
was laid out in 1750-80 and later named after

the Italian unification hero, Guiseppe Garibaldi,
who was born in Nice in 1807 and whose statue
stands in the centre.

On the seafront west of the rivermouth, the
promenade des Anglais is 19th-century
Nice's most famous landmark. It started off as a
simple footpath leading to the western suburb
of New Borough, then popular with wintering
British. Getting safely across it through manic
traffic can be a challenge, and the palm trees
ain't what they used to be, but the grandiose
belle époque and art deco palaces that line it –
such as the **Hôtel Negresco** and the **Musée
Masséna** – are a joy. Shortly before the Musée
Masséna, the **Palais de la Méditerranée**, an
art deco jewel built by American millionaire
Frank Jay Gould in 1929, was shamefully
gutted in the 1990s, preserving only the facade,
but looks set for resurrection in 2003 as a
luxury hotel, flats and casino. To the west, a
couple of blocks back, the **Musée des Beaux-
Arts** has a delightful collection. A kilometre
further on is the **Musée International d'Art
Naïf Anatole Jakovsky**, while just before
the airport, the **Musée des Arts Asiatiques**
nestles among the botanical species and giant
hothouse of the **Parc Floral Phoenix**.

The beach itself, though long, is not
particularly spectacular: pebbly, and not
sparklingly clean (though it's OK to swim).

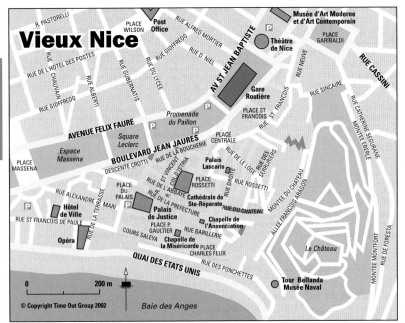

While some stretches are open to anyone and have attractions ranging from parascending and volleyball pitches to kids' sandpits, other parts of it are carved up by private beach concessions, some run by hotels for their guests and some open to paying customers. One of the nicest of the latter is **Castel Plage**, across the street from the *vieille ville*. It's got comfy mattresses, bronzed pretty people and some artsy local celebs playing chess over coffee in a friendly, relaxed ambience.

Slicing north-west through the new town from place Masséna, **avenue Jean Médicin** is Nice's prime shopping street, and home to every chain store imaginable. At its northern end is the main train station, to the west of which, across boulevard Gambetta, stands the **Cathédrale St-Nicolas**, the Russian church that, thanks to its flow of visiting Russians, is Nice's most-visited attraction.

Cathédrale St-Nicolas (Eglise Russe)

bd du Tzarewich (04.93.96.88.02). **Open** *June-Sept* 9.30am-noon, 2.30-6pm daily; *Oct-May* 9.30am-noon, 2.30-5pm daily. **Admission** €2.50; free under-12s.
The five brilliantly coloured onion-domed cupolas of Nice's Russian Orthodox cathedral, built 1903-12, are a startlingly surreal sight against the flat red-tile rooftops of the central western suburbs. If you visit only one church, go and see this beautiful pink and grey marble oddity, filled with intricate carving, icons and frescoes, and a marvellous iconostasis.

Musée des Arts Asiatiques

405 promenade des Anglais (04.92.29.37.00/ www.arts-asiatiques.com). Bus 9, 10, 23. **Open** *May to mid-Oct* 10am-6pm Mon, Wed-Sun; *mid-Oct to Apr* 10am-5pm Mon, Wed-Sun. **Admission** €5.35; €3.80 14-18s; free under-14s.
This impressive minimalist glass and metal structure, designed by Japanese architect Kenzo Tange overlooking the duck pond in the Parc Floral Phoenix, boasts a small but stunning collection of rare pieces that range from a 12th-century Japanese Buddha and bronze winged lions from Vietnam to the latest in oriental high-tech design. Don't miss the tea pavilion under the ginko trees, with a display of ceremonial clay bowls.

Musée d'Art Moderne et d'Art Contemporain (MAMAC)

promenade des Arts (04.93.62.61.62/www.mamac-nice.org). **Open** 10am-6pm Mon, Wed-Sun. **Admission** €3.80; free under-18s.
The city's sprawling, multi-level marble home of European and American art from the 1960s on stages first-rate seasonal shows. In addition to a new room with a diverse collection from the Nice school (Arman, César, Klein and Sosno), the museum's most recent pride and joy is artist Niki de Sainte Phalle's exceptional donation of 170 of her works.

Cathédrale St-Nicolas: Moscow on sea.

Musée des Beaux-Arts

33 av des Baumettes (04.92.15.28.28). **Open** 10am-noon, 2-6pm Tue-Sun. **Admission** €3.80; free under-18s.
Built for a Ukrainian prince, this Genoese-inspired villa houses an unmissable collection of 17th- to early 20th-century art. Highlights include works by Niçois pastel artist and pioneering lithographer Jules Cheret, canvases by Van Dongen, Sisley and Dufy, and newly acquired paintings by Signac and Kisling.

Musée International d'Art Naïf Anatole Jakovsky

Château Ste-Hélène, av de Fabron (04.93.71.78.33). Bus 9, 10, 12. **Open** 10am-noon, 2-6pm Mon, Wed-Sun. **Admission** €3.80; free under-18s.
Once the home of perfume creator René Coty, this lovely pink villa now houses a private collection that traces the history of naive art from the 18th century to the present, including Bombois, Séraphine, Rimbert and Grandma Moses. Great for kids, who will enjoy spotting the canvases that could have been done by a child of three.

Musée Masséna

65 rue de France (04.93.88.11.34). **Open** closed until 2004. **Admission** ring for details.
Closed for renovation until 2004, the Masséna's Empire salons contain an eclectic mix of Nice primitive painters and water-colourists, armour and Napoléon's coronation robe and death mask.

The Riviera

Villa Arson

20 av Stephen Liegeard (04.92.07.73.73/www.villa-arson.org). Bus 4, 7. **Open** *2-7pm Mon, Wed-Sun.* **Admission** *free.*

The cutting edge of adventurous, young and contemporary avant-garde art, with plenty of performance art, and a related art school.

Cimiez

To the north of the centre, Cimiez is Nice's best-heeled suburb, an affluent hillside swathed in large villas and sweeping *belle époque* hotels. Just off the lower reaches of boulevard de Cimiez is the **Musée National Message Biblique Marc-Chagall**. At the top of the hill, the **Musée Matisse** stands in an olive-tree dotted park behind the ruins of the Roman amphitheatre, site of the summer jazz festival, and the **Musée d'Archéologie**, which charts Nice's history from prehistoric times. The nearby church of **Notre-Dame-de-l'Assomption** and its 16th-century Franciscan monastery are flanked by a glorious rose-perfumed garden and a cemetery where Matisse and Dufy are buried. Lower down on rue Grammont, take a look at Nice's most unusual church, **Eglise Ste-Jeanne d'Arc**, a radical 1930s reinforced-concrete structure nicknamed 'the egg'.

Eglise Notre-Dame-de-l'Assomption (Musée Franciscain)

pl du Monastère (04.93.81.00.04). Bus 15, 17. **Open** *church 9am-noon, 2-6pm daily; museum 10am-noon, 3-6pm Mon-Sat.* **Admission** *free.*

At the edge of the gardens of Cimiez, this church is a heavy-handed 19th-century reworking of a 16th-century building. Inside, two Louis Bréa altarpieces survive. The adjoining 16th-century monastery includes a couple of pretty cloisters – one with some strange, perhaps alchemical murals – as well as the Musée Franciscain, where the uncomfortable ends of Franciscan martyrs are documented.

Musée d'Archéologie

160 av des Arènes (04.93.81.59.57). Bus 17, 20. **Open** *museum & ruins Apr-Sept* 10am-1pm, 2-6pm Tue-Sun; *Oct-Mar* 10am-noon, 2-5pm Tue-Sun. **Admission** €3.80; free under-18s.

The smart archeological museum charts Nice's history from 1100BC up to the Middle Ages through an impressive display of ceramics, sculpture, coins, jewellery and tools. Outside are the first- to fourth-century ruins on the ancient site of Cemenelum, with vestiges of the Roman public baths, paved streets and a 4,000-seat stone amphitheatre that once served as the playground for gladiators and now is a concert venue during the Nice Jazz Festival.

Musée Matisse

164 av des Arènes (04.93.81.08.08). Bus 17, 20. **Open** *Apr-Sept* 10am-6pm Mon, Wed-Sun; *Oct-Mar*

10am-5pm Mon, Wed-Sun. **Admission** €3.80.

This renovated 17th-century villa, with a modern extension houses a fascinating collection, tracing Matisse's development from his dark, brooding early works through his archaic-style sculptures, Pointillisme and Lautrec-like graphic simplicity on to his fluid line-drawings, languid odalisques and colourful paper cut-outs. One room is devoted to massive sketches for the Chapelle du Rosaire.

Musée National Message Biblique Marc-Chagall

av du Dr Menard (04.93.53.87.20). Bus 17, 20. **Open** *10am-6pm Mon, Wed-Sun.* **Admission** €5.50; free under-18s.

This long-time Riviera resident Chagall at his best, a purpose-built space with a stunning selection of large paintings on Old Testament themes, notably the Song of Songs. Chagall provided stained glass, mosaics and sketches for the gallery, which holds frequent temporary shows on Jewish art.

Arts, entertainment & sport

For music and theatre listings, pick up the weekly French-language *Semaine des Spectacles* available from newsagents.

Acropolis

1 esplanade Kennedy (04.93.92.83.00).
A modern mega-structure that hosts special events, conventions, concerts, ballet and opera.

Casino Ruhl

Hôtel Le Méridien, 1 promenade des Anglais (04.97.03.12.33). **Open** *10am-5am daily.* **Admission** *free.* **Credit** AmEx, DC, MC, V.

A gamblers' paradise: a modern expanse of gaming rooms with French and English roulette, blackjack, punto banco, craps and clanging slot machines.

Cinémathèque de Nice

3 esplanade Kennedy (04.92.04.06.66/www.cinematheque-nice.com). **Films** *2.30pm, 8pm Tue-Thur; 2.30pm, 10pm Fri, Sat; 3pm Sun.* **Tickets** €3; €6 three-film pass.

Offers an international selection of classics and quality recent films in their original version.

Galerie Françoise Vigna

3 rue Delille (04.93.62.44.71). **Open** *3-7pm Tue-Sat.* **Admission** *free.*

On Nice's artsy gallery row, Vigna shows a mix of young and established contemporary artists.

Galerie Soardi/Espace d'Art Contemporain

8 rue Desiré Niel (04.93.62.32.03). **Open** *9am-7pm Mon-Sat.* **Credit** AmEx, DC, MC, V.

This was once the atelier of Henri Matisse, and it

From top left: Palais Maeterlinck, promenade des Anglais, old town promenade, place St-François fish market.

was here that he sketched *La Danse* with a long pole and charcoals. Today, it's a private gallery presenting innovative seasonal shows featuring the Ecole de Nice. It also sells lithographs, frames and arty gift items. The gallery also offers superb cultural excursions around Matisse's Nice and Vence (€25 half-day, €50 full day, incl coach and lunch).

Opéra de Nice
4 rue St-François-de-Paule (04.92.17.40.00/ www.ville-nice.fr). **Box office** 10am-5pm Mon-Sat. **Tickets** €6-€67. **Credit** MC, V.
A small 19th-century gem of an opera house, done out in sumptuous red velvet with crystal chandeliers and lashings of gold. The Opéra attracts top-notch visiting artists for symphonies, ballet and opera.

Palais Nikaïa
163 rte de Grenoble (04.92.29.31.29/ 08.20.02.04.06/www.nikaia.fr). **Box office** 1-6pm Mon-Fri. **Tickets** vary. **Credit** V.
Inaugurated in 2001 by Nice's honorary resident, Sir Elton John, this massive state-of-the-art modular concert hall-cum-stadium hosts crowd-pleasing rock and classical stars, plus sporting events.

Palais des Sports Jean Bouin
esplanade de Lattre de Tassigny (04.93.80.80.80). **Open** hours vary Mon-Sat. **Admission** *pool* €3.50-€4.30; *ice rink* €3.15-€4.30. **No credit cards.**
A vast municipal sports complex with a well-kept indoor Olympic-sized pool and covered ice rink.

Théâtre de Nice
promenade des Arts (04.93.13.90.90). **Box office** 9am-7pm Tue-Sat. **Tickets** *grande salle* €7-€28.20, *petite salle* €18.20. **Credit** AmEx, DC, MC, V.
One of the most important theatres in the South of France (with Marseille's La Criée) is now directed by Daniel Bunoin. This impressive venue stages high-profile productions of French and foreign classics and varied contemporary plays.

Théâtre de la Photographie et de l'Image
27 bd de Dubouchage (04.92.04.99.70). **Open** 10am-noon, 2-6pm Tue-Sun. **Admission** free.
A recently restored pink *belle époque* theatre, now a vast space for big-name photography shows, lectures, an Internet archive and a convivial coffee bar.

Restaurants & brasseries

Acchiardo
38 rue Droite (04.93.85.51.16). **Open** noon-1.30pm, 7-9.30pm Mon-Fri; noon-1.30pm Sat. Closed Aug. **Average** €13. **No credit cards.**
This family-run, check-tableclothed Niçois dining spot is a long-standing *vieille ville* favourite for the budget-minded. Daily specials might include homemade *ravioli au pistou*, *merda de can* (dog-turd shaped pasta swirls – delicious once you get over the resemblance), *daube de boeuf* and ratatouille.

L'Auberge de Théo
52 av Cap de Croix (04.93.81.26.19/www.auberge-de-theo.com). **Open** noon-2pm, 7pm-10.30pm Tue-Sat; noon-2pm Sun. Closed 20 Aug-10 Sept. **Menus** €18.29-€25.92. **Credit** V.
Set in a residential part of Cimiez, this charming Italian trattoria with an open-air patio is a perfect place for pasta, pizza or grilled fish on your way to or from the Chagall and Matisse museums.

Bistrot du Port
28 quai de Lunel (04.93.55.21.70). **Open** noon-2.15pm, 7.40-10.30pm Mon, Thur-Sun. **Menus** €13-€32.55. **Credit** DC, MC, V.
At this big yellow brasserie on the old port, excellent specialities include warm lobster salad with olive *tapenade* and pigeon in a flaky crust with foie gras, to be followed by superb Grand Marnier soufflé or decadent moist chocolate cake. Friendly service and top-notch affordable wines.

Bouillon de Pub
24 rue François Guisol (04.92.04.02.99). **Open** noon-2pm Mon; noon-2pm, 7-9.30pm Tue-Sat. **Menus** €22-€30. **Credit** AmEx, V.
A friendly neighbourhood favourite by the Old Port with a cheery retro ad decor and tasty daily specials like fresh grilled swordfish and seafood pasta.

Le Chantecler
Hôtel Negresco, 37 promenade des Anglais (04.93.16.64.00). **Open** 12.30-2pm, 8-10pm daily. Closed mid-Nov to mid-Dec. **Menus** €75-€100. **Credit** AmEx, DC, MC, V.
Chef Alain Llorca is a key player in the new generation of Provençal cooks. He specialises in bold and authoritative combinations of texture and flavour. Don't miss his startlingly original tomato *tarte Tatin* served with candied black-olive ice-cream. Excellent service and a very good wine list add to the pleasure.

La Cigale
7 av de Suède (04.93.88.60.20). **Open** 10am-midnight daily. **Menus** €23-€38. **Credit** AmEx, DC, MC, V.
Perfect for an affordable lunch on designer boutique row. Try the yummy chicken chawarma or the mixed assortment of Middle Eastern salads, and the scrumptious honey-soaked pastries. Check out the lively atmosphere on weekend nights when a belly-dancer performs.

Le Grand Café de Turin
5 pl Garibaldi (04.93.62.29.52). **Open** 8am-10pm daily. **Menus** €25-€55. **Credit** AmEx, DC, MC, V.
Situated on a perfect people-watching corner, this classic Niçois shellfish haunt, opened in 1910, is always jammed with oyster-slurping locals. Service can be testy but the atmosphere is the real thing.

Indyana
11 rue Gustave Deloye (04.93.80.67.69). **Open** noon-2.30pm, 7pm-midnight Mon-Sat. **Average** €38. **Credit** AmEx, DC, MC, V.
Thirty- and fortysomething hipsters finally have

The Riviera

their own stylish but affordable dining spot, run by enterprising brothers Christophe and Pascal Ciamos, whose 'fusion cuisine' menu matches the eclectic New York loft meets art deco, Asian and Moroccan decor. Global dishes range from sushi and Japanese duck to more classic beef and fish platters with potato or courgette gratin, and scrumptious fruit tarts.

Karr
10 rue Alphonse Karr (04.93.82.18.31). **Open** noon-2.30pm, 7.30-10pm Mon-Sat (bar 7.30am-11pm). **Menus** €10-€38. **Credit** AmEx, MC, V.
This chic new contemporary eatery, on a quiet pedestrian street near the upmarket boutiques, is where London-imported chef Philippe Soublet dishes up an ever-creative menu that goes beyond Provençal. Try the mouthwatering lobster lasagne or coquilles St Jacques with raisins and cauliflower.

Kf'bis
8 rue Defly (04.93.80.02.22). **Open** 11am-3.30pm, 5.30pm-2.30am Tue-Sat; 11am-2.30pm Sun. **Menus** €12-€31. **Credit** AmEx, DC, MC, V.
In keeping with the increasing 'just like home' dining trend, this attractive boutique/gallery, lined with paintings, furniture, *objets d'art* and fashion, doubles as an intimate restaurant. More for the magical atmosphere than the less-than-remarkable homemade dishes. Nice for Sunday brunch.

La Merenda
4 rue de la Terrasse (no phone). **Menus** €22.90-€27.45. **Open** lunch and dinner Mon-Fri. Closed three weeks Aug. **No credit cards.**
Chef Dominique Le Stanc shed his three-star perch at the Negresco for this rustic hole-in-the-wall not far from the Cours Saleya market in 1996; he serves a full repertoire of Niçois classics such as stuffed sardines, *stockfissa* (salt cod with tomatoes and olive oil) and *daube de boeuf.* Though it's crowded and hot, the food is delicious. Book (in person) if you can.

La Mousson
167 promenade des Flots Bleus (04.93.31.13.30). **Open** noon-2.30pm, 6.30-10.30pm Mon, Thur-Sun. **Menus** €16-€32. **Credit** AmEx, MC, V.
Exquisite Thai cuisine, a stone's throw from the airport at the seaside port of St-Laurent-du-Var. Highlights include the spicy sautéed squid and chicken dish, mouthwatering Thai ravioli, steamed fish wrapped in banana leaves, and a creamy coconut flan. Best bargain lunch menu in town.

La Part des Anges
17 rue Gubernatis (04.93.62.69.80). **Open** noon-2pm Mon-Thur; noon-2pm, 7-9.30pm Fri, Sat. **Average** €21. **Credit** AmEx, DC, MC, V.
The captivating aroma as you walk past this intimate wine cellar and bistro draw you inside, where owner and sommelier Olivier Labarde offers expert advice on his superb selection of local and rare vintages. The delicious home-cooked south-western specialities served at five tables at the back are one of the best gastronomic bargains in town. Book.

La Petite Maison
11 rue St-François-de-Paule (04.93.85.71.53/ www.lapetitemaison.net). **Open** noon-2pm, 7.30-10pm Mon-Sat. **Average** €45. **Credit** AmEx, MC, V.
This venerable restaurant draws colourful locals at noon, top models and cinema stars by night. Start with the Niçois hors d'oeuvres – *pissaladière*, stuffed vegetables, courgette and aubergine *beignets*, etc – and then have sea bass cooked in a salt crust. The house ice cream is the best in town. Wear something Champagne-proof, since *patronne* Ruby tends to spray customers when in a playful mood.

Le Safari
1 cours Saleya (04.93.80.18.44). **Open** noon-3.30pm, 7-11pm daily. **Menu** €24.39. **Credit** AmEx, DC, MC, V.
The Safari's terrace fills quickly on market days, but it's pleasant inside, too. Food on offer includes pizzas cooked in a wood oven, Niçois specialities such as ravioli stuffed with braised beef in beef stock, a salade Niçoise that defines the term and the Cascade Safari starter, an assortment including grilled red peppers, *accra*, artichoke salad and squid *beignets*.

La Table Alziari
4 rue François Zanin (04.93.80.34.03). **Open** noon-2pm, 7.30-10pm Tue-Sat. Closed one week Aug, one week Dec. **Menus** €13.72-€21.34. **Credit** MC, V.
From the family that sells the best local olive oil in town (*see p241,* **Shopping**), this low-key but authentic Nissart bistro hidden on a sidestreet off rue Pairolière offers home-style cooking with the freshest ingredients. Don't miss the stuffed sardines, delicate courgette flower *beignets* or *morue Niçoise.*

Terres des Truffes
11 rue St-François-de-Paule (04.93.62.07.68). **Open** noon-2pm, 8-10pm Mon-Sat. **Menus** €16-€45. **Credit** AmEx, MC, V.
Nice's recently-opened fast-food truffle bar, created by celeb chef Bruno Clément (*see chapter* **The Var Heartland**), combines a stylish wood-panelled bistro with a gourmet shop and serves everything from truffle sandwiches and delectable truffle-studded warm brie to caramelised truffle ice cream.

L'Univers de Christian Plumail
54 bd Jean Jaurès (04.93.62.32.22). **Open** noon-2pm, 7.30-10pm Mon-Fri; 7.30-10pm Sat. **Menus** €16.77-€57.17. **Credit** AmEx, MC, V.
Renowned Niçois chef Christian Plumail has transformed this former brasserie into an unpretentious haven for simple yet refined Mediterranean cuisine at surprisingly affordable prices. Regulars rave about dishes such as purple artichoke salad with parmesan, grilled fish with coriander, rabbit stew and macaroons with pine nuts and mascarpone.

La Zucca Magica
4 bis quai Papacino (04.93.56.25.27). **Open** noon-2.45pm, 7-10.30pm Tue-Sat. **Menus** €13.72-€19.82. **No credit cards.**
In 1996, Marco Folicardi, Rome's best vegetarian

Provençal People: Ben

While old-established artists like Picasso and Cocteau were taking advantage of the swinging 60s on the Côte d'Azur, a new, more experimental group of artists was emerging. The Ecole de Nice became an internationally recognised centre for a body of artists, among them Yves Klein, César, Raysse, Arman and Ben (all featured at MAMAC), whose styles included *nouveau réalisme* (the French equivalent of Pop) and Fluxus.

Ben dabbled with *nouveau réalisme*, which he considered a movement 'where you took things out of the world and signed them. So I took everything and signed it and they kicked me out.' Instead he joined Fluxus, a group heavily involved in performance art – along with Yoko Ono, John Cage and Robert Filliou – where he did things to change and provoke, or even provoke change.

Born in Naples in 1935, Ben Vautier was adopted by the Niçois and Nice, which has been his home and place of work since 1949. Heavily influenced by Duchamp and dada, Ben combines the 'ready-made' with statements, questions and truisms written in his trademark childlike scrawl on a black background. When Ben paints text on discarded objects or on a canvas, like Duchamp's urinals they too become art, while his texts 'rien n'existe pas', 'il y a trop art', or 'l'art est inutile' force you to question what is 'art'?

In Nice in the late 1950s Ben opened *Magasin*, a shop and huge work in progress, from which he sold bric-a-brac and where he first encountered Yves Klein. Aware of the trend for abstraction, he sought a form unused by anyone else: Mondrian had the square, Ben chose the banana. When Klein came into his shop, Ben asked his impression of the banana works. Klein said 'The bananas are "after-Kandinsky". Exhibit your giant poems in Chinese ink, they are much more authentic.' While Klein was developing art actions, Ben used performances to surprise. At his exhibition openings he has sat naked in a gallery window and signed autographs from a bathtub, 'it was a way not to be bored with a glass in my hand like the others,' he said.

It's the combination of text and object that have pride of place in museums. *Magasin*, deconstructed and reconstructed, is now part of the collection at the Centre Pompidou in Paris. His installation *Cambra* (room in Niçois dialect), a fairytale array of goodies, is on display at MAMAC, and a new shop, which he says will be 'one of my biggest pieces ever',

is going to Documenta in Germany, followed by the Tate Liverpool in 2002.

Ben is a prolific writer. He publishes his own newsletter, now on www.ben-vautier.com, with his views on art, politics, the media and his true passion, ethnic cultures – not distant minorities, but those within Europe whose traditions are dying, like the Bretons, the Corsicans and the Niçois.

The house where he lives on route de St-Pancrace (9km from central Nice) is another incredible piece of work. He's decorated the east side and is now on the north side, which is visible from the road: 'it's not in any guidebook but I often enjoy seeing Japanese tourists taking photographs from tour buses that have included it in their programme', he said. If you'd prefer to spend time inside one of his works, he also decorated one of the 'artists' bedrooms' at the Hôtel Windsor (*see p244*), where colourful graffiti fills the walls with the words of his dreams. A little book for you to record your dreams sits by the bed, once more provoking the viewer to respond to his work.

All the herbs and spices of the south at **cours Saleya** market. *See p232.*

chef, set up shop at this grotto-like tavern by the old port, where he serves a remarkable lunch menu that may be the best bargain in the city. You drink the house wine – it's all there is – and you eat what Folicardi serves you: the bounty goes from lasagne with ricotta, asparagus and lemon zest, and cheese-and-aubergine 'meatballs' in tomato sauce to cherry flan.

Cakes & ice cream

Fennocchio
2 pl Rossetti (04.93.80.72.52). **Open** 10am-11.30pm Tue-Sun. Closed Dec, Jan. **Credit** MC, V.
The terrace of this ice cream maker in Vieux Nice is a fine destination on a warm afternoon. Settle in at a table overlooking the fountain and choose from a superb range of ice cream and sorbets, including what's surely the world's best peach ice cream.

Pâtisserie Cappa
7-9 pl Garibaldi (04.93.62.30.83). **Open** 7.30am-7.30pm Tue-Sun. Closed Sept. **Credit** MC, V.
Venture under the arches for heavenly pastries, mousse cakes and *tourte de blettes* – a sweet Niçois tart of swiss chard, pine nuts and raisins – to take away or consume in the miniature tea room.

Bars & cafés

Le Bar des Oiseaux
5 rue St-Vincent (04.93.80.27.33). **Open** noon-2pm Mon; noon-2pm, 7-11pm Tue-Fri; 7-11pm Sat. Closed Aug. **Credit** MC, V.
Lots of local atmosphere at this popular restaurant, bar and theatre. Live bands and live birds, too – in cages, most of the time – and uproarious comic sketches written by proprietor Noëlle Perna, whose plays target the Niçois and city politics.

Blue Boy Enterprise
9 rue Spinetta (04.93.44.68.24/www.blueboy.fr). **Open** 11pm-dawn, days vary. **Credit** DC, MC, V.
The best-known gay disco in town draws a big crowd. Young boys prance and dance, grand old Riviera queens cosy up or bitch and the rest hit the booze and the dancefloor.

Le Blue Whales
1 rue Masconinat (04.93.62.90.94). **Open** 5.30pm-4.30am Tue-Sun. **Credit** V.
A relaxed, congenial thirtysomething crowd frequents this better-than-most pub where you can shoot pool and dance to live bands ranging from jazz funk to salsa.

Le Bull Dog Pub
16 rue de l'Abbaye (04.93.85.04.06/ www.bulldogpub.com). **Open** 8pm-2.30am daily. **Credit** MC, V.
Plenty of decibels, free munchies with cocktails and 25 brands of beer at this rosbif hangout. Live pop and rock bands play to a 25- to 35-year-old crowd.

Café Borghèse
9 rue Fodéré (04.92.04.83.83). **Open** 9am-10.30pm Mon-Fri; 11am-2pm, 7-10pm Sat. **Credit** MC, V.
Located behind the church of the Vieux Port, this is the place for cappucino, apéritifs, delicious antipasti platters and copious portions of gnocchi and ravioli.

La Casa del Sol
69 quai des Etats Unis (04.93.62.87.28). **Open** *mid-May to Sept* 6.30pm-2.30am daily; *Oct to mid-May* 7pm-2.30am Tue-Sat. **Credit** MC, V.
This before- and after-hours tapas bar in the arcades between the seafront and cours Saleya has a lively atmosphere and a Spanish-Latino beat (DJs Thur-Sat). Dress cool, clean and casual to get past the door.

Cherry's Café
36 rue des Ponchettes (04.93.13.85.45). **Open** noon-midnight Mon, Fri-Sun; 4pm-midnight Tue, Wed. **Credit** AmEx, MC, V.
This popular gay bar/restaurant (menus €12.20-€26.68) has an inviting miniature terrace overlooking the promenade des Anglais; it offers a variety of salads and an affordable *plat du jour*.

Chez Pipo
13 rue Bavastro (04.93.55.88.82). **Open** 5.30-10pm Tue-Sun (daily July & Aug). Closed Nov. **No credit cards.**
A lively port-side spot, with a huge wood-burning oven and long tables where old-timers gossip in Niçois dialect. The perfect place for an early evening snack on *socca* and a glass of local *rosé*.

Wayne's
15 rue de la Préfecture (04.93.13.46.99/ www.waynes.fr). **Open** noon-1am daily. **Credit** AmEx, MC, V.
This buzzing live-music pub with a decent-sized stage, is a magnet for English students and Sophia Antipolis high-tech workers. Drinks can be pricey, especially during the summer.

La Havane
32 rue de France (04.93.16.36.16). **Open** 4pm-2.30am Mon, Sun, 11am-2.30pm, 4pm-2.30am Tue-Sat. **Credit** AmEx, MC, V.
No one can resist dancing in this recently opened restaurant/bar (restaurant closed Mon), where a hot Cuban group plays nightly. Great place for cocktails and one of the liveliest spots in the centre of town.

The Klomp
6 rue Mascionat (04.93.92.42.85). **Open** 5.30pm-2.30am Mon-Sat. **Credit** DC, MC, V.
Jazz-oriented dive with draught Guinness, presided over by English barman Russell.

Mezzanine
5 rue Barillerie (04.93.80.10.68). **Open** 4.30pm-12.30am daily. **Credit** MC, V.
There are only four consoles in this tiny bar in the *vieille ville*, but it's the hippest Internet café in town (free for 15 mins with a drink), with chilled music and a modest-priced but tasty menu of salads and pasta. A good place to find party flyers.

Nocy-Be
4-6 rue Jules Gilly (04.93.85.52.25). **Open** 4pm-midnight Mon, Wed-Sun.
If you're looking for ethnic bric-a-brac or unusual handcrafted lamps, this cosy boutique, which dou-

bles as a Moroccan tea room, is a place where you can literally shop till you drop… on to a comfortable floor cushion, for invigorating mint tea and pastries.

Oliviera
8 bis rue du Collet (04.93.13.06.45). **Open** *May-Oct* 10am-10pm Mon-Sat; 10am-3pm Sun; *Nov-Apr* 10am-8pm Mon-Sat; 10am-3pm Sun. **No credit cards.**
In the thick of the Old Town, this new boutique/café sells a variety of Mediterrean olive oils and is also the perfect spot for a quick salad or pasta dish (€7-€13), prepared with top-quality products.

Clubs & music venues

For concerts see also *p237*, **Palais Nikaia**.

Dizzy Club
26 quai Lunel (04.93.26.54.79). **Open** 11.30pm-5am Wed-Sun. **Credit** MC, V.
One of the few clubs where you can actually have a conversation at the bar. Sleek decor, piano-bar, a dancefloor with live bands, working out from jazz to electro, and DJs draw pretty people from 25 to 50.

Le Ghost House
3 rue Barillerie (04.93.92.93.37). **Open** 8pm-2.30am Mon-Sat. **Admission** free. **Credit** DC, MC, V.
Trip-hop, drum 'n' bass and house fans flock to this tiny club in the old town, which leads the way on the Nice electronic scene.

Le Grand Escurial
29 rue Alphonse Karr (04.93.82.37.66). **Open** 9pm-5am Fri, Sat. **Admission** €16 (incl 1st drink). **Credit** MC, V.
Under new ownership, this cavernous disco has added a cozy mezzanine restaurant/lounge.

Le Saramanga
45 promenade des Anglais (04.93.96.68.00). **Open** 11pm-6am Fri, Sat and eves before public holidays. **Admission** €12 (incl 1st drink).
The rebaptised Forum is still the favourite haunt of the under-25 clubbers. Expect red velvet curtains, huge dancefloor and mega decibels.

Shopping

Department store Galeries Lafayette, book and record emporium Fnac and countless clothing chains line avenue Jean Médecin. Luxury labels congregate on rue Paradis (Chanel, Emporio Armani, Kenzo, Sonia Rykiel), avenue de Suède (Yves Saint-Laurent, Rolex, Louis Vuitton) and avenue de Verdun (Cartier, Hermès).

Agnès b
17 rue des Ponchettes (04.93.62.32.39/ www.agnesb.fr). **Open** 10am-7pm Mon-Sat. **Credit** AmEx, MC, V.
An oasis of beautifully cut stylish but sober classics for women and kids, on the edge of the *vieille ville*. Her cult menswear is on 5 impasse Longchamp.

And all that jazz

The jazz tradition in Nice dates back to 1974, when francophile American George Wein (founder of the Newport Festival) created the Grande Parade de Jazz, drawing jazz lovers to the Côte d'Azur with artists such as Cab Calloway, Lionel Hampton, Ray Charles, Ella Fitzgerald and Miles Davis. Since 1994, assorted French promoters have added a more commercial world and pop mix, but failed to break even financially. Fortunately, the festival's latest organiser, Viviane Sicnasi, a former assisant of Wein, has finally reinstated the original spirit, an eclectic mix of traditional and modern sounds and a prestigious international lineup. Scheduled over one week in July, the record-breaking crowds in 2001 seem to prove that the festival's diverse thematic formula – seven different musical atmospheres – will keep Nice on the jazz map. Set in the Arena Gardens in the historic hills of Cimiez, concert-goers wander between simultaneous concerts on three separate stages. The *bon enfant* atmosphere is a cross between a Gallic Woodstock and a musical fair: families en masse with pushchair, grandma and the dog picnic under the century-old olive trees, where piping hot *socca* and sandwiches are also sold. The 4,000 seat arena stage once served as the playground for the javelin-throwing gladiators, and sometimes gets just as wild.

Nice Jazz Festival

(www.nicejazzfest.com). See also chapter, **The Festive South**.

Alziari

14 rue St-François-de-Paule (04.93.85.76.92). **Open** 8.15am-12.30pm, 2.15-7pm Tue-Sat. **Credit** MC, V.
Since 1879, the Alziari family has been producing a superb nutty olive oil, sold in distinctive yellow and blue tin drums. There is also a selection of other natural products. Don't miss their green *tapenade* or the gorgeous lavender, honey and olive oil soap.

L'Atelier des Jouets

1 pl de l'Ancien Sénat (04.93.13.09.60). **Open** 10.30am-7pm Mon, Tue-Sat; 2-7pm Wed. **Credit** AmEx, DC, MC, V.
A charming old-fashioned toy shop on a pretty square in the old town, packed with everything from soft toys, puzzles and puppets to stocking fillers.

Blanc d'Ivoire

17 rue de la Préfecture (04.93.85.57.43). **Open** 10am-1pm, 2-7pm Mon-Sat. **Credit** AmEx, DC, MC, V.
The first outlet of the Parisian homeware brand to open in the provinces has hand-stiched Provençal quilts, curtains, sweet-smelling bath salts and soaps.

Boutique 3

3 rue Longchamp (04.93.88.35.00). **Open** 10am-1pm, 2-7pm Mon-Sat. **Credit** AmEx, MC, V.
Designer Jacqueline Morabito creates creamy linen tablecloths, flowing white shirts, shawls, ceramic dishware, and over a shelf of gourmet goodies handpicked by Chantacler chef Alain Llorca.

The Cat's Whiskers

30 rue Lamartine (04.93.80.02.66). **Open** 2-6.45pm Mon; 9.30am-6.45pm Tue-Fri, 9.30am-noon, 3-6.30pm Sat. **Credit** AmEx, MC, V.
A small but smart selection of English books.

Façonnable

7, 9, 10 rue Paradis (04.93.87.88.80). **Open** 10am-7pm Mon-Sat. **Credit** AmEx, DC, MC, V.
What began as a small Nice-based menswear label in this small shop now has stores in every major international city, selling elegantly preppy sportswear, suits and ties. Womenswear at No.10.

Fayences de Moustiers

18 rue du Marché (04.93.13.06.03). **Open** 9.45am-1pm, 2-7pm Mon-Sat. **Credit** AmEx, MC, V.
The only shop in Nice with delicately hand-painted porcelain from Moustiers; everything from cream jugs to fruit bowls. Pricey, but the real thing.

Marché de la Brocante

cours Saleya. **Open** 8am-5pm Mon. **Credit** varies.
Antiques galore at this inviting outdoor market, where you'll find vintage phonographs, blue seltzer bottles, old linen tablecloths, art deco jewellery, assorted attic junk and dazzling silver cutlery.

Matarosso Bookstore/Gallery

2 rue Longchamp (04.93.87.74.55). **Open** 10am-12.30pm, 4-7.30pm Tue-Sat. **Credit** MC, V.
This pioneer Niçois gallery also stocks contemporary art books, original editions and engravings.

Hôtel Negresco: luxury froth.

Village Ségurane

main entrance on rue Ségurane (no phone). **Open**
10am-noon, 3-6.30pm Mon-Sat. **Credit** AmEx, MC, V.
When Elton John went on a decorating spree for his
villa in Mont Boron, this is where he shopped: a two-
storey miniature village of antiques shops, stacked
together on one square block.

Where to stay

Luxury

Hôtel Negresco

36 promenade des Anglais (04.93.16.64.00/
www.hotel-negresco-nice.com). **Double** €213-€460.
Suite €556-€1,410. **Credit** AmEx, DC, MC, V.
You can't miss this pink and white wedding cake of
a palace, built by Eduoard Niermans, known as the
Offenbach of architecture. The parking valet with
tailcoat and breeches sets the mood. In the lobby, the
modern world pales beside the glitter of a crystal
chandelier, Aubusson carpet and a dazzling glass
and metal dome designed by Gustave Eiffel. Considered a folly at the time when Cimiez was the chic
place to be, the Negresco eventually drew everyone,
from crowned heads to the stars of stage and screen.
Sumptuous bedrooms range from oriental splendour
to Louis XIV and Napoléon III pomp, though many
bathrooms are oddly Las Vegas. There isn't a pool
but there is a private beach.

Hôtel Palais Maeterlinck

30 bd Maurice Maeterlinck (04.92.00.72.00/
www.palais-maeterlinck.com). Closed mid-Jan to mid-
Mar. **Double** €225-€390. **Suite** €388-€1,100.
Credit AmEx, DC, MC, V.
Once a villa belonging to Belgian writer Count Maurice Maeterlinck, this renovated modern structure –
a sprawling 'neo-classic style' palace – on the edge
of the sea on the Basse Corniche, is now a hotel
boasting luxurious rooms, an excellent restaurant
and lovely outdoor pool. The atmosphere is somewhat stiff and formal, but the views are superb.

Hôtel West End

31 promenade des Anglais (04.92.14.44.00/
www.hotel-westend.com). **Double** €170-€610.
Credit AmEx, DC, MC, V.
Built in 1842, the recently renovated West End was
the first grand hotel on the Baie des Anges. There
are lovely salons and a listed bar downstairs, but the
repro Gainsboroughs and Fragonards in the corridors are a crime. This is where Isabelle Adjani stays
and where Tony Blair touched down for the Nice
Summit. Private beach and plans to add a pool.

Moderate & inexpensive

Hostellerie du Petit Palais

17 av Emile Bieckiert (04.93.62.19.11/www.hotel-
petit-palais.com). **Double** €66-€124. **Credit** AmEx,
MC, V.
Set back on a quiet street in hilly Cimiez, this 25-
room *belle époque* hotel in the house where actor-
playwright Sacha Guitry lived in the 1930s may not
be the dernier cri in decor, but the panoramic view
and lush breakfast garden make up for the rest.

Hôtel Atlantic

12 bd Victor Hugo (04.93.88.40.15). **Double** €114-
€175. **Credit** AmEx, MC, V.
Beyond the sumptuous *belle époque* stained-glass
lobby – used by François Truffaut as a location in
Day for Night – the modern, renovated rooms are
spacious and comfortable.

Hôtel Beau Rivage

24 rue St-François-de-Paule (04.92.47.82.82).
Double €119-€152.50. **Credit** AmEx, DC, MC, V.
Thoroughly modernised since the days when
Matisse had a seafront apartment here, this com-
fortable 1930s hotel has its own private beach and
excellent restaurant across the street.

Hôtel Les Camélias

3 rue Spitalieri (04.93.62.15.54). **Double** €64.
Closed Nov. **Credit** MC, V.
This kitsch haven of faded splendour next to the
Nice Etoile mall has a lobby filled with artificial
flowers and a palm-shaded patio. Low-budget charm.

Hôtel Château des Ollières

39 av des Baumettes (04.92.15.77.99/
www.chateaudesollieres.com). **Double** €129-€335.
Credit AmEx, MC, V.

Only steps from the Musée des Beaux-Arts, this turretted *belle époque* palace, formerly owned by a Russian prince, is an ornate mini-museum of marble statues, stained glass, crystal chandeliers and tapestries, with excellent cuisine and friendly staff.

Hôtel Excelsior
19 av Durante (04.93.88.18.05/ www.excelsiornice.com). **Double** €70-€90. **Credit** AmEx, MC, V.
An impressive turn-of-the-century building on a quiet street, with clean, old-fashioned rooms and a small garden where breakfast is served.

Hôtel Le Floride
52 bd de Cimiez (04.93.53.11.02/www.hotelfloride.fr). Closed three weeks Jan. **Double** €44-€60. **Credit** AmEx, MC, V.
Only a ten-minute walk from the centre of town and right near the Chagall museum, this modest small hotel even has a view on the top floor.

Hôtel Gounod
3 rue Gounod (04.93.16.42.00/www.gounodnice.com). Closed mid-Nov to mid-Dec. **Double** €85-€120. **Credit** AmEx, DC, MC, V.
A lovely dusty-rose *belle époque* exterior and chic but standard modern rooms with balconies. Guests can use the rooftop pool next door at Hôtel Splendid.

Hôtel Le Grimaldi
15 rue Grimaldi (04.93.16.00.24/www.le-grimaldi.com). **Double** €75-€145. **Credit** AmEx, MC, V.
An elegant, upmarket bed and breakfast, offering guests the kind of personalised hospitality often lacking in the glitzy Riviera palaces. All the rooms are different, tastefully decorated with countrified furnishings and Provençal fabrics.

Hôtel Oasis
23 rue Gounod (04.93.88.12.29/www.hotel-oasisnice.com.fr). **Double** €60-€84. **Credit** AmEx, MC, V.
Centrally located, and slightly set back from the street, this tranquil hotel once lodged illustrious Russians including Chekhov and Lenin. The biggest rooms (nos. 110, 124 and 210) look over the splendid shady garden.

Hôtel La Perouse
11 quai Rauba-Capeu (04.93.62.34.63). **Double** €124-€305. **Credit** AmEx, MC, V.
This bright, airy hotel, ideally situated between the port and *vieille ville*, has an unbeatable sea view and a rooftop garden and spill-over pool.

Hôtel Windsor
11 rue Dalpozzo (04.93.88.59.35/ www.hotelwindsornice.com). **Double** €70-€120. **Credit** AmEx, MC, V.
An arty oasis with its own exotic garden, aviary and pool. The spacious rooms are all individually decorated by renowned contemporary artists, including Ben, Peter Fend and Lawrence Weiner; there's also a lovely Moroccan-style *hammam* and small gym.

Essentials

Getting there

From the airport
Bus no.99 runs every 30 minutes between the airport and the main SNCF station: the fare is €3.51. A taxi costs about €31 to the city centre.

By car
Leave the A8 at exit no.54 or no.55, but it's more scenic to take the N7 or N98 along the coast.

By train
The main SNCF station is at 3 av Thiers, served by frequent trains from Nice and Marseille. Local services to Menton also stop at the smaller Gare Riquier, which is handy for the port and the old town. The closest station to the airport is the Gare St Augustin. The private Gare de Provence, just north of the main station, is the departure point for the narrow-gauge Var Valley Train des Pignes.

By bus
The *gare routière* (04.93.85.61.81) on promenade du Paillon is the hub for most Côte d'Azur coach services, including international buses running Rome-Nice-Barcelona and Venice-Milan-Nice.
Phocéens Cars (04.93.85.66.61) runs three buses daily (Mon-Fri) to Marseille via Cannes and Aix, only one on Sun, and two buses daily Mon-Sat from place Masséna to Toulon, via Cannes and Hyères.

Getting around

By bus
Local services are run by **Sunbus**, 10 av Félix Fauré (04.93.13.53.13; open Mon-Sat). Tickets cost E1.30. Bus-hop passes cost €4 (one-day), €12.96 (five-day) and €16.77 (seven-day), available from Sunbus, tabacs and newsagents.

By taxi
Nice taxis are notoriously expensive. To order a taxi, call Central Taxi Riviera (04.93.13.78.78).

Tourist information
All museums are free the first Sunday of the month. The **Passe-musées** (€8.08 one day; €15.24 three days) gives free entrance.
Webstore (12 rue de Russie, 04.89.06.90.80) is an internet café with 15 terminals.

Office du Tourisme et des Congrès
5 promenade des Anglais (04.92.14.48.00/ www.coteazur.org). **Open** 9am-6pm daily.
Branches: Aéroport Nice Côte d'Azur, Terminal 1 (04.93.21.44.11); Gare SNCF, av Thiers (04.93.87.07.07).

Police & lost property
Police Municipal, 10 cours Saleya (04.93.54.10.32).
Open 8.30am-5pm Mon-Thur; 8.30am-3.45pm Fri.

The Riviera

The Corniches

The Corniches wind round and tunnel through the Riviera coast, offering dizzy vistas, ancient ports and the follies and foibles of the very, very rich.

The Corniches are the quintessence of the Riviera. The name refers to three roads – high, middle and low – between Nice and Menton, and, by extension, to the strip of coastline in between. But it also conjures up visions of sun-bronzed boys and babes speeding along in convertible sports cars. Unfortunately, the reality is more prosaic. In summer the traffic often slows to a crawl – which at least gives you time to admire the glorious panoramas.

The Basse Corniche (N98 – also known as the Corniche Inférieure) hugs the coast, passing through all the towns and resorts; most of the year it is a vehicle-packed nightmare. To take some of the strain, the wider Moyenne Corniche (N7) was hacked through the mountains in the 1920s. The highest route – the Grande Corniche (D2564) – follows the ancient Roman Aurelian Way, and is the most spectacular of the three.

The glamour of the Corniches has its tragic side, too. On 13 September 1982, a car carrying Princess Grace of Monaco and her daughter Stéphanie swerved off the N53, a treacherous descent full of hairpin bends that leads from the

Grande Corniche to the Moyenne Corniche. Stéphanie survived; her mother didn't. There's no memorial, but a bunch or two of fresh flowers can generally be seen by the roadside.

The Basse Corniche

Villefranche-sur-Mer

Founded in the 14th century by Charles d'Anjou II as a duty-free port, Villefranche's steep narrow streets and stacked up dusty-rose, ochre and apricot houses with *trompe l'oeil* frescoes redefine the term 'picturesque'. On the tiny cobblestoned port, you might still see old women mending fishing nets. In the old town rue Obscure, a dark and eerie vaulted passageway, has changed little since the Middle Ages. And the **Combat Naval Fleuri**, held on the Monday before Ash Wednesday, is a surreal sight as dozens of fishing boats bedecked with flowers invade the harbour.

The **Baie de Villefranche**: heavily built up since its duty-free past.

The Riviera

The deep harbour between the headlands of Mont Boron to the west and Cap-Ferrat to the east was used as a US naval base until France withdrew from the military wing of NATO in 1966. The quayside has settled down since the days when it used to service sailors; lined with restaurants and brasseries, it overlooks a strip of beach. At the western end of the old port is the postage stamp-sized **Chapelle de St-Pierre-des-Pêcheurs** – once a storehouse for fishing nets. In 1957, Jean Cocteau covered the walls with lively frescoes recounting the life of St Peter. At the summit of the old town, the **Eglise St-Michel** (04.93.01.73.13, open 9am-7pm daily) is a handsome 18th-century Italianate church that boasts an impressive organ built in 1790 by the Niçois Grinda brothers, still played during Sunday mass.

To the west, the 16th-century **Citadelle** was built by the Dukes of Savoy, complete with drawbridge. It now houses the voluptuous female figurines of local sculptor Antoniucci Volti in the **Musée Volti** and 100 minor works by artists, such as Picasso, Hartung, Picabia and Miró in the **Musée Goetz-Boumeester** .

Chapelle de St-Pierre-des-Pêcheurs

pl Pollonais (04.93.76.90.70). **Open** *July-Sept* 10am-noon, 4-8.30pm Tue-Sun; *Oct-Feb* 9.30am-noon, 2-5pm Tue-Sun; *Mar-June* 9.30am-noon, 2-7pm Tue-Sun. Closed 15 Nov to 15 Dec. **Admission** €2, free under-12s.

Musée Volti & Musée Goetz-Boumeester

Citadelle, av Sadi Carnot (04.93.76.33.33). **Open** *June-Sept* 10am-noon, 2.30-7pm Mon, Wed-Sat; 2.30-7pm Sun; *Oct-May* 9am-noon, 2-5.30pm Mon, Wed-Sat; 1.30-6pm Sun. **Admission** free.

Where to stay & eat

The newly renovated **Hôtel le Welcome** (1 quai Amiral Courbet, 04.93.76.27.62, closed 12 Nov-22 Dec, double €99-€290) is a splendid pink- and green-trimmed portside hotel, and though it unfortunately bears little resemblance to the hotel of the same name where Jean Cocteau fraternised with young sailors amid opium fumes in the 1920s, the artist's spirit lives on in the decor. Many of the small but airy rooms have sunny balconies that give on to the port. **La Mère Germaine** (7 quai Corbet, 04.93.01.71.34, closed 12 Nov-22 Dec, menu €34), just a few metres from the cobblestoned quay, is the best bet for traditional fish soup. Up a steep alley, **L'Echalote** (7 rue de l'Eglise, 04.93.01.71.11, open dinner only, closed Sun and 15-30 Jan, menus €23-€35) serves tasty dishes such as heavenly vegetable and parmesan tarts and pork sirloin with figs. For great squid salad

and wonderful *bouillabaisse*, book a table on the terrace at family-run **La Trinquette** (Port La Darse, 04.93.01.71.41, closed Tue, Wed, menus €20-€30). **Le Cosmo Bar** (pl Amelie Pollonais, 04.93.01.84.05, menus €13-€25) is not just a friendly local café, but offers top-quality fish specials and one of the best *salades niçoises* on the Riviera. Great for breakfast before the Sunday antiques market.

Tourist information

Office de Tourisme

Jardin François Binon, 06230 Villefranche-sur-Mer (04.93.01.73.68/www.villefranche-sur-mer.com). **Open** 9am-noon, 2-6pm Mon-Sat.

Cap-Ferrat

This lush, secluded peninsula jutting out between Villefranche and Beaulieu is a millionaires' paradise of high-hedged, security-gated mansions (part-time residents include Hubert de Givenchy and Andrew Lloyd Webber), but it is also a walker's dream, with a rocky 10km path (*see p223*) that winds around the Cap en route to the Plage des Fosses, a pebbly beach that is ideal for small children.

The approach to the Cap is dominated by the **Villa Ephrussi-de-Rothschild**, an Italianate extravaganza built for Béatrice de Rothschild in the early 1900s. Inside, Béatrice had appropriate settings recreated for her immense collection, which focuses on the 18th century, along with Impressionist paintings and Oriental knick-knacks. The villa is surrounded by seven hectares of Spanish, Japanese and Italian gardens and fountains.

On the eastern side of the peninsula, luxury yachts have replaced fishing boats at **St-Jean-Cap-Ferrat**, which remains a pleasant enough town, good for an evening drink followed by a stroll along the marina. Further west, the **Zoo du Cap-Ferrat** is a miniature tropical park with 300 species, from flamingos and talking cockatoos to Himalayan bears and Siberian tigers – all more likely to impress tots, however, than adult animal-lovers.

Villa Ephrussi-de-Rothschild

1 av Ephrussi-de-Rothschild (04.93.01.45.90/ www.villa-ephrussi.com). **Open** *mid-Feb to June, Sept, Oct* 10am-6pm daily; *Nov to mid-Feb* 2-6pm Mon-Fri; 10am-6pm Sat, Sun; *July, Aug* 10am-7pm daily. **Admission** €8; €6 7-18s; free under-7s.

Zoo du Cap-Ferrat

117 bd du Général de Gaulle (04.93.76.07.60/ www.zoocapferrat.com). **Open** *Apr-Oct* 9.30am-7.30pm daily; *Nov-Mar* 9.30am-5.30pm daily. **Admission** €9.80; €6.50 3-10s; free under-3s.

The world's a balloon from David Niven's former garden at **Cap Ferrat**. *See p250.*

Where to stay & eat

You almost expect to see gentlemen in top hats strolling through the manicured gardens of the stately **Grand Hôtel du Cap-Ferrat** (71 bd Général de Gaulle, 04.93.76.50.50/www.grand-hotel-cap-ferrat.com, closed Jan & Feb, double €230-€1,100), hidden near the tip of the peninsula. Non-guests can eat at the classically elegant Le Cap restaurant (menus €69-€90) or stop for a drink at its Somerset Maugham Bar, where the writer occasionally wandered from his nearby home to meet friends for *gin tonics*; for a €54 entrance fee, you can also take the funicular to Le Club Dauphin, a spectacular spill-over pool at the water's edge. Set on a hill inland, the more affordable **Hôtel le Panoramic** (3 av Albert 1er/www.hotel-lepanoramic.com, 04.93.76.00.37, closed 11 Nov-20 Dec, double €101-€137) has airy rooms with terraces and a dazzling harbour view. **La Voile d'Or** (av Jean Mermoz, 04.93.01.13.13/www.lavoiledor.fr, closed mid-Oct to Mar, double €291-€741) by Port St-Jean might be mistaken for an impressive family villa. The excellent traditional cuisine (menus €58-€91) and 1950s decor may not be trendy, but starlit nights at its breezy terrace restaurant make up for any stuffiness. The **Royal Riviera** (3 av Jean Monnet, St-Jean-Cap-Ferrat, 04.93.76.31.00/www.royale-riviera.com, closed 15 Dec-15 Jan, double €180-€640, menu €45) was recently revamped by designer guru

Grace Leo Andrieu; the pink *belle époque* palace is now a mix of Etruscan inspiration and third millenium chic, with a splendid pool, fitness centre and garden. If you can't afford to stay there, go for the delicious lunch buffet at La Pergola, the poolside restaurant. **Hôtel Brise Marine** (58 av Jean Mermoz, 04.93.76.04.36/hotel-brisemarine.com, closed Nov-Jan, double €119-€134) is an ochre- and turquoise-trimmed villa with a tangled garden, near La Paloma beach. **Résidence Bagatelle** (11 av Honoré Sauvan, 04.93.01.32.86, closed Nov-Mar, double €53-€91), on a quiet backstreet linking St-Jean and Beaulieu, has modestly priced rooms and an overgrown citrus garden where breakfast is served.

Tourist information

Office de Tourisme

59 av Denis Semeria, 06230 St-Jean-Cap Ferrat (04.93.76.08.90/fax 04.93.76.16.76). **Open** *June-Aug* 8.30am-6.30pm daily; *Sept-Apr* 8.30am-noon, 1-5pm Mon-Fri.

Beaulieu-sur-Mer

A charming *belle époque* resort that was long a favourite with holidaying Russian and British aristocrats, Beaulieu still has an old-world feel, with its neat rows of genteel but non-designer boutiques and ubiquitous palms. Well-heeled Sunday strollers and their yapping dogs jostle each other for space on **promenade Maurice**

Rouvier, a paved seaside path linking the port of Beaulieu to St-Jean-Cap-Ferrat via the late David Niven's pink castle; go early in the morning or at sunset to get the best of the view.

Gustave Eiffel (he of the tower) and Gordon Bennet, legendary director of the *New York Herald Tribune*, lived here. So did archaeologist Theodore Reinach, who was so enamoured of Ancient Greece that he built a fastidious and not-to-be-missed reconstruction of a fifth-century BC Athenian house. Situated in front of the Baie des Fourmis – so called because of the ant-like black rocks dotted about – the **Villa Kerylos**, is now a museum, with sunken marble bath, reclining sofas and antique-looking frescoes galore (plus some hidden modern amenities such as showers, loos and pianos).

The **Casino**, a small turn-of-the-century jewel on the seafront offering roulette, blackjack and baccarat for the staid, wealthy Cap-Ferrat crowd, is deliciously retro. So, too, is the **Tennis Club de Beaulieu-sur-Mer** (4 rue Alexandre 1ᵉʳ de Yougoslavie, 04.93.01.05.19, non-members €16 per day), a quaint club with eight clay courts.

East of Beaulieu, the Basse Corniche continues towards Monaco through the nondescript ribbon development of Eze-Bord-de-Mer and on to Cap-d'Ail, which would have little to recommend it were it not for a splendid (and well-signposted) pebbly beach, **Plage la Mala**, a democratic favourite equally prized by the Monaco jetset and Italian day-trippers. It's only a ten-minute walk from the Basse Corniche, but be prepared for a considerable trek down (and up!) the stone steps. Top up your energy reserves with the surprisingly good food at the beach shack.

Casino

4 rue Fernand Dunan (04.93.76.48.00/www.partouche.com). **Open** 11am-4am daily.

Villa Kerylos

impasse Gustave Eiffel (04.93.01.01.44/www.villa-kerylos.com). **Open** *Feb-June, Sept, Oct* 10.30am-6pm daily; *July, Aug* 10.30am-7pm daily; *Nov-Jan* 2-6pm Mon-Fri; 10am-6pm Sat, Sun. **Admission** €7; €5.50 7-18s; free under-7s.

Where to stay & eat

Relaxed yet stylish bistro **Les Agaves** (4 av Maréchal Foch, 04.93.01.13.12, closed Mon, lunch Tue and all Feb, menu €28) in the Palais des Anglais opposite the station is popular with locals for ravioli, steaks and aïoli. The Italianate **Le Métropole** (15 bd Leclerc, 04.93.01.00.08/www.lemetropole.com, closed mid-Oct to mid-Dec, rates €280-€690) has its own flower-lined walkway by the sea and an excellent restaurant

(average €76) serving an inspired mix of classic and Provençal dishes by chef Christian Metral. The *fin de siècle* Florentine **Hôtel La Réserve** (5 bd Leclerc/www.reservebeaulieu.com, 04.93.01.00.01, closed Nov, double €149-€732), where celebrities and royalty once flocked, is a discreetly elegant landmark, recently refurbished in sumptuous marble to match the refined but pricey Mediterranean cuisine (menus €46-€73) orchestrated by chef Christophe Cussac. **Hôtel Le Havre Bleu** (29 bd du Maréchal Joffre, 04.93.01.01.40/www.hotel-lehavrebleu.fr, double €45-€70) is a Victorian-style villa with simple, clean rooms, some with terraces. The seven-room **Auberge du Soleil** (av de la Liberté, Basse Corniche, Eze, 04.93.01.51.46, closed Nov, double €69.60, menus €19.82-€38.11) may not be glam but it's smack in front of the beach. Now under new ownership, its restaurant serves Mediterranean specialities and fresh fish.

The **Pâtisserie Lac** (35 bd Marioni, 04.93.01.35.85, closed Wed) is a must for sweet fiends: try its famous featherlight *fraisier*, a divine strawberry mousse cake. The retro-colonial **L'African Queen** (port de Plaisance, 04.93.01.10.85, average €34) is always lively; it offers standard brasserie fare plus a chance to rub elbows with stars like Jack Nicholson or Bono, who occasionally turn up for dinner.

In **Villa Kerylos** Reinach rebuilt Ancient Greece and added some fancy plumbing, too.

Tourist information

Office de Tourisme

pl Georges Clemenceau, 06310 Beaulieu-sur-Mer (04.93.01.02.21/www.ot-beaulieu-sur-mer.fr). **Open** *July-Sept* 9am-12.15pm, 2-5.30pm Mon-Sat; 9am-12.30pm Sun; *Oct-May* 9am-12.15pm, 2-5.30pm Mon-Sat.

The Moyenne Corniche

Eze

Perched photogenically on a pinnacle of rock 430 metres above sea level, Eze started life as a Celto-Ligurian settlement, passing over the ages from Phoenicians to Romans and from Lombards to Saracens. The village's glorious vistas inspired Nietzsche, who would stride up here in the 1880s from his Eze-Bord-de-Mer home, composing the third part of *Thus Spake Zarathustra* in his head. The steep mule path he followed (now called **sentier Frédéric-Nietzsche**) snakes through olive and pine groves. Allow an hour and a half for the upward slog.

Eze, where Zarathustra first spake.

Eze hosts the **Eze d'Antan Festival** in the third week of July, when the village is swamped by sword-toting knights and colourful pageantry. Cutesy Provençal boutiques go some way to marring Eze's charm the rest of the year, but a place where donkeys still haul groceries up the steep lanes can't be entirely ruined (unless, of course, they're financed by the tourist board).

In what remains of Eze's castle, at the summit of the village, the **Jardin Exotique** is a prickly blaze of flowering cacti and succulents, offering a sweeping panorama over the village's red-tiled roofs to the coast.

Jardin Exotique

rue du Château, Eze (04.93.41.10.30). **Open** *Mar-Apr* 9am-6.30pm daily; *May, June* 9am-7pm daily; *July, Aug* 9am-8pm daily; *Sept-Feb* 9am-5pm daily. **Admission** €2.50; free under-12s.

Where to stay & eat

Nestling beneath the castle ruins, the **Nid d'Aigle** (rue du Château, 04.93.41.19.08, closed Wed & Jan and dinner Nov-Apr, menus €21-€34) is an informal, family-run restaurant specialising in Provençal dishes does a tasty *daube niçoise*. The sumptuous rooms at the **Château de la Chèvre d'Or** (rue du Barri, 04.92.10.66.66/ www.chevredor.com, closed Nov-Feb, double €260-€720) have sweeping views along the coast, and there's a pool, too. At the Château's gourmet restaurant (menus €58-€180), chef Jean-Marc Delacourt specialises in classic Med-inspired dishes; if you're not up to the splurge, put on your finery and sip cocktails at sunset in the very romantic bar. **Château Eza** (rue de la Pise, 04.93.41.12.24, closed Nov-Mar, double €350-€700), a mini-castle at the top of endless crooked steps, has pricey rooms bordering on kitsch, with a choice of medieval armour or chintz; the highlight is the outdoor terrace restaurant (closed Nov-25 Dec, menus €45-€90) with romantic balconies for two, a sublime panorama and exquisite food. The **Auberge du Troubadour** (rue du Brec, 04.93.41.19.03, closed Mon & Sun and 17 Nov-20 Dec, end Feb & beg July, menus €28-€39) lacks a view, but offers reliable regional specialities and an extensive choice of wines.

Tourist information

Office de Tourisme

pl Général de Gaulle, 06360 Eze (04.93.41.26.00/ www.eze-riviera.com). **Open** *May-Sept* 9am-7pm Mon-Sat; 2-7pm Sun; *Oct-Apr* 9am-6.30pm Mon-Sat; 9.30am-1pm, 2-6.30pm Sun.

The Riviera

The Grande Corniche

Built under Napoléon along the route of the Aurelian Way (known in this stretch as the Via Julia Augusta), the Grande Corniche winds for 32km along the breathtaking precipices of the Alpes-Maritimes. It's a favourite recreational route for wannabe Formula One drivers, masochistic cyclists, scenery-lovers who don't suffer from vertigo and *To Catch a Thief* fans.

Dominating the road is **La Turbie** (from *tropea*, Latin for trophy), a spectacularly located village that is often shrouded in mountain mist. Basking in sleepy charm, it consists of little more than a row of ancient ochre houses, two town gates and an 18th-century church, **St-Michel-Archange**, with a host of 'attributed to' and 'school of' works. What puts the village on the map is the Roman **Trophée des Alpes**, a partly restored curve of white Doric columns set in a hilltop park. The Trophée was erected in 6BC to celebrate the victories of Augustus' troops over rowdy local tribes who had benefited from the confusion after the death of Julius Caesar to overrun the place; a copy of an inscription praising Augustus can be seen on the trophy, though the huge statue of the victor that once adorned it has long since gone. Inside the adjoining museum is a scale model of the original, and diverse artefacts unearthed from the site.

If it's sport, not history, you're after, the **Monte-Carlo Golf Club** is an 18-hole course with a vertiginous view. Star-gazers should head for the **Eze Astrorama**, a wildly popular astronomical show (planetarium, telescopes, videos), north of La Turbie.

Eze Astrorama
Rte de la Revere (04.93.41.23.04). **Open** *July, Aug* 6-10pm Mon-Sat; *Sept-June* 6-10pm Fri, Sat. **Admission** €6; €4.50 children.

Monte-Carlo Golf Club
rte du Mont Agel (04.92.41.50.70). **Open** *June-Sept* 8am-8pm daily; *Oct-May* 8am-6pm daily. **Price** €85 Mon-Fri, €100 Sun.

Trophée des Alpes
18 av Albert 1ᵉʳ (04.93.41.20.84). **Open** *mid-Sept to Mar* 10am-5pm Tue-Sun; *Apr to mid-June* 9.30am-6pm daily; *mid-June to mid-Sept* 9.30am-7pm daily. **Admission** €4, free under-18s.

Where to stay & eat

Besides offering pleasant rooms, La Turbie's **Hôtellerie Jérome** (20 rue de Compte de Cessole, 04.92.41.51.51, double €82) boasts a restaurant (closed Mon & Tue, menu €29-€40) in which chef Bruno Cirino concocts great country recipes with a Ligurian twist, such as roast chicken with chestnut stuffing and candied fennel, and caramelised apples with ricotta. Hanging off a cliff off the Grande Corniche, the **Roquebrune Vista Palace** (04.92.10.40.00/www.vistapalace.com, closed Feb to mid-Mar, double €197-€370) is an architectural eyesore of monstrous proportions; inside, however, the vast triangular rooms have a luxury-liner feel, with countless spellbinding vantage points. Its restaurant, **Le Vistaero** (open dinner only May-Sept, closed Feb to mid-Mar, menus €53-€90) cultivates classic French cuisine with a hint of Provençal whimsy.

Tourist information

La Mairie
06320 La Turbie (04.92.41.51.61). **Open** 9am-noon, 2-5pm Mon-Fri; 9am-noon Sat.

▶ Getting There & Around

▶ By car
From the Vieux Port in Nice, bd Carnot becomes the Basse Corniche (N98). Corniche André de Joly from pl Max Barel roundabout in Nice becomes the N7 Moyenne Corniche, which climbs to Eze via the Col de Villefranche. For the Grande Corniche take A8 autoroute exit no.57or bd Riquier north Nice and turn right at the sign marked Grande Corniche. From Roquebrune, follow signs to the Grande Corniche from the Basse or Moyenne Corniches.

▶ By train
Stations at Villefranche, Beaulieu, Eze-Bord-de-Mer and Cap-d'Ail are served by regular trains from Nice, some of which continue on to Ventimiglia in Italy. Beaulieu is also served by faster Italian trains on the Nice-Genova run, but not by French TGVs which go direct from Nice to Monaco. Shuttle buses connect Eze-Bord-de-Mer railway station and Eze village.

▶ By bus
Broch and **RCA** (04.93.85.61.81) run buses along the Basse Corniche between Nice and Menton every 20min. RCA's fairly frequent Nice-Beausoleil service (no.112) stops in Eze (and terminates there on Sun); three buses daily (Mon-Sat) run between Nice and Peille via La Turbie.

Monaco & Monte-Carlo

The Riviera bolt-hole for the very, very rich is so ridiculous that it has to be experienced to be believed.

Controlled by the Grimaldi family since 1297, the principality of Monaco is the last European state – apart from the Vatican – with an autocratic ruler. It's a perfect set-up: the prince holds benevolent but absolute sway over 32,000 residents – of whom only 6,000 are Monégasque citizens – and they, in return, are happy to barter democracy for tax breaks.

One look at the square in front of the casino – lined with Ferraris, Lamborghinis and Rolls-Royces (many hired just for the stay), with white-gloved *gendarmes* directing traffic – and you know this is a world apart. Here you can indulge your dress-code daydreams: from sables to labels, you can never be too ostentatiously rich. As for jewels, the bigger the better, and if they're real, never fear: there's a policeman for every 60 residents and some 300 surveillance cameras – in trees, at traffic lights, in lifts – guard the two-kilometre-square realm.

It wasn't always like this. When Menton and Roquebrune were whisked away from Grimaldi control in 1848, Europe's poorest state lost its main source of revenue: a tax on lemons. Then-ruler Charles III called in financier François Blanc, who set up the Société des Bains de Mer (SBM) to operate a casino on a hill named after the prince: Monte-Carlo. The crown took 10% of SBM profits. Blanc gave the French government a 4.8-million franc loan so it could finish building the Paris Opéra; in return, he got the Opéra's architect, Charles Garnier, to design the casino, plus a French-built railway to ship in gamblers. So fruitful was the venture that in 1870 the flourishing principality abolished taxes for nationals and anyone meeting certain residence requirements, and for companies based and trading here. That rule still stands, much to the delight of the world's top earners and tax-dodgers (*see p257*, **Banco**).

Nowadays, Monaco has a government of sorts, the 18-member National Council elected by Monégasque citizens (not residents). The Council's main job is to pass French legislation on to the reigning prince: if he approves, it becomes law in Monaco, too; if he doesn't, it doesn't. Apart from a tiff with France in 1962, when Paris tired of its richer citizens taking tax-refuge in Monaco and stationed troops along the border, relations between the principality and its bigger neighbour run pretty smoothly.

Everybody wants a piece of **Le Rocher**.

Much more smoothly, indeed, than the affairs of the Grimaldi family. Dapper Rainier III's 1956 marriage to Hollywood star Grace Kelly was a fairy tale that came to a tragic end when Princess Grace was killed in a car accident in 1982. Princess Caroline's first marriage ended disastrously, and her second husband was killed in 1990 in a speedboat race; she has since united the European blue-bloods by wedding Prince Ernst-August of Hanover. Her sister Stéphanie was stung by scandal when former-bodyguard husband Daniel Ducruet was photographed in a compromising position with a Belgian stripper, and is still a media magnet for her less-than-royal choice of suitors (recently a Swiss circus elephant trainer). The real pressure, though, seems to be on Prince Albert, who has been properly groomed to inherit his father's tiny kingdom, but so far remains single and has produced no heir.

Palais Princier: a fantastical exercise in total control.

Sightseeing

Glitzy Monte-Carlo is just one of Monaco's five districts. It packs in the **Casino**, with its **Salle Garnier** opera house, most of the shops and hotels and the slightly creepy **Musée National Automates et Poupées** doll museum.

Fontvieille is a concrete sprawl of high-rise, high-price apartments, many built on reclaimed land. It has some rather antiseptic museums, plus a lovely rose garden dedicated to Princess Grace and the cactus-filled **Jardin Exotique**.

Le Rocher – or Monaco-Ville – is the medieval town, dominated by the **Palais Princier**. Le Rocher abounds in shops purveying touristic paraphernalia. The neo-Byzantine **Cathédrale de Monaco** is the final resting place of many Grimaldi princes and of Princess Grace. More Grimaldis can be seen in the **Historial des Princes de Monaco** waxworks museum. Head for the infinitely more fascinating **Musée Océanographique** or the old masters housed in the **Musée de la Visitation**.

La Condamine, the harbour area, has a good daily food market, the **Eglise Ste-Dévote** and industrial lofts that have been turned into ateliers for a select group of international artists – Arman, Botero, Sosno, Adami and Matta. This Cité des Artistes boasts an art gallery and a brasserie where creative ideas can be swapped over an apéritif. If you're on the celebrity watch, **Larvotto**, the eastern strip where Monaco's beaches are located, is your best bet: you may glimpse residents Boris Becker, Ringo Starr or Claudia Schiffer at **Le Sporting Club**.

Cathédrale de Monaco
av St Martin (00.377-93.30.87.70). **Open** 8.30am-7pm daily. **Admission** free.
Built in 1875, this Romanesque-y, Byzantine-y cathedral has a 15th-century altarpiece by Louis Bréa, a grandiose marble altar, tombs of the princes of Monaco, and a simple pavement slab for Princess Grace.

Collection des Voitures Anciennes
terrasse de Fontvieille. (00.377-92.05.28.56).
Open 10am-6pm daily. **Admission** €6; €3 8-14s; free under-8s.
Prince Rainier's vintage car collection, from a 1903 De Dion Bouton to a 1986 Lamborghini Countach.

Eglise Ste-Dévote
pl Ste Dévote (00.377-93.50.52.60). **Open** 8am-6.30pm daily. **Admission** free.
This portside church was built in 1870 on the site where, according to legend, Monaco's patron saint was guided ashore by a dove after surviving a shipwreck off Africa. Medieval pirates stole the saint's relics; they were caught, and their ship burnt. A replica goes up in flames in front of the church every 26 January.

Jardin Animalier
terrasse de Fontvieille (00.377-93.25.18.31).
Open *Oct-Feb* 10am-noon, 2-5pm daily; *Mar-May* 10am-noon, 2-6pm daily; *June-Sept* 9am-noon, 2-7pm daily. **Admission** €4; €2 under-14s.
After a visit to Africa in 1954, Prince Rainier procured countless varieties of monkeys and sundry other wild beasts and exotic birds for this mini-zoo.

Jardin Exotique et Grotte de l'Observatoire
62 bd du Jardin Exotique (00.377-93.15.29.80).
Open *mid-May to mid-Sept* 9am-7pm daily; *mid-Sept*

to mid-May 9am-6pm daily. Closed mid-Nov to Dec. **Admission** (incl Musée d'Anthropologie Préhistorique) €6.40; €3.20 6-18s; free under-6s.

Inaugurated in 1933, this succulent wonderland of nearly 7,000 bizarrely shaped tropical specimens has everything from giant Aztec agaves to ball-shaped 'mother-in-law's' cushion' cacti. The grotto inside the garden contains a stalactite- and stalagmite-lined Neolithic dwelling 60 metres underground.

Musée d'Anthropologie Préhistorique

bd du Jardin Exotique (00.377-93.15.80.06). **Open** *mid-May to mid-Sept* 9am-7pm daily; *mid-Sept to mid-Nov to mid-May* 9am-6pm daily. Closed mid-Nov to Dec. **Admission** (incl Jardin Exotique and Grotte de l'Observatoire) €6.40; €3.20 6-18s; free under-6s.

Relics of Stone Age life on the Riviera when mammoths, elephants and hippos ruled. Bones galore of extinct animal species and impressive Cro-Magnon skeletons, all found in the Grimaldi caves (which can be visited in Balzi Rossi, just over the border in Italy).

Musée de la Chapelle de la Visitation

pl de la Visitation (00.377-93.50.07.00). **Open** 10am-4pm Tue-Sun. **Admission** €3.05; €1.52 6-14s; free under-6s.

This 17th-century chapel houses religious paintings by Rubens, Zurbaran and Italian Baroque masters.

Musée des Cires Historial des Princes de Monaco

27 rue Basse (00.377-93.30.39.05). **Open** *Feb-Sept* 10am-6pm daily; *Oct-Jan* 11am-5pm daily. **Admission** €3.80; €2 8-14s; free under-8s.

Everything you've ever wanted to know (and probably rather more) about the Grimaldi dynasty in wax, with life-sized figures in full regalia.

Musée National Automates et Poupées

17 av Princesse Grace (00.377-93.30.91.26). **Open** *Apr-Sept* 10am-6.30pm daily; *Oct-Mar* 10am-12.15pm, 2.30-6.30pm daily. **Admission** €5; €3.05 6-14s; free under-6s.

18th- and 19th-century dolls and mechanical toys, set into motion several times daily.

Musée Naval

terrasse de Fontvieille (00.377-92.05.28.48). **Open** 10am-6pm daily. **Admission** €4; €2.50 8-18s; free under-8s.

Prince Rainier's scale models of famous sea vessels.

Musée Océanographique

av St-Martin (00.377-93.15.36.00/www.oceano.mc). **Open** *Apr-June* 9am-7pm daily; *July-Aug* 9am-8pm daily; *Oct-Mar* 10am-6pm daily. **Admission** €4; €2.50 8-18s; free under-8s.

Founded in 1910 by Albert I, the aquarium contains nature's most bizarre creatures, plus bream circling endlessly in their cylindrical tank like bored Monégasque millionaires. A live coral reef and a giant shark lagoon are a guaranteed thrill for kids.

Musée des Souvenirs Napoléoniens et Collection des Archives Historiques du Palais

pl du Palais (00.377.93.25.18.31). **Open** *June-Sept* 9.30am-6.30pm daily; *Oct, Nov* 10am-5pm daily; *Dec-May* 10.30am-12.30pm, 2-5pm daily. Closed 12 Nov-16 Dec. **Admission** €4; €2 8-14s; free under-8s.

Bonaparte buffs will enjoy the vast display of objects and documents from the First Empire, while the more Monaco-smitten can peruse an exhibit of historic charters and Grimaldi medals.

Musée des Timbres et des Monnaies

terrasse de Fontvieille (00.377-93.15.41.50). **Open** *July, Aug* 10am- 6pm daily; *Oct-June* 10am-5pm daily. **Admission** €3; €1.50 12-18s; free under-12s.

More conspicuous money in this coin and stamp display covering four centuries of Monégasque minting.

Palais Princier

pl du Palais (00.377-93.25.18.31). **Open** *June-Sept* 9.30am-6.20pm daily; *Oct* 10am-5pm daily. Closed Nov-May. **Admission** €4; €8-14s; free under-8s.

The sugary palace, built over a 13th-century Genoese fortress, is closed to the public when the prince is in residence – signalled by a red and white banner. The 30-minute tour takes in the frescoed gallery, sumptuous bedrooms, state apartments with Venetian furnishings, the throne room and the mosaic courtyard. The changing of the guard takes place at 11.55am daily in the palace square.

Arts & entertainment

Le Cabaret du Casino

pl du Casino (00.377-92.16.36.36). **Shows** 10.30pm Tue-Sun. **Admission** €40. **Credit** AmEx, DC, MC, V.

Slick cabaret shows *pour touristes* offer an alternative to gambling, including Parisian import Le Crazy Horse with its famous 'art of the nud'e dancers, in a red-velvety nightclub atmosphere.

Casino de Monte-Carlo

pl du Casino (00.377-92.16.23.00). **Open** (over-21s only, ID essential). *Salons européens* noon-late daily; slot machines 2pm-late daily; *Salons privés* 3pm-late; *Club anglais* 10pm-late. **Admission** €10 (plus €10 for Salons privés & Club anglais).

The ornate gambling house was dreamed up by Monaco's prince in 1863, to generate new revenue. When his early attempts failed, he turned it over to businessman François Blanc, who sought out star architect Charles Garnier to build the new casino, and founded the now all-powerful Société des Bains de Mer (SBM) to run it. In 1962, Prince Rainier III made the state the principal shareholder. Old-fashioned precepts still apply: no clergymen or Monégasque citizens are allowed into the gaming rooms, and a sports jacket and a tie are de rigueur. Roulette has a €5 minimum bet, stakes are higher in the Salons privés and the Club anglais, which offer chemin de fer, trente-et-quarante, blackjack, and craps.

The Riviera

Grimaldi Forum

10 av Princesse Grace (00.377-99.99.30.00/ www.grimaldiforum.com). **Open** noon-7pm Mon-Sat. **Admission** varies.

This vast ultramodern exhibition and cultural centre is the Principality's state-of-the-art jump into the new millennium: a multi-levelled modular glass and steel complex with everything from concert halls, seasonal art and trade shows to a cybercafé.

Monte-Carlo Beach Club

av Princesse Grace (04.93.28.66.66). **Open** *Apr-Oct* 9am-7pm daily. **Admission** €50 mid-Apr to mid May & mid-Sept to mid-Oct; €75 mid-May to mid-Sept. **Credit** AmEx, DC, MC, V.

The favoured summer playground for Hermès-towel-toting socialites. Most of the action is by the huge heated seawater pool where Princess Stéphanie does her laps. Extras include jet-skiing, parasailing, water-skiing and windsurfing.

Monte-Carlo Country Club

155 av Princesse Grace (04.93.41.30.15/ www.mccc.mc). **Open** *July, Aug* 8am-9pm daily; Sept-June 8am-8.15pm daily. **Admission** one-day €36; €26 under-18s. **Credit** AmEx, DC, MC, V.

The swankiest club on the Riviera has clay tennis courts, squash, and a heated open-air pool (open May-Oct) with airjets, waterfalls and a counter-current basin for aquatic workout enthusiasts.

Salle Garnier

pl du Casino (00.377-92.16.23.67). **Box office** 10am-5.30pm Tue-Sun. **Tickets** €15-€110. **Credit** MC, V.

Within Monaco's splendid Casino, Garnier's chocolate-box opera hall, replete with frescoed ceilings and wreath-toting sculpted cherubs is currently closed for renovation. In the meantime, opera and ballet – including the innovative performances of Ballet de Monte-Carlo's Jean-Christophe Maillot – are mainly in the Grimaldi Forum.

Stade Louis II

7 av des Castelans (00.377-92.05.40.11). **Open** guided tours by appointment at 2.30pm & 4pm Mon, Tue, Thur, Fri. **Admission** €3.81; €1.91 under-12s.

This unsightly circular concrete block houses a gigantic sports complex with gyms, an athletics track, a pool – and the soccer pitch where AS Monaco play their home games. Football is not high on most Monégasques' priorities: when they won the French league in 1997, Prince Albert, ringleader of the hardline fans, had to bus in 2,000 schoolchildren for the victory party, and despite being one of the wealthiest clubs in the league, the 2001-02 season has seen them languishing in the nether regions.

Stade Nautique Rainier III

quai Albert I (00.377-93.30.64.83). **Open** *May-June, Sept-Oct* 9am-6pm daily; *July, Aug* 9am-8pm daily. **Admission** €4. **No credit cards.**

This beautiful Olympic-sized seawater outdoor pool is a great place for serious swimming. Leave your designer swimsuits behind: no one's watching.

Théâtre du Fort St-Antoine

av de la Quarantaine (00.377-93.25.66.12). **Box office** one hour before show. **Shows** July, Aug. **Tickets** €4.57-€9.15. **No credit cards.**

This lovely stone theatre-in-the-round was built on the ruins of an 18th-century fortress overlooking the sea and is magical for open-air concerts or theatre productions on starry summer nights.

Les Thermes Marins de Monte-Carlo

2 av de Monte-Carlo (00.377-92.16.40.40). **Open** 8am-8.30pm daily. **Credit** AmEx, DC, MC, V.

A luxurious temple of thalassotherapy with state-of-the-art fitness centre and heated seawater pool. Special packages include quit-smoking cures and a back-in-shape programme for new mothers. A one-day package with four treatments costs €125.

Restaurants & brasseries

Bice

17 av Spelugues (00.377-93.25.20.30). **Open** noon-2.30pm, 8pm-11.30pm daily. **Average** €50. **Lunch menu** €30. **Credit** AmEx, MC, V.

This chic business lunch spot has Principality prices, but the authentic Italian dishes, such as veal ossobuco and tiramisu, are good.

Bar et Boeuf

av Princesse Grace (00.377-92.16.60.60/www.alainducasse.com). **Open** 8pm-1am daily. Closed Oct-Apr. **Average** €92. **Credit** AmEx, DC, MC, V.

Ducasse's conceptual contemporary food revolves around *bar* (sea bass) and *boeuf* (beef), in all sorts of

A whale of a time at the **Musée Océanographique**. *See p255.*

world-influenced preparations, served in a refreshing, Philippe Starck-designed setting. High tables and bar stools allow you to be both visible and approachable: high priorities in Monaco.

Le Café de Paris

pl du Casino (00.377.92.16.25.54). **Open** 7am-1am daily. **Average** €38. **Credit** AmEx, DC, MC, V.
The renowned turn-of-the-century brasserie next to the casino has a sprawling outdoor terrace so perfect for people-watching that it compensates somewhat for the pricey espresso. The reliable fare ranges from oysters and grilled fish to *hamburger-frites*. Try the crêpe Suzette, inadvertently invented here in the 1900s when a creation by Escoffier caught fire.

Castelroc

pl du Palais (00.377-93.30.36.68). **Open** *mid-June to mid-Sept* noon-2.30pm, 7.30-11pm Mon-Fri, Sun; *mid-Sept to mid-June* noon-2.30pm Mon-Fri, Sun; Closed Dec-Jan. **Menus** €19.82-€37.35. **Credit** AmEx, MC, V.
Don't be put off by the touristy air of the outdoor terrace smack in front of the palace: this affordable family-run bistro is an established local haunt for seafood such as stockfish and steamed scampi.

La Coupole

Hôtel Mirabeau, 1 av Princesse Grace (00.377-92.16.65.65). **Open** noon-2.30pm, 8-10pm daily. **Menus** €55-€77. **Credit** AmEx, DC, MC, V.
Under chef Michel de Matteis, this restaurant has become a mecca for enlightened gastronomes. Specialities include ravioli stuffed with lobster, Swiss chard and ricotta, coquilles St-Jacques in truffle sauce, and a divine caramelised apple soufflé.

Louis XV

Hôtel de Paris, pl du Casino (00.377.92.16.38.40/ www.alain-ducasse.com). **Open** noon-2pm, 8-10pm Mon, Thur-Sun (plus 8-10pm Wed in July, Aug). Closed two weeks in Feb and Dec. **Menus** €76-€150. **Credit** AmEx, DC, MC, V.
This jewel box of a dining room offers the ultimate Riviera gilt trip and one of the most glamorous outdoor terraces in the world. This was Alain Ducasse's first restaurant and it's still his best, although he flies in to supervise, among his many other concerns. The food is a contemporary update of the sturdy, peasant food native to the coast and hinterlands from Nice to Genoa, including superb vegetable and fish dishes, complemented by a remarkable cellar.

La Rose des Vents

Lavarotto Beach (00.377-97.70.46.96). **Open** 8am-midnight Tue-Sat; 8am-3pm Sun. **Menus** €10-€60. **Credit** AmEx, MC, V.
Dine on fresh homemade pasta with your toes in the sand at this recently opened Italian family-style restaurant next to the Grimaldi Forum. The copious portions of grilled swordfish, scampi and tuna are brought in daily from the local fishermen, and the desserts – a divine coffee *panna cotta* or amaretto flan – are the real thing from across the border.

Banco

Monaco's financial institutions have been in a flurry of late, thanks to American legislation demanding that all banks outside the USA, including offshore or so-called tax havens, submit information on all American citizens and concerns maintaining accounts with them.

Desperate to prove its good faith, the principality invited the Banque de France to examine the situation. The team headed by Arnaud de Montebourg, an eminent lawyer and politician (the same tracker of tricky practices who wanted to bring Jacques Chirac to court over Paris' public housing schemes) resulted in a certain panic among Monaco's private banks, who brought in independent experts to oversee their internal auditing. Just how independent these experts really were is doubtful.

Perhaps Monaco is not the haven of honesty and integrity it likes to present. As recently as 2000, the Banque Gothard, an independent Monegasque bank (largely Grimaldi-owned), was brought to trial for having accepted large deposits in cash – literally in suitcases – without questioning too closely the origin, which resulted in two of its directors receiving prison sentences. Another scandal saw an American investment advisor set up shop in luxurious premises in the port area, fleecing hundreds of would-be market-players before fleeing with their millions.

Nonetheless, you can't complain, particularly in Monaco where trade unions are virtually nonexistant, along with the right to demonstrate, whatever the cause. It's best not to disturb the smooth running of the money-machine, which makes a show of maintaining public security with highly visible uniformed police and some 300 video surveillance cameras placed all over the city, as proof that the city's high-flyers are getting their money's worth. Cameras cover all ways in and out of the territory, including the railway station and bus terminals, and tracking even the workers who commute from Nice or Menton, ensuring that nobody escapes the all-pervading electronic eyes. If so much attention is given to the surveillance of the ordinary mortal, surely the same intense scrutiny must be given to the principality's biggest money earner, its banks.

Bars & nightlife

Sass Café
11 av Princesse Grace (00.377-93.25.52.00). **Open** 8pm-late daily. **Admission** free. **Credit** AmEx, DC, MC, V.
A hotspot offering live music and pricey international dishes, with the quintessential Monte-Carlo mix of Eurotrash, club-hoppers and dressed-to-kill women who'll be dancing on the tables by 2am.

Le Sporting Club
av Princesse Grace (00.377-92.16.22.77). **Open** 10.30pm-late daily. **Admission** €46 (incl 1st drink). **Credit** AmEx, DC, MC, V.
This six-hectare seaside complex is frequented by royalty, models, pop stars, Middle Eastern princes and mini-skirted demoiselles in Cartier. Jimmy'z (00.377-92.16.36.36, open Apr-Nov 11.30pm-dawn Wed-Sun), the disco for beautiful people, requires chic dress and an amply stuffed wallet. Le Sporting d'Eté, a multi-level entertainment complex, hosts big-name crooners.

Stars & Bars
6 quai Antoine 1ᵉʳ (00.377-97.97.95.95). **Open** *July, Aug* 10am-5am daily; *Sept-June* 11am-midnight Mon-Thur; 11am-2am Fri-Sun. **Credit** AmEx, MC, V.
This portside American-style sports bar is packed with locals – plus racing drivers and the odd rock or film star. There's Tex-Mex food, a kids' playroom, a video games room and a small upstairs club (admission €3-€8) with live bands.

Le Rocher: surrounded by a few miles of road for would-be racing drivers.

Zebra Square
Grimaldi Forum, 10 av Princesse Grace (00.377-99.99.25.50). **Open** *bar* noon-6am; *restaurant* noon-3pm, 8pm-midnight daily. **Credit** AmEx, DC, MC, V.
The hot new after-hours lounge and restaurant atop the Grimaldi Forum has lots of high-tech, low-light atmosphere and oversized cushioned booths. The nouveau-Provençal cuisine is uneven, but the terrace is a wonderfully romantic spot for summer dining. In the wee hours top models, Middle Eastern princes and visiting screen idols can be found tucking into a cold buffet after an evening at Jimmy'Z.

Shopping

Luxury knows no bounds in Monte-Carlo, from the rash of jewellery shops near the casino to the designer boutiques along the boulevard des Moulins and avenue Princesse Grace. In the place du Casino, the Galerie du Metropole is an upscale three-storey mall. Rue Grimaldi offers the flip, hip side of fashion. True Monégasques shop in the Centre Commerciale in Fontvieille, a large mall with mega-supermarket.

Where to stay

Hôtel Columbus
23 av des Papalins (00.377-92.05.90.00). **Doubles** €190-€285. **Credit** AmEx, DC, MC, V.
Launched by Ken McCulloch, founder and former owner of the wildly successful Malmaison chain, this hip new lifestyle hotel is putting a contemporary spin on Monaco's stuffy, old-world image. On the harbour of Fontvieille, the 153 rooms and 31 suites are decked out in soft lavenders and creamy beiges, with luxurious leather upholstered beds, feather duvets and a cabinet equipped with a CD player and Internet. The bar is a favorite haunt of Formula One drivers, presided by part-owner, David Coulthard.

Hôtel Helvetia
1bis rue Grimaldi (00.377-93.30.21.71). Closed two weeks Dec. **Double** €54-€68. **Credit** AmEx, MC, V.
A stone's throw from the port, this clean, affordable hotel has unremarkable decor but friendly staff.

Hôtel Hermitage
sq Beaumarchais (00.377-92.16.40.00/www.sbm.mc). **Double** €340-€590. **Credit** AmEx, DC, MV, V.
A *belle époque* landmark of understated elegance, with a stained-glass-domed *jardin d'hiver* designed by Gustave Eiffel. Comfortable modern rooms; the more expensive ones have balconies with harbour views. Its rooftop restaurant **Le Vista Mar** (00.377-92.16.27.72, menus €39-€55) offers exquisite seafood.

Hôtel de Paris
pl du Casino (00.377-92.16.30.00/www.sbm.mc). **Double** €365-€685. **Credit** AmEx, DC, MC, V.
The most luxurious of the three hotels owned by the Grimaldi-run Société Bains de Mer, this rococo-

Fireworks over the Port Hercule in Monaco's **Fête Nationale** in November.

style palace built in 1865 was frequented by every-one from Sarah Bernhardt to Churchill. Majestic grandeur still prevails – if funds are short, soak up the atmosphere in its old-world bar.

Monte-Carlo Grand Hôtel

12 av des Spélugues (00.377-93.50.65.00/ www.montecarlograndhotel.com). **Double** €230-€520. Closed Dec-Feb. **Credit** AmEx, DC, MC, V. This high-rise hotel built over the sea may be glitz-less and efficiently modern, but it's also family-friendly, with a choice of restaurants and bars, a fitness centre, rooftop swimming pool and casino.

Essentials

The international phone code for Monaco is 00 377. If you're calling from France, dial 00 377 then the number. When phoning a Monégasque number from inside the principality, omit the code. To call abroad – including France – from Monaco, use the international prefix 00 then the country code (33 for France). Letters from Monaco must bear Monégasque stamps. Although not part of the Europian Union, the euro is now the official currency.

Getting there

By helicopter

Heli-Air Monaco, Fontvieille (00.377-92.05.00.50). A seven-minute flight from Nice airport costs €77; €38.50 under-12s; free under-2s.

By car

Leave the A8 autoroute at exit no.57 or no.58 or by N98 (Basse Corniche), the coast road from Nice to the west and Cap Martin and Menton in the east.

By train

Monaco-Monte-Carlo station is served by regular trains on the Cannes-Nice-Menton-Ventimiglia line, as well as a few TGVs direct from Paris.

By bus

From Nice *gare routière* **RCA** and **Broch** (information 04.93.21.30.83) run services every 15 min Mon-Sat (every 20min Sun) along the Basse Corniche road between Nice and Menton, stopping at Monaco.

Tourist information

Seven public lifts and a number of escalators ferry people from car park sea-level areas up to Monaco-Ville and Monte-Carlo.

Direction des Tourismes et des Congés de la Principauté de Monaco

2A bd des Moulins, 98000 Monaco (00.377-92.16.61.16/www.monaco-congres.com). **Open** 9am-7pm Mon-Sat, 10am-noon Sun.

Postes et Télégraphes

Palais de la Scala, 1 av Henri Dunant (00.377-97.97.25.25). **Open** 8am-7pm Mon-Fri; 8am-noon Sat.

Roquebrune to Menton

Millionaires hide themselves away on the wild Cap-Martin coast, while gardening aficionados flock to Menton's botanical wonders.

(see p225)

Roquebrune-Cap-Martin

Wedged between Monaco and Menton, **Cap-Martin** is one of the Riviera's loveliest stretches of wild coast, cloaked in pines, firs, olive and mimosa trees and studded with luxury hideaways, most of them hidden from mere mortal view in the millionaires' row of the *domaine privé du Cap-Martin*. Empress Eugénie, Churchill, Coco Chanel, Le Corbusier and WB Yeats lived (and, in the case of the latter two, died) here, as did Emperor Bokassa. A white rocky seaside footpath, the Sentier Douanier, winds around the peninsula (*see p225*), passing by **Le Cabanon**, Le Corbusier's tiny modular beach cottage (call tourist office for visits Tue & Fri), set just before the Pointe de Cabbé. West of here, the curved beach of the **Plage du Golfe Bleu** is a favourite landing spot for hang-gliders.

The architect, who drowned while swimming here in 1965, had the foresight to design himself an impressive memorial in the cemetery (open 10am-noon, 2-5pm daily) in the old village of **Roquebrune**, which rises above the Cap-Martin peninsula. Carved into the rock above the Grande Corniche, this handsome *village perché* started life in the tenth century as a fortified Carolingian fiefdom. For five centuries, from 1355, it belonged to the Grimaldis. Up the steep stairways at the top of the village is the **Château de Roquebrune**, which was almost fairy tale-ified by an English owner in the 1920s until the locals kicked up a stink. It now has four floors of historical displays, lordly armour galore and a tenth-century dungeon. On the chemin du St-Roch, not far from the cemetery, stands one of the oldest trees in the world: the *olivier millénaire* 1,000-year-old olive tree.

For the energetic, the Sentier Massolin is little more than a giant staircase leading from Roquebrune village down to the coast via **Carnolès**, the much less exclusive seaside suburb of the Cap, whose holiday flats sprawl eastwards until they merge into Menton.

Château de Roquebrune

pl du Château (04.93.35.07.22). **Open** July-Aug 10am-12.30pm, 3-7.30pm daily; Sept, Apr-June 10am-12.30pm, 2-6.30pm daily; Oct, Feb-Mar 10am-12.30pm, 2-6pm daily; Nov-Jan 10am-12.30pm, 2-5pm daily. **Admission** €3.50; €1.60 7-18s; free under-7s.

Where to stay & eat

In Cap-Martin is a small, reasonably priced gem on the water's edge, the **Hôtel Westminster** (14 av Louis Laurens, 04.93.35.00.68/ www.westminster06.com, closed mid-Nov to mid-Feb except Christmas/NewYear, double €45-€78), with a glorious view and a secluded cove just down the street. In old Roquebrune, **Au Grand Inquisiteur** (18 rue du Château, 04.93.35.05.37, closed Mon & Tue and Nov to mid-Dec, menus €24-€35F), once the château's sheep pen, serves classic southern French dishes and a whopping assortment of cheeses. For a breathtaking view, dine on the terrace of the **Hôtel-Restaurant des Deux-Frères** (pl des Deux Frères, 04.93.28.99.00, double €90), an impeccably run inn on the esplanade at the foot of the village; its restaurant serves traditional cuisine (closed Mon, plus dinner Sun Sept-June and 15 Nov-15 Dec, menus €21-€49); stylish dinner, too. Across the square, atmospheric café **La Grotte** (3 pl des Deux Frères, 04.93.35.00.04, closed Wed and Nov, average €16) is hollowed out of the rock face. The food is simple: salads, hot *plats du jour* and pretty good pizzas.

Tourist information

Roquebrune Office de Tourisme

218 av Aristide Briand, 06190 Roquebrune (04.93.35.62.87). **Open** May-June, Sept 9am-12.30pm, 2-6.30pm Mon-Sat; July-Aug 9am-1pm, 3-7pm daily; Oct-Apr 9am-12.30pm, 2-6pm Mon-Sat.

Menton

Menton, last stop on the Côte before the Italian border, has preserved a certain geriatric charm. It claims to have the mildest climate on the Riviera, with 316 cloudless days a year. Lemon trees thrive here and the humble fruit – juiced, iced, painted on plates or amassed in gigantic kitsch floats for the annual Fête du Citron in February – is slowly replacing the zimmer frame as Menton's official symbol.

After more than six centuries of Monégasque domination, Menton voted to become French in 1860. With invasion or takeover no longer a threat, the town expanded beyond its fortified walls and over the terraced green hillsides. In

Menton's *vieille ville* has plenty of stairs to keep pensioners healthy.

1860, British physician Henry Bennet recommended Menton as the ideal site for a seaside health resort. Before long, wealthy Britons and Russians began gracing its shores, bringing tea rooms and botanical gardens (*see p263*). Writers, artists and musicians – among them Monet, Maupassant, Flaubert and Liszt – also sojourned in the lemon-scented city.

The sea air wasn't always restorative. Tuberculosis sufferers like Robert Louis Stevenson (who discovered the virtues of opium in Menton) and Katherine Mansfield, holed-up in her tiny villa Isola Bella, found that the seaside dampness only worsened their condition.

The tone of present-day Menton is still set by its dilapidated *belle époque* villas and the public **Jardin Biovès** with its bitter orange trees, and by historic tropical gardens. But there's modernity, too: Jean Cocteau left his mark, as did architect Eileen Gray, whose miniature 1930s cube-house, later owned by painter Graham Sutherland, is visible on route de Castellar.

Menton has few nocturnal hotspots, and the gambling at the casino is low-key. Year-round, however, smartly dressed Italians can be seen strolling along the seafront **promenade du Soleil**, scooping up fruit every morning in the covered market that sits behind the quays beneath the *vieille ville*, or sunbathing topless on the uninspiring pebbly beach. Indeed, border-hopping is a favourite pastime here: less-welcome visitors include cigarette smugglers and would-be illegal immigrants, while Mentonnais head into Italy for bargains at Ventimiglia market on Friday or down the

coast for ice cream at San Remo.

The **Musée des Beaux-Arts**, an 18th-century former summer retreat for the Princes of Monaco, has European paintings ranging from Italian primitives to a beautiful *Virgin and Child* by Louis Bréa, and works by contemporary artists including Graham Sutherland, an honorary Mentonnais. The palace is surrounded by the **Jardin des Agrumes**, an extravaganza of 400 citrus trees.

The *salle des mariages* (registry office) of the **Hôtel de Ville** was decorated by Jean Cocteau in the 1950s. It features splendid murals of swirling seas, a fish-eyed fisherman and his straw-hatted bride, as well as kitsch palm tree candelabras and a mock panther-skin carpet – perhaps not the most auspicious background for a wedding: the bride's mother looks royally pissed off, as does the groom's angry ex-wife and her well-armed brother. There's more Cocteau in a fortified stone bastion on the waterfront, where the **Musée Cocteau** contains works donated by the artist, ranging from beach-pebble mosaics and Aubusson-inspired tapestries to ceramic vases and pastels.

Two blocks north of the Hôtel de Ville, the **Musée de Préhistoire Régionale** shows what life was like on the Riviera a million years ago, with remains from Vallonet, Lazaret and the Grimaldi caves. East of here, the Italianate *vieille ville*, a largely pedestrian zone, climbs uphill to the Baroque **St-Michel** church (open 10am-noon, 3-5pm Mon-Fri, Sun; 3-5pm Sat), which has a gilded marble interior with *trompe l'oeil* dome and altarpiece of St Michael slaying the dragon.

The Riviera

The 1,000-year-old olive tree in Roquebrune is the oldest resident of all.

The pretty square in front hosts Menton's long-established **Festival de Musique** each August (*see chapter* **The Festive South**).

Higher still in the *vieille ville* is the **Cimetière du Vieux-Château**, a terraced cemetery with great views, where artist Aubrey Beardsley and the Reverend William Webb Ellis – credited with being the first person to pick up a soccer ball and run with it, thus inventing rugby – rest in peace, along with a lot of Russian dignitaries. Heading east, promenade de la Mer leads into **Garavan**, a leafy quarter of romantic villas. Just off the promenade, the **Jardin Val Rahmeh** (*see p263*) is a tropical garden founded in 1905 by Lord Radcliffe.

Hôtel de Ville
17 rue de la République (04.92.10.50.00). **Salle des mariages open** 8.30am-noon, 1.30-5pm Mon-Fri. **Admission** €1.50.

Musée des Beaux-Arts
Palais Carnolès, 3 av de la Madone (04.93.35.49.71). **Open** 10am-noon, 2-6pm Mon, Wed-Sun. **Admission** free.

Musée Cocteau
Le Bastion, quai Napoléon III (04.93.57.72.30). **Open** 10am-noon, 2-5pm Mon, Wed-Sun. **Admission** €3; free under-18s.

Musée de Préhistoire Régionale
rue Loredan-Larchey (04.93.35.84.64). **Open** 10am-noon, 2-6pm Mon, Wed-Sun. **Admission** free.

Where to stay & eat

The *belle époque* **Hôtel Aiglon** (7 av de la Madone, 04.93.57.55.55/ www.hotelaiglon.net, closed 5 Nov-15 Dec, double €62-€134) is the epitome of old Riviera charm. It has a garden lined with towering banana palms and rooms with frescoes and mouldings. It also boasts a good pool-side restaurant (menus €29-€45.80). **Hôtel des Ambassadeurs** (3 rue des Partouneaux, 04.93.28.75.75, double €91-€122) is a faded mini-palace with a central location.

In the heart of the old town, stone-vaulted **Braijade Meridiounale** (66 rue Longue, 04.93.35.65.65, closed Wed except July-Aug, and end Nov, menus €21-€40) is a favourite for local specialities, such as *brochettes* grilled over an open fire, tripe and *aïoli*. **Le Darkoum** (23 rue St-Michel, 04.93.35.44.88, closed Mon & Tue and Jan & Mar, menus €15-€21) is a small family-run Moroccan restaurant; try the *briouates de keftas* (crisp fried pastry filled with beef and coriander). **Le Lion d'Or** (7 rue des Marins, 04.93.35.74.67, closed Nov, average €45) is reputed for its classic regional cuisine and seafood, with fish of the day delivered straight from the town's fishing boats. Surrounded by lemon and avocado trees on a lush hillside by the Italian border, **Restaurant Mirazur** (30 av Aristide Briand, 04.92.41.86.86, closed Jan, menus €30-€40) has been tranformed from 40s café into an ultra-modern, glass and chrome, three-storey bistro and bar. Beyond the dazzling sea view, it boasts refined Mediterranean fare under the wing of part-owner, celebrated Grasse chef, Jacques Chibois.

Tourist information

Menton Office de Tourisme
Palais de l'Europe, 8 av Boyer, 06500 Menton (04.92.41.76.76/www.villedementon.com). **Open** Oct-May 8.30am-12.30pm, 1.30-6pm Mon-Sat; June-Sept 8.30am-6pm Mon-Sat; 10am-noon Sun.

Office du Patrimoine
Hôtel d'Adhemar de Lartagnac, 24 rue St-Michel (04.92.10.33.66). **Open** 9am-noon, 2-5pm Mon-Fri. Visits of historic sights and private gardens.

North of Menton

From Menton, a series of narrow roads fans out northwards through dramatic mountain scenery to a cluster of *villages perchés*.

Gorbio sits on a hilltop surrounded by olive groves, which used to provide the town's only livelihood. It now makes money from tourists, too, who are attracted to its narrow arched streets, especially during the Procession des Limaces (snails) on the feast of Corpus Christi

Gardens of Eden

The real estate-scarred seafront and traffic-snarled coast roads make it hard to see the Côte d'Azur as the Garden of Eden. Yet miraculously, most of the extraordinary gardens created here in the mid-19th and early 20th centuries still exist, many hidden in the incubator-like hills around Menton.

Serre de la Madone in the Gorbio valley was created in the 1920s by the English gardener Lawrence Johnston, of Hidcote Manor fame. He planted species from his travels over five continents, resulting in a garden for all seasons; look out for the rare mahonias from the Far East. The three landscaped hectares of the estate go from open spaces to enclosures, creating an atmosphere of suspense, while the three hectares left wild blend graciously with the man-made patterns.

Nearby **Les Colombières** was conceived by painter and landscape gardener Ferdinand Bac in the 1920s. A fine colourist, Bac played with the greens and greys of cypress and olive trees, using their shapes to frame Alp and sea views. For more exotica, **Jardin Val Rahmeh** is a steamy botanical garden founded in 1905 by Lord Radcliffe and now an annexe of the Muséum National d'Histoire Naturelle. Among 700 tropical and subtropical species are the Easter Island pagoda tree, Sophora toromiro, passiflora and avocadoes.

The revered **Clos du Peyronnet** was acquired in 1915 by Derrick and Barbara Waterfield. Despite covering only half an hectare, the estate is an inexhaustible source of exotic plants, including rare species of acacia and oreopanax. A series of basins grow larger as they descend like a water stairway to a pool mirroring the sea, and a

Chinese wisteria is in such robust health that one of its branches broke a stone column of the Clos' 19th-century villa, home to botanist William Waterfield.

With Italy just next door, it would be a shame not to skip over the border to the **Giardino Botanico Hanbury**. There are fabulous rose gardens and passionflower displays, an Australian forest, Mexican cypresses and Atlantic blue cedars – some date from the estate's origins in the 1870s. Perhaps most impressive is the area left wild in a rare sweep of indigenous coastal *maquis*.

Le Clos du Peyronnet
av Aristide Briand, Menton (04.93.35.72.15). **Open** contact tourist office for visits.

Les Colombières
372 rte de Super Garavan, Menton (04.92.10.97.10). **Open** by appointment. **Admission** €5.

Jardin Val Rahmeh
av de St Jacques, Garavan (04.93.35.86.72). **Open** 10am-12.30pm, 3-6pm daily (closes 5pm Oct-Apr). **Admission** €4; €2 under-18s.

Giardino Botanico Hanbury
Pont San Luigi, La Mortola, Italy (00.39-0184-229507). **Open** Mar-Oct 10am-6pm daily; Nov-Ferb 10am-5pm Mon, Tue, Thur-Sun. **Admission** €6; €3.50 6-18s; free under-6s.

Serre de la Madone
74 rte du Val de Gorbio, Menton (04.93.57.73.90). **Guided visits** *July-Aug* 10am, 5pm Tue-Sun; *Sept-June* 2.30pm Tue-Sun. **Admission** €8; free under-15s.

The Riviera

in June. Don't expect a live snail race, however: it's a procession of villagers carrying snail shells that have been turned into tiny oil lamps. The 17th-century Baroque church of **St-Barthélémy** has a striking black marble holy water stoop.

Up the tortuous D22 road from Menton, scenic **Ste-Agnès** hangs from the rock at 780m above sea level. The narrow cobblestoned streets have succumbed to the inevitable quaint shops selling tourist-oriented clutter. But the spectacular panorama of the Italian and French coastline is reason enough for a visit. The **Fort Maginot**, built in the 1930s when the village was a strategic point in Riviera defences, has some impressive cannons.

Castillon, known as the 'artists' village', is a regrettably prettified town whose modern Arcades du Serre along the main square and the rue Haute contain Disneylandish crafts boutiques. Its main redeeming feature, in fact, is an exit: the ancient mule trail through the lemon and olive groves to Ste-Agnès, which makes for a lovely two-hour hike.

After skirting the *vieille ville* of Menton, the route de Castellar (D24) winds uphill through lemon groves to the tiny medieval fortressed village of **Castellar**, a *village perché* without a trace of cute gentrification. Once the home of the illustrious seigneurs of Lascaris-Vintimille, it now attracts Sunday lunchers from Menton. The pretty Baroque church of **St-Pierre** has a pink facade and onion-domed bell tower.

Fort Maginot

Ste-Agnès (04.93.35.84.58). **Open** *July-Sept* 3-6pm daily; *Oct-June* 2.30-5.30pm Sat, Sun. **Admission** €3.05; €1.52 7-15s; free under-7s.

Where to stay & eat

In Gorbio, the **Restaurant Beau-Séjour** (pl de la République, 04.93.41.46.15, closed Wed all year and dinner Oct-June, menus €21-€29) dishes up tasty specialities such as courgette flower fritters, fried ravioli stuffed with swiss chard, cheese and rice, and marjoram-sautéed rabbit. **Hôtel St-Yves** (rue des Sarrasins, 04.93.35.91.45, closed 20 Nov-20 Dec, double €30) in Ste-Agnès offers small but comfortable rooms. For typical Franco-Italian regional fare, such as vegetable *tourtes* and ravioli, try the bar/restaurant **Le Logis Sarrasin** (rue des Sarrasins, 04.93.35.86.89, lunch only except July-Aug, closed Mon and 15 Oct-15 Nov, menus €13-€19). In Castillon, **Hôtel La Bergerie** (chemin Strauss, 04.93.04.00.39, closed Nov, double €72) has rustic rooms, and a moderately priced restaurant (closed Mon-Fri from Sept to Easter & all Nov, menu €23). In

Castellar, the **Hôtel des Alpes** (1 pl Clemenceau, 04.93.35.82.83, closed mid-Nov to mid-Dec, double €38-€43) has cheerful rooms with views of the coast and Provençal dishes (closed Fri, menus €14-€17). More rustic is the **Palais Lascaris** (58 rue de la République, 04.93.57.13.63, closed Mon and Oct, menus €14-€19), with its Ligurian and Provençal peasant cooking.

Tourist information

Castillon Syndicat d'Initiative

rue de la République, 06500 Castillon (04.93.04.32.03). **Open** 10am-noon, 2.30-5.30pm daily.

Gorbio Office de Tourisme

Hôtel de Ville, 30 rue Garibaldi, 06500 Gorbio (04.92.10.66.50/fax 04.92.10.66.59). **Open** 8.30am-12.30pm Mon, Thur; 8.30am-12.30pm, 1.15-5.30pm Tue, Wed, Fri.

Ste-Agnès Office de Tourisme

Espace Culturel des Traditions, 51 rue des Sarrasins, 06500 St-Agnès (04.93.35.87.35). **Open** 9.30am-1pm, 2-5pm Tue-Sun.

▶ Getting There & Around

▶ By car

Leave the A8 at exit no.58 and follow the Grande Corniche down to Roquebrune, or exit no.59 for Menton (last exit before Italy), or one of the three Corniches from Nice (*see p247*, **The Corniches**). Gorbio is 9km northwest of Roquebrune-Cap-Martin on the narrow D23. For Ste-Agnès, take rte des Castagnins from Menton, which becomes the D22 (13km). Castillon is 10km up the D2566 Sospel road from Menton. For Castellar is 6km up the D24.

By train

Local trains on the Nice-Ventimiglia line stop at Roquebrune-Cap-Martin (just before the headland), Carnolès (just beyond) at Menton and Menton-Garavan stations. There are also daily TGV connections between Paris and Menton.

By bus

RCA Menton (04.93.21.30.83) runs a regular daily service along the Basse Corniche to Nice, stopping at Carnoles, Roquebrune and Monaco, and a reasonably frequent shuttle bus service from Carnolès station to Roquebrune village. **Breuleux Cars** in Menton (04.93.35.73.51/ www.autocarsbreuleux.com) runs services to Castellar, Gorbio and Ste-Agnès.

Inland Alpes Maritimes

Grasse & the Gorges du Loup

Sniff out the world capital of perfume before exploring a landscape of dramatic waterfalls, dripping caves and high-tech businesses.

Grasse

In the old days, Grasse (from *grâce*, as in grace, rather than *gras*, as in fat) was a bustling fortified city known for its tanning industry. Prosperity arrived when Henri II's wife, Catherine de Medici, suggested that these hills, whose balmy micro-climate ensures that flowers flourish year-round, would be a good place to turn out the perfumed gloves that were essential to the fashion conscious of the time. Grasse's inhabitants became *parfum-gantiers* and, when gloves went out of fashion, the Grassois continued to perfect the art of perfume-making (captured in all its pungent detail in Patrick Suskind's novel *Perfume*). Now Grasse bustles in a more tourist-oriented way and boasts easily toured factories that continue to extract precious essences of jasmine, rose, orange, tuberose, jonquil, violet, mimosa and lavender, which get transformed into fragrances for Dior, Chanel, Yves Saint Laurent and other fashion houses.

Within the busy boulevards and industrial zones, the medieval old town retains a workaday atmosphere, despite droves of hard-sell souvenir shops and tourist-trap restaurants. Every morning except Monday, the flower and fresh produce market in **place aux Aires** is good for stocking up on picnic fare. The cobbled square, surrounded by winding streets and stairways, has elbow-to-elbow pavement cafés from which to admire the 1802 market clock, as well as the wrought-iron balconies of the Hôtel Isnard (1781) at No.33. The Hôtel du Dauphin at No.27 for a long time was the city's only inn. Wandering down rue Droite (crooked, despite its name), takes you to the Maison Doria de Roberti at No 24 which has a remarkable Renaissance stairwell. The street ends in the place des Herbes, which was once (and on occasion still is) Grasse's herb and vegetable market. Nearby a portal and Gothic window of the old Oratory Chapel have been incorporated into the facade of the Monoprix supermarket. The **Musée Grasse d'Antan** reconstructs 19th-century Grasse with 150 miniature figures in mini town and landscape sets.

Place du Petit Puy is dominated by the **Cathédrale Notre-Dame-du-Puy**. A prime piece of the Lombard-influenced Romanesque, it was mauled in the 17th and 18th centuries. In the right aisle are several paintings by a very young Rubens painted for a church in Rome. There is also *The Washing of the Disciples' Feet*, a rare religious subject by local boy Fragonard, and a triptych by Louis Bréa. Across the square, the Hôtel de Ville occupies the old bishop's palace and incorporates the tenth-century watchtower the Tour de Guet.

Just past the cathedral, the **Musée d'Art et d'Histoire de Provence** charts high-class Provençal life in the 1800s. The **Musée Provençal du Costume et du Bijou** is housed in the magnificent 18th-century home of the Marquise de Clapiers-Cabris, sister of the flamboyant Revolutionary politician Mirabeau. It now houses a quaint collection of 18th- and 19th-century costumes and jewellery. D'Artagnan, musketeer to Louis XIV, stayed down the road at No.14. Nearby, the **Musée International de la Parfumerie** provides an indispensable introduction to the area's chief industry, explaining the manufacture of perfume essence by distillation, *enfleurage* (in which the raw materials are sandwiched between layers of animal fat that absorb the scent) and by extraction using solvents. Other treasures include Dior's 1950s New Look Bar Dress and Paco Rabanne's 1960s futuristic plastic dress, plus perfume bottles dating from classical Greece to the present and the chance to test your sense of smell in lush greenhouses.

At the far end of the Jardin Public stands the **Villa-Musée Fragonard**, the elegant 17th-century country house where artist Jean-Honoré Fragonard (1732-1806) sought refuge when he fell from favour with the Revolutionary powers. The son of a not particularly successful glove-maker, Fragonard took himself to Paris at a young age to study painting. In the capital, he offered four paintings representing the steps of amorous conquest to Louis XV's favourite, the Comtesse du Barry: the *Rendez-Vous, Pursuit, Letters* and *The Lover Crowned*. Replicas of

Flower power: **Grasse** is always greener.

these are in this museum (the originals are in the Frick Collection in New York). Fragonard's chocolate-box works were all the rage, but were little liked by the children of the Revolution who, in any case, had decapitated most of his clients. The villa has trompe l'oeil wall and ceiling paintings by Fragonard's 13-year-old son Alexandre and, upstairs, original sketches and etchings by Fragonard himself.

The 18th-century Hôtel Pontevès-Morel houses the **Musée de la Marine**, dedicated to Admiral François Joseph Paul (1722-88), Count of Grasse, whose defence of Chesapeake Bay during the siege of Yorktown helped bring the American War of Independence to an end.

Flowers are at the heart of Grasse's perfume success, celebrated in the Expo-Rose in May and the annual Jasmine Festival the first weekend of August, when there are processions, swathes of flowers and the election of Miss Jasmine. The **Jardin de la Princesse Pauline** has not only a spectacular view but offers jasmine, roses and other aromatic plants. For a more informative tour, visit the gardens of the **Domaine de Manon** whose plants find their way into Chanel N°5, Guerlain's Jardin de Bagatelle and Patou's Joy.

Domaine de Manon

36 chemin du Servan, Plascassier (04.93.60.12.76/ www.4acf.com/domaine_manon). **Open** *May-mid June roses* 2-5pm daily; *Aug-Oct jasmine* 8am-10am daily. **Admission** €5; free under-12s.

Musée d'Art et d'Histoire de Provence

2 rue Mirabeau (04.93.36.01.61/ www.museesdegrasse.com). **Open** *June-Sept* 10am-7pm daily; *Oct-May* 10am-12.30pm, 2-5.30pm Mon, Wed-Sun. Closed Nov. **Admission** €3.05; €1.90 12-16s; free under-12s. **Credit** MC, V.

Musée Grasse d'Antan

3 rue des Moulinets (04.93.40.07.29/ www.grasseparfums.com). **Open** *Mar-Sept* 10am-noon, 2-6pm daily; *Oct-Feb* 3-6pm daily. **Admission** €3.80; €1.91 12-16s; free under-12s. **Credit** MC, V.

Musée International de la Parfumerie

8 pl du Cours Honoré Cresp (04.93.36.44.73/ www.museesdegrasse.com). **Open** *June-Sept* 10am-7pm daily; *Oct-May* 10am-12.30pm, 2-5pm Mon, Wed-Sun. **Admission** €3.80; €1.91 12-16s; free under-12s. **No credit cards.**

Musée de la Marine

2 bd du Jeu de Ballon (04.93.40.11.11). **Open** *June-Sept* 10am-7pm daily; *Oct-May* 10am-5.30pm Mon-Sat. Closed Nov. **Admission** €3.05; €1.52 12-16s; free under-12s. **No credit cards.**

Musée Provençal du Costume et du Bijou

2 rue Jean Ossola (04.93.36.44.65/ www.fragonard.com). **Open** *Sept-June* 10am-12.45pm, 2-6pm daily. **Admission** free.

Villa-Musée Fragonard

23 bd Fragonard (04.93.40.32.64/ www.museesdegrasse.com). **Open** *June-Sept* 10am-7pm daily; *Oct-May* 10am-12.30pm, 2-6.30pm daily. Closed Nov. **Admission** (incl gardens) €3.50; €1.90 12-16s; free under-12s. **Credit** MC, V.

Where to stay & eat

Jacques Chibois is one of the hottest chefs on the Riviera; his **Bastide St-Antoine** (48 av Henri Dunant/www.jacques-chibois.com, 04.93.70.94.94, menus €42-€114), set in a century-old olive grove below Grasse has 11 elegant rooms (double €159-€419). Truffles and mushrooms are a speciality. **La Voûte & Côté Place Café** (rue du Thouron-pl aux Aires, 04.93.36.11.43, menus 89F-135F) is a great place to people watch from a cosy, well-decorated patio, and has a very nice lunch menu. **Les Moulin des Paroirs** (7 av Jean XXIII, 04.93.40.10.40, closed Sun & Mon and 1-15 Nov, 1-15 July, menus €19-€30.50) serves a superbly tender *pigeon à la royale.* **Le Gazan**

(3 rue Gazan, 04.93.36.22.88, closed dinner, menus €12.84-€30) is a slightly kitsch spot with a popular terrace but the cooking is spot on. **Le Coin Swisse** (1 pl Cesar Ossola, 04.93.36.44.44, closed Sat lunch & Sun, menus €10-€16.50) is an inexpensive fondue joint. Bar-*tabac* **Le Celtic** (4 cours Honoré Cresp, 04.93.36.06.78) has a shady terrace and is a great place for a quick snack (the house speciality is toasted bread moistened with olive oil and topped with tomato, ham and grilled red peppers). **L'Indiana's** in the Casino de Grasse (bd Jeu de Ballon, 04.93.36.91.00) has a certain LasVegas style that's hard to ignore. Despite the name, the food is anything but Tex-Mex, offering weekly themes from Chinese to Indian, friendly service and a huge upstairs terrace. Cyber café **Le Petit Caboulot** (escalier Maximim Isnard, 04.93.40.16.01, closed Sun) is reasonable at €4.57/30 mins, and has a good terrace too; most Grassois prefer that and the crêpes to its technological offerings.

La Bellaudière (av Pierre Ziller, 04.93.36.02.57, double €86.29-€89.34) has been completely refurbished, perhaps with more enthusiasm than style, and is friendly, clean and close to all amenities. The quiet **Auberge La Tourmaline** (381 rte de Plascassier, 04.93.60.14.44 , double €53-€61) is a little out of the way but has great views. The friendly **Hôtel des Parfums** (1 rue Eugène Charabot, 04.92.42.35.35/www.hoteldesparfums.com, closed Nov-Jan, double €75.46-€121.20) has a jacuzzi and gym as well as fabulous views from rooms geared more to travelling salesmen than to tourists. **Le Victoria** (7 av Riou Blanquet, 04.93.40.30.30/www.le-victoria-hotel.com, closed Jan, €60-€76) is a mid-sized hotel with a nice gym and a reasonable restaurant. If you prefer to pitch a tent, try the **Camping Municipal** (27 av de Rothschild, 04.93.36.28.69, closed Dec-Jan, two people €12.50) or the **Camping de la Paoute** (160 rte de Cannes, 04.93.09.11.42, closed mid-Sept to mid-June, two people €17).

The Nose have it

Once tonnes of flower petals have been reduced to their few precious drops of essence, it is just the start of a process of sniffing and blending. Perfumes contain only 10%-25% of essence, eau de cologne 2%-6%, and aftershave as little as 0.2%. The secret behind a bestselling perfume – along with clever design and a hefty dose of marketing – is the art of *Le Nez* or Nose. To reach the final product, the Nose assembles some 100 different ingredients. Noses are trained to smell over 3,200 different scents and good ones are a rare commodity. Many perfume houses share a Nose, who often works in secret, though you can watch one in action at the **Parfumerie Fragonard**. You can test your olfactory prowess and mix your own perfume at the Fragonard, Galimard and **Molinard** parfumeries. At **Parfumerie Galimard** you can take an initiation course and, under the advice of Le Nez, mix up something fabulous.Your exclusive creation will be funnelled into a charming glass bottle and the formula registered on Galimard's computer; you can have further supplies whipped up on demand and sent to you anywhere in the world.

Parfumerie Fragonard

17 rte de Cannes-Les Quatre Chemins (04.93.77.94.30/www.fragonard.com). **Open** *Mar-Sept* 9am-6pm daily; *Oct-Feb* 9am-12.30pm, 2-6pm daily. **Admission** free.

Parfumerie Galimard

73 rte de Cannes (04.93.70.36.22/ www.galimard.com). **Open** *May-Oct* 9am-6pm daily; *Nov-Apr* 9am-12.30pm, 2-6pm Mon-Sat. **Admission** free; *studio des fragrances* €34.

Parfumerie Molinard

60 bd Victor Hugo (04.93.36.01.62/ www.molinard.com). **Open** *Mar-Oct* 9am-6pm; *Nov-Feb* 9am-12.30pm, 2-6pm. **Admission** free.

Tourist information

Grasse has an Olympic-size outdoor pool (Altitude 500, rte Napoléon, 04.93.36.42.51) and a year-round indoor pool (Harjès, av de St Exupéry, 04.93.36.20.89) and four golf courses in the area, including Le Claux-Amic (rte des Trois Ponts, 04.93.60.55.44) in Grasse itself.

Office de Tourisme
22 cours Honoré Cresp, 06130 Grasse (04.93.36.66.66/fax 04.93.36.03.56). **Open** 9am-12.30pm, 1.30-6pm daily.

Oily comeback

Thanks to the popularity of a healthy Mediterranean-style diet, olive-growing is making a comeback: proud of its 400,000 olive trees, 27 mills and 2,000 growers, the Alpes-Maritimes *département* aims match the 1.6 million hectares it had under cultivation at the start of the 20th century. There are five very active mills around Grasse, which process oil and eating olives from the 'olive de Nice', which was recently awarded its own *appellation d'origine côntrolée*.

Olive lovers can follow an olive trail around the Grasse area. The harvest begins September-October, with pressing from early November to the end of February. To see the *moulins* in action, you have to go during pressing season, though most have shops open year round.

Moulin de la Brague
2 rte de Châteauneuf, Opio (04.93.77.23.03). **Open** 9am-noon, 2-6.30pm Mon-Sat. Closed 15-30 Oct.

Moulin à Huile Baussy
rue Bourboutel, Speracèdes (04.93.60.58.59). **Open** 8am-noon, 2.30-7pm Mon-Sat.

Moulin à Huile Conti
Josephe Conti, 138 rte de Draguignan, Grasse (04.93.70.21.42). **Open** 8am-noon, 1.30-6.30pm Mon-Sat (closed Mon Mar-Sept).

Moulin à Huile de St-Cézaire
100 rte de St-Vallier, St-Cézaire (04.93.60.29.59). **Open** by appointment.

Moulin à Huile du Rossignol
41 chemin des Paroirs, Grasse (04.93.70.16.74). **Open** by appointment.

West of Grasse

A surprising hinterland awaits along the Route Napoléon north-west out of Grasse. About 12km along lies the medieval village of **St-Vallier-de-Thiey**, a good vantage point for spotting *bories*, stone igloos once occupied by shepherds. The village offers activities from horse riding (try La Celle, 04.93.09.06.89) to cross-country bicycle rallies. Nearby is the **Souterroscope de Baume Obscure**, where underground waterfalls crash past stalactites, stalagmites and other natural phenomena. Bring a sweater, as it's a constant 12°C. South towards Cabris are the **Grottes des Audides**. This cave system, inhabited in prehistoric times, was discovered by a shepherd in 1988. Dioramas illustrate the lives of the original inhabitants.

Perched above the river Siagne lies unspoiled medieval **St-Cézaire-sur-Siagne**. Abundant harvests earned the village the title of 'Caesar's storehouse' and Julius Caesar was so thrilled with the views that he set up an observation post at the top. A Gallo-Roman sarcophagus can be seen in the entrance to the 12th-century cemetery chapel. Most visitors come to see the **Grottes de St-Cézaire**, caves whose stalagmites and stalactites are a rusty red. Some, when struck, emit an eerie musical sound.

Grottes des Audides
1606 rte de Cabris (06.64.95.74.11). **Open** *15 Feb-30 June, Sept* 2-5pm Wed-Sun; *July-Aug* 10am-noon, 12.30-6pm daily. Closed 1 Oct-14 Feb. **Admission** €5; €3 4-11s; free under-4s. **No credit cards.**

Grottes de St-Cézaire
9 bd du Puit d'Amon (04.93.60.22.35). **Open** *June, Sept* 10.30am-noon, 2-6pm daily; *July-Aug* 10.30am-6.30pm daily; *Oct-May* 2.30-4.30pm Sun. Closed Jan, Dec. **Admission** €5; €2.05 5-11s; free under-5s. **No credit cards.**

Souterroscope de Baume Obscure
Chemin Ste-Anne, St-Vallier-de-Thier (04.93.42.61.63). **Open** *May-Sept* 10am-5pm daily; *Oct-Apr* 10am-5pm Tue-Sun. Closed 15 Dec-15 Feb. **Admission** €7.62; €3.81 4-12s; free under-4s. **Credit** MC, V.

Where to stay & eat

Le Relais Impérial in St-Vallier-de-Thiey (85 rte Napoléon, 04.92.60.36.36/ www.relaisimperial.com, double €37-€65) is cosy and clean. **Le Préjoly** (pl Rougière, 04.93.42.60.86/www.hostellerieleprejoly.com, closed 15 Nov-1 Feb, double €30-€69, average €27) is a welcoming country inn with 17 rooms and a restaurant. **L'Hostellerie des Chênes Blancs** (2020 rte de St-Vallier, 04.93.60.20.09/ www.chenes-blancs.com, closed 1-15 Jan, double €45-€105) outside town has a pool,

St-Cézaire-sur-Siagne – 'Caesar's storehouse' – still has plenty in store for visitors.

tennis courts and restaurant (menus €15-€20). For regional cooking try **L'Auberge le Jardin de Curé** (1 av Fontmichel, 04.93.42.69.70, closed Mon & Sun, and mid-Nov to Jan, menus €15-€21) or the budget **Bistrot du Pré** (27 rue de l'Hôpital, 04.92.60.03.69, menus €15-€21).

In Cabris, **L'Horizon** (100 promenade St-Jean, 04.93.60.51.69, closed mid-Oct to 30 Mar, rates €54-€106) has a pool, terrace and renovated bedrooms. **Le Vieux Château** (pl du Panorama, 04.93.60.50.12, www.auberge-vieux-château.com restaurant closed Mon & Tue, double €59-€98, menu €23-€34) is a charming hotel/restaurant carved out of the old castle, with Provençal food and four double rooms: reserve well ahead. **Le Petit Prince** (15 rue Frédéric Mistral, 04.93.60.63.14, average €17) serves great rabbit with lavender and raspberry vinegar.

Tourist information

Cabris

Office de Tourisme, 4 rue Porte Haute, 06530 Cabris (04.93.60.55.63/www.mairie-cabris.fr.st). **Open** 9.15am-12.15pm, 1.30-5.15pm Mon-Sat.

St-Cézaire

Office de Tourisme, 3 rue de la République, 06530 St-Cézaire (04.93.60.84.30). **Open** *May-Oct* 10am-noon, 2-7pm Tue-Fri, 10am-noon Sat, Sun; *Nov-Apr* 10am-noon, 3-6pm Tue-Fri; 10am-noon Sat, Sun.

St-Vallier-de-Thiey

Office de Tourisme, 10 pl du Tour, 06460 St-Vallier-de-Thiey (04.93.42.78.00/www.stvallierdethiey.com). **Open** 9am-noon, 3-5pm Mon-Sat (and July-Aug 10am-noon Sun).

The Gorges du Loup

Built on a rocky peak surrounded by precipices, medieval **Tourrettes-sur-Loup** produces so many violets (celebrated in the early-March Fête des Violettes) that it has earned the name 'Violet Village'. In the 1920s it became a meeting place for artists and writers. Today, more than 30 workshops and galleries make Tourrettes a high spot for arts and crafts. The Grand'Rue is lined with shops, most more earnest (and more expensive) than their souvenir-oriented cousins in nearby St-Paul-de-Vence. It is also the home of the award-winning mutt Flo, named best truffle-finder in France in 2000.

Le Bar-sur-Loup has all the authentic charm of a well-kept medieval village. The Gothic church of St-Jacques contains a 15th-century altarpiece, as well as a famous *Danse Macabre*, which portrays tiny courtly dancers being shot by Death, their souls being judged unworthy by St Michael and hurled into hell. When he's in the area, a less saintly Michael – Schumacher – takes a spin at **Fun Kart**.

Tortuous bends and overhanging cliffs, accompanied by the sounds of crashing waterfalls, lead you into the **Gorges du Loup** where hiking and canyoning are a must. Canyoning is dangerous so organise a private guide (Destination Nature, 04.93.32.06.93 is affordable and reliable); if you must try it on your own, consult *Les Guides Randoxygène*, updated each year and free at tourist offices.

Along the D6, amid lush vegetation, a huge monolith marks the entrance to the **Saut du Loup**. The waters of the Loup swirl furiously through this enormous cauldron, gushing down through moss and vegetation petrified by the lime carbonate of the spray.

Perched between Grasse and the Loup Valley lies **Gourdon**, a medieval citadel which kept watch for marauding Saracens. The 13th-century **Château de Gourdon** blends French and Italian Romanesque influences and has gardens by Le Nôtre. It houses the **Musée Historique**, with the usual weaponry and torture implements plus a Rembrandt, a Rubens and Marie Antoinette's writing desk, plus the **Musée de la Peinture Naïve** with Douanier-Rousseau-type daubs and one example of the real thing.

Château de Gourdon

(04.93.09.68.97). **Open** *June-Sept* 11am-1pm, 2-7pm daily; *Oct-May* 2-6pm Mon, Wed-Sun. **Admission** €4; €2.50 12-16s; free under-12s. **No credit cards**.

Fun Kart

Plateau de la Sarée, rte de Gourdon *(04.93.42.72.27)*. **Open** 9.30am-dusk daily. **Rates** €16/10 mins; *kids' karts* €6/5 mins. **Credit** MC, V.

Where to stay & eat

In Tourrettes-sur-Loup **Chez Grande Mère** (pl Maximin Escalier, 04.93.59.33.34, closed Wed, lunch Sat and Nov, menus €14.50-€16.75) makes a fabulous lentil soup and has a cosy fireplace. Reserve. **Le Petit Manoir** (21 Grand'Rue, 04.93.24.19.19, closed Mon & Tue and 15-30 Nov, menus €15-€34) is a local favourite with a great vegetarian selection. **Le Mas de Cigale** (1673 rte des Quenières, 04.93.59.25.73/www.mascigale.online.fr, closed Nov-15 Mar, double €77) is a lovely bed and breakfast with six large, well-decorated rooms, hearty breakfasts plus a pool and tennis courts. The **Auberge de Tourrettes** (11 rte de Grasse, 04.93.59.30.05/www.aubergedetourrettes.fr, closed end Nov to beg Feb except Christmas/New Year, double €65-€104) has six cosy rooms and a lovely terrace; its restaurant (average €40) is quickly acquiring a well-deserved reputation for its innovative menu.

Restaurant delights are slim in Le Bar: try **La Jarrerie** (av Amiral de Grasse, 04.93.42.92.92, closed Mon Oct-Apr, all Tue, dinner Wed May-Sept and all Jan, menus €19-€43), which serves hearty Provençal fare. In Gourdon, the **Auberge de Gourdon** (04.93.09.69.69, closed Nov, menu €14.94-€19.36) is a bar-*tabac*-restaurant with local charm, heavy Provençal accents and simple, honest dishes. If you have a tent, the **Camping Rives du Loup** (2666B rte de la Colle, Pont du Loup 04.93.24.15.65, two people €18.29) is a well-organised site in a lovely setting, with caravans and mobile homes to rent.

Who's afraid of the **Gorges du Loup**?

Tourist information

Le Bar-sur-Loup

Office du Tourisme, pl Francis Paulet, 06620 Le Bar-sur-Loup (04.93.42.72.21/www.bar-sur-loup.com). **Open** 9am-12.20pm, 2-5pm daily.

Gourdon

Syndicat d'Initiative, pl de l'Eglise, 06620 Gourdon (tel/fax 04.93.09.68.25/www.gourdon-france.com). **Open** *July-Aug* 9am-7pm; *Sept-June* 10am-6pm.

Tourrettes-sur-Loup

Office de Tourisme, 5 rte de Vence, 06140 Tourrettes-sur-Loup (04.93.24.18.93/ www.tourrettessurloup.com). **Open** 9.30am-12.30pm, 2.30-6.30pm Mon-Sat (daily May-Aug).

Valbonne & Sophia-Antipolis

Unlike most villages in Provence, **Valbonne** was planned on a chequerboard design by the monks of Lérins, clearly inspired by the plans of Roman towns. The village is surrounded by 'rampart houses' with an entrance gate on each of its four sides, and was built as part of a bid by Augustin de Grimaldi, Bishop of Grasse, to repopulate a region that had been devastated by plague. Today it has several glass workshops, notably for perfume flasks. At the heart of the village is the 17th-century place des Arcades, where the Fête du Raisin celebrates the late-ripening servan grape at the end of January.

The parish church is part of the former Chalaisian Abbey which also contains the small **Musée des Arts et Traditions Populaires**. Below the village, the Sentier Découverte de la Brague follows the river Brague.

In the shadow of ancient Valbonne lies **Sophia-Antipolis**, the Riviera's 15,000-hectare bid for high-tech power and prestige on a truly Californian scale, where 20,000 people from more than 60 countries work in R&D-intensive companies – keeping the already high property prices in the surrounding area bubbling over. Work on this perfectly landscaped, perfectly soulless science park began in 1969; today 1,300 high-tech companies share the site, which is set to double in size over the next decade. Information technology, telecoms, electronics and biotechnology are the main sectors; the University of Nice also has a research faculty. The park has been described as 'Milton Keynes on the Riviera' – not least because of its lack of a centre and its endless roundabouts. The managing consortium, SAEM, maintains a website at www.saem-sophia-antipolis.fr.

South-west of Valbonne, **Mouans-Sartoux** draws contemporary art pilgrims. The Renaissance château was converted into the **Espace de l'Art Concret** in 1990 by artist Gottfried Honegger with a striking minimalist extension. The permanent collection includes works by Honnegger, Albers, André, LeWitt and Morellet, exhibited along with three- or four-month theme shows dedicated to geometrical abstraction and minimalist art.

Espace de l'Art Concret

Château de Mouans-Sartoux (04.93.75.71.50).
Open *June-Sept* 11am-7pm Mon, Wed-Sun; *Oct-May* 11am-6pm Mon, Wed-Sun. **Admission** €2.30; free under-12s.

Musée des Arts et Traditions Popularires

rue Paroisse, Valbonne (04.93.12.96.54).
Open *May-Sept* 3-7pm Tue-Sun; *Oct-Apr* 2-6pm Tue-Sun. Closed 17 Dec-23 Jan. **Admission** €2; free under-12s.

Where to stay & eat

La Cigale (27 rte de Nice, 04.93.12.24.43, doubles €49-€71, closed 21 Dec-4 Jan and 1-17 Feb) has eight smallish rooms, and very welcoming staff. The **Hôtel Les Armoiries** (pl des Arcades, 04.93.12.90.90, doubles €79-€199) is a 17th-century building surrounded by four golf courses. Just outside Valbonne, the **Château la Bergude** (rte de Roquefort Les Pins, 04.93.12.37.00/www.chateaubergude.com, closed 25 Nov-26 Dec, double €68.60-€167.69) is a lovely restored manor with 34 rooms, some

overlooking a golf course, and English-speaking staff. The simply named **Bistro de Valbonne** (11 rue de la Fontaine, 04.93.12.05.59, closed Sun & Mon and Thur lunch mid-June to mid-Sept, menus €23.63-€29) serves French classics and some superb smoked wild Baltic salmon with dill sauce and blinis. **La Bergerie** (18 rue d'Opio, 04.93.12.94.74, closed lunch Thur-Sat, menus €21-€30) is a great place to listen to softly played guitar and get romantic. Some of Valbonne's best food is to be found at **Lou Cigalon** (4-6 bd Carnot, 04.93.12.27.07, closed Mon, Sun, two weeks Jan, menus €44-€69). Owner-chef Alain Parodi specialises in simple Provençal cuisine with a light, modern spin; booking advised.

Tourist information

Office de Tourisme

11 av St Roch, 06560 Valbonne (04.93.12.34.50/ www.alpes-azur.com/vsa). **Open** *15 June-14 Sept* 9am-6pm Mon-Fri; 9am-12.30pm, 3-6pm Sat; 9am-12.30pm Sun; *15 Sept-14 June* 9am-5pm Mon-Fri; 9am-12.30pm Sat.

▶ Getting There & Around

▶ By car

The N85 goes from Cannes to Grasse continuing to St-Vallier-de-Thiey, or take the more scenic D3 to Grasse via Valbonne. From Nice take the D2085 at Cagnes towards Le Bar-sur-Loup and Grasse. For Cabris, take the D4 out of Grasse, then D13 to St-Cézaire. The D2210 winds from Vence towards Grasse via Tourrettes-sur-Loup and Le Bar, with side roads turning off up the Gorges du Loup.

▶ By bus

Rapides du Côte d'Azur (RCA 04.93.36.37.37) runs buses Mon-Sat between Cannes and Grasse (No.600), between Nice Airport and Grasse (No.500), between Grasse and St-Cézaire, some of which stop at Cabris, and between Grasse and St-Vallier-de-Thiey (Mon-Sat). For the Gorges du Loup, take RCA's No.511 from Grasse to Pont-sur-Loup. Bus No.510 runs three times a day Mon-Fri during school term time between Grasse and Vence. **TACAVL** (04.93.42.40.79) operates several services (Mon-Sat) between Grasse and Le Bar-sur-Loup. **STCAR** (04.93.12.00.12) bus No.3VB runs from Cannes direct to Valbonne about every hour (less on Sun) and the No.5VB (four buses Mon-Fri) goes via Sophia-Antipolis.

Vence & St-Paul

From Matisse's master-strokes to Maeght's Modernist manna, art has always been the dove that lays the golden egg in this mountainous nest.

St-Paul-de-Vence & La Colle-sur-Loup

Due north from Cagnes, St-Paul-de-Vence might have been just another picturesque *village perché*. Instead, St-Paul-de-Vence has become a regional *quartier général* of modern art, helped along by a heritage of illustrious artistic visitors and the presence of one of the most important modern art museums in France, the Fondation Maeght.

St-Paul flourished in the Middle Ages thanks to its vines, figs, olives and orange trees, as well as hemp and linen. The almost-intact ramparts were put up in 1540 by François 1er, in thanks for the town's role in beating off his arch-enemy, Emperor Charles V. The town went into a decline until the 20th century, when an influx of artists gave it a much-needed makeover. Picasso, Matisse, Braque and Dufy were just some of the impoverished daubers who pitched up here after World War I, paying for their board and lodging at the town's only inn, **La Colombe d'Or**, with paintings that still adorn the hostelry's walls. In the 1960s, art dealer-collectors Aimé and Marguerite Maeght created the Fondation Maeght, a remarkable container for their remarkable private collection.

St-Paul's narrow medieval lanes are lined with bougainvillea, jasmine and geraniums along with hard-sell artists' studios and shops selling antiques, crafts and souvenirs. In the **Eglise Collégiale** on place de la Mairie (open 8am-8pm daily), only the choir remains from the original 12th-century building; later adornments include the Baroque stucco masterpiece of St Clément's chapel and a painting of St Catherine of Alexandria, attributed to Tintoretto. From a café in the place de Gaulle, observe France's most famous *terrain de boules*, shaded by plane trees. Celebrities line up to challenge local champions and Japanese players travel huge distances for regional tournaments, but rookies are welcome (*boules* can be rented from the tourist office at €3/hour per set). The walk around the ramparts affords spectacular views from the Alps to the sea. The Porte de Nice leads to the **cemetery** (open June-Sept 7.30am-8pm; Oct-May 8am-5pm) where Chagall lies beneath a slab of stone adorned with pebbles, coins, twigs and acorns, placed there by fans.

In a pinewood just north-west of St-Paul, the **Fondation Maeght** is one of the Côte's star attractions. Opened in 1964, this extraordinary low-slung construction set in grounds bristling with artworks was designed by Catalan architect José Luis Sert to house Aimé and Marguerite Maeght's collection. As you prepare to join the 200,000 people who visit each year, it helps to throw away any preconceptions of what a gallery should look like. The Fondation is a maze, with no fixed route and nothing resembling a hanging plan. Some works do have places of their own, by virtue of being part of the fabric of the place: Giacometti figures in the courtyard; a Miró labyrinth peopled with sculptures and ceramics, including the half-submerged *Egg*; mural mosaics by Chagall and Tal-Coat; the pool and stained-glass window by Braque; Pol Bury's fountain; Calder's bobbing mobiles. But the Fondation's more moveable Braques and Légers, Kandinskys and Mirós, Bonnards and Chagalls shift places or disappear into storage to make way for temporary exhibitions, including the annual summer show.

The more modern, commercial **Galerie Guy Pieters** was opened by the Belgian gallery owner in July 2000, showing American Pop and French *nouveau réalisme*, including Christo, Niki de Saint Phalle, Arman and Robert Indiana. For art which is truly state-of-the-art, head into town where **Galerie Catherine Issert**, opened nearly 30 years ago, has a seriously contemporary feel and a fine line in installation.

Southwest of St Paul-de-Vence, unspoiled **La Colle-sur-Loup** has an attractive 17th-century church, but is best known for antiques. The main drag of antique shops on rue Yves Klein is open daily 4-6pm, and an antiques market is held every second Sunday of the month. The recently opened **Maison des Arts** offers weekly residential courses in a beautiful 18th-century house. What really puts La Colle on the map is **L'Abbaye**, a 12th-century monastery built around a 10th-century chapel and now a stunning hotel/restaurant (*see p276*), where guests have included Brigitte Bardot and Roger Moore.

Fondation Marguerite et Aimé Maeght

chemin des Trious (04.93.32.81.63). **Open** *Oct-June* 10am-12.30pm, 2.30-6pm daily; *July-Sept* 10am-7pm daily. **Admission** €7.62; €6.08 10-18s; free under-10s.

Matisse considered Vence's stunning **Chapelle du Rosaire** to be his masterpiece. *See p277.*

Galerie Catherine Issert

2 rte des Serres (04.93.32.96.92/www.galerie-issert.com). **Open** 11am-1pm, 3-7pm Mon-Sat.

Galerie Guy Pieters

chemin des Trious (04.93.32.06.46/ www.guypietersgallery.com). **Open** *June-Oct* 10am-7pm Mon-Sat; *Nov-May* 10am-1pm, 2-6pm Mon-Sat.

Where to stay & eat

Accommodation is expensive in St-Paul, but the **Hostellerie les Remparts** (72 rue Grande, 04.93.32.09.88, double €39-€80) in the centre of the old town combines style and value. Its nine charming rooms have a medieval feel and its restaurant (closed Mon lunch all year and dinner Tue-Thur & Sun Nov-Mar, menu €26) serves regional specialities such as *beignets de fleurs de courgette* and *petits farcis*. Book well ahead for a meal or a bed if you're hoping to get even a glance inside **La Colombe d'Or** (pl des Ormeaux, 04.93.32.80.02/www.la-colombe-dor.com, closed 29 Nov-21 Dec, ten days in Jan, double €244-€282). The artworks left here in lieu of payment by penniless clients of the hostelry's founder Paul Roux – including works by then-unknowns Picasso, Modigliani, Miró, Matisse and Chagall – are only on view to guests. A meal on the celebrated, fig-shaded terrace (average €57) is pleasant enough but it's art and atmosphere that count here. **Le St-Paul** (86 rue Grande, 04.93.32.65.25, double €170-€560) is a 16th-century mansion with four-poster beds. Chef Frédéric Buzet offers a modern Provençal menu and a fine list of local wines (menu €43, closed Tue lunch and Jan & Dec). For light meals in cosy surroundings, check out **Comme à la Maison** (montée de l'Eglise, angle rue Grande, 04.93.32.87.81, dishes €9.15-€19.80), a poetry café with vegetarian tendencies. In the old town, the tiny **Couleur Pourpre** (7 rempart Ouest, 04.93.32.60.14, closed lunch Wed, all Mon, Sat, Sun and mid-Nov to Dec, €30.50) offers refined local fare including wonderful desserts. The **Café de la Place** (pl de Gaulle, 04.93.32.80.03, closed 11 Nov-25 Dec) is the prime spot for watching the *boules* action and serves a wholesome *plat du jour* (€8.50). Chagall once stayed at **Hôtel le Hameau** (528 rte de la Colle, 04.93.32.80.24/ www.le-hameau.com, closed mid-Nov to mid-Feb except Christmas & New Year, double €93-€128), which oozes charm and has pretty rooms, a pool and terraced garden with fruit trees. **La Ferme de St-Paul** (1334 rte de La Colle, 04.93.32.82.48, closed all Tue & lunch Wed from Nov to Apr, menu €28) serves fine, classic Provençal cuisine in a converted 18th-century farmhouse, with a delightful but noisy terrace. Set in an eight-hectare park with views to the Med, **Le Mas d'Artigny** (20 rte de la Colle, 04.93.32.84.54/www.mas-artigny.com, double €109-€420) has rooms, suites, self-catering apartments and a heated outdoor pool open all year, plus a venerable restaurant that has been given a new direction by chef Francis Scordel

(menus €43-€72). The 14 rooms at **L'Abbaye**
(541 bd Honoré Teisseire, La Colle-sur-Loup,
04.93.32.68.34, double €84-€199, restaurant
closed all Mon, lunch Tue, menus €29-€75) are
simple, but it's the lounge, cloisters, pool and
restaurant which make it special. Roger Moore
took over the hotel for his step-daughter's
wedding party and Church of England
marriages can be arranged in the achingly
charming chapel. Menus are good value for a
special occasion, but the speciality of sea bass
cooked in a salt crust will make you ditch the
prix-fixe for the *à la carte*.

Tourist information

La Colle-sur-Loup Office du Tourisme

*8 av Maréchal Foch, 06480 (04.93.32.68.36/
www.lacollesurloup.com).* **Open** *July, Aug* 9am-7pm
Mon-Fri; 9am-12.30pm 4-7pm Sat, Sun. *Sept-June*
9am-12.30pm, 2-6pm Mon-Fri; 9am-12.30pm, 3.30-
6pm Sat, Sun.

Maison des Arts

*10 rue Maréchal Foch, La Colle-sur-Loup
(04.93.32.32.50/www.maisondesarts.com).* **Courses**
1,067/week (incl tuition, accommodation, meals).

St-Paul-de-Vence Office de Tourisme

*2 rue Grande, 06570 (04.93.32.86.95/
www.stpaulweb.com).* **Open** *June-Sept* 10am-7pm
daily; *Oct-May* 10am-6pm daily.

Vence

When the Emperor Augustus led his jack-
sandalled hordes into what they were to call
Vintium, it had long been inhabited by a
Ligurian tribe. Set in a strategic position 10km
back from the sea, Vence was a bishopric from
the fourth to 19th centuries, and boasts two
patron saints. The first was fifth-century bishop
Véran, who organised the town's defences
against Visigoth invaders (though Saracens
would later succeed where the Barbarians had
failed, razing the cathedral and much of Vence
to the ground). 12th-century bishop Lambert
defended the town's rights against its rapacious
new baron, Romée de Villeneuve, setting a trend
of rivalry between nobility and clergy that was
to last until the bishopric was dissolved after
the Revolution. Perhaps Vence's most popular
prelate – though this one was never canonised –
was 17th-century bishop Antoine Godeau, a
gallant dwarf, poet and renowned wit who was
a founding member of the Académie Française.

In the 1920s, Vence became a popular pitstop
for artists and writers, including Paul Valéry,
André Gide and D H Lawrence, who died here
in 1930. A simple plaque in Vence cemetery
marks the place where Lawrence lay for five

Solace for body and soul in the 12th-
century cloisters of **l'Abbaye.**

years before the family moved his grave to
South America, though his ashes are said to
have been scattered off the Côte d'Azur.

Walls still encircle some of the vieille ville,
Vence's medieval heart, which manages to
retain its old-world feel despite the modern
sprawl outside. Outside the western Porte
Peyra, one of five original gates into the town,
the place du Frêne is named after its giant ash
tree planted to commemorate Pope Paul III's
visit to Vence in 1538. The porte leads into
place Peyra, site of the Roman forum. Between
the two squares, the 17th-century **Château de
Villeneuve** now hosts modern art exhibitions.
At the centre of the *vieille ville*, the **Ancienne
cathédrale Notre-Dame de la Nativité**
(open 9am-6pm daily) was built over a Roman
temple of Mars, a column from which can be
seen in place Godeau. A fifth-century church
was replaced by a Romanesque one, which has
itself been reworked over the centuries. The
Roman legacy can be seen in inscriptions worked
into the Baroque facade on place Clemenceau and
in the pre-Christian sarcophagus (third chapel on
the right) in which St Véran is said to have been
buried. There's a Chagall mosaic of Moses in
the bulrushes in the baptistry, and some
charmingly irreverent 15th-century carvings by
Jacques Bellot on the choir stalls. Three
stairways lead from the centre towards
boulevard Paul André, which follows the old
ramparts and offers sweeping views to the Alps.

Leave the medieval town through place du Grand Jardin, edged with cafés from which you can watch the *boules* players and visit the daily morning farmers' market. It never looks truly busy until July when Vence's biggest event, the **Nuits du Sud** music festival, brings four raunchy weeks of Latin, salsa, jazz and French-Arabic music, waking Vence from its slumber.

Vence's biggest tourist attraction, the **Chapelle du Rosaire**, lies slightly north of the *vieille ville*. In 1941, Matisse took refuge in Vence from the Allied bombs that were raining down on Nice. He fell ill, and was nursed back to health by the town's Dominican sisters, and designed the chapel to repay the favour. Matisse himself always maintained that this chapel, entirely conceived and created between 1947 and 1951, was his masterpiece, the result of a lifetime devoted to the search for truth. Though not a believer, the elderly artist threw himself wholeheartedly into this project for the nuns who had nursed him through illness. Bedridden, he splashed out the designs for his towering figures using a paintbrush tied to a bamboo pole. From the outside, the chapel looks traditional, but inside, it is an icebox of stark white tiles disturbed only by the scrawled, black, faceless figures of St Dominic, the Virgin and Child, and the Stations of the Cross. Stained glass windows fill the chapel with a glowing light which is at its best in the morning.

Slightly north of the old centre is **Galerie du Centre d'Art VAAS**, a commercial exhibition space for contemporary art, which takes its name from the first letters of the Latin for truth, love, art and spirituality. It was the studio of Jean Dubuffet 1955-70, though sadly none of his work remains. Southwest of town is the **NALL Association** where you can see artists in action. Students, some in rehab, others gaining credits towards their degree, work as assistants to Nall, the artist-founder, while painters, sculptors, writers and musicians hire cottages within the extensive grounds to work on their personal projects. The house, completely built and decorated by Nall, is a work of art in itself.

West of Vence on the Grasse road, the **Galerie Beaubourg** is more museum than private gallery, a gem of an exhibition of contemporary works housed in a château. Terraced sculpture gardens dotted with pieces by Niki de Saint Phalle, Arman and Julian Schnabel are part of a permanent collection assembled by former Parisian gallery owners Marianne and Pierre Nahon, which also continues inside. The pièce de résistance is the Jean Tinguely chapel, featuring his weird and wonderful *Grande odalisque*.

To the north-east of Vence, **St-Jeannet** is a wine-making village dominated by the dramatic rock outcrop known as le Baou, which can be ascended by a waymarked path. 15km east of Vence, **La Gaude** is comparatively dull, but a well preserved and friendly little perched village dating from 189BC. It's a good place to start a pedestrian exploration of the surrounding countryside: there are six marked walks, the one to Vence taking an hour and ten minutes, and the one to le Baou an hour and a half. The tourist office has maps.

Chapelle du Rosaire

466 av Henri Matisse (04.93.58.03.26). **Open** 10-11.30am, 2-5pm Tue, Thur; 2-5.30pm Mon, Wed, Sat; *mass* 10am Sun. Closed Nov to mid-Dec. **Admission** €2.50; €1 6-16s; free under-6s.

Galerie Beaubourg

Château Notre Dame des Fleurs, 2618 rte de Grasse (04.93.24.52.00/www.galeriebeaubourg.com). **Open** *Apr-Sept* 11am-7pm Mon-Sat; *Oct-Mar* 12.30-5.30pm Tue-Sat. **Admission** €4.60; €2.30 12-18s; free under-12s.

Galerie du Centre d'Art VAAS

2 rue des Portiques, Vence (04.93.58.29.42). **Open** *Apr-Oct* 11am-1pm, 2.30-6.30pm Tue-Sat; *Nov-Mar* 2-6pm Tue-Sat. **Admission** free.

The best An abbey to lay your head

L'Abbaye: a celebrity retreat in chapel and cloisters, near Vence. *See p278.*

Hôtel des Augustins: soaring Gothic vaults in Aix-en-Provence. *See p157.*

Hostellerie du Prieuré: spiritual seclusion in Bonnieux, in the Luberon. *See p119.*

Hôtel du Cloître St-Louis: perfectly cloistered, with Nouvel additions, in Avignon. *See p95.*

Hostellerie de l'Abbaye de la Celle: religious foundation turned Ducasse gastronomic destination. *See p189.*

Abbaye de la Ste-Croix: luxury pitstop in a 12th-century abbey and Roman burial site in the Crau. *See p67.*

Couvent Royal: a cell of your own in the royal abbey at St-Maximin-la-Ste-Baume. *See p191.*

Inland Alpes-Maritimes

Château de Villeneuve Fondation Emile Hugues

2 pl du Frêne, Vence (04.93.24.24.23). **Open** *July-Oct* 10am-6pm Tue-Sun; *Nov-June* 10am-12.30pm, 2-6pm Tue-Sun. **Admission** €4.57; €2.29 12-18s; free under-12s.

NALL Art Association (Nature, Art & Life League)

232 bd de Lattre, Vence (04.93.58.13.26). **Open** *May-Sept* 3-6pm Mon, Sat, Sun. **Admission** €3.05.

Where to stay & eat

Super-chef Jacques Maximin at **Restaurant Jacques Maximin** (689 chemin de la Gaude, Vence, 04.93.58.90.75, closed dinner Apr-Sept, and all Mon & Tue Oct-Mar, menus €37-€88) is a Provençal legend and you'll see why once you tuck into a starter like his salad of artichoke hearts, broad beans, squid, penne and parmesan, or the classic autumnal salad of ceps and scallops. It's pricey, but worth it, especially when they're serving outdoors in the lush subtropical garden. Recently renovated **La Closerie des Genêts** (4 impasse Marcellin Maurel, 04.93.58.33.25, double €35.06-€59.46) has 12 chintz-draped rooms. **Hôtel Miramar** (167 av Bougearel, 04.93.58.01.32, double €60-€125, closed 15 Nov-15 Dec) on the eastern edge of Vence, is a delightfully converted ancient manor with pool, terrace and lovely views of St-Jeannet, while the inexpensive **Hôtel Le Provence** (9 av Marcellin Maurel, 04.93.58.04.21, double €38-€68) has a central location and pretty rooms. Slightly out of the centre, **Hôtel Villa Roseraie** (av Henri Giraud, 04.93.58.02.20, closed 15 Nov-15 Feb, double €82-€133) has a magnificent garden with pool. The **Château du Domaine St-Martin** (av des Templiers, 04.93.58.02.02/www.chateau-st-martin.com, rates €230-€790), under the same ownership as the Cap Eden Roc, offers elegant accommodation and stunning views plus an excellent restaurant (menus €49-€89). Best of all, you can cut out all those winding roads by availing yourself of the hotel's private helipad. **L'Auberge des Templiers** (39 av Joffre, 04.93.58.06.05, closed Mon, menus €31.25-€58.69) has great mod-Med cuisine cooked up by internationally trained (but Vence-born) chef Stéphane Demichelis in a pretty setting with tables in the garden in summer. Live and dine like a medieval lord in the 15th-century **Auberge des Seigneurs** (pl du Frêne, 04.93.58.04.24, closed 13 Jan-11 Feb, closed Nov to mid-Mar, double €80-€90), an inn since 1895; its restaurant (open dinner Tue-Sun, menu €37.35) specialises in roast meats. In the heart of Vence's old town, **Le P'tit Provençal** (4 pl Clemenceau, 04.93.58.50.64,

closed Wed, Thur and 7 Nov-6 Dec, end Feb-beg Mar, menus €19-€25) offers foie gras with figs and rabbit casserole with thyme. At the nearby **La Terrasse du Clemenceau** (22 pl Clemenceau, 04.93.58.24.70, closed Mon & dinner Sun, menu €22.90) staff often ignore you, but pasta dishes and lamb cooked in a wood oven, devoured on the loveliest terrace in the square, are worth the hassle. For a blowout meal, head for the hills to **La Table de Marc** (269 chemin des Salles, 04.93.58.28.63, closed one week Feb, menu €23), for six, pre-determined courses, using fresh local ingredients (cheeses produced by a neighbouring poet-shepherd) with a good selection of well-priced wines.

In St-Jeannet, join hepcats from all over the Côte at **La Seguinière** (rte de St-Laurent, 04.93.24.42.92, closed Tue, Wed, dinner Sun and Feb, average €30) for simple food along with live music on Friday and Saturday nights. Rest up before or after a hike at the **Hôtel du Baou** (le plan du Bois, 04.93.59.44.44, double €56-€89) in La Gaude, which has a swimming pool.

Tourist information

Vence market is Tuesday and Friday mornings.

La Gaude Syndicat d'Initiative

20 rue Centrale, 06610 La Gaude (04.93.24.47.26/www.mairie-lagaude.fr). **Open** *mid-June to mid-Sept* 9am-12.30pm, 3-6pm Tue-Fri; 9am-4pm Sat; *mid-Sept to mid-June* 9.30am-12.30pm, 2.30-5.30pm Tue-Fri; 9am-4pm Sat.

St-Jeannet Syndicat d'Initiative

35 rue de la Soucare, 06640 St-Jeannet (04.93.24.73.83/www.saintjeannet.com). **Open** *June-Sept* 9am-6pm daily; *Oct-May* 9.30am-noon, 2.30-5pm Tue-Sat.

Vence Office de Tourisme

8 pl du Grand Jardin, 06140 Vence (04.93.58.06.38/www.ville-vence.fr). **Open** *July-Aug* 9am-7pm Mon-Sat; 9am-1pm Sun; *Sept-June* 9am-12.30pm, 2-6pm Mon-Sat.

▶ Getting There & Around

▶ By car

A8 autoroute, Cagnes-sur-Mer exit (no.48), then D7 to St-Paul-de-Vence via La Colle-sur-Loup or D36 to Vence. From Vence, D2210 east to St-Jeannet, then D18 to La Gaude.

▶ By bus

The TAM bus no.400 goes from Nice to Vence via Cagnes and St-Paul-de-Vence 27 times a day Mon-Fri, 15 on Sat, 13 on Sun. Varmer bus no.13 departs from Vence to St-Jeannet 12 times a day Mon-Sat.

The Arrière-pays

Nice's back country is an olive-infested wilderness where quiet villages and a few strange saints seem a world apart from the hectic coast.

Ask any full-time Riviera residents where they spend their weekends, and they're likely to tell you that they head for the hills. Once out of the the industrial suburbs of Nice, these backlands, known as the *arrière-pays*, are a mini-wilderness of olive groves, pine woods, wild flowers and *villages perchés*, offering spectacular panoramas, pristine cool breezes in the summer months and rustic cuisine based around local produce such as olive oil and goat's cheese.

Once a Roman settlement, **Contes**, 18km north of Nice on the D2204/D15, juts out from a steep slope overlooking the Paillon de Contes torrent. The village found itself in the limelight in 1508 when the bishop of Nice was called in to rid the place of a nasty plague of caterpillars. At the **Site des Moulins** olives are still pressed (Dec-Mar) in a 17th-century water-powered mill. Olive oil, salted olives and olive paste are on sale at **Gamm-Vert** agricultural cooperative (rte de Châteauneuf, 04.93.79.01.51, closed Sun). From **Châteauneuf-de-Contes**, a tiny village 4.5km west of Contes, there is a good 30-minute walk to the atmospheric, abandoned ruins of **Vieille Châteauneuf.**

Continuing upvalley from Contes, the D15 leads to **Coaraze**, the self-styled *village du soleil* (village of the sun). On the main square, the outer walls of the *mairie* (town hall) are decorated with dazzling modern sundials by Jean Cocteau and other artists. The village is a maze of vaulted passageways and cypress-lined gardens and fountains. At the top of the village is the old cemetery, with cement boxes for burials because the rocks are too hard even for pickaxes. The name Coaraze, locals will tell you, derives from *caude rase* (cut tail): wily medieval inhabitants caught Old Nick napping and grabbed hold of him, obliging him to shed his lizard-like tail to escape; a modern pavement mosaic commemorates the event.

Only 16km from Nice on the D2204/D21, isolated on a rocky spur above olive groves, **Peillon** has not a single quaint boutique, the wise residents having banned all touristic upscaling. To compensate, there are narrow cobblestoned streets, russet pantiled roofs and an unbeatable panorama of the valley. Not to be missed is the miniscule **Chapelle des Pénitents Blancs** at the entrance of the village. The chapel is kept closed to protect the 15th-

What a drop at **Coaraze**.

century frescoes of the Passion attributed to artist Giovanni Canavesio, but the works can be viewed through a grating with coin-operated lights. Further upstream – or a lovely one-and-a-half-hour ridge walk from Peillon – **Peille** is a quiet village with some handsome Romanesque and Gothic doors, windows and fountains and a ruined feudal castle at the top. Peille's feisty inhabitants, who accepted numerous excommunications in the Middle Ages rather than pay taxes to the bishop, speak a dialect all their own known as *pelhasc*.

At the bottom of the main Paillon Valley, the agricultural township of **L'Escarène** was once an important staging post on the *Route du sel* (salt road) from Nice to Turin; for once, a piece of modern engineering – the arched viaduct of the Nice-Sospel railway – complements the view of the old town. The ornate Baroque church of **St-Pierre**, renowned for its 18th-century organ, is generally closed, but the mayor's office

Inland Alpes-Maritimes

(04.93.91.64.00) can sometimes be prevailed on to produce a key. The **Association ADO** (Amis de l'Olivier) located across from the post office (19 bd du Dr Roux, 04.93.91.44.29, closed Sat, Sun) takes great pride in its superb extra-virgin olive oil, and offers a tasting initiation, a tour of the town's oil mill, a hike through the groves and a traditional Niçois olive-centric feast at a nearby restaurant. Further up the *Route du sel*, the fortified medieval crossroads of **Lucéram** is worth a detour for the 15th-century **Eglise Stes-Marguerite-et-Rosalie** (rue de l'Eglise, closed Mon & Tue), which has a striking Italianate onion-domed yellow and pink bell tower. Don't miss the silver reliquary and outstanding *rétables* by the Bréa school that recount the story of Ste Marguerite, a third-century shepherdess-martyr burned at the stake, who was one of Joan of Arc's favourite voices-in-her-head.

Where to stay & eat

In Contes, **Le Cellier** (3 bd Charles Alunni, 04.93.79.00.64, double €28-€35, restaurant closed Sun, menus €10.50-€22), in the lower, modern end of town, dishes up tasty family-style cuisine; there are also a few rooms. One of the most quietly celebrated *arrière-pays* destinations is the **Auberge du Soleil** (04.93.79.08.11, closed Nov to mid-Feb, double €59-€82, menus €18-€22) in Coaraze, where the bucolic vista from the dining room bay window is a treat for city-sore eyes. Try the *giboulette de lapin* (rabbit stew) and heavenly nougat ice cream. Rooms are simple but comfortable, and overlook the valley. In Peillon, the **Auberge de la Madone** (04.93.79.91.17, closed three weeks Jan, mid-Oct to mid-Dec, restaurant closed Wed, dinner by reservation, double €93-€155, menu €27) is a long-standing romantic hideaway with lovely antique-filled rooms, the best with loggias overlooking the village. There is very little room service in the hotel, but the restaurant features refined Nissart specialities. The view from the flower-lined terrace makes up for the slightly overpriced fare. In Peille, stop for a *pastis* and *pissaladière* at the café **Chez Cauvin** (5 pl Carnot, 04.93.79.90.41, closed dinner Mon, Thur & Sun, lunch Fri & Sat, and all Tue & Wed, menu €18).

Getting there

By car
The starting point for all these villages is the D2204 Paillon Valley road, which begins at the Acropolis roundabout in Nice as bd J-B Verany.

By train/bus
The Nice-Sospel line (four-six trains daily) winds up the Paillon valley, stopping at Peillon, Peille and

L'Escarène, but only L'Escarène has a station within easy reach of the town; Peillon and Peille are a 5km walk from their respective stations. There are buses from Nice to Peillon and Peille (three daily Mon-Sat), to L'Escarène and Lucéram (four daily Mon-Sat), and to Contes and Coaraze (two Mon-Sat); for details ring Nice *gare routière* (04.93.85.61.81).

Tourist information

Coaraze Office du Tourisme
Office de Tourisme, 7 pl Ste-Catherine, 06390 Coaraze (04.93.79.37.47/fax 04.93.79.31.73). **Open** *Apr-Sept* 10am-noon, 2-5pm daily; *Oct-Mar* 10am-noon, 2-5pm Mon, Tue, Thur, Fri.

Contes Syndicat d'Initiative
pl du Dr Olivier, 06390 Contes (04.93.79.13.99/fax 04.93.79.26.30). **Open** 2-6pm Mon-Fri.

Lucéram Maison du Pays
la Placette, 06440 Lucéram (04.93.79.46.50). **Open** 9am-noon, 2-6pm Tue-Sat.

Peille Syndicat d'Initiative
Mairie, pl Carnot, 06440 Peille (04.93.91.71.71/fax 04.93.91.71.78). **Open** 9am-noon Mon-Fri.

Peillon Syndicat d'Initiative
Mairie, 672 av de l'Hôtel de Ville, 06440 Peillon (04.93.79.91.04/fax 04.93.79.87.65). **Open** 8.30am-noon, 2-5pm Mon-Fri.

Peillon: just cobbled together, *see p279*.

Into the Alps

Away from the glitz of the Riviera, the *département* of the Alpes-Maritimes also hosts some of the most spectacular mountain scenery in France.

Less than an hour's drive north of Nice, olive groves make way for some serious Alpine crags, dominating the deeply scored valleys of the Roya, the Vésubie, the Tinée and the Haut Var. Walking, skiing, canyoning and mountain biking bring visitors in droves, but there are more sedate reasons to come up here: the views, the cool summer evenings and Renaissance frescoes hidden in out of the way chapels.

The flora- and fauna-rich **Parc National du Mercantour** covers a huge swathe of territory near the border with Italy, and offers some 600km of waymarked footpaths. Here, as well as free-roaming, bell-clanking sheep and goats, you may well see chamois and marmots, rare imperial eagles, eagle owls, snow grouse, the recently reintroduced lammergeyer, a bearded vulture that lives mainly on bones, as well as Alpine ibex or *bouquetin* which roam between the Mercantour and the adjacent Parco Naturale delle Alpi Marittime in Italy (officially twinned with its French cousin since 1987). Less welcome to some locals are the wolves that have made their way back over the border from Italy and have been blamed for excessive sheep consumption. The park is efficiently and even aggressively run, with strictly enforced bans on dogs, camping, firearms, gathering of plants, fires and off-road driving. There's an information office in Nice (23 rue d'Italie, 04.93.16.78.88) as well as local information offices at Tende, St-Martin-Vésubie, St-Sauveur-sur-Tinée, St-Etienne-de-Tinée, Valberg, Entraunes, Allos and Barcelonnette. The Parc also has one of the area's more unusual sights – the rock-hewn Bronze Age engravings of the **Vallée des Merveilles**. And, though the region is short on luxury pitstops, it does at least offer rustic hospitality of a kind (and at a price) that's sadly lacking on the coast.

The Roya & Bévéra Valleys & the Vallée des Merveilles

When the rest of the county of Nice devolved to France in 1860, the upper valleys of the Roya and its tributary the Bévéra stayed Italian – the reason being that King Vittorio Emanuele II liked to go hunting there. It was not until 1947 that the French-speaking inhabitants of these most Mediterranean of Alpine valleys were allowed to decide which side of the border they wanted to be on – and after 20 years of Mussolini and five of total chaos, it was hardly surprising that they plumped en masse for France. The Italian influence makes itself felt in colourful village houses and churches and in the valleys' artistic legacy – notably the remarkable frescoes in the chapel of Notre-Dame-des-Fontaines near the village of La Brigue.

Sospel, a sleepy, sprawling town that hangs over the olive groves beside the river Bévéra, is the mountain gateway to the Roya valley, and a Mecca for soft-core ramblers who prefer classic hilly countryside to jagged peaks. It is also a great place to stock up on the outstanding local olive oil. The streets abound with charming squares and sculpted fountains, but the main highlight is the **Eglise St-Michel** (open 3-6pm daily) on place St-Michel, with its peach and frothy stucco facade, trompe l'oeil murals and François Bréa's splendid early 16th-century *Immaculate Virgin* surrounded by angels. The tourist office, in the tower that once served as a tollgate, halfway across the 11th-century hump-backed bridge, provides useful hiking maps. On the edge of Sospel, the **Musée du Fort St-Roch** is a fascinating memory of the Maginot line. Built in 1932, this underground world was a marvel of 30s technology, and from what appears to be the entrance to a garage on the side of a cliff, the visitor finds himself embarking on a trip through seemingly endless galleries, containing officer's quarters, munitions, a hospital and, this being France, some impressive kitchens and even a *cave à vin*. Another curiosity are some original carriages from the Orient Express, stationed at the Gare.

Northwest of Sospel, the narrow D2566 climbs alongside the Bevera to the 1,604m **Col de Turini**, a popular spot for hiking and skiing (*see p287* **White Out**) at the edge of the Parc National du Mercantour. Goats clamber up mountain paths amid the stark ruins of L'Authion, Napoleonic military barracks.

The alternative route north of Sospel, the D2204 climbs over the 879m Col de Brouis before dropping into the Roya valley proper at **Breil-sur-Roya**. A tranquil village of red-tiled pastel houses surrounded by olive trees, Breil has also become an internationally known centre for canyoning, rafting and kayaking. Visit the flamboyantly ornate 18th-century church of **Sancta-Maria-in-Albis** (open 9am-noon, 2-5pm daily), which has a fine gilded organ from the 17th century. Organs are big news in the churches of the Roya-Bévéra area: there are no fewer than seven historic, finely decorated instruments made by Tuscan or Lombard craftsmen, all in perfect working order and put into service in Les Baroquiales Baroque music festival every summer (*see chapter* **The Festive South**).

Saorge is the most spectacular Roya village: a cluster of Italianate houses and bell towers with shimmering fish-scale tile roofs, clinging to the side of a mountain at the entrance to the breathtaking Roya Gorge. A narrow cobbled street winds up to the 15th-century church of St-Sauveur, with another of those magnificent carved organs. South of the village is the not-to-be-missed **Couvent des Franciscains**, whose lovely rectangular cloister is filled with painted sundials and 18th-century frescoes depicting the life of St Francis of Assisi. Beyond the monastery's cypress-lined terrace, an old mule track leads to **Madone del Poggio**, a ruined, isolated Romanesque abbey (closed to public).

As one approaches **Tende**, 20km on, the surrounding peaks become seriously Alpine.

The dark, narrow streets and grey slate houses of this frontier town offer little distraction for the wandering tourist. At the end of an alley on rue de France, however, the 15th-century stucco facade of **Notre-Dame-de-l'Assomption** (open 9am-6pm daily) adds a surprising splash of colour. Anyone intending to visit the Vallée des Merveilles (*see below*) should not miss the **Musée des Merveilles**, which has a diorama and interactive exhibits explaining these prehistoric scratchings, as well as an array of hunting tools and fossils from the Bronze Age.

Downstream from Tende, a pretty side road leads east to **La Brigue**. Postcard picturesque, the village boasts no fewer than three Baroque churches, of which **La Collégiale St Martin** (La Place, open 9am-6pm daily), with some fine primitive paintings of the Nice school, is the only one open to the public. The real cultural treat, though, lies a little further east, where the mountain chapel of **Notre-Dame-des-Fontaines**, the site of which has been a place of pilgrimage since antiquity, conceals a series of frescoes that has earned it the moniker of 'Sistine of the Alps'. The nave frescoes by Giovanni Canavesio push beyond the Gothic into a touching, though still primitive, foretaste of the Renaissance. Don't just turn up: visits are arranged through the tourist office in La Brigue.

Come up and see my etchings

Is it a long-horned cow? Is it a beetle? Is it a woman giving birth? The great thing about the prehistoric rock engravings of the Vallée des Merveilles, a magnificent, rock-strewn valley dominated by the 2,872m Mont Bego, is that they allow us all to become amateur archaeologists: the scholarly debate on the meaning and purpose of these prehistoric leavings is as wide-ranging as it is inconclusive. Over 50,000 engravings have been catalogued, most dating from 2500BC to 500BC, although there are more recent interlopers (crucifixes, Napoleonic slogans, and local ritual signs made in the 16th-18th centuries). The Bronze and Iron Age shepherds who grazed flocks here chipped away at the red rocks (the colour is caused by the lichen that once grew on them, and is only skin deep) to depict apparently familiar objects – cattle, ploughs, field systems. A few, though, seem clearly ritual in intent. One of the most famous – and a symbol of the Vallée des Merveilles – is the so-called Sorcerer, a bearded giant who appears to be shooting lightning bolts from his hands. For

some, the engravings are markers on a processional way leading to the sacred Mont Bego; for others, they are simply doodles.

It is possible to visit the engravings in a day from Nice, but it's more rewarding to spend the night in one of the refuges administered by the **Club Alpin Nice** (04.93.62.59.99/ http://cafnice.free.fr, refuges open May-Sept, bed in dorm around €12). Or hire a guide from the **Bureau des Guides du Val des Merveilles** (11 av du 16 septembre 1947, 04.93.04.77.73, closed Mon, Tue) to see some of the less-known engravings. The valley is reached from St-Dalmas-de-Tende, 5km south of Tende (the **Association des Taxi Accompagnateurs**, 04.93.04.60.31, can provide transport), where a paved mountain road branches west to Casterino, jumping-off point for two waymarked footpaths – the direct route via the **Refuge de Fontalbe**, the only refuge accessible by car and then a 30-minute walk, or the longer northern route via the **Refuge de Valmasque**. Western access is from Madone de Fenestre in the Vésubie valley, via the high-altitude **Refuge de Nice**.

The **Roya valley**: an eyrie for eagles.

Couvent des Franciscains

Saorge (04.93.04.55.55). **Open** *Apr-Oct* 10am-6pm
Mon, Wed-Sun; *Nov-Mar* 10am-noon, 2-5pm daily.
Admission €4; free under-18s.

Musée du Fort St Roch

16 pl Guillaume Tell, Sospel (04.93.04.00.70). **Open**
Apr, May, Sept, Oct 2-6pm Sat, Sun; *June-Aug* 2-6pm
Tue-Sun. **Admission** €5; €3 5-13s; free under-5s.

Musée des Merveilles

*av du 16 Septembre 1947, Tende (04.93.04.32.50/
www.museedesmerveilles.com).* **Open** 10am-6pm Mon,
Wed-Fri, Sun; 10.30am-9pm. Closed two weeks in Mar,
two weeks in Nov. **Admission** €4.55; €2.30 7-18s;
free under-7s.

Where to stay & eat

At Sospel, although it looks as if it has seen
better days, the leisurely Bel Acqua restaurant
of the **Hôtel des Etrangers** (9 bd de Verdun,
04.93.04.00.09, closed Nov-Feb, double €49-
€64, menus €20-€34) is a local institution and
the food, including a winning *tête de veau* and a
tank of justifiably worried trout, is first class.

In Breil-sur-Roya, the reasonably priced
bistro **L'Etoile 'Chez Camolio'** (19 bd
Rouvier, 04.93.04.41.61, closed Wed & May,
menus €14) offers simple home cooking. Out of
town beside the Roya on the N204, the **Hôtel
Restaurant Castel du Roy** (04.93.04.43.66,
closed Nov-Easter, double€53-€69), has
comfortable rooms and a rustic restaurant
(closed lunch Mon & Tue, menus €17-€26)

looking out on to grassy parkland. The
exquisitely served regional cuisine (sea perch
with a Provençal *tian*, local trout with mustard
sauce) is well worth a trip from the coast.

In Saorge, the restaurant **Le Bellevue** (5 rue
Louis Périssol, 04.93.04.51.37, closed lunch Tue
& all Wed Sept-June and end Nov to mid-Dec,
menus €15-€21) has a panoramic view. There
are no hotels in Saorge but trekkers flock to the
Gîte Bergiron (04.93.04.55.49, €27 per person
incl dinner) behind the Franciscan monastery.

In Tende, **L'Auberge Tendasque** (65 av du
16 Septembre 1947, 04.93.04.62.26, closed Tue,
menus €11.50-€20) serves the famous *truite au
bleu*, where the fish hardly pauses from tank to
plate. In nearby St-Dalmas-de-Tende, the **Hôtel
Restaurant Le Prieuré** (av Jean Médecin,
04.93.04.75.70, closed Dec, double €42.70-€59,
restaurant closed Mon & dinner Sun Nov-Mar,
menus €10-€21) offers a comfortable stop for
those allergic to mountain refuges.

At La Brigue, **La Cassoulette** (20 rue du
Général de Gaulle, 04.93.04.63.82, closed all Mon
& dinner Sun and Mar, menus €16-€25) is a
tiny convivial bistro, chock-a-block with kitsch
statuettes of barnyard birds; it also offers
divine foie gras, duck confit and mouthwatering
desserts (book). **Hôtel Restaurant Le Mirval**
(3 rue Vincent Ferrier, 04.93.04.63.71, closed
Nov-Mar, double €40-€53, menus €14-€20) is
prettily positioned across a bridge and has
utilitarian but quite spacious modern
accommodation; it also organises four-wheel-
drive excursions into the surrounding valleys.

Inland Alpes-Maritimes

Pile them high: architecture at **Saorge**

Tourist information

Market day in Breil is Tuesday, in Sospel is Thursday, in Tende is Wednesday.

Breil-sur-Roya Office de Tourisme

17 pl Bianchéri, 06540 Breil-sur-Roya (tel/fax 04.93.04.99.76). **Open** *Apr-Sept* 9am-noon, 1.30-5pm; 9am-noon Sun; *Oct-Mar* 9am-noon, 1.30-5pm Mon-Fri.

La Brigue Office de Tourisme

Mairie, pl St-Martin, 06430 La Brigue (04.93.04.36.07/fax 04.93.04.36.07). **Open** 9am-noon, 1.30-5pm Mon-Sat.

Sospel Office de Tourisme

Le Pont-Vieux, 06380 Sospel (04.93.04.15.80). **Open** *July, Aug* 9am-12.30pm, 2-6pm daily; *Sept-June* 9.30am-noon, 2.30-6.30pm daily.

Tende Office de Tourisme

av du 16 septembre 1947, 06430 Tende (04.93.04.73.71). **Open** *Oct-May* 9am-noon, 2-5.30pm Mon-Sat; *June-Sept* 9am-noon, 2-6pm daily.

The Vésubie valley

The best way into the high mountains of the Vésubie is the D19 out of Nice, which rises almost imperceptibly past villas and pastures to the village of **Levens**, an atmospheric cluster of stone houses with an excess of burbling

fountains. Beyond Levens the mountains begin with a vengeance as the road clings to the side of the Gorges de la Vésubie – which can also be negotiated on the lower D2565 route. Soon after the two roads meet is the turn-off for **Utelle**, another *village perché*, whose church has a pretty Gothic porch and doors carved with scenes from the life of local boy St Verain. The shrine of **Madone d'Utelle** stands on a barren peak 6km further on; try to visit in the morning, as the clouds often roll up here later in the day. A plain terracotta-red barn of a church, it owes its existence to a ninth-century shipwreck on the patch of sea that – on a clear day – can be seen far down below. Saved from drowning by the Virgin, who appeared on the mountainside bathed in light, the grateful mariners climbed up here to set up a rudimentary shrine.

The road up to St-Martin-de-Vésubie continues past **Lantosque** to **Roquebillière**, a crumbling old village with a modern offshoot opposite, built after a landslide in 1926 that claimed 17 lives. Down by the river on the same side as the modern village is the unusual church of **St-Michel-de-Gast-des Templiers**. Built by the Knights Templars and later taken over by the Knights of Malta, it is full of abstruse Templar symbolism; on one ancient capital there is even a carving of the Egyptian baboon god Thot. The key is kept by the voluble Madame Périchon, who can be found in the house opposite the church.

St-Martin-Vésubie is a good place to refuel and pick up supplies and information. The pocket-sized place Félix Faure, home to a couple of tempting patisseries, links the main valley road with rue Cagnoli, St-Martin's pedestrian backbone. A little paved channel of water runs the whole way down the steeply inclined street. Known as a *gargouille*, this is a rare feature today; the only other example is in Briançon.

The road west to the church of **Madone de Fenestre** criss-crosses a mountain stream that offers plenty of excuses for a paddle, a picnic or some serious raspberry-picking. But it's worth pushing on to the end, where a large mountain refuge and a tin-roofed church stand in a spectacular position, surrounded by a cirque of high peaks. The church is only two centuries old, but its miraculous icon of the Madone de Fenestre (kept down in St-Martin in winter) dates from the 12th century. Allow at least an hour and a half for the rewarding walk up past a lake to the Col de Fenestre on the Italian border. Madone de Fenestre also gives access to the Vallée des Merveilles (*see p282*, **Come up and see my etchings**).

Perched on a rocky spur overlooking St-Martin, **Venanson** is home to the tiny chapel of Ste-Claire, with its lively 15th-century frescoes

Inland Alpes-Maritimes

of the life of St Sebastian. If it's closed, ask
Roger the butcher (opposite) for the key.

West of St-Martin, the D2565 continues up to
the Col St-Martin (1,500m), which links the
Vésubie and Tinée valleys. Just below the pass
is the aspiring resort of **La Colmiane**, where,
in June and July, you can career down the
mountain on a *trottinerbe* – a sort of kid's
scooter with huge soft tyres – from the top of
the Pic de Colmiane lift. The charms of **St-
Dalmas-de-Valdeblore**, the first village over
the pass, are more sedate. The **Eglise de
l'Invention de la Ste-Croix**, a fine
Romanesque church with its very own piece of
the Holy Cross, once belonged to a powerful
Benedictine priory. St-Dalmas was a local grain
basket and market centre in the Middle Ages,
when many traders preferred the high Alpine
routes to the pirate- and brigand-infested coast.

Where to stay & eat

Just above Utelle on the Madone d'Utelle road,
Le Bellevue (04.93.03.17.19, only open July &
Aug, double €35-€48) has a pool and views
that live up to the name. Its restaurant is open
all year (closed Mon, menus €11-€24.40). In
Lantosque, **L'Ancienne Gendarmerie** (Le
Rivet, 04.93.03. 00.65, closed Nov-Mar, double

€76-€114, restaurant closed Mon & dinner Sun,
menu €27) really was a police station – hence
the sentry box outside – and offers eight rooms
and a small swimming pool perched above the
river. Up in the village, the **Bar des Tilleuls**
(04.93.03.05.74) is a good place for a *pastis* or
light lunch under the eponymous lime trees.

In St-Martin-Vésubie, **La Treille** (68 rue
Cagnoli, 04.93.03.30.85, closed Wed & Thur
except in school holidays and Dec & Jan, menus
€17-€20.50), towards the top of the main street,
is a friendly restaurant with good wood-fired
pizzas (dinner only), classic meat and fish
dishes and a panoramic terrace at the back. **La
Trappa** (pl du Marché, 04.93.03.21.50, closed
Mon & dinner Sun, menus €17-€20) specialises
in pasta and fondues, and has tables in the
pretty square. **La Bonne Auberge** (La Place,
04.93.03.20.49, closed 15 Nov-15 Feb, double
€38-€47, menus €16-€23) lives up to its name,
offering solid mountain hospitality in a cheerful
building overlooking the valley. The slightly
more luxurious **Edward's Parc Hôtel La
Chataigneraie** (04.93.03.21.22, closed Oct-
May, double €55-€69), set in a park of chestnut
trees, is a little frayed but is still a good place to
relax, with the aid of a heated outdoor
swimming pool and mini-golf.

The imposing **Refuge de la Madone de
Fenestre** (04.93.02.83.19, closed Mon-Fri from
Oct to mid-June) has 62 dormitory beds (€10)
and is a good place to stop for lunch; don't miss
the home-baked tarts.

Tourist information

St-Martin-Vésubie Office de
Tourisme

*pl Félix Faure, 06540 St-Martin-Vésubie (tel/fax
04.93.03.21.28).* **Open** *June-Sept* 9am-noon, 3-7pm
daily; *Oct-May* 10am-noon, 2.30-5.30pm Mon-Sat.

Bureau des Guides du Mercantour

rue Cagnoli, St-Martin-Vésubie (04.93.03.26.60).
Can arrange guided walks in the mountains, as well
as canyoning, climbing and parascending courses.

The Tinée valley

Most niçois see this road as a bit of scenery on
the way to the ski resorts of Isola 2000 or
Auron, but the upper reaches of the Tinée
Valley are worth a visit in their own right,
though less precipitous than the Vésubie. The
Tinée flows into the Var just where the latter
changes direction to head south to Nice. A few
side roads even wind their way up to the
villages perchés of **La Tour** – which has some
vivacious 15th-century scenes of vices and
virtues in the **Chapelle des Pénitents-**

Sleeping stones at Levens.

The road to the Alps: walking might almost be easier.

Blancs and an ancient but still-working oil mill – and the well-preserved medieval village of **Clans**, where the **Chapelle de St-Antoine** has frescoes of the life of the saint. The last of this trio of villages on the east side of the valley, **Marie**, is a pretty hamlet of only 60 inhabitants with an excellent hotel/restaurant.

Approaching **St-Sauveur-sur-Tinée**, the iron-rich cliffs turn a garish shade of puce – quite a sight at sunset. St-Sauveur is a one-horse town, strung out along the road, with little to detain the visitor, but it is also the jumping-off point for a spectacular route west via the ski resort of **Valberg** into the Haut Var valley, whose source lies just below the Col de Cayolle, one of the most rewarding of all the gateways into the Mercantour.

Above St-Sauveur, the Tinée valley heads north through the **Gorges de Valabre** before broadening out below **Isola**, a siesta of a village amid chestnut groves, with a solitary 15th-century bell tower and – rather incongruously, given the pace of life around these parts – a covered fun pool, **Aquavallée** (04.93.02.16.49, open daily). Further incongruities lie in wait up the side road that ascends the Chastillon torrent to the ski resort of **Isola 2000**. The 1970s British design of this blight on the landscape has not aged well, and the only reasons to come up here in summer are to walk up into the high peaks that surround the resort or to continue by car over the Col de la Lombarde pass into Italy.

St-Etienne-de-Tinée, near the head of the valley, is a surprisingly lively market town of

tall, pastel houses and Gothic portals, which celebrates its shepherding traditions in the Fête de la Transhumance on the last Sunday in June. The town has a cluster of interesting churches, though you need to go on a tour organised by the Maison de Tourisme to see the Chapelle de St-Sébastien, with frescoes (1492) by Jean Canavesio and Jean Baleison, the Chapelle des Trinitaires, which has a marvellously graphic 17th-century depiction of the Venetian naval Battle of Lepanto, or the Chapelle de St-Maur, with 16th-century frescoes so rustic you can almost smell the hay.

Prize for the most unexpected sight in the Maritime Alps goes to the **Chapelle de St-Érige** (collect key from tourist office) in the lively ski resort of **Auron**. This little wooden chapel – commissioned by wealthy parishioners in the 15th century, when this upland plain was covered in summer cornfields – is almost overwhelmed by the faux-Swiss chalet hotels, ski-lifts and roller discos that surround it. Inside, though, it's another story – a series of stories, in fact, told in vivid frescoes dating back to 1451. Scenes of the life of Mary Magdalene alternate religious mysticism with the secular spirit of the troubadour poets.

North of St-Etienne the D2205 soon becomes the D64 to Barcelonnette, the highest paved road in Europe. When the pass is open (June-Sept) bikers, motorists and even cyclists slog up to the **Col de la Bonette**, where the road loops to encircle the bare peak of Cime de la Bonette. From the highest snack bar in Europe (2,802m), a short path takes you up to the viewing table at 2,860m for a spectacular 360° panorama. Alternatively leave the D2205 north of St-Etienne and head left to the ravishingly pretty mountain village of **St-Dalmas-le-Selvage**. Most of the houses still have their original *bardeaux de mélèze* larchwood roofs, open under the eaves where the corn was laid out to dry. The parish church has two early 16th-century altarpieces, and inside the tiny Chapelle de Ste-Marguerite in the centre of the village are frescoes by Jean Baleison, which were discovered behind the altar in 1996.

Where to stay & eat

It's worth planning a lunch or dinner stop in Marie, where the relaxing family-run hotel-restaurant **Le Panoramique** (pl de la Mairie, 04.93.02.03.01, double €32-€41, closed Thur, menus €14-€30) provides five scenic rooms and fine meals, including seasonal game. In Isola (the village, not the ski resort), **Au Café d'Isola** (pl Jean Gaïssa, 04.93.02.17.03, menus €12-€23) does decent pizzas, salads and full meals; it also 'welcomes bikers' – attracted, no doubt, by the flowers and the baby-blue décor. Sheep-crazed St-Étienne-de-Tinée is hardly crawling with three-star chefs, but the restaurant at the comfortable **Le Régalivou** hotel (8 bd d'Auron, 04.93.02.49.00, closed May & mid-Oct to mid-Dec, double €46-€61, menus €12-€21) serves up solid regional dishes. The town also has a well-run municipal **campsite** on a small watersports lake a three-minute walk from the centre (Plan d'Eau, 04.93.02.41.57, €8.50 two people). **L'Auberge de l'Etoile** (04.93.02.44.97, closed mid-Oct to mid-June, open Sat & Sun and school holidays Dec to mid-June by reservation, average €23) in St-Dalmas-le-Selvage hides not a little sophistication beneath its rustic décor, which is enlivened by fake Van Goghs courtesy of Paul – half of the laidback young couple that runs the place. Booking is essential. There is also a homely **Gîte d'étape** (04.93.02.44.61, dormitory €9.15) in the village, designed for walkers doing the GR5 long-distance path, but open to all-comers.

Tourist information

Auron Maison du Tourisme

Grange Cossa, 06660 Auron (04.93.23.02.66/fax 04.93.23.07.39). **Open** 8.30am-12.30pm, 1.30-6.30pm Mon-Fri; 8.30am 6.30pm Sat, Sun.

Isola 2000 Chalet d'Acceuil

06420 Isola (04.93.23.15.15/www.isola2000.com). **Open** *school holidays* 8.30am-7pm daily; *rest of year* 9am-noon, 2-6pm Mon-Fri.

White out

Never mind the heart-stopping blue of the Mediterranean, for avid skiers the white of snow-capped mountains is the only colour that counts. With numerous ski resorts, the Alpes-Maritimes has something to suit even the most demanding taste and budget.

Beginners might want to consider a stay at **Valberg**, 86km from Nice, with 90km of skiable terrain. Arguably the most attractive features for the novice skier are the inflated balloon-like safety stops, strategically placed for crashing into. Advanced skiers may enjoy the challenge of the 12 high-difficulty-level black runs. Ski passes go from €19.82 on weekdays to €28.97 for a weekend pass that also includes the smaller, next door resort, **Bueil**, which has 12 more black runs and 12km of cross-country pistes.

Intermediates may appreciate the intimacy and charm of smaller resorts **Gréolières** (04.93.60.45.40) or **La Colmiane** (04.93.23.25.90), with smaller skiable areas and correspondingly lower rates. **Turini** (04.93.03.60.52) in the Parc National du Mercantour is mainly for cross-country skiers, as is **St-Dalmas-le-Selvage**, the highest village in the Alpes-Maritimes, with over 35km of pistes. Passes cost €5-€15/day for adults. Snowshoe or skidoo excursions are also available.

For advanced and multi-level skiers, the larger resorts provide the widest choice of options. **Auron**, at 1,600m altitude, offers 130km of pistes and 25 assorted téléphériques, télésièges and téléskis to get to them, as well as Surf-land, a huge playground for snowboarders, with a half-pipe and runs for beginners. The purpose-built resort **Isola 2000** offers 48 runs, including 5 blacks, heli-skiing, and one of the largest snowboarding and mini-skiing clubs in France. Prices range from €18.60 during the week to €21.65 at weekends. And if 70s concrete is not your style, try the rustic chalets north of the station.

The ski season usually starts with snow in December and ends when it melts, around April. Most medium to large resorts have snow machines to create snow when it is lacking and due to an odd depression in the Gulf de Gènes, huge snowstorms often hit the Mercantour; check with Météo de Routes et des Pistes (04.93.59.70.12) or Météo Neige (08.36.68.10.20).

St-Etienne-de-Tinée Maison du Tourisme
1 rue des Communes de France (04.93.02.41.96/fax 04.93.02.48.50). **Open** 9am-noon, 2-5pm daily.

The Upper Var valley

The river Var flows into the Mediterranean just next to Nice airport at St-Laurent-du-Var, but in the upper reaches it offers Alpine scenery and perilously perched villages. Although you can follow the route by N202 from Nice airport, this is one place where the train trip on the **Train des Pignes** is worth the journey in itself. Built 1891-1900 between the Gare de Provence in Nice and Digne-les-Bains in the sparsely populated Alpes de Haute-provence, it was part of an ambitious plan to provide a direct rail link between the Alps and the Côte d'Azur. The one-metre narrow gauge railway runs over 31 bridges and viaducts and through 25 tunnels, climbing to an altitude of 1,000m. Beyond **Plan du Var** the mountains close in on either side at the forbidding **Défilé de Chaudan**, beyond which the Var abruptly changes direction, heading west. **Villars-sur-Var** is a *village perché* with some good Renaissance art in the church of St-Jean-Baptiste; but its main claim to fame is as the centre of the tiny Bellet wine appellation, which occupies a mere 43 hectares; the white is definitely worth trying. At **Touët-sur-Var**, space is so tight that the village church straddles a mountain stream. The valley opens out a little at **Puget-Théniers**, an old Templar stronghold and the birthplace of Auguste Blanqui, one of the leaders of the Paris Commune of 1870, who is commemorated by a stirring Aristide Maillol monument on the main road.

Cradled in a curve of the river, **Entrevaux** is a handsome fortified village. Perched way above on a perilous ridge is a fortress built by Louis XIV's military architect Vauban in the 1690s. Until 1860, this was a frontier town between France and Italy. The twin towers that guard the entrance to the village across a single-arched bridge are almost Disney-picturesque, but once inside it is a sturdily practical place, with tall houses, narrow lanes and a 17th-century cathedral built into the defensive walls. The castle itself is a steep, appetite-building climb from the town up a zigzag ramp; it's an atmospheric old pile, with dungeons and galleries to explore.

Beyond Entrevaux, the Train des Pignes continues towards Digne-les-Bains via the old town of **Annot**, where the houses are built right up against huge sandstone boulders, and **St-André-les-Alpes** on the Lac de Castellane. The Var valley backtracks again in a route that can be traced by the D2202 along the dramatic red schist Gorges de Dalious to its source way north in the Parc de Mercantour.

Tourist information

Puget-Theniers Maison de Pays
2 rue Alexandre Borety, 06260 Puget-Theniers (04.93.05.05.05). **Open** *Mar-Oct* 9am-noon, 2-6pm daily; *Nov-Feb* 9am-noon, 2-5pm daily.

Train des Pignes
(04.97.03.80.80). Trains depart from the Gare de Provence in Nice (4bis rue Alfred Binet) and terminate at the Gare Digne-les-Bains. There are four daily departures in each direction; Nice to Digne takes just over three hours and costs €17.38 (€8.69 4-12s) one-way; Nice to Entrevaux takes an hour and a half and costs €8.69. Trains are modern, with two carriages, but steam trains still ply the route on Sunday from May to October.

> ## ▶ Getting There & Around
>
> ### ▶ By car
> For the Roya and Bevera valleys take the D2566 from Menton to Sospel, then the D2204 north for Breil-sur-Roya. Alternatively, the Roya valley can be ascended from Ventimiglia in Italy on the S20, which crosses into France at Olivetta San Michele, 10km before Breil. The N202 follows the Var valley from Nice airport; the D2565 branches off here along the Vésubie valley (also reached by D2566/D70 from Sospel via the Col de Turini), the D2205 follows the Tinée valley.
>
> ### ▶ By train
> Around five trains a day travel the picturesque Nice-Cuneo line stopping at Menton, Sospel, Breil-sur-Roya and Tende. For the Train des Pignes from Nice to Digne, *see left*, **Upper Var valley**.
>
> ### ▶ By bus
> Bus travel is limited in this area; **Autocars Rey** (04.93.04.01.24) runs services between Menton and Sospel and between Sospel and other destinations in the Roya valley. **TAM** (04.93.89.47.14) buses run twice daily between Nice and St-Martin-Vésubie, Mon-Sat, and once daily Sun. In summer, one a day continues to La Colmiane, only Sunday in winter. Infrequent buses also serve Le Boréon and Madone de Fenestre in summer. **Santa-Azur** (04.93.85.92.60) runs daily services between Nice, St-Etienne-de-Tinée and Auron, and between Nice, Isola and Isola 2000.

Directory

Directory

Getting There & Around

Airlines

Air France (*UK 0845 084 5111/ USA 1-800 237 2747/France 08.20.82.08.20/www.airfrance.com*) operates flights from Paris to Nice, Marseille, Avignon, Montpellier and Nîmes. There are direct flights from London Heathrow to Nice.

Air Inter (*France 08.02.80.28.02*) Hourly *navettes* (shuttle flights) run from Paris Orly to Marseille, Nice, Avignon, Nîmes, Montpellier and Toulon-Hyères.

Air Lib (*France 08.03.80.58.05/ www.airlib.fr*) flies from Paris Orly to Toulon-Hyères, and Nice.

bmibaby (*UK 0870 264 2229/ France 01.41.91.87.04/ www.flybmi.com/bmibaby*) flies from East Midlands airport to Nice.

British Airways (*UK 0845 773 3377/US 1-800 247 9297/ France 08.25.82.54.00/ www.britishairways.com*) flies to Marseille and Montpellier from Gatwick, and Nice from Heathrow, Gatwick and Manchester.

British Midland (*UK 0870 607 0555/France 01.48.62.55.65/ www.flybmi.com*) flies direct to Nice from Heathrow and East Midlands, and via either of these two airports from Aberdeen, Belfast, Edinburgh, Glasgow, Leeds, Manchester and Teeside.

Buzz (*UK 0870 240 7070/ France 01.55.17.42.42/ www.buzzaway.com*) runs budget flights from Stansted to Lyon, Toulon and Marseille and April to October to Montpellier.

Easyjet (*UK 0870 600 0000/ France 08.25.08.25.08/ www.easyjet.com*) runs low-cost flights to Nice from Luton and Liverpool.

Go (*UK 0870 607 6543/ www.gofly.com*) fly low-cost from Stansted and Bristol to Nice.

Ryanair (*UK 0870 156 9569/ France 08.25.07.16.26/ www.ryanair.com*) has two daily low-cost flights from Stansted to Nîmes. From the USA, most flights involve a Paris connection.

Delta (*US 1-800 241 4141/France 08.00.35.40.80/ www.delta.com*) has a daily flight from New York JFK to Nice.

Major airports

Marseille International Airport

(*04.42.14.14.14/ www.marseille.aeroport.fr*). Situated in Marignane, 28km north-west of the centre. Buses run every 20 mins to Marseille rail station, and every 30 mins to Aix-en-Provence.

Aéroport Montpellier Méditerranée

(*04.67.20.85.00/recorded flight times 04.67.20.85.85/www.montpellier.aero port.fr*). One terminal serves all regional and international flights.

Nice International Airport

(*04.93.21.30.30/recorded flight times 08.36.69.55.55/www.nice.aeroport.fr*). 7km west of the centre, Nice is the second largest airport in France. Most flights arrive and depart from Terminal 1; Air France (Paris flights), Air Lib uses Terminal 2.

Minor airports

Avignon

(*04.90.81.51.51/ www.aeroport.avignon.fr*). 8km south of town; buses from the Lycée Agricole.

Nîmes

(*04.66.70.49.49*). 10km SE of Nîmes, linked by shuttle bus.

Toulon-Hyères

(*04.94.00.83.83*). Near Hyères port.

Helicopter services

Air St-Tropez

(*04.94.97.15.12*). Helicopters between Nice and St-Tropez. Cost €762 for five people.

Héli Air Monaco

(*00.377.92.05.00.50*). Return Nice-Monaco around €120 per person.

Nice Hélicoptères

(*04.93.21.34.32*). Cannes-Nice return approx €120 per person.

There are international trains from Spain, Italy, Switzerland, Germany and the Benelux countries. From the UK, the Eurostar runs to Lille and Paris Gare du Nord. The French TGV (high-speed train) departs for the South from Paris Gare de Lyon and Lille, running south to Avignon, where it splits west to Nîmes and Montpellier and east to Aix-en-Provence, Marseille, Toulon, St-Raphaël, Cannes, Antibes, Nice, Monte-Carlo and Menton (not all trains stop at all stations). Note that the highest-speed track currently only reaches Marseille and Nîmes. Eight TGVs per day depart from Paris Gare de Lyon for Nice (approx 5 hours 30 minutes), 18 a day for Marseille (approx 3 hours), 12 a day for Avignon (approx 2 hours 40 minutes), 7 a day for Aix-en-Provence (approx 3 hours), 12 a day for Nimes (approx 3 hours).

LOCAL TRAINS

All these stations connect with the local train network, which is most extensive in the Rhône valley and along the coast. Regional rail maps and timetables are on sale in *tabacs* and free in stations. Local bus services stop everywhere; out-of-town stations usually have a connecting *navette* (shuttle bus) to the town centre. Sometimes SNCF runs buses (indicated as Autocar in timetables) to stations where the train no longer stops; rail tickets and passes are valid on these. Métrazur runs along the coast, stopping at all stations between Marseille and Ventimiglia in Italy. Two mountain lines depart from Nice: the Roya valley line via Sospel, and the private Train des Pignes.

TICKETS

In the UK, tickets for through travel can be booked from any mainline station or travel centre. Alternatively, try the International Rail Centre, Chase House, Gilbert St, Ropley, Hampshire SO24 0BY (0196 277 3646/ www.international-rail.com) or the Rail Europe Travel Shop 179 Piccadilly, London W1V 0BA (0870 584 8848/ www.raileurope.co.uk).

In France, call SNCF on 08.36.35.35.35 (open 7am-10pm daily). For rail information in English call 08.36.35.35.39. You can buy tickets in all SNCF stations from counters or automatic ticket machines; some travel agents also sell tickets. The TGV can be booked up to two months ahead, or, if there are seats available, up until the time of departure. Internet bookings can be made at **www.sncf.com** or **www.tgv.com**. You must have seats reserved for the TGV, and you must *'composter votre billet'* – date-stamp your ticket in the orange *composteur* machine on the platforms before starting your journey.

DISCOUNTS & PASSES

A Eurodomino pass allows unlimited travel on France's rail network for three- to eight-day duration within one month, but must be bought before travelling to France. Discounted rates are available for children aged between four and 11, young people between 12 and 25 and for the over-60s. Passes for North Americans include Eurailpass, Flexipass and Saver Pass, which can be purchased in the USA. SNCF offers many discounts on early reservations and for families

and couples. Fares vary according to whether you travel in peak hours or seasons; discounts are sometimes still available within these times; first-class travellers pay the same rate at all times. There are discounts if you purchase tickets at least eight or 30 days in advance; couples are entitled to a *'Découverte a deux'* 25% reduction for return journeys. You can also save on fares by purchasing special discount cards for 12-25 yr olds, over-60s and a child under 12 with up to four adults. Children under four travel free.

BICYCLES

For long-distance train travel bicycles need to be transported separately, and must be registered and insured. They can be delivered to your destination, though this may take several days. On Eurostar services bikes can be transported as has hand luggage in a bike bag, or checked in at the station's goods depot up to 24 hours in advance of your journey.

SLEEPERS

For long-distance journeys you can travel overnight by *couchette* (bunk-bed sleeping car shared with up to five others) or *voiture-lit* (more comfortable sleeping compartment for up to three people). Both services are available for first- and second-class travellers, and must be reserved in advance.

By bus

LONG-DISTANCE BUSES

Eurolines (UK 01582 404511/France 08.36.69.52.52/ www.eurolines.fr/) has regular coach services from London Victoria Station to Avignon, Marseille, Toulon and Nice.

LOCAL BUSES

The coastal area is reasonably well served by buses,

especially around the main towns, and city centres have good regular services. In the country, services are more limited and generally run by a galaxy of small local companies. Most towns of any size have a bus station or *gare routière*, often near the train station. In remote rural areas buses are often linked to the needs of schools and working people, so often there may be only one bus in the morning, one in the evening and none at all during school holidays.

By car or motorbike

Remember that much of Europe heads south in the summer, when motorways and coast roads, especially around St-Tropez or between Cannes and Menton, can become heavily congested. You often only have to drive a few miles inland to find peace and quite again (except at beauty spots), though bear in mind that much of the region is mountainous and travel can be slow on narrow, twisty roads.

The school holidays take up July and August, and the roads are at their worst on Saturdays and around the 14 July and 15 August public holidays. It's worth remembering that the hallowed French lunch break is still widely observed, so it can be a good time to travel. Special scenic diversions attempt to reduce summer traffic by using back roads; look out for the small green BIS (*Bison Futé*) signs.

From Calais to Nice is 1,167km; from Caen to Nice 1,161km. Dieppe to Avignon is 854 km, Calais to Avignon 965km. Journey times depend on routes; for Provence, the quickest route from Calais is via Paris (though avoid the Périphérique ring road at rush hour) and on the A6 Autoroute du Soleil to Lyon and the

Directory

Rhône valley. A less-trafficked route to western Provence is the A10-A71-A75 via Bourges and Clermont-Ferrand. All autoroutes have *péage* toll-booths, where payment can be made by cash or credit card. From Calais to Menton, expect to spend around €76 on tolls. Websites: **www.iti.fr** or **www.mappy.fr** (route planners); **www.autoroutes.fr** (motorway info).

MOTORAIL

A comfortable though pricey option is the Motorail; put your car on the train in Calais or Paris and travel overnight down to the coast. *Couchettes* are obligatory. For UK bookings, contact Rail Europe (0870 584 8848/ www.frenchmotorail.com).

PAPERWORK

If you bring your car to France, you will need to bring the relevant registration and insurance documents and, of course, your driving licence. New drivers need to have held a licence for at least a year.

ROADS & TOLLS

French roads are divided into *autoroutes* (motorways, marked A8, A51, etc), *routes nationales* (national 'N' roads, marked N222, etc), *routes départementales* (local 'D' roads) and tiny, often unpaved rural *routes communales* ('C' roads). Autoroutes are toll (*péage*) roads, although some sections – especially around major cities – are free. There are service stations (*aires*) with 24-hour petrol service approximately every 20 km and, more frequently, well-designed parking and picnic areas, with toilets and sometimes showers. The tolls can work out quite expensive: Nice to Monaco costs €3.81, Aix to Nice €13.72.

SPEED LIMITS

In normal conditions, speed limits are 130km (80 miles) per hour on autoroutes, 110 km (69 miles) per hour on dual carriageways, and 90 km (56 miles) per hour on *routes nationales*. In heavy rain and fog, these limits are reduced by 20 km on autoroutes, by 10 km on other roads. The speed limit within towns and built-up areas is 50km (28 miles) per hour, with 30km (17 miles) per hour in some districts.

BREAKDOWN SERVICES

The AA or RAC do not have reciprocal arrangements with French organisations, so it's best to take out additional breakdown insurance cover, for example with Europ Assistance (in the UK 01444 442211). Local 24-hour breakdown services include Dépannage Côte d'Azur, which offers a 24-hour service (04.93.29.87.87). Autoroutes and *routes nationales* have emergency telephones every two km. Police stations and *gendarmeries* can give information about the nearest breakdown service or garage. For what to do in the case of an accident, *see page 299* **Emergencies**.

DRIVING TIPS

● At intersections where no signposts indicate the right of way, the car coming from the right has priority. Roundabouts follow the same rule, though many now give priority to those on the roundabout: this will be indicated either by stop markings on the road or by the message '*Vous n'avez pas la priorité*'. A yellow diamond sign indicates that you have priority; the diamond sign with a diagonal black line indicates that you do *not* have priority.
● Drivers and all passengers must wear seat belts.
● Children under ten are not allowed to travel in the front of a car, except in special baby seats facing backwards.
● You should not stop on an open road; pull off to the side.
● When drivers flash their lights at you, this means that they will not slow down and are warning you to keep out of the way. Oncoming drivers may also flash their lights to warn you when there are *gendarmes* lurking on the other side of the hill.
● Carry change, as it's quicker to head for the exact-money line on *péages*; but cashiers do give change and *péages* accept credit cards.
● Motorbikes must have headlights on while in motion, and cars must have their headlights on in poor visibility. All vehicles have to carry a full spare set of light bulbs and drivers who wear spectacles or contact lenses must carry a spare pair with them.
● The French drink-driving limit is 50mg alcohol per 100ml of blood, about the equivalent of two glasses of wine.
● *Cédez le passage* = give way.
● *Vous n'avez pas la priorité* = you do not have right of way.
● *Passage protégé* = no right of way.
● *Rappel* = reminder. This reminds drivers of a restriction or danger previously signposted.

FUEL

Since January 2000, French petrol stations have no longer sold leaded petrol. It has been replaced by a substitute unleaded petrol that can be used in leaded fuel vehicles. Petrol on autoroutes is the most expensive; most French drivers fill up at supermarkets.

PARKING

Parking along the coast in high season is difficult; you'll have to get up very early to get a parking space at the beach. In small French towns it is pretty difficult, too, especially in medieval town centres with narrow streets. Some highly touristed villages now have compulsory car parks. In most towns, parking meters have been replaced by *horodateurs*, pay-and-display machines, which take either coins or cards, available from *tabacs*. Many towns now have marked blue zones where you can park free for an hour.

CAR HIRE

Hiring a car in France is expensive. Consider fly-drive packages, or arranging car hire before leaving home, which can work out a lot cheaper. Most airlines offer fly-drive packages and SNCF offers a train/car rental scheme, in assocation with Avis.

To hire a car you must normally be 25 or over and have held a licence for at least a year. Some hire companies will accept drivers aged 21-24, but a supplement of €8-€15 per day is usual (USIT travel do good deals for this age group, *see below*). Take your licence and passport with you. Ensure you have all the relevant information and telephone numbers in case of an accident or a breakdown.

There are often good weekend offers (Fri evening to Mon morning). Week-long deals are better at the bigger hire companies – with Avis or Budget, for example, it's around €244 a week for a small car with insurance and 1,700km included. Members of auto clubs may get a discount. Most international companies will allow the return of a car in other French cities or other countries. Low-cost operators may have a high excess charge for dents or damage.

Car hire companies

ADA *01.55.46.19.99/ www.net-on-line.net/ada*
Avis *08.02.05.05.05/ www.avis.com*
Budget *08.00.10.00.01/ www.budget.com*
Europcar *08.03.352.352/ www.europcar.com*
EasyCar (No phone reservations)

www.easycar.com
Hertz *01.39.38.38.38/ www.hertz.com*
Rent A Car *08.36.69.46.95/ www.rentacar.fr*
Usit Connections *04.93.87.34.96/ www.usitconnections.com*

Motorbike & moped hire

see also below, **Holiday Bikes**.

Harley-Davidson Factory

8 rue Boyer, 06300 Nice (04.92.00.08.41/www.hdrentals.com). Rentals. You must be over 21 years old and a licence holder for at least two years. Prices start at around €136 per 24 hours.

By ferry

The ferry is a good option if you're travelling by car.
Hoverspeed (France 08.20.00.35.55/ www.hoverspeed.com) operates between Dover-Calais and Newhaven-Dieppe.
Brittany Ferries (08.03.82.88.28/ www.brittanyferries.fr) sail between Cherbourg-Poole, Roscoff-Plymouth, St-Malo/Caen-Portsmouth.
P&O Stena Line (08.20.01.00.20/www.posl.com) Calais-Dover.

By bicycle

Cycling is an excellent way to see Provence at the right pace. You'll get plenty of support from hotels and repair shops, but if you have a foreign-made bike, be sure to bring spare tyres with you, as French sizes are different. You can travel with your bike on many local trains; look out for the bicycle symbol in timetables. For bike transport on long-distance trains, *see p291*. Bikes can be rented from many SNCF stations (around €11 a day plus €152 deposit), and returned to any station in the scheme. You can reserve in advance; see the SNCF brochure *Guide Train + Vélo*. For tours and specialist holidays, *see p304* **Sport & activity holidays**.

Holiday Bikes

www.holiday-bikes.com Franchise network with 20 branches along the Côte d'Azur, between Bandol and Menton, plus Avignon and Forcalquier. Bicycles, scooters and mopeds can be hired at individual agencies or on the web. Prices start at €21 per 24 hours. Note prices vary from branch to branch.

On foot

Provence is a wonderful place to explore on foot. It is criss-crossed by several well-signposted *sentiers de grande randonnée* (GR), long-distance footpaths (including nos.4, 5, 6, 9, 51 and 99) as well as local paths, all described in the excellent *Topo* guides, available from bookshops and newsagents.

Although much of the coast is built up, some of the most beautiful *caps* (headlands) have waymarked coast paths (*see Walk on the Wild Side, pp222-225*), while walking in the Calanques (*see Les Calanques, pp162-163*) gives access to spectacular unspoilt beaches that are inaccessible to cars.

The best times for walking are spring and autumn, and access may be limited in high fire-risk areas in high summer. At all times, make sure you have plenty of water and sun protection.

For walking holidays, *see page 305* **Sport & activity holidays**.

Hitch-hiking

People do hitch-hike (*faire l'autostop*) in France, but it's safer and more reliable to arrange lifts with an agency.

Allô-Stop

8 rue Rochambeau, Paris (01.53.20.42.42). **Open** 10am-1pm, 2-6.30pm Mon-Fri, 10am-1pm, 2-6pm Sat. **Credit** MC, V. Call several days ahead to be put in touch with drivers. There's an agency fee of €4.50-€10.50 depending on distance; you then pay €0.33 per 10km to the driver (Paris to Nice would cost around €31).

Directory

Accommodation

There is a huge variety of accommodation available in the South, from the grandest seafront Palace hotel to the simplest mountain refuge; in between you can rent villas or gîtes, camp, or stay in a wide range of country auberges and chambres d'hôtes. In summer it is obviously advisable to book, and essential if you want to stay on the coast, but outside the peak period of mid-July and mid-August, when the French head south en masse, you should not have too much trouble finding accommodation. Many hotels close from November to February, and most campsites close in winter. Tourist offices in many areas offer a free booking service and, if you arrive in peak season without accommodation, will usually know which hotels have last-minute vacancies.

Camping

French campsites (les campings) can be surprisingly luxurious. Many are run by local councils. Prices range from €6 to around €15 per night for a family of four, with car, caravan or tent. Camping rough (camping sauvage) is discouraged but you may be given permission if you ask. Be very careful camping in areas that may have a fire risk.

FACILITIES

Campsites are graded from one-star (minimal comfort, water points, showers and sinks) to four-star luxury sites that offer more space for each pitch and above-average facilities. To get back to nature look out for campsites designated Aire naturelle de camping where facilities will be absolutely minimal, with prices to match. Some farms offer camping pitches under

the auspices of the Fédération Nationale des Gîtes Ruraux – these are designated Camping à la ferme, and again facilities are usually limited.

INFORMATION

The Guide Officiel of the French Federation of Camping and Caravanning (FFCC) lists 11,600 sites nationwide, and indicates those that have facilities for disabled campers. The Michelin Green Guide – Camping/Caravanning France is informative, and lists sites with facilities for the disabled.

Chambres d'hôtes

Chambres d'hôtes are the French equivalent of bed and breakfast, in private homes. Sometimes lunch or dinner en famille is also offered. Regulating standards are not as strict as hotels; however, this is often a fairly upmarket (and pricey) option and many are beautifully decorated rural farmhouses or even châteaux.

The following guides, available from French Government Tourist Offices, provide listings, and most tourist offices will have a local list, but it is also worth simply looking out for roadside signs, especially in rural areas (we also list selected chambres d'hôtes in the **Where to stay** sections). Gîtes de France (see right) has some chambres d'hôtes on its books as well as self-catering accommodation.
Chambres et tables d'hôtes – listings for 14,000 French B&Bs.
Chambres d'hôtes Prestige – a selection of 400 luxury B&Bs, plus 100 luxury gîtes.
Châteaux Accueil – a selection of B&B in private chateaux.
Thomas Cook Welcome Guide to Selected Bed & Breakfasts in France – 500 personally inspected B&Bs.

B&B Abroad

5 Worlds End Lane, Orpington, Kent BR6 6AA (01689

857838/www.hotelsabroad.com).
A straight-forward B&B booking service for either a single destination or various stops around the region; service can include ferry bookings.

Gîtes d'Etape & refuges

Gîte d'Etape accommodation – which is often found in mountain areas, or along long-distance footpaths – is intended for overnight stays by hikers, cyclists, skiers or horse-riders. These gîtes are often run by the local village and tend to be spartan, with bunks and basic facilities. Reservations are recommended. Gîte de neige, Gîte de pêche and Gîte équestre are all variations on the Gîte d'étape, for skiers, anglers and horse riders respectively.

Mountain refuges (shelters) range from large and solid stone houses to basic huts. All have bunk beds; many offer food – often of surprisingly high quality. Many are open only June-September; they should always be booked in advance. Prices vary between €6 and €14 per person. Lists of refuges are available from local tourist offices or from the Club Alpin Français (see p304).

Hotels

Hotels in France are generally very reasonably priced. Hotels are graded from no stars to four star and four star luxe, according to factors such as room size, lifts and services, but the star system does not necessarily reflect quality or welcome: an old building may lack a lift but be otherwise charming. For this reason we do not list star-ratings.

Prices & reservations

You can usually get a decent room with an adequate bathroom for around €38-€46, though prices are higher on the coast. Prices are usually given per room rather than per person, and will be posted on the back of the door. We quote the price for double rooms, but many hotels will also have triples, quadruples or suites suitable for families, or can provide an extra bed or cot for a child (there may be a supplement). Breakfast is not normally included: expect to pay from €5 in a budget hotel to €25 in a luxury hotel. In the peak season hotels often insist on *demi-pension* (with lunch or, more usually, dinner included). All hotels charge an additional room tax (*taxe de séjour*) of €0.15-€1 per person per night. When booking, you may be asked for a deposit; most will accept a credit card number; some may be satisfied with a confirming fax. When booking a room, it is normal to look at it first; if it doesn't suit, ask to be shown another (rooms can vary enormously within the same hotel).

Hotel groups

Various catalogues can be obtained from the French Government Tourist Office *(see p307)* in person or by post

or direct from the following:
Châteaux & Hotels de France (01.40.07.00.20/ www.chateauxhotels.com). A group of independent, upmarket hotels, ranging from moderate to luxury, plus a few B&Bs in private châteaux.
Logis de France (Fédération Nationale des Logis et Auberges de France, 83 av d'Italie, 75013 Paris, 01.45.84.70.00/www.logis-de-france.fr). France's biggest hotel network acts as a sort of quality-control stamp for over 5,000 private, often family-run, hotels, all with restaurant, in the countryside or small towns, most are one or two star.
Groupe Accor *(www.accorhotels.com)*. This is the biggest hotel group in the world, ranging from luxury Sofitel group to budget Etap and Formule 1 chains, which may be in industrial estates or by motorways, via the mid-range Hôtel Ibis and Novotel and upmarket Mercure, generally situated in towns.
Relais du Silence (01.44.49.79.00/ www.silencehotel.com). Peaceful hotels in châteaux or grand houses.
Relais & Châteaux *(01.45.72.90.00/*

www.relaischateaux.com*). A consortium of luxury hotels and restaurants in France and abroad.

Bon Weekend en Villes

(03.20.68.50.31/www.bon-week-en-villes.com). A tourist office promotion offering two nights (either Fri-Sat or Sat-Sun) for the price of one at selected hotels in participating cities. The offer is usually valid between November and March, and all year round in some towns. Marseille qualifies all year, Aix, Arles, Avignon and Nimes from November to March (in 2002). You need to book at least eight days in advance and mention the scheme when booking.

Youth hostels

To stay in most *auberges de jeunesse* you need to be a member of the International YHA or the **Fédération Unie des Auberges de Jeunesse** (27 rue Pajol, 75018 Paris, 01.44.89.87.27 /www.fuaj.org).

Gîtes & holiday rentals

If you want to experience the Provençal lifestyle, there are plenty of opportunities to rent self-catering accommodation. Rentals normally run Saturday to Saturday; book well ahead for July and August. Gîtes are self-catering (in some cases you will be expected to supply your own bed linen), but most have owners living nearby who will tell you where to buy local produce (or even provide it).

Best-known organisation is the **Fédération des Gîtes Ruraux de France** (Maison des Gîtes de France, 59 rue St-Lazare, 75009 Paris, 01.49.70.75.85/www.gites-de-france), which was set up 40-odd years ago, offering grants to owners to restore rural properties and let them out as holiday homes. *Gîtes* are an inexpensive way of enjoying a rural holiday in regional France. Properties range from simple farm cottages to grand manor houses and even the odd château. Note that some will be off the beaten track and the use of a car, or at the very least a bicycle, is usually essential. Prices average €180-€270 per week in August for a two- to four-person *gîte*. Properties are inspected by the Relais Départemental and given an *épi* (ear of corn) classification according to level of comfort. Brittany Ferries is the UK agent for Gîtes de

France, although the list in its brochure is only a small selection; bookings can be made through The Brittany Centre, Wharf Road, Portsmouth PO2 8RU (0870 536 0360).

Clévacances (05.61.13.55.66/ www.clevacances.com) is a more recently established association of holiday flats, houses and *chambres d'hôtes*, which exists in some *départements*, and is reputed for its more up-to-date rating system.

On the coast, rental accommodation also abounds, ranging from luxury villas near St-Tropez to purpose-built (and often cramped) holiday flats or Résidences de Tourisme in the newer coastal resorts. Rentals are usually by the week or month. Individual tourists offices usually have information; specialist agencies include **French Affair** (UK 020 7381 8519/www.frenchaffair.com), which lets villas and houses in Provence, and **Riviera Retreats/Kestrel Travel** (UK 01672 520651/ France 04.93.24.10.70/ www.kestreltravel.com), specialising in upmarket villas and yachts in the Var and Alpes-Maritimes. **Alastair Sawdray's Special Places to Stay French Holiday Homes** (www.specialplacestostay.com) is a selective guide to holiday rentals all over France.

Resources A-Z

Banks & money

The euro

Since 1 January 2002 the euro is
the official currency in France
and the ten other participating
European Union nations. If you
have leftover French francs,
they can be exchanged free of
charge at most banks and post
offices, until 30 June 2002
(€1 = 6.55957F). Thereafter,
only the Banque de France
will offer free exchanges (coins
until 2005, notes until 2012).
Foreign debit and credit cards
can be used to withdraw and
pay in euros.

Euro currency

The euro notes and coins are:
Coins
1, 2, and 5 euro cents (copper pieces)
10, 20 and 50 euro cents (gold pieces)
1 euro (silver piece with gold rim)
2 euros (gold piece with silver rim)
Notes
5, 10, 20, 50, 100, 200 and 500 euro
notes.

Useful euro addresses

Freephone official helpline
08.00.01.20.02 (in service until
November 2002).

www.euro.gouv.fr Official
website, with helpful information,
updates and an online converter.

Banque de France (Information:
www.banque-france.fr).

Branches: *8 bd Croisette, 06400
Cannes (04.92.99.57.00).* **Open**
8.45am-12pm, 1.30-4pm Mon-Fri.
*18 rue 4 Septembre, 13100 Aix-en-
Provence (04.42.93.66.33).* **Open**
9.15am-12.15pm, 2-3.30pm Mon-Fri.

Bank hours & rates

French banks usually open 9am-5pm
Monday-Friday (some close for lunch
12.30-2.30pm); some banks also open
on Saturday. All are closed on public
holidays (actually closing at noon on
the previous day). Note that not all
banks have foreign exchange
counters and not all offer cash
advance on a credit card. Commission
rates vary between banks. The state
Banque de France usually offers
good rates. Most banks accept
travellers' cheques.

Bank accounts

To open an account (*ouvrir un
compte*), you need proof of identity,
regular income and an address in
France. You'll probably have to show
your passport or *carte de séjour*, a
utility bill in your name and a payslip
or a letter from your employer.
Students need a student card and may
need a letter from their parents.
Most banks don't hand out a *Carte
Bleue*/Visa until several weeks after
you've opened an account. A
chequebook (*chéquier*) is usually
issued in about a week. *Carte Bleue*
transactions are debited directly
from your current account, but you
can choose for purchases to be
debited at the end of every month.
French banks are tough on
overdrafts, so try to anticipate any
cash crisis in advance and work out a
deal for an authorised overdraft
(*découvert autorisé*) or you risk being
blacklisted as *interdit bancaire* –
forbidden from having a current
account for five years. Depositing
foreign-currency cheques is slow, so
use wire transfer or a bank draft in
euros to receive funds from abroad.

Credit cards & cash machines

Major international credit cards are
widely used in France. Visa (linked to
the French Carte Bleue) is the most
readily accepted; American Express
coverage is more patchy. French-
issued cards have a security
microchip (*puce*) in each card. The
card is slotted into a card reader; the
holder keys in a PIN to authorise the
transaction. Occasionally, UK/US
cards with magnetic strips cannot be
read by French machines. Most
retailers understand the problem. If
you come across one who doesn't,
explain that the card is valid and that
you would be grateful if the
transaction could be confirmed by
phone, by saying: '*Les cartes
internationales ne sont pas des cartes
à puce, mais à bande magnétique.
Ma carte est valable et je vous serais
reconnaissant d'en demander la
confirmation auprès de votre banque
ou de votre centre de traitement.*'
  In case of credit card loss or theft,
call the following 24-hour services,
which have English-speaking staff:

● **American Express** *01.47.77.72.00*
● **Diners' Club** *01.49.06.17.17*
● **MasterCard** *01.45.67.84.84*
● **Visa** *08.36.69.08.80*
If your cash withdrawal card carries

the European Cirrus symbol,
withdrawals in euros can be made
from bank and post office cash
machines bearing the same symbol
by using your card's PIN. The
specific cards accepted are marked
on each machine, and most give
instructions in English. Credit card
companies charge a fee for cash
advances, but rates are often better
than bank rates.
  Note that cash machines are
widespread in major cities and
towns, but can be few and far
between in rural areas.

Beauty spas

Seawater spas are popular
with the French, who will often
spend an entire vacation
seeking 'thalassotherapy'–
therapeutic water massage and
seaweed treatment. Six days is
the recommended stay, though
you can usually just visit for
the day.
  The atmosphere at spas is
seriously health-focused, and
children are generally not
welcome (although some
centres do offer babysitting
services and postnatal
packages).
  Most cost around €46 to
€76 per day depending on
treatments and facilities.
Inland there are thermal spas
at Aix-en-Provence and
Gréoux-les-Bains. Grape cures
are also available in the
Vaucluse wine region (contact
Avignon Office de Tourisme
on 04.90.82.65.11). Most spas
have associated hotels offering
treatment and accommodation
packages.

Thalassa Hyères

*allée de la Mer à la Capte, Hyères
(04.94.58.00.94).*

Thalazur Antibes

*770 chemin des Moyennes
Bréguières, 6600 Antibes
(04.92.91.82.00).*

Thermes de Gréoux-
les-Bains

*av des Thermes, Gréoux-les-Bains
(04.92.70.40.01).*

Directory

Thermes Marins de Monte-Carlo

2 av de Monte-Carlo
(00.377.92.16.40.40).

Thermes Sextius

55 cours Sextius, Aix-en-Provence
(04.42.23.81.81).

Business

The most important thing to know about doing business in France, especially in the South, is that people will invariably prefer to meet you in person. You will often be expected to go in and see someone, even if it's to discuss something that could easily have been dealt with over the phone. And the three-course, three-hour lunch remains a sacred ritual.

Most major banks can refer you to lawyers, accountants and tax consultants; several US and British banks provide expatriate services.

For business and financial news, the French dailies *La Tribune* and *Les Echos*, and the weekly *Investir*, are the tried and trusted sources. *Capital*, its sister magazine *Management* and the weightier *L'Expansion* are worthwhile monthlies. *Défis* has tips for the entrepreneur, *Initiatives* is for the self-employed.

BFM on 96.4 FM is an all-news business radio station. *Les Echos* gives stock quotes on www.lesechos.com, as does **www.boursorama.com**. Business directories *Kompass France* and *Kompass Régional* also give company details and French market profiles on **www.kompass.fr**.

The standard English-language reference is *The French Company Handbook*, a list of all companies in the 120 Index of the Paris Bourse, published by the *International Herald Tribune* (01.41.43.93.00). It can be ordered for £50 from Paul Baker Publishing, 37 Lambton Road, London SW20 OLW (0176 568 8236).

Institutions

Banque Populaire de la Côte d'Azur

International Branch, 22 bd Victor Hugo, 06000 Nice (04.93.82.81.81/www.cotedazur.banq uepopulaire.fr). Banking advice in English.

British Chamber of Commerce

25 bis bd Carnot, Nice 06300 (04.97.08.11.30). By appointment only.

Centre de Ressources Côte d'Azur

Chambre de Commerce et d'Industrie Nice Côte d'Azur, 20 bd Carabacel, Nice 06000 (04.93.13.74.36/ www.businessriviera.com). Information centre for business resources and facilities.

Conference centres & trade fairs

Acropolis

1 esplanade Kennedy, Nice (04.93.92.83.00).

Centre de Congrès Auditorium

bd Louis II, Monte-Carlo, Monaco (00.377.93.10.84.00).

Centre de Rencontre Internationale

13 bd Princesse Charlotte, Monte-Carlo (00.377.93.25.53.07).

Palais des Congrès

Parc Chanot, 2 bd Rabatau, Marseille (04.91.76.16.00).

Palais des Festivals

La Croisette, esplanade George Pompidou, Cannes (04.93.39.01.01).

Miscellaneous

Accents

Pauline Beaumont, 120 chemin des Serres, 06510 Gattières (04.93.08.38.38/pauline.beaumont@ worldonline.fr). Translation service.

DHL

(Freephone 0800.20.25.25.25). International delivery service.

FedEx

(Freephone 0800.12.38.00). International delivery service.

Gale Force

13 av St-Michel, Monte-Carlo (00377.93.50.20.92/www.galeforce.c om). Computer sales and servicing in English.

Loca Centre

1330 av Guilibert de la Lauzière, Europarc de Pichaury, Bâtiment B5, 13865 Aix-en-Provence (04.88.71.88.35/www.locacentre.com Rentals of laptops, PCs, printers and scanners. Branch in Marseille.

Children

The beach and the sea are the easiest way to amuse children and private beach concessions with sunloungers and parasols are the easiest of all; just book your parasol close to the shore and watch the kids make sandcastles. Inflatables are often provided and there are sometimes bouncy castles, too. Main resorts and beaches have surveyed beaches with lifeguards in summer. But do be careful with the intense midday sun – most French families leave the beach between noon and 3pm and the southern tradition of a siesta is not just for sleeping off all that wine. Even small villages will often have a playground with a slide or climbing frame, and this can often be a good place to meet other families. Sightseeing is only likely to be difficult in steep hill villages, which can be hard to negotiate with a pushchair.

Eating out with children is a normal part of the French lifestyle, and children, as long as they are reasonably well behaved are generally welcome. It's especially easy during the day: just choose a restaurant or café with a terrace and they can run around while you have another glass of wine. Many restaurants offer a children's menu or will split a *prix-fixe* menu between two children or even give you an extra plate to share your own meal. Most hotels have family rooms so children do not have to be separated from parents and a cot (*lit bébé*) can often be provided for a supplement; check availability in advance.

Disposable nappies (*couches jetables*) are easy to find, and French baby food is often of gourmet standard, especially the puréed artichoke – though watch out for added sugar.

When hiring a car, be sure to book baby seats in advance – though larger hire companies usually have a few ready to go.

Crime & police

Police in urban and rural areas come under two different governmental organisations. The **Gendarmerie nationale** is a military force serving under the *Ministère de la Défense* and its network covers minor towns and rural areas. The **police nationale** serve under the *Ministère d'Intérieur* in main cities.

Watch out in particular for crime from cars. Police advise leaving nothing visible in parked cars. In Nice, there has also been a spate of 'car jackings' – car theft as people are parking – and petrol theft is not unknown in rural areas.

If you are robbed, you will need to make a statement at the police station or gendarmerie for your insurance claim.

Customs

There are no limits on the quantity of goods you can take into France from another EU country for personal use, provided tax has been paid on them in the country of origin. However, Customs still has the right to question visitors. Quantities accepted as being for personal use are:

● up to 800 cigarettes, 400 small cigars, 200 cigars or 1kg loose tobacco.

● 10 litres of spirits (over 22% alcohol), 90 litres of wine (under 22% alcohol) or 110 litres of beer.

For goods from outside the EU:

● 200 cigarettes or 100 small cigars, 50 cigars or 250g loose tobacco.

● 1 litre of spirits (over 22% alcohol) and 2 litres of wine and beer (under 22% alcohol).

● 50g perfume.

Visitors can carry up to €7600 in currency.

See also **Tax refunds** *below*.

Disabled travellers

Eurotunnel (UK 0870 535 3535/ Disabled inquiries 0130 327 3747/France 01.43.18.62.22/www.eurotunnel .com). The Channel Tunnel car-on-a-train service is good for disabled passengers; you may stay in your vehicle and are offered a 10% discount.
Eurostar trains (UK special requests number 020 7928 0660) give wheelchair passengers first-class travel for second-class fares. Most **ferry companies** will offer facilities if contacted beforehand. Cars fitted to accommodate disabled people pay reduced tolls on autoroutes, and most motorway aires and service stations have disabled toilet facilities.

But once you get there, France in general, and the South in particular, is not as sensitive to the needs of disabled travellers as it might be. In small hill villages with cobbled streets, wheelchairs are simply not feasible. In bigger cities there is usually reasonably good provision – especially in newer museums – and in small towns and cities disabled parking is provided and indicated with a blue wheelchair sign; the international orange disabled parking disc scheme is also recognised in France. (Don't forget to bring the disc with you.) Even if places claim to have disabled access, it's wise to check beforehand. Many places are accessible to wheelchair users but do not have accessible toilets. If you

need to hire a wheelchair or other equipment, enquire at the local pharmacy.

In Nice, part of the public beach has been adapted for wheelchairs with ramp access and a concrete platform on the shingle.

TAXIS
If you are disabled, taxi drivers cannot legally refuse to take you. They must help you into a taxi; they are also required to transport guide dogs for the blind.

An autoroute guide for disabled travellers (*Guides des Autoroutes à l'usage des Personnes à Mobilité Réduite*) is available free from:

Ministère des Transports
Direction des Routes, Service du Contrôle des Autoroutes, La Défense, 92055 Cedex, Paris (01.40.81.21.22).

CAR HIRE
Location de Véhicules Equipés et Automatiques *51 rue Celony, 13100 Aix-en-Provence (04.42.93.54.59/www.lvea.fr)* Rents specially adapted cars for disabled drivers. Rates are approximately €102 per day.

HOLIDAYS & ACCOMMODATION
Gîtes Accessibles à Tous lists *gîte* accommodation equipped for the disabled. It is available from Maison des Gîtes de France, 59 rue St-Lazare, 75009 Paris (01.49.70.75.85/ www.gites-de-france.fr). The *French Federation of Camping and Caravanning Guide* indicates which campsites have facilities for disabled campers. It's available from Deneway Guides and Travel Limited, Manor Garden, Burton Bradstock, Bridport, Dorset, DT6 4QA (0130 889 7809), price £9 plus postage and packing. The *Michelin Green Guide – Camping/Caravanning France* lists sites with facilities for the disabled.

Useful addresses

Association des paralysés de France *17-19 bd Auguste-Blanqui, 75013 Paris (01.40.78.69.00).* **Open** 9am-12.30pm, 2-6pm Mon-Fri.
Comité national de liaison pour la réadaptation des handicapés (CNRH) *236 bis rue de Tolbiac, 75013 Paris (01.53.80.66.85/ www.handitel.org).*
RADAR (Royal Association for Disability & Rehabilitation) *Unit 12 City Forum, 250 City Road, London EC1V 8AF (0207 250 3222/Minicom 0207 250 4119/www.radar.org.uk).*

Information department can give specialist advice (lines open 10am-4pm Mon-Fri), and sells *Getting There*, a guide to facilities in airports. Price £5; send an SAE.

Local information

Office de Tourisme
4 La Canebière, Marseille (04.91.13.89.00). Can provide a list of sights and areas accessible to the disabled, and a list of suitable hotels.

Groupement pour Insertion des Handicapés Physiques (GIHP) *(04.91.11.41.000).* Information on disabled transports.

Ulysse *23 bd Carlone, 06200 Nice (04.93.96.09.99).* Will organise transport from airport, tourist visits, find accommodation and provide general assistance.

Drugs

Possession of drugs is illegal in France. Officially there is no legal distinction between 'hard' and 'soft' drugs and possession of even a small amount of marijuana or cannabis for personal use could land you in jail and incur a large fine.

Electricity & gas

Electricity in France runs on 220V, so visitors with British 240V appliances can simply change the plug or use a converter (*adaptateur*), available at better hardware shops. For US 110V appliances, you will need to use a transformer (*transformateur*), available at the Fnac and Darty chains.

Gas and electricity are supplied by the state-owned EDF-GDF (Electricité de France-Gaz de France). Contact them about supply, bills, or in case of power failures or gas leaks . Look under *Urgences* in the phone book for a local number or on line at www.edf.fr or www.gazdefrance.fr.

Note that Butane gas is widely used for cooking (and sometimes water and heating) in towns and villages without mains gas supply. If you stay

in rented accommodation, you may need to change the cylinder and buy new ones, from a garage or local shop.

Remember that in rural areas electricity sometimes flickers or cuts out altogether; you will need a good supply of candles and torches. You also need computer back-up and some form of surge control.

Embassies & consulates

Before going to an embassy or consulate, phone and check opening hours. You may need to make an appointment. The answerphone will usually give an emergency contact number. There's a full list of embassies and consulates in the *Pages Jaunes* under *Ambassades et Consulats* or on line at *www.pagesjaunes.fr*. For general enquiries or problems with passports or visas, it is usually the consulate you need. You are advised to contact the consulate in the first instance and staff will advise you whether your problem can be dealt with by them, if you need the embassy in Paris, or if it can be dealt with by a local honorary consul.

Consulates in the South

British *24 av du Prado, 13006 Marseille (04.91.15.72.10).*

US *12 bd Paul Peytral, 13286 Marseille (04.91.54.92.00).*
7 av Gustave V, 06000 Nice (04.93.88.89.55).

Canadian *10 rue Lamartine, 06000 Nice (04.93.92.93.22).*

Irish *152 bd JF Kennedy, 06160 Cap d'Antibes (04.93.61.50.63).*

Paris embassies & consulates

Australian Embassy *4 rue Jean-Rey, 15th (01.40.59.33.00). Mº Bir-Hakeim.* **Open** 9am-5pm Mon-Fri; *visas* 10am-noon Mon-Fri.

British Embassy *35 rue du Fbg-St-Honoré, 8th (01.44.51.31.00). Mº*

Concorde. **Open** 9.30am-1pm, 2.30-6pm Mon-Fri. **Consulate** *18bis rue d'Anjou, 8th (01.44.51.33.01/01.44.51.33.03). Mº Concorde.* **Open** 9.30am-12.30pm Mon,Wed,Thur,Fri; 9.30am-4.30pm Tue.

Canadian Embassy *35 av Montaigne, 8th (01.44.43.29.00). Mº Franklin D Roosevelt.* **Open** 10am-5pm Mon-Fri. **Visas** *37 av Montaigne (01.44.43.29.16).* **Open** 8.30am-11am Mon-Fri.

Irish Embassy *12 av Foch, 16th.* **Consulate** *4 rue Rude, 16th (01.44.17.67.00). Mº Charles de Gaulle-Etoile.* **Open** 9.30am-noon Mon-Fri; *by phone* 9.30am-1pm, 2.30-5.30pm Mon-Fri.

New Zealand Embassy *7ter rue Léonard de Vinci, 16th (01.45.00.24.11). Mº Victor-Hugo.* **Open** 9am-1pm, 2-5.30pm Mon-Fri; *visas* 9am-12.30pm Mon-Fri.

South African Embassy *59 quai d'Orsay, 7th (01.53.59.23.23). Mº Invalides.* **Open** 8.30am-5.15pm Mon-Fri, by appointment. **Consulate** 9am-noon.

US Embassy *2 av Gabriel, 8th (01.43.12.22.22). Mº Concorde.* **Open** 9am-5pm Mon-Fri, by appointment. **Consulate/ visas** *2 rue St-Florentin, 1st (01.43.12.22.22). Mº Concorde.* **Open** phone 2-5pm Mon-Fri for appointment; *passport service* 9am-12.30pm, 1-3pm Mon-Fri.

Emergencies

See also below, **Health.**

Police 17.
Fire (Sapeurs-Pompiers) 18.
Ambulance (SAMU) 15.
Emergencies from mobile phone 112.

Gay d'Azur

France is a generally gay-tolerant country and the Riviera has long been a stomping ground for pink people – plenty of beach cruising, sun to soak up and same-sex action. Your first pick-up, however, should be a copy of local free gay listings magazine *Ibiza*.

Despite a large gay population, the Côte d'Azur lacks a gay infrastructure to match. Bars and saunas abound in Nice, Toulon,

Directory

Marseille and Avignon, but helplines, self-help groups and drop-in centres, struggle by despite the highest HIV/AIDS infection rates in France outside Paris.

Lesbians are almost invisible on the Côte d'Azur, though St-Tropez is home to high-profile gay girl couple Amélie Mauresmo and Sylvie, to be found singing of a summer evening in **Le Gorille**.

Café terraces are always busy with wandering eyes, and the boardwalks and beaches are a mecca for Mediterranean man. Gay beaches are eye-popping day-trip destinations. Reaching the designated area can resemble a Famous Five adventure along winding cliff paths or hopping across rocks, as is the case at the 24-hour Nice cruising point, **Coco Beach**. Other gay beaches include the ritzy **Plage de St-Laurent-d'Eze** and Plage St-Aygulf at Fréjus. **La Batterie**, just outside Cannes towards Antibes, is a straight and gay nude beach.

Associations

Centre Gai et Lesbien
11 rue Regal, 30000 Nîmes (04.66.67.10.59). **Open** 7-9pm Thur. Support and advice.

All EU nationals staying in France are entitled to use of the French Social Security system, which refunds up to 70% of medical expenses (but sometimes much less, for example for dental treatment). To get a refund, British nationals should obtain form E111 before leaving the UK (or E112 for those already in treatment). Nationals of non-EU countries should take out insurance before leaving home. Fes and prescriptions have to be paid for in full, and are reimbursed, in part, on receipt of a completed *fiche* (form).

If you undergo treatment in France, the doctor will give you a prescription and a *feuille de soins* (statement of treatment). The medication will carry *vignettes* (stickers) that you must stick on to your *feuille de soins*. Send this, the prescription and form E111 to the local Caisse Primaire d'Assurance Maladie (in the phone book under *Sécurité Sociale*). Refunds can take over a month to come through.

Contraception & abortion

For the pill (*la pilule*) or a coil (*stérilet*) you will need a prescription. Visit a GP (*médecin généraliste*) – look in the *Pages Jaunes* (www.pagesjaunes.fr) or ask at a pharmacy for a recommendation. In France, women usually go direct to specialists for contraception and help with gynaecological problems. You can buy condoms and spermicides from pharmacies. French pharmacies also dispense the morning-after pill (*pilule du lendemain*) without a prescription. If you need an abortion, either consult a gynaecologist or look for the local *Planning Familial* centre in the telephone directory.

Doctors & dentists

A complete list of practitioners is in the *Pages Jaunes* under *Médecins Qualifiés*. To get a Social Security refund, choose a doctor or dentist registered with the state system; look for *Médecin Conventionné* after the name. Consultations cost at least €17.50, of which a proportion can be reimbursed – if you are entitled to use the French Social Security system (*see above*). A *médecin généraliste* is a general practioner, though you are also free to go to the specialist of your choice – who may also be *conventionné* but whose fees may be two or three times higher.

Helplines & house calls

● In cases of medical emergency, dial 15 to call an ambulance or ring the Service d'Aide Médicale d'Urgence (SAMU), which exists in most large towns and cities – the numbers will be given at the front of telephone directories. The fire brigade (sapeurs-pompiers) also have trained paramedics.

Alcoholics Anonymous South of France
(04.93.82.91.10). Local contacts and meetings.

Centre Anti-Poisons
(04.91.75.25.25).

Nice Médecins
(04.93.52.42.42). The local doctor service for home visits.

SIDA Info Service
(08.00.84.08.00). **Open** 24 hours daily. Confidential AIDS information in French (some bilingual counsellors).

SOS Médecins
(08.10.85.01.01). Covers the whole region and will give another number for another locality if necessary. Can send a doctor on a house call. A home visit before 7pm starts at €38 if you don't have French Social Security, €22 if you do; fee rises after 7pm.

Hospitals

For a complete list, consult the *Pages Blanches* (www.pagesblanches.fr) under *Hôpital Assistance Publique*. The following all have 24 hour casualty departments.

Centre Hospitalier Géneral Joseph Imbert
quartier Haut de Fourchon, Arles (04.90.49.29.29).

Centre Hospitalier H-Duffaut
305 rue Raoul-Follereau, Avignon (04.32.75.33.33).

Hôpitaux La Conception
144 rue St-Pierre, Marseille (04.91.38.30.00).

Centre Hospitalier du Pays d'Aix Urgences
av Tamaris, Aix-en-Provence (04.42.33.90.28).

Hôpital de Draguignan
route de Montferrat, Draguignan (04.94.60.50.00).

Hôpital St-Roch
5 rue Pierre Dévoluy, Nice (04.92.03.77.77/www.chu-nice.fr).

Pharmacies

Pharmacies sport a green neon cross. They have a monopoly on issuing medication, and also sell sanitary products. Most open from 9am or 10am to 7pm or 8pm. Staff can provide basic medical services such as disinfecting and bandaging wounds, attending to snake or insect bites (for a small fee) and will indicate the nearest doctor on duty. French pharmacists are highly trained; you can often avoid visiting a doctor by describing your symptoms and seeing what they suggest. They are also qualified to identify mushrooms, so you can take in anything you aren't sure about. Towns have a rota system of *pharmacies de garde* at night and on Sundays. Any closed pharmacy will have a sign indicating the nearest open pharmacy. Otherwise, you can enquire from the *Gendarmerie*. Toiletries and cosmetics are usually cheaper in supermarkets.

Opticians

Any optician will be able to supply new glasses, but remember to bring your prescription. Also remember that drivers are required by law to carry a spare pair.

Complementary medicine

Most pharmacies also sell homeopathic medicines and can advise on their use. For alternative medicine practitioners, ask in the pharmacy, or look them up in the *Pages Jaunes* (www.pagesjaunes.fr).

Legal advice

Mairies (town halls) may be able to answer legal enquiries. Phone for details and times of free *consultations juridiques*. Or they will be able to recommend a local *notaire*. (lawyer). Note that lawyers are always addressed as *'Maître'*.

Living & working in the South

Anyone from abroad coming to live in France should be prepared for a long and tiring struggle with bureaucracy, whether acquiring a *Carte de séjour* (resident's permit), opening a bank account, reclaiming medical expenses or getting married. Among documents regularly required are a *Fiche d'état civil* (a sort of identity card consisting of

essential details translated from your passport by an embassy/consulate) and a legally approved translation of your birth certificate (embassies will provide lists of approved legal translators). You will need to be able to prove your identity to the police at all times, so keep your passport/*Carte de Séjour* or a photocopy with you.

Carte de séjour

Officially, all foreigners, both EU citizens and non-Europeans in France for more than three months, must apply at the local *mairie* (town hall) for a *Carte de séjour*, valid for one year. Those who have had a *Carte de séjour* for at least three years, have been paying French income tax, can show proof of income and/or are married to a French national can apply for a *Carte de résident*, valid for ten years.

Working

All EU nationals can work legally in France, but must apply for a *Carte de Séjour* (*see above*) and a French social security number from the nearest social security office (*Caisse Primaire d'Assurance Maladie*). Some job ads can be found at branches of the *Agence National Pour l'Emploi* (ANPE), the French national employment bureau. This is also the place to sign up as a *demandeur d'emploi*, to be placed on file as available for work and to qualify for French unemployment benefits. Britons can only claim unemployment benefit if they were signed on before leaving the UK. If you also have a *Carte de Séjour*, you can get free French lessons (*perfectionnement de la langue française*), although these are not aimed at complete beginners. Offices are listed under *Administration du Travail et de l'Emploi* in the *Pages Jaunes*, or get a list from ANPE (33-39 bd des Provinces-Françaises, Nanterre; 01.55.51.18.50). There is also a European Employment Service (EURES) network, which aims to put job seekers in touch with job offers (details available in local employment offices in member countries). In the UK, the Employment Service (Overseas Placing Unit, Level 2, Rockingham House, 123 West Street, Sheffield S1 4ER; 0114 259 6051) publishes information on working in France. The South is part of the expanding Mediterranean high-tech sunbelt, focused on the technopark of **Sophia-Antipolis** near Valbonne,

where a number of international high-tech companies are based. Seasonal work is available mainly in the tourist industry, though this is notoriously badly paid. The main openings are in hotels, restaurants, bars, ski resorts and outdoor activity centres. You will need to speak decent French and ensure you have the correct papers. Other possibilities are gardening, house-sitting and teaching English, which can be well paid, especially if you have a TEFL qualification. Foreign students in France can get a temporary work permit (*autorisation provisoire de travail*) for part-time work in the holidays. PGL Young Adventure Ltd (Alton Court, Penyard Lane, Ross-on-Wye; Herefordshire/ 01989 764211) has activity centres in France and recruits temporary chalet staff and sports instructors. Grape and fruit picking is another possibility, but very difficult to set up in advance. A good Internet job search engine is www.pacajob.com.

Accommodation

Rented accommodation is plentiful in France. For short-term rentals, tourist accommodation can often be found at very reduced rates out of season (Oct-Mar). As always in France, contacts are the thing, as well as rental agencies, which can be found under *Agences de Location et de Propriétés* in the *Pages Jaunes*. Other sources include local newspapers and English-language magazines (eg the *Riviera Reporter – see* **Media** *below*), advertisments in shop windows, supermarkets, petrol stations and colleges and club, church and expatriate newsletters.

Those intending to buy should survey the market carefully; there will be great variations in price between small inland villages and coastal resorts, though fashionable inland areas like the Luberon and Alpilles can also be in the millionaire bracket. As always, get good legal advice. There are several English-language magazines devoted to French property-buying including *Property France* and *French Property News*, which are good sources of information, advice and properties for sale. Check French property website *www.immoneuf.com* for regularly updated sales offers.

Rental laws

The legal minimum period for a rental lease (*bail de location*) is three years for an unfurnished apartment and one year for a furnished flat. Both are renewable. During this period the landlord can only raise the rent in line with the official construction inflation index. At the end of the lease the rent can be

Directory

readjusted to any level, but tenants can object before a rent board if it seems exorbitant. Tenants can be evicted for non-payment, or if the landlord wishes to sell the property or use it for his own residence.

Before accepting you as a tenant, agencies or landlords will probably require you to present a dossier with pay slips (*fiches de paie/bulletins de salaire*) showing three to four times the amount of the monthly rent; foreigners may also be required to furnish a financial surety. When taking out a lease, payments usually include the first month's rent, a deposit (*une caution*) equal to two months' rent and an agency fee, if applicable. It is customary for an inspection of the premises (*état des lieux*) by a bailiff (*huissier*) at the start and end of the rental to assess the flat's condition; the cost of this inspection (around €150) should be shared equally between landlord and tenant. Landlords may try to rent their flats *non-declaré*, without a written lease, and get rent in cash. This can make it difficult for the tenant to establish their rights. Note that all important communications to one's landlord must be sent by registered letter.

Useful addresses

Riviera Insurance Brokers

rue de la Paroisse, Valbonne (04.93.12.36.10).

Union Nationale des Accueils des Villes Françaises

Relations Internationales, Secrétariat Administratif, 3 rue de Paradis, 75010 Paris (01.47.70.45.85). This national volunteer organisation welcomes and supports new arrivals with free advice and information. Consult them for local addresses.

Lost & stolen property

To report a crime or loss of belongings, visit the local *gendarmerie* or *commisariat de police* (*see p298* **Crime**). If you want to make an insurance claim, you will need a police report anyway. Telephone numbers are given at the front of local directories; in an emergency dial 17. If you lose a passport, report it first to the police, then to the nearest

consulate (*see above* **Embassies & consulates**).

Maps

Tourist offices can usually provide free town maps. The large-format Michelin Atlases or sheet maps are good for driving. Michelin Carte Routiére et Touristique No.245 is the best all-purpose map for the Provence Côte d'Azur area. For walking or cycling, the Institut Géographique National (IGN) maps are invaluable. The Top 100 (1:100,000, 1cm to 1km) and Top 50 (1:50,000, 2cm to 1km) maps have all roads and most footpaths marked. For even greater detail, go for the IGN blue series 1:25,000 maps.

Good map sources in the UK include:

Stanfords International Map Centre *12-14 Long Acre, London WC2E 9LP (020 7730 1354).*

The Travel Bookshop *13 Blenheim Crescent, London W11 2EE (020 7229 5260/ www.thetravelbookshop.co.uk).*

World Leisure Marketing *11 Newmarket Court, Derby DE24 8NW (freephone 0800 83 80 80).* IGN agent, offers a mail order service.

Natural hazards

Insects

For every tourist there is at least one mosquito in the South, particularly in the Camargue. Plug-in vaporisers are a good defence and are available in most French supermarkets. Campers should beware a spider that bites exposed skin at night, producing a scratchy rash. Huge summer flies are harmless. Black scorpions are around too, appearing in late spring and lasting well into autumn, so be careful.

Fire

Fire is a major risk during the dry summer period, and each

year there are usually several serious fires, some of them caused deliberately. Always be careful when walking or cycling on open mountain or in woodland; note that campfires are strictly banned and that certain paths (eg. in the Calanques) are closed in high summer or on windy days.

Opening times

The sacred lunch hour is still largely observed, which means that most shops and offices will close at noon or 1pm and may not reopen till 2 or 2.30pm. Many shops also close on Monday morning or all day Monday. Hypermarkets (*grandes surfaces*) usually stay open through lunch and till 7pm or 8pm. Most shops close on Sundays, though *bureaux de tabac* (cigarettes, stamps) and *maisons de la presse* (newsgents) are often open Sunday mornings, and *boulangeries* (bakers) may be open every day.

Banks are usually open 9am-noon and 1.30-5pm Mon-Fri, though these times can vary.

Petrol stations usually open at 8.30 am, close for lunch noon-2pm or 2.30pm and close around 9pm except on motorways; those attached to supermarkets may stay open for credit card sales only.

Museums: except during July and August, many museums close for lunch from noon to 2pm. They also close on certain public holidays, notably 1 January, 1 May and 25 December. National museums are usually closed on Tuesday.

Public offices usually open 8.30-noon, then 2-6pm. *Mairies* (town halls) will also close for lunch and in smaller places may only open in the morning.

Post & fax

Postes or PTTs (post offices) are generally open 9am-noon, 2-6pm Monday-Friday, and

9am-noon Saturday. In small villages, they may open only in the morning. Inside major post offices, individual counters are marked according to the services they provide; if you just need stamps, go to the window marked *Timbres*. If you need to send an urgent letter overseas, ask for it to be sent *par exprès*, or through the Chronopost system, which is faster but much more expensive. Chronopost is also the fastest way to send parcels within France; packages up to 25kg are guaranteed to be delivered within 24 hours.

For a small fee, you can arrange for mail to be kept *poste restante* at any post office, addressed to *Poste Restante, Poste Centrale* (for main post office), then the town postcode and name. You will need to present your passport when collecting mail.

Stamps are also available at tobacconists (*bureaux de tabac*) and other shops selling postcards and greetings cards. For standard-weight letters or postcards (up to 20g) within France and the EU, a €0.46 stamp is needed.

Telegrams can be sent during post office hours or by telephone (24-hours); to send a telegram abroad, dial 08.00.33.44.11.

Fax and photocopying facilities are often available at major post offices and *maisons de la presse* (newsagents). Many supermarkets have coin-operated photocopiers.

Press

English-language newspapers

Most of the major British and a few American papers can be picked up from newsagents (*maisons de la presse*) in the centre of the major towns, at train stations and airports, and along most of the coast in summer. Supply goes with demand; even in tiny Luberon villages, one can normally find one or two British papers. The Paris-based *International Herald Tribune* is widely available, especially during tourist season. *The Riviera Reporter* is an English-language magazine aimed at local foreign residents, carrying local information, news and small ads; it can be picked up at English-language bookshops and other outlets in the Riviera area (or call Riviera Reporter, 56 chemin de Provence, 06250 Mougins, 04.93.45.77.19).

French newspapers

As well as the French national dailies *Le Monde* (centre-left), *Libération* (left), *Le Figaro* (right), and sports daily *L'Equipe*, the French are attached to their local papers: *Nice Matin* (www.nicematin.fr), *La Provence* (www.laprovence-presse.fr), *Var Matin* (www.varmatin.com), *Le Dauphiné Vaucluse* and *La Marseillaise* cover most of Provence and the Côte d'Azur.

Public holidays

On public holidays, banks, post offices and public offices will be closed. Food shops – in particular *boulangeries* (bread shops) – will still open, even on Christmas Day. It is common practice, if a public holiday falls on a Thursday or Tuesday, for French businesses to *faire le pont* (bridge the gap) and take Friday or Monday as a holiday, too. The most fully observed public holidays are 1 May, 14 July and 15 August. Foreign embassies/consulates observe both French public holidays and their own.

1 January New Year's Day (Nouvel an).

Easter Monday (Lundi de Pâques)

1 May Labour Day (Fête du Travail)

May Ascension Day (Ascension), on a Thursday 40 days after Easter.

8 May Victory Day (Fête de la Libération) to commemorate the end of World War II.

May/June Pentecost (Pentecôte), ten days after Ascension.

14 July Bastille Day (Quatorze Juillet).

15 August Assumption Day (Fête de l'Assomption)

1 November All Saints' Day (Toussaint).

11 November Armistice Day (Fête de l'Armistice).

25 December Christmas Day (Noël).

Radio

FM radio

Note that for many stations, wavelengths vary from area to area.

87.8 France Inter State-run, MOR music and international news.

91.7/92.1 France Musique State classical music channel with concerts and jazz.

93.5/93.9 France Culture Highbrow state culture station; literature, poetry, history, cinema and music.

105.5 France Info 24-hour news, economic updates and sports. Repeated every 15 minutes, so good for learning French.

BFM Business and economics. Wall Street in English every evening.

RTL Most popular French station mixing music and talk.

Europe 1 News, press reviews, sports, business and good weekday breakfast news broadcast.

NRJ enormously popular pop channel.

Nostalgie golden oldies.

Rire et chansons French comedy acts mixed with pop, to be heard to be believed.

Local FM stations

88.8 FM Radio Grenouille. Marseille station, with hip coverage of culture, events and new music.

98.8 FM Radio Monte Carlo.

106.3 & 106.5 FM Riviera Radio parochial English-language radio with small ads and local gossip.

BBC World Service

Between **6.195** and **12.095** MHz shortwave.

Religion

The history of the British in the South of France over the past two centuries means there are several Anglican churches. For more information on churches and chaplains in France, including seasonal chaplaincies, contact:

Intercontinental Church Society *1 Athena Drive, Tachbrook Park, Warwick CV34 6NL (0192 643 0347/www.ics-uk.org).*

Holy Trinity Church *rue du Canada, Cannes (04.93.94.54.61).* Service 10.30am Sun.

Monaco Christian Fellowship *9 rue Louis Notari, Monaco (00.377.93.30.60.72).* Service 11am Sun.

St Michael's Anglican Church
*11 chemin des Myrtes, Beaulieu
(04.93.01.45.61).* **Service** 10am Sun.

Removals/relocation

For international removals you should use a company that is a member of the International Federation of Furniture Removers (FIDI) or the Overseas Moving Network with experience in France. They will advise on the customs formalities and documentation required.

Overs International *Unit 8, Abro Development, Government Road, Aldershot GU11 2DA (01252 343646).*
Weekly service to Côte d'Azur.

Tooth Removals *107 rte de Plan, 06130 Le Plan de Grasse (04.93.77.90.15/ UK 01784 251 252).*
Between London and the Côte d'Azur.

Smoking

Despite health campaigns and a 1991 law that insists restaurants provide non-smoking areas (*zones non-fumeurs*), the French remain enthusiastic smokers and happily smoke in public places. Though smokers should note that tobacconists are hard to find late at night or on Sunday.

Sport & activity holidays

Not everyone goes to the South of France to lie on the beach; there is a huge range of sports and activities to choose from. Even beach bums can indulge in windsurfing, water-skiing and jet-skiing.

The sea is usually warm enough for swimming from June to September. Almost every town also has a municipal pool, though it may only be open during school holidays. Even small villages often have a tennis court,

though you may have to become a temporary member to use it – enquire at the local tourist office or *mairie* (town hall), which will also provide details of all other local sporting activities.

Inland Provence and the mountains offer walking, riding, cycling and climbing, river rafting and canoeing, and skiing in the winter months. At certain times of the year it is possible to fulfill that urban dream of sunbathing on the beach in the morning and going for a ski after lunch.

Information on sports and activities can be had from local tourist offices, national organisations or from the Centre Régional Information Jeunesse Côte d'Azur (19 rue Gioffredo, Nice; 04.93.80.93.93/ fax 04.93.80.30.33). Many UK tour operators offer holidays tailored to specific activities.

Climbing

The Conseil Général des Alpes-Maritimes publishes several excellent guides for climbers and trekkers, *Les Guides Randoxygène* (available from main tourist offices), with detailed trails in the region. Dozens of climbing clubs provide beginners' courses, plus guides and monitors for day outings. There are also a few protected climbing routes, equipped with pitons and wire handrails and known as '*via ferrata*', in the Alpes-Maritimes.
Club Alpin Français
14 av Mirabeau, Nice (04.93.62.59.99/ www.cafnice.free.fr) or 3 rue St Michel, Avignon (04.90.82.34.82).
For climbing information.

Canoeing & kayaking

Options include sea-kayaking or canoeing in the Gorges du Verdon. Some clubs organise day outings accompanied by guides.
Fédération Française de Canoe-Kayak et des Sports Associés en Eau-Vive *87 quai de la Marne, 94340 Joinville-le-Pont (01.45.11.08.50).*
Ligue Régionale Alpes-Provence *14 av Vincent Auriol, 30200 Bagnols-sur-Cèze (04.66.89.47.71).*

Cycling

Taking your own bike (*vélo*) to France is relatively easy and once there, they can be carried free on most ferries and trains (*see* **Getting There & Around**). Some youth hostels rent out cycles and arrange tours with accommodation in hostels or under canvas. For more info, contact the YHA. Package cycling holidays are offered by various organisations, with campsite or hotel accommodation; luggage is normally transported each day to your next destination. It is advisable to take out insurance before you go. Obviously, the normal rules of the road apply to cyclists (*see* **Getting Around**). The IGN 906 Cycling France map gives details of routes, cycling clubs and places to stay (*see above* **Maps**). Advice and information can be obtained from the Touring Department, **Cyclists Touring Club** (Cotterell House, 69 Meadrow, Godalming, Surrey GU7 3HS; 01483 417217/www.ctc.org.uk). Its service to members includes competitive cycle and travel insurance, free detailed touring itineraries and general information sheets about France, while its tours brochure lists trips to the region, organised by members. The club's French counterpart, **Fédération Française de Cyclotourisme**, is at 12 rue Louis-Bertrand, 94207 Ivry-sur-Seine, Cedex (01.56.20.88.88).

Golf

Provence has some excellent golf courses, and the weather means golf can be played all year round. Most clubs provide lessons with resident experts. **Cordon Rouge Villas** (01253 739749) and **French Golf Holidays** (01277 824100/www.golf-france.co.uk) offer golf holiday packages out of the UK. For more information, contact the following:

Fédération Française de Golfe *68 rue Anatole France, Le Vallois, Perret 92309 (01.41.49.77.00).*

Ligue de Golf Provence-Alpes-Côte d'Azur *Domaine de Riquetti, Chemin départemental 9, 13290 Les Milles (04.42.39.86.83).*

Horse riding

Horse riding and pony trekking are popular activities, with *centres équestres* all over the region, in rural areas, the mountains, less inhabited parts of the coast, and the Camargue. **Equestrian Travellers Club** (0208 3878076) and **Foxcroft Travel** (01509 813252) offer French equestrian tours and holidays out of the UK. For further information, contact:

Association Drôme à Cheval *(04.75.45.78.79./www.drome-a-cheval.com)*

Ligue Régionale de Provence de Sports Equestres *298 av du club Hippique, 13090 Aix-en-Provence (04.42.20.88.02).*

Skiing

There are several large ski resorts in the Maritime Alps within a few hours of the coast; the three with the best facilities are Auron, Valberg and Isola 2000 (*see p287*).

Fédération Française de Ski *50 av des Marquisats, 74011 Annecy Cedex (04.50.51.40.34/www.ffs.fr).*

Watersports

All along the coast you can water-ski, windsurf or scuba dive; surfing, too, is possible on certain beaches when the mistral is blowing. Antibes and Cannes are major watersports centres, and the Iles de Lerins, the Iles de Hyères and the *calanques* offer some of the best diving in the Mediterranean. For detailed listings pick up the *Watersports Côte d'Azur* brochure from main tourist offices or go online to www.france-nautisme.com.

Comité Régional de Voile Alpes-Provence *46 bd Kraemer, 13014 Marseille (04.91.11.61.78).*

Comité Régional de Voile Côte d'Azur *Espace Antibes, 2208 rte de Grasse, 06600 Antibes (04.93.74.77.05).*

Fédération Française d'Etudes et de Sports Sous-Marins *24 quai Rive-Neuve, 13284 Marseille (04.91.33.99.31).*

Walking

Walking holidays are extremely popular in France, and there is an extensive, well-signposted network of *sentiers de grande randonnée* (long-distance footpaths). For information on maps *see* **Maps**. Each *département* has its own ramblers' organisation that arranges guided walks of a day or more, as well as walks to see local flowers and wildlife. The Club Alpin Français in Nice (*see above* **Climbing**) organises day-long hikes at various levels with coach/minibus transport from Nice. For local information contact the relevant tourist office, or:

Fédération Française de Randonnée Pédestre *14 rue Riquet, 75019 Paris (01.44.89.93.90/www.ffrp.asso.fr).*

Study & students

Cultural exchange & language courses

Central Bureau for Educational Visits & Exchanges
10 Spring Gardens, London SW1A IBN (020 7389 4004).

Centre des Échanges Internationaux
1 rue Golzen, 6th, Paris (01.40.51.11.71). Sporting and cultural holidays and educational tours for 15-30-year-olds. Non-profit-making organisation.

Socrates-Erasmus Programme
In Britain *UK Socrates-Erasmus Council, RND Building, The University, Canterbury, Kent CT2 7PD (0122 776 2712/www.erasmus.ac.uk/Contact erasmus@ukc.ac.uk).* **In France** *Agence Erasmus, 10 pl de la Bourse, 33081 Bordeaux Cedex (05.56.79.44.02/ www.socrates-france.org/ Contact mj.bio.ndini@ socrates-fr.org).* This scheme enables EU students with a reasonable standard of written and spoken French to spend a year of their degree following appropriate courses in the French university system. The UK office publishes a brochure and helps with general enquiries, but applications must be made through the Erasmus co-ordinator at your home university.

Souffle
Espace Charlotte, La Crou, 83260 (04.94.00.94.65). An umbrella organisation for courses in French as a foreign language.

Language courses

Actilangue *2 rue Alexis Mossa, 06000 Nice (04.93.96.33.84/fax 04.93.44.37.16/www.actilangue.com).* French courses and cultural activities.

Alliance Française *310 rue de Paradis, 13008 Marseille (04.96.10.24.60); 2 rue de Paris, 06000 Nice (04.93.62.67.66).* Branches of the highly regarded non-profit French language school, offering both beginners' and specialist courses.

Azurlingua *25 bd Raimbaldi, 06000 Nice (04.93.62.01.11/ www.azurlingua.com).* Language holidays.

Centre International d'Antibes

38 bd d'Aguillon, Antibes 06600 (04.92.90.71.70/www.cia-France.com). French tuition.

ELFCA (Institut d'Enseignement de la Langue Française sur la Côte d'Azur) *66 av de Toulon, 83400 Hyères (04.94.65.03.31/www.elfca.com).* French tuition.

International School of Nice *15 av Claude Debussy, 06200 Nice (04.93.21.04.00/04.93.21.84.90).*

Universities

For the **University of Aix-Marseille**, which has faculties in the two cities (arts, humanities, law in Aix; science, mathematics in Marseille) contact CROUS (Centre Régional des Oeuvres Universitaires et Scolaires) on 04.91.62.83.60 (Marseille) or 04.42.93.47.70 (Aix).

For the **University of Nice**, contact CROUS on 04.92.15.50.50. Contact the **Institut d'Etudes Françaises pour Etudiants Etrangers** (23 rue Gaston de Saporta, Aix-en-Provence, 04.42.21.70.90) about university courses for foreign students

Discounts

A wide range of student discounts are on offer. To claim discounts in museums, cinemas and theatres you need an **International Student Identity Card** from **CROUS** (*see above*) or from travel agents specialising in student travel. ISICs are only valid in France if you are under 26. Under-26s can also get discounts of up to 50% on trains with the **Carte 12/25**. The **Carte Jeune** (€18.29 from **Fnac**) gives discounts on museums, cinema, theatre, travel, sports clubs, restaurants, insurance and some shops.

Tax refunds (Détaxe)

Non-EU residents can claim a refund (average 15%) on value-added tax (TVA) if they spend over €183 in any one shop. At the shop ask for a *détaxe* form and when you leave France have it stamped by customs. Then send a stamped copy back to the shop, which will refund the tax, either by bank transfer or by crediting your credit card. *Détaxe* does not cover food, drink, antiques or works of art.

Telephones

After decades in the dark ages, the French telephone system is actualy now very efficient, and you can usually find operational telephone boxes (*cabines publiques*). Telephone numbers are always ten figures, written and spoken in sets of two, for example – 01.23.45.67.89. If you want numbers to be given singly rather than in pairs as is customary, ask for them *chiffre par chiffre*.

Regional telephone numbers are prefixed as follows **Paris, Ile de France region** 01; **North-west** 02; **North-east** 03; **South-east and Corsica** 04; and **South-west** 05. **Mobile phones** start 06.

When dialling from abroad, omit the zero. The country code for dialling France is 33; for Monaco it is 377.

Public phones

Public phone boxes use phone cards (*télécartes*), which are available from post offices, stationers, stations, some cafés and *bureaux de tabac*. To make a call from a public phone box, lift the receiver, insert the card, then dial the number. To make a follow-on call, do not replace the receiver but press the green *'appel suivant'* button and dial.

Calls from metred cabins in cafés, shops or restaurants are generally more expensive.

If you need to make a phone call in rural areas, or villages with no public phone, look out for the blue *téléphone publique* plaque on private houses. This means the owner is officially appointed to allow you to use the phone and charge the normal amount for the call.

You cannot reverse charges within France but you can to countries that will accept such calls. Go through the operator and ask to make a 'pcv' ('pay-say-vay') call. Incoming calls can only be received at boxes displaying the blue bell sign.

International calls

Dial 00 followed by the country's international call number, found in the front of the *Pages Jaunes* section of the *annuaire* or listed in a phone box. For operator calls to abroad, dial 31.23.

International codes

Australia *00 61*
Canada *00 1*
Ireland *00 353*
Monaco *00 377*
New Zealand *00 64*
South Africa *00 27*
UK *00 44*
US *00 1*

Special rate numbers

Numbers starting with the following prefixes have special rates:
0800 Numéro vert freephone.
0801 Numéro azur €0.11 first 3 mins, then €0.04/min.
0802 Numéro indigo I €0.15/min.
0803 Numéro indigo II €0.23/ min.
0867 €0.23/min.
0836/0868/0869 €0.34/min.

Cheap rates

For calls within France, the cheapest times to telephone are weekdays 7pm to 8am and weekends.

Mobile phones

France has three mobile phone operators (Bouygues, France Telecom/Orange and SFR) offering myriad subscriptions and prepaid card systems.

Misterrent

(01.44.88.76.80/ www.misterrent.com). Internet-based company finds the nearest franchise outlet in a nationwide network, which will then bike the phone to you.

Phone directories

Phone directories are found in post offices and in most cafés. The *Pages Blanches* (*White Pages*) lists people and businesses alphabetically. *Pages Jaunes* (*Yellow Pages*) lists businesses and services by category. Both are available on www.pagesjaunes.fr.

24-hour services

French directory enquiries (*renseignements*) **12**.
International directory enquiries **32 12** then country code (eg. 44 for UK, 1 for USA).
Telephone engineer **13**.
International news (French recorded message, France Inter) dial **08.36.68.10.33** (€0.34/min).
To send a telegram (all languages): international **08.00.33.44.11**, within France **36.55**.
Speaking clock **36.99**.

Television

Terrestrial channels

France has six terrestrial channels. The biggest, **TF1**, features movies, game shows, soaps and news with star anchors Patrick Poivre d'Arvor and Claire Chazal. State-run **France 2** mixes game shows and cultural chat. **France 3** has news, sports, wildlife documentaries and Cinema de Minuit with classic films in the original language (VO *version originale*). **Canal+** is a subscription channel with movies, exclusive sport and late-night porn. **Arte** is a Franco-German hybrid specialising in intelligent arts coverage and films in VO. Its wavelength is shared with educational channel, **La Cinquième** (6.45am-7pm). **M6** rotates music videos and magazine programmes.

Cable TV & satellite

The cable and satellite network is well-established, although satellite has been opposed by some local authorities who see the dishes as eyesores. Channels include **LCI** for 24-hour news, documentary **Planète**, woman's channel **Téva** with *Ally McBeal* and other sitcoms in VO, **Mezzo** for classical music, **Eurosport** for sport, and **Canal Jimmy**, **13e Rue**, **Série Club** and **TMC** for sitcoms, as well as a range of specialist film channels. Foreign-language channels include **BBC World**, **BBC Prime** and **CNN**.

Time

France is one hour ahead of Greenwich Mean Time (GMT) and six hours ahead of New York. The 24-hour clock is frequently used in France when giving times: 8am is 8 heures, noon (midi) is 12 heures, 8pm is 20 heures, and midnight (minuit) is 0 heure.

Tipping

By law a mandatory service charge of 10-15% is included in the bill in all restaurants; leave a small extra tip of €0.50-€2 on the table if you are particularly pleased. Service is also usually included in taxi fares, though an extra €0.50 to €2 tip will be appreciated. The same amount is also appropriate for doormen, porters, guides and hairdressers. In bars and cafés, it is usual just to leave small change as a tip.

Toilets

Anyone may use the toilet in a bar or café whether they are a customer or not, although it's polite to at least have a café at *le zinc*. (Ask for *les toilettes* or *le WC* – pronounced 'vay say'.) Public toilets vary considerably and some are still old-fashioned squat jobs. Men and women sometimes use the same facilities.

Tourist information

France has an efficient network of tourist information offices (Office de Tourisme or Syndicat d'Iniative), often present in even the tiniest village.

All will be able to provide information on hotels, restaurants, *gîtes* and other rented accommodation, sporting facilities, cultural attractions and guided visits; some also have hotel booking and ticket reservation services.

For general information on the region and hotels before you travel, there are French Government Tourist Offices in the UK (178 Piccadilly, London W1; 0906 824 4123) and USA (444 Madison Avenue, NY NY 10022; 212 838 7800). You can also consult the French Government Tourist Office's official Internet site, www.franceguide.com.

Videos

Due to different transmission standards, British and US TVs and video recorders won't work in France, so videos on the PAL system won't work unless you have a multi-standard TV and video, which most of the French now do.

Visas

To visit France, you need a valid passport. Non-EU citizens require a visa, although USA, Canada, Australia or New Zealand citizens do not need a visa for stays of up to three months. If in any doubt, check with the French consulate in your country. If you intend to stay in France for more than 90 days, then you are supposed to apply for a *carte de séjour*.

Weather

Most of the South of France is hot and dry, except for spring, when there may be heavy rainfall, and November, which can be blustery, cold and wet. The coast has a gentle Mediterranean climate with mild winters, daytime temperatures rarely lower than 10°C/50°F degrees, and hot summers with temperatures often rising above 30°C/86°F. Although summer is generally dry (see above Fire), there are often dramatic thunderstorms along the Riviera in late August. Average sunshine on the French Riviera is six hours in January and 12 hours in July. Late January and February can be a wonderful time to visit, when there are few other tourists, but most museums are open and the cafés have tables outside.

Provence has similar conditions, mitigated by the dreaded mistral – a harsh, cold wind that blows down the Rhône Valley. It howls through the streets of Arles, Avignon and Marseille, bringing the temperatures down dramatically and clearing the air. It usually lasts three or four days, but can go on as long as ten days. The area has also seen dramatic storms in recent years, causing major floods and damage. The high mountains usually have snow from November to March.

Information

In English 08.36.70.1.2.3. For local forecasts dial 08.36.68.12.34 followed by the *département* number. *www.lachainemeteo.com* French and European weather updates.

Women

Women need feel no more threatened in the South of France than in any other European country; indeed women alone will be more comfortable than in many places. Women often go to the beach alone, and you will be welcomed graciously in restaurants. The usual safety precautions should be taken in big cities at night. Be careful on trains, especially sleepers, where the rates of assault have risen, and always lock car doors when driving alone. You may receive compliments – more a cultural difference than sexual harrassment. A polite 'N'insistez pas!' (don't push it) should turn off any unwanted attention. For contraception and abortion, *see p300*.

International Women's Club of the Riviera

(04.93.14.93.62). Coffee mornings for newcomers.

Service des Droits des Femmes

10-16 rue Brancion, 75015 Paris (01.40.56.60.00). This service of the Minstère de l'Emploi et de la Solidarité was created to promote women's rights and implement equal opportunity legislation. In each département contact the Préfecture for a local representative.

SOS Viol Informations

08.00.05.95.95. Freephone in French dealing with rape.

Essential Vocabulary

In French, as in other Latin languages, the second person singular (you) has two forms. Phrases here are given in the more polite *vous* form. The *tu* form is used with family, friends, young children and pets; you should be careful not to use it with people you do not know sufficiently well. You will also find that courtesies such as monsieur, madame and mademoiselle are used much more than their English equivalents. See page 305 for information on language courses and page 30 for Provençal menu terms.

General expressions

good morning/good afternoon, hello *bonjour*
good evening *bonsoir*
goodbye *au revoir*
yes *oui*; no *non*; OK *d'accord/ça va.*
hi (familiar) *salut*
How are you? *Comment allez vous?/vous allez bien?*
How's it going? *Comment ça va?/ça va?* (familiar)
Sir/Mr *monsieur (M)*; Madam/Mrs *madame (Mme)*
Miss *mademoiselle (Mlle)*
please *s'il vous plaît;*
thank you *merci;* thank you very much *merci beaucoup*
sorry *pardon;* excuse me *excusez-moi*
Do you speak English? *Parlez-vous anglais?*
I don't speak French *Je ne parle pas français*
I don't understand *Je ne comprends pas*
Speak more slowly, please *Parlez plus lentement, s'il vous plaît*
Leave me alone *Laissez-moi tranquille*
how much?/how many? *combien?*
Have you got change? *Avez-vous de la monnaie?*
I would like… *Je voudrais…*
I am going *Je vais;* I am going to pay *Je vais payer*
it is *c'est;* it isn't *ce n'est pas*
good *bon(ne);* bad *mauvais(e)*
small *petit(e);* big *grand(e)*
beautiful *beau/belle*
well *bien;* badly *mal*
expensive *cher;* cheap *pas cher*
a bit *un peu;* a lot *beaucoup;* very *très;* with *avec;* without *sans;* and

et; or *ou;* because *parce que*
who? *qui?;* when? *quand?;* which? *quel?;* where? *où?;* why? *pourquoi?;* how? *comment?*
at what time/when? *à quelle heure?*
forbidden *interdit/défendu*
out of order *hors service/en panne*
daily *tous les jours (tlj)*
except Sunday *sauf le dimanche*

On the phone

hello (telephone) *allô;* Who's calling? *C'est de la part de qui?/Qui est à l'appareil?*
Hold the line *Ne quittez pas/Patientez s'il vous plaît*

Getting around

When is the next train for…? *C'est quand le prochain train pour…?*
ticket *un billet;* station *la gare;*
train station *gare sncf;* platform *le quai;* bus/coach station *gare routière;* bus/coach *autobus/car*
entrance *entrée;* exit *sortie*
left *gauche;* right *droite;*
interchange *correspondence*
straight on *tout droit;* far *loin;* near *pas loin/près d'ici*
street *la rue;* street map *le plan;* road map *la carte*
bank *la banque;* is there a bank near here? *est-ce qu'il y a une banque près d'ici?*
post office *La Poste;* a stamp *un timbre*

Sightseeing

beach *une plage;* bridge *pont;* cave *une grotte;* church *une église;*
market *marché* or *les halles;*
museum *un musée;* mill *un moulin;*
town hall *l'hôtel de ville/la mairie;*
exhibition *une exposition;* ticket (for museum) *un billet;* (for theatre, concert) *une place;* free *gratuit;* reduced price *un tarif réduit*
open *ouvert;* closed *fermé*

Accommodation

Do you have a room (for this evening/for two people)? *Avez-vous une chambre (pour ce soir/pour deux personnes)?*
full *complet;* room *une chambre*
bed *un lit;* double bed *un grand lit;* (a room with) twin beds *(une chambre) à deux lits;* with bath(room)/shower *avec (salle de) bain/douche;* breakfast *le petit déjeuner;* included *compris*
lift *un ascenseur;* air-conditioned *climatisé;* swimming pool *piscine*

At the café or restaurant

I'd like to book a table (for three/at 8pm) *Je voudrais réserver une table (pour trois personnes/à vingt heures)*
lunch *le déjeuner;* dinner *le dîner*
coffee (espresso) *un café;* white coffee *un café au lait/café crème;*
tea *le thé;* wine *le vin;* beer *la bière;*
a draught beer *une pression*
mineral water *eau minérale;* fizzy *gazeuse;* still *plate;* tap water *eau du robinet/une carafe d'eau*
the bill, please *l'addition, s'il vous plaît*

Behind the wheel

give way *céder le passage*
it's not your right of way *vous n'avez pas la priorité;* no parking *stationnement interdit/stationnement gênant;* deliveries *livraisons;* residents only *sauf riverains.*
pedestrian *pieton;*
toll *péage;* speed limit 40 *rappel 40*
petrol *essence;* unleaded *sans plomb;* diesel *gasoil.*
traffic jam *embouteillage/bouchon;*
speed *vitesse*
dangerous bends *attention virages*

Numbers

0 *zéro;* 1 *un, une;* 2 *deux;* 3 *trois;* 4 *quatre;* 5 *cinq;* 6 *six;* 7 *sept;* 8 *huit;* 9 *neuf;* 10 *dix;* 11 *onze;* 12 *douze;* 13 *treize;* 14 *quatorze;* 15 *quinze;* 16 *seize;* 17 *dix-sept;* 18 *dix-huit;* 19 *dix-neuf;* 20 *vingt;* 21 *vingt-et-un;* 22 *vingt-deux;* 30 *trente;* 40 *quarante;* 50 *cinquante;* 60 *soixante;* 70 *soixante-dix;* 80 *quatre-vingts;* 90 *quatre-vingt-dix;* 100 *cent;* 1,000 *mille;* 1,000,000 *un million.*

Days, months & seasons

Monday *lundi;* Tuesday *mardi;* Wednesday *mercredi;* Thursday *jeudi;* Friday *vendredi;* Saturday *samedi;* Sunday *dimanche.*
January *janvier;* February *février;* March *mars;* April *avril;* May *mai;* June *juin;* July *juillet;* August *août;* September *septembre;* October *octobre;* November *novembre;* December *décembre.*
Spring *printemps;* summer *été;* autumn *automne;* winter *hiver.*

Further Reference

Books

History & archaeology

Maurice Agulhon, Noël Coulet
Histoire de la Provence
A short, scholarly account of the region's political and economic history, in French. Que sais-je? PUF, 4th edition, 2001.

James Bromwich
The Roman Remains of Southern France
Leaves no stone unturned in its tour of Roman Provence. Routledge, 1996.

Provençal identity

John Ardagh
France in the New Century
Few journalists writing in English know France as well as Ardagh. This book updates his earlier *France in the 1980s* to take in the rapid changes of the last two decades. Penguin, 2000.

Alphonse Daudet
Letters from my Windmill
French 19th-century version of *A Year in Provence*, for escapist Parisians. Penguin (out of print).

Frédéric Mistral, tr George Wickes
Memoirs
The 19th-century prophet of Provençal regionalism relives the events that inspired his passion for the region. Alyscamps Press, 1994.

Laurence Wylie
Village in the Vaucluse
A readable sociological account of life in the village of Roussillon in the 1950s. Harvard UP, 1976.

Art, architecture & gardens

La Côte d'Azur et la Modernité
This French exhibition catalogue offers an excellent, well-illustrated account of the South's crucial place in modern art. RMN, 1997.

Charles Bilas & Lucien Rosso
French Riviera the 20s and 30s
Glossy architectural survey of the villas, hotels and apartment buildings along the coast between Hyères and Menton. Telleri, 1999.

Eileen Gray
Eileen Gray
Memoirs of the Irish architect and furniture designer Eileen Gray. Her two Modernist houses on the Riviera near Menton – the only buildings she ever designed – earned her a cult following. Thames & Hudson, 1998.

Louisa Jones
Gardens of the French Riviera; Gardens in Provence
Two glossy, highly illustrated coffee-table tomes for garden-lovers. Flammarion, 2002.

Ed Ronald de Leeuw
Letters of Van Gogh
Van Gogh is often pigeon-holed as art's mad genius, but his letters show a perceptive, engaged and engaging observer. Penguin, 1997.

John Richardson
The Sorcerer's Apprentice: Picasso, Provence and Douglas Cooper
Gossipy, first-hand account of the Riviera lifestyle of Picasso and his main dealer, the exuberant Douglas Cooper, from the artist's multi-volume biographer. Cape, 1999.

Bogomila Welsh-Ovcharov
Van Gogh in Provence and Auvers
Well-documented study of the earless one's Provençal jaunt. Hugh Lauter Levin, 1999.

Emigrés

Sybille Bedford
Jigsaw
Wry autobiographical account of itinerant childhood, with eccentric parenting and neighbours in Sanary-sur-Mer. Penguin, 1999.

Mary Blume
Côte d'Azur – Inventing the French Riviera
An entertaining, informed account of the decline and fall of the Riviera myth, and the emigrés who fuelled it. Thames & Hudson, 1992.

Lawrence Durrell
Caesar's Vast Ghost
Durrell's last work is a dithering mélange of historical essay and earnest reflection, interspersed with some fairly bad poetry. Faber & Faber, 1990.

Graham Greene
J'Accuse: the Dark Side of Nice
Impassioned exposé of corruption in the regime of former Nice mayor Jacques Médecin. Penguin, 1982 (out of print).

Peter Mayle
A Year in Provence
Surprisingly readable advertising copy with a few insights among the clichés. And you have to admire the royalties. Penguin, 1989.

Tobias Smollett
Travels through France and Italy
Cantankerous letters of Scottish novelist and doctor from his tour of the Mediterranean. Oxford World's Classics, 1999.

Fiction & poetry

J G Ballard
Super-Cannes
Ballard lands an expat couple in a murder mystery revolving around a fictional Provençal business park, Eden-Olympia. Flamingo, 2001.

Alexandre Dumas
The Count of Monte Cristo
A ripping yarn of prison, buried treasure and revenge in the post-Napoleonic South. Various editions.

F Scott Fitzgerald
Tender is the Night
Wealth and mental health gone wrong on the Riviera, based on the lives of American socialites Sara and Gerald Murphy. Various editions.

Jean Giono
The Man who Planted Trees
Eco-fable for grown-ups:
a good introduction to the work of this gritty Southern writer. Harvill, 1992.

Jean-Claude Izzo
One Helluva Mess (Total Khéops)
The first of Izzo's detective series *La Trilogie Noire* is a gritty, atmospheric tale, starring cop Fabio Montale, set in multi-racial Marseille. Arcadia, 2001.

J M G Le Clézio
Le Procès Verbal
A classic when published in the 1960s, the Nice writer's best-known novel is a mysterious, anonymous chronicle of inactivity. Poche, 1973.

Marcel Pagnol
The Water of the Hills: Jean de Florette & Manon of the Springs
Dour Provençal peasants bicker with incomers about the water supply. As a special bonus, the book comes *sans* Gérard Depardieu. Picador, 1989.

W Somerset Maugham
Collected Short Stories
Including the unforgettable 'Three Fat Ladies of Antibes'.

Patrick Süskind
Perfume
If a mysterious character asks if they can kill you to extract your scent, Just Say No. A smelly thriller set in the 18th-century Grasse perfume trade. Picador, 1989.

Emile Zola
La Fortune des Rougon
The opening episode of Zola's vast Rougon-Macquart saga is set in Plassans, a loosely disguised Aix-en-Provence. Plassans also features in *L'Oeuvre*, Zola's tale of a struggling artist (a mix of Manet and Cézanne), which broke the author's friendship with Cézanne. Penguin Classics.

Food & wine

The A-Z of French Food
A useful bilingual glossary of French gastronomy. Editions Scribo, 1999.

Alain Ducasse
Flavours of France
The seven-star chef's classic first cookbook. Artisan, 1998.

Ed Hugh Johnson
Touring in Wine Country: Provence
Essential companion for those serious fact-finding tours of Southern vineyards. Mitchell Beazley, 1993.

Dixon Long
The Markets of Provence
Seven produce markets in the *départements* of Vaucluse and Bouches-du-Rhône, with recipes and lavish photos. Collins US, 1996.

Mort Rosenblum
Olives
US newsman buys a farm in Provence, saves its olive trees and gets hooked on the little green fruit. Absolute Press, 1997.

Films

La Baie des anges (1963)
Jeanne Moreau plays a charismatic compulsive gambler who seduces Claude Mann and leads him on a dance of death in Jacques Demy's ravishingly shot New Wave film set in Nice and Monte Carlo.

To Catch a Thief (1955)
Hitchcock classic starring Cary Grant and Grace Kelly caught in a crime riddle on the Riviera.

Et Dieu créa la femme (1956)
Director Roger Vadim's classic launched the career of a scantily clad teenage Brigitte Bardot, with St-Tropez posing in the background.

Daddy Nostalgie/These Foolish Things (1990)
Bertrand Tavernier directs Dirk Bogarde and Jane Birkin in father and daughter weepie on the Riviera.

The French Connection (1971)
Gene Hackman stars as a tough New York cop brought to the Riviera on the trail of a drug smuggling ring. See also the sequel, set in Marseille, **French Connection II** (1975).

Gazon Maudit/French Twist (1995)
Ménage à trois with a twist when Riviera housewife Loli (Victoria Abril) falls for butch Marijo (Josiane Balasko), with Alain Chabat as the philandering husband.

Les Gendarmes et les extraterrestres (1978)
Aliens in St-Tropez, *see box p175.*

Goldeneye (1995)
Bond (Pierce Brosnan) at his most politically correct takes part in a spectacular car chase in the hills above Monaco before cashing in his chips at the casino.

Herbie goes to Monte-Carlo (1977)
Disney's chirpie VW beetle is all tuned up for the Paris to Monte-Carlo road race but falls for a pert little Lancia. Sunshine all the way.

Jean de Florette and Manon des Sources (1986)
Based on Marcel Pagnol's novel *L'Eau des Collines*, these romantic epics wafted the scent of Provence into cinemas around the world.

Marius, Fanny and **César** (1931, 1932, 1936)
Scripted by Marcel Pagnol, this 1930s trilogy set in Marseille's *vieux port* pays sentimental homage to the characters, traditions and accents of France's second city.

Marius et Jeanette (1997)
Local director Robert Guédiguian's (*see p36*) delicate portrait of a working-class friendship in Marseille's L'Estaque suburb.

Rebecca (1940)
Hitchcock's adaptation of Daphne du Maurier's novel begins with the fateful meeting of the future Mrs de Winter (Joan Fontaine) and 'Maxim' (Laurence Olivier) in Monte Carlo, and their marriage on the Riviera.

Taxi (1998)
Stunts galore in the Luc Besson-scripted and produced car chase caper through streets of Marseille.

Two for the Road (1967)
Stanley Donen's sophisticated tale of marital crisis on the Riviera starring Albert Finney and Audrey Hepburn.

Websites

www.artists-stories.com
Titled Irony and Rude Questions, this Provence-run site invites artists to submit their tales of the weird and wonderful in the art world.

www.cityvox.com
Lively urban city guides with club, restaurant and bar info, largely compiled from readers opinions.

www.festivals.laregie-paca.com.
The region's countless summer festivals.

www.fnac.com
The French CD and book superstore on the web, with online ticket agency.

www.franceguide.com
The French Government Tourist Office's info-packed official site.

www.luberon-news.com
Local Luberon site with listings of restaurants and hotels and info on wines, markets, events and property.

www.marseille.webcity.fr
A savvy guide to bars, pubs and cinemas in Marseille. Also sites for Nice and Nîmes.

www.meteo.fr
State meteorological service.

www.nicematin.fr
News and columnists from the French regional daily and its sister paper *Var Matin.*

www.pages-jaunes.com/
www.pages-blanches.com
The indispensable web versions of the French telephone directory, yellow and white pages.

www.pitchoun.com
What's on: restaurants, clubs, gay, shops and sports on the Côte from Antibes to Nice.

www.provence-beyond.com
Excellent independent English website, with illustrated in-depth information on all the big towns and tiny villages plus insights into local folklore and transport systems.

www.provenceguide.com
Départemental tourist guide to the Vaucluse.

www.provenceweb.fr
French site listing several hundred villages and towns, with hotels, restaurants and brief descriptions, plus cycle routes with map refs.

www.rivieragenda.com
Comprehensive listings for everything from bistros to beaches, all along the coast.

www.riviera-reporter.com.
Offshoot of the English-language expat magazine with an rchive of past storeis, events lisstings and good links.

www.sncf.fr
Information, timetables and online reservations for French railways.

www.visitprovence.com
Official government tourist website (French and English) for the Bouches du Rhône with events features and info on where to stay, eat and visit.

Index

Page numbers in italics indicate illustrations, page numbers in **bold** indicate main references.

Index

Index

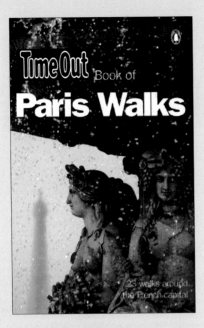
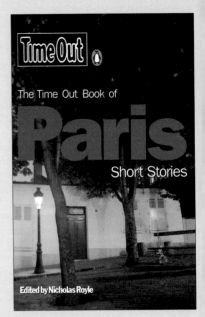

Maps

The South of France

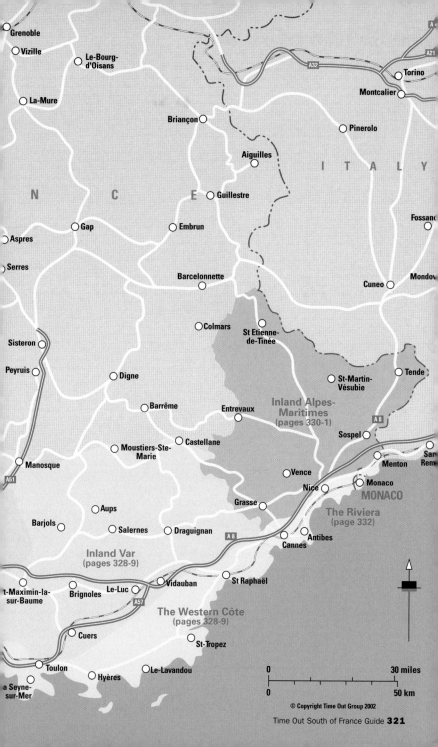

The Rhône Delta

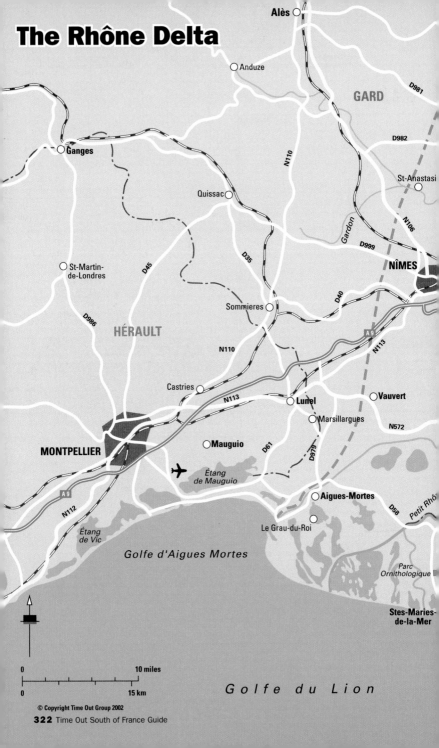

Alès

Anduze

GARD

D981

D982

Ganges

St-Anastasi

Quissac

N110

Gardon

D999

NÎMES

D35

St-Martin-
de-Londres

D45

N106

D986

HÉRAULT

Sommieres

D40

A 9

N113

Castries

N110

Vauvert

N113

Lunel

Marsillargues

N572

MONTPELLIER

Mauguio

D61

D979

Étang
de Mauguio

Aigues-Mortes

D58

Petit Rhô

A 9

Le Grau-du-Roi

N112

Étang
de Vic

Golfe d'Aigues Mortes

Parc
Ornithologique

Stes-Maries-
de-la-Mer

N

0   10 miles

0   15 km

Golfe du Lion

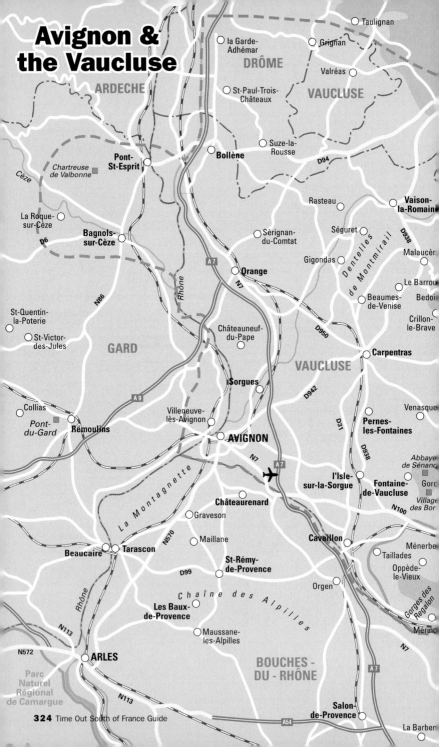

Avignon &
the Vaucluse

ARDECHE

DRÔME

Taulignan

la Garde-
Adhémar

Grignan

Valréas

St-Paul-Trois-
Châteaux

VAUCLUSE

Suze-la-
Rousse

Bollène

D94

Pont-
St-Esprit

Chartreuse
de Valbonne

Cèze

Rasteau

Vaison-
la-Romaine

La Roque-
sur-Cèze

Séguret

D938

Malaucèr

D6

Bagnols-
sur-Cèze

Sèrignan-
du-Comtat

Gigondas

Le Barrou

Bedoi

Dentelles de Montmirail

A7

Orange

Beaumes-
de-Venise

Crillon-
le-Brave

N86

N7

St-Quentin-
la-Poterie

Châteauneuf-
du-Pape

D950

Carpentras

St-Victor-
des-Jules

GARD

VAUCLUSE

A9

Sorgues

D942

Venasque

Collias

Pont-
du-Gard

Rémoulins

Villeneuve-
lès-Avignon

D31

Pernes-
les-Fontaines

D938

AVIGNON

Abbaye
de Sénan

N7

A7

l'Isle-
sur-la-Sorgue

Fontaine-
de-Vaucluse

Gor

Village
des Bor

Châteaurenard

N100

Graveson

La Montagnette

Cavaillon

Ménerbe

N570

Maillane

Taillades

Beaucaire

Tarascon

St-Rémy-
de-Provence

Oppède-
le-Vieux

D99

Orgen

Gorges des Regalon

Les Baux-
de-Provence

Chaîne des Alpilles

Rhône

N113

Maussane-
les-Alpilles

Mérino

N7

N572

ARLES

BOUCHES -
DU - RHÔNE

Parc
Naturel
Régional
de Camargue

N113

A7

Salon-
de-Provence

A54

La Barber

0   10 miles

0   15 km

Nyons

D994

HAUTE - ALPES

A51

Buis-les-Baronnies

Ouvèze

N974

▲ Mont Ventoux

D974/D19

Aurel

Montagne de Lure

Sault

Monieux

N942

Gorges de la Nesque

Plateau d'Albion

HAUTE - PROVENCE

Plateau de Vaucluse

D30

Banon

D950

D51

N96

Simiane-la-Rotonde

Forcalquier

N100

Roussillon

D4

Rustrel

Mane

Colorado de Rustrel

St-Michel-l'Observatoire

D13

ND de Salagon

Goult

Apt

Saignon

Lacoste

Buoux

N100

Abbaye St-Hilaire

Bonnieux

D36

▲ Mourre Nègre

D907

N96

Manosque

Montagne du Luberon

D943

Lourmarin

Parc Régional du Luberon

la Bastide-des-Jourdans

Lauris

Cucuron

Grambois

Cadenet

Ansouis

D956

A51

La Roque-d'Anthéron

Abbaye de Silvacane

N973

La Tour-d'Aigues

N7

D543

Pertuis

Durance

VAR

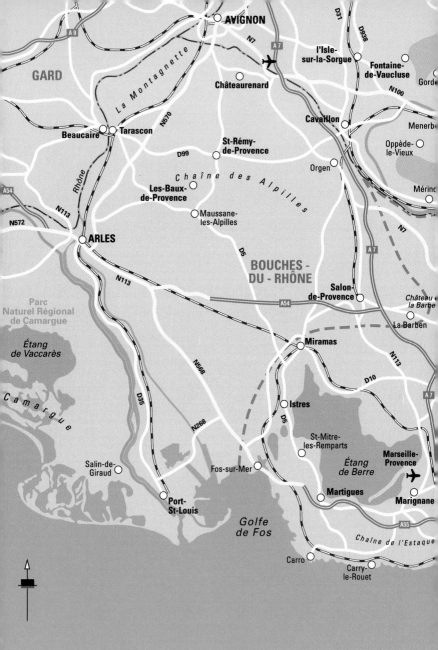

Marseille &
Aix-en-Provence

VAUCLUSE

Roussillon

D4

Apt

Lacoste

Bonnieux

N100

HAUTE - PROVENCE

N100

Manosque

Montagne du Luberon

Parc Régional
du Luberon

Lourmarin

Cucuron

D956

Cadenet

Ansouis

La Tour-
d'Aigues

La Roque
d'Antheron

Abbaye de
Silvacane

N973

A51

Pertuis

Durance

Lambesc

Rognes

N7

N96

Peyrolles

D29

Puyricard

Rians

Oppidium
d'Entremont

Vauvenargues

D3

AIX-EN-PROVENCE

Montagne St Victoire

Puylaubier

Le Tholonet

D17

D23

Pourrières

D543

N7

D560

VAR

D9

D6

Les Milles

Jardins
d'Albertas

D67

A51

Gardanne

St-Maximin-
la-Ste-Baume

A7

A52

N560

A8

MARSEILLE

Auriol

D1

Tourves

D5

La Roquebrussanne

Massif de la Ste Baume

A50

Aubagne

N8

Signes

D2

Méounes-lés-
Montrieux

D559

Les Calanques

Cassis

N8

Ile de Riou

A50

La Ciotat

Le Lecques

0   10 miles

0   15 km

© Copyright Time Out Group 2002

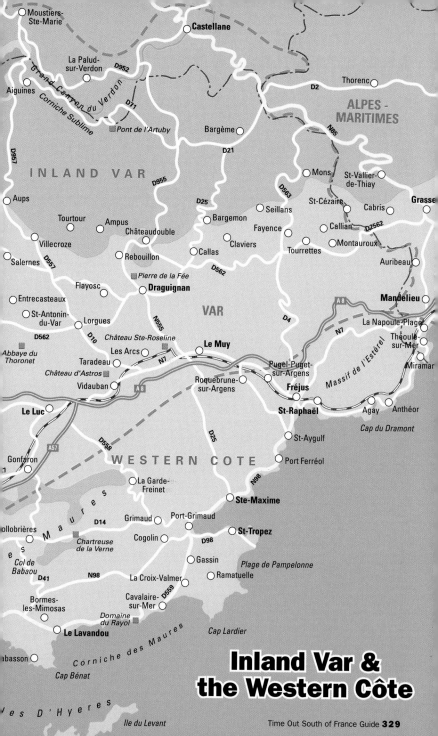

Inland Var &
the Western Côte

Inland
Alpes-Maritimes

Barcelonnette

HAUTE - PROVENCE

Col de la
Bonette

D64

St-Dalmas-
le-Selvage

St-Etienne-
de-Tinée

Auron

D2205

Iso

Parc National
du Mercantou

D2202

Guillaumes

Valberg

D30

Roubio

St-Sauveu
sur-Tinée

A l p e s   d e   P r o v e n c e

D902

Var

**ALPES -
MARITIMES**

Annot

N202

Puget-
Théniers

N202

Touët-sur-V

Entrevaux

Route Napoléon

N85

Villars-sur-Var

Castellane

M o n t a g n e   d u   C h e i r o n

Thorenc

D2

Coursego

*Oppidum
Castelleras*

Gréolières

Cipières

*Gorges du
Loup*

Bargème

N85

Tourettes-
sur-Loup

Ven

Gourdon

St-Vallier-
de-Thiey

Le Bar-
sur-Loup

D2210

**St-Paul-
de-Vence**

Mons

Route Napoléon

D2085

D563

VAR

Cabris

Grasse

Seillans

Calliar

Valbonne

Biot

Bargemon

Fayence

Montauroux

D2562

Mouans-
Sartoux

Sophia-
Antipolis

Châteaudouble

Claviers

Tourrettes

N85

Vallauris

Anti

Callas

Mougins

Rebouillon

Le Cannet

D562

Mandelieu

Juan-les-Pins

CANNES

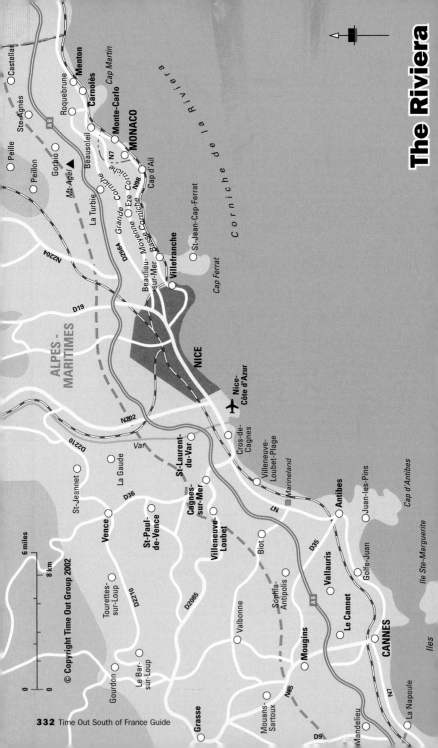

The Riviera

Castellar

Menton
Ste-Agnès
Roquebrune
Carnolès
Cap Martin

Peille
Gorbio
Beausoleil
Monte-Carlo
MONACO

Peillon
Mt-Agel
La Turbie
Èze
Cap d'Ail

Grande Corniche
Moyenne Corniche
Basse Corniche

Corniche de la Riviera

St-Jean-Cap-Ferrat
Villefranche
Beaulieu-sur-Mer
Cap Ferrat

N2204

D19

ALPES-MARITIMES

D2564

NICE

Nice-Côte d'Azur

N202

Var
St-Jeannet
La Gaude
St-Laurent-du-Var
Cros-de-Cagnes
Villeneuve-Loubet-Plage
Marineland

D2210

D36
Cagnes-sur-Mer
Antibes
Cap d'Antibes

Tourettes-sur-Loup
Vence
St-Paul-de-Vence
Villeneuve-Loubet
Biot
Juan-les-Pins

D2210

D2085

Valbonne
Sophia-Antipolis
Vallauris
Golfe-Juan
Île Ste-Marguerite

Gourdon
Le Bar-sur-Loup
Mougins
Le Cannet
Îles

Grasse
Mouans-Sartoux
CANNES

Mandelieu
La Napoule

D35

N7

A8

N85

D9

6 miles
8 km

© Copyright Time Out Group 2002